PICTORIAL HISTORY
1900 TO THE PRESENT DAY

FOREWORD BY LORD BRIGGS
CHIEF CONTRIBUTOR NEIL WENBORN

REVISED AND UPDATED

The material in this book has previously been published under the titles
Pictorial History of the Twentieth Century,
101 Years A Pictorial History
Text and pictures have been revised and updated especially for this edition.

Chief contributor: Neil Wenborn

Other contributors: Helen Dore, Jake Douglas, Ian Jackman, Tony
Kingsford, Alan McIntosh, Brian Murphy, Sonia Porter, Pat Pierce

Foreword: Live Aid Concert, July 1985
(Syndication International)

First published in 1989 by Hamlyn.
This edition published in 2003 by Chancellor Press,
an imprint of Bounty Books,
a division of Octopus Publishing Group Ltd.,
2-4 Heron Quays, London, E14 4JP.

Updated 1990, 1991 (twice), 1993, 1995, 1997, 1999, 2000, 2001, 2002
© Copyright 1989, 1990, 1991, 1993, 1995, 1997, 1999, 2000, 2001, 2002, 2003
Octopus Publishing Group Ltd.

A CIP catalogue record for this book is available at the British Library

ISBN 0 7537 0859 0

Printed in Slovenia

Foreword

It is now possible to have some idea of the shape of the twentieth century as a whole. The decades have fallen into place. We can produce balance sheets of gains and losses and we can discern long-term trends that lead us into the future.

More of the history of the last century has been recorded in pictures than the history of any other century before it. The invention of the motion picture in the late ninteenth century has revolutionised communication. This volume presents a panorama of our century, focusing both on events and themes. Every picture tells a story.

As a result of the communications revolution — a continuing revolution that is still barely through its first phases — many of the pictures recording events in distant parts of the world were transmitted instantaneously. They have become the staple of news, news from all round the world. From our present vantage point, however, we can convert news into history. We can know what happened next. This fascinating volume enables events to be seen as sequences. It also relates one cluster of events to another.

The main themes are clear. This has been a century of unprecedented change, much of it unanticipated, and not all the changes have been easily acceptable. Some of them have met with resistance. The map of the world has changed as old empires have broken up and new nations have been created. Much of the change has been a result of war, world war and local war. Yet there has been a powerful technological thrust based on science. Ours is the age of the computer. It is already difficult to conceive of life without it.

A greater global sense has at last come to be associated with a concern for what is happening to the planet, and we know far more about how our planet is related to the other planets than our ancestors did. The concern, ecological and environmental, distinguishes us from our recent ancestors, but it is still not strong enough to save us from disaster and destruction.

Many questions will be provoked by the material set out in the pages that follow. Why do we have so many problems? What has been the role of leadership on the twentieth century? What happened to ethics and to religion? What are the limits to political — and to economic — progress? Will science, which has saved life and raised expectations, continue to threaten destruction?

For every question there will be different answers. History does not provide single answers: it is an invitation to intelligent and informed argument. This book is valuable not only because it provides indispensable information, but because it opens up debate.

Asa Briggs

1900–1909

The 1900s

The first decade of the new century – a century that was to see more far-reaching changes than any previous period in human history – began with celebrations of stability. For the traditional ruling classes of Europe it was to be the last decade of relative peace and security before the cataclysm which was to engulf the Western world in August 1914. Already, though, the strains were beginning to show beneath the apparently unruffled surface of empire. In the Tsar's Russia the first stirrings of revolution were already claiming lives on the streets of Moscow and St Petersburg. In Great Britain the Victorian sunset lingered on to light the comfortable imperialism of the Edwardian era, while at home the birth of the Labour Representative Committee and overseas the conflict in South Africa pointed the way to uncertainty and change. In Germany the Kaiser began a programme of naval rearmament which was watched with growing unease by her European neighbours. Meanwhile, the USA attained her industrial maturity and stood poised to enter the world stage as a major international power.

The international scene

As the new century dawned a fifth of the world's entire land-mass was covered by the British Empire, which had expanded during the last years of the nineteenth century to encompass some 400 million people, 300 million of them in India alone. Queen Victoria, who numbered Empress of India amongst her regal titles, was still on the throne after a reign of 63 years, during which hitherto unparalleled changes had been made to the fabric of the country as the consolidation of the industrial revolution turned Britain into 'the workshop of the world'. At the same time, there were rumblings of discontent at home and abroad. The same industrialisation that had made Britain a watchword of prosperity had also created a class of urban poor for whom no organised system of financial relief existed outside the centuries-old Poor Laws. The decade was to see the first beginnings of the Labour Party, with support amongst the urban proletariat, and the rise of the women's suffrage movement in the face of male opposition.

The United States began the century with an empire of almost four million square miles and some 85 million people. The first decade was to be a period of rapid change, with the conservatism of President McKinley and his predecessors jolted into self-questioning by an assassin's bullet and the accession of Theodore Roosevelt. It was a time of unprecedented industrial growth, with the expansion of the railway, oil, steel and financial sections placing the US in the first rank of industrial nations.

The Russian empire too was feeling the first shocks of change. There were riots and strikes in major Russian cities as revolutionary fervour found its echo in the dissatisfaction of a working class long smarting under the yoke of an autocratic monarchy. In St Petersburg any remaining belief in the Tsar as the friend and father of his people was brutally dispelled when his forces fired on a crowd of peaceful protestors outside the Winter Palace in 1905. There were mutinies amongst army and naval forces who had tasted humiliation and defeat at the hands of the Japanese in Korea and Manchuria. The Duma, a short-lived experiment in partial democracy, was convened and suspended, many of its deputies ending up in prison.

In Germany Kaiser Wilhelm II, nephew of the new King of England, Edward VII, began to build up his naval forces. While the inter-related Royal families of Europe engaged in displays of dinner-party diplomacy, the seeds of the First World War were being sown.

Science and technology

The first decade of the century also saw startling advances in the scientific world, as new discoveries opened up previously undreamt-of possibilities and new theories challenged old assumptions about the nature of the world. Marconi transmitted his first transatlantic wireless signal, and Wilhelm Roentgen won the first ever Nobel Prize for Physics for his discovery of X-rays. Nobel Prizes were also awarded to the Curies for their discovery of radium and to Ernest Rutherford for his work in radioactivity and atomic physics. Conceptions of the physical universe were shaken to their foundations by Max Planck's Quantum Theory and Albert Einstein's Theory of Relativity. The world of the mind was remapped too, with the publication in 1900 of Sigmund Freud's *The Interpretation of Dreams*, one of the cornerstones of the new science of psychoanalysis.

Technological developments also led to a revolution in modes of transport, with the epoch-making flights of the Wright Brothers and Louis Bleriot, the formation of the Ford Motor Company and Rolls-Royce and the appearance on the streets of motor cars whose names were to remain familiar for the rest of the century. In Russia the trans-Siberian railway was completed, and in London and New York the first electrically powered underground trains carried commuters.

Literature and the arts

The decade saw the death of many figures associated with the artistic world of the Victorian age and the birth of new and influential movements. Oscar Wilde died in Paris, the great critic John Ruskin in the Lake District. The wider artistic world saw the deaths of such nineteenth century giants as Cézanne, Grieg, Ibsen, Zola and Chekhov. In their place came artists such as Matisse, Dérain and Dufy, known as Les Fauves (the Wild Beasts) for their daring use of colour, and the young Spanish painter Picasso, whose first exhibitions shocked and stimulated many. In England, George Bernard Shaw took the London stage by storm and in Dublin there were riots after the first performances of J. M. Synge's *The Playboy of the Western World*.

Left: The San Francisco earthquake and fire of 1906.

1900

Jan	1	British protectorates are set up in Nigeria		20	German Ambassador assassinated in Peking by Boxers
	5	Redmond, Irish Nationalist leader, calls for uprising		27	Opening of London Underground Central Line
	20	John Ruskin, writer and art critic, dies	Jul	1	Maiden flight of airship built by Count von Zeppelin
	24	Boers defeated at Spion Kop		29	King Umberto of Italy assassinated
Feb	9	Dwight Davis creates Tennis Cup	Aug	14	Allied troops relieve besieged embassies in Peking
	27	Labour Party founded in UK		25	Friedrich Nietzsche, German philosopher, dies
Mar	13	British Army captures Bloemfontein		31	End of Taff Vale railway strike in S Wales
	14	US goes on Gold Standard		31	British Army occupies Johannesburg
Apr	4	Prince of Wales shot at in Belgium	Sep	19	Alfred Dreyfus pardoned in Paris
	14	World Exhibition opens in Paris	Oct	16	Tories win British General Election
	30	Hawaii officially becomes US territory		25	Britain annexes Transvaal
May	14	Second Olympic Games open in Paris	Nov	6	McKinley wins US election for Republicans
	17	British Army relieves Mafeking		22	Operetta composer Sir Arthur Sullivan dies
	19	Britain annexes Tonga Islands		30	Oscar Wilde dies in Paris
	24	Britain annexes Orange Free State			*The Arts*
	31	Boxer rebellion in China			George Bernard Shaw's *Three Plays for Puritans*
Jun	4	Rodin Exhibition opens in Paris			Anton Chekhov's play *Uncle Vanya*
	5	British Army takes Pretoria, capital of the Transvaal			Joseph Conrad's novel *Lord Jim*
	5	German liner *Deutschland III* sets new speed record			Sigmund Freud's study *The Interpretation of Dreams*
	19	Republicans nominate Roosevelt as US Vice-President			Puccini's opera *Tosca*

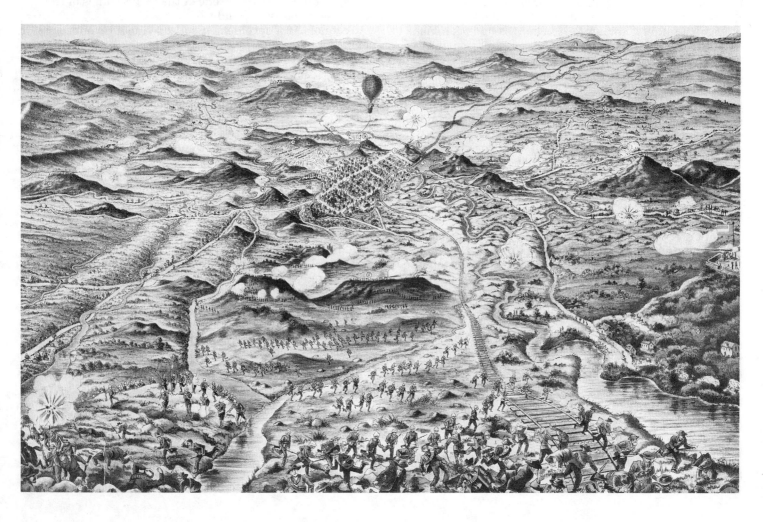

On his way to relieve Ladysmith, Buller inflicted heavy casualties at Spion Kop, a hill 24 miles west of the town.

Many Boxers were severely punished for their part in the rising. Here, a Boxer leader is decapitated in public.

The Boer War

Relations between the Boers, descendants of the original Dutch settlers in South Africa and more recent arrivals, mainly British, had been deteriorating for some years. The British government was also apprehensive of the Boer tendency to expand into areas they considered properly theirs. The tensions between the two sides exploded into war in October 1899. In the beginning the British were disadvantaged in numbers, weaponry and, most important, intimate knowledge of the terrain they were to fight over. The arrival of massive reinforcements soon rectified the first two of these but they were never able to match the Boers in the third. Their ponderous equipment, out-dated order of battle and Crimean tactics meant that the lightly armed, khaki-clad and nimble Boer horsemen could run rings round the sweating British redcoat, and they did so to great effect. But the British, with their overpoweringly superior reserves, were bound to win in the end, although they suffered many humiliating setbacks.

In their attempt to beat the Boer, the British were both relentless and harsh. Kitchener, Commander-in-Chief since November 1900, had Boer farms ruthlessly destroyed and his setting up of concentration camps for Boer women and children (disease and neglect killed 20,000) was to have chilling repercussions 30 years later.

Left: Ladysmith, an important rail junction in Natal, was besieged by the Boers on November 2nd 1899 and was relieved by General Buller on February 28th 1900.

The Boxer Rising

Throughout the nineteenth century, less populous but better managed countries had exploited the fragmented and almost helpless giant China, whose weakness had been increased by disabling internal quarrels. Countries like Japan, the United States and most of the great European states had carved out often conflicting spheres of interest through a complicated series of treaties with little respect for long-established Chinese susceptibilities. These foreign interventions occasioned a deep and growing resentment among Chinese of all classes. This became focused in the Boxers, a group of volunteer Chinese militiamen who were encouraged by the Chinese authorities, sometimes openly, sometimes secretly, to oppose the depredations of the 'foreign devils'. This opposition had already manifested itself in the occasional murder of foreign missionaries, but it flared into general violence in Peking with the murder of the German minister, Baron von Ketteler on June 20th, and the siege of the foreign legation.

The affronted foreign powers immediately formed an international expedition, well armed and commanded, which relieved the besieged legations on August 14th. The dowager Empress and her Court, who had encouraged the Boxers, fled from Peking on the arrival of the expedition and soon accepted the terms of the foreign powers. These included the punishment of 96 senior officials, large reparations in gold, the acceptance of a strategic string of foreign forts and expressions of regret.

The first of the many

The motor car was a wonderful new toy for the wealthy. All had to be custom-built – their engines by engineers and their coachwork by craftsmen whose proper trade was making phaetons and landaus. Of course they found it hard to shed old habits – one provided a whip-holder for the driver, while another firm claimed that it was not cruel to drive their automobiles fast uphill! Here, enthusiasts gather in Edinburgh for the start of the Automobile Club's 1,000-mile trial run round Britain.

Transport in 1900

While the motor car was fun for the few, the horse-drawn vehicle was still the reality for most people. In 1900, horses reigned supreme on the roads of the world and a huge stabling, watering, shoeing and feeding infrastructure existed to serve them.

The Interpretation of Dreams

In October 1900, the Austrian psychiatrist Sigmund Freud (1865–1939) published his seminal book. Although it was only read by a few specialist psychiatrists at first, the insights it contained were so new and profound that in time it would change the whole way in which human beings saw themselves and their psyches. Freud's psychoanalytic techniques of free association and interpretation of dreams have been developed by many different schools, but his ideas remain basic to them all. He is seen here with his eldest son.

In 1938, following the Nazi occupation of Austria, and the persecution of Jews, he left Vienna for London.

A revolutionary thinker

Max Planck (1858–1947) shown here in old age, first formulated his quantum theory in 1900. It was to have as profound an effect on physics as was Einstein's theory of relativity which he published five years later.

Ruskin dies

On January 20th, John Ruskin (1819–1900), the great British art critic and social reformer, died at his home in the Lake District. While none of his social theories was ever put into practice, they profoundly influenced the thinking and actions of more practical social reformers.

The art nouveau style

The new graceful curves of art nouveau, initiated and developed in France, were soon to decorate artefacts of every kind. This bed, made by Pérol Frères, was exhibited at the Paris Exhibition of 1900. It was expensive even then, being made of oak and mahogany with inlays of Hungarian ash, satinwood, sycamore and holly, and applied carvings in sabicu (Cuban hardwood).

Study for *The Burghers of Calais*

Auguste Rodin (1840–1917) established his reputation as a sculptor at his 1900 Exhibition in Paris where this study appeared. Conventional taste had been shocked by his *Balzac* of 1897 and would be again by his *Victor Hugo* in 1901.

Genius at work

Pablo Picasso (1881–1973) showed his virtuosity at a very early age. He was already an accomplished draughtsman as an adolescent and was producing excellent academic portraits at the age of 16. Very few of his early drawings survive but this rare, undated self-portrait comes from about the turn of the century. It shows none of the violent distortions that were to outrage his detractors a few years later with the launch of Cubism in the shape of his *Demoiselles d'Avignon* (see page 37).

In the course of his long career he went on to develop many other styles, including Surrealism, Expressionism and Abstractionism.

1901

Jan	1	Commonwealth of Australia comes into being
	10	World's largest oil strike in Texas
	22	Queen Victoria dies
Feb	2	Queen Victoria's funeral
	5	Pierpont Morgan has near monopoly of US steel industry
	14	King Edward VII opens his first parliament
	22	Mail steamer sinks in San Francisco Harbour
Mar	4	Inauguration of President McKinley
	12	Whitechapel Art Gallery opens in London
	19	Boer leader Botha rejects Kitchener's terms
Apr	24	200 killed in chemical explosion at Griesheim, Germany
May	13	PM Lord Salisbury attacks Irish home rule
	24	78 miners die in Caerphilly pit disaster in S Wales
Jun	17	Lloyd George condemns concentration camps in S Africa
	24	First Picasso exhibition in Paris
	26	*Lusitania* wrecked off Newfoundland – 350 rescued
Jul	2	400 die in New York heatwave
	4	Taft, US Republican, appointed Governor of Philippines
Aug	1	UK parliament votes extra £12.5 million for munitions
	4	Gold strike in S African Rand
	9	Colombian troops invade Venezuela
	12	British Govt defeated on Bill to limit working hours
	21	Cadillac car company formed in Detroit, Michigan
Sep	4	Taff Vale judgement: UK unions liable for strike losses
	6	President McKinley shot by anarchist
	7	Boxer rebellion ends in Peking treaty
	9	French painter Toulouse-Lautrec dies
	14	Vice-President Roosevelt becomes President of the US
	25	Britain annexes Ashanti kingdom in Africa
Oct	2	Vickers launches Britain's first submarine
	16	Black teacher dines with President Roosevelt
	23	General Buller sacked in S Africa for indiscretion
	28	34 die in race riots over dinner at White House
	29	McKinley's killer Czolgosz executed
Nov	10	North West Frontier province incorporated into India
	25	Japanese prince seeks Korean concessions from Russia
Dec	2	First safety-razor blades launched by Gillette in US
	10	First Nobel prizes awarded
	12	First transatlantic radio transmission made by Marconi

The Arts

Anton Chekhov's play *Three Sisters*

Rudyard Kipling's novel *Kim*

Thomas Mann's novel *Buddenbrooks*

Rachmaninov's *Piano Concerto No. 2*

August Strindberg's play *Dance of Death*

Queen Victoria dies

A distraught courtier greeted a familiar portly figure: 'What shall we do, Sir, the Queen is dead?', to receive a cool but firm reply, 'But the King is alive!' Both the new Edward VII and the courtier had a point. Their entire lives had been spent in the shadow of a woman who had been on the throne for so long (63 years) that she seemed like a force of nature. She had come to personify an age which as late as the 1980s could still be instanced as a time of vigorous enterprise and moral rectitude. So the courtier was right in that it was impossible to see how the new century would develop without her reassuring presence. But the King was right too in that things would carry on very much as before. Neither King nor courtier could foresee the coming catastrophe which would extinguish Victorian certainties for ever.

The early years of her reign had seen the full flowering of the industrial revolution, culminating in the profusion of artefacts displayed at the Great Exhibition of 1851. The middle years of her reign saw Britain established as the greatest industrial and military power in the world. The end of her reign would see Britain beginning to be overtaken by the more powerful economies of the United States and Germany.

This lithograph by William Nicholson would not have amused the Queen.

Victoria had gone into a much criticised semi-retirement on the death of her husband Albert in 1861. Even so, she maintained a firm grasp of events and was never averse to expressing her point of view strongly to her Prime Ministers, of whom she had ten, some serving her several times.

Her nine children married into many of the royal houses of Europe and her children and grandchildren were established on the thrones of Germany, Russia, Sweden, Spain, Norway and Romania. Many of the dwindling band of royalty today are her direct descendants.

The word 'Victorian' still excites powerful emotions among politicians and historians, who have yet to arrive at a consensus about this powerful woman and her extraordinary times.

Kaiser Wilhelm II of Germany, seen standing beside Edward VII at Queen Victoria's funeral, was her grandson

through her eldest daughter, Princess Victoria, who had married Prince Frederick of Prussia.

Edward VII was 59 when he ascended the throne. He only reigned nine years before dying suddenly of pneumonia.

HMS *Hyacinth* goes to sea

Britain's Royal Navy presented Germany with her greatest challenge. The growing industrial strength of Germany was reflected in the desire to catch up with and surpass Great Britain in every respect, and the comparative strengths of their navies was the most tangible yardstick. Britain was consistently ahead in naval innovation, here evidenced by a new kind of warship, although Germany was consistently superior in engineering, the technical quality and constructional strength of her ships; a situation curiously repeated in both World Wars. The years between 1900 and the beginning of the First World War were to witness the greatest naval arms race the world has ever seen.

First transatlantic wireless transmission

On Thursday December 12th, the Italian physicist Guglielmo Marconi (1874–1937) received the first transatlantic wireless signals at St John's, Newfoundland. A continuous transmission of the three-dot Morse code for the letter S was sent from his station at Poldhu in Cornwall and received at Signal Hill, overlooking St John's Harbour, at 12.30 p.m., 1.10 p.m. and 2.20 p.m. Bad weather had interrupted previous attempts, in which the aerial had been raised by balloon. The successful attempt used kites (left).

Ending and beginning

William McKinley (1843–1901), 25th President of the USA, was in his second term of office when he was assassinated at the Pan-American Exhibition in Buffalo, New York State.

McKinley, born in Niles, Ohio, enlisted in the Union Army as a private and was a major when the Civil War ended. An able speaker, he studied law and served as a Congressman before becoming governor of Ohio and in 1896 being elected President. He was following the mood of the people rather than leading them when in 1898 he committed his nation to war with Spain over the matter of Cuban independence. Under McKinley the USA acquired the epithet 'imperialist', Puerto Rico, Guam, the Philippines, Hawaii, and a taste for international power politics.

None of that motivated his assassin, the anarchist Leon Czolgosz, who shot McKinley in the stomach at point-blank range with a revolver hidden in a handkerchief.

Gospel of wealth

The American iron and steel magnate Andrew Carnegie (1835–1918) sold the Carnegie Steel Company to the US Steel Corporation for $447,000,000 – big money at any time, and in 1901 unprecedented. From that year he went into a new business: systematic philanthropic endowment.

Carnegie's life story embodies classic American ideals. Born in Dunfermline, Scotland, the son of a weaver, he emigrated with his parents and settled in Allegheny County, Pittsburgh, Pennsylvania. He was an assiduous self-improver. His skill as a telegrapher started his rise with the Pennsylvania Railroad, and gradual investments – sleeping cars, oil, iron and steel – led to the creation of his vast enterprise.

In 1901 he set up the Carnegie Trust for the Universities of Scotland. Then came the Carnegie Institution, Washington (1902) and numerous others.

Popular movement

The first year of the 20th century was the start of a decade in American history unparalleled, in at least one respect, either before or since. It was to be the decade when immigration into the USA was at its peak, the high spot of what has been called the greatest migration in history.

The poor, the hungry, and the oppressed were leaving in hundreds of thousands from eastern and southern Europe: Russia, Poland, Austria-Hungary, the Balkans, Italy . . . Between 700,000 and 900,000 a year passed through Ellis Island, America's major immigration station from 1892 until 1943. The immigration process at Ellis Island is still an acute if mixed memory for millions of Americans.

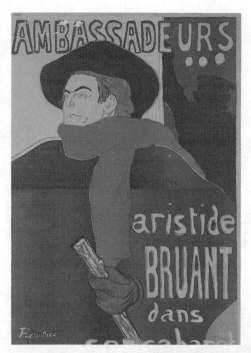

Toulouse-Lautrec dies

Henri de Toulouse-Lautrec (1864–1901) has come to typify the Bohemian artist, mixing with the dancers, entertainers and whores, the absinthe drinkers and others who lived in Montmartre and who formed much of his subject matter.

He was born at Albi but soon moved to Paris, where his instinct for low life drew him to Montmartre, and it was here that he produced his most typical and finest work. He was commissioned to produce posters for the music halls which abounded in the area and his first appeared in 1891, when he was 26. He went on producing them, alongside more conventional paintings and drawings, until the end of his life. The poster of Aristide Bruant, (left) is typical of his work.

Toulouse-Lautrec was of distinctly odd appearance, with a body too big for his stumpy little legs, the result of an accident in his youth when he broke both thighs.

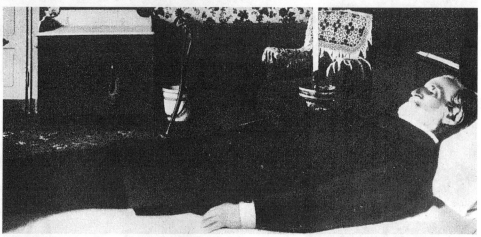

Leopold II, King of the Belgians

This year saw growing controversy over King Leopold II's personal ownership of the Congo Free State.

Verdi dies

Giuseppe Verdi (1813–1901), composer of some of the world's greatest operas, died on January 27th. His first major opera *Nabucco* was produced in 1842; his last, *Falstaff*, in 1893.

South African gold

Thousands of men rushed to the Rand after gold was discovered there on August 4th.

1902

Jan	1	El Greco exhibition held in Madrid
	18	US Commission chooses Panama as site of canal
Feb	1	Women's foot binding abolished in China
	6	Italian govt calls up railwaymen to prevent strike
	15	Berlin's first underground railway opened
	25	Boers rout British Army at Klerksdorp
Apr	7	Texaco oil company formed in US
	8	Russia agrees to withdraw troops from Manchuria
	13	New car speed record of 74 mph set in France
May	1	Tornado kills 416 in Dacca, India
	12	Miners' strike in US
	28	British march against the 'Mad Mullah' in E Africa
	31	Peace of Vereeniging ends Boer War
Jun	18	Death of British writer and satirist Samuel Butler
	23	Albert Einstein starts work in Swiss patent office
	23	Germany, Austria-Hungary and Italy renew Triple Alliance
	24	King Edward VII has appendicitis. Coronation delayed
Jul	12	Arthur Balfour becomes Conservative PM
	12	Kitchener receives hero's welcome in London

Aug	1	100 miners die in pit explosion in Wollongong, Australia
	9	King Edward VII crowned in Westminster Abbey
	18	Shah of Persia visits Britain
	29	Over 9,000 die from cholera in Egypt
	30	Labour MP Keir Hardie protests at Taff Vale decision
Sep	14	20,000 in Dublin demonstrate against British govt
	28	15,000 requests a week for S African goldmining permits
	29	Emile Zola, French novelist, dies
Oct	15	Roosevelt's threat to send troops in ends miners' strike
	23	Irish MPs in violent scenes in British Parliament
Dec	9	Swiss Parliament agrees to build Simplon railway tunnel
	10	First Aswan Dam on Nile completed
	18	1st meeting of Committee of Imperial Defence in London

The Arts

Joseph Conrad's novella *Heart of Darkness*

Rudyard Kipling's *Just So Stories*

Auguste Rodin's sculpture *Romeo and Juliet*

Henry James's novel *The Wings of the Dove*

Arthur Conan Doyle's *The Hound of the Baskervilles*

The Empire builder

Cecil John Rhodes (1853–1902) died on March 26th in a small cottage by the sea near Cape Town. In his short life – he was only 48 when he died – Rhodes had made a large fortune, been Prime Minister and had had a country named after him. He was a man of enormous drive and energy, ambitious for himself and his country, and willing to spend all his time and money in achieving his ends. He wanted to bring large tracts of Africa under the British flag and he succeeded.

The diamond industry

English by birth, he first went out to South Africa in 1870 because of ill health. He made his fortune by gaining effective control of the diamond industry of South Africa under the name of the British South Africa Company. This he founded in 1889, although his activities as head of De Beers Consolidated Mines and Goldfields of South Africa Ltd. had already made him rich and powerful years before. He had been granted mineral rights in Matabeleland by King Lobengula in 1888 and, with the encouragement of a royal charter, immediately began to put pressure on Transvaal. He became Prime Minister of Cape Colony in 1890 but six years later he resigned through his connection with the notorious Jameson Raid into the Transvaal, which was intended to start a revolt against Kruger, the Boer leader.

Rhodesia

Undoubtedly Cecil Rhodes' greatest gift to the British Empire was his creation of Rhodesia in 1895 when the territories south of the Zambesi River controlled by the British South Africa Company were formally accepted into the Empire under his own name. Today he is equally well remembered for the Rhodes scholarships which were founded at Oxford under the terms of his will.

Kitchener wins

Although Lord Roberts claimed that he had won the Boer War in September 1900, the Boers simply ignored him and went on winning battles and killing British soldiers. Roberts was quietly recalled in November, and was succeeded as Commander-in-Chief by his chief of staff Lord Kitchener who quickly summed up the situation, asking for more men and supplies so that he could finally defeat the Boers.

Kitchener was very popular in Britain. His defeat of the Mahdi at Omdurman in 1898 had avenged the death of General Gordon at Khartoum and restored the reputation of the British Army. He had returned from the Sudan as a hero and he did not intend to return from South Africa as anything less.

Concentration camps

He countered the Boers' highly successful hit-and-run tactics by erecting a line of blockhouses and barbed wire fences across the Boer lines of advance and retreat. He burned their farms and collected all their women and children into concentration camps,where thousands died of sickness. Most effective of all, he had a quarter of a million men in action against the Boers' 40,000. The odds in men and the sheer weight of the British military machine began to tell upon the Boers, and their more realistic leaders realised that they could not win.

Peace

They asked for peace and Kitchener accepted their surrender at Pretoria. At the last hour before midnight on the 31st May, the Boer war was finally over with the signing of the Treaty of Vereeniging. Kitchener duly got his victory triumph (right) on his return to Britain.

Krupp dies of a stroke

Friedrich Krupp (1854–1902), head of the great German steel and armament company, died very suddenly on November 22nd at the early age of 48. His father Alfred, who had founded the company, died in 1887 and so Friedrich had been in charge since he was 33.

Alfred, a trained metallurgist, had designed every detail of the great hammer shown here himself, and it first went into operation as early as 1861. It was primarily designed to forge huge cast-steel ingots weighing up to 50,000 pounds and was used to make propeller shafts and similar ultra-heavy artefacts.

Although a shock, the death of Friedrich made no great difference to the Krupp dynasty. He was succeeded by his daughter Bertha whose husband changed his name to Krupp and took over the running of the family firm. They went on to make armaments for the Kaiser including 'Big Bertha' – named after Bertha Krupp – the 98-ton howitzer that shelled Verdun. Later, they supported Adolf Hitler and the Nazis into the Second World War. The company is still in business today.

No death in Venice

On July 15th, Venetians woke up to a strange new skyline. The ancient bell tower which had dominated their famous city for almost exactly a thousand years was no longer there. It had quietly collapsed the previous day and was now no more than a heap of rubble in St Mark's Square.

Cracks had been seen in the 324-foot high structure for some time, and there had been concern about its stability, but no one was expecting such a total disaster. In fact, a team of architects was engaged in a survey of the tower when the collapse occurred.

Joseph Conrad

Joseph Conrad (1857-1924), published his novella *Heart of Darkness* this year. Born Teodor Józef Konrad Korzeniowski in the Ukraine, Conrad became a merchant seaman, landing in Britain in 1878. Although he spoke no English on arrival, he gained a master mariner's certificate in 1886 and took British nationality. He started his writing career in 1894 and published a number of novels in English which vividly depict man's psychological isolation, life at sea, and exotic countries.

The Lotus Lamp

Art nouveau was the dominant decorative style of the early years of the century. Designers, art studios and manufacturers imposed it on a variety of furnishings and decorations, some bizarre, some stunningly beautiful. This lamp from the Tiffany Studios of New York shows the art nouveau style at its splendid best.

Just So Stories

Rudyard Kipling (1865–1936) was an established author by the turn of the century. He started his writing career as a journalist on an Indian newspaper, and published his first book on his Indian experiences, *Plain Tales from the Hills* in 1888 – followed by *Barrack Room Ballads* in 1892. The immensely popular *Jungle Book* appeared two years later. Kipling was also an accomplished illustrator, as this picture from the *Just So Stories*, published in 1902, shows.

Charles Rennie Mackintosh

Mackintosh (1868–1928), who worked almost entirely in Scotland, translated the fashionable art nouveau style into his own unique architectural idiom. His most famous building was the Glasgow School of Art, built in 1900, although his Willow Tea Rooms, also in Glasgow, are about equally well known. The house in the picture, which dates from 1902 and is typical of his work, is the Hill House, Helensburgh, seen from the south east.

Mackintosh was a meticulous designer and took great care that the interiors of his houses, and their decorations and furnishings, were in tune with the exterior appearance.

30,000 die in seconds

An incandescent cloud of poisonous gas wiped out the entire population of St Pierre, capital of the island of Martinique in the French West Indies. The gas came from the exploding peak of a nearby volcano, Mount Pelée, that everyone believed was dormant. But enormous pressures had built up inside the volcano and these had been released in a titanic explosion that blew the entire peak away. There was, in fact, a sole survivor of the disaster: a prisoner arrested for drunkenness and held in a cell deep inside a thick-walled prison.

1903

Jan	1	King Edward VII proclaimed Emperor of India		31	Reports of atrocities by all sides in the Balkans
	22	US signs treaty with Colombia to build canal at Panama	Sep	1	Macedonian rebels blow up Hungarian steamer; kill 29
	24	Joint US–UK commission to decide Alaskan frontier		8	Turks massacre 50,000 Bulgarians
Feb	3	British capture Kano from Nigerian rebels		8	UK Trades Union Congress opposes govt's tariff policy
Mar	3	Scott in the Antarctic reaches furthest point south		17	Joseph Chamberlain resigns over tariff reform
	14	US Senate ratifies construction of canal at Panama		17	Turks massacre 10,000 in Macedonia
	18	Anti-clerical French govt dissolves all religious orders	Oct	13	US: First baseball World Series won by Boston Red Sox
Apr	2	Bloody clashes between students and police in Spain	Nov	2	President Roosevelt sends three gunships to Panama
	6	Dreyfus documents are proved army forgeries in France		3	Colombian rebels proclaim Panama's independence
	14	Bulgarians massacre 165 Muslims in Macedonia		6	US government recognises Panama as independent State
	16	Scores of Jews massacred in pogrom in Bessarabia		12	10,000 Chinese troops move into Manchuria
May	1	Edward VII visits France		18	US and Panama sign canal treaty
	21	Chamberlain launches 'Tariff League'	Dec	10	Pierre and Marie Curie awarded Nobel Prize for physics
Jun	4	Russian decree restricts Jewish ownership of property		17	Wright brothers make first heavier-than-air flight
	10	Army officers kill King and Queen of Serbia			*The Arts*
	16	Socialists make big gains in German general election			Samuel Butler's novel *The Way of All Flesh*
Jul	3	UK and Japan demand that Russians leave Manchuria			Henry James' novel *The Ambassadors*
Aug	9	Pope Pius X crowned before a crowd of 70,000 in Rome			Jack London's novel *The Call of the Wild*
	12	Colombian Senate rejects US treaty for canal at Panama			George Bernard Shaw's play *Man and Superman*

Man takes to the air

There had been many attempts to get a heavier-than-air machine off the ground over the years, but the aeroplanes so carefully constructed were all either underpowered or aerodynamically unsound. It took the engineering skill and the design genius of Wilbur (1867–1912) and Orville (1871–1948) Wright to finally get a machine into the air at Kittyhawk, North Carolina on December 17th.

Although their aircraft looks primitive and rickety it was, in fact, a highly sophisticated piece of engineering design, well-balanced aerodynamically, with efficient control surfaces and a powerful engine.

The impression is sometimes given that the Wright brothers were small town engineers who got it right by chance. This is far from the truth, and the famous first flight (seen below) was very carefully prepared. Both were skilled and experienced inventors, and Orville, who actually made the first flight, had tested their flying machine in a home-made wind tunnel before risking it to the air.

A Balkan assassination

The King and Queen of Serbia were assassinated by a group of disaffected army officers. King Alexander and Queen Draga, hiding in a cupboard in their bedroom, were shot by officers, enraged both by the Queen's unsavoury reputation and the King's determination to impose a more repressive government on his country. The King's marriage to a woman with a past had deeply offended his people and the final straw was his decision to move the Serbian War School from Belgrade. However, the causes of the assassination went much deeper. Alexander (above) was succeeded by King Peter.

Edward, Emperor of India

Lord Curzon, Viceroy of India, proclaimed King Edward VII Emperor of India at a magnificent ceremony on the plains outside Delhi on January 1st. The ceremony, known as the Imperial Durbar saw a hundred Indian princes, resplendent in their bejewelled uniforms and accompanied by their State elephants, swear eternal loyalty to their faraway master in England. Above, the Maharajah of Bundi is seen making his ceremonial obeisance to Lord Curzon.

Ford Motor Company founded

Almost as important historically as the world's first heavier-than-air flight was Henry Ford's decision to go into the automobile business. Ford (1863–1947), who had built his first car in 1893, transformed the car, then a hand-crafted luxury for the wealthy few, into the means of travel for the many. And his invention and development of the mass production line altered the face of industry. Ford founded his company in 1903 to produce cars like the one on the left (notice the flat back tyre). He was backed by a group of businessmen from Detroit who believed there might be something in the horseless carriage, and put the money up to start his factory. Ford became Vice President of the company as well as its chief engineer. He also owned a quarter of the shares.

Nobel Prize for discoverers of radium

Pierre and Marie Curie shared the Nobel Prize for Physics with another French scientist, Henri Becquerel for their work on radioactivity. Marie Curie (1867–1934) was the first woman ever to be honoured in this way. She is seen here with her husband in their laboratory. The couple first discovered that uranium was radioactive and then went on to isolate polonium – named after her native Poland – and radium in 1898. She won a second Nobel Prize for chemistry in 1911.

South Sea painter dies

Paul Gauguin (1848–1903) died in the Marquesas Islands in the South Pacific. He had earlier given up a career as a prosperous stockbroker to become a full-time painter, although he had never attended art school or had any formal training as an artist. He had abandoned his wife and family for a life of art and although his friends and acquaintances were outraged by his action, he believed that he had something special to offer the world as a painter. Time has proved him right. This self-portrait is typical of his work. The halo is an ironic joke.

578 die in Chicago theatre fire

On the last day of the old year, celebrations to welcome 1904 quickly turned to tragedy as the Iroquois Theatre in Chicago was swiftly enveloped in flames. A variety show was in progress when a fire was noticed backstage. The asbestos safety curtain was jammed and flames quickly spread through the theatre as panic-stricken people fought to escape. Many were trampled to death. Others died when they jumped from the balcony or from crowded fire escapes. It was found later that the theatre had violated many safety regulations. Chicago has a bad reputation for fires: the entire city had been burned to the ground in 1871.

A new Pope

Pope Leo XIII, who had been in office since 1878, died on July 20th at the age of 93. He had entered the priesthood in 1837 and became Bishop of Perugia in 1846. He was seen as a moderate rather than a reforming pope and spent much of his papacy trying to reduce class warfare. He was succeeded by Pope Pius X who was enthroned before a crowd of 70,000 people in Rome on August 9th. Above: a rare picture of the new Pope returning from an outing in his carriage.

Newgate Prison closed

The grim old prison at Newgate, London, finally closed its doors to be demolished. The first prison on the site was opened as early as 1190 but had been rebuilt and extended several times before being burned down in the Gordon Riots of 1780. The new Newgate, completed in 1783, was the scene of many executions. Anything saleable, such as the doors (above), was put up for public auction.

1904

Jan	11	British troops massacre 1,000 Dervishes in Somaliland
	12	Henry Ford sets new car speed record of 91.37 mph
	22	Norwegian city of Ålesund burnt down: 12,000 homeless
Feb	3	Irish Nationalist leader Redmond calls for home rule
	5	US withdraws forces from Cuba
	6	Maryland disenfranchises black voters
Mar	5	New enquiry into Dreyfus case in France
Apr	8	UK and France sign Entente Cordiale
May	4	US Army engineers begin work on Panama Canal
	4	Charles Rolls and Henry Royce agree to make cars
Jun	7	Fire destroys paddle steamer in New York: 693 dead
	23	US: President Roosevelt nominated for another term
	28	Immigrant steamer *Norge* wrecked off Iceland: 700 die
Jul	1	3rd Olympic Games open in St Louis, US
	15	Anton Chekhov, Russian writer, dies
	21	Trans-Siberian Railway completed
	28	Russian Interior Minister von Plehve assassinated
Aug	7	Railway bridge collapses in Colorado, US: 125 die

Sep	1	Helen Keller graduates from Radcliffe College, US
	20	US Army rejects heavier-than-air flying machines
Oct	3	African tribes rise against Germans in SW Africa
	10	Kurdish tribesmen massacre Armenians in Turkey
	21	Russian Baltic Fleet sinks two Hull trawlers
	24	Four French officers charged with lying in Dreyfus case
	27	Subway opens in New York
	31	John Fleming at London University invents radio valve
Nov	8	Theodore Roosevelt wins US presidential election
	18	Gold discovered in Rhodesia
	28	Rebels beaten by German troops in SW Africa
	30	Japanese lose 12,000 troops in capture of Port Arthur

The Arts

J. M. Barrie's play *Peter Pan*

Joseph Conrad's novel *Nostromo*

Anton Chekhov's play *The Cherry Orchard*

Giacomo Puccini's opera *Madam Butterfly*

Henry James's novel *The Golden Bowl*

Blitzkrieg!

Towards the end of the 19th century Japan had emerged from centuries of international isolation and remodelled its state and military on western lines. Japanese ambition for influence on the Asian mainland, especially in Korea, collided with Russia's eastward expansion. In 1898 Russia had secured the ice-free port of Port Arthur on the North China coast and had then linked Vladivostok to the Trans-Siberian Railway.

Unable to settle differences with Russia by negotiation, in February 1904 Japan made a surprise attack on the Russian fleet at Port Arthur, and occupied Seoul in Korea. Russia faced tremendous logistical problems in the ensuing war, forced to move men and materiel along the single-track Trans-Siberian Railway from the west. Enormous numbers of troops were involved attacking entrenched positions. The intricately-organised defences of Port

Arthur fell only on January 1st 1905, with 60,000 Japanese casualties. Below left: Japanese sailors practising gunfire at sea. Right: a Russian post in Manchuria.

In an attempt to swing the balance of naval forces, Russia dispatched its Baltic fleet, much of it having to sail around the Cape. On the way they sank two British fishing trawlers off the Dogger Bank in the North Sea, thinking they were Japanese warships.

The British Army enters Tibet

The British had their own problems in the Far East. A British expeditionary force sent to Tibet was met with unexpected hostility and asked to withdraw. This unthinkable suggestion was firmly rejected and the expedition pushed on to be met with active resistance from Tibetans armed with swords and pistols. A few brisk engagements with British troops firing Maxim guns soon put an end to resistance. The Dalai Lama fled and British troops entered Lhasa on August 2nd.

Herzl dies

Theodor Herzl (1860–1904), founder of modern Zionism, died on July 3rd. He was born in Hungary and spent almost all his adult life engaged in the fight to establish a national home for the Jewish people. He published a famous book *The Jewish State* in 1896 and was the convenor of a number of Zionist Congresses. The sixth, the last one before he died, was held in Basle, Switzerland. Here it was decided that only Palestine could ever be accepted as the Jewish homeland (Uganda and Palestine, among others, had been suggested as possible sites).

St Louis blues

The Great World Fair, at St Louis, USA, finally closed its doors on December 1st, having been visited by millions of people from all over the world. Its displays of modern technology, such as the Palace of Mines and Metallurgy (above) had aroused great interest.

Broadway to City Hall

The New York subway opened a line with electric trains between Broadway and City Hall. This contemporary engraving shows the method of construction.

Dribbling dogs

Ivan Pavlov (1849–1936), the distinguished Russian physiologist, was awarded the Nobel Prize for his work on the digestive system. It was, however, his work on conditioned reflexes that won him world fame. His experimental animals were dogs. Every time he fed them he would ring a bell. After repeating this process many times he found that the dogs had come to associate the sound of the bell with food and would begin to salivate at the sound of the bell itself. He had thus demonstrated that the reflex of salivation could be conditioned and, by inference, that other reflexes could be similarly conditioned.

More Russian riots

The cities of Russia were no strangers to riots but there was a particularly violent one in St Petersburg (above) when a charge of mounted police seriously injured more than 50 people. The Tsar had continually promised better living conditions for his people, especially the peasants, but his failure to keep his promises led to much unrest. The débâcle of the war with Japan made the position even worse. Many of the riots were fomented by university students, most of whom were violently anti-monarchist and easily influenced by the revolutionaries who were becoming more active both in Moscow and St Petersburg.

Dvořák dies

The Czech composer Antonin Dvořák (1841–1904), died on May 1st at the age of 62. Although he was a master of most forms of classical music and composed symphonies, chamber music and tone poems, he was a great admirer of the folk music of his native Bohemia and used folk tunes as a basis for much of his own music.

The boy who wouldn't grow up

J. M. Barrie's (1860–1937) famous play had its first performance in Britain on December 27th, making Christmas happier not only for its initial audiences, but for generations of children afterwards. The tale of a little boy who refused to grow up, *Peter Pan* quickly became a classic.

Helen Keller graduates

Helen Keller (1880–1968), who had been deaf and blind since a childhood illness at the age of two, graduated with honours from Radcliffe College in the USA. She was now qualified as a doctor. Helen Keller had escaped from her dark, silent world through the dedication of an inspired teacher, Anne Sullivan Macy. In 1902 she published *The Story of My Life*, which won her world fame.

1905

Jan	1	Trans-Siberian Railway officially opened
	1	Russians surrender Port Arthur to Japanese
	19	75,000 Russian workers strike – growing disturbances
	21	US govt agrees to run affairs of Dominican Republic
	22	Russian strikers' march fired on: 500 die
	25	Tsar Nicholas II promises reforms
Feb	2	Maxim Gorky, Russian writer, released from prison
	17	An assassin's bomb kills Grand Duke Sergei in Moscow
Mar	3	Tsar Nicholas II agrees to form a Consultative Assembly
	24	French writer Jules Verne dies
	30	President Roosevelt asked to mediate in Far East War
	31	Conan Doyle resurrects fictional Sherlock Holmes
Apr	2	Simplon tunnel through Alps officially opened
	4	Indian earthquake kills 10,000 in Lahore district
	8	Reservoir collapses in Madrid, Spain: 400 killed
	30	Tsar Nicholas II guarantees freedom of conscience
May	24	Anti-semitic riots in Warsaw: many Jews are killed
	25	Europe's first flight of heavier-than-air machine
	27	Russian fleet annihilated by Japanese
Jun	3	Cossacks charge rioting crowds in St Petersburg

	7	Norway decides on independence from Sweden
	23	Tsar Nicholas II breaks promise re: elected Assembly
	27	Mutiny on Russian battleship *Potemkin*: officers killed
Jul	1	Albert Einstein propounds Theory of Relativity
	3	Separation of Church and State in France
	8	The crew of the *Potemkin* surrender to Rumania
	10	Parliamentary reshuffle means 22 fewer Irish MPs
Sept	5	Hundreds die in clashes between Armenians and Tartars
	5	Russians and Japanese sign peace treaty
	9	Thousands die in earthquake in Calabria, Italy
	12	Japanese navy's flagship *Mikasa* sinks: 544 die
Oct	5	Wright brothers make record flight of 38 minutes
Nov	18	Prince Carl of Denmark chosen to be King of Norway
Dec	30	Revolt in Moscow brutally put down

The Arts

Claude Debussy's three symphonic sketches *La Mer*

E. M. Forster's novel *Where Angels Fear to Tread*

Franz Lehar's operetta *The Merry Widow*

Henri Rousseau's painting *The Hungry Lion*

Edith Wharton's novel *The House of Mirth*

Problems in Russia

Bloody Sunday

In Russia, widespread civil discontent erupted into revolution. On January 22nd, a crowd intending to present a petition of grievances to Tsar Nicholas II, led by a young priest, Father Gapon (above left), was fired upon by troops. Hundreds died, most trampled to death in the panic. Following the massacre, Tsarist Russia was shaken by a series of strikes in many towns. There were also demands for some form of parliamentary system from workers, and the small political community, alike. Peasants began to seize land from their landlords and troops were repeatedly needed to suppress revolts in the countryside.

Parts of the military too displayed revolutionary zeal. The crew of the battleship *Potemkin* mutinied and sailed the battleship around the Black Sea, an event commemorated by Sergei Eisenstein's film. (The *Potemkin* is shown below left.)

Many political organisations sprang up to represent particular sections of society including new political parties, noble associations and illegal trades unions. In St Petersburg workers elected a *Soviet* ('Council' in Russian) which publicly debated such matters as working conditions, pay and workers' representation.

The Russo–Japanese war

Events to the west led to a loss of confidence in Russia's ability to continue the war against Japan. In the first half of 1905 Russia suffered two reverses. The Battle of Mukden in March, involving 750,000 men, although militarily inconclusive, was a serious reverse with over 70,000 Russians killed. (Above the town of Mukden is seen in flames.) When the Baltic fleet finally arrived in May, it was immediately destroyed off Tsushima Island. (Opposite is the bridge of the triumphant Japanese flagship *Mikasa*.)

The October Manifesto

The failure to defeat Japan further undermined the prestige of the monarchy. To answer the clamour for a popular voice in government the Tsar announced the October Manifesto, promising to establish an elective Parliament (*Duma*) with substantial legislative powers.

The Fundamental Laws of May 1906 set up the parliamentary mechanism without making the Cabinet responsible to the Duma as many had demanded. The Duma was frequently dissolved when it showed signs of fractiousness. The small electorate, changed by successive manipulations of the franchise, produced an assembly increasingly out of tune with many of the more radical demands of workers and peasants. The limited concessions and the loyalty of the bulk of the armed forces had, however, provided the Tsar with a platform from which to attempt to build a new political consensus for ruling the Russian Empire.

Princess Mary's diamond

Princess Mary of Teck, later Queen Mary, had been engaged to the Duke of Clarence before his death in 1892, and a year later married his younger brother, later George V. Here she is seen wearing the principal stone from the Cullinan diamond, the biggest ever, found in the Transvaal in January 1905. It was presented to Edward VII in 1907 and cut into several large stones. It is now in the Royal Sceptre.

Nobel Prize for discovering tubercular bacillus

World-famous bacteriologist Robert Koch (1843–1910) won the Nobel Prize for Medicine for identifying the bacillus that caused the scourge of tuberculosis. Koch was already renowned for his discoveries in the field of anthrax, cholera, sleeping sickness and bubonic plague and this latest discovery crowned a life dedicated to the eradication of disease. Koch is shown (bottom left) towards the end of his life.

Norway becomes independent

The Norwegians had long been dissatisfied with their Swedish overlords and on June 7th they dissolved the Swedish-Norwegian Union and declared their independence. A referendum on August 13th found that 80 per cent of the Norwegian people wanted this. They also wanted a new King and they chose Prince Carl, the second son of King Frederick of Denmark. He renamed himself King Haakon and is seen (below) with Queen Maud, daughter of King Edward VII, and the young Crown Prince Olaf.

1906

Jan	1	General von Moltke is new head of German armed forces		15	Edward VII visits Kaiser Wilhelm II in Germany
	2	New French Darraq racing car breaks record at 108 mph		18	Massive earthquake in Chile kills hundreds
	4	US dancer Isadora Duncan banned by Belgian police	Sep	9	100 Jews murdered in Siedlce, Poland
Feb	2	530 injured in Paris in dispute over Church property		20	Launch of British liners *Mauretania* and *Adriatic*
	3	Japan decides to double size of its navy by 1908		28	US Secretary of War William Taft intervenes in Cuba
	7	Liberal landslide in British General Election	Oct	3	'SOS' adopted as international distress signal in Berlin
Mar	2	Tsar Nicholas II gives Russian Parliament some power		5	1,000 prisoners a day exiled to Siberia in Russia
	11	1,200 miners die in explosion at pit in N. France		9	Joseph Glidden, US inventor of barbed wire, dies
	14	British Parliament accepts principle of old age pensions		24	11 suffragettes jailed for demonstrations in London
	20	Russian soldiers kill officers at Sebastopol, Crimea		25	Georges Clemenceau becomes French PM
Apr	7	Eruption of Vesuvius, Italy, kills hundreds	Nov	2	Leon Trotsky, Russian revolutionary, exiled to Siberia
	18	Severe earthquake in San Francisco		15	Launch of world's biggest battleship in Japan, *Satsuma*
May	10	1st Duma (Russian Parliament) meets in St Petersburg		26	President Roosevelt returns from historic trip to Panama
	12	Duma against Tsar over amnesty for political prisoners	Dec	6	Self-govt granted to Transvaal and Orange River Colony
Jun	5	German naval bill provides for more battleships		10	Leopold II of Belgium denies abuse of Congo workers
	5	Peter Stolypin becomes Russian PM		14	1st submarine, U1, enters German navy
	7	*Lusitania*, world's biggest liner, launched in Glasgow		30	Josephine Butler, British social reformer dies
	17	Russian officials admit they planned Bielostock pogrom			*The Arts*
	23	UK: Representatives of women press PM for vote			Winston Churchill's *Life of Lord Randolph Churchill*
Jul	12	Alfred Dreyfus awarded French Legion of Honour			John Galsworthy's novel *The Man of Property*
	21	Duma dissolved and martial law declared in Russia			Jules Massenet's opera *Ariane*
	23	Exiled Duma calls on Russians to refuse to pay taxes			Georges Rouault's painting *At the Mirror*
Aug	4	Italian liner *Sirio* wrecked off Spain: 200 drowned			Upton Sinclair's novel *The Jungle*

Labour's first leader

James Keir Hardie (1856–1915) was born into a poor Scottish mining family and became a miner himself. It soon became clear to the miners he worked with that he was a man of exceptional talents and he rapidly advanced in the Scottish Miners' Federation and in the infant Labour movement; he was elected to Parliament in 1892. In January 1893, the Independent Labour Party was formed with Keir Hardie as its leader and in February 1900 the Labour Representation Committee (soon to become known as the Labour Party) came into being to attempt to elect Labour MPs to Parliament. Ramsay MacDonald was appointed Organising Secretary, although there was some confusion as to what his exact responsibilities would be, and Keir Hardie remained very much in command.

When, in February 1906 the Liberals won a landslide victory at the General Election, they were accompanied by 29 new members of the Labour Representation Committee. The

triumphant Liberals did not realise that they had unwittingly let a Trojan horse into Parliament. Within half a lifetime the Labour Party would have replaced them as the main party of opposition. This was all too clearly demonstrated at the local elections later that year when the Liberals lost not only to the Conservatives but, significantly, to a growing number of Labour candidates who described themselves as Socialists. In April Keir Hardie introduced a Bill to give the vote to women, but it was not voted on in Parliament, much to the chagrin of the growing suffragette movement. The same Bill was decisively defeated in March of the next year.

Keir Hardie was a republican, although not a very vocal or active one, and the following year there was much speculation when he was not invited to a Royal Garden Party for Members of Parliament. He was still active in 1911 when there was a strike of dockers, railwaymen and transport workers, addressing many meetings. He died in 1915 at the age of 59.

Left: A contemporary cartoon of Hardie by Spy, in *Vanity Fair*.

Record flight in France

Alberto Santos-Dumont, the Brazilian aviator, made a record flight of 235 yards in his flying machine in France on November 12th. Santos-Dumont, who started his flying career as a balloonist, then began to construct dirigible airships. In 1901 he won the Deutsch de la Meurthe prize of 100,000 francs by becoming the first man to fly a dirigible airship for half an hour. He then turned to heavier-than-air machines and in 1906 built one on the principle of the box kite. One of the great pioneers of early flying, he committed suicide in 1932, having become depressed over the military uses of aircraft.

Ibsen dies

Henrik Ibsen (1828–1906), the great Norwegian playwright, died on May 23rd, aged 78. He had suffered a stroke in 1900 and had not written since. Opposition to his work drove him into exile for many years and plays such as *A Doll's House* and *Hedda Gabler* outraged audiences all over the world. By the time of his death, however, he was recognised as Norway's greatest living writer.

Vesuvius erupts

On April 7th the volcano Vesuvius suddenly erupted, and a lava flow enveloped the town of Ottaviano, killing and injuring many hundreds of Italians. Naples was blanketed with cinders and many more people were killed when roofs became overloaded and collapsed.

Cézanne dies

Paul Cézanne (1839–1906), the greatest of all French Post-Impressionist painters, died on October 22nd at the age of 67. He had lived in France all his life and never tired of painting the subjects he most admired, especially the landscape around his home in Provence.

Moors ambush French in North Africa

The French Army experienced considerable trouble with its disaffected colonial subjects in North Africa, not only in Algeria, which was a colonial possession, but in the neighbouring state of Morocco where it claimed a special interest. This was opposed by the Germans who claimed a special interest of their own. France was backed by Britain, Spain and Italy, all countries with an involvement in North Africa, while Germany was backed only by Austria.

The illustration above from *Le Petit Journal* – a contemporary magazine – depicts an incident in which a French army detachment was ambushed by Moors at Tidj Kardje, where two officers and two NCOs were killed. Minor attacks like this were a continuous embarrassment to the French.

The master politician

In 1906 Theodore Roosevelt (1858–1919) became the first American to be awarded a Nobel prize for his successful intervention in the Russo-Japanese war, acting as mediator and persuading both sides to open peace negotiations, resulting in the Treaty of Portsmouth. US influence in world affairs advanced substantially during Roosevelt's presidency (1901–9) and at home he was a masterly, though often controversial politician, with a reforming zeal that alarmed the more conservative elements of his party.

It was his zeal for reform that led to his nomination as McKinley's running mate in 1900. As Republican Governor of New York, his campaign against corruption had embarrassed influential political bosses who thought that he would be less threatening to vested interests as Vice-President. However, after McKinley's assassination in 1901, 'Teddy' Roosevelt became the 26th President of the US.

He already had considerable political experience: three terms in the New York assembly, six years on the Civil Service Commission and two years as Police Commissioner of New York, as well as his term as Governor. He had worked a ranch in the Dakota Territory and served in the Spanish-American war (on the far right of the photograph) and his record captured the popular imagination. As President, he soon won a name for 'trust-busting' and championing the 'little man'. He was energetic and versatile and in 1904 his re-election on a large majority was a foregone conclusion. His prestige throughout his presidency was so great that at the end of his term he was able to choose his successor, William Howard Taft.

Upton Sinclair

The Jungle, published this year, was Upton Sinclair's sixth novel and the most successful of the 80 books he wrote in his lifetime. The idea for the story came when Sinclair was in Chicago, investigating conditions in the stockyards, for a weekly Socialist newspaper. The novel tells of an immigrant Lithuanian family and their sufferings as employees at the stockyards. The book incidentally brought about the passing of food inspection laws, of processed meat. Sinclair had paid for the book's publication after it was rejected by several publishers and it quickly became a best-seller.

A long series of other topical novels followed, including *Oil*, (1927), based on a scandal about US oil reserves, and *Boston*, (1928), inspired by the Sacco and Vanzetti case of the two radicals executed after allegedly committing a hold-up murder.

San Francisco devastated

The earthquake and fire of April 18th 1906 took more than 500 lives and devastated 3000 acres in the heart of San Francisco. The shock brought down buildings, snapped overhead power lines and gas mains. The fire that followed caused far more damage than the quake itself; it took three days to bring the flames under control and over 490 blocks were destroyed. The rebuilding programme was prompt and impressive but the threat from San Francisco's position on the San Andreas fault remains. Seismologists believe that a quake on the same scale as 1906 could result in 23,000 deaths.

Jan	14	Earthquake devastates Kingston, Jamaica	Jul	12	Alfred Dreyfus resigns from French army
	19	Mohammad Ali Mirza becomes new Shah of Persia		20	471 miners killed in Japanese pit disaster
	22	Strike by music hall artistes disrupts London's theatres		25	Japan makes Korea a protectorate
	23	UK: Lloyd George advocates reducing power of Lords		26	US author Mark Twain receives Honorary Doctorate
	26	Strauss's opera *Salome* banned as obscene in New York		29	Robert Baden-Powell launches Boy Scout movement
	28	164 miners die in pit explosion at Saarbrücken, Germany		30	British troops sent in to quell unrest in Belfast
Feb	3	King Edward VII and Queen Alexandra visit Paris	Aug	1	US Army forms 1st military air force
	6	HMS *Dreadnought* is fastest from Gibraltar to Trinidad		4	French fleet bombards Moroccan port of Casablanca
	12	Home rule for Ireland on British Liberal govt's agenda		13	4 civilians killed by troops in Belfast
	21	Liner *Berlin* wrecked off Holland: 144 drown	Sep	4	Norwegian composer Edvard Grieg dies
Mar	5	2nd Duma meets in St Petersburg	Oct	4	Riots in India blamed on MP Keir Hardie's visit
	8	UK: Women's Enfranchisement Bill defeated		14	3rd Duma formed in St Petersburg
	12	French battleship *Jena* explodes at Toulon, killing 118	Nov	16	Oklahoma admitted as 46th US State
	22	Gandhi starts civil disobedience campaign in S. Africa	Dec	10	Rudyard Kipling awarded Nobel Prize for literature
	22	75 suffragettes jailed in Britain for refusing to pay fines		31	167 Duma deputies jailed for treason in Russia
Apr	25	Channel Tunnel Bill killed by British govt			*The Arts*
May	2	King Edward VII visits French President in Paris			Joseph Conrad's novel *The Secret Agent*
	2	Riots break out in Rawalpindi and East Bengal, India			Maxim Gorky's novel *Mother*
	21	Irish Home Rule Bill attacked in Dublin and London			Pablo Picasso's painting *Les Demoiselles d'Avignon*
Jun	6	British govt says it will never leave India			Henri Rousseau's painting *The Snake Charmer*
	14	British govt Bill to curb power of House of Lords			J. M. Synge's play *The Playboy of the Western World*
	16	Duma dissolved with charge of treason in Russia			George Bernard Shaw's play *Major Barbara*

Lawyer breaks law

Mohandas Gandhi (1869–1948), a brilliant young Indian lawyer practising in South Africa, announced that he intended to break a new law about to be imposed by the government of Transvaal which would require all Indians living there to be finger-printed and to carry a special certificate at all times.

Talks with Churchill

Gandhi had already been to London to talk to the Colonial Secretary, Winston Churchill, who had told him that the British government would not agree to this new racial law. But as the Transvaal would shortly become self-governing, this reassurance was not much use: the Transvaal government had made it clear that they intended to go ahead with the law the moment they became independent. Gandhi did as he said he would, and refused to be finger-printed. He was promptly jailed. But (as often happened later in his life) he was more of an embarrassment inside prison than out.

Discussion with Smuts

General Smuts, then State Attorney for Transvaal, was a sensible man and immediately realised this. He took steps to undo the mischief that the provincial government had done. Gandhi was summoned to a secret meeting to discuss the matter. He was ready to compromise on one or two minor matters and Smuts then freed him.

In later years, in India, Gandhi was not to be so accommodating to his captors, and they came to learn that putting him in prison was one thing, but getting him out again was quite another.

The world's most powerful warship

The launch of HMS *Dreadnought* in Britain, only a few months after her keel was laid, made every other battleship in the world obsolete. She is seen here at sea, fully armed and kitted out, in 1907. Her ten 12-inch, turret-mounted guns meant that she outranged and outgunned every other battleship. More particularly, she represented a direct threat to Germany, whose obvious and immediate response was an accelerated naval construction programme to build her own fleet.

Grieg dies

Edvard Grieg (1843–1907), Norway's most famous composer, died at Bergen on September 4th. His Piano Concerto (1869) and incidental music for Ibsen's *Peer Gynt* (1876) had brought him world fame, and have continued firm favourites ever since.

Be prepared

Robert Baden-Powell (1857–1941), hero of the siege of Mafeking in the Boer War, founded the Boy Scouts in order to give British boys a sense of discipline and self-sacrifice so that they could better serve the British Empire.

Birth of Cubism

The French artist, Georges Braque (1881-1963), painted in the Fauve style until the arrival of the Cubist art form around 1907-8. Although Picasso is usually credited with inventing Cubism, Braque was the first to exhibit a Cubist painting.

Taxi! Taxi!

Motor taxis were beginning to appear on London streets in increasing numbers, as this taxi rank in Knightsbridge clearly shows. These early cabs were mechanically unreliable and there were many breakdowns, but they were popular as a novelty to London's travelling public. They were highly unpopular with London's hansom cab drivers who said that they frightened the horses, and there were many attempts to sabotage the new motor taxis. Almost certainly economic considerations were the major cause of the trouble.

Royalty at Windsor

This nostalgic photograph shows European royalty en masse at a reception given by King Edward VII and Queen Alexandra. Seen here are the Emperor of Germany, Wilhelm II with the Empress Augusta; King Haakon VII and Queen Maud of Norway with Crown Prince Olaf; the Grand Duke Vladimir of Russia, King Alfonso XIII of Spain, Prince Arthur, Duke of Connaught, and the Prince of Wales; as well as dozens of other royal notabilities. Few of them were to preserve their crowns after the First World War.

The Victoria and Albert Museum

This splendid Victorian establishment, which houses the major collection of decorative arts in Britain, had seen some changes. Originally opened as the Museum of Ornamental Art in 1852 in the aftermath of the Great Exhibition, it was merged with the South Kensington Museum in 1857. Queen Victoria laid the foundation stone to the present building, designed by Sir Aston Webb, in 1899. In the final stages of completion in 1907, it was officially opened by King Edward two years later.

American suffragettes

The American Woman Suffrage Association had been established as early as 1869. By the early years of the 1900s suffragettes were using increasingly militant tactics, and had gained the vote for women in 11 states before the First World War.

1908

Jan	1	State of Georgia, US, introduces alcohol prohibition
	6	2,000 textile workers strike in Oldham, Lancashire
	8	Count von Zeppelin to build airship to hold 100 people
	22	British Labour Party decides to adopt socialism
	30	General Smuts frees Gandhi in S. Africa
Feb	1	King Carlos I and Crown Prince murdered in Portugal
	13	Tsar Nicholas II said to encourage anti-semitism
	18	Emmeline Pankhurst tells of British prison miseries
	20	General Stossel to die for surrendering to Japanese
Mar	7	1st German dreadnought battleship launched
	21	Frenchman Henri Farman pilots 1st passenger flight
Apr	8	Herbert Asquith becomes new British Liberal PM
	13	Floods in China kill 2,000
	27	International Congress of Psychoanalysis in Austria
May	7	British old age pensioners to get 5 shillings a week
	15	Monet destroys painting worth £20,000
	23	Famine in Uganda kills 4,000
	26	State of North Carolina, US, adopts alcohol prohibition
Jun	11	Rotherhithe Tunnel under Thames opened
	20	Russian composer Rimsky-Korsakov dies
	22	Six blacks accused of murder are lynched in Texas, US
	24	Former US President Grover Cleveland dies
Jul	7	US: Death of J. C. Harris, author of *Uncle Remus*
	8	World navy list shows Germany catching up with UK
	27	4th Olympic Games open in London
Aug	19	Belgian Parliament to annex Congo from Leopold II
Sep	16	US: Buick and Oldsmobile firms form General Motors
Oct	1	'Model T' Ford goes on sale for first time in US
	5	Bulgaria proclaims independence from Ottoman Empire
	5	Austria formally annexes Bosnia and Herzegovina
	14	Chicago Cubs win World Series
	31	Wilhelm II attacks UK in *Daily Telegraph* interview
Nov	3	William Taft elected President of US
	5	Cullinan diamond cut for Queen Alexandra
	7	UK Navy launches biggest battleship, HMS *Collingwood*
Dec	2	Child Emperor Pu Yi ascends Chinese throne aged two
	28	Messina, Sicily, wrecked by earthquake

The Arts

Marc Chagall's painting *Nu Rouge*

E. M. Forster's novel *A Room With a View*

Kenneth Grahame's novel *The Wind in the Willows*

Claude Monet's painting *The Ducal Palace, Venice*

The Baby Emperor

The little boy standing on the right became Emperor Pu Yi of China at the age of two. Not surprisingly, the real power lay with the Regent, his father Prince Chun, who is seen next to him. Little Pu Yi ascended the throne on the death of the Dowager Empress Tz'u-hsi, who had effectively controlled the throne through a number of dynastic shuffles.

She had been the concubine of the Emperor Hsien-feng and when he died in 1861 she grabbed the throne for her son, the Emperor Tsai-ch'un, ruling with him as co-regent. He died childless in 1875 and she immediately replaced him with her nephew, the Emperor Kuang-hsü who died very shortly after the Dowager Empress in mysterious circumstances.

The Dowager Empress was a powerful woman and the two Emperors that she reigned with were merely puppets. She kept the reins very firmly in her own hands and made all the important decisions. She had encouraged the Boxers and had to flee from Peking on their defeat, but after she had made her peace with the Western powers and Japan, she returned to Peking and took up command again.

Pu Yi was not to last very long as Emperor. There were powerful nationalist and republican forces at work in China and they surfaced violently in 1911. Pu Yi abdicated in 1912 at the age of five and the long reign of the Manchu emperors was over.

Winston Churchill marries his Clementine

On August 15th, Winston Churchill, recently appointed to the British Cabinet as President of the Board of Trade, announced his engagement to Miss Clementine Hozier, and on September 12th they were duly married.

W. G. Grace is finally out

Dr W. G. Grace (1848–1915), the redoubtable English sportsman, finally hung up his cricketing boots and retired from first-class cricket at the advanced age of 59. His unbroken career began in 1865 and during it he scored 54,211 runs and took 2,808 wickets. His final game was for the Gentlemen of England against Surrey on Easter Monday, in which he scored 15 and 25. He died in 1915 at the age of 67. He is seen here with a colleague, C. W. Alcock.

Portuguese King assassinated

King Carlos I and his son Crown Prince Luis were shot in Lisbon on February 1st. He was succeeded by his younger son, 19-year-old Don Manuel.

A forgotten figure

Florence Nightingale (1820–1910), who became famous for her nursing activities in the Crimea, was awarded the Freedom of the City of London on March 16th at the age of 87.

Jack Johnson wins world title

Texan boxer Jack Johnson became the first black man to win boxing's most coveted title – the world heavyweight – when he knocked out Tommy Burns in Sydney, Australia, on December 22nd.

Earthquake destroys Messina

On December 28th, Sicily's second biggest city was struck by one of the most violent earthquakes ever recorded in Europe. Very few buildings remained standing and more than half of Messina's 150,000 inhabitants were feared killed, plus many more in areas around the city.

'Model T' Ford appears

Henry Ford's promise to produce a car that everyone could afford was fulfilled on August 12th when the first ever 'Model T' came off his production line in Detroit. His new assembly line method of production meant that cars could be mass produced cheaply and efficiently. The first 'Model T' sold at 900 dollars.

London Olympic Games open

London's new 'White City' was the venue for the 1908 Olympic Games which opened in July. It was built as part of the great Anglo-French Exhibition which had been opened on May 14th by the Prince of Wales.

March of the unemployed

Workless men on the march brought home to the government the unacceptable level of unemployment in Britain. On October 21st, the Prime Minister, Herbert Asquith, announced practical measures to reduce unemployment by recruiting men into the Post Office, the dockyards and the Army Special Reserve.

1909

Jan	5	Colombian govt recognises independence of Panama
	5	Riots between Hindus and Muslims in Calcutta, India
	9	Ernest Shackleton's expedition gets closest yet to S Pole
	11	4 murderers guillotined publicly at Béthune, N France
	12	Turkey accepts cash for loss of Bosnia and Herzegovina
	21	State of Tennessee, US, adopts alcohol prohibition
Feb	8	British Navy to get 6 more dreadnought battleships
	17	Royal Commission suggests reforms to British poor laws
Mar	4	William Taft inaugurated as US President
	12	New Naval Bill reflects British alarm at German Navy
	15	Selfridges store opens in Oxford Street, London
	25	Madame Papova arrested for 300 murders in Russia
Apr	3	Keats and Shelley memorial unveiled in Rome
	6	US Commander Robert Peary reaches N Pole
	10	Algernon Charles Swinburne, British poet, dies
	18	Joan of Arc beatified in Rome
	23	Muslim fanatics massacre 30,000 Armenians in Turkey
May	18	George Meredith, British novelist, dies
	23	US police break up lecture by anarchist Emma Goldman
Jun	1	Opening of Seattle World Fair, US
	11	Earthquake in Provence, France, kills 60
	26	Edward VII opens Victoria & Albert Museum, London
	29	120 suffragettes arrested outside Houses of Parliament
Jul	1	Indian terrorist kills Anglo-Indian Sir Curzon Wylie
	16	Revolution in Persia places 12-year-old prince on throne
	24	Aristide Briant becomes French PM
	25	Louis Blériot makes first flight across English Channel
Aug	22	5 US workers die in steel industry riots
	30	Floods in Mexico kill 1,400
Sep	4	1st Boy Scouts parade at Crystal Palace, London
	21	Catholic Truth Conference speaks against socialism
	25	Scott buys ship *Terra Nova* for S Pole expedition
	28	Officially confirmed that suffragettes are being force-fed
Oct	9	Lloyd George attacks Lords in Newcastle speech
	13	Ferren, leader of anti-clerical party, executed in Spain
	16	President Taft meets Mexican President Diaz at El Paso
	20	Prince Ito of Japan assassinated by Korean terrorist
Nov	24	British bishops to abstain in Lords' Budget vote
Dec	17	Albert I becomes King of the Belgians

The Arts

Production of Sergei Diaghilev's *Les Sylphides*

Gustav Mahler's *Symphony No. 9*

Henri Matisse's painting *The Dance*

H. G. Wells' novel *Tono-Bungay*

Frank Lloyd Wright's Robie House, Chicago

The People's Budget

When he was appointed British Chancellor of the Exchequer by Herbert Asquith in April 1908, David Lloyd George (1863–1945), the leading light of liberal reform, faced some daunting tasks. There was an enormous deficit due to the greatly expanded naval construction programme and recent social legislation. And there was the prospect of a fight with the House of Lords who were bitterly opposed to any radical changes, especially those involving increased taxation.

But Lloyd George was not a man to be frightened by a challenge and he devised the most radical budget that Parliament had ever seen – the famous 'People's Budget'. It effectively shifted the burden of taxation from the producers of wealth to its possessors, combining a number of progressive taxes on income, inherited wealth and unearned income. It imposed heavy taxes on monopolies such as licences for alcohol. It caused joy to its supporters and consternation to its opposers – and these were, of course, the people who would be hardest hit by the taxes. Many of them sat in the House of Lords. And this is where Lloyd George met his most formidable opposition.

The battle in the House of Commons was fierce but Lloyd George had a majority and could force the Budget through on a vote. As was expected, the Lords threw his Budget out. Asquith angrily denounced the Lords for their rejection of the people's will and held an election largely on the issue of the Lords' veto.

As it happened, the Liberals lost some power in the Commons but still maintained a majority. And they were now even more determined to see the measure through. The bill again failed to get through the Lords and Asquith went to the country once more, gaining an unsatisfactory two seats. He now threatened to cut this Gordian knot by persuading the new King George V to create enough new peers to ensure the passage of the bill through the Lords. This threat finally convinced the Lords that he meant business and the Parliament Bill limiting the Lords' veto finally went through in 1911.

The Kaiser inspects his troops

The German army was powerful, well trained and with effective modern arms and equipment. Moreover, the German General Staff was the finest in the world, with an excellent grasp of military tactics and strategy. The army was backed by an equally powerful industrial base capable of providing it with all the weapons necessary for a successful war.

Alcohol banned

Prohibition was spreading rapidly in America and many states were 'dry'. Groups of fanatical women often raided bars armed with pistols and hatchets. Many fierce fights took place.

A new saint

On April 18th in Rome, Joan of Arc was beatified by the Pope, 478 years after the English burned her at the stake at Rouen.

Poverty in Britain

Workhouses like the London one shown above were still the last resort of the destitute, hated and feared by millions of poor Britons. A Royal Commission reporting in February recommended that children should be excluded and cared for in other ways. Workhouses were finally abolished in 1925, although the Poor Law system did not finally disappear until the National Assistance Act of 1948. Some of Britain's older hospitals were originally built as workhouses.

Blériot flies the Channel

On July 25th, the French pilot, Louis Blériot, became the first man to fly across the English Channel. The flight, from take-off near Calais to landing at Dover Castle took him 43 minutes. He thus won the thousand pound prize offered by the *Daily Mail*.

Ballets Russes

The first production of Sergei Diaghilev's Russian Ballet, founded in 1909, caused a major sensation in the artistic world. The Russian dancers, led by Nijinsky and Anna Pavlova, gave a brilliant performance.

Death of Geronimo

On February 17th, the old Apache Chief Geronimo died in an Indian reservation, far from his homeland. With his fellow-chief Victorio he had led the Apaches from Arizona and New Mexico in their final uprising against the Americans from the east in 1882. By 1886 it was all over.

North Pole conquered

On April 6th, Commander Robert Peary (top left) of the United States Navy reached the North Pole. This was his sixth attempt. He had sailed to Greenland by ship and then had to cross 90 miles of mountains before the final trek to the Pole itself.

Old age pensions

In Britain, Chancellor Lloyd George's 'People's Budget' in April raised taxes to pay for the new 'old age pensions' which had been introduced on the first day of the year. The weekly pension was five shillings for people over 70, and it was universally welcomed as a right rather than an act of charity.

1910–1919

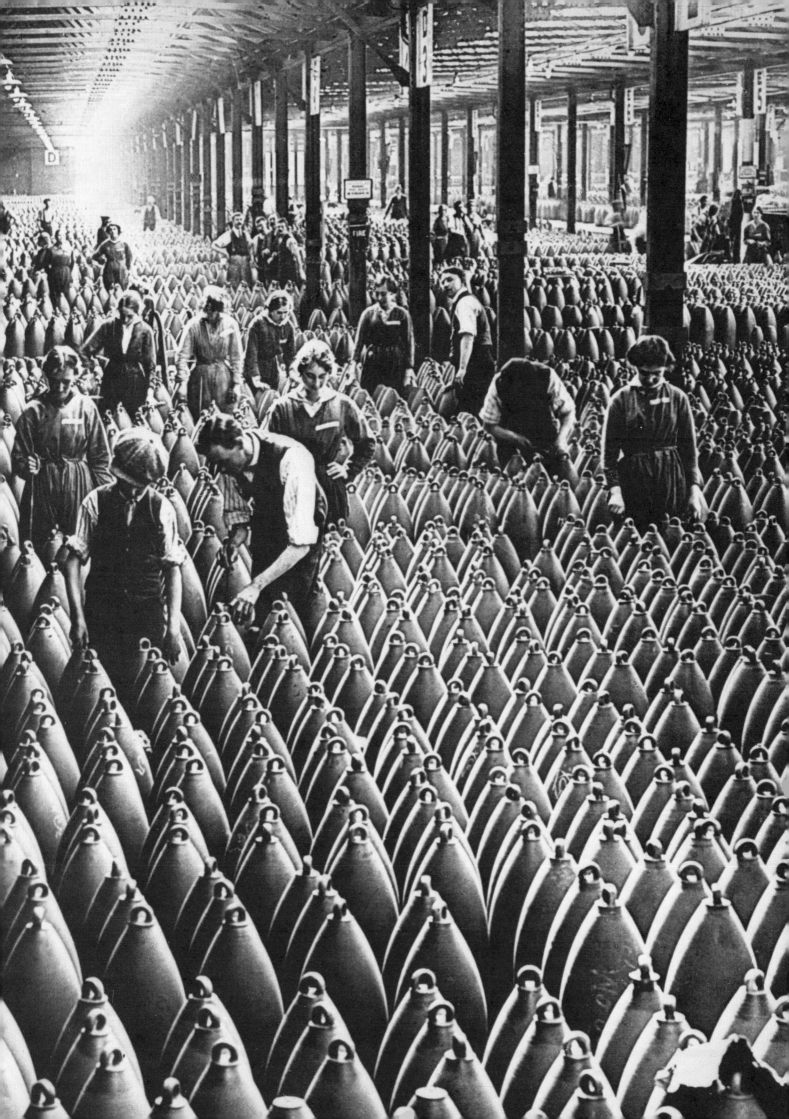

The 1910s

Above all else, the second decade of the twentieth century was the decade of the Great War. After 1918, when the four years of carnage finally drew to a close – years that had robbed Europe of the flower of its young men and all but bankrupted the Western economies – the world could never be the same again.

Seen by some liberals, including such influential figures as Bertrand Russell, as an upsurge of primitive bloodlust, the War was nonetheless viewed by the majority of people in Britain, France and Russia, at least at the outset, as a patriotic crusade against the tyranny of the Kaiser. Young men volunteered for the armed forces in their thousands, little thinking that their dream of service to King and country would all too soon dissolve in the nightmare of the Western Front and the trenches.

In Russia the War proved the catalyst for revolutionary changes that were to redraw the political map of the world. In Europe the treaty which ended the bloodbath sowed seeds of resentment that were to blossom over the next 20 years into the dark flower of Nazism and the Second World War. With the economies of the Western European powers in tatters, the United States of America emerged onto the world stage in a position of unprecedented influence.

Prelude to war

The years 1910 to 1914 were years in which the tensions that were to erupt into world war underlay ways of life that seemed superficially little changed since the nineteenth century. Few people seemed fully to appreciate the dangers to world peace posed by the Balkan Wars or the threat to the stability of the British–Russian–French alliance from Kaiser Wilhelm II's relentless build-up of naval and military strength. In the British Cabinet Winston Churchill's calls for greater expenditure on the Navy were met by charges of war-mongering.

The shot that killed the Archduke Franz Ferdinand at Sarajevo in 1914 is often spoken of as the first shot of the First World War. In fact, though, it was only the last of a number of shots that had destabilised the balance of power in the Balkan states and amongst their allies since King Nicholas of Montenegro declared war on Turkey in 1912. But if Austria's declaration of war against Serbia in 1914 was merely a diplomatic manoeuvre, it was one doomed to plunge Europe into the abyss. As the Great Powers mobilised for war, war itself became inevitable.

The war to end all wars

Britain declared war on Germany when the Kaiser's forces, following a plan laid down some years before, invaded Belgium, whose neutrality Britain had sworn to defend. There were scenes of enormous patriotic fervour as young men flocked to the recruiting offices and embarked for the front. Within weeks, though, the so-called 'war of movement' was over and the opposing armies were locked into a tragic stalemate, facing one another across a no-man's land of mud and shell-craters, dug into trenches defended by machine gun emplacements and barbed wire. While the generals gave their orders from behind the lines, wave after wave of men went over the top to their deaths. Perhaps the most poignant symbol of the futility of it all was the first Christmas Day on the Western Front, when German and British soldiers left their trenches and met in no-man's land to play football and exchange cigarettes before the shooting began again. The average life expectancy of a second lieutenant on the Western Front was two weeks.

The human cost of the war was almost unimaginably high. Some 10 million people died and many millions more were injured. It seemed as if an entire generation had been lost.

Revolution in Russia

In October 1917 the unrest that had been fermenting in Russian society for many years finally erupted in fully-fledged revolution. With the Bolsheviks' seizure of power in Petrograd a new era of world politics began. The immediate effect of the revolution was to take Russia out of the war with a separately negotiated peace and to plunge the country into a civil war of its own. The long term effect was to create a model for Communist revolution and to establish for the first time a major power bloc dedicated to Marxist ideology. The shock waves from the revolution were felt throughout the West and there were fears that Bolshevism would spread through Europe like wildfire.

Versailles and after

The Treaty of Versailles was finally signed by Germany in June 1919. The terms imposed upon her were harsh in the extreme. She was to give up her armies, cede vast areas of territory to her neighbours, pay war reparations of billions of marks and suffer partial occupation. There was concern in the Allied camp that the extent of this humiliation was ill-judged. Lloyd George's fear that if these terms were forced upon Germany the world would have to fight another war in 25 years was to prove tragically prophetic.

The United States

Perhaps the true victor of the First World War was the United States. Having joined the war late, her casualties were fewer and the cost to her exchequer less crippling than for most of the European powers. For the first time America emerged onto the world stage as a power rich in natural and industrial resources and capable of political influence on an international scale. Of the great imperial powers of the nineteenth century only Britain surfaced from the war with her empire more or less intact. For the United States of America the empire of influence was just beginning.

Pages 46–7: Filling shells in a munitions factory.

1910

Feb	8	US Boy Scouts founded
	19	Railway to be built through St Gotthard Pass
	20	Egypt's Christian Premier assassinated by Nationalist
	23	Chinese troops occupy Tibet, forcing Dalai Lama to flee
Mar	8	French Baroness de Laroche becomes 1st woman pilot
	10	D. W. Griffith makes 1st Hollywood film
	27	Major eruption of Mount Etna in Sicily
Apr	2	German scientist creates artificial rubber
	21	Mark Twain, US author, dies
	25	King Albert I opens World Exhibition in Brussels
May	5	Earthquake in Nicaragua kills 500
	18	1st Air Traffic Conference opens in Paris
	21	Union of S. Africa formed, headed by Botha as PM
	31	Theodore Roosevelt made Freeman of the City of London
	31	Girl Guides founded by Baden-Powell's sister Agnes
Jun	1	Scott's 2nd Polar expedition leaves for Antarctica
	17	Severe floods in Central Europe: 1,000 die in Hungary
	22	Paul Ehrlich announces salvarsan as syphilis treatment
Jul	1	S Africa becomes a Dominion of the British Empire
	12	Charles Rolls of Rolls-Royce killed in air crash
Aug	3	Muslim Druzes massacre 100 Jews in Palestine
	14	Fire at Brussels World Exhibition destroys paintings
	22	Japan formally annexes Korea
	28	Prince Nicholas of Montenegro takes the title of King
	29	Dr Crippen charged with wife's murder in London
Sep	2	French painter Henri Rousseau dies
	7	International Court settles Canadian fishing dispute
	7	Marie Curie first isolates radium
	21	Rosa Luxemburg shouted down at Socialist Congress
Oct	4	Revolution in Portugal; King Manuel II flees to England
	7	New Lisbon govt abolishes monarchy
	20	UK launches SS *Olympic*, biggest ship afloat
	30	Death of Jean Dunant, Swiss founder of Red Cross
Nov	28	New French law allows pregnant women 8 weeks' leave
	30	House of Lords rejects Asquith's Budget
Dec	4	Death of Mary Baker Eddy, founder of Christian Science
	10	Irish home rule & abolition of Lords on Liberals' agenda
	13	Antarctic explorer Ernest Shackleton knighted
	16	Nicaraguan President forced to resign by US Marines
	29	Grand Vizier resigns in Constantinople

The Arts

Henri Rousseau's painting *Yadwiga's Dream*

Bertrand Russell's *Principia Mathematica*

Elgar's *Violin Concerto*

Stravinsky's ballet *The Firebird*

Edward VII dies

King Edward did not ascend the throne until he was 59, and his short reign lasted only nine years. He was succeeded by his son, who became George V. Edward's reign had seen the beginning of the Entente Cordiale with France, so soon to be called into action, and the beginning and development of the great naval arms race between Britain and Germany. Edward was a tubby, kindly man but his long years of waiting in the shadow of his imperious mother Queen Victoria had made him capricious and self-indulgent, and he liked to surround himself with amusing and entertaining people rather than with politicians and advisers. Many royal personages in Europe were his cousins, nephews and nieces, and he could claim blood relationships with the houses of Germany, Norway, Sweden, Romania, Spain and Russia. He is seen (below) walking in Biarritz, his favourite French resort. His son George and nephew Wilhelm II of Germany appear in the colonel's uniform of each other's armies.

Holman Hunt dies

On September 7th, William Holman Hunt (1827–1910), the last surviving Pre-Raphaelite painter, died. Founded in 1848 by Holman Hunt, John Everett Millais and Dante Gabriel Rossetti with the intention of replacing the vulgar opulence of contemporary art with a return to ancient simplicities, the Pre-Raphaelite movement favoured biblical subjects such as *The Boyhood of Jesus*, *The Discovery of our Saviour in the Temple* and *The Scapegoat*. Their paintings were received with much derision when they appeared. Although to the modern eye they appear highly idealised, Victorian critics found them stark and ugly, and their models in particular came in for much abuse as being loutish and repellent. This painting of Holman Hunt's, *Early Britons Sheltering a Missionary* (left), is typical of the Pre-Raphaelites' archaic and romantic style, with every detail lovingly recorded.

Girl Guides founded

The Girl Guide movement was formed on May 31st, just three years after the Boy Scouts came into being. Co-founded by Sir Robert Baden-Powell and his sister Agnes, the Girl Guides was to be run very much on the lines of the Boy Scouts with much emphasis on discipline, physical fitness and cleanliness of body and mind. The idea of a special organisation for girls had been much discussed since the previous year: a suitable uniform was devised with jacket, skirt, tie, a broad-brimmed hat, and black shoes and stockings. A system of Girl Guide troops was set up, with patrols, guide mistresses and merit badges for every conceivable feminine skill, with much concentration on cookery, child care and needlework. The Girl Guides were soon very popular and within a few years there were hundreds of troops all over the country. Above: Chief Guide Lady Baden-Powell (centre) and some of her followers a few years after the Guides were founded.

It takes two to tango

The daring new South American dance, the tango, instantly became popular with younger people everywhere, although their elders found its close bodily contact and sensuous gliding movement highly offensive, indecent and immoral. Not surprisingly, this made it even more popular and it rapidly spread from the theatres where it was first demonstrated to all sections of society. Here, two Argentinians demonstrate the new dance.

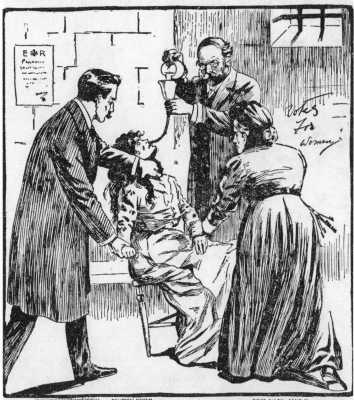

TORTURING WOMEN IN PRISON

PUBLISHED BY THE NATIONAL WOMEN'S SOCIAL AND POLITICAL UNION, 4 CLEMENTS INN, STRAND, W.C. & PRINTED BY DAVID ALLEN & SONS L⁰ 100 FLEET ST E.C

VOTE AGAINST THE GOVERNMENT

Industrial unrest in Britain

1910 saw much industrial unrest in Britain. In July the railwaymen came out. In September the shipbuilders were locked out. Troops were sent against striking Welsh miners in November. These miners (above) are in one of the crude lifts used to carry men and coal to the surface.

Suffragettes force-fed

Doctors and warders hold down suffragettes on hunger strike in a British prison and force sustenance down their throats through tubes (above right). This degrading procedure gave much offence, as this poster shows.

Tolstoy dies

On November 10th, the great Russian novelist Leo Tolstoy (1829–1910) died at Astapova railway station near his home at Yasnaya Polyana. His two greatest novels were *War and Peace* (1864–9) and *Anna Karenina* (1873–5). During the last years of his life he gave up owning property and tried to live as a Russian peasant while his home became a place of pilgrimage.

1911

Jan	3	Soldiers kill 3 anarchists in Sydney Street, London
	11	18 killed in riots in Bombay, India
	16	Big oil strike in Borneo
	25	US Cavalry sent to Rio Grande in Mexican Civil War
Feb	6	King George V opens his first Parliament
	6	Large area of Constantinople destroyed in fire
	22	Canada votes to remain in British Empire
	24	German Reichstag increases army by half a million men
Mar	2	Lords' Veto Bill gets 2nd reading in House of Commons
	31	British shopworkers win fight for 60-hour week
May	4	Lloyd George introduces National Health Insurance Bill
	16	King George V unveils Victoria Memorial
	18	Gustav Mahler, Austrian composer, dies in Venice
	23	PM Asquith opens Imperial Conference in London
	25	Mexican dictator Porfirio Diaz ousted after 45 years
	30	W. S. Gilbert, collaborator with Arthur Sullivan, dies
Jun	13	1st performance of Stravinsky's ballet *Petrushka*
	22	Coronation of King George V
Jul	13	Investiture of Edward Prince of Wales
	20	9 rioters shot by troops in Wales
	22	King promises enough peers to pass Lords' Veto Bill
	28	French Chief of Staff resigns over Dreyfus affair
Aug	1	Germany decides to fortify Heligoland in N Sea
	8	50,000 troops assemble to fight riots in Liverpool
	10	House of Lords passes Parliament Bill
	14	S Wales miners lift strike after 10 months
	22	*Mona Lisa* stolen from the Louvre in Paris
Sep	4	100,000 die in Yangtse River floods in China
	6	British TUC condemns use of troops in strikes
	14	Russian hardline Premier Peter Stolypin shot
	23	Edward Carson heads opposition to Irish home rule
	29	Italy declares war on Turkey
Oct	9	Launch of *King George V*, Britain's biggest battleship
	10	Canada: Robert Borden succeeds Wilfred Laurier as PM
	23	Winston Churchill appointed First Sea Lord
	30	Chinese Emperor Pu Yi grants a constitution
Nov	1	1st ever aerial bombing by Italians in Tripolitania
	12	George V presides at Coronation Durbar in Delhi
	14	Amundsen reaches S. Pole ahead of Scott
	29	US journalist Joseph Pulitzer dies
		The Arts
		Elgar's *Symphony No. 2*
		Richard Strauss's opera *Der Rosenkavalier*
		Rupert Brooke's *Poems*
		Georges Braque's painting *Man with a Guitar*

Ramsay MacDonald elected chairman of the British Labour Party

On February 6th Ramsay MacDonald (1866–1937) succeeded Keir Hardie as the Chairman of the Labour Party and made an impressive debut as leader in a speech supporting the Liberals in their struggle against the intransigent House of Lords.

Ramsay MacDonald was the illegitimate son of a Scottish farm worker. In spite of early troubles, he grew up to be a talented and active man with a gift for oratory. He first encountered left-wing ideas in the Social Democratic Federation, and subsequently joined the Fabian Society. By 1900 he had become the first secretary of the Labour Representation Committee, the predecessor of the Labour Party.

First Labour Prime Minister

One of the first Labour MPs (elected in 1906) his performance in parliament made him the natural choice for chairman when Keir Hardie resigned. Eleven years later he was elected leader of the Labour Party itself. The General Election of 1923 ended in a stalemate, with the Tories gaining the greatest number of seats, but not enough to form a government. As the party with the next largest number of MPs in the House of Commons, Labour became the second choice, and on January 22nd 1924, King George V asked Ramsay MacDonald to form a government – just 24 years after its formation, the Labour Party found itself in power.

Royalty robed

The children of the new king prepare for his coronation. King George V and Queen Mary were crowned on June 22nd. Prince Edward of York, shortly to be created the new Prince of Wales and his sister Victoria Mary are robed for the ceremony. Prince Edward went on to become Edward VIII and, after his abdication, the Duke of Windsor. His sister married Viscount Lascelles in 1922, and ten years later she became the Princess Royal.

Gold from the sea bed

In a terrible storm on October 9th 1799, the British warship HMS *Lutine* sank off Holland with a fortune in gold on board. Salvage operations soon started but much of the gold could not be reached. Further attempts were made in the 1850s, but with little success. In 1911 a new salvage technique using a kind of enormous vacuum cleaner sucked up sand from round the wreck, put it through a wire sieve and recovered much of the remaining treasure. Fresh attempts in 1938 recovered some further gold bars (top left).

Lost city of the Incas

Exploring a remote mountain area of Peru, Dr Hiram Bingham of Yale University made one of the greatest archaeological discoveries of all time. Reaching the edge of a steep cliff he found himself looking down on the ruins of a great city at 6,700 feet. Built around 1500 AD, Machu Picchu had been lost to all human knowledge for hundreds of years. It is now one of the most famous tourist attractions in Peru.

Amundsen reaches South Pole first

Roald Amundsen, the Norwegian explorer (1872–1928), beat British Captain Scott in the race to the South Pole, arriving at his destination a whole month earlier, a shattering disappointment to the British. Scott and his team were to perish on the return journey. Amundsen's success was due to careful planning and leaving nothing to chance. He had chosen to simplify his journey by using only dog teams rather than the cumbersome sequence of tractors, ponies and man-handled sledges favoured by his rival. He even carried his own food on the hoof – some of the dogs were eaten on the way back. Amundsen (left) is seen inspecting ice fields near the South Pole.

Mexico's 'Robin Hood' in action

Francisco 'Pancho' Villa, half bandit, half politician, was one of the forces that finally helped Francisco Madero bring down the Mexican dictator General Porfirio Diaz, who had been in power for 34 years. Villa was a thorn in everyone's side – he attacked his own people, which gave him a power base in the north of Mexico, and he attacked the Americans, which brought swift retribution when he was thrashed by a detachment of the US cavalry under General Pershing. He was finally bought off by the Mexican authorities by the gift of a large estate. He was assassinated there in 1923. Some of the weapons captured from him after one skirmish are shown (left).

The siege of Sidney Street

The streets of London's East End echoed to gunfire on January 3rd as the police and army units battled with three armed anarchists holed up in a house in Sidney Street, off the Mile End Road. The anarchists, who had already killed three policemen, fired on the armed police who came to arrest them, badly wounding one of them. Reinforcements were sent for and arrived under the personal leadership of the Home Secretary, Winston Churchill. After thousands of rounds of ammunition were fired the house caught fire and was burned to the ground. Only two charred bodies were found and there was much speculation about the whereabouts of the third.

1912

Jan	3	UK: Ulster Unionists pledge to ignore home rule
	6	New Mexico becomes 47th US State
	17	Scott reaches S Pole to find Amundsen has beaten him
	30	UK: House of Lords reject Irish Home Rule Bill
Feb	14	Arizona becomes 48th US State
Mar	1	US: Albert Berry makes 1st successful parachute jump
	3	Martial law is declared in Peking
	10	China: Yuan Shi-kai provisional President of Republic
Apr	4	Chinese Republic is proclaimed in Tibet
	15	The *Titanic* liner sinks in N Atlantic on maiden voyage
May	5	First issue of revolutionary Russian paper *Pravda*
	14	Swedish dramatist August Strindberg dies
	26	UK: Transport strike paralyses the country
	28	US: *Titanic* enquiry gives verdict of negligence
	31	US Marines land in Cuba to quell slave revolt
Jun	22	William Taft nominated for 2nd term as US President
	23	Bridge over Niagara Falls collapses, killing 47
Jul	1	Morocco is declared a French protectorate
	2	Woodrow Wilson nominated for US Presidency
	22	Royal Navy patrols N Sea to counter German build-up
	23	US: Modesty League protests against tight dresses
	30	Japanese Emperor Meiji Tenno dies, Yoshihito succeeds
Aug	11	Morocco: Sultan Mulai Hafid abdicates
Sep	1	Uprising in Morocco quelled by French troops
	30	Russia mobilises forces in response to Balkan unrest
Oct	1	Greece, Bulgaria and Serbia prepare to fight Turkey
	8	Montenegro declares war on Turkey
	14	Turkey invades Serbia
	18	Italy and Turkey sign peace treaty at Lausanne
	19	Bulgarian and Allied armies invade Turkey
Nov	5	Woodrow Wilson elected US President
	27	Spain and France sign treaty over Morocco
	28	Albania declares its independence
	30	Bulgaria and Turkey sign armistice
Dec	4	Turkey and Balkan allies (except Greece) sign armistice
	4	Albania: First Cabinet formed
	16	Start of Balkan peace conference in London
	25	Italy sends troops to Albania to deal with uprising
		The Arts
		M. Duchamp's painting *Nude Descending a Staircase*
		C.J. Jung's study *The Theory of Psychoanalysis*
		Amadeo Modigliani's sculpture *Stone Head*
		George Bernard Shaw's play *Pygmalion*
		Richard Strauss's opera *Ariadne auf Naxos*
		First news film produced by Charles Pathé

The unsinkable ship sinks

On April 15th, the mighty *Titanic*, pride of the White Star Line, struck an iceberg off Newfoundland, was fatally holed and sank with the loss of over 1,500 passengers. The ship had been proclaimed unsinkable because of her 16 watertight compartments but apparently too many of these were opened up by the collision and the ship was doomed. The *Titanic* was on her maiden voyage and carried many rich and famous passengers. But she did not carry enough lifeboats and many of those which were launched were not full: people foolishly opted to stay on the great ship rather than entrust their lives to them. Much heroism was displayed. The ship's orchestra played on almost until the very last. Millionaire John Jacob Astor chivalrously put his bride into a lifeboat but stayed on board himself. He was never seen again.

The first ship on the scene of the sinking was the liner *Carparthia* which picked up some hundreds of survivors. But the icy waters of the North Atlantic would have meant a speedy death for anyone immersed in it so that lifebelts and life rafts were of little use.

The wreck of the *Titanic* was finally discovered in 1985 in two pieces, two and a half miles beneath the surface.

Progress continued on the construction of the Panama Canal. This huge lock at Pedro Miguel was the biggest of all. It was begun in 1912. Still one of the world's greatest engineering feats, the Canal offers ships a 50-mile passage between the Atlantic and Pacific Oceans. Ships started using it in 1913 (above), although it was not officially completed until 1920.

Fossilised skull fragments 'discovered' in Piltdown, Sussex were believed to be the earliest human remains found in Europe, but in 1953 'Piltdown Man' was exposed as a hoax.

Queen Alexandra, the widow of King Edward VII, started Alexandra Rose Day in aid of hospitals in June 1912. It has been held each year in Britain ever since.

Suffragettes had to suffer the indignity of prison dress when they were jailed. Here, Mrs Pankhurst and her daughter Christabel demonstrate what it was like.

The costumes and décor designed by the Russian artist Leon Bakst for Diaghilev's *Ballets Russes* caused a sensation. Above: Nijinsky's costume for *L'Après-midi d'un faune*.

In Italy, excavations at Pompeii, the Roman city buried when Vesuvius erupted in 79 AD, were continuous, and discoveries were made all the time. In 1912 this pathetic group of bodies was found, struck down by poisonous gases as the volcano erupted and preserved by the cinders which engulfed them.

1913

Jan	9	Turkey breaches armistice with attacks on Bulgaria
	13	UK: National Insurance Act offers sickness benefits
	17	Serbian troops massacre Muslims
	22	Turkey accepts ceasefire ultimatum
Feb	2	Grand Central Station opens in New York
	3	Bulgaria restarts Balkan War
	7	Turkish/Bulgarian battle leaves 5,000 Turks dead
	9	Felix Diaz, nephew of ex-President, seizes Mexico City
Mar	2	Suffragettes attacked by mob in Hyde Park, London
	4	Woodrow Wilson inaugurated as US President
	18	Greek King assassinated in Salonika
	26	Bulgarians capture Adrianople from Turks
	31	Death of Pierpont Morgan, US banker
Apr	16	Turkey signs armistice with Bulgaria
	21	Launch of *Aquitania*, world's largest liner, in Scotland
	22	Scutari falls to Montenegrins after six-month siege
May	30	Turks sign Balkan Peace Treaty
Jun	26	Bulgaria signs defensive pact with Austro-Hungary
Jul	1	Zanzibar incorporated into British E Africa

	3	Rumania orders mobilisation
	10	Russia declares war on Bulgaria
	11	Rumania invades Bulgaria
	12	Turkey seizes Adrianople
Aug	7	Conscription introduced in France
	10	Balkan Peace Treaty signed in Bucharest
Sep	1	Louis Blériot 'loops the loop' for the 1st time
	8	1st flight of Germany's biggest Zeppelin
	21	Turkey and Bulgaria agree on new frontier
	24	Ulster Unionists block Irish home rule
Oct	17	Serbia invades Albania
	21	Royalist rising fails in Portugal
Nov	17	1st ship through Panama Canal
Dec	14	Greece annexes Crete

The Arts

D. H. Lawrence's novel *Sons and Lovers*

Marcel Proust begins *A La Recherche du Temps Perdu*

Sargent's *Portrait of Henry James*

Woolworth building, New York: world's tallest

The two nations

Although Britain continued to be one of the world's most prosperous nations – 'The best country in the world for a rich man to live in' as Winston Churchill said at the time – wealth was concentrated in the middle and upper classes. There was an enormous poverty-stricken underclass living in the slums that festered in the middle of all of Britain's big cities. Poor families were often large (bottom left), without money or food (bottom two pictures): the appearance of the baker's cart could provoke a rush (below). A number of charities and bodies like the Salvation Army and Dr Barnardo's tried to rescue the destitute, but the government was slow to acknowledge the problem.

Heroic failure

The heroic failure of Robert Falcon Scott and his companions to win the race to the South Pole, and their death on the return journey, has entered the world of myth. Scott is seen below by himself, leading the sledge party that he hoped would take him to the South Pole ahead of Amundsen. In retrospect, Scott's attempt was ill-founded and over-complicated: too many things could (and did) go wrong. Nevertheless, the heroism and dogged determination of Scott, Wilson, Oates, Bowers and Evans will never be forgotten. Their bodies were found on February 10th just 11 miles from a food depot. They remain there today under a cairn erected over their last resting place.

Scandal and tragedy

Isadora Duncan (1878–1927), the pioneer of modern dance seen here (left) with her troupe of pupil dancers, had scandalised the world both by the passion and eroticism of her dancing and the irregularity of her private life – she had children by two different fathers. Tragedy struck when both children and their nurse were drowned in the Seine on April 20th.

Suffragette's funeral

On June 14th, the suffragette movement buried its first martyr. Emily Davison had been killed when she grabbed the reins of the King's horse during the Epsom Derby.

The world's biggest railway station

The impressive portico of Grand Central Station, New York, opened on February 2nd, is overshadowed today by the Chrysler Building, opened in 1930.

1914

Jan	3	British suffragette Sylvia Pankhurst re-arrested
	8	*Figaro* accuses French Finance Minister of corruption
Mar	10	Suffragette slashes Velasquez's *Rokeby Venus*
	16	French Finance Minister's wife shoots editor of *Figaro*
	30	UK: 100,000 Yorkshire miners strike
Apr	17	Suffragette bomb destroys pier at Yarmouth, England
May	6	House of Lords rejects Women's Enfranchisement Bill
	25	Irish Home Rule Bill gets third reading
Jun	28	Archduke Franz Ferdinand of Austria assassinated
Jul	23	Austro-Hungarian ultimatum to Serbia
	28	Austria-Hungary declares war on Serbia
	30	Jean Jaurès, French Socialist leader, murdered in Paris
	30	British govt shelves Irish home rule
Aug	2	Germany occupies Luxembourg
	3	Germany declares war on France
	4	Germany invades Belgium
	4	Britain declares war on Germany
	8	British troops land in France
	23	Japan declares war on Germany
	28	British Navy raids Heligoland Bight
	31	Russian troops defeated at Tannenberg
Sep	2	Turkey mobilises
	3	New Pope, Benedict XV, elected in Rome
	6–14	Battle of the Marne forces Germans to retreat to Verdun
	7	Carson urges Ulster Unionists to join British Army
	22	3 British cruisers sunk in North Sea
	23	British troops retreat from Mons after heavy casualties
	23	British airmen bomb Zeppelin shed at Düsseldorf
	27	Russian troops invade Hungary
Oct	1	Turkey closes the Dardanelles
	11	Bombs dropped on Paris
	14	Canadian troops land in Britain
	17	Royal Navy sinks 4 German destroyers in North Sea
Nov	1	British fleet defeated at Battle of Coronel, Chile
	5	Britain annexes Cyprus
	21	Indian troops occupy port of Basra on Persian Gulf
Dec	8	Admiral Sturdee sinks German squadron off Falklands
	17	British Protectorate proclaimed in Egypt
	17	Anzac troops occupy Samoa and German New Guinea
		The Arts
		James Joyce's stories *Dubliners*
		Edgar Rice Burroughs' novel *Tarzan of the Apes*
		Braque's painting *The Guitarist*
		Joseph Conrad's novel *Chance*
		Ralph Vaughan Williams's *A London Symphony*

The Irish trouble

Amidst mounting international tension in Europe, the running sore of Ireland continued to infect British politics. Sir Edward Carson (1854–1935), seen below addressing a rally, led the movement in Ulster to resist Home Rule and a United Ireland, by armed force if need be (he suspended it on the outbreak of war later in the year). In the south of Ireland, the tension in Dublin exploded in a rising on July 26th. The funeral of those shot in the street battles attracted a crowd of tens of thousands (below). The deepening shadows of approaching war allowed the British government to abandon its plans for the implementation of Home Rule and in late July the whole question was shelved. But the Irish were not prepared to let the issue lie dormant and it exploded into violence again less than a year later.

A date with death

The Archduke Franz Ferdinand of Austria is seen leaving the train that carried him and his wife to their fatal appointment with their assassin on the streets of Sarajevo on June 28th. This event was to cause the loss of millions of lives, the disappearance of many familiar names from the map of Europe, and the eventual emergence of new nations such as Yugoslavia and Czechoslovakia. Gavrilo Princip, the student who fired the fatal shots, was a Serbian nationalist, but the result would have been the same had he come from any of the subject-states of the Austro-Hungarian Empire that Franz Ferdinand was heir to. A Czech daily newspaper carries the news of the assassination.

Suffragettes try to reach the King

On May 22nd a band of more than 50 suffragettes stormed Buckingham Palace in an attempt to deliver a petition to King George V. They failed, and are seen here being arrested.

The First Lord of the Admiralty arrives

Winston Churchill, First Lord of the Admiralty since 1911, saw the advantages of aircraft for the Royal Navy very early on. He is seen here arriving by air for a meeting at Plymouth.

The Western Front

In September, following the Battle of the Marne, the opposing forces of the German Army and the British Expeditionary Force dug themselves into the first trenches of the War. The formation of the Western Front, running from Switzerland to the coast, bogged down the British hopes of an early victory in a sea of mud and established the pattern according to which the War was to be waged for the next four years. Above: German field guns in the Champagne area.

'Old contemptibles'

Kaiser Wilhelm II referred to 'Britain's contemptible little army' but the regular British soldiers soon adapted to trench warfare and dug-outs.

Kitchener Needs You!

War minister Lord Kitchener's famous recruitment poster was quite unnecessary at this point – young men were flocking to the colours.

1914

Lille falls

The war did not go well for the Allies in its earliest stages. The well-prepared German Army, working to an excellent strategic plan, swept into Belgium and France, pushing back the Allied forces and taking many prisoners. On August 20th they crossed the River Meuse and captured the town of Lille (right), just across the French border. The French and British, still hastily trying to work out a co-ordinated plan, were unprepared for the German assault, but the courage and tenacity of their troops soon checked the German advance and the war settled down to the trench warfare which, on the Western Front, was to be its main characteristic.

Serbia at war

It was strongly suspected that Serbia was implicated in the assassination on June 28th of the Austrian Archduke Franz Ferdinand and his wife in the Bosnian capital of Sarajevo: his assassin claimed that his motive was to draw attention to the oppression of the Serbian people. Austria used it as an excuse to issue Serbia an ultimatum on July 23rd, demanding that Serbia join her in putting down nationalist movements. It required a reply within two days, and there was never the slightest chance of its acceptance. It made a European war certain, and mass mobilisation immediately began in all the European countries concerned. Here (right) Serbian troops march to the coming battle front.

Austria goes to war

The 98th Austro-Hungarian Infantry Regiment musters at Vysoke Myto in eastern Bohemia (now Czechoslovakia) before leaving for the front. As the European Great Powers became involved in the deepening crisis following Serbia's rejection of Austria's insulting ultimatum, diplomatic manoeuvres were replaced by war. Everyone expected a short war which would be over by Christmas. Austria and the whole of Europe duly got their war.

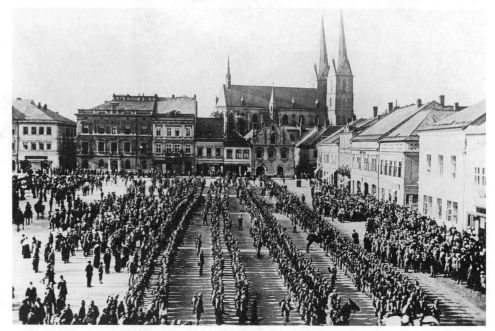

The price of war

The Belgian refugees finding sanctuary in neutral Holland were part of the terrible cost of war for the nations involved in it. Their homes had been destroyed by the advancing German Army, and they had no choice but to take to the road, with what few possessions they could carry with them. Similar scenes could be observed on every fighting front where civilians became innocently involved in the struggle, merely because they were there.

Allies blockade Germany

The successful Allied blockade of Germany soon deprived her of much of the food she normally imported from abroad. Shortages became common and a strict form of rationing had to be introduced. Here (left) German housewives and their families queue for ration books at the beginning of the war. In spite of severe shortages and occasional food riots, Germany managed to survive until the very end of the war, when violent rioting caused by semi-starvation broke out in many parts of the country.

Dirty work for women

Before the beginning of the war, many people believed that women were weak, half-helpless creatures, only capable of light and undemanding physical work such as typing, shopkeeping and millinery. The war and its concomitant shortage of men soon changed all that. Women were soon successfully engaged in some of the hardest and toughest physical labour – cleaning and greasing locomotives, humping heavy loads about and, as in this photograph, working as chimney sweeps. Previous generations who had seen women used as beasts of burden in the mines, labouring alongside their men in the fields, or at looms in textile factories, would have known that they had always been capable of work traditionally reserved for men.

Actress loses leg

Sarah Bernhardt (1844–1923), the great French actress who dominated the theatre of her day, had to have a leg amputated but did not let this minor inconvenience interrupt her career. As soon as she had been fitted with an artificial leg, she was back on stage.

Pygmalion

Mrs Patrick Campbell (1865–1940) starred as cockney flower-girl Eliza Doolittle, the role specially written for her by George Bernard Shaw in his new play *Pygmalion*. Sir Herbert Tree played opposite her as Professor Higgins. The play was famous for Eliza's phrase 'Not bloody likely!'

The Tsarina's evil genius

Many Russians feared the influence of the monk Rasputin over the Tsarina, the German-born wife of Nicholas II, after he had claimed to be able to stop her haemophiliac son's bleeding. In 1916 he was finally shot and dumped in the River Neva in Petrograd.

A great athlete

Jim Thorpe, whose Indian name was *Wa-Tho-Huk*, meaning Bright Path, was working as a backfield coach at Indiana University when he was asked to join the Canton Bulldogs as a professional football player. He had won gold medals in the 1912 Olympics, but was stripped of them when it later emerged that he had played baseball on a semi-professional basis.

Charlie Chaplin

Charlie Chaplin (1889–1977) made his film debut in 1913 in *Making a Living* and, as the little tramp with moustache, bowler hat, and cane, starred in many short films throughout the war years. He became enormously popular with the Allied troops, and the showing of his films in hastily constructed cinemas behind the lines was an invaluable morale builder. Chaplin's later masterpieces include *The Gold Rush*, *The Great Dictator*, *Modern Times* and *Monsieur Verdoux*.

1915

Jan	1	German submarine torpedoes HMS *Formidable*		15	200,000 Welsh miners strike for more pay
	12	US Congress defeats Bill for Women's Suffrage		27	Revolution in Haiti
	24	German battle cruiser *Blücher* sunk by Royal Navy	Aug	5	German Army takes Warsaw
Feb	4	Execution of Sarajevo conspirators in Bosnia		6	New Allied landings in Gallipoli
	17	German Army captures Polish port of Memel		29	UK sends £55,000,000 in gold to pay for US munitions
	26	UK: Clydeside armament workers strike for more pay	Sep	28	UK defeats Turks at Kut-El-Amara in Mesopotamia
Mar	11	British impose naval blockade of Germany	Oct	5	Allied troops land at Salonika, Greece, to help Serbia
	11	HMS *Bayano* sunk off Scotland: 200 casualties	Nov	13	UK: Churchill resigns from Cabinet over Dardanelles
	14	Royal Navy sinks German battleship *Dresden*	Dec	16	General Haig is new British C. in C. in France
Apr	20	President Wilson says US is strictly neutral		19	Allied troops pull out from Gallipoli
	22	Germans first use poison gas at Ypres on Western Front		30	Liner *Persia* sunk by U-Boat: 400 drowned
	24	Ottoman Turkish government massacres Armenians			*The Arts*
May	1	US ship *Gulflight* sunk without warning by U-Boat			Gustav Holst's symphonic suite *The Planets*
	15	Admiral Sir John Fisher resigns as First Sea Lord			D. H. Lawrence's novel *The Rainbow*
	22	Train crash at Gretna Green, Scotland, kills 158			W. Somerset Maugham's novel *Of Human Bondage*
	23	Italy enters war on Allied side			Pablo Picasso's painting *Harlequin*
Jun	16	UK: Lloyd George appointed 1st Minister for Munitions			John Buchan's novel *The 39 Steps*
Jul	9	All German forces in SW Africa surrender to Botha			D. W. Griffith's film *The Birth of a Nation*

Gallipoli

Winston Churchill's idea of a landing in the Dardanelles to take the pressure off the Russo–Turkish front in the Caucasus and to threaten Constantinople was strategically brilliant, but its execution was badly botched. The British and French fleets bombarded the Dardanelles in February. In March 18 warships tried to force the narrows but four were promptly mined and they withdrew in confusion. The Turks and their German advisers were now fully aware of the planned landing at Gallipoli. They hurried an extra 100,000 men to the area and dug them in, as well as concentrating artillery there.

This meant that when the allied force arrived on April 25th, they were outnumbered, overlooked and outgunned – the classical sitting target. In spite of this, they landed and established beachheads under a hail of fire, but were never able to secure more than a tenuous foothold.

Here troops and stores are confined to a narrow strip of beach on Anzac Bay (named after the Australian and New Zealand Army Corps who fought there).

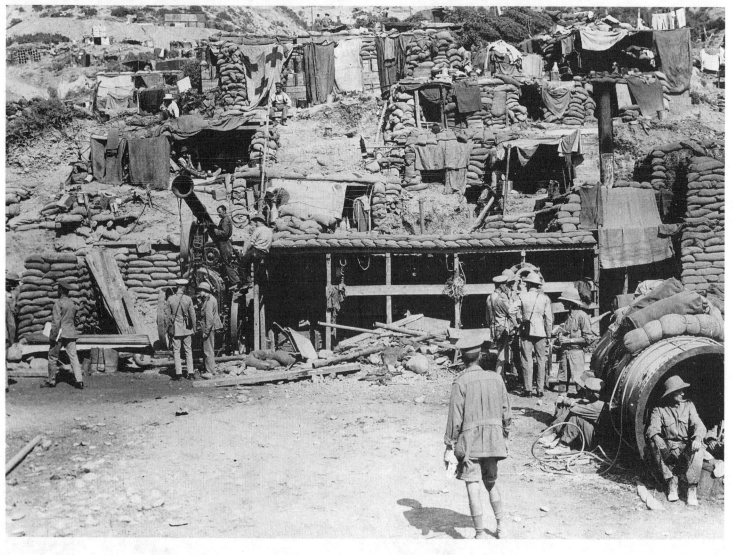

Poison gas

German scientists were recruited to produce war weapons, and the Allies were not far behind them. One of the nastiest new weapons was poison gas. It was an unreliable front-line weapon because it depended for its effectiveness on predicting the direction of the wind. All too often the wind changed and blew the poison gas back across the lines it was discharged from.

Right: Herr Professor Schrefeld, Head of the German National Institute, at work in his laboratory in Berlin experimenting on poison gases. Above: The theoretical work of the professor and his colleagues is put into practice as a German regimental chemist and his assistants actually manufacture poison gas in a makeshift front-line laboratory, assisted by a Russian prisoner of war. Top: A line of British soldiers blinded by mustard gas line up outside a dressing station – a chilling reminder of the effects of this vicious substance.

Top left: The landing at Anzac Cove.
Bottom left: A corner of the Anzac position.

A psychological blunder

The German authorities shot Nurse Edith Cavell (1865–1915) on the morning of October 12th for helping fugitive British, French and Belgian soldiers to escape to Holland. By applying military law so rigidly the Germans made the fatal error of giving the Allies a perfect martyr.

British women go to work

The demand for a constant supply of young men to go to the Western Front meant that British factories, workshops and service industries soon began to feel an acute shortage of workers. The government had not anticipated this difficulty. And since there was no provision for exempting key workers from military service, many industries became critically short-staffed. Happily, and to the considerable surprise of both management and government, women were found to be more than capable of replacing male workers. They were very adaptable, learned quickly and came into every branch of industry in greater and greater numbers.

Here (left) a bus conductress shows that she could easily do what was traditionally considered a man's job. (The role of women in the workforce re-emerged in the Second World War and has been maintained ever since.)

Women took on the most demanding and dangerous jobs in the arms industry, such as manufacturing and filling shells (below). One curious and unforeseen advantage of employing women was that they did not spend their high wages on drink, thus rendering themselves unfit for work. Men did. The problem of excessive drinking by men plagued the government throughout the war years and they made many attempts to solve it by limiting public house opening hours and increasing the price of beer.

French resist German advance in Champagne

Although the strength and speed of the initial German advance caught the Allies off-balance and resulted in much loss of territory, they soon recovered and even managed to mount a powerful counter-attack on the plains east of the Paris basin, in Champagne. But this quickly petered out in the face of formidable German resistance. A German heavy gun emplacement during the campaign is shown (above).

The French Army used dogs to carry messages in the early part of the war; the dog kennels (right) took the form of small dug-outs.

HELP TO STOP THIS!

Crude anti-German posters pleased civilians if not the soldiers.

'Britain's Call to Arms' by Frank Brangwyn (1867–1956) shows that even distinguished artists could be infected by the 'Hate Germans' campaign.

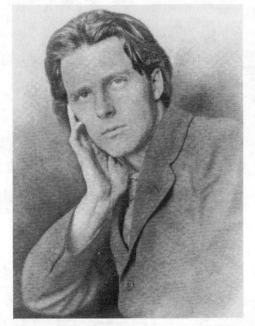

Rupert Brooke

Brooke (1887–1915) became known as the romantic poet-hero of the early part of the war, although his active service was limited. He travelled widely in America, New Zealand and the Pacific, joined the Naval Division as an officer in 1914 and fought at Antwerp. On April 23rd 1915 he died of blood-poisoning on board a French hospital ship on the way to the Dardanelles and was buried on the Greek island of Skyros. Although much of his verse may not have stood the test of time in comparison with other First World War poets like Wilfred Owen or Isaac Rosenberg, his most famous lines will never be forgotten:

'If I should die, think only this of me:
That there's some corner of a foreign field
That is for ever England.'

Sentimental postcards like this one were very popular with the troops. Though the words seem clichéd the sentiments are genuine.

The *Lusitania* Medal was struck by the Germans to commemorate the sinking of the famous liner on May 7th when 1,198 died.

1916

Jan	14	Zuider Zee dam in Holland collapses, causing flooding
	29	France: 1st Zeppelin raid on Paris
Feb	8	German food shortages cause riots in Berlin
	11	Kaiser Wilhelm II orders stepping up of U-Boat war
	22	Russia: Tsar Nicholas II opens Duma
	25	General Pétain to command 2nd French Army
	28	US: Author Henry James dies
Mar	9	US: Pancho Villa leads attack into New Mexico
	15	Admiral von Tirpitz resigns as head of German Navy
	15	US Army invades Mexico on punitive expedition
	20	Rationing in Germany as food becomes scarce
	21	Austrian soldiers kill 10,000 Serbian civilians
	22	China: Death of Yuan Shi-kai
Apr	14	Allies bomb Constantinople
	24	Easter Rising in Dublin
	29	Mesopotamia: British-held Kut-al-Amara falls to Turks
May	8	Australian and New Zealand troops arrive in France
	12	Irish rebels executed after Easter Rising
	31	British and German fleets engage in Battle of Jutland

Jun	9	Sherif Hussein of Mecca leads revolt against Turks
Jul	1	Beginning of Somme offensive
	2	Hundreds die in race riots in St Louis, US
Aug	19	German warships bombard English coast
	20	Allies begin offensive in Mesopotamia
	28	Italy declares war on Germany
	30	Paul von Hindenburg as German Chief of General Staff
Sep	4	British troops take Dar-es-Salaam in E Africa
Oct	16	Allies occupy Athens
Nov	7	Janet Rankin is 1st woman member of US Congress
	7	Woodrow Wilson re-elected as US President
	21	Emperor Franz Joseph of Austria-Hungary dies
	22	US: Author Jack London dies
Dec	7	Lloyd George becomes British PM
	13	New British offensive in Mesopotamia
		The Arts
		Charlie Chaplin in film *The Pawn Shop*
		D.W. Griffiths' film *Intolerance*
		J. Joyce's novel *Portrait of the Artist as a Young Man*

Haig takes over

The war on the Western Front had become one of trenches and barbed wire, artillery and machine guns. Each side would launch offensives which would result in heavy casualties but never gain more than a few thousand yards. By the end of 1915, when General Sir Douglas Haig took over the command of the British Expeditionary Force from Sir John French, the question was how to break the stalemate. Haig believed in all-out offensives, and more and more divisions were sent to France for his big attack. Gas had first been used by the Germans in May 1915, and by the British at Loos in September. Here, German soldiers advance through a wood in gas masks.

The Somme

The flower of British – and much of German and French – young manhood was destroyed in the mud of the Somme in northern France between July 1st and November 18th. The British High Command expended tens of thousands of young lives by flinging masses of infantry against unbroken German barbed wire and untouched German machine guns in an effort to gain a few hundred yards of torn-up and useless territory – on the first day alone the British lost 60,000 (including 19,000 dead).

Above left: British troops of the 17th London Regiment struggle through the mud.

Left: German dead lie round a machine gun post at Guillemont.

Above right: An eight-inch howitzer of the Royal Garrison Artillery in the Fricourt-Mametz Valley.

Right: A dressing station on the Somme.

The Battle of Verdun

What the Somme did to the British Army, Verdun did to the
French and German Armies – only for longer (February 21st–
December 18th). At the end of 1915 both the French and German
High Command were certain that the war would be decided on
the Western Front and, more precisely, on the French Front to the
south of Flanders and the Somme, which was the main area of
British occupation. Because the Germans had been successful on
the Eastern Front they were able to reinforce their troops on the
Western Front by almost 500,000 men and the German generals
chose Verdun as their point of attack. They concentrated 1,400
guns on a front of only eight miles on the eastern bank of the
Meuse and after bombarding it with shells they took Fort
Douaumont on February 25th.

This outraged the French who started a series of enormous and
costly counter-offensives, with great loss of life on both sides.
Despite the heavy losses sustained by their own forces, the
Germans almost achieved their objective of bleeding the French
Army dry at Verdun.

Vaux

German technical superiority and French difficulty in getting
enough troops into the narrow area which they occupied slowly
gave the German Army the advantage. The Germans captured
the Fort of Vaux on June 2nd and the fortification at Thiaumont
on June 23rd. The front then stabilised, although the mass
slaughter continued. Finally, between October and December, the
French recaptured the forts, which had become a symbol of defeat
or victory for both sides.

The butcher's bill

At the end of the year neither side had made very much progress.
But in the meantime, conservative estimates were that the
French had lost 350,000 men, and the Germans rather less. No
nation could afford losses of this magnitude for long, and there
were mutinous mutterings among the French troops.
Left: A French soldier at Verdun is masked against poison gas.
Above: The town of Verdun after bombardment.

The Irish problem

On Easter Monday 1916 a Nationalist rising was staged in Ireland. As a military exercise it was a fiasco; Anglo-Irishman Sir Roger Casement was captured as he tried to land 20,000 German-supplied weapons, and of the original plan only the seizure of strategic points in Dublin was achieved.

From the steps of the Dublin Post Office Padraic Pearse proclaimed the Irish Republic. Using artillery, British soldiers regained control, destroying much of the centre of Dublin in the process. British troops are shown (above) standing guard, and manning a barricade in Dublin.

The political effects were more substantial. The execution of a number of Republican leaders, including Casement, whose funeral is shown (left), and the internment of large numbers of Nationalists in prison camps on the mainland, gained them much support among Irish people.

The wreckage of a Zeppelin airship brought down and burned out at West Mersea in Essex, south-east England. Though they were frightening, Zeppelins caused little fundamental damage either to Britain's industry or its fighting spirit.

Conscription soon brought men of all ages into the British forces. New recruits are being given a medical examination.

Women were to be found in every kind of occupation. Here, three English farmworkers hoe a field at Bentley, Suffolk.

This British howitzer factory employed both men and women in the production of these vital weapons.

The French munitions factory shown here, was typical of the many factories manufacturing weapons of mass destruction.

1917

Jan	31	Germany announces unrestricted naval warfare policy
Feb	7	Germany: All US citizens held as hostages
	10	Weizmann and British govt discuss Jewish Homeland
	12	No US/German talks until U-Boat warfare restricted
Mar	8	US Marines land in Cuba to help civil authorities
	11	British capture Baghdad
	16	Tsar Nicholas II abdicates in Pskov
	19	France: Alexandre Ribot forms cabinet
	21	Ex-Tsar and his family are arrested
	31	US purchases Virgin Islands from Denmark
Apr	6	US officially enters the war
	16	Food strikes in Berlin
	20	US severs relations with Turkey
May	4	Widespread mutiny among French regiments at Front
	18	Selective conscription introduced in US
Jun	3	Italy declares protectorate over Albania
	4	Brazil declares war on Germany
	10	Sinn Fein uprising in Dublin
	14	First bombing of London by German aircraft
	15	Ireland: Prisoners held since Easter Rising released
	16	First Congress of Soviets meets in Russia
	19	British Royal Family renounce all German titles
Jul	16	Bolsheviks fail to take over Petrograd
	17	UK: Churchill returns as Minister for Munitions
	19	Mutinies break out in German Navy
	19	German Reichstag passes motion to end war
	31	Third battle of Ypres begins
Sep	15	Russia proclaimed a Republic with provisional govt
	26	Painter Edgar Degas dies
	30	Former Tsar and family sent to Siberia
Oct	20	4 Zeppelins shot down over France after raids in UK
	27	US troops in France fire first shots
	28	Vittorio Orlando becomes Italian Premier
Nov	6	British and Canadian troops capture Passchendaele
	7	Bolsheviks assume power in the name of the Soviets
	16	Georges Clemenceau heads new French govt
	17	British troops under Allenby capture Jaffa in Palestine
Dec	1	German E Africa cleared of German troops
	6	Finland proclaims its independence; is now a Republic
	17	Death of W. F. Cody – 'Buffalo Bill'
		The Arts
		Picasso designs sets for Diaghilev's ballet *Parade*
		J. M. Barrie's play *Dear Brutus*
		T. S. Eliot's poems *Prufrock and Other Observations*
		Sergei Prokofiev's *Classical Symphony*

The Russian Revolution

On March 16th, Nicholas II abdicated on behalf of himself and his sickly heir Alexei as he was about to be ousted. Russia became a Republic when Nicholas's brother Michael declined to assume the throne.

Power passed to a provisional government of Duma politicians and the reconstituted Petrograd Soviet. The atmosphere was one of debate and excitement. The provisional government, headed first by Prince Lvov and from July by the Socialist lawyer Alexander Kerensky (1881–1970), attempted to continue to fight the war. Opposition to this and the increasingly desperate economic situation was capitalised upon by the Bolsheviks who were characterised by their vehement opposition to the provisional government.

Lenin and the Bolsheviks

Exiled Bolsheviks returned, Lenin travelling across German territory in the famous sealed train to reach Petrograd by April. He is seen (above) addressing a rally soon after his return, with Trotsky at his side. The Bolshevik Party was, however, very small and their success depended upon the outright failure of the provisional government and the increasing radicalism of the Army at the front, especially after a disastrous summer offensive.

Lenin had to be patient, fleeing to Finland in August after a non-Bolshevik demonstration against the provisional government led to orders for his arrest. An attempted right-wing coup by General Kornilov, the Commander in Chief, convinced many that the dangers were from the Right and Bolshevik influence increased.

The Winter Palace

Despite grave doubts expressed by many Bolsheviks, Lenin pressed for a revolutionary seizure of power. In the early hours of November 7th (October 25th old style), the Bolsheviks' Military-Revolutionary Committee occupied strategic points in Petrograd, and the following day the Winter Palace, with the government inside, was captured.

Other radicals protested at the Bolsheviks' assumption of government as the Council of People's Commissars. They were in a weak position – outnumbered on the Left by Socialist revolutionaries and under immediate threat from domestic and international enemies. The October Revolution was seen by many as only a temporary aberration.

Above left: A demonstration in front of St Isaac's Cathedral in Petrograd (as St Petersburg was renamed during the war).

Left: A crowd in Petrograd is scattered by gunfire during the days of uncertainty between the February and October Revolutions.

Top: Alexander Kerensky reviewing troops during his brief period of tenure as head of the provisional government.

Above: Buildings damaged by gunfire in Moscow in the course of the Revolution.

Above right: Women soldiers on the march.

Right: A Bolshevik postcard with soldiers and sailors under a banner reading 'Long Live the Revolution.'

The War in the West

The war on the Western Front was not going well for the Allies. While the German General Staff had very clear intentions, there was considerable disagreement between the British and the French commanders. The new French commander Robert Nivelle wanted a great French attack towards Laon, aided by the British, while the British commander Douglas Haig wanted a British attack in Flanders, aided by the French. The German commander Erich von Ludendorff meanwhile straightened his front line. There were a number of serious local battles but the picture at the end of the year was essentially unchanged.

Above: This wood in France shows the effect of continuous heavy shelling on the landscape.

Left: A heavy British eight-inch howitzer in action over the Messines Ridge. The stop at the rear is to prevent the gun from running off its chocks.

Right: A Mark II tank in trouble behind the lines at the Battle of Arras.

Underwater menace

In both World Wars, the British Admiralty was obsessed with battleships, despite the fact that surface ship engagements were extremely rare and the real menace lay in Germany's U-Boats. In both conflicts, Germany came frighteningly close to defeating Britain by cutting her supply lines.

The German government formally announced a submarine blockade of Britain on February 4th 1915. The torpedoing of the *Lusitania*, on May 7th 1915, killed 139 Americans. And this, combined with the loss of more American lives in further sinkings, led to a crisis in German-American relations which brought America into the war by April 1917.

German U-Boats increased their pressure on Britain's supply ships, and by the end of 1916, 120 of their submarines were sinking 300,000 tons of shipping a month. In April 1917, they sank no less than 875,000 tons.

At this point Lloyd George brought in the convoy system. Losses in shipping soon began to fall while the number of U-Boat sinkings increased. Here, a German U-Boat surfaces.

An American call to arms

This powerful poster (very reminiscent of the famous 'Kitchener' poster of the early days of the war) brought tens of thousands of patriotic young American men into their country's armed services. The huge influx of new, vigorous and optimistic troops decisively tipped the balance towards the Allies and against Germany – both of the armies having been bled nearly white in the trenches of the Western Front.

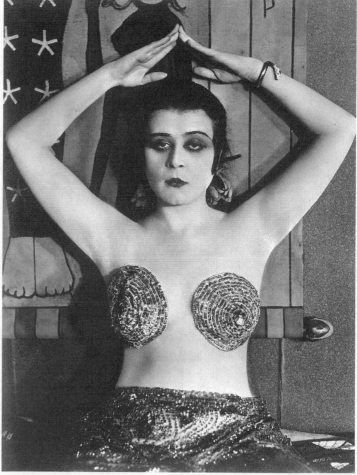

Theda Bara

Even in 1917, Hollywood publicity writers had the power to turn nice, ordinary young women into exotic and seductive temptresses. The dark-eyed Theda Bara (1890–1955), shown here in *Cleopatra*, was no exception. Not only a new name but new parents and an extraordinary new history were invented for her. She went on to make a number of films in which she played scarlet women with great conviction and success.

1918

Jan	8	President Wilson states his 14 Points	Oct	1	British and Arab armies take Damascus
	28	Workers' strike begins in Berlin		17	Yugoslavia gains independence from Austria-Hungary
Feb	9	Ukraine signs separate peace treaty with Germany		20	Germany stops U-Boat warfare
	18	Germans launch big offensive on Russian Front		30	Turkey signs armistice with Allies
	21	Australian troops take Jericho from Turks	Nov	1	Anglo-French troops take Constantinople
Mar	3	Treaty of Brest-Litovsk between Russia and Germany		3	German fleet mutinies at Kiel
	23	German gun 'Big Bertha' shells Paris from 75 miles		11	Austria-Hungary signs armistice with Allies
	23	Lithuania declares itself an independent Republic		6	Republic proclaimed in Poland
Apr	9	Latvia declares itself an independent Republic		9	Kaiser Wilhelm II abdicates
	29	German 'Big Push' on Western Front peters out		11	Fighting ceases on the Western Front
May	7	Rumania signs peace treaty with Germany		14	German fleet surrenders
	23	Georgia proclaims independence from Russia	Dec	1	Iceland becomes independent of Denmark
Jun	13	Turkish offensive in Palestine is halted		6	Allied troops occupy Cologne
Jul	16	Execution of Tsar Nicholas and family		14	President Wilson arrives in Paris for peace talks
	18	Foch launches counter-offensive on the Western Front			*The Arts*
Aug	2	Japanese invade Siberia			Lytton Strachey's biography *Eminent Victorians*
	15	US breaks off relations with Bolshevik govt			Béla Bartók's opera *Bluebeard's Castle*
Sep	22	Turkish resistance in Palestine collapses			Pirandello's play *6 Characters in Search of an Author*
	29	Bulgaria signs armistice with Allies			C. Chaplin in films *Shoulder Arms!* and *A Dog's Life*

Stalemate broken in the West

Although the contending armies had moved backwards and forwards on the Western Front, expending more than a million men in the process, the position had not changed significantly since late 1914. But the German High Command realised that the arrival of large numbers of fresh American troops would inevitably turn the tide against them. Their only hope was to win a decisive victory in France before the Americans arrived. They therefore planned an enormous offensive in the West.

The Germans knew that the French Army was desperately tired and that a great mutiny had only just been put down by draconian methods. They knew that the British were concerned about the Russian Bolshevik régime's signing of an armistice with Germany in December 1917 and the possible consequences of this. But they also knew of the growing weariness of their own population – and of the German Army itself. A quick, overwhelming victory was vital.

The much-disputed Chemin des Dames, running between Soissons and Berry-au-Bac, after the Germans recaptured it.

Top: Walking wounded Australian troops march down the Menin Road in Belgium past a casualty station on their way back from the Front.

Left: German soldiers relax in their dug-out on the Western Front. Soon the time for relaxation will be over.

Above: British prisoners taken by the German Fourth Army at the Battle of Amiens. They would not be in captivity for long.

Above right: A mass of victorious British soldiers rest on the captured St Quentin Canal in northern France.

Below right: American troops of the 30th Division are shown with Mark V tanks carrying 'cribs' for crossing trenches and ditches.

Progress of the Revolution

Lenin's priority was to get Russia out of the war and Germany took advantage of the chaos by demanding severe peace terms in the Treaty of Brest-Litovsk which finally ended Russian participation in March.

The Revolution was threatened with obliteration: counter-revolutionary 'White' armies were active in many areas against the Bolsheviks; the Czech Legion, an army of liberated POWs, occupied vast tracts of Siberia; and 'Green' bands challenged any central authority.

Foreign interference

Internal opposition was compounded by the attention of Russia's former allies. The Czech Legion became nominally a part of the French Army as France and Britain encouraged opposition to the Bolsheviks. In the east 70,000 Japanese troops occupied Vladivostok to keep an eye on the situation and US forces were sent to keep an eye on the Japanese.

Trotsky, as Commissar for War, built the Red Army from scratch and used Tsarist officers, with Bolshevik Political Commissars ensuring their loyalty. By October 1920, five and a half million men had been mobilised.

Denied control of so much of the country, Lenin, shown (bottom) with his wife Krupskaya, faced huge problems. The hopes for a fundamental transformation of Russian society were sacrificed to the more basic aim of feeding the population. A public food distribution point is shown (below). Raiding parties were dispatched from the cities to seize grain from peasants unwilling to sell.

Left: The Tsar's daughters, murdered with the rest of their family at Ekaterinburg on the orders of the Urals Soviet.

The war ends in Germany

The great German offensive on the Western Front in March had much initial success. The British line was broken and the British Army was driven back 40 miles. Shortly afterwards another great blow was delivered at Messines Ridge and the British line was again broken south of Ypres. However, lack of reserves made it difficult for the Germans to exploit this breakthrough. A third blow caught the French by surprise at the Chemin des Dames and the French Army was driven back some 13 miles on the first day.

This success encouraged the German commander, Ludendorff, to switch the thrust of his attack to this new front. But the Americans now appeared in force. A mighty Allied counter-attack began and the spent German forces had to retreat. They would never advance again.

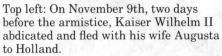

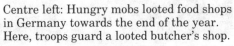

Top left: On November 9th, two days before the armistice, Kaiser Wilhelm II abdicated and fled with his wife Augusta to Holland.

Centre left: Hungry mobs looted food shops in Germany towards the end of the year. Here, troops guard a looted butcher's shop.

Above: German Red Cross workers collect clothes for families made destitute by the war.

Bottom left: The closing days of the war in Germany saw revolutionary and Communist crowds meeting in the squares and streets of the towns.

The armistice

The armistice signed on November 11th was a cause for great celebrations on the streets of Britain's towns and villages and there were almost universal spontaneous demonstrations of joy from the war-weary people. Unlike the Second World War, the civil population had not suffered very much – although they sincerely believed they had. They therefore had little understanding of the horrors and hardships suffered by the soldiers, who generally celebrated the end of the war in much more sombre mood.

The British Empire had lost over three-quarters of a million dead, the French nearly a million and a half, the Germans and the Russians well over a million and a half each. Within two years, the ill-thought-out Treaty of Versailles had rendered all their sacrifice useless, by setting the stage for future conflict.

Above left: The new Women's Royal Air Force show their pleasure on the streets of London.

Left: Children's street parties like this one took place in thousands of towns and villages all over Britain, to celebrate the armistice.

Death of a hero

The legendary German flying ace Manfred von Richthofen (1892–1918) was shot down behind British lines in the closing months of the war.

Lawrence of Arabia

T. E. Lawrence (1888–1925) had a brilliant war, leading Arab tribesmen in many successful guerrilla raids against the Turks, and capturing Damascus in 1918.

1919

Jan	5	Theodore Roosevelt, former US President, dies
	5	Spartacus League initiates week of revolt in Berlin
	5	National Socialist (Nazi) Party formed in Germany
	11	Rumania annexes Transylvania
	21	Sinn Fein Congress claims Irish independence
	23	Socialists win German election
	25	Peace Conference adopts principle of League of Nations
Feb	1	Portugal declares for monarchy
	3	President Wilson presides at first League of Nations
	3	International Socialist Congress meets in Berne
	11	Friedrich Ebert elected President of Germany
	23	Benito Mussolini founds Fascist Party in Italy
	28	US diplomat Lodge speaks against League of Nations
Mar	22	Bela Kun declares Hungary a Soviet Republic
Apr	5	Eamon de Valera elected President of Sinn Fein
	8	Red Army invades Crimea
May	3	Fighting breaks out between Britain and Afghanistan
	6	Peace Conference shares out German colonies
Jun	3	Fresh British troops arrive at Archangel in Russia

	6	Finland declares war on Russia
Jul	27	Large-scale race riots in Chicago
	31	Germany adopts Weimar Constitution
Aug	31	US Communist Party founded
Sep	15	China ends war with Germany
	22	Big steel strike in US
	25	Spitzbergen given to Norway by Paris Peace Conference
Oct	6	Norway adopts alcohol prohibition
	12	British troops pull out of Murmansk in Russia
	13	Dock strike in New York
Nov	13	US Senate rejects Wilson's peace treaty proposals
	15	Red Army captures Omsk
	28	Latvia declares war on Germany
Dec	16	German troops leave Latvia and Lithuania
		The Arts
		W. Somerset Maugham's novel *The Moon and Sixpence*
		Pablo Picasso's painting *Pierrot and Harlequin*
		Bernard Shaw's play *Heartbreak House*
		Elgar's *Cello Concerto*

The Treaty of Versailles

Never have hopes of peace been so high as in the Treaty of Versailles, here shown in full session in the Hall of Mirrors in Louis XIV's great palace. The Germans had been assured that American President Woodrow Wilson's 14 points would form the basis of a settlement: the Americans had intended to initiate a League of Nations.

Both were bitterly disappointed – the Germans became victims of the conflicting greeds of the European Allied powers, and the Americans found that politicians at home had withdrawn their support. So although the Treaty was signed on June 28th, with the Germans making no secret of their profound opposition to its terms, it soon came to nothing. Within weeks, the Treaty of Versailles was being denounced throughout Germany and one agitator found it a most useful political weapon. His name was Adolf Hitler.

This American cartoon is one of many similar expressions of hope, all destined to be cruelly dashed.

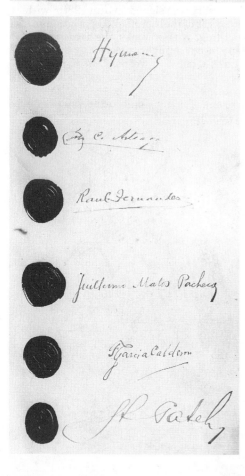

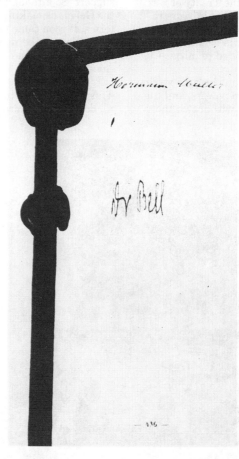

Signed and sealed

The politicians who signed the Treaty of Versailles had all achieved their common purpose in the defeat of Germany. However, none of them had properly worked out what they wanted then, apart from vague threats made during the war itself, such as Lloyd George's famous promise to 'squeeze Germany until the pips squeak'.

In fact their common purpose was dissipated in widely differing policies that simply could not be reconciled. Lloyd George wanted a moderate peace but was stuck with unfortunate election promises to bring war criminals to trial; Georges Clemenceau wanted revenge and reparation; Vittorio Orlando wanted Italy's territorial claims against Austria realised.

Top left: Woodrow Wilson, Georges Clemenceau, Arthur Balfour and the Italian Foreign Minister Sidney Sonnino arrive at the Peace Conference.

Top right: The Allied Women's delegation arrives.

Centre left: The German delegation.

Above right: The Conference in session.

Left: The signatures on the Treaty itself.

Post-war Germany

Any thoughts of magnanimity towards a defeated enemy were entirely absent from the post-war settlement and an impoverished Germany was made even poorer by the imposition of heavy reparations payments. No opportunities to exploit her were missed. Children unborn at the time were to pay a high price for this short-sighted folly which sowed the seeds of the Second World War.

Top left: Empty cattle pens are a clear indication of Germany's destitution.

Top right: In Munich more than 30,000 Germans protest against the Versailles decision.

Above left: German troops return home over the Rhine.

Above right: German tanks are broken up outside Berlin.

Meanwhile back at the Ritz

These British merrymakers celebrate their country's victory over their defeated enemy with champagne and party hats at the Ritz Hotel in London.

The Cenotaph

There were lengthy deliberations on the placing of Britain's most solemn memorial to her fallen sons, but a site in Whitehall was eventually chosen. The site is shown (above left) some ten years before the Cenotaph was built. It was in the heart of London, near the Houses of Parliament, the Admiralty and the War Office, and close to Westminster Abbey and Buckingham Palace. The Cenotaph, designed by Sir Edwin Lutyens (1869–1944), is seen (above right).

Rosa Luxemburg

Rosa Luxemburg (1871–1919), a Polish-Jewish Marxist, and a superb orator and organiser, was murdered by the extreme right wing in post-war Germany.

Nancy Astor

American born Lady (Nancy) Astor (1879–1964) (right) was Britain's first woman Member of Parliament.

Auguste Renoir

The great French Impressionist painter, Auguste Renoir (1841–1919), died at his villa in Cannes on December 3rd at the age of 78. He painted almost until the end.

First non-stop Atlantic flight

On June 15th, a Vickers-Vimy biplane bomber piloted by Captain John Alcock (1892–1919) and navigated by Lieutenant Arthur Whitten Brown (1886–1948) landed in Ireland after the first non-stop flight across the Atlantic. Unfortunately, the nose of the plane dug into the ground on landing, but the two heroes were unhurt and both received knighthoods.

The end of the German fleet

On June 21st, the German fleet scuttled itself at Scapa Flow in the Orkney islands. It was the final act of defiance of a fleet that had never been defeated in battle, but the scuttling solved an embarrassing problem for the British who had been wondering what to do with the ships. Here, the hulk of the battle cruiser *Moltke* is towed into Rosyth.

Violent strikes in Britain

Nationwide strikes for a shorter working week in many industries, including rail and iron workers, miners, and even the police, caused much bad feeling. Here, a strike-breaker at King's Cross, London, has been attacked.

Jack Dempsey

Jack Dempsey (1895–1983) beat Jess Willard in the world heavyweight boxing championship on July 4th.

1920–1929

The 1920s

Perhaps the most enduring images of the 1920s are those of the Jazz Age – the 'flappers', the Charleston, the decadent frantic world of *The Great Gatsby*. But behind the marathon dancing and the scandalous new fashions more sinister movements were at work. In the war-devastated countries of Europe the spectre of extreme nationalism grew larger and darker with the rise of Mussolini's Fascist Party in Italy and of Hitler's Nazis in Weimar Germany. In the Soviet Union the ruthless revolutionary fervour of Lenin and Trotsky gave way to the equally ruthless power-play of Joseph Stalin.

In Britain, at the beginning of the decade, men who had returned from the bloodbath of the Great War formed one third of the million or so unemployed in the land that was to have been made fit for heroes to live in. Overseas the most serious challenge yet to the power of the British Empire was posed by the civil disobedience campaign in India.

In the United States the outward-looking administration of Woodrow Wilson, whose hand was so evident in the peace settlement of 1919, was replaced by the isolationist governments of Warren Harding and the taciturn Calvin Coolidge. Domestic problems loomed large as gangs spawned by prohibition brought lawlessness to the streets of major cities and the growing ranks of the Ku Klux Klan preached militant white supremacy in the southern states. Throughout it all, a stock market boom fuelled by ever-increasing speculation threatened to overreach itself and plunge the country into economic disaster. The last months of the decade saw the Wall Street Crash, which ended the fragile economic growth of the 1920s and sounded the first blast of the Great Depression that was to follow.

The rise of Fascism

Resentment against the terms of the Treaties of Versailles and Trianon, which extorted a heavy penance from the defeated Germany, proved a fertile breeding ground for the extreme nationalism of the National Socialist German Workers' Party. Led after 1921 by an Austrian ex-Corporal and former freelance artist, Adolf Hitler, the Nazi movement, with its fanatical hatred of Bolshevism and the Jews, rapidly gained support in a country racked by hyper-inflation and political disintegration. From being a small movement on the fringes of politics at the beginning of the decade the Nazis emerged by 1929 as a fully-fledged party of almost 200,000 members, poised for the major electoral successes they were to achieve the following year.

In Italy, Fascism was making even more momentous gains. The former socialist agitator turned nationalist, Benito Mussolini, declared himself leader of the National Fascist Party in 1921. The following year his black-shirted supporters staged the famous March on Rome and Mussolini became head of the Italian government. In 1924, amidst accusations of intimidation and electoral fraud, a landslide victory in the polls confirmed the Fascists' hold on power.

The rise of Stalin

An ideological mirror-image of the growth of Nazism and Italian Fascism was working itself out in the Soviet Union during the decade. Lenin's death in 1924 created a power vacuum at the top of Russian politics which Josef Stalin moved rapidly to fill. The nature of Communist thinking changed from Trotsky's 'permanent revolution' to Stalin's 'Socialism in one country'. Trotsky himself was exiled and other leading opponents were purged by Stalin's secret police. The experiment in collectivisation of Soviet agriculture, which was to become one of the greatest human tragedies of the century, had already begun as the decade drew to a close.

Science and technology

Developments in the sciences during the 1920s were to have far-reaching consequences for the lives of ordinary people. In the field of medicine Alexander Fleming discovered penicillin and insulin was isolated by scientists working in Canada. There were giant strides in flight technology, with the development of civil airship programmes, the first helicopter and the first liquid-fuelled rockets. Niels Bohr was awarded a Nobel Prize for his work in atomic physics, the full implications of which were not to become clear for many years. In London the first birth control clinic was opened by Dr Marie Stopes and the first flickering images were transmitted by John Logie Baird through a new medium – television – which was to make almost unprecedented changes in the social habits of millions of people.

Literature and the arts

The decade saw the publication of such experimental works as T. S. Eliot's long poem *The Waste Land* and James Joyce's stream-of-consciousness novel *Ulysses*. The Bloomsbury group first came to the notice of the reading public, and in Ireland the grand old man of Irish letters, the poet and dramatist W. B. Yeats, was awarded the Nobel Prize for Literature. In music, a whole new form – jazz – gave its name to the age. To the disapproval of an older generation and the wild enthusiasm of the young, the innovative sounds of jazzmen like Jelly Roll Morton, King Oliver and Duke Ellington spread the word from New Orleans and Chicago to the rest of the Western world. In the visual arts, the bizarre images of Dada laid the groundwork for surrealism, while the theories of Walter Gropius and the Bauhaus school made their mark on public and domestic architecture alike. Meanwhile, from the studios of the United States, the march of the movies continued, creating new popular heroes in the likes of Charlie Chaplin, Rudolf Valentino and Douglas Fairbanks.

Pages 96–7: A scene from My Lady of Whims *(1925), starring Clara Bow.*

1920

Jan	5	Radio Corp. of America formed for world broadcasting
	10	Treaty of Versailles takes effect
	16	League of Nations holds first meeting
	16	Prohibition becomes law in US
	25	Death of Italian painter Modigliani
Feb	2	Estonia signs peace treaty and claims independence
	7	Bolsheviks execute White Admiral Kolchak
	8	Bolsheviks capture Odessa
	27	Russian peace offer rejected by US
Mar	7	Bolshevik offensive on Polish Front
	10	Ulster votes to accept Home Rule Bill
	16	Constantinople occupied by Allies
	19	US Senate definitively rejects Treaty of Versailles
	19	In Germany, Socialists rebel and capture Essen
Apr	1	Birth of Nazi Party in Germany
	30	Britain abolishes conscription
May	8	Poles and Ukrainians capture Kiev
Jun	24	Riots in Londonderry put down by British Army
Jul	6	Russia opens big offensive against Poland

Jul	10	Canada: Arthur Meighen becomes PM
	21	Sinn Fein and Ulster Unionists riot in Belfast
	23	Poland seeks peace with Russians
	31	Russians postpone peace talks and march on Warsaw
Aug	1	Foundation of British Communist Party
	19	Russian Army defeated by Poles at Warsaw
	28	Women get the vote in US
Sep	1	Lebanon wins independence from France
Oct	16	US Marines kill Haitian rebel leader
Nov	2	Warren Harding becomes President of US
	14	Sebastopol captured by Red Army
	15	Danzig declared free city
	16	Counter-revolution ends in Russia
Dec	23	N and S Ireland to have own Parliaments
		The Arts
		Colette's novel *Chéri*
		Henri Matisse's painting *The Odalisque*
		Eugene O'Neill's play *Beyond the Horizon*
		Sinclair Lewis's novel *Main Street*

More Irish problems

Politicians in Westminster were now unable to control events in Ireland. Support for the Republican cause grew; Sinn Fein, the political arm of Catholic Irish Nationalism, superseded Redmond's Parliamentarians at the 1918 election, winning 73 seats which they refused to take up in Westminster.

Meanwhile the military elements, the Irish Republican Brotherhood (later the IRA) and the 'Irish Volunteers' stockpiled arms in readiness. A dead Irish Volunteer and a wounded British soldier are seen (below). The two modes of protest had been united when the President of the Volunteers, de Valera, became Sinn Fein President in 1917. De Valera spent much time in the USA raising support and money through the Irish-American organisation Clan na Gael.

Ulster Unionists hoped for the permanent exclusion of the north from any Home Rule settlement and were prepared to seize control of Ulster should any attempt be made to introduce a Parliament in Dublin with authority over the whole of Ireland. By 1920 the cycle of violence had escalated into a terrorist war.

Civil war in Ireland

The British government had alienated much Irish opinion by executing the leaders of the Easter Rising, interning many Republicans and attempting to introduce conscription.

The crisis became civil war on January 21st 1919 when Irish Volunteers shot two policemen dead at Soloheadbeag. On the same day 37 Sinn Fein MPs established the *Dail Eireann* (an Irish Parliament) and proclaimed the establishment of an Irish Republic. The British government had been thrown a direct challenge over Irish sovereignty.

The war was characterised by brutal violence on both sides. The IRA had the upper hand until the introduction in 1920 of ex-servicemen known as 'Black and Tans' (because of the colour of their uniforms) and 1,000 former Royal Irish Constabulary officers. Between January 1919 and May 1921 there were 622 killings and a breakdown in law and order.

Home Rule Bill

In December 1919 a new Home Rule Bill was introduced proposing Parliaments in Dublin and Belfast and an Irish Council to handle all-Irish affairs. The system would be complex and Ireland would remain part of the Empire with Dominion status.

Unionists believed they could maintain the north's British status. By the end of 1920 Prime Minister Lloyd George had accepted the notion of separate treatment for Ulster and now had to persuade Republican politicians of the need for Partition, representing the victory of Unionism and the notion of a divided Ireland.

Above: Unionist workers chase Sinn Fein supporters along York Street in Dublin.

Left: Republican suspects are interrogated by British soldiers.

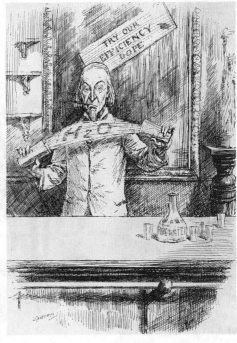

Finish your drinks, please

On January 16th, the Volstead Act, prohibiting the manufacture and distribution of alcohol, went into effect in America. There had been a long-standing groundswell of opinion in favour of prohibition and by the beginning of the First World War, two-thirds of the States were 'dry'. But it took a National Act to complete the job.

Above left: Federal agents pour whisky down the drain.

Above right: A cartoon of the time.

Left: Federal agents destroy barrels of illicit beer.

Birth pangs of Communism

Russia remained in turmoil. The State had been greatly expanded to manage newly nationalised industries and to attempt to secure food for the cities, but it could not immediately resurrect a shattered economy. In a new era of change, debates and demonstrations, such as that pictured (left), were commonplace as the workers found themselves excluded from the decision-making process.

Amid the chaos there were visions of a new society. For some, the breakdown of old ways heralded the arrival of genuine Communism.

Revolutionary art, such as the poetry of Vladimir Mayakovsky, flourished, while Yevgeny Zamyatin, who had been a Bolshevik, produced a novel *We*, a critique of totalitarianism which influenced both Aldous Huxley and George Orwell.

Blood flows before the Reichstag

The atmosphere in Germany was tense as Left and Right factions clashed on the streets and squares of her towns. Sometimes the most innocent occurrences could be misread: a massive but peaceful march turned into a massacre in the centre of Berlin in January, when agitators encouraged some of the marchers to try to get into the Reichstag. The armed police guarding the building (left) fired on the crowd with rifles and machine guns, wounding and killing many as they attempted to flee from the forecourt.

Expensive firewood

One of the provisions of the Treaty of Versailles was that Germany was to have no submarines or military aircraft. Disposing of submarines was quite easy: they could simply be taken to sea and scuttled. But disposing of aircraft scattered over airfields the length and breadth of Germany was more difficult. Here (left), a German woodman and his son have found one solution – they have simply sawed up the propellers for firewood. Memories of these sights were to fester in the minds of Germans for years.

The Kapp *putsch*

There were still many royalist sympathisers in Germany and on March 13th there was an attempt at a royalist coup in Berlin, led by Dr Wolfgang Kapp. The rebels were able to occupy some government buildings, forcing the government to retreat to Stuttgart, but the German workers were infuriated, and immediately called a general strike. In the face of this the rebels were helpless, and had to flee. The coup failed after only a few days. The photograph (left), taken from a hotel in Munich, shows troops sympathetic to Dr Kapp on the march.

The miners want more money

Britain's miners walked out on October 18th over a claim for two shillings more per week. They did not return to work until November 3rd.

Modigliani dies

The Italian painter Amedeo Modigliani (1884–1920) died on January 25th at the age of 35. This drawing dates from the early years of the First World War.

Charlie Chaplin

Charlie Chaplin (1889–1977) remained the most popular film star of his day. Here, he is seen with Jackie Coogan in *The Kid*.

'The world's sweetheart' marries

On March 29th Mary Pickford (1893–1979) 'the world's sweetheart' married Douglas Fairbanks, the world's most eligible bachelor.

When the laughter stopped

Roscoe 'Fatty' Arbuckle was a popular American film comedian, but a charge of rape and murder, of which he was found not guilty, effectively ended his career.

1921

The great British coal strike

British miners hated and feared the mine-owners and had welcomed the wartime takeover of the pits by the government because it meant continuity of work and wages, and a stringent observance of safety regulations. But now the government decided to hand back the mines and refused to nationalise them. In protest against this, the miners came out on a national strike on March 31st and refused to return until July 1st, after the government had promised to subsidise the coal industry. Their strike had become a lockout. Their traditional allies, the railway and transport unions, failed to support them and in the end they were obliged to settle on terms imposed by the owners that were shameful and humiliating. Wage reductions in other industries followed: and neither Lloyd George nor the Liberals ever received another chance to 'make Britain a fit country for heroes.'

Below: As the strike begins, pit ponies are brought to the surface.

Babe Ruth

In 1921, 'Babe' Ruth (right) scored 177 runs, a major league baseball record that still stands. Lou Gehrig (left) was another outstanding player. His 184 RBIs in 1931 is an American League record.

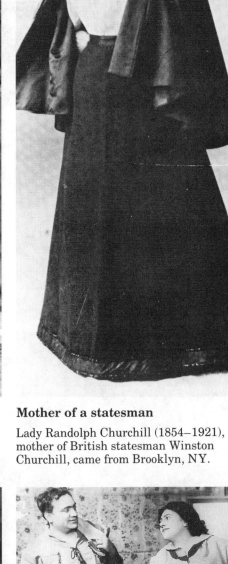

Mother of a statesman

Lady Randolph Churchill (1854–1921), mother of British statesman Winston Churchill, came from Brooklyn, NY.

A flawed administration

Warren G. Harding (1865–1923), inaugurated as the 29th President of the US in 1921, was kindly and popular but widespread corruption flourished in his administration. He is seen (above) with his wife.

Caruso dies

Enrico Caruso (1873–1921), the Italian operatic tenor was one of the first singers whose fame was broadened by recordings.

The Irish Free State

With a truce in mid-year, the focus of the Irish conflict returned to London. Lloyd George met Republican leaders. Above right: IRA leader Michael Collins and Sinn Fein representative Arthur Griffith arrive at Number 10.

In December 1921 a treaty was signed which provided for an Irish Free State within the Empire with a Boundary Commission to decide the areas of jurisdiction of the Northern and Southern Parliaments.

Ulster opted out of the Free State and the six Counties were separated. Whilst Republicans felt this was only temporary, Ulster Unionists were determined that it should be permanent. Above left: Crowds in Downing Street await developments.

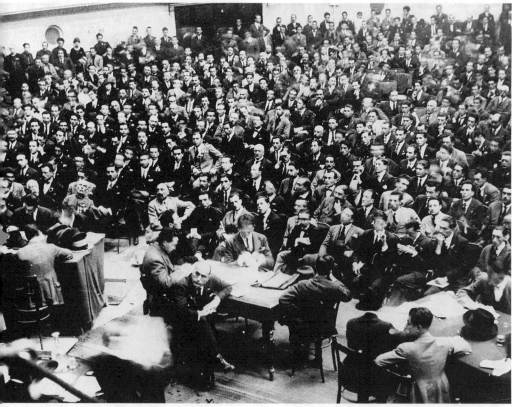

Hitler and Mussolini

Two extreme nationalist political agitators took their first steps towards power during the year, one in Weimar Germany and the other in Italy. Adolf Hitler (seen above in the first political photograph taken of him) shook off his life as an aspiring artist and

unemployed ex-corporal to become leader of the National Socialist German Workers' Party, where he turned his newly-discovered gift for oratory to good account. Meanwhile in Italy, Benito Mussolini, ousted from his editorship of a socialist

newspaper, took the path to fascism. His party gained 35 seats out of more than 500 in the parliamentary elections in May.

Lenin's 'New Economic Policy'

At the Tenth Party Congress in March, Lenin announced the first elements of the 'New Economic Policy'. Grain seizure was to be replaced by a tax, and private trade would gradually be legalised to revitalise the economy and improve the food supply.

At the same Congress, Lenin (above left) sent the Red Army out against the sailors of Kronstadt. These sailors had been part of the revolutionary vanguard in 1917, and were now staging a revolt, condemning the lack of democracy and popular

participation in the new regime. Many people had hoped for mass involvement in the running of the State, but these aspirations were now shattered. Above: Caricatures erected outside the Kremlin during the Congress.

War between Turkey and Greece

The defeat of Turkey in the First World War gave the Greeks the opportunity to seize territory from their old enemy and, encouraged by Lloyd George and his allies, they advanced into Turkey to claim territory on the Aegean coast of Asia

Minor. The Turks resisted fiercely under their new leader, Mustafa Kemal (left). He realised that stopping the Greeks was a matter of survival, not only for him, but for his country too, and he made desperate efforts to hold them back, sometimes

succeeding in fierce counter-attacks. But the Greek Army, seen (right) moving their headquarters, continued their relentless advance until they were decisively defeated by the Turkish Army the following year.

A land fit for heroes

The plight of unemployed ex-servicemen in Britain was terrible. In spite of promises by Lloyd George and other politicians, the government made no real effort to create jobs, and many able-bodied men found themselves out of work or forced to accept humiliating jobs well below their capacity, as in the case of these ex-servicemen, starting work as street pedlars.

Sacco and Vanzetti

On July 14th, a jury in Massachusetts found two Italian anarchists Nicola Sacco and Bartolomeo Vanzetti guilty of murder, although it was obvious that the trial was rigged. In spite of many appeals and a wealth of evidence which pointed to their innocence, they finally went to the electric chair in August 1927.

Birth of a legend

Mysterious footprints in the Himalayan snow started the legend of Big Foot that, like the Loch Ness Monster, was to keep the newspapers happy for years.

Prince Hirohito

Crown Prince Hirohito paid Britain his first official visit in May. Six months later he ascended the throne as Regent due to his father King Yoshihito's mental illness.

Birth control

In March, Dr Marie Stopes (1880–1958) opened her first birth control clinic in London. Most clergymen and many doctors opposed it because they feared it would encourage promiscuity.

1922

Resilient Turks fight back

The Turkish Army had been demoralised by its defeat in 1918 and the Greeks had taken advantage of the situation to advance against their ancient Ottoman adversary. The old Turkish High Command was discredited too, with its heavy reliance on German advice and weaponry.

But the Turks had an advantage in the person of Mustafa Kemal Pasha (1881–1938), seen here inspecting his troops before battle – a military leader of outstanding ability who had taken over in 1920. There was not much he could do at first: the advancing Greeks were being almost openly encouraged by Lloyd George. But he soon had the resilient Turks fighting back.

The Allies, suddenly concerned about the extent of the Greeks' success, had forbidden them to take Constantinople, but in August Kemal suddenly counter-attacked and inflicted a disastrous defeat on the Greeks who fled in confusion. He followed his success by capturing Smyrna which was promptly burned down by his marauding troops.

The burning of Smyrna

The speed and violence of the Turkish advance took not only the Greek Army but the overseeing Allies completely by surprise. No one was over-concerned by a minor Greek invasion into Turkish territory although some limits were recognised, as when the Greeks approached Constantinople and were told that this was not to be taken. This pious hope was rudely shattered by the sudden reversal of Greek fortune and the victorious reoccupation of lost territories by the Turks. The terrified inhabitants of Smyrna are seen (left) leaving the burning port in whatever vessels will carry them. The Allied leadership was in some confusion but Lloyd George was too committed to the Greek cause to do nothing and he appealed to his Allies to join him in defending the Straits against the Turks.

British intervention fails

Lloyd George received a cool response to his plea for aid in the Dardanelles. The French and the Italians were not interested. And among the Dominions only the Australians and New Zealanders offered any support – although they had vivid memories of the Straits from their experiences at Gallipoli six years earlier. A joint force under the British general Sir Charles Harington was occupying Chanak in the Straits with the intention of confining the Turkish advance and keeping the Dardanelles as an international waterway. But there was no political support from the Allied powers and this intervention was ineffective. Left: The victorious Turkish Army and its supply train of camels camp outside Smyrna.

The Turks get their way

The Allies decided that they had had enough and there was a conference which in October resulted in the Treaty of Mudania by which Turkey regained Eastern Thrace and Adrianople while guaranteeing the Straits as an international seaway. This was presented as a reasonable compromise but, in fact, it was a considerable diplomatic and military triumph for the Turks, seen (left) celebrating their triumph round a giant flag outside Smyrna. The Treaty was ratified the next year in the Treaty of Lausanne by which Turkey gave up all the non-Turkish territory she had gained in the World War but recovered much other territory, including Smyrna and Eastern Thrace. The Aegean had finally settled down and Kemal could get on with the real task of transforming Turkey into a modern industrial state.

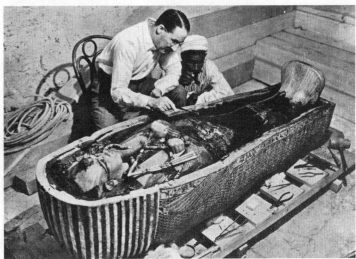

Tutankhamen

Archaeologist Howard Carter and his patron Lord Carnarvon had been searching for years in the Valley of the Kings (in Luxor) for an unrobbed Egyptian royal tomb. Most of the tombs had been desecrated and looted comparatively soon after they had been sealed. Even the Great Pyramid at Giza with all its elaborate seals and devices was empty by the time of the Ancient Greeks. But in November, in an obscure part of the valley, an Arab worker discovered some steps under a pile of rubble. When the rubble was removed a sealed door was revealed. Behind this was the greatest archaeological discovery of all time – the tomb of the boy King Tutankhamen.

Above left: Carter and Carnarvon and their party pose outside the steps of the newly discovered tomb.
Above right: Howard Carter at work inside the tomb.
Left: A gilt wooden statue of the King on a raft holding a harpoon.
Above: Carter examines the sarcophagus of the King.

Oxford bags

These wide-legged trousers were all the rage for every man in fashion.

The 'It' girl

Clara Bow (1905–1965), Hollywood's first sex symbol, became known as the 'It' girl.

The darling of the music halls

Marie Lloyd (1870–1922), famous for her insinuating songs, died this year.

Mussolini

Known to his fellow countrymen as 'Il Duce', the dictator Benito Mussolini (1883–1945) formed Italy's first National Fascist government in 1922. He went on to lead his unprepared country to universal defeat in the Second World War. He was executed on April 28th 1945 after the German collapse.

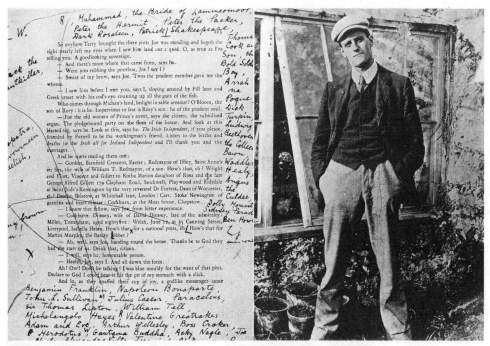

James Joyce

The great Irish writer was born in Dublin, and although he left Ireland at the age of 22 to live the rest of his life on the Continent, his boyhood memories of his native city colour all his work. His masterpiece, *Ulysses*, published in 1922, tells the story of a day in the life of Dubliner Leopold Bloom, with a host of colourful characters and minutely portrayed events. It was at first almost universally banned for what was then regarded as its obscenity. Other famous books by Joyce include a collection of short stories, *Dubliners* (1914), an auto-biographical novel, *Portrait of the Artist as a Young Man* (1916) and his last and most complex and difficult work, *Finnegans Wake* (1939).

Far left: Joyce's amendments to the page proofs of *Ulysses*.

London calling

The British Broadcasting Company was formed on October 18th (it became the British Broadcasting Corporation in 1927) and set up its studios in Savoy Hill off the Strand in London. From here the new Company made its first broadcast on November 14th. News programmes and music played a central role and have continued to do so in radio ever since.

The recording and broadcasting equipment in this early studio (left) would make a modern electronics engineer smile but this was the most advanced technology available at the time. The first newscasters had to wear dinner jackets when they addressed the nation as the General Manager, John Reith, believed that wearing casual clothes for so important a job might incline them to casual habits.

Louis Armstrong

The jazz age produced many great jazz players and among the greatest of them all was Louis ('Satchmo') Armstrong (1900–1971), seen here with an early jazz band. Born in New Orleans, he developed his particular trumpet style during the 1920s, became famous in the 1930s and was an extremely popular figure. Not only was he one of the world's greatest trumpeters, but he became the first solo jazz virtuoso. His deep 'gravelly' singing voice became equally well known and he invented 'scat' singing. He appeared in a number of films such as *High Society* as his inimitable self. Behind all the exaggerated gestures and wisecracks he remained a superb musician, totally in control of his technique and his instrument.

1923

Jan	1	French pilot sets new air speed record of 217 mph
	9	New Zealand: Writer Katherine Mansfield dies
	10	US withdraws last troops from Germany
	11	French and Belgian troops occupy Ruhr in Germany
	13	US Senate agrees to take in 25,000 Armenian orphans
Mar	3	US Senate rejects International Court of Justice
	14	Allies recognise Vilna and East Galicia as Polish
Apr	26	UK: Duke of York marries Lady Elizabeth Bowes-Lyon
	30	US only permits alcohol on ships 3 miles out at sea
May	8	English batsman Jack Hobbs scores 100th century
	21	UK: Stanley Baldwin is new PM as Bonar Law resigns
Jun	4	Spanish Archbishop of Saragossa murdered
	8	UK: Law allows wives to divorce husbands for adultery
	10	Switzerland and Liechtenstein form Customs Union
	15	20,000 dead in Persian earthquake
Jul	6	Suzanne Lenglen wins Wimbledon for 5th time running
	10	All non-Fascist parties in Italy abolished
	25	100 killed in Bulgarian train crash
Aug	2	US President Harding succeeded by Calvin Coolidge
	6	Gustav Stresemann becomes German Chancellor
	13	Mustafa Kemal elected President of Turkey
	15	Eamon de Valera arrested by Irish Free State
	31	Italian govt seizes Greek island of Corfu
Sep	2	Adolf Hitler in fierce attack on Weimar Republic
	3	US recognises Mexican government
	3	Greece appeals to League of Nations over Corfu
	10	Irish Free State joins League of Nations
	27	Martial law decreed in Germany
	28	Ethiopia joins League of Nations
Oct	12	Turkish capital moved from Istanbul to Ankara
	15	New York Yankees win World Series
	25	US: Teapot Dome oil reserves scandal
	29	Mustafa Kemal proclaims first Turkish Republic
Nov	8	Hitler's coup in Munich fails
	11	Hitler arrested in village outside Munich
	25	First UK-US wireless broadcast
Dec	7	UK: 8 women now MPs
	13	Lord Alfred Douglas jailed for libelling Churchill
	17	Greek Army deposes King George II
	27	Hirohito, Regent of Japan, escapes assassination
		The Arts
		Sergei Eisenstein's film *Battleship Potemkin*
		F. Scott Fitzgerald's stories *Tales of the Jazz Age*
		Dorothy L. Sayers' novel *Whose Body?*
		Sigmund Freud's study *The Ego and the Id*

Growth of the Ku Klux Klan

The early 1920s saw spectacular growth in the membership of the Ku Klux Klan, an American secret society dedicated to white supremacy, anti-Roman Catholicism and anti-semitism. The Klan, which took its name and structure from those of a white supremacist organisation of the 1860s, was founded in Georgia in 1915 by 'Colonel' William J. Simmons, an ex-Minister, who styled himself Imperial Wizard of the Invisible Empire. From its origins in the southern States, it quickly became a powerful force in Texas, Oklahoma, Indiana, Oregon and Ohio. By 1923, under the leadership of Simmons' successor, Hiram Wesley Evans, a dentist from Dallas, it claimed to have a million members throughout the United States.

By day the Klansmen were often respectable members of their local community – small-town businessmen and politicians sharing the post-war xenophobia of many of their countrymen. But at night, behind the anonymity of their sinister peaked hoods, white robes and fiery crosses, they entered a world of mysterious rituals, silent processions and secret greetings as the Grand Goblins, Great Titans and Kleagles of their order. In many towns the Klan operated as a law unto itself in dealing with its enemies, and there were numerous stories of beatings, tarrings and featherings, brandings and even murder.

Earthquake in Tokyo

More than 100,000 people were killed and over two million were made homeless by an earthquake which flattened the Japanese capital city of Tokyo just before noon on September 1st. Only the hilltop and suburban areas of the city survived. The quake was followed by widespread flooding and cholera, and martial law was declared. Hundreds of thousands of refugees abandoned their ruined homes and fled to the countryside in search of food and shelter.

J'Y SUIS—J'Y RESTE.

French occupation of the Ruhr

Despite opposition from the American and British governments, the French President Raymond Poincaré ordered the occupation of the Ruhr Basin, and in January more than 100,000 French and Belgian troops marched into Germany's industrial heartland. The move was intended to force repayment of German war reparations. In fact it led to a campaign of civil unrest, with violent demonstrations, and accelerated the catastrophic fall in the value of the Deutschmark.

Hyper-inflation in Germany

1923 saw the value of the German Mark plummet uncontrollably. At the beginning of 1923 it had been worth 2.38 US dollars, but by the summer one American exchanged 7 dollars for 4,000 million Marks. At the height of the crisis inflation was running at 2,500 per cent a month. Workers were paid twice a day and by the evening a loaf of bread could cost what a house had been worth in the morning. Children played with the worthless notes in the street. A cartoon in *Punch* shows the 'Exchange Asylum'.

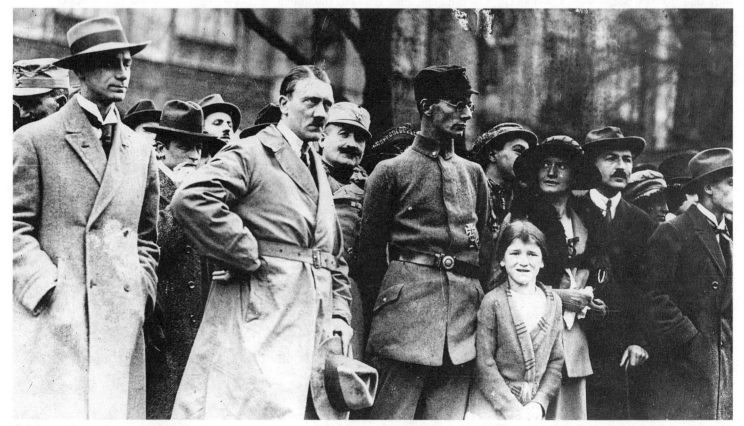

Hitler's Munich beer-hall *Putsch*

Adolf Hitler, leader of the little-known National Socialist German Workers' Party, staged an abortive *Putsch* in a Munich beer-hall on November 8th. This attempt to overthrow the Republican government of Germany (with the support of Field Marshal von Ludendorff) failed when local military and political leaders withdrew their proclamation of national revolution as soon as Hitler's paramilitary brownshirts released them. Hitler served nine months in prison where he wrote *Mein Kampf*.

Elections in Ireland

William Cosgrave's Cumann na nGaedheal party won the first general election to be held in the newly formed Irish Free State, with 63 out of the 153 seats contested. The Nationalist Party Sinn Fein won 44.

First performance of Edith Sitwell's *Façade*

On June 12th, the poet Edith Sitwell (1887–1964) staged the first public performance of her and William Walton's musical entertainment *Façade* at London's Aeolian Hall. Hidden behind a curtain, she chanted the poetry through a megaphone.

Royal wedding

On April 26th, Lady Elizabeth Bowes-Lyon, the 22-year-old daughter of the 14th Earl of Strathmore, married his Royal Highness Prince Albert Frederick Arthur George, Duke of York, at Westminster Abbey. The future Duchess of York is seen leaving her parents' London house in Bruton Street, which had been besieged by press reporters and photographers since news of the engagement became public in January. The royal couple spent the first days of their honeymoon at Polesden Lacy in Surrey.

Prohibition in the United States

Bootlegging of illicit alcohol continued to be big business in the United States after ratification in 1919 of the 18th Amendment to the American Constitution, forbidding the manufacture, sale, import or export of intoxicating liquor. Police hauls like this one in Georgia failed to contain the ever-growing network of illegal stills, warehouses and speakeasies.

'Empress of the Blues'

Bessie Smith (1894–1937), America's 'Empress of the Blues', made her first recordings in New York City.

Lenglen's fifth British success

In July the French tennis star Suzanne Lenglen (1899–1938) won the British women's singles for the fifth time.

Hobbs' 100th 100

English cricketer Jack Hobbs made his 100th century while playing for Surrey against Somerset at Bath.

1924

Jan	21	China: Kuomintang Congress admits Communists	16	French agree to leave Ruhr in Germany within 1 year
	22	USSR: Stalin joins forces with Zinoviev and Kamenev	Sep 1	Dawes Plan settling German reparations takes effect
	23	UK: Ramsay MacDonald becomes first Labour PM	18	India: Mahatma Gandhi fasts in bid to end riots
	27	Italy and Yugoslavia sign treaty: Fiume ceded to Italy	Oct 2	USSR: Trotsky takes command of Red Army in Georgia
Feb	3	Woodrow Wilson, former US President, dies	10	Washington Senators win World Series 4-3
	4	India: Mahatma Gandhi is freed from prison	12	Death of French writer Anatole France
	19	Shah Ahmad of Persia is deposed	13	China: Northern Faction's HQ in Shanghai falls
Mar	25	Greece: Parliament deposes King George II	29	UK: Conservative victory in general election
Apr	1	Germany: Hitler sentenced to 5 years' imprisonment	Nov 4	Calvin Coolidge is elected US President
	6	Italy: Fascists win overwhelming victory in election	26	USSR: Trotsky is denounced by Communist Party
	28	US sends troops to Honduras in case of election unrest	29	Italian composer Giacomo Puccini dies
May	1	Greece proclaims a Republic	Dec 2	UK and Germany sign commercial pact
	4	8th Olympic Games opens in Paris	20	Germany: Adolf Hitler is released from jail on parole
	26	US: Bill signed to limit immigration and bar Japanese	24	Albania is declared a Republic
	31	China recognises the USSR		*The Arts*
Jun	2	US grants full citizenship to American Indians		Noel Coward's play *The Vortex*
	13	G. Doumergue succeeds Millerand as French President		E. M. Forster's novel *A Passage to India*
	17	S Africa: Nationalists led by Hertzog win elections		George Gershwin's music *Rhapsody in Blue*
Jul	11	India: Hindus and Muslims riot in Delhi		Cecil B. de Mille's film *The Ten Commandments*
Aug	6	UK and USSR make trade agreement		Puccini's opera *Turandot*

Lenin dies

Lenin, the greatest revolutionary of them all, died on January 21st at the age of 53, after a long illness. He had been weakened by three strokes over the previous two years and had been out of touch with the day-to-day running of the mighty Communist State he had created. Not surprisingly, the will he left was above all a political document.

His elder brother Alexander had been shot in 1887 for his part in an attempt to assassinate Tsar Alexander III when the young

Vladimir Ilyich Ulyanov (Lenin's real name) was a youth of 17. This experience turned Lenin into a dedicated revolutionary whose only objective was to get rid of the regime that had killed his brother and replace it with a proletarian dictatorship. This could only be done through the seizure of power by an ideologically single-minded group of revolutionaries. That he was able to achieve this objective while still in his 40s is a tribute both to his energy and his dedication to the Communist cause.

Keeping death off the roads

When there were very few cars on the roads, traffic control systems were unnecessary and accidents few and far between. But as the number of vehicles increased most countries found it essential to institute some means of regulating the flow of traffic. A number of schemes were initiated, including one-way roads, traffic lights and the introduction of a number of traffic signs. The importance of these systems was soon recognised, and more and more were introduced.

Malcolm Campbell breaks record

This headline became increasingly familiar to the British and indeed the whole world as the indefatigable Captain Malcolm Campbell (1885–1949) again and again broke the world land speed record in ever bigger and faster cars. Campbell was ruthlessly single-minded and devoted his life to gaining and holding the record for Britain. Here, he is making small adjustments to the engine of one of his earlier speed-record cars. He broke the current record with it, and went on to break the record in 1927, at 174 mph; in 1928, at 206 mph; in 1931, at 245 mph; in 1932, at 253 mph; in 1933 at 274 mph; and in 1935 at 276 mph and, later in the year, at the magic 301.1 miles per hour.

Mallory & Irvine leaving the North Col on their Last Climb, 6 June 1924

Mallory and Irvine lost on Everest

On June 9th, the experienced mountaineer George Mallory and the young climber Andrew Irvine of Merton College, Oxford, died attempting to reach the as yet unconquered summit of Mount Everest. It was Mallory's third attempt, a previous expedition in 1922 having brought him to a record height of 26,985 feet.

When the party left base camp at Rongbuk glacier, conditions seemed ideal, but the expedition soon encountered the worst Himalayan storms in living memory and was twice beaten back to base camp. On the morning of June 8th, Mallory and Irvine set off on their final assault. They were last glimpsed at 12.50 p.m. the following day, only 800 feet from the summit, when they disappeared into a snowstorm and were never seen again.

Britain's first airline

Imperial Airways, Britain's first national airline, was formed in March. It began with 13 aircraft flying in and out of Croydon, London's only airport at the time. Although flying was very expensive in the early days the premier London to Paris route was always popular. The aircraft were short-range at first but custom-built aeroplanes, capable of flying much longer distances, soon became available.

Government policy was to use Imperial Airways as an instrument of Empire, linking all the dominions to the mother country. Within a few years, Imperial Airways airliners like this one at Gwadar (in what is now Pakistan) would be carrying passengers all over the British Empire.

The flying Scot

Eric Liddell refused to run in the 100-metres relay at the Olympics because it was held on a Sunday. Instead he set a new record in the 400-metres. He was made famous in the film *Chariots of Fire*.

Ireland

With Ulster ruled from Stormont Castle and the Irish Free State struggling to establish itself, the Irish question remained unresolved and the situation volatile as this cartoon shows.

Nathan Leopold and Richard Loeb

These two American students were sentenced to life imprisonment for murdering a 14-year-old boy. They came from very wealthy families in Chicago and murdered their victim for 'thrills'.

The British Empire Exhibition

Wembley Stadium and the Empire Swimming Pool are the only remaining buildings from the great Exhibition of 1924. Here, Queen Mary is escorted to the Burma Pavilion. Some people, including the newly appointed Master of the King's Musick, Sir Edward Elgar, found the flag-waving offensive, but Londoners flocked to the Exhibition.

Lloyd George electioneering

The great Liberal British Prime Minister was famous for his brilliant oratory. But all his eloquence could not save him from defeat in the crucial 1922 general election – a time of crisis and a turning point for the country. He is seen here speaking during the 1924 election, when the Conservatives gained office.

The Zinoviev letter

The Conservatives won the election by producing a forged letter from Soviet revolutionary Grigory Zinoviev inciting Communist revolt in Britain.

George Gershwin

1924 saw two of the legendary Gershwin's (1898–1937) most famous compositions: the musical *Lady Be Good*, and the haunting *Rhapsody in Blue*. Gershwin wrote innumerable hit songs, but he was also an important composer of serious works.

A Passage to India

E. M. Forster's (1879–1970) most celebrated work, *A Passage to India*, was published this year. He had published four other famous novels: *Where Angels Fear to Tread* (1905), *The Longest Journey* (1907), *A Room with a View* (1908) and *Howard's End* (1910).

Celluloid hero

Famous for his dare-devil, swashbuckling image, Douglas Fairbanks (1883–1939) made some of his best films in the 1920s, including *Thief of Baghdad* in 1924.

Pola Negri

This gloomy, broodingly sensual star of the silent screen (1894–1987) made a number of films with Ernst Lubitsch, among them *Forbidden Paradise* in 1924.

Franz Kafka

Kafka's (1883–1924) disturbing, enigmatic novels, of which *The Trial* (1925) and *The Castle* (1926) are best known, express the *angst* of 20th-century society.

1925

Jan	1	Norway: Capital Christiania is renamed Oslo
	3	Italy: Mussolini assumes full dictatorial control
	5	Italy: Mussolini forms new Cabinet
	5	Wyoming: Mrs Ross is 1st woman governor in US
	16	USSR: Trotsky is removed from Soviet Military Council
	20	UK and China make Treaty of Peking
Feb	14	Germany: Ban on Nazi Party lifted in Bavaria
	27	Hitler speaks at Nazi meeting in Munich beer hall
	28	Turkey: Kurdish anti-government uprising
Mar	4	US: Calvin Coolidge is sworn in as President
	12	China: Kuomintang leader Dr Sun Yat-sen dies
	12	General Chiang Kai-shek is new Kuomintang chief
	23	US: Tennessee law prohibits teaching of evolution
	29	Japan passes Bill for universal male suffrage
Apr	10	France: Paul Painlevé succeeds Herriot as Premier
	16	Turkey: Kurdish rebellion ends
	23	Morocco: French territory invaded by rebels
	25	Germany: Paul von Hindenburg is elected President
May	1	Cyprus is declared a British colony
	4	Arms conference begins in Geneva, Switzerland
	8	S Africa: Afrikaans becomes official language
	13	Britain returns to the Gold Standard
	30	British police fire on anti-imperialist crowd in China
Jun	25	Greece: General T. Pangalos takes power in coup
Jul	13	French troops start to withdraw from the Rhineland
	18	Insurrection by Druze in Syria
Aug	8	US: Big Ku Klux Klan march in Washington
	26	Henri Pétain in command of French troops in Morocco
	28	UK and Mexico resume diplomatic relations
Oct	5	Locarno Conference re German border and Rhineland
	12	USSR and Germany make commercial treaty
	18	Syria: French fleet bombs Damascus
	22	Balkans: Greece and Bulgaria in border conflict
	27	Czechoslovakia and France make treaty of mutual aid
	29	Greece obeys League; withdraws troops from Bulgaria
	31	Persia: Riza Khan Pahlavi deposes the Shah
Nov	5	Italy: Mussolini bans all left-wing parties
Dec	1	UK, France, Germany and Italy make Treaty of Locarno
	3	Border settled between N Ireland and Irish Free State
	18	USSR adopts policy of 'socialism in one country'

The Arts

Virginia Woolf's novel *Mrs Dalloway*

Scott Fitzgerald's novel *The Great Gatsby*

Franz Kafka's novel *The Trial*

Pablo Picasso's painting *Three Dancers*

Charlie Chaplin in film *The Gold Rush*

The Great Paris Exhibition

France startled the world yet again with a fascinating new international art exhibition which opened in April and ran along both banks of the River Seine in Paris. It was not so much the exhibits themselves but the new style which permeated them – a tamed version of Cubism which moved away from the curves and curlicues of art nouveau towards an exotic and unfamiliar way of handling textures and colour. It was later to become known as 'art deco'. The office (below left) and the reception hall (below right) are typical of the new art deco style.

The exhibition, which included architecture, interior design, ceramics, furniture, glass and high fashion was a major artistic event in the post-war period. There were gowns by Poiret, Lanvin and Chanel, textiles by the painter Dufy, furniture by Ruhlman and crystal by René Lalique (above right).

René Lalique

Lalique (1860–1945) was one of the designers whose work was exhibited at the Paris Exhibition. Above: His clock *Le Jour et La Nuit* (Day and Night). Right: The fountain, over 50 feet high, designed by Lalique specially for the Exhibition.

The Girl of the straight legs. "IT'S A PITY YOU DON'T CHARLESTON, AUDREY. YOUR KNEES ARE SIMPLY MADE FOR IT."

The Charleston

This fast and furious new dance was born in the South Carolina town from which it took its name. It aroused a storm of protest from clergymen, politicians and sundry busybodies. It was immoral, it was unladylike, it was likely to lead the young astray.

Predictably, it immediately became hugely popular with the young, who danced it whenever they could. The Charleston cut across all social boundaries; it was danced by working-class girls in dance halls, and at all the expensive nightclubs. Eventually even society matrons and their partners could be found enthusiastically indulging in the new craze from the USA. Above and left: Contemporary cartoons from *The Sketch* and *Punch*.

Mussolini consolidates

Having won a landslide victory in Italy in the previous year's election, Mussolini was very firmly in power. But he still felt the need to strengthen his position and therefore embarked on a programme to advance his friends and punish his enemies. He moved against his political opponents by removing them from public office, from government and from other positions of influence and authority. The police force were instructed to carry out mass arrests and destructive house searches. In a wider context, Mussolini abolished freemasonry, disbanded political clubs and associations, and shut down meeting halls.

Most effective of all, Mussolini (himself a former journalist and editor) moved against the Italian press. Newspapers which printed 'lies' (i.e. stories critical of the Fascists) were taken over, closed down and their journalists arrested. Mussolini also insisted that a Fascist appointee should serve on the board of every newspaper. Through these actions, he removed all freedom of the press.

Left: Mussolini is seen in conversation with the Italian poet-politician Gabriele d'Annunzio.

The booze war

Although the Federal authorities tried to enforce the law against alcohol, a torrent of illicit beer and whisky flowed through every town in the USA. Murderous gangsters like Capone, Moran and O'Banion were soon making fortunes distilling 'whisky' and 'persuading' speakeasies to buy it. This enormous illicit still was found in a Chicago office building.

Soviet persecution of religion

As part of the official assault on religion, the Soviet authorities began publication of the newspaper *Bezbozhnik* (*The Atheist*). Its first cover (above), entitled *The Storming of Heaven*, shows a worker confronting the major figures of the Islamic, Jewish and Christian faiths above a scene of industrial activity and ruined churches. During the purges, many thousands of believers were sent to labour camps.

Princes and paupers

With high levels of unemployment and coal industry employers demanding longer working hours for lower wages, class divisions in Britain remained as rigid as ever in the land that the First World War was to have made 'fit for heroes to live in'. Despite the Chancellor Winston Churchill's claims of economic recovery in his April Budget, poverty was still deeply entrenched in British society in the 1920s.

Left: King George V smiles for the camera as a beggar runs alongside the royal carriage.

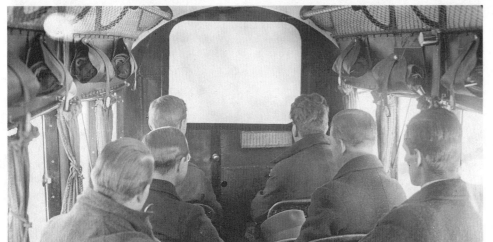

First in-flight movie

One of the more modest 'firsts' of aviation history was achieved above the English Channel on April 6th. The passengers on a scheduled Imperial Airways flight from London to the Continent became the first air travellers to be treated to a motion picture show as part of their in-flight entertainment. The film, which was shown in the aircraft's passenger saloon (left), was First National's production of Sir Arthur Conan Doyle's *The Lost World*.

Hindenburg elected President

The veteran First World War commander General Paul von Hindenburg succeeded to the German presidency on the death of Friedrich Ebert.

Buster Keaton goes west

Buster Keaton (1896–1966), the deadpan comic genius, directed and starred in the classic silent film *Go West*.

Gentlemen Prefer Blondes

American authoress Anita Loos (1893–1981) scored a notable success with her bestselling novel *Gentlemen Prefer Blondes*.

George Bernard Shaw

Born in Dublin, Shaw (1856–1950) became one of the great Socialist thinkers of his day and a founder of the Fabian Society. An outstanding critic and speaker, he became best known as a dramatist, using his brilliantly witty plays as vehicles for his concern with important contemporary intellectual and moral issues, particularly the English class system and social and political reform. This special blend of seriousness and comedy was unique to Shaw, whose plays included *Arms and the Man* (1894), *Major Barbara* (1905), *Man and Superman* (1903), *Pygmalion* and *Androcles and the Lion* (1913), *St Joan* (1923) and *The Apple Cart* (1929).

In 1925 Shaw was awarded the Nobel Prize for literature. He is depicted here by Bernard Partridge, the eminent illustrator and cartoonist, who was knighted in the same year. Partridge (who had begun his career as an actor) worked as a stained-glass artist before joining *Punch* in 1891, remaining with the magazine until his death in 1945.

Josephine Baker charms Paris

The stunning dancer from St Louis took Paris by storm in the Revue Nègre. She stayed in Paris for the rest of her life (1906–1975) starring at the Folies-Bergère, and endearing herself to all with her warm, witty personality as well as her glamour. She worked for the French Resistance in the Second World War.

P. G. Wodehouse

The British-born comic novelist (1881–1975) is shown at home in the USA, in the country house setting which features so often in his hilarious novels as a backdrop for the antics of Bertie Wooster, Gussie Finknottle and other young men about town. One of his most popular novels, *Carry on Jeeves* – Wooster's preferred instruction to his immortal manservant – was published this year.

1926

Jan	5	UK: Widows' pensions issued for first time at Post Office
	8	New King Ibn Saud renames Hejaz Saudi Arabia
	12	Pasteur Institute says it has found anti-tetanus serum
	27	UK: Logie Baird demonstrates his new invention: TV
	30	British troops withdraw from Rhineland
Feb	12	Italy: Strikes are made illegal
Mar	11	Ireland: Eamon de Valera resigns as head of Sinn Fein
Apr	2	India: More rioting between Hindus and Muslims
	4	Martial law declared in Calcutta to quell rioting
	7	Italy: Benito Mussolini survives assassination attempt
	25	Riza Khan is crowned Shah of Persia
May	1	UK: Miners go on strike
	3	UK: TUC calls general strike in support of miners
	7	US troops arrived in Nicaragua following coup
	12	Poland: Military coup led by Joseph Pilsudski
	13	Polish President Wojciechowski arrested by Pilsudski
	20	UK: Miners' conference decides to continue with strike
	23	Morocco: French seize Rif; rebel Abd el Krim surrenders
	23	France declares Lebanon a Republic
	31	Portugal: Coup led by Gomes da Costa
Jun	1	Poland: Joseph Pilsudski assumes dictatorial powers
	12	Brazil leaves League of Nations
	19	UK: 100,000 women march for peace
	28	Canada: Liberal Premier Mackenzie-King resigns
Jul	9	Portugal: General de Fragoso Carmona ousts da Costa
	23	France: Coalition govt formed with R. Poincaré as head
Aug	6	US woman is first to swim English Channel
	22	Greece: Theodoros Pangalos is overthrown in coup
Sep	6	China: Chiang Kai-shek captures Hankow
	8	Germany to join League of Nations
	11	Spain leaves League in protest at Germany joining
Oct	1	Alan Cobham makes round-the-world flight in 58 days
	7	Italy: All political opposition to Fascism is banned
	23	USSR: Trotsky and Zinoviev ousted from Politburo
	31	Death of US magician Houdini
Nov	19	UK: Miners end strike after 6 months
Dec	3	UK: Mystery novelist Agatha Christie goes missing
	25	Japan: Hirohito becomes Emperor on death of his father

The Arts

Marc Chagall's painting *Lovers' Bouquet*

Franz Kafka's novel *The Castle*

Fritz Lang's film *Metropolis*

A. A. Milne's stories *Winnie-the-Pooh*

Henry Moore's sculpture *Draped Reclining Figure*

Ramon Novarro in film *Ben Hur*

The general strike

The wheels of industry ground to a halt for nine days in May in the greatest concerted national strike ever seen in Great Britain. The action was taken in support of Britain's coalminers, two-thirds of whom had been locked out by their employers for refusing to accept the lower wages proposed by the Samuel Commission. Talks between the government, the Trades Union Congress (TUC) and the mine-owners broke down on May 2nd and the general strike began at midnight on May 3rd. The response was overwhelming. Within 24 hours there were no trains, trams or buses, no newspapers appeared on the streets, the iron and steel industries shut down and the docks lay idle.

More than 300,000 volunteers, mainly from the professional, middle and upper classes, rallied to the government cause. Society figures took on roles as lorry-drivers or telephonists. Hundreds of students helped drive buses and man signal boxes; and troops with machine guns were sent in to break the strike at the docks. On May 12th, the TUC called the strike off unconditionally, but the miners stayed out until November, when they were forced to return to work on the employers' terms.

Top: This overturned tram is a sign of how far some strikers were prepared to go in bringing transport to a halt. Trams were driven by volunteers who were highly unpopular with the striking tram drivers.

Above left: Londoners today are used to traffic jams, but they were almost unknown in 1926. Here, the sudden absence of all public transport has brought large numbers of cars on to the road with predictable results.

Above right: Some strange things happened in strange places during the general strike. For instance, Hyde Park served as a milk pool where shopkeepers and dairies sent their carts to pick up the milk that was normally delivered to them.

Left: Striking miners play cards near their silent pit at Prestonpans near Edinburgh. Many workers enjoyed an unexpected holiday during the general strike.

Top: Workers' marches like this one through the streets of London went on almost every day during the general strike. They were generally peaceful and good-natured.

Above left: Barricades were built by the Army to protect some essential services from possible disruption. Here, hastily erected barricades protect the meat market at Smithfield in London.

Above right: Armoured cars were an unusual sight on the streets of London in peacetime, but the Army was taking no chances. In this example, soldiers escort a convoy carrying essential foodstuffs.

Right: Even the Royal Navy was called in to maintain essential services. Here, sailors work as temporary dockers on the River Thames.

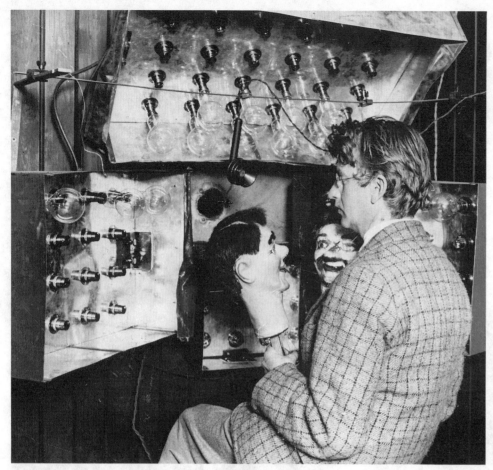

Early television pictures

In 1923 J. L. Baird in England and C. F. Jenkins in the USA devised a crude television system consisting of a series of moving black and white silhouettes. A couple of years later they were able to transmit moving pictures in half-tones.

Alan Cobham

Air ace Alan Cobham (1894–1973) completed his London–Cape Town return flight on March 13th.

Metropolis

The epic, silent film took two years to make and was the most expensive Germany ever produced. The futuristic fantasy is set in a Big Brother society of the year 2000. The director, Fritz Lang, conceived the idea for the film on seeing the Manhattan skyline during a visit to America in 1924.

Winnie-the-Pooh is born

Winnie-the-Pooh, shown here with his friend Piglet in an illustration by E. H. Shepard, was born this year in a series of stories by A. A. Milne (1882–1956).

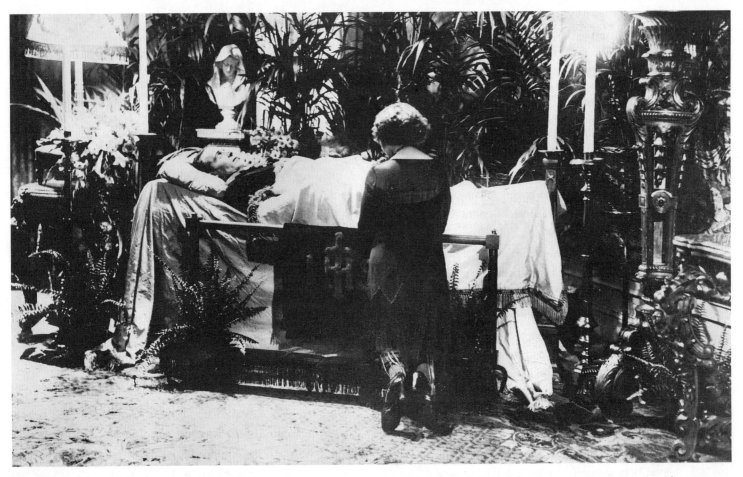

Death of an icon

Rudolf Valentino (1895–1926), the greatest screen lover that Hollywood had ever known, died on August 23rd at the age of 31. He had gone into hospital five days earlier with a ruptured appendix but complications set in and he could not be saved. A whole generation of women mourned, and the funeral of 'The Sheik' was marred by scenes of mass hysteria.

Stalin

Stalin was on his way to ousting Trotsky from the party over the struggle to bring full socialism to Russia.

Death of Monet

Claude Monet (1840–1926), regarded by many as the greatest of the French Impressionists, died this year. He is particularly noted for his series of pictures of a single subject painted under varying conditions of light, his most famous being *Rouen Cathedral*, *Water Lilies* and *The Houses of Parliament*.

1927

Jan	1	China: Kuomintang establishes govt at Hankow	
	5	US: Fox Studios show 'Movietone' sound-on-film process	
	29	Germany: Wilhelm Marx becomes Chancellor	
	31	Germany: Allied military control ends	
Feb	3	Portugal: Revolt against dictator General Carmona	
	13	Portuguese uprising defeated	
	18	Shanghai: Chinese protest at presence of foreign troops	
Mar	21	China: Chiang Kai-shek's Nationalists take Shanghai	
	24	China: US and British warships attack Nanking	
	24	China: Communists capture Nanking	
	29	Henry Seagrave sets land speed record over 200 mph	
Apr	15	China: Chiang Kai-shek sets up new govt in Hankow	
	18	Kuomintang split between Nationalists and Radicals	
May	2	Economic Conference opens in Geneva with 52 nations	
	13	Germany's economic system collapses	
	21	Charles Lindbergh completes first solo Atlantic flight	
	27	UK severs diplomatic relations with USSR	
Jun	20	Naval Disarmament Conference: UK, US and Japan	
Jul	15	General strike and Socialist riots in Vienna	

Aug 4	Naval Disarmament Conference ends – no settlements
7	Opening of Peace Bridge between Canada and the US
12	Ireland: Eamon de Valera takes seat in the *Dail*
23	Egypt: Nahas Pasha becomes leader of Wafd Party
24	US: Sacco and Vanzetti executed for murder
Sep 2	Mustafa Kemal makes Turkey a single party State
22	Sierra Leone abolishes domestic slavery
Oct 17	Norway elects first Labour govt
28	Pan Am launches world's first international flight
Nov 11	France and Yugoslavia make friendship treaty
15	USSR: Communist Party expels Trotsky and Zinoviev
22	Albania makes defensive alliance with Italy
Dec 14	China and USSR break off diplomatic relations

The Arts

Cecil B. de Mille's film *King of Kings*

Herman Hesse's novel *Steppenwolf*

Virginia Woolf's novel *To the Lighthouse*

Florenz Ziegfeld's musical *Show Boat*

Sinclair Lewis's novel *Elmer Gantry*

Lindbergh's solo triumph

By 1927 the Atlantic had been crossed by air many times, both ways, but always with large and multi-engined aircraft and crews of two or more. Only one great prize remained – the solo, non-stop flight. On May 21st, Charles Lindbergh (1902–1974), a 26-year-old pilot from Minnesota achieved this final goal, winning too the $25,000 prize money offered.

He took off at dawn from Long Island on May 20th and headed east with his Ryan monoplane *Spirit of St Louis* loaded down with petrol. He arrived at Le Bourget airport, Paris, 33 hours later and was a world hero from the moment he touched down. He is shown here arriving at Croydon airport, London, after his record-breaking flight.

Lindbergh's end was not as happy as his beginning. In later life he became a Nazi sympathiser and a powerful supporter of American isolationism. He also lost his baby son in 1932 in a tragic kidnapping and murder case.

Campbell wins again

Malcolm Campbell is shown here, breaking the land speed record yet again in one of his famous series of specially built cars, all called *Bluebird*. This year the speed he achieved was 174 miles per hour. He was to break it a year later on the beach at Pendine Sands in Carmarthenshire, Wales. However this speed was to prove inadequate in later years, and Campbell decided to move to the more spacious flatlands of America.

Riots in Vienna

There was violent unrest in Austria (especially in Vienna) during the summer months, with much bloodshed. The established classes felt exposed and threatened by Communism or, indeed, by any left-wing or socialist manifestations and the courts were inclined to be lenient to right-wing activists – on occasion, even condoning murder. It was the acquittal of anti-Communist thugs that started the worst rioting in Vienna when several public buildings were set on fire: there were many armed clashes between police and rioters. Here, a crowd is shown fleeing from police bullets before the burning law courts.

Revolution in Mexico

The Mexican government's strong anti-clerical stance caused violent opposition among the country's millions of devout Roman Catholics and the early months of the year saw a revolt in which many people were killed. The government put the revolt down fairly easily and took some distinguished prisoners. Here, one of the prisoners, General Alfredo Ruodo Quijana faces a firing squad in the courtyard of the military prison in Mexico City. He died bravely, eyes open and telling the firing squad to shoot straight.

Trouble in China

Shanghai, with its numerous enclaves of foreigners, had always been a trouble spot in China. Ever since the Boxer risings of 1900, substantial bodies of foreign troops had been stationed there. Now anti-foreigner demonstrations, such as the one shown here, gave worried foreign governments the excuse to ship in even more armed troops. The British sent 12,000 extra men under Major General Duncan, to protect the British inhabitants among the 40,000 foreigners in China's most cosmopolitan city.

Paul Klee

Klee (1879–1940), a highly innovative and influential artist, taught at the Bauhaus in Weimar for six years before he was dismissed as a degenerate by the Nazis and returned to his native Switzerland.

Founder of the Bauhaus

Especially well known as a pioneer of modern 'functional' architecture, Walter Gropius (1883–1969) reorganised the Weimar School of Art, which he had directed from 1915, as the Bauhaus in 1919, and remained as its Director until 1928, when he was succeeded by Mies van der Rohe. Gropius emigrated from Germany to the USA in 1937.

The Bauhaus aimed to produce artist-craftsmen, with none of the traditional distinction between the two. Students were trained under an apprenticeship system in special workshops.

Noel Coward

Coward's (1899–1973) string of sophisticated stage comedies began with *Hay Fever* in 1925. He was also a brilliant writer of witty songs, musicals and fiction, and a talented performer in his own right.

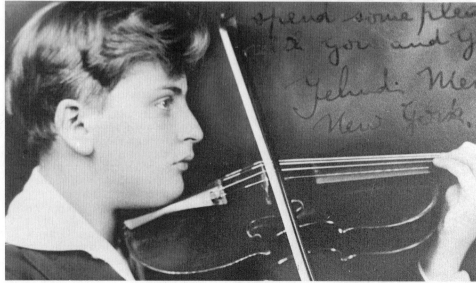

Yehudi Menuhin

Menuhin (1916–   ), the distinguished virtuoso violinist, began his career as a child prodigy in the 1920s.

The Legendary Garbo

Greta Garbo (1905–1990), whose hallmark was her inscrutability, made some of her most memorable silent films in the 1920s.

The Jazz Singer

Al Jolson (1886–1950), became one of America's top entertainers in the 1920s, best known for his black minstrel singing roles. His film *The Jazz Singer* (1927) had the first ever live dialogue.

Duke Ellington

'The Duke' (1899–1974), one of the most important figures in the history of jazz, was highly influential in his orchestral direction and composition of innovative music.

The flapper

This dizzy creature is the quintessential symbol of the Jazz Age, immortalised in particular in the novels of Scott Fitzgerald.

Mae West

The great actress (1892–1980) was famous for her glamour and suggestive wit, often expressed in one-line quips like 'When I'm good I'm very good but when I'm bad I'm better.'

1928

The Arts

Sergei Eisentein's film *October*

George Gershwin's music *An American in Paris*

D. H. Lawrence's novel *Lady Chatterley's Lover*

Maurice Ravel's music *Bolero*

Evelyn Waugh's novel *Decline and Fall*

Weill and Brecht's musical *The Threepenny Opera*

Hurrah for Hoover

Calvin Coolidge did not choose to run again for the American presidency in 1928. Instead, he backed the Republican nomination of his Secretary of Commerce, Herbert Clark Hoover (1874–1964), who won an easy victory (444 electoral votes to 87) over the Democrats' candidate, New Yorker Alfred E. Smith.

Hoover, orphaned son of Quakers from West Branch, Iowa, had graduated from Stanford University as a mining engineer and earned a sizeable fortune from mining work on several continents. He had a reputation as an administrator and humanitarian, partly as a result of work on famine relief and aid programs.

It was the jazz era. To most Americans 1928 seemed a good year. Sales of automobiles and consumer goods were expanding on the economies and techniques of mass production, wages were growing, bootleggers were thriving. So was Wall Street: stock prices were booming on speculation. Americans confidently expected a continuation of conservative Republican laisser-faire capitalism and – over-confidently – of prosperity. The Crash, the beginning of the Great Depression, was still a year away.

Flying Scotsman

In 1928 the London and North Eastern Railway offered their customers a revolutionary service, running their principal express trains non-stop from London to Edinburgh, a distance of 392¾ miles – a landmark in the history of rail travel. The train truly earned its nickname – the Flying Scotsman.

Amelia Earhart

American aviator Amelia Earhart (1898–1937) became the first woman to fly across the Atlantic this year. In 1932 she flew trans-Atlantic again, solo.

Sir Alexander Fleming

Fleming (1881–1955) discovered penicillin – by accident – in 1928, thus making one of the greatest contributions to medicine. He became a Nobel prizewinner in 1945.

King Zog

Ahmed Bey Zogu (1895–1961) had entered Tirana in Albania from Belgrade towards the end of 1924, following serious political upheavals in Yugoslavia. He had assumed absolute power under the title of President of the Republic: Albania became a monarchy in 1928, when he was proclaimed King Zog I on September 1st – a crucial event in Balkan politics. His reign lasted until 1939, when he was deposed and Mussolini made Albania an Italian Protectorate.

Hirohito

On November 10th the Emperor Hirohito of Japan (1901–1989) was enthroned according to traditional ceremony in the ancient Japanese capital of Kyoto.

Thomas Hardy

Hardy (1840–1928) died this year after a long and distinguished writing career. His Wessex novels and short stories are classics of English fiction, including such masterpieces as *Under the Greenwood Tree* (1872), *Far From the Madding Crowd* (1874), *The Return of the Native* (1878), *The Mayor of Casterbridge* (1886), *Tess of the d'Urbervilles* (1891) and *Jude the Obscure* (1895). For the last 30 years of his life he devoted himself to writing poetry.

Ellen Terry

Ellen Terry (1847–1928), one of the English theatre's greatest stars, died. She began her stage career as a young actress, working as Irving's leading lady from 1878 to 1902 and bringing distinction to her portrayals of Shakespearian heroines.

Labour Day

May 1st was the day appointed by British trade unions, socialist political parties and labour organisations to make demonstrations of solidarity with public celebrations, in line with similar events on May Day in the Soviet Union. In North America, Labor Day, an important date in the calendar, falls on the first Monday in September.

Mickey Mouse

The well-loved mouse was the most famous of Walt Disney's cartoon characters – rivalled only by Donald Duck. Both are immortalised in the Disneyland theme park in California. Disney (1901–1966) experimented initially with animated cartoons, then made his first successful sound picture, *Steamboat Willie*, in 1928. He went on to make full-length cartoon classics.

Prohibition

During the Prohibition years in the USA one way of transporting illicit gin was to strap the containers to your legs and wear an all-concealing coat!

Floods

Children had to be rescued from their homes after the river Thames burst its banks above London. Heavy rain had caused serious floods – the worst for several hundred years.

Laurel and Hardy

Stan Laurel (1890–1965) and Oliver Hardy (1892–1957) rate as one of the funniest and most enduring of comic partnerships. They joined forces in the 1920s and made a host of comic films, including four in 1928 alone.

1929

The Arts

First musical sound film *Broadway Melody*

Ernest Hemingway's novel *A Farewell to Arms*

Remarque's book *All Quiet on the Western Front*

Shaw's play *The Apple Cart*

Wall Street crash

Perhaps the greatest disaster ever to strike the financial world occurred in October when prices on the American stock market suddenly fell after years of rising share values. The Wall Street crash, which wiped out millions of dollars of investments at a stroke, heralded the beginning of the Great Depression.

Over the previous 18 months the bull market had seemed unstoppable. Some major industrial stocks had more than doubled in value as speculators rushed to the market in ever-increasing numbers to make quick profits. At times more than five million shares were traded each day. Vast funds were moved out of less profitable sectors as investors ploughed their money into the stock market. European funds also flooded into the United States, and banks lent some eight billion dollars to brokers trading shares on the New York Stock Exchange. Despite newly elected President Herbert Hoover's attempts to control the market by refusing to lend money to banks that financed speculation, values continued to escalate, reaching an all-time high on September 3rd, when over eight million shares were traded.

In the same month prices began to fluctuate for the first time, but experts and government statements assured the public that there was no cause for alarm. They were wrong. On October 24th, the bottom dropped out of the market. Panic broke out on Wall Street when prices fell an average of 18 points. Tickertape machines failed to keep up with the pace of trading as investors scrambled to sell before prices fell still further. More than 12 million transactions were recorded on October 24th alone, and a consortium of banks acted swiftly to contain the situation. But it was only a temporary delay. Share prices soon resumed their relentless fall, plummeting by an unprecedented average of 40 points on October 29th. With the value of some leading stocks slashed by over two-thirds, thousands of Americans had seen their entire life savings wiped out in a matter of days.

BROOKLYN DAILY EAGLE
And Complete Long Island News

★ NEW YORK CITY, THURSDAY, OCTOBER 24, 1929 ★

WALL ST. IN PANIC AS STOCKS CRASH

Attempt Made to Kill Italy's Crown Prince

Maiden flight of R101

Britain's first rigid airship made its maiden flight from Cardington in Bedfordshire, England, on October 14th. The R101, which measured 732 feet in length and held five million cubic feet of hydrogen, was built by the Air Ministry to carry a large payload on intercontinental flights. Only two of the five diesel engines were working during the flight, which lasted five and a half hours, and doubts about the ship's safety were expressed in some quarters.

King Alexander of Yugoslavia

King Alexander, who acceded to the throne of the kingdom of the Serbs, Croats and Slovenes in 1922, declared himself absolute ruler of the country which he officially renamed Yugoslavia. He led the Serbian forces in both the Balkan War of 1912 and the First World War, but during the 1920s he faced growing unrest among his subjects, particularly as a result of Croatian demands for autonomy. In 1929 he dismissed the Yugoslavian Parliament, abolished the constitution and outlawed all political parties in an attempt to impose unity on his troubled kingdom, but this only led to further bitterness among the separatist minorities. He is seen (left) in happier times after the christening of his son and heir, Peter.

© CASTERMAN, FLIGHT 714

Tin-Tin's first adventure

This year saw the birth of one of the most enduringly popular characters in children's literature with the publication of the first Tin-Tin cartoon. Tin-Tin, a cub reporter with a distinctive quiff of red hair and a fearless taste for adventure, was the creation of Hergé, otherwise known as the Belgian artist Georges Rémi. The comic-strip hero, seen here with his familiar cohorts, went on to be reprinted all over the world, nothing apparently being lost in translation except the name of his faithful dog Milou, who became Snowy in English.

Farewell to the Rhine maidens

As part of the evacuation of the Rhineland agreed with the German leader Gustav Stresemann, the last British troops stationed there left their base at Wiesbaden on October 12th.

Rallies in Nuremberg

The economic depression of 1929 attracted mass support to the Nazi Party. In Nuremberg enormous gatherings of the party faithful were roused by Hitler's magnetic oratory.

St Valentine's Day massacre

In one of the grisliest and most cold-blooded murders of America's gangster years, seven members of Chicago's O'Banion gang were mown down by mobsters working for Al Capone. The O'Banion gang, under the leadership of George Bugs Moran, had been hijacking whisky from consignments earmarked for Capone.

On the morning of February 14th, Moran's men were lined against a wall and raked with machine gun fire. The whole exercise took eight minutes to execute.

The 1930s

After the economic recovery of the 1920s – a recovery proved illusory by the Wall Street Crash of 1929 – the 1930s witnessed depression and unemployment throughout the Western world. The ways to economic health proved steep and costly. In the United States, unemployment remained at previously unimagined levels, seldom falling below eight million despite the expensive reconstruction programme of Roosevelt's New Deal. In Germany, the cost of recovery was higher still – too high, by 1939, to be borne any longer.

Over the whole decade there hung, like a darkening cloud, the spectre of war. In the Far East the conflict between Japan and China claimed thousands of lives as Japan brought the techniques of modern warfare to its territorial claims on Manchuria and the South of China. In China itself the Nationalist government and the Communist Red Army were locked in internecine combat. In Africa the imperial ambitions of Benito Mussolini ranged the tanks and poison gas of the Italian army against the tribesmen of Haile Selassie's Ethiopia. And in Spain the Republican government fell after almost three years of bloody conflict with the Nationalist forces of General Francisco Franco.

Hitler's Germany

From the beginning of the 1930s the rise of the Nazi party under its charismatic leader, Adolf Hitler, was meteoric. Gathering its support not only from the disenchanted urban unemployed, but also from big business, who saw in its nationalist policies a bulwark against the spread of Bolshevik revolution, the party registered its first significant electoral successes in 1930. By 1932 the Nazis were the largest party in the Reichstag, and at the beginning of 1933 Hitler became Chancellor of the German Reich. It was the beginning of the end, not only for German democracy but also for peace in Europe.

Following the convenient burning down of the Reichstag, the Nazis lost little time in showing what life in the Third Reich would be like. All civil liberties were suspended, absolute power was vested in the Führer and the anti-Semitism of so many of Hitler's rabble-rousing speeches began to enshrine itself in law. Those deemed enemies of the Reich – Communists, Social Democrats, trade unionists, Jews – began to disappear, many of them into the new concentration camps set up by Heinrich Himmler. By the end of the decade the Jewish population of the territories under German control had been deprived of all economic and personal rights. Totalitarianism and technology met as the resources of a modern industrial state were harnessed to the 'final solution' of genocide.

Expansionism and appeasement

The tearing up of the hated Treaty of Versailles was one of the Nazi Party's most popular rallying cries. Accordingly, demands for living space – *Lebensraum* – became one of the main planks of German foreign policy as Hitler sought to reclaim territories ceded to Germany's neighbours under the terms of the 1919 peace settlement. As Mussolini's Italian forces invaded the kingdom of Ethiopia, Hitler too looked for colonies. The Saar, the Rhineland, Austria, the Sudetenland were all assimilated, while Britain and France, anxious to avoid another full-scale European conflict, pursued their policies of appeasement. Finally, with the annexation of Czechoslovakia and the invasion of Poland, war became inevitable.

The Spanish Civil War

The 1930s saw Spain in a state of turmoil. The unrest in which the Republic was born, and which continued after its declaration, boiled over into civil war in 1936. It was a war that was to be prolonged by intervention, as Spain became the stage on which the international ambitions of Germany, Italy and the Soviet Union played themselves out. For many Western intellectuals it was a war of ideologies. The International Brigades harnessed the idealism of thousands of young people who saw in the battle against Franco the struggle of liberty against Fascism. For the people of Spain it was a living nightmare.

Stalin's Russia

While Hitler strengthened his grip on power in Germany, Stalin was consolidating his position in the Soviet Union with equal ruthlessness. The terror which ensued was hardly glimpsed in the West. Few if any knew the full extent of the purges with which Stalin rid himself of his political opponents or the scale of the human tragedy involved in his collectivisation of agriculture. It was not until very many years later that the death toll from his determination to stamp out the *kulak* class, or the cost in human life of the show trials and the labour camps, was seen to rank with the worst excesses of Nazi Germany.

Depression and recovery

Unemployment soared in most countries during the course of the decade, and with it the evils of poverty and social unrest. The number of people out of work in Britain, Germany and the United States reached record levels. In America the problem was made still worse by an almost unprecedented drought in the Mid-West, which reduced many farmers to penury and created an internal refugee problem as families fled the dust bowl states. In Britain the Labour government of Ramsay MacDonald gave way to a National Government as financial crisis loomed; in the United States President Roosevelt was swept to power on the back of a promised recovery programme that was to become known as the New Deal. In Germany Hitler offered Nazism as the only solution to the economic ills of the country. The politics of the Great Depression became the politics of the approach of war.

Pages 146–7: Hitler and Mussolini stride out in Rome, followed by Ribbentrop, Ciano, Goebbels and Goering.

1930

Jan	3	Stalin collectivises all farms in USSR
	28	Spanish dictator Primo de Rivera resigns
Feb	3	First ever 'untouchables' elected to local council in India
	13	US: Hughes replaces Taft as Chief Justice
	18	New planet discovered beyond Neptune is named Pluto
Mar	2	English novelist D. H. Lawrence dies
	8	Former US President Taft dies
Apr	16	Rioting in India – police fire on crowds
	24	Amy Johnson first woman to fly from UK to Australia
May	4	India: Gandhi arrested by British authorities
	20	UK: Mosley leaves Labour govt; replaced by Attlee
Jun	30	Last Allied troops leave Rhineland
Jul	10	Communist armed forces attack Hankow, China
	21	Maxim Litvinov becomes Soviet Foreign Minister
	30	Fascist National Union Party formed in Portugal
Aug	4	Soviet troops kill 200 strikers in Odessa
	5	Douglas MacArthur appointed US Chief of Staff
	7	UK: 2,000,000 unemployed
	7	Canada: Conservative R. B. Bennett becomes PM
	25	Joseph Pilsudski forms new govt in Poland
	25	Military coup in Peru
Sep	2	Rebels take power in Peking under Yen Hsi-chan
	14	Nazis win 100 seats from moderates in German elections
	15	Hitler denied seat because he is Austrian, not German
Oct	1	Irish demand independence at London conference
	4	Brazilian revolution; Getulio Vargas becomes President
	16	France plans Maginot Line along frontier with Germany
	20	British demand halt on Jewish immigration to Palestine
	22	China: Rebels massacre 8,000 in Shanghai
	27	Mussolini wants Versailles Treaty revised
Nov	2	Haile Selassie becomes Emperor of Ethiopia
	9	Social Democrats win Austrian election
	12	Indians demand Dominion status in London talks
	14	Attempted assassination of Hamaguchi, Japanese PM
	30	Germany: Nazis win Bremen in municipal elections
Dec	12	Germany: Last Allied troops leave the Saar
	12	Spanish revolution begins
	12	US writer Sinclair Lewis wins Nobel literary prize
	16	General strike in Spain

The Arts

W. H. Auden's *Poems*

Dashiell Hammett's novel *The Maltese Falcon*

Lewis Milestone's film *All Quiet on the Western Front*

Josef von Sternberg's film *The Blue Angel*

Evelyn Waugh's novel *Vile Bodies*

The Depression

Hunger and poverty were growing on both sides of the Atlantic. There were more than four and a half million unemployed in the United States by the end of the year, and over two million in Britain. Demonstrations were held in major cities and food was handed out to patient queues of jobless as in the Chicago street (above). President Hoover set up a committee to devise ways to create jobs and called for the cooperation of both public and private agencies.

In Britain, apart from demonstrations, hunger marches were organised. Three hundred and fifty marchers, including for the first time a women's contingent (below), converged on London from Scotland, Wales and all corners of the country for a great demonstration in Hyde Park on May 1st. This march was generally peaceful, but scuffles between police and demonstrators broke out on other occasions during the year.

Collectivisation

Soviet agriculture was radically transformed in the years after 1928. The 'collectivisation' of village plots into huge farms was designed to produce a more reliable food supply. Farmland and implements were to be used jointly and private trade was outlawed.

At first, collectivisation was voluntary, but in 1929 Stalin began to establish it by force. He saw the Kulaks (better-off peasants) as an obstacle and decided that they should be 'liquidated' as a class. This is mentioned in the banner (above), when the dislocation and destruction caused by collectivisation were at their most extreme. Stalin later told Churchill that the policy had cost ten million Kulak lives, commenting, 'What is one generation?'

By 1938 over 25 million individual farms had been reduced to 250,000 collectives. There was intense hardship in rural areas, and the supposed bounty of the reorganised countryside, as shown in this official, idealised painting, was a myth.

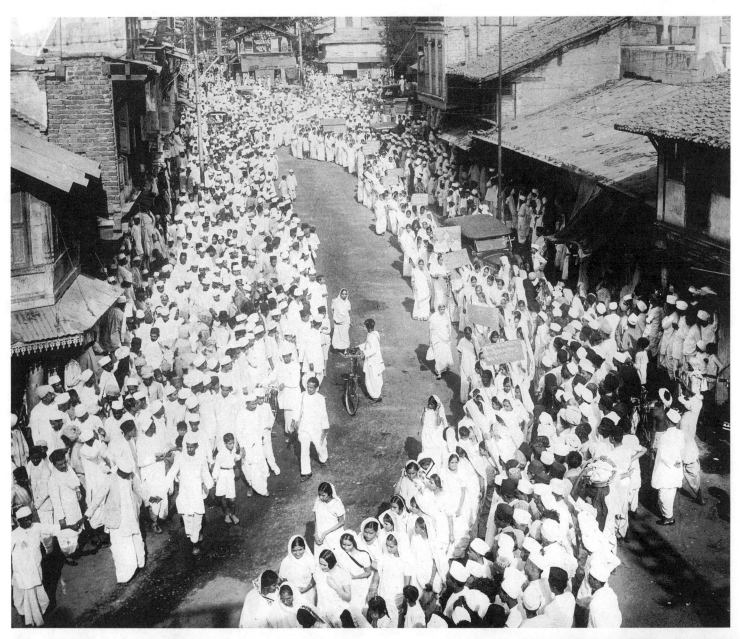

Gandhi arrested

In March Mahatma Gandhi, the Indian Nationalist leader, launched his campaign of *satyagraha* or peaceful civil disobedience. His immediate target was the British government's salt laws, which established a government monopoly on salt and levied a tax on its purchase. In a widely reported act of defiance, Gandhi and 79 of his followers left his *ashram* to march the 240 miles to the coast at Dandi, where Gandhi symbolically collected salt from the seashore. The march, which was greeted by crowds of well-wishers, led to widespread gatherings in defiance of the salt laws, such as the one on the Maidan esplanade at Bombay (right).

A boycott of liquor and foreign cloth was also launched, with large-scale demonstrations such as the one near Gandhi's Karadi headquarters (above). The situation became more serious for the authorities when violence broke out in India's North-West Frontier Province, and on May 4th Gandhi himself was arrested while sleeping under a mango tree near Dandi.

Rioting in Egypt

In July serious anti-British rioting broke out in Mansurah and other major Egyptian cities. Police and rioters battled in the streets (above) following the dismissal of the Nationalist Premier Nahas Pasha. The former Premier himself narrowly escaped death in the unrest when a soldier's bayonet thrust was diverted by his deputy.

Resignation of Primo de Rivera

In January the resignation of the President of the Republic of Spain, General Miguel Primo de Rivera, ended more than six years of military dictatorship.

Bradman triumphs

Australian cricketer Don Bradman (1908–2001) is applauded after his Test Match record-breaking score of 334 runs against England at Headingley, Leeds.

The raising of the *Hindenburg*

After 11 years and two previous attempts, the giant German battlecruiser the *Hindenburg* was salvaged by a team led by Mr Ernest Cox on July 22nd. The 700-foot-long *Hindenburg* (above) was the largest of the German fleet scuttled by its crew in Scapa Flow on June 21st 1919.

The Emperor's bride

Resplendent in his imperial robes, Ethiopia's new Emperor Haile Selassie (1892–1975) poses with his wife, Empress Menen, shortly after their marriage.

A regal couple

King George V and Queen Mary travel in state, the King wearing ceremonial military uniform and the Queen in elegant fur and veiled hat.

1931

Jan	2	Panamanian government ousted
	10	Molotov announces collectivisation of Soviet agriculture
	26	Gandhi released from prison for talks with government
	27	Pierre Laval becomes French Premier
Feb	2	Nazis demand Germany's withdrawal from League
	5	UK: Campbell breaks land speed record in *Bluebird*
	16	Indian Viceroy receives Gandhi for first time
	28	UK: Oswald Mosley forms 'New Party'
Mar	1	Navy stages coup in Peru
	3	Viceroy agrees to withdraw salt tax in India
Apr	5	Germany forms customs union with Austria
	12	Big victory for Republicans in Spanish elections
	14	King Alfonso abdicates; Spain declared a Republic
May	11	Austrian bank failure starts panic in Middle Europe
Jun	1	US to build 90 steel plants in USSR
	11	Martial law in 7 Spanish cities
	13	German bank failure forces closure of all German banks
	19	Second Five-Year Plan announced in USSR
Jul	31	Chiang Kai-shek beats Communists in N China

Aug	24	Russo-French non-aggression pact
	25	UK: MacDonald forms National Government
	28	UK: MacDonald sacked as Labour leader
Sep	2	Mussolini makes pact with Vatican
	15	UK: Royal Navy mutiny at Invergordon
	18	Japan besieges Mukden in invasion of Manchuria
	21	Britain comes off Gold Standard
Oct	11	Big march against pay cuts in London
	25	France and US agree to keep Gold Standard
Nov	10	US scientists discover secrets of atomic nucleus
	15	Germany: Nazi Party wins State election in Hesse
	20	Spanish King charged with high treason
Dec	11	British Dominions granted sovereignty
	11	Japan goes off Gold Standard
	30	Nazi Party formed in Holland
		The Arts
		Pearl Buck's novel *The Good Earth*
		Salvador Dali's painting *Persistence of Memory*
		Eugene O'Neill's play *Mourning Becomes Electra*

Japanese invasion of Manchuria

On the night of September 18th, in a surprise attack, the Japanese army invaded Manchuria. The Kwantung army, which had made a previous attempt to wrest power in the province from the Chinese in 1928, launched its assault after an incident in which trucks on the South Manchurian Railway were blown up just outside the Chinese garrison at Mukden. The garrison itself was stormed and occupied by the Japanese after heavy shelling, the Chinese putting up no resistance. The invasion was the result of a plot by officers in the Kwantung Army, but seems to have had the support of military leaders in Tokyo.

Spain declared a Republic

There were enormous demonstrations in Spain after the country became a Republic in April. Huge crowds marched through the streets of Madrid (top left) and gathered at the Spanish Republicans' tomb to express their support for the Republic. Months of constitutional uncertainty, which had their roots in the death of the dictator Primo de Rivera the previous year, finally led to the fall of the Monarchy on April 14th. King Alfonso XIII (1886–1931) (above, second from left) left Spain for Britain, after the Republicans gained a majority in the *Cortes* (the Spanish parliament) and it became clear that he could no longer rely on the support of the cities. In a broadcast address, the new President, the landowner Alcalá Zamora, spoke of the birth of the Republic as 'a peaceful revolution'.

Riots in India

Throughout 1930 the Civil Disobedience movement in India gained strength under the leadership of Mahatma Gandhi as demands grew for independence from British rule. In March 1931, however, the Indian city of Cawnpore was swept by one of the worst outbreaks of intercommunal violence in the country's history. Hundreds were killed in savage rioting after Moslem shopkeepers ignored Hindu demands that they stop work as an act of mourning for Bhagat Singh of Punjab, who had been executed by the authorities for shooting a young English police officer. Men, women and children were clubbed or hacked to death and many houses and places of worship were burned as mobs rampaged through the streets of the city. Observers reported that some thoroughfares in Cawnpore looked as if they had been hit by an earthquake (above).

National Government

The new National Government in Britain received the overwhelming support of the electorate when it was returned to power in the General Election of October 29th. The coalition had taken over in August when the Labour Prime Minister Ramsay MacDonald (above, right) failed to obtain the backing of his cabinet colleagues for a far-reaching package of public spending cuts. The drastic measures were proposed after pressure from financiers in the City of London, who feared that declining gold reserves and a run on the pound would soon plunge Britain into economic disaster. Following consultations with King George V, MacDonald, the Conservative leader Stanley Baldwin (1867–1947) (above, left) and the Liberals formed a new National Government in order to contain the situation. The political complexion of the administration was radically changed when Britain went to the polls in October. While Ramsay MacDonald remained at the head of the government, the Labour Party won only 52 seats, as against the 289 with which it had come to power only two years before. The Conservatives won 471.

Sir Oswald Mosley

In February the maverick British politician Sir Oswald Mosley (1896–1980) (seen above speaking to a crowd in London's Trafalgar Square) announced the formation of a new political party, called simply the New Party. Mosley, who resigned from the Labour government in May 1930, was formally expelled from the Labour party shortly after launching his new venture. The New Party was routed at the polls in October.

Support for Nazis

In a speech made in December Adolf Hitler (seen above with his Nazi colleagues Joseph Goebbels and Hermann Göring) claimed that the National Socialist Party, formed in 1919 with just seven members, could now count on the support of 15 million people in Germany. Earlier in the year the party had decided to take up its seats in the Reichstag and try to force the government of Dr Brüning to resign.

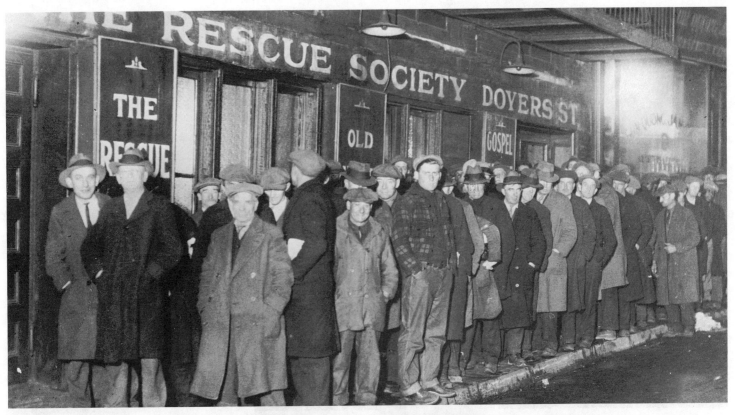

Unemployment

The USA

The number of people out of work rose sharply in most countries during the course of the year. The leader of the American Workers' Federation warned in July that if the industrial situation failed to improve, 7,000,000 people would be out of work by the end of the year. As he spoke, the total number of unemployed throughout America stood at 5,200,000. Within six months it had outpaced even his predictions, to reach a catastrophic 8,300,000. With no general system of unemployment insurance in operation, many of the unemployed were reduced to dependence on charity in order to survive, and at Christmas hungry men could be seen lining up outside hostels in New York City.

Britain

There was a similar picture in Britain (left), where there were ever-lengthening queues at employment exchanges as the number unemployed or laid off reached two and three quarter million in August. It was to remain at or around this level for the rest of 1931.

Germany

In Germany soup kitchens were opened for the unemployed (bottom left) as the numbers registered as out of work soared from 3,962,000 in June to 5,057,000 in November. The Chancellor Dr Brüning warned that the total could reach seven million during the winter. By January 1932 there were almost six million people out of work, of whom less than half were receiving financial support.

Al Capone

FBI agents finally arrested the US gangland leader Al Capone (above), who had dominated the Chicago underworld since the St Valentine's Day massacre in 1929. The only charges brought against him were for tax evasion.

The Empire State Building

The world's tallest building, the Empire State Building in New York City (above), was officially opened on May 1st. The concrete and glass skyscraper had 102 floors and stood 1,250 feet high.

Pavlova

The death was announced in London of the Russian-born ballerina Anna Pavlova (1881–1931), a few days before her 50th birthday. She had been a member of Diaghilev's legendary troupe and had danced with Nijinsky.

Thomas Edison

Thomas Edison (1847–1931), the man whose inventions changed the face of the twentieth century, died in October at his home in New Jersey at the age of 84. Amongst more than 1,000 inventions patented during his long career were the movie projector, the carbon telephone transmitter, the phonograph, the electric light bulb and an electric safety lamp for miners. His work on sound and vision also contributed to making talking pictures possible.

Stratosphere flight

Professor Auguste Piccard (1884–1962) became the first man to reach the stratosphere during his balloon flight on May 27th. Piccard took off from Augsburg in Germany and rose to a height of nine and three quarter miles.

1932

Jan	2	Japanese proclaim Manchukuo Republic in Manchuria		16	Germany lifts ban on Nazi stormtroopers
	4	Gandhi arrested in India as Congress Party outlawed	Jul	5	Salazar establishes Fascist regime in Portugal
	15	France finally pacifies French Morocco		17	Chiang Kai-shek starts anti-Communist drive
	22	Communist uprising in N Spain smashed		25	USSR, Poland and Japan in non-aggression pact
	28	China: Shanghai attacked by Japanese		31	War declared between Bolivia and Paraguay
Feb	6	*Coup d'état* by Fascists in Memel, Lithuania		31	Nazis win 230 seats in Reichstag, but are stalemated
	16	Irish elections give majority to Republicans	Aug	4	Nazi versus Communist riots in Berlin
	22	Nazis choose Hitler as presidential candidate		13	Hitler turns down Vice-Chancellorship under von Papen
Mar	9	Ex-Emperor Pu Yi made President of Manchukuo		30	Hermann Goering elected President of Reichstag
	9	Eamon de Valera elected President of Ireland	Sep	12	Von Papen dissolves Reichstag
	13	Hindenburg defeats Hitler in German elections	Oct	4	Hungary: Nationalist, anti-Semitic government formed
Apr	13	Nazi paramilitary SA and SS banned in Germany		9	Rebels control most of Manchuria
	24	Nazis win elections in 4 States	Nov	17	Hitler refuses Chancellorship when von Papen resigns
May	6	President Doumer of France assassinated		29	Non-aggression pact between USSR and France
	16	Hindu–Muslim clash in Bombay – hundreds killed	Dec	27	South Africa quits Gold Standard
	19	Irish *Dail* votes against loyalty to British Crown			*The Arts*
	21	A. Earhart is first woman to fly solo across Atlantic			Frank Borzage's film *A Farewell to Arms*
	31	Von Papen replaces Brüning as German Chancellor			Ernest Hemingway's novel *Death in the Afternoon*
Jun	14	Hitler promises to co-operate with von Papen			Aldous Huxley's novel *Brave New World*

Roosevelt landslide

In November Franklin Delano Roosevelt (1882–1945) the charismatic Governor of New York, swept to victory in the Presidential elections in one of the greatest landslides in American electoral history. His opponent, the Republican President Herbert Hoover, won only six states. The electoral vote was 472 to 59 in favour of the Democratic candidate, who won more than 22 million popular votes. The new President, who had fought a dynamic campaign on policies including repeal of prohibition, cuts in government spending and a balanced budget, pledged himself to 'a new deal for the American people'.

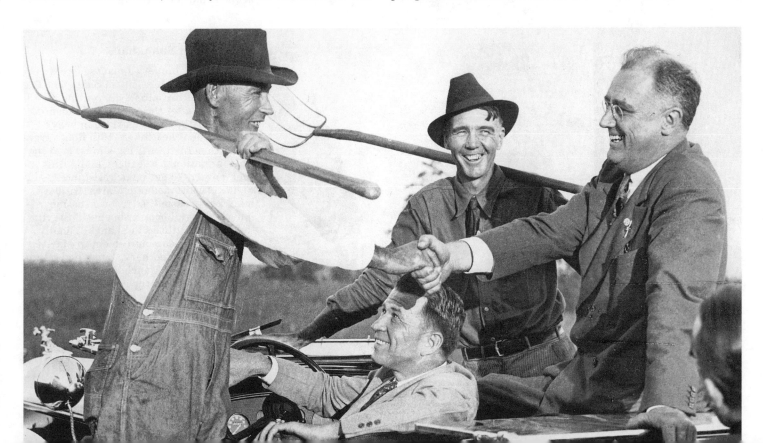

Defeat for Hitler

In the elections for the Presidency of the German Reich in April Field-Marshal Paul von Hindenburg defeated two other candidates, including the Nazi leader Adolf Hitler, to be re-elected in a second ballot. Hindenburg (seen, left, with the man whose challenge he dismissed) won a majority of nearly six million votes over Hitler. The third candidate, the Communist Ernst Thälmann, won only 3,706,388 votes to Hitler's 13,417,460. The result represented an increase of two million votes for Hitler over his showing in the first ballot, with a total of just under 37 per cent of the vote going to the Nazis. He had fought the campaign on a platform of strong opposition to the Treaty of Versailles, but Socialists claimed that his election would result in civil war and the end of personal liberties.

Unrest in Spain

There was continuing unrest in Spain after the formation of the Republic the previous year. Despite moves by the new Republican government to promote reform in areas such as education and the agricultural system, Spanish politics were still riddled with factionalism and regional problems. Communists staged demonstrations and hoisted the Red Flag in cities such as Bilbao (left), while Monarchists within the military sought to reinstate the King in a coup – the so-called *pronunciamiento* – led by General José Sanjurjo in Seville on August 12th. Regionalist demands led to the official recognition of Catalonian autonomy by the government in September. Moderate supporters of the Republic were driven into opposition by the government's actions against the Roman Catholic church, such as the expulsion of the Jesuits.

Japanese in Shanghai

At the end of January Japanese forces attacked the Chinese city of Shanghai. The Kwantung army, already in control of Manchuria after the so-called Mukden incident of 1931, was engaged in heavy combat when the Chinese 19th Route army under General Ts'ai T'ing-k'ai ignored the Chinese nationalist leader Chiang Kai-shek's orders to put up no resistance. Fighting continued into March, with hundreds of casualties reported as Japan launched aerial bombardments of the city (left). The hostilities in Shanghai finally ended after a peace agreement in May. Meanwhile, in February, Japan had set up a puppet state in Manchuria, to be called Manchukuo, under the nominal leadership of the ousted Chinese emperor Pu Yi.

Hunger marches

There were ugly scenes in London's Hyde Park in October when scuffles broke out between police and demonstrators against unemployment in Britain. The gathering of some 20,000 people came as the climax to a hunger march comprising seven contingents from many parts of the country, but particularly from those worst affected by rising levels of unemployment.

The march was organised by the Communist-led National Unemployed Workers' Movement and included a women's contingent, here seen making their way from Holloway to Hyde Park in the rain (above). Six platforms were erected in the park for speeches, and there was a heavy police presence. The trouble seems to have started amongst groups not attached to the main march but quickly flared up into rioting. Order was only restored after mounted police were deployed in baton-charges against the demonstrators (left).

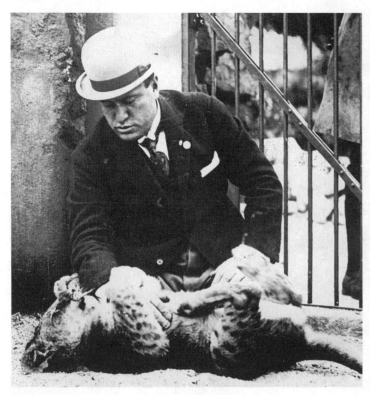

Il Duce

The Italian Fascist leader Benito Mussolini, seen with his pet lion cub in Rome Zoo, met Pope Pius X for talks at the Vatican in February on the tenth anniversary of the latter's inauguration. Mussolini, an avowed atheist, recognised the Vatican as an independent state within Italy in 1929.

The Vicar of Stiffkey

Mr Harold Davidson, the Norfolk vicar who was defrocked by the Church of England in October following accusations of sexual impropriety, took to earning a living by very unclerical means, including lion-taming in Skegness, England, where he was mauled to death shortly after this photograph was taken.

'Babe' Didrikson

One of the best all-round American sportswomen of all time, Mildred Didrikson (1914–1956) won her 80-metres hurdles title this year at the Los Angeles Olympics.

Marlene Dietrich

Marlene Dietrich, the German–American film actress who came to prominence in *The Blue Angel* in 1930, starred in Josef von Sternberg's *Shanghai Express* and *Blonde Venus*.

Nancy Mitford

Nancy Mitford (1904–1973), the English novelist and daughter of Lord Redesdale, confirmed the success of her first novel *Highland Fling* (1930) with a new work of fiction, *Christmas Pudding*.

John Galsworthy

The 65-year-old English novelist and playwright John Galsworthy (1867–1933) was awarded the Nobel Prize for Literature. Galsworthy was best known for his novels about the fictional Forsyte family.

Brave New World

The English writer Aldous Huxley (1894–1963) published his stark vision of the future in the novel *Brave New World*. His anti-Utopia was a world dehumanised by technology and political repression.

De Valera

Eamon de Valera (1882–1975) came to power in the Irish Free State when his Fianna Fail Party defeated William Cosgrave's Cumann na nGaedheal in the elections of February 16th. On March 9th he formed an administration.

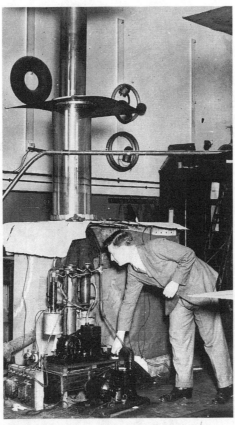

Atom split

John Cockcroft (1897–1967) became the first man to split the atom by mechanical means. The breakthrough came as a result of his work with Ernest Walton at the Cavendish Laboratory in Cambridge.

Lindbergh baby kidnap

Tragedy struck Charles Lindbergh (1902–1974), known as the Lone Eagle after his 1927 solo flight from New York to Paris, when his baby son was kidnapped from his home in New Jersey. The child was found murdered two months later.

1933

Jan	8	Anarcho-syndicalist uprising in Barcelona, Spain
	30	Adolf Hitler becomes German Chancellor
Feb	10	Hitler attacks democracy in speech in Berlin
	23	Japan now occupies all China north of the Great Wall
	27	Japan announces withdrawal from League of Nations
	27	Germany: Reichstag building razed in arson attack
Mar	1	Nazis begin mass arrests of political opponents
	4	US: Roosevelt inaugurated as President
	6	Poland occupies free city of Danzig (now Gdansk)
	6	US banks close for 4 days because of financial crisis
	7	Chancellor Dollfuss suspends Austrian Parliament
	20	Nazis open first concentration camp at Dachau
	23	Enabling Law gives Hitler dictatorial powers
Apr	1	Nazis seize Jewish bank accounts
	25	Canada comes off Gold Standard
	30	US also comes off Gold Standard
May	2	Nazis suppress German trade unions
	3	Ireland: *Dail* abolishes loyalty to British Crown
	7	Jews and Fascists fight in West End of London
	10	Paraguay formally declares war on Bolivia
	28	Nazis win elections in Danzig
Jun	19	Dollfuss bans Nazi Party in Austria
Jul	4	Gandhi jailed for a year for anti-British activity
	14	Nazis ban all other political parties in Germany
	22	Wiley Post completes first solo flight round world
	25	Leon Trotsky is granted asylum in France
Oct	14	Germany leaves League of Nations
Nov	10	Dollfuss declares martial law in Austria
	12	Nazis win huge vote of confidence in German plebiscite
	16	President Vargas of Brazil given dictatorial powers
Dec	5	US: Prohibition repealed
	12	New Reichstag meets but adjourns indefinitely
	29	Ion Duca, Rumanian Premier, murdered by Iron Guard

The Arts

Greta Garbo in film *Queen Christina*

George Orwell's *Down and Out in Paris and London*

Ernest Schoedsack's film *King Kong*

Leon Trotsky's study *History of the Russian Revolution*

Chancellor Hitler

The last nail was driven into the coffin of parliamentary democracy in Germany on January 30th when Adolf Hitler became Chancellor. The post was offered to him by the veteran President Paul von Hindenburg, who had denied him the Chancellorship two months earlier in favour of General Kurt von Schleicher. Hitler was already leader of the largest party in the Reichstag, where the Nazis had won almost 12 million votes in the elections the previous November. Immediately upon his accession he moved to consolidate his power. That evening there was a massive torchlight procession of his followers through Berlin. Within days he had given the government unlimited rights to ban all public meetings and control the press.

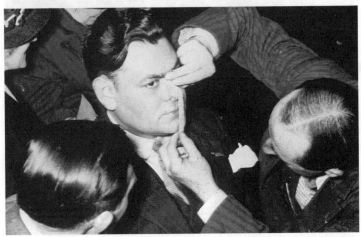

Persecution of the Jews

Hitler lost little time in using his power to legislate against the Jewish population of Germany, who had been the subject of Nazi attacks, both verbal and physical, since Hitler imbibed his racialist theories in pre-War Vienna. Jewish shops were boycotted (top) and suspected Jews subjected to degrading tests of racial purity (above, left). In retaliation, there were demonstrations against the Nazi régime by Jews in Britain and elsewhere (above, right).

In April the British Fascist leader Sir Oswald Mosley met Mussolini in Rome (above).

Burning of books

In a ceremony reminiscent of the excesses of the Inquisition, thousands of books deemed to be 'un-German' were burned in an enormous public bonfire in Berlin's Opera House Square on May 10th (left). Similar conflagrations were held in other major German cities and official figures claimed that a million volumes had been destroyed in these cultural purges.

The Reichstag fire

On the night of February 27th the Reichstag building in Berlin was burnt out, apparently by a young Dutchman. Amidst rumours that the fire was started by the Nazis themselves, Hitler enacted wide-ranging powers curtailing personal liberties.

Labour Corps

Members of the Henlein Party Labour Corps (above) at Toplitz–Schoenau. These young German-speaking Czechs, lead by Konrad Henlein, received military training as part of the campaign to unite Czech Sudetenland with the German Reich.

Nuremberg

There were extraordinary scenes in Nuremberg as thousands of Nazis gathered in the city (left) for the party convention, described as a 'Congress of Victory' by Rudolf Hess in his opening speech. On September 2nd Hitler addressed some 200,000 people on the Zeppelin Field (above), promising that the party would meet in Nuremberg for 100 years.

The New Deal

During his election campaign in 1932 Franklin Roosevelt had promised a 'new deal' for the American people. Within days of his inauguration as President the machinery was put into motion for achieving economic recovery in the depression-hit United States. A flood of new initiatives passed through Congress between March and June in what became known as 'The Hundred Days'. Amongst these measures, the National Industrial Recovery Act, described by the President as 'the most important and far-reaching legislation ever enacted by the American Congress', set up the National Recovery Administration (NRA), whose work was celebrated by an enormous parade in New York in September (left). The NRA established codes of practice for industry and commerce, banning child labour, limiting working hours, setting minimum wages and giving employees rights of collective bargaining. Within weeks thousands of businesses were displaying the NRA's blue eagle insignia, with its legend 'NRA – we do our part'.

Bodyline

There was controversy during England's cricket tour of Australia over the aggressive bowling techniques of England's Bill Voce and Harold Larwood.

The Prince of Wales

Prince Edward made a tour of Britain's distressed areas to see the way of life of the less fortunate amongst his future subjects.

Jean Harlow

Twenty-two-year-old platinum blonde, Jean Harlow (1911–1937) Hollywood's first screen sex goddess, fresh from her success in *Red Dust*.

Movie audiences gasped in terror as King Kong showed Fay Wray the New York City skyline.

1934

Jan	20	Mosley argues for Fascist dictatorship in UK	Sep	9	Fascists and their opponents clash in London
	30	All Austrian parties banned except 'Fatherland Front'		18	USSR joins League of Nations in anti-Nazi move
Feb	16	Trade treaty signed between UK and USSR		22	262 miners die in Welsh pit disaster
	17	Socialist revolt in Austria brutally crushed	Oct	16	Mao Tse-tung's 'Long March' begins
Mar	1	Pu Yi ascends throne as Emperor of Manchukuo		24	Nazi labour movement formed
	24	US promises independence for Philippines		24	Gandhi leaves Indian Congress Party
	26	Driving tests become mandatory in UK	Nov	26	Mustafa Kemal bans hereditary titles in Turkey
Apr	7	Gandhi suspends campaign of civil disobedience		28	UK: Churchill warns of growing German air strength
	29	Italian Parliament gives Mussolini dictatorial powers		30	Egyptian constitution suspended
May	16	UK: Wimbledon officials allow women to wear shorts	Dec	1	Assassination of Kirov sparks purges in USSR
	23	US gangsters Bonnie and Clyde killed by police		5	Italy and Ethiopia clash on Somaliland frontier
Jun	14	Meeting between Hitler and Mussolini in Venice		14	Mustafa Kemal gives vote to Turkish women
	23	Italy invades Albania		20	Stalin arrests Zinoviev and Kamenev
Jul	25	Dollfuss assassinated in failed Nazi coup in Austria		29	Japan renounces Washington Naval Treaty of 1922
	30	Kurt Schuschnigg is new Austrian Chancellor			*The Arts*
Aug	2	Hindenburg dies, leaving free hand for Hitler			Robert Graves's novel *I Claudius*
	2	US: Nazi rally in New York City draws crowd of 9,000			Henry Miller's novel *Tropic of Cancer*
	19	Germans vote to give Hitler dictatorial powers			Rachmaninov's *Rhapsody on a Theme of Paganini*
	20	US joins International Labour Organisation			Sholokhov's novel *And Quiet Flows the Don*

Stalin's 'purges'

While many Western intellectuals were impressed by Stalin's apparent attempts to remedy the enormous economic problems of the Soviet Union, few saw the stark reality behind the Five Year Plans and the personality cult. Little information leaked out to the West about the gigantic human cost of Stalin's forced collectivisation of agriculture and his ruthless consolidation of power. Millions of peasants were killed as Stalin sought to liquidate the Kulak class. Political opponents were arrested and tried by 'purge' committees (below) or summarily executed. By 1934 some 10 million people were believed to be in concentration camps in the Soviet Union. Between 1929 and 1936 the same number again may have been eliminated.

'I have conquered Germany'

As the German President Field-Marshal Paul von Hindenburg (below) lay dying in Neudeck, Hitler's Cabinet enacted a law combining the offices of President and Chancellor in one. Thus, on the old man's death on August 2nd, Adolf Hitler became Führer of the Third Reich.

This final consolidation of personal power came at the end of two months of political bloodshed in Germany and Austria. On June 30th, in what became known as the 'Night of the Long Knives', Hitler put paid to the ambitions of his former associate, the SA leader Ernst Röhm (seen left, with Rudolf Hess), who was rounded up with other eminent Brownshirts at a hotel in Wiessee and shot. Many others were murdered in the internal coup, which further strengthened Hitler's hold over the Nazi party.

The following month the Austrian Chancellor Dr Engelbert Dollfuss (1892–1934) was shot by a gang of SS men who burst into the Chancellery in Vienna and occupied it for several hours. There was an international outcry. Above: Dollfuss's funeral.

King of Yugoslavia assassinated

There were dramatic scenes in the streets of Marseilles when King Alexander I of Yugoslavia (1888–1934) was shot dead during a state visit to France. The assassination occurred only minutes after the King's arrival in Marseilles. He was driving through the Place de la Bourse with the French Foreign Minister Louis Barthou when a shabbily dressed man broke through the cordon of police holding back the crowds that lined the route and leapt onto the running board of his car. The gunman, who was later identified as Petrus Kaleman, a 35-year-old Croatian, fired a number of shots into the vehicle, fatally wounding the King and M. Barthou. A Colonel in the King's escort of mounted soldiers immediately cut the man down with his sabre (left), but a number of bystanders were injured as Kaleman continued firing randomly with his automatic rifle. He was savagely set upon by the crowd and died shortly afterwards of his injuries.

Strikes in Spain

The troubled Republic of Spain was swept by a wave of industrial and regional unrest during the year as Gil Robles's ruling Confederation of Autonomous Rightist Parties (CEDA) set about reversing the reforming policies of the previous administration.

Political groups increasingly looked to direct action to further their policies. The Socialist leader Francino Largo Caballero, together with Communist and Anarchist organisers, encouraged strikes amongst industrial workers in October. Support in Madrid for a general strike call was patchy, but in the Asturias striking miners took control of the provincial capital Oviedo. They held out for two weeks, defending their Workers' Commune with explosives, before the military, under General Francisco Franco, were sent in to crush them. There was widespread bloodshed during the operation, which involved four columns of troops, including Spanish Foreign Legionnaires. Those who had taken part in the rising were rounded up by the Civil Guard (above left) and there were rumours of torture.

At the same time, an Independent Catalan Republic was proclaimed in Barcelona. This too was put down by police and the military with many arrests (above right).

Sir Edward Elgar

The grand old man of English music, Sir Edward Elgar (1857–1934), died on February 23rd. A master of orchestral colour, he left two symphonies, a violin concerto, a cello concerto and many chamber and choral works.

The Long March begins

In October some 90,000 troops of Mao Tse-tung's Communist Red Army broke out of a Nationalist blockade in the Kiangsi-Fukien area of China to begin a trek in search of refuge through some of the least hospitable terrain in the world.

Pu Yi

The 28-year-old former Emperor of China Henry Pu Yi (1906–1967) was enthroned as Emperor K'ang Teh of the Japanese puppet State of Manchukuo on March 1st in a replica of Peking's Temple of Heaven.

Eric Gill

The controversial British sculptor and artist Eric Gill (1882–1940) was commissioned to work on an extension to the new Moorfields Eye Hospital in London. This photograph shows him working on the sculpture *Christ Giving Sight to Bartemus*.

Gloria Vanderbilt

Poor little rich girl Gloria Vanderbilt, (1924–   ), 10 years old, preferred living with her aunt Mrs Harry Payne Whitney. In a court case, the mother, also Gloria, was ruled unfit for custody of the child and her $2.8 million trust fund.

Bonnie and Clyde

The American bank robbers Bonnie Parker and Clyde Barrow died in a hail of police bullets in May when their four-year partnership in crime ended in an ambush on a road in Louisiana.

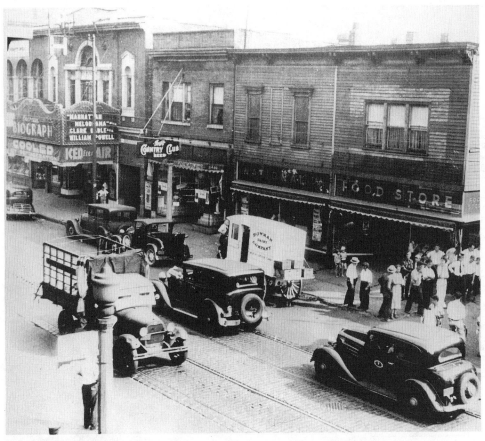

John Dillinger

Bank robber John Dillinger became one of the most notorious criminals of the Depression in the United States, capturing the public imagination with his daring bank raids and escapes. He was wanted in several states for murder and armed robbery and had escaped imprisonment several times. He was eventually run to ground and shot by the FBI in Chicago in 1934, after leaving a cinema. He had been 'shopped' by his girlfriend's landlady.

Claudette Colbert

French-born actress Claudette Colbert (1905–1996) enchanted audiences with her witty, sophisticated performances in a host of films. She made three in 1934 alone – *Cleopatra*, *Imitation of Life*, and *It Happened One Night*.

Eros and advertising: London's Piccadilly Circus in January.

1935

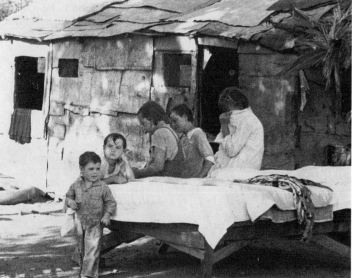

The Dust Bowl

Catastrophic dust storms swept the Mid-Western states of America in April, doing severe damage to one of the world's main corn-growing regions.

The storms followed a summer of unprecedented drought in the United States, after a heat wave causing temperatures of up to 120 degrees in places had claimed 1,200 lives and cost hundreds of millions of dollars in lost crops and cattle. Fields which should have held ripening corn were reduced to arid plains and millions of tons of topsoil were scoured off by the wind in the worst affected states. Farmers in North and South Dakota, Nebraska, Kansas, Oklahoma, Minnesota, Iowa, Missouri, Montana, Wyoming, Colorado, Texas and New Mexico saw their livelihoods destroyed as cattle died in the fields for lack of water. As some 70,000 refugees fled the dust bowl states (above), meteorologists warned that the abnormal conditions could last for two or three years.

The Second New Deal

Following the successes of the Hundred Days, the Roosevelt administration launched a new stage in its national recovery program. The so-called Second New Deal set out not just to treat the symptoms of the nation's economic decline but to attack the root causes.

On May 6th the Works Progress Administration (WPA) was set up to help create jobs for some of the eight to 10 million unemployed (left). By the end of the year it had recruited some 2,700,000 people and had begun an enormous programme of public works, ranging from roadbuilding (above) to health services. A National Youth Administration was formed to provide part-time work for young people in families on welfare without their having to leave school. In August the Social Security Act was passed, creating a system of pensions, unemployment insurance, financial help for the disabled and needy and public health provision.

Invasion of Ethiopia

The invasion of the African kingdom of Ethiopia by Mussolini's forces on October 2nd came after a long period of preparation and military build-up. The first Italian troops had left for Italian Eritrea on the Ethiopian border on February 1st, and further mobilisations had taken place throughout May, June and July. In August Mussolini called up 40,000 men as Ethiopia braced itself for the coming conflict. As Italian infantrymen crossed the border, bombers flew over, attacking first the frontier town of Adowa.

The Emperor of Ethiopia, Haile Selassie (top right), protested to the League of Nations, but despite an international outcry only limited sanctions were imposed against Italy. While Britain and France sought to negotiate a compromise solution, the full force of Italy's modern army, with its tanks, air power and poison gas, was mobilised against the poorly armed Ethiopian tribesmen (above). By the end of the year Mussolini's forces were estimated at some 650,000 (top left).

The Long March

October 20th saw the end of one of the most remarkable feats of military endurance in the history of the twentieth century. A year after their escape from the Nationalist blockade at Kiangsi, the Communist forces of Mao Tse-tung finally took refuge in the province of Shensi in the north west of China. In the intervening time the 20,000 men had marched some 6,000 miles through the mountains of Western China, fighting both Nationalist and provincial forces as they went. Many had died in the process, while others had been left behind to establish the bridgeheads of revolution. The Long March came to occupy a central place in the mythology of the Communist Revolution, forming the theme of many songs, paintings and tapestries (left).

UK unemployment

While unemployment continued to fall slowly in most countries throughout the year, the numbers of people out of work remained at distressingly high levels. In Britain there were still more than two million people registered as unemployed at the end of 1935. Faced with scenes of human misery such as out-of-work miners scrabbling through slag heaps in the hope of finding scraps of coal to heat their homes (left), the government introduced legislation to establish a system of unemployment insurance. Under the terms of a Bill put before the House of Commons in December, three-quarters of a million people were expected to benefit from payments of up to 14 shillings a week in return for weekly contributions of up to 4½ pence a week. The benefits were to be payable after 20 contributions had been made.

The Saar plebiscite

There were scenes of jubilation in the towns of the Saar Basin (left) after a plebiscite held on January 13th produced a massive 90 per cent vote in favour of a return to the German Reich. The turn-out was equally overwhelming, comprising almost all of those who were registered to vote. Speaking in characteristically messianic tones from his home in Bavaria, the German leader Adolf Hitler claimed that 'the voice of the blood has spoken its mighty word' and welcomed the end of a 'wrong which has lasted for 15 years'. However, some 2,000 refugees were reported to have fled to France on news of the result. On March 7th the Saar territories were officially reunited with Germany and later the same day Hitler and other Nazi ministers addressed a large demonstration in Saarbrücken.

Queen Astrid of the Belgians

Queen Astrid of Belgium, 29, was killed on August 29th when a car driven by her husband King Leopold III careered off a road near Lucerne, crashing into a tree.

Clement Attlee

Major Clement Attlee (1883–1967) MP for the London constituency of Limehouse, became leader of the British Labour Party on October 8th following the resignation of George Lansbury.

John Steinbeck

The 33-year-old American novelist John Steinbeck (1902–1968) received great critical acclaim for his novel about the Spanish-speaking poor of Monterey, *Tortilla Flat*.

Trans-Pacific pioneers

Pan American World Airways pioneered the first regular trans-Pacific mail and passenger flights. During the summer flying-boat bases were built and equipped as stages for the flights on Guam and on the barren and hitherto uninhabited atolls of Midway and Wake. Regular mail flights from San Francisco to Manila in the Martin M-130 flying boat, *China Clipper*, started in November.

1936

Jan	20	Death of King George V
	22	Laval's government falls in France over Italian policy
Feb	16	Victory for the Left in Spanish election
	26	Hitler launches Volkswagen motorcar
Mar	3	Mussolini nationalises Italian banks
	23	Austria, Hungary and Italy sign Rome Treaty
	25	UK, France and US sign London Naval Pact
	29	Nazis win 99 per cent of vote in German elections
Apr	1	Austria brings in conscription
	28	King Farouk ascends Egyptian throne
May	5	Italians win Ethiopian war by occupying Addis Ababa
	7	German troops reoccupy the Rhineland
Jun	4	France: Socialist Leon Blum forms Popular Front govt
Jul	6	German airship *Hindenburg* crosses Atlantic in 46 hours
	17	Civil war begins in Spain after military revolt
Aug	1	11th Olympic Games opened by Hitler
	4	Badajoz captured by Franco's Nationalist forces
	11	Chiang Kai-shek enters Canton, China
	25	Stalin executes 16 senior Communists

Sep	27	Switzerland, France and Holland come off Gold Standard
Oct	6	UK Labour Party refuses affiliation to Communist Party
	22	Martial law in Belgium to control Fascists
	27	Mrs Wallis Simpson divorces her husband Ernest
Nov	1	Mussolini announces Rome–Berlin Axis
	3	Roosevelt re-elected as US President
	18	Germany and Italy recognise Franco's Spain
	24	Anti-Comintern Pact signed by Germany and Japan
Dec	8	Somoza elected President of Nicaragua
	10	King Edward VIII abdicates
	12	Chiang Kai-shek declares war on Japan
	22	Trotsky leaves Norway for Mexico
	30	US: Striking workers at General Motors close 7 plants
		The Arts
		Charlie Chaplin's film *Modern Times*
		Sergei Prokofiev's music *Peter and the Wolf*
		Vladimir Nabokov's novel *Despair*
		Margaret Mitchell's novel *Gone with the Wind*
		Piet Mondrian's painting *Composition in Red and Blue*

Civil war in Spain

The turbulence and lawlessness which had riven Spain since the declaration of the Republic in 1931 finally erupted into full-scale civil war in July. There was widespread violence following the election in February of the left-wing Popular Front government. On July 11th, the leading right-wing politician Calvo Sotelo was found murdered, supposedly by government security forces. With the country rapidly degenerating into anarchy, a section of the army under Generals Franco and Mola rose against the Republican government on July 17th. The coup failed to take the country at a stroke, but after fierce fighting the rebels established a Nationalist government at Burgos in northern Spain, where Franco took the oath as supreme Head of State (below).

Spanish Nationalist successes

The outbreak of civil war in Spain was marked by massacres on both sides as the rebel generals sought to consolidate their hold over the country. Harrowing reports of atrocities multiplied and thousands died as the Nationalist forces mounted mopping-up operations in Spanish towns and villages (top and middle). In November the rebels, who were joined by forces sent to Spain by Hitler and Mussolini, reached the outskirts of Madrid (above). The government moved to Valencia, but Republican forces, backed by Soviet tanks and aircraft, succeeded in holding the city against the Nationalist onslaught.

German occupation of Rhineland

Germany unilaterally tore up the Locarno Pact when Hitler's troops marched into the demilitarised Rhineland. Nineteen infantry battalions and 13 batteries of artillery were deployed in the occupation of the towns of Cologne, Coblenz, Frankfurt and Mainz (above) as Hitler announced the restoration of the Reich's sovereignty over the Rhineland, which had been ceded by Germany under the terms of the Treaty of Versailles after the First World War. There was widespread condemnation of the move in Europe.

Abdication of Edward VIII

Constitutional crisis erupted in Britain over the King's plans to marry the American divorcee Mrs Wallis Simpson (1896–1986) (seen together, left, on an Adriatic cruise). Rumours of the association had been rife since Edward VIII's accession to the throne on the death of his father George V in January (top). High-level political discussions led to the announcement by the Prime Minister Stanley Baldwin in the House of Commons on December 10th that the King was intending to abdicate. The Abdication Act was signed the next day, and in the evening the former King made a farewell broadcast to the nation from the Augusta Tower at Windsor Castle (above). In a moving address he told how he had 'found it impossible to carry the heavy burden of responsibility and discharge my duties as King as I would wish to do without the help and support of the woman I love.' He was succeeded by his brother the Duke of York, whose first act as King George VI was to create him Duke of Windsor.

Joltin' Joe

In the 1936 World Series the New York Yankees took the Series four games to two. Joe DiMaggio, the Yankee Clipper, batted .346 in his first Series appearance. In all he spent 13 seasons with the Yankees, during which time they won nine World Series. His consecutive game hitting streak of 56 is possibly the safest record in the major leagues. Joe had a lifetime batting average of .325, with 361 home runs, and was considered one of the great center-fielders.

Fall of Ethiopia

As Mussolini's Italian army advanced rapidly towards the Ethiopian capital Addis Ababa, people began to load their possessions onto carts and horses in preparation for evacuation of the city (left). Fierce fighting was reported during April as area after area fell to the well-equipped invading forces. During the night of May 1st the Emperor Haile Selassie left Addis Ababa with his family and advisors. His departure was the signal for widespread rioting in the capital as mobs looted the Imperial Palace which had been thrown open to the people on his orders. Order was only restored with the arrival in the city of the Italian forces on May 5th. Later that same day, Mussolini announced to jubilant crowds in the Piazza Venezia in Rome that 'Ethiopia is Italian'.

The Jarrow March

In October some 200 unemployed men began what was to be the most celebrated of the protest marches from the distressed areas of Britain in the 1930s. The march began in the shipbuilding, iron and steel town of Jarrow, near Newcastle-upon-Tyne in the north east of England, which had been badly hit by unemployment during the economic depression.

The protestors, who called themselves the Jarrow Crusade, arrived in London at the beginning of November (left), having walked almost 300 miles, often in very poor weather conditions. The Prime Minister, Stanley Baldwin, refused to receive them at No 10 Downing Street.

Stay-down strike

Miners from Fernhill Colliery, Wales, emerge after a 12-day stay-down strike by 60 men over a minimum wage dispute. The idea of such a protest came from Hungary where, in 1934, 1,000 men stayed down.

Crystal Palace fire

On November 30th the Crystal Palace, originally built in Hyde Park in 1851 for the Great Exhibition, was completely destroyed by fire. The blaze, in Sydenham, South London, was visible for many miles.

Shirley Temple

The eight-year-old child star Shirley Temple (1929–   ) (above) reached the pinnacle of her profession with four films, including *Poor Little Rich Girl* and *Dimples*.

Hitler's Games

On August 1st the Olympic Games in Berlin were formally opened by Adolf Hitler as the last of a chain of runners from Mount Olympus in Greece lit the Olympic flame in the Führer's presence. The star of the games was to be the black American athlete Jesse Owens (above, right), who won gold medals in the 100 metres, the 200 metres, the long jump and the 400 metres relay, much to the discomfiture of Hitler and his Aryan theories of the 'master race'.

1937

Jan	7	Poland signs pact with Danzig	
	15	Austrian amnesty for Nazis	
Feb	20	Paraguay leaves League of Nations	
	25	Italian-Yugoslavian non-aggression pact	
Mar	2	Oil nationalised in Mexico	
	18	US: 500 die in Texas school fire	
Apr	2	S Africa bans political activity by foreigners	
	22	Austrian Chancellor Schuschnigg meets Mussolini	
	26	Basque town of Guernica destroyed by Nazi bombers	
May	6	German airship *Hindenburg* explodes in New Jersey	
	23	John D. Rockefeller, US capitalist, dies	
	26	Egypt joins League of Nations	
	28	UK: Neville Chamberlain becomes PM	
	31	German fleet bombards Spanish port of Almería	
Jun	12	Stalin shoots 12 Russian generals	
	18	Franco's forces take Bilbao	
Jul	11	American composer George Gershwin dies	
	17	Naval pact signed by Britain and Germany	
Jul	18	US aviator Amelia Earhart vanishes in flight	
	28	Japanese troops take Peking	
Aug	1	Nazis open Buchenwald concentration camp	

	2	Zionists endorse Peel Plan to partition Palestine
	11	Assassination of Bakr Sidqui, Iraqi dictator
Sep	8	Pan-Arab Conference rejects Peel Plan
	26	British Commissioner for Galilee murdered by Arabs
Oct	13	Belgian safety guaranteed by Germany
	16	Fascists form Nazi Party in Hungary
	17	Sudeten Nazis riot in Czechoslovakia
	22	Duke and Duchess of Windsor welcomed by Nazis
	28	Spanish government removed to Barcelona
Nov	6	Anti-Comintern Pact joined by Italy
	8	Shanghai falls to Japanese
Dec	11	Italy leaves League of Nations
	12	Japanese Army captures Nanking with many atrocities
	14	Brazil bans political parties
	24	Japanese troops capture Hankow in China
	29	Irish Free State becomes Eire

The Arts

J. R. R. Tolkien's fantasy novel *The Hobbit*

Pablo Picasso's painting *Guernica*

Jean Renoir's film *La Grande Illusion*

Hemingway's novel *To Have and Have Not*

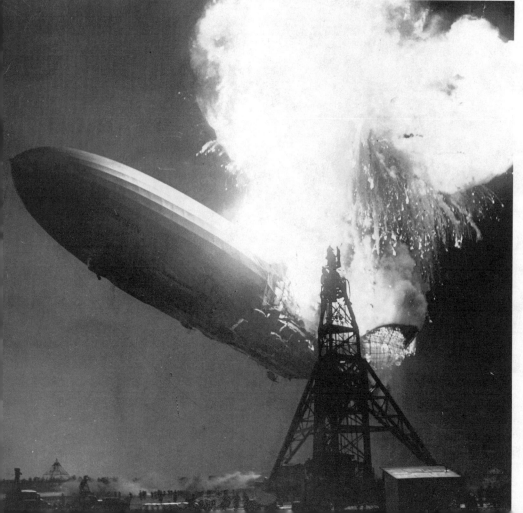

The *Hindenburg* tragedy

Thirty-three people died and many others were injured when the giant German airship the *Hindenburg* exploded and burst into flames on May 6th.

The tragedy occurred as the airship, which was the largest in the world, was coming in to land at Lakehurst, New Jersey after completing its first flight of the year from Frankfurt-am-Main with a total of 97 people on board. The 972-foot long ship, weighing 110 tons, suddenly burst into flames as it was 300 feet above the ground (left). People below watched helplessly as the seven million cubic foot hydrogen envelope was almost instantly engulfed and the blazing framework crumpled to the ground. One reporter wept openly as he gave a running commentary on the disaster.

An inquiry launched to discover the cause of the fatal explosion found that a freak combination of circumstances had conspired to produce the tragedy. A build-up of hydrogen in the rear of the ship had been ignited by an electrical storm, ground electricity from which was conducted along wet mooring ropes to the framework of the ship, a layer of rain on the fabric of the envelope having converted the whole structure into a giant electrical condenser.

Spanish Civil War

The death toll mounted and the cost in human misery soared as war-wracked Spain became an arena for international conflict on an ever-increasing scale. The Fascist powers, Germany and Italy, supplied men and equipment to General Franco's Nationalist forces. Stalin's Soviet Union supplied the Republican forces and, together with the Communists within Spain, helped organise the International Brigades which brought thousands of young left-wing idealists to the country to fight in what they saw as the struggle against fascism. During the course of the war some 35,000 people fought with the International Brigades, including 5,000 from Britain and the United States.

Guernica

On April 26th, in perhaps the single most remembered event of the war, 43 aircraft of the German Condor Legion under Colonel Wolfgang von Richthofen bombed and strafed the ancient Basque cultural centre of Guernica. At least 1,000 people, most of them civilians, were believed to have died in the raid, which outraged liberal opinion throughout the West and formed the inspiration for one of Picasso's most famous paintings (top).

Franco's Nationalists

Despite offensives by the Republicans, Franco's armies, which began the year in control of half of Spain, gradually extended their grip on the country, capturing the major centres of Bilbao and Santander. With the fall of Gijou on October 21st the Republicans lost their last remaining stronghold in the north of the country. The fighting and continuing atrocities by both sides created floods of refugees (left) and the conflict threatened to escalate still further with attacks on neutral shipping in the Mediterranean. The League of Nations was powerless to intervene.

Lebensraum

Hitler used the occasion of the fourth anniversary of the beginning of the Nazi revolution on January 30th to make a major speech on Germany's foreign policy. Speaking at a special sitting of the Reichstag, which confirmed the extension of full powers to the government for a further term of four years, he spoke of his desire to remain on friendly terms with his European neighbours. At the same time, though, he staked a claim for greater 'living space' – *Lebensraum* – asserting that 'the possession of colonies is essential to Germany' for 'economic purposes'. It was a theme to which he returned at the Nazi party's annual rally at Nuremberg in September and at a mass meeting in Augsburg in November (left), where his demands were greeted with wild enthusiasm.

Bombing at Shanghai

At least 1,000 people were believed to have died in one of the most tragic episodes of the Sino–Japanese conflict when Chinese aircraft accidentally bombed Shanghai on August 14th. The raid had been intended to sink Japanese warships, including the flagship *Izumo*, in the harbour, but the bombs fell short and caused havoc and destruction in the International Concession (left). Most of the casualties were amongst the Chinese population, who had crowded into the area for safety. Britain and France made urgent plans to evacuate their citizens from Shanghai as a massive Japanese land, sea and air offensive began the following day.

The Tennessee Valley Authority

One of the most important bodies set up under President Roosevelt's New Deal was the Tennessee Valley Authority (TVA), whose work aroused considerable interest both in the United States and overseas.

The TVA was formed in May 1933 with, in the President's words: 'the broadest duty of planning for the proper use, conservation and deployment of the natural resources of the Tennessee River drainage basin . . . for the general social and economic welfare of the nation'. Under its authority the Tennessee River became the most thoroughly controlled river in the world. Twenty new dams were built (left), 650 miles of navigable waterways provided and various reforestation programs begun. The TVA also had authority to generate and sell electricity, an activity which entangled it in legal battles with private power companies.

The Duke of Windsor

The Duke of Windsor and his new American wife, for whom he had given up the throne of England the previous year, made a controversial visit to Germany in October. The Duke and Duchess, who were married in France on June 3rd, were entertained by Adolf Hitler and other Nazi leaders, in Berlin and at the Berghof, Hitler's villa at Berchtesgaden in the Bavarian Alps. There was criticism of the trip both in Britain and elsewhere.

George VI crowned

On May 12th King George VI (1895–1952) and his wife Queen Elizabeth (1900–) were crowned in a colourful traditional ceremony at Westminster Abbey in London. Crowds of people had gathered from the early hours of the morning to watch the royal procession from Buckingham Palace. After the coronation, which was attended by representatives from all parts of the Empire, the royal family, including the young princesses Elizabeth and Margaret, acknowledged the cheers of the crowd from the balcony at Buckingham Palace (above).

Haves . . .

Crowds of the well-to-do queued at Lord's cricket ground in London, waiting to gain admission to the annual match between premier British public schools Eton and Harrow (above).

San Francisco Oakland Bay Bridge

Traffic flows over the San Francisco Oakland Bay Bridge (above), opened the previous year. At eight-and-a-quarter miles, the two-deck bridge was the longest in the world and had cost more than $77 million to complete.

. . . and have-nots

With unemployment in the United States running at over 8,000,000, the destitute of Cleveland, Ohio, lined up for hand-outs of potatoes and cabbages. In May relief funds ran out for some 78,000 people in the city.

1938

Anschluss

At 10.00 p.m. on March 12th German troops crossed the border into Austria, thus tearing up Article 88 of the Treaty of Versailles under which the union of Austria and Germany – *Anschluss* – was forbidden. The move came after the Reich issued ultimata to the Austrian Chancellor, Dr von Schuschnigg, demanding the postponement of a planned plebiscite and the installation of a Nazi régime in Austria under the chancellorship of Dr Seyss-Inquart. Schuschnigg stepped down and within hours the Swastika appeared on public buildings in Vienna and other cities. Following Seyss-Inquart's invitation to the Germans to enter Austria, Hitler himself flew back to his home country to be greeted by cheering crowds in Vienna.

Republic in retreat

With 1938 the long civil war in Spain entered its last full year. The Nationalist forces of General Franco made sweeping territorial gains. The Republicans mounted a brief counter-offensive in June, but with the withdrawal of Soviet and French aid it was clear that they could not hold out much longer. By the end of the year Franco's men were at the gates of Barcelona and the war was all but over. Loyalist Republicans continued to flee the country (left), escaping a conflict which, by the time it ended three months later, would have claimed some half a million dead.

Anti-Semitism

Hitler's invasion of Austria was followed by attacks on Jewish property throughout the country as the anti-Semitic Aryan laws were imposed. All Jewish judges and State attorneys were immediately forced out of their jobs and Jews were forbidden to leave the country or to vote in the plebiscite which took place in April. In Vienna Nazi stormtroopers watched in amusement as elderly Jews were forced to scrub the streets (left). In the upsurge of anti-Semitic violence which engulfed the Reich in November thousands of Jews were arrested in Vienna alone. The elderly were forced to leave old people's homes and were driven into the streets. Many were sent to concentration camps. By the end of the year draconian laws had been introduced depriving Jews of almost all their remaining personal and economic rights.

Bombing of Canton

In a new development in the Sino–Japanese conflict, the South Chinese city of Canton was subjected to a series of bombing raids by Japanese aircraft which left some 5,000 people dead and thousands more wounded (left). The daily raids by wave after wave of bombers virtually paralysed the city's life and were strongly criticised in the West. On October 12th Japanese troops landed in force on the Chinese mainland and began a swift advance on Canton, which fell after only minimal resistance on October 21st. By then the centre of the city was a burnt-out ruin, the Chinese having completed the work begun by the Japanese air force by setting fire to all military and industrial facilities before withdrawing. China's six largest cities – Canton, Hankow, Nanking, Peking, Shanghai and Tientsin – were now under Japanese control.

Appeasement

On September 29th the leaders of Britain, France, Italy and Germany met in Munich at a conference designed to solve the problem of Hitler's claim to the Sudeten territories in Czechoslovakia and to hold back the looming spectre of war.

Benito Mussolini, Edouard Daladier and Neville Chamberlain (top left) met Hitler for talks lasting from lunchtime into the early hours of the morning, when they emerged with a settlement. Under the terms of their agreement, the Sudetenland would be ceded to Hitler on October 1st. The Czech Prime Minister accepted the proposed plan, but described it as 'the most tragic moment of my life.'

'Peace in our time'

The French, Italian and British leaders were received in their own countries with enthusiasm bordering on ecstasy. British Prime Minister Chamberlain was met at Heston aerodrome by the Lord Mayor of London, the entire Cabinet and thousands of cheering people. He waved in the air the famous piece of paper which, he said, would guarantee 'peace in our time' (top right). From there he was driven to Buckingham Palace where he appeared on the balcony with the King and Queen to tumultuous applause from the crowds gathered in the Mall. Five days later Hitler led his troops into the Sudetenland (above, left and right).

Kristallnacht

In November widespread anti-Jewish violence broke out in Germany. In what became known as *Kristallnacht* – the night of broken glass – synagogues were bombed or burned out, Jewish shops and homes were ransacked and Jews were subjected to mob violence in the streets while the police stood idly by. Some 35,000 Jews were arrested throughout the Reich.

British troops in Palestine

Following a serious escalation in terrorist violence in Palestine, the largest continent of British troops assembled since the First World War was despatched to the mandated territory. Effective martial law was imposed on October 18th and the next day the troops stormed and occupied the Old City of Jerusalem (above), evicting the Arabs who had been holding it.

Around the world in less than four days

On July 14th Howard Hughes and four companions landed at New York in their plane the *New York World Fair* (above) after a record-breaking around-the-world flight lasting three days, 19 hours and 17 minutes.

Snow White

Walt Disney, the animator and film producer, released his first full-length cartoon feature film, *Snow White and the Seven Dwarfs*, to enormous popular acclaim. The film, a musical, took three years to complete.

Bette Davis

Bette Davis (1908–1989), the film star Lowell, Massachussetts whose screen career began in 1931, won an Academy Award for her performance in *Jezebel*.

War of the Worlds?

A young actor shot to fame with a radio broadcast convincing enough to cause panic amongst thousands of Americans. Orson Welles (1915–1985) was reporting a Martian invasion in a dramatisation of H.G. Wells's novel *The War of the Worlds*.

Carmen Miranda

Carmen Miranda (1913–1955), the flamboyant Brazilian screen star with the fruity taste in hats, on the threshold of a new career with Hollywood's Twentieth Century-Fox studios.

Britain prepares itself for the worst . . .

1939

Jan	26	Franco captures Barcelona with help of Italians
	28	Irish poet W.B. Yeats dies
Feb	27	Britain and France recognise Franco
Mar	2	New Pope Pius XII
	15	Germany marches into Bohemia and Moravia
	16	Slovakia becomes German protectorate
	16	Hungary annexes Ruthenia
	21	Germany annexes part of Lithuania
	28	Surrender of Madrid to Franco ends Spanish Civil War
Apr	7	Albania invaded by Italy
	11	Hungary leaves League of Nations
	16	USSR suggests mutual defensive deal with Britain
	27	Britain calls up all men of 20 and 21
	30	New York World's Fair opens
May	4	Molotov succeeds Litvinov as Soviet Foreign Minister
	8	Spain leaves League of Nations
	22	Hitler and Mussolini sign 'Pact of Steel'
Jun	7	Estonia, Latvia and Germany sign non-aggression pact
Jul	9	Military pact with USSR urged by Churchill
Aug	23	Germany and USSR sign non-aggression pact

	25	Britain signs assistance pact with Poland
Sep	1	Germany invades Poland
	3	Britain and France declare war on Germany
	5	Jan Christian Smuts becomes Premier of South Africa
	17	German Army reaches Brest-Litovsk
	17	USSR invades Poland from the east
	19	Aircraft carrier HMS *Courageous* sunk by U-Boat
	19	Royal Air Force begins leaflet raids on Germany
	30	British Expeditionary Force sails to France
Oct	6	Britain and France reject Hitler's peace bid
	8	Nazis incorporate western Poland into Germany
	10	Nazis deport Polish Jews to Lublin ghetto
Nov	4	Roosevelt lifts US embargo on sale of arms for war
	30	USSR invades Finland
Dec	14	USSR expelled from League of Nations

The Arts

John Steinbeck's novel *The Grapes of Wrath*

James Joyce's *Finnegans Wake*

Bertolt Brecht's play *Mother Courage*

John Ford's film *Stagecoach*

The war that had to come

The seeds of the Second World War were sown by the Treaty of Versailles which ended the First World War 20 years earlier. The Treaty, signed on June 28th 1919, imposed constraints on the development of post-war Germany which were to be deeply resented there and provided fertile soil for the Nazis' nationalist ideals in the late 1920s and early 1930s. It is no coincidence that in 1940 Hitler forced the French to sign their surrender in the same railway carriage in which the armistice was signed in 1918. The Allies' conditions for German surrender after the First World War were a simmering humiliation for the German people. Hitler's Reich, with its territorial successes and its rhetoric of racial superiority, represented for many a resurgence of national pride and sense of identity.

Europe on the eve of the Second World War was riven by political and military tensions. In Britain the government of Neville Chamberlain clung to its policy of appeasement in the face of ever-more blatant German expansionism. The French supported Chamberlain at Munich, believing themselves secure behind fortifications which were all too soon to prove outmoded and misconceived. Italy was meanwhile pursuing its own expansionist aims, notably against the almost defenceless African country of Ethiopia. In Spain, Italy, Germany and the Soviet Union had played their part in the long and devastating bloodbath that was the Spanish Civil War. The Soviet Union, over which Stalin had spent the 1930s ruthlessly consolidating his personal power, looked to the West with distrust. Woodrow Wilson's cherished dream of a League of Nations was proving at every turn a powerless illusion.

In 1938, as Chamberlain spoke of 'Peace in our time', the stage was already set for the coming conflict. The legacy of the Great War, the war that was meant to end all wars, was about to take its final terrible toll.

Far left: Hitler reviews his troops at his birthday parade in April.
Above left: Britain wakes up to the need to prepare for war.
Above right: Cheerful patriotism was the norm in the early days.
Left: President Roosevelt discusses the grim European situation with Secretary of State Cordell Hull.

Invasion of Poland

The opening shots of the Second World War were fired on the morning of September 1st when German troops crossed the Polish frontier. Typically, the Nazis staged a 'provocation' as the actual cause of the invasion although the massing of German columns on the border of Poland left no one in any doubt as to Hitler's intentions.

The Polish Army (above) put up a bitter resistance but was no match for the massive and well-oiled Nazi war machine. In a number of gallant but hopeless actions, including the use of cavalry against tanks (above left), the Poles were smashed to pieces. Moreover, the Polish rear was left in disarray by the use of terror bombing raids against civilians (below left).

Danzig

Danzig (Gdansk) was annexed by the Germans on the first day of the war, although isolated pockets of resistance held out for some time. The Westerplatte Garrison, for instance, held out for 11 days before the Germans were able to raise the flag of victory over it (right). But by then the issue was not in doubt.

On September 17th, German forces reached Brest and on the same day the Soviets invaded from the east. At the time, this appeared to be simply a stab in the back for a nation already defeated. However, with hindsight, it gave the Soviet Union an extra defensive cordon against an inevitable future onslaught. Warsaw, the Polish capital, fell on September 28th and Hitler had achieved his objective at little cost in less than a month.

Allied reaction

The Allies had seen the formidable German blitzkrieg (or 'lightning war') in action but learned little from it. The French sat behind their Maginot Line of forts and anti-tank defences running along the German frontier between Switzerland and Luxembourg, not realising that it could be rendered useless by an attack through Belgium. The British expeditionary force, with inferior tanks and artillery, mustered in northern France. For reasons now hard to explain, the Allies appear to have believed that Hitler would respect the neutrality of Belgium, Holland and Luxembourg – a belief that was to be shattered within a few months.

The British home front

Within hours of war with Germany being declared on September 3rd, air raid sirens sounded in many parts of Britain. It was a false alarm but a grim reminder that, as Guernica and a dozen other Spanish towns had proved, in this war the civilians were in the front line from the beginning. But unlike August 1914, the citizens of Britain in 1939 were well prepared for the ordeals which lay ahead. They had been issued with gas masks, fortunately never needed. They had dug trenches, seen important buildings sandbagged and public air raid shelters built. The fat and silver shapes of hundreds of barrage balloons loomed overhead.

Air raid wardens

Air raid wardens knew what they should do when the bombs began to fall. Auxiliary firemen, soon to be severely tested, knew how to tackle big fires and everyone knew how to extinguish an incendiary bomb with a stirrup pump. Even the policeman's familiar helmet was replaced by a tin hat. The signs of active war were present everywhere.

Rationing

At a more mundane level, the government had printed and issued the millions of ration books necessary to allocate fairly the food for a nation at war. Most of this food had to be imported by dangerous sea lanes. Not surprisingly, a flourishing black market soon emerged. Many women were already doing work usually reserved for men: soon they would be employed in the factories, shipyards and railway sheds on the heavy jobs that had been previously allocated to big, muscular men.

Petrol rationing was immediately introduced, with a severity that made many people take their cars off the roads for the duration of the war – removing the wheels and propping the axles on bricks. What few cars still ran had their headlights reduced to thin, shaded pencils of light which meant that night-time driving was hazardous to pedestrians and fellow drivers alike.

Blackout

And there was, of course, the universal blackout. The tiniest hint of light from the edge of a window prompted an angry shout of 'Put that light out', with the possible consequence of fine or prison sentence and the lively suspicion that you were an enemy agent signalling to German aircraft. Beneath the blackout curtains, and on buses and other public transport, glass windows were heavily taped to prevent flying glass. Everyone was exhorted to grow food in their allotment, garden or even window box. On the 'home front' Britain went to war in good heart.

Most children in big cities were evacuated to the country or small towns. There was often mutual culture shock.

In a major industrial effort, the government offered every household in the big cities an Anderson shelter, to be erected in the garden.

Most groceries were rationed and in quantities that got smaller and smaller as the war went on. One egg a week was allowed.

Some people found ingenious ways to stretch their rations. This lady's toy-like car used little petrol – but it was unique.

Trees, kerbs and lamp-posts were marked with white to help in the blackout. Here, steps at Alexandra Palace in North London make a pleasing pattern.

Women took on supposedly masculine skills with the greatest ease – but had to relinquish them, however unwillingly, when the war ended and the men wanted their jobs back.

German occupation forces in Austria

Following Hitler's March 1938 annexation of Austria, the country was assimilated into the German Reich as the province of Ostmark. This emboldened Hitler for further flexing of military muscles with the invasion of Poland in 1939. In the meantime, swapping one totalitarian regime for another, Austrians accommodated themselves with varying degrees of enthusiasm to the omnipresence of the occupying German forces (above).

Most famous film ever made

The three-hour movie masterpiece *Gone with the Wind* was released this year, winning nine Oscars. Set in the period of the American Civil War and its aftermath, it has since proved to be one of the most popular movies ever made. Following a highly-publicised search to fill the starring roles, an almost unknown English actress, Vivien Leigh, was chosen for the much-envied part of Scarlett O'Hara playing opposite Hollywood's leading man, Clark Gable.

Epstein's 'Adam'

This notorious statue, the work of British sculptor Jacob Epstein (1880–1959), caused great controversy when it was first publicly shown in 1939.

New land speed record

On August 23rd, the British driver John Cobb (1900–1952) drove his Railton Special at 368.85 mph at the Salt Flats, Bonneville, Utah – a new land speed record. The car shown here, with (inset) John Cobb in the cockpit and the designer Reid Railton at his side, had its transmission brakes cooled by ice.

Graf Spee scuttled

The powerful German pocket battleship the *Graf Spee* was finally cornered at Montevideo in Uruguay by three British cruisers shortly before Christmas. The Uruguayan government, anxious not to be involved in the war, refused to give her sanctuary and Hitler subsequently ordered her to be scuttled rather than surrender to the British. On December 17th she moved into the seaway outside Montevideo and blew herself up. Her captain, Hans Landsdorf, shot himself.

1940–1949

The 1940s

The 1940s were the decade in which the contours of today's political world map were drawn. It was a decade which began with the great European powers locked in military struggle and ended with relations between the world superpowers – the United States and the Soviet Union – frozen in the no less entrenched positions of the cold war. As the political battle-lines were drawn up in Berlin – the city from which Hitler had sought to spread his Reich throughout Europe – a new power bloc was formed by the signing of the North Atlantic Treaty. Just as the First World War had given birth to the League of Nations, so the Second provided the crucible for its successor, the United Nations.

Outside Europe and the United States, too, momentous changes were taking place in traditional patterns of power. In China Mao Tse-tung emerged victorious from the long drawn out civil war between the Nationalists and the Communists. In Asia the death knell of colonialism was sounded by the granting of independence to India after more than 160 years of British rule. And in the Middle East the seeds of a new and lasting conflict were sown by the formation of the Jewish state of Israel.

But perhaps the most momentous change of all occurred with the dropping of the first atomic bomb on Japan. As the mushroom cloud rose over Hiroshima, the world could never be the same again. From that moment forward international politics would be conducted under the shadow of the Bomb.

The War

Scarcely one generation after the 'war to end all wars', the world found itself plunged once again into bloody conflict. The scale and technological sophistication of the fighting were unprecedented, as were the number of casualties. While Britain, France and Italy lost fewer dead than in the Great War, the losses elsewhere were staggering. Some five million Germans died in the fighting, as did two million Japanese. China, in some ways the forgotten victim of the war, may have lost as many as 10 million people, Poland more than five million, the vast majority of them civilians. The greatest human cost, however, was borne by the Soviet Union, where some 20 million people died – a tragedy that was to leave an indelible mark on the national psyche. In addition to those who died as a result of the conflict between nations, millions of Jews were murdered by the Nazis in the territories under their occupation. By the end of the war, as the full horrors of the Holocaust were revealed to the advancing Allies, only a small minority of the Jewish population of Europe remained alive.

The Iron Curtain

In March 1946 Churchill spoke of an Iron Curtain that had descended across Europe. It was perhaps the most telling image of the new confrontation which emerged from the Second World War – the political stand-off between the United States and her allies on the one hand and the Soviet Union and her newly-acquired satellite states on the other – a confrontation which came to be known as the cold war. In the aftermath of the agreements at Yalta and Potsdam, which divided the war-ravaged territories of Europe between the great powers along lines reflecting the military position on the eve of victory, Stalin acquired Bulgaria, Romania, Hungary, Poland and Yugoslavia. Russian forces remained in Prague, Vienna and Berlin. The guiding force of American foreign policy, which had been isolationist for so many years, shifted to fear of Russian expansionism. Berlin became the front line of this new battle. In 1948 the West defeated a Russian blockade of the divided city by mounting an historic airlift of supplies. In 1949 NATO was born.

India

After years of unrest and struggle, the people of India won independence from British rule in 1947. It was the first major loss to an Empire which at the beginning of the century had covered a fifth of the earth's land mass and a fitting symbol of the waning of British influence in a world now dominated by Russia and the United States. It was also the beginning of a new era of conflict on the Indian sub-continent itself. With the former British territory partitioned between India and Pakistan, independence lent fuel to the bitter intercommunal struggle between Hindus and Moslems.

Israel

The appalling sufferings of European Jewry under Nazi rule gave new political impetus to Zionist demands for a Jewish homeland. In 1948 the state of Israel was created in the former British mandated territory of Palestine. It was a birth preceded by acts of terrorist violence and was to prove the cause of many more in the years to come. With the creation of a Palestinian refugee problem of enormous dimensions, the foundations were laid for a struggle that was to change the relatively stable Middle East into a political powderkeg. A new focus of international tension was already developing.

The shadow of the Bomb

In August 1945 the United States dropped the first atomic bombs on the Japanese cities of Hiroshima and Nagasaki. The immediate effect was to bring the Pacific War to a sudden end and to shift the balance of international military power conclusively in favour of the Americans. In the longer term, the face of world politics was changed irrevocably. The wheels of the nuclear arms race had been put in motion, and with them the development of a weapon system which, for the first time in history, would give mankind the power to destroy itself. The relationship between political and military power had entered a new and terrible phase. The nuclear age had begun.

Pages 202–3: The atom bomb explodes at Bikini Atoll, 1946.

1940

Jan	8	Sugar, butter and bacon rationed in Britain
Feb	1	Death of British writer John Buchan
	11	Russia attacks Finnish Mannerheim Line
Mar	12	Finland signs peace treaty with Russia
Apr	9	Denmark and Norway invaded by Germany
	14	British naval forces land in Norway
May	2	British forces leave Norway
	10	Chamberlain resigns in Britain, replaced by Churchill
	10	German army enters Holland, Belgium, Luxembourg
	15	Dutch army surrenders
	21	German army takes Amiens and Arras in France
	28	Belgium surrenders to German forces
Jun	10	Italy declares war on Britain and France
	14	German army enters Paris
	16	Pétain takes over in France
	17	Russians take over Latvia, Estonia and Lithuania
	22	French make peace with Germany
	27	Russia invades Rumania
Jul	2	First German daylight bombing raid on London

	3	Royal Navy bombards French navy at Oran
	5	Vichy Government severs relations with Britain
	9	RAF begins night bombing-raids on Germany
Aug	21	Trotsky assassinated in Mexico
	23	Blitz on London begins
Sep	16	Italian Army advances to Sidi Barrani, Western Desert
	22	Japan enters Indo-China
Oct	7	Germans capture Rumanian oilfields
	12	Germans take Bucharest
Nov	5	Roosevelt re-elected as President in US
	11	British air attack on Italian fleet at Taranto
Dec	15	British Army drives Italians back across Libyan border
	21	Death of US writer Scott Fitzgerald

The Arts

Arthur Koestler's novel *Darkness at Noon*

Graham Greene's novel *The Power and the Glory*

Ernest Hemingway's novel *For Whom the Bell Tolls*

Walt Disney's film *Fantasia*

Chaplin's film *The Great Dictator*

The evacuation of Dunkirk

In an operation showing remarkable military discipline, thousands of British and French troops were safely evacuated as the advancing German army swept through northern France.

The evacuation was completed on the night of June 3rd/4th, the final stages being conducted under fire from German machine guns. In all, some 335,000 British and French troops were safely landed, in what Sir Winston Churchill described as 'a miracle of deliverance'. Paying tribute to the determination and heroism of the men involved, he nonetheless recognised that the retreat from France was 'a colossal military disaster'.

The Blitz

Despite greatly increased production of fast and powerfully armed fighter planes like the Hurricane and Spitfire, the Royal Air Force in 1940 was markedly inferior in numbers to the German Luftwaffe. Many fighters had additionally been lost in France and in protecting the British withdrawal from Dunkirk. The Germans had begun to build up large numbers of barges and to concentrate troops on the coast opposite Britain, and an early invasion seemed not only probable, but inevitable. Britain awaited the onslaught with determination, but with real doubt as to the outcome.

The expected German air attacks soon began. At first they concentrated on British shipping in the English Channel, but soon switched to airfields in the southeast where British defensive air strength was concentrated. In spite of all the efforts of the young British pilots, these attacks began to have a catastrophic effect on Fighter Command, and the British reserves began to diminish and almost disappear.

It was at this point that the Luftwaffe switched its targets yet again, away from the RAF's sorely pressed airfields to the easier target of London. The Blitz was the salvation of the RAF, which now had time to train more pilots and build up essential stocks of aircraft. But in the meantime much damage and suffering was inflicted on the buildings and people of London, Bristol, Manchester, Liverpool, and many other British towns and villages.

Coventry

One of the worst hit was Coventry which was to suffer a concentrated attack on the night of April 11th 1941. The German bombers devastated the town, reducing much of it to rubble and destroying the beautiful medieval cathedral. This unexpected attack caused panic in the city and many of its citizens fled the town in the expectation of a repeat hammering.

London

London lost many famous buildings and familiar landmarks; St Paul's, the Houses of Parliament and Buckingham Palace were all damaged. The City and the East End of London were also severely hit. But the morale of Londoners, although shaken, was never broken, and they were heartened when Bomber Command began to inflict damage on German cities. These, in fact, were to suffer incomparably greater damage than that inflicted on British cities by the Luftwaffe.

These photographs (left) show some of the damage inflicted on famous landmarks in London and Coventry. The King and Queen walk among the ruins of Buckingham Palace.

Nazis invade Norway and Denmark

Indignant complaints from neutral Norway about the laying of mines by the British Navy in her waters to discourage shipments of iron ore from Narvik to Germany were overtaken by events when the Germans invaded Norway and Denmark the next day, April 9th. The Germans (above) soon had both countries under their control.

The Italians strike in North Africa

Under the Fascist leader Benito Mussolini, Italy had joined the Germans in the war in June 1940 in the hope of quick conquests. She immediately attacked British troops in Egypt from her colonies in Libya and Ethiopia. Here, African troops fire field guns on British Army positions. After initial successes, the Italians were forced back, with great losses in prisoners.

The British Bulldog's indomitable fighting spirit

Winston Churchill tries out a Tommy gun during an inspection tour of defences in the north-east.

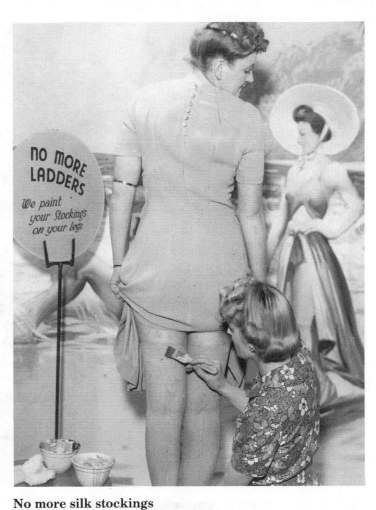

No more silk stockings

Many familiar goods disappeared from British shops early in the war. This London store showed ingenuity in painting a customer's legs to simulate silk stockings.

The war in the desert

British soldiers in Egypt were very thin on the ground in the early days of the North African war.

Friendly enemies

After the fall of France, the British authorities feared a 'fifth column' of enemy agents. Thousands of German and Italian nationals were rounded up as 'enemy aliens' and interned. Ironically, many had been victims of the Nazis.

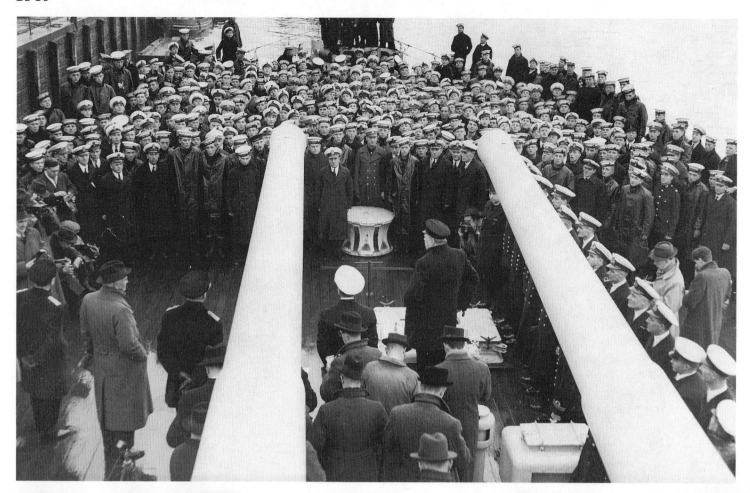

Churchill takes over

Churchill had been a great success as First Lord of the Admiralty. He had taken some credit for the destruction of the German battleship *Graf Spee*, and he was not slow in taking advantage of this when he welcomed home the crew of the victorious cruiser *Exeter* (above) after their epic battle.

The British Parliament and people were disillusioned with Chamberlain (right) and his conduct of the war; the hasty withdrawal from Norway had removed his last remaining shred of credit. In a stirring speech in the House of Commons a senior member of his own party, Leo Amery, told him in no uncertain terms that he must go. Chamberlain's feeble response ensured his downfall and he resigned on May 10th.

There was little doubt about his successor and Winston Churchill (left) formed his National Government the same day with Clement Attlee, leader of the Labour Party, as Lord Privy Seal; A. V. Alexander as First Lord of the Admiralty; and Ernest Bevin as Minister of Labour and National Service. It was not a minute too soon. The very same day the Germans smashed their way into Belgium, Holland and Luxembourg.

Battle of Britain

'Never in the field of human conflict was so much owed by so many to so few.' These were the words of Winston Churchill describing the desperate courage of a few hundred young RAF pilots who saved Britain from invasion between July 10th and October 31st, despite the Luftwaffe's advantage in numbers of aircraft. For the Germans, losing the Battle of Britain was a serious setback; for Britain it would have been the final catastrophe.

A fighter is seen here from the nose of a Heinkel 111, the main German bomber at the time.

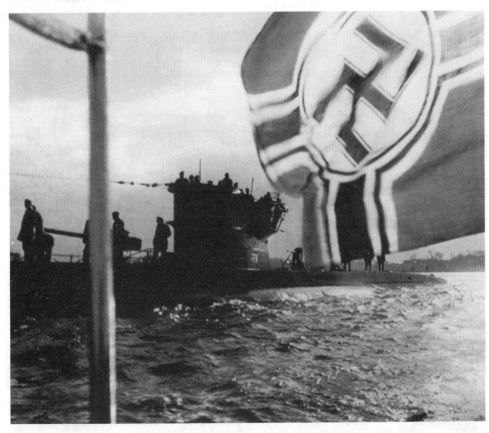

U-Boats

The German U-Boat (or submarine) was the major threat to Britain's survival in the early years of the war. Their 'wolf packs' inflicted enormous damage on shipping in the Atlantic and they were not finally brought under control until 1943. During the war as a whole they sank more than 2,700 merchant ships, two battleships, six aircraft carriers and almost 100 other British warships. The U-Boat shown (above) is entering its base at Lorient in north-west France.

The attack on Norway

The Germans attacked Norway both from the sea and the air. They quickly realised the importance of seizing the airfields – one of their priorities in the brief Norwegian campaign. Here, a German signaller tells an S2 carrying troops that it is safe to land.

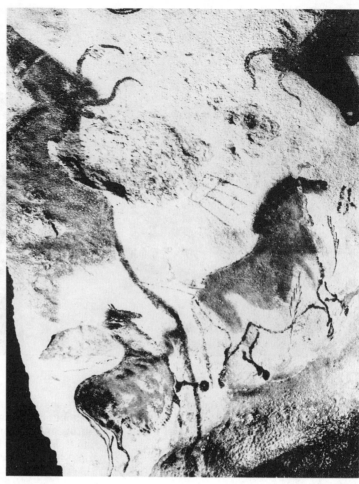

Shelter from the Blitz

Thousands of Londoners regularly slept on Underground station platforms to get away from all sight and sound of the Blitz. The Underground scenes inspired sculptor Henry Moore to do a series of evocative drawings of the sleeping crowds.

Lascaux

These spectacular prehistoric rock paintings were discovered by four boys searching for a dog at Lascaux in France's Dordogne region. The cave is believed to have long served as a centre for the performance of hunting and magical rites.

Trotsky

Leon Trotsky, the exiled Bolshevik, was killed on August 21st, 1940, in Mexico City with an ice pick. The assassin, Ramon Mercader, was apparently acting on orders from Joseph Stalin.

Jane

'Jane' the British strip cartoon ran in the *Daily Mirror* from 1932–1959, but it was during the War that she had her greatest following, boosting morale amongst troops. She went into battle painted on aircraft and stuck to doors of ships' lockers. In 1959 she sailed into the sunset with boyfriend Georgie, only to reappear in 1985 – minus Georgie – in the *Mirror* where she's still stripping away merrily.

Jan	6	Roosevelt sends Lend–Lease Bill to Congress
	10	HMS *Southampton* sunk off Crete
Feb	6	British Eighth Army captures Benghazi in Libya
Mar	7	British Army enters Ethiopia
	11	US Congress agrees Lend–Lease Bill
	19	Luftwaffe resumes Blitz on London
	27	British Army takes Keren and Hasara in Ethiopia
	28	Royal Navy sinks three Italian cruisers
Apr	5	British Army captures Addis Ababa, Ethiopia
	6	German army invades Yugoslavia
	7	British army abandon Benghazi
	11	Heavy air raid on Coventry, England
	13	German Afrika Corps recaptures Bardia
	17	Yugoslavia surrenders
	20	Afrika Corps under Rommel attacks Tobruk, Libya
	22	British forces leave Greece
May	10	London: Luftwaffe destroys House of Commons
	10	Rudolf Hess, Hitler's Deputy, lands in Scotland
	20	German paratroops invade Crete
	24	HMS *Hood* sunk by *Bismarck* off Greenland
	27	Royal Navy sinks *Bismarck*
Jun	8	Free French and British invade Syria
	22	German army invades Russia
	27	Hungary declares war on Russia
	28	German Army captures Minsk
Jul	1	Auchinleck succeeds Wavell in Western Desert
	7	US troops take over from Britain in Iceland
	12	Anglo–Soviet pact signed in Moscow
	27	German Army enters Ukraine
Aug	11	Churchill and Roosevelt sign Atlantic Charter
	25	Britain and Russia invade Iran
Sep	19	German Army takes Kiev in USSR
Oct	13	RAF raid on Nuremberg
	17	Japan: General Tojo appointed PM
Nov	12	HMS *Ark Royal* sunk off Gibraltar
Dec	7	Japanese attack US base at Pearl Harbor
	8	Britain and the US declare war on Japan
	10	HMS *Prince of Wales* and *Repulse* sunk by Japanese
	11	US declares war on Germany and Italy
	25	Hong Kong surrenders to Japanese

The Arts

Rex Warner's novel *The Aerodrome*

Benjamin Britten's *Violin Concerto*

Edward Hopper's painting *Nighthawks*

Orson Welles's film *Citizen Kane*

Operation Barbarossa

On June 22nd 1941 Hitler launched 'Operation Barbarossa': the invasion of the Soviet Union. Barbarossa was envisaged as the swift demolition of the supposedly inferior Slav enemy and Hitler felt confident enough to leave 54 Divisions in the west. Belief in Soviet weakness was abetted by Stalin's faith in the Nazi–Soviet Non-Aggression Pact of August 1939. Stalin insisted that nothing should be done to provoke Germany even as British and Soviet Intelligence warned of German intentions. In addition, the Soviet leader's desire for political uniformity had purged the upper echelons of the military of many of its ablest members, notably Marshal Tukhachevsky, and ensured that strategic and logistical planning were prejudiced. Soviet forces were under-equipped and devoid of contingency plans in the event of invasion. The order issued in response to the attack, 'Directive Number 3', merely called for Soviet forces to advance.

The Eastern Front

Substantial gains were made by German troops as the Soviet front line was caught utterly unawares. Most of the antiquated air force was destroyed by the Luftwaffe on the ground – planes had been parked unconcealed in serried ranks on their airfields. Within six months much of the economic heartland of the Soviet Union had fallen – areas producing 60 per cent of its coal, pig-iron and aluminium production and containing 40 per cent of its population. However, rapid redeployment of economic resources east of the Urals and the institution of effective decision-making systems, maintained the necessary economic base for the war of attrition that German plans had not considered.

Here German troops advance through Rostov-on-Don in the south of the USSR.

The Russian winter

The German supply-line became classically over-stretched, exacerbated by the different gauge and fuel requirements of Soviet railways, which ensured that 70 per cent of the Wehrmacht had to walk into battle. Left: Protected by a tank, German troops advance towards the Soviet capital. German hopes that Soviet citizens would view them as liberators were proved groundless. And whilst resistance slowed the advance, winter temperatures of −40 degrees halted it, freezing the blood of many ill-clothed German soldiers (right). The Germans suffered enormous losses in both men and materiel. Above: They make desperate efforts to move a gun through the snowy terrain. In the spring of 1942 the advance resumed and Sebastopol, the great Crimean port, finally fell. Top: What was left of the city after the eight-month siege.

The Balkans

The Germans invaded Yugoslavia and Greece (the only two countries that were fully on the Allied side) in the spring. Britain sent a force of 60,000 men to Greece under General Wilson but they were no match for a German Army superior in manpower and firepower, and they had to be evacuated by the British Navy in April. German troops are shown (above left) approaching Mount Olympus in Greece.

The Battle of the Atlantic

The war at sea continued, with U-Boats sinking merchant ships in the Atlantic almost at will, though German surface raiders caused more excitement than trouble. The appearance of Germany's great battleship *Bismarck* occasioned much alarm until she was sunk in the Atlantic – but not before she had destroyed the pride of the British Navy, HMS *Hood*, seen (above) in her last photograph.

War in the desert

The desert war went in favour of Germany, with General Erwin Rommel (1891–1944) displaying tactical mastery with insolent ease first against General Wavell and later General Auchinleck. It was not until General Alexander (1891–1969) and Lt General Bernard Montgomery (1887–1976) appeared in August 1942 with greatly increased resources that Rommel was finally defeated.

The opposing air forces were fairly evenly matched because the Allies had larger numbers of inferior aircraft and the Luftwaffe a much smaller number of superior aircraft like the camouflaged Messerschmitt 109 (left).

St Paul's Cathedral and surroundings after the Blitz, May 1941.

Partisans in Yugoslavia

On April 6th Germany invaded Yugoslavia and on 17th the Yugoslav Royal Army surrendered. While the Axis powers divided the country amongst themselves, Communist partisans waged a determined war of resistance under the leadership of the previously little known Tito (1892–1980). Left: Tito in his mountain hideout. Right: A German watch tower.

The Atlantic Charter

The Big Two – President Roosevelt and Prime Minister Churchill – after a series of highly secret meetings between August 9th and 12th aboard warships in the Atlantic Ocean, agreed to a joint US–British declaration of fundamental principles for the post-war world. The pact, named The Atlantic Charter, listed eight principles which included: agreement not to seek territorial gains, restoration of the rights of those sovereign nations which have lost them by force, the right of peoples to choose their own form of government, freedom of the seas, the 'final destruction of Nazi tyranny', and that after the war 'all men shall be enabled to live in freedom from fear and want'. By September 15th, 15 Allied nations had endorsed the Charter.

President Roosevelt was the initiator of the meetings and it was assumed that practical help was offered to Britain in the war effort. It was seen too by many as a move closer towards America's entry into the War.

Gassing!

Even if the gossip gets garbled, invasion scares remind everyone to make sure their anti-gas respirators are always at hand.

The spirit of London

As shown here, the indomitable spirit of Londoners survived the worst that the Luftwaffe could do. These citizens (and later, in even worse circumstances, those of Berlin) proved that aerial bombardment can destroy buildings but not courage.

Amy Johnson

Amy Johnson (1904–1941) was one of the small, brave band of British women pilots who ferried aircraft from factory to airfield. She is seen here in happier days, just after her 19½-day solo flight from England to Australia in 1930. She was killed ferrying an aircraft in 1941.

Marlene Dietrich

The famous actress Marlene Dietrich (1904–1992) had never concealed her hatred and contempt for the Nazis who had taken over the country of her birth, and had renounced her German citizenship to become an American citizen in January. She spent an exhausting war entertaining Allied troops wherever she could.

Virginia Woolf

One of Britain's most distinguished novelists and critics, Virgina Woolf (1882–1941) had received great acclaim for books such as *Mrs Dalloway* and *To the Lighthouse*. However, she was subject to fits of deep depression and mental illness, and drowned herself on March 28th.

Attack on Pearl Harbor

On December 7th, Japanese aircraft carriers launched 360 fighters, bombers and torpedo planes in a surprise attack on the American Pacific Fleet in Pearl Harbor, Hawaii, which finally brought America into the war. The Japanese succeeded in sinking or damaging five battleships and 14 other ships, as well as destroying over 200 aircraft (see damage, above).

Luckily for the Americans, most of their aircraft carriers were safely at sea, and these were to form the nucleus of their later naval warfare. Japanese forces also struck at Malaya and Hong Kong and a few days later opened a full-scale assault on all Britain's colonial possessions in the Far East, forcing Western nations out of the area.

1942

Jan	10	Japanese invade Dutch East Indies
	11	Japanese capture Kuala Lumpur, Malaya
	19	Japanese advance into Burma
	21	German troops go on offensive in Western Desert
Feb	1	British Army retreats to Singapore
	15	Singapore falls to Japanese
	28	Japanese invade Java, Indonesia
Mar	10	Japanese capture Rangoon, Burma
	28	Royal Air Force raid on Lübeck, Germany
Apr	9	Japanese capture Bataan in the Pacific
May	1	Mandalay, Burma, captured by Japanese
	5	Battle of Coral Sea, Pacific
	6	Japanese capture Corregidor, Philippines
	31	Gestapo chief Heydrich assassinated by Czechs
Jun	3	Battle of Midway in Pacific
	6	Nazis massacre villagers at Lidice, Czechoslovakia
	21	Tobruk, Libya, captured by German Afrika Corps
	25	1,000 RAF bombers raid Bremen, Germany
	28	Eighth Army retreat to El Alamein, N Africa

Jul	3	Germans capture Sebastopol, USSR
	10	Remains of Convoy PQ-17 reach Archangel
	28	Germans capture Rostov-on-Don, USSR
Aug	7	US troops invade Guadalcanal in the Pacific
	17	First US bombing raid in Europe
	19	Heavy Allied casualties on Dieppe raid
Sep	13	Germans begin massive assault on Stalingrad
Oct	3	New US price law freezes wages, rents, farm prices
	23	Eighth Army attack starts El Alamein battle
Nov	4	Rommel retreats in North Africa
	8	Allies land in French North Africa under Eisenhower
	9	German Army marches into unoccupied France
	13	British recapture Tobruk, Libya
	19	Soviet Army surrounds Germans at Stalingrad
Dec	21	Eighth Army take Benghazi, Libya

The Arts

Albert Camus's novel *L'Etranger*

Igor Stravinsky's *Danse Concertante*

Shostakovich's *Seventh (Leningrad) Symphony*

German advance in the Soviet Union

After the setback of the early winter of 1941, the Germans continued their advance into the Soviet Union, gaining further tracts of territory, especially in the centre and the south where they got as far as the mountains of Caucasus. In the summer, when the roads were dry, German armoured and motorised columns could move easily and their superior generalship and gunnery gained them many battles, except when they were held up or pushed back by sheer weight of Soviet numbers.

But things were no longer going entirely according to plan. A new generation of Soviet generals – Zhukov, Chuikov, Rokossovsky – was emerging, tough, battle-hardened and professional. The superb T34 tank was appearing in large numbers and the Soviet soldiers, traditionally hardy and stoical, were now armed with automatic weapons and supported by powerful and accurate artillery.

The balance was slowly turning against the Germans and their more experienced generals knew this. They began to think about shortening their lines and conserving men, supplies and equipment. But Hitler was only interested in advancing and would never willingly give up territory he had gained.

Increasing numbers of German prisoners made their way to a harsh captivity (below).

The swastika on this German tank identified it to German aircraft flying over the Soviet Union.

Nazi soldiers wore women's furs to keep warm in the Soviet winter.

A young German Stormtrooper cautiously approaches a Soviet house.

The RAF retaliates

The British people had suffered two years of bombing raids from the Luftwaffe. Now, with a degree of satisfaction, they heard that the German cities were going to get some of their own medicine. Thousand-bomber raids were directed at Cologne, Essen and Bremen in May and June.

Crucially, a new generation of four-engined bombers, capable of carrying heavy bomb loads, was replacing the obsolete Hampdens and Wellingtons of the early war years. These Stirlings, Halifaxes and, especially, Lancasters could carry out raids anywhere in Germany and the capital, Berlin, soon became a prime target.

Severe damage was inflicted on the industrial Baltic port of Rostock (below), while the devastation visited on Cologne destroyed about 85 per cent of the city (left).

Fires raged for two days, about 20,000 homes were destroyed or damaged and about 2,000 commercial properties were wrecked. Communications came to a standstill for two weeks, nearly 500 people died and about 500,000 were left homeless. Curiously, the famous cathedral remained unharmed throughout the war years.

The Western Desert

Rommel at El Alamein

Rommel, shown consulting with his staff officers at El Alamein (left) was nearing the end of his resources in the summer of 1942. He was short of petrol and the Allied air and naval forces were destroying many of his supply convoys from Europe.

The Australian Infantry

Although the British had numerical superiority in North Africa, they were strengthened by troops from many parts of the Commonwealth – Australia, New Zealand, India and South Africa. These soldiers were bold and resilient, particularly the Australians (below left) who were often used to spearhead an attack.

A new broom

The arrival of General Montgomery in mid-August soon changed everything. He enjoyed Churchill's support and British code-breakers were able to give him a full outline of Rommel's tactical plan. Montgomery carefully fostered his resources so that when he finally attacked Rommel's weakened forces in the crucial battle on October 23rd, he was certain of success.

Montgomery is seen (below right) leaving a conference in London.

Panzers in action

The German tanks outgunned their Allied counterparts throughout the Western Desert campaign. Here (above right) they manoeuvre on a Libyan hillside.

War on two fronts

On November 8th an Anglo-American invasion force commanded by General Dwight Eisenhower (1890–1969) landed in North Africa and was soon in action. The French troops there joined in at once. French and American generals and relatives are seen in Casablanca, Morocco, (below right) honouring French and American soldiers who fell in North Africa.

Bogart and Bergman

Casablanca brought together two superstars, Humphrey Bogart (1889–1957) and Ingrid Bergman (1917–1982), in a film that has stood the test of time. It caught the mood of the era – heroism against a background of turmoil and treachery and the faint beginnings of hope. Contrary to universal belief, Bogart does not say 'Play it again, Sam' in this scene from the film.

Duke of Kent killed

The Duke of Kent (1902–1942), youngest brother of King George, was killed in a flying accident on his way to Iceland on August 24th. A qualified RAF pilot, the Duke was 39 and the only member of the royal family to be killed in the war. He had just celebrated the birth of his third son. His coffin is shown on its way to Windsor.

Battle of the Solomons

After almost six months of unstoppable Japanese expansion across the Pacific Ocean, the Americans were beginning to strike back. The Japanese had established a seaplane base on Tulagi in the Solomon Islands. On August 7th American Marines landed on the nearby island of Guadalcanal, and in spite of repeated Japanese attacks over several months they refused to be budged.

Later in the year, on November 12th, the American Navy intercepted a heavily armed transport convoy, bringing 13,000 Japanese troops in an attempt to recapture the island. The Americans gained a decisive victory, sinking all the transport ships and sinking or severely damaging all the escort vessels. The next two days saw several air battles.

Gandhi

India's nationalist Congress party leader, Mahatma Gandhi, led a protracted civil disobedience campaign (including several 'fasts unto death') for which he was frequently arrested. In 1934 he decided to give up politics and withdrew to his *ashram* at Wardha. However, with the outbreak of World War II he renewed his demands for independence from British rule. On August 9th, 1942, shortly after Congress had passed a resolution for immediate British withdrawal and were about to launch a huge civil disobedience campaign, the British authorities arrested the entire Congress leadership, including Nehru.

Nehru

Seen here with Gandhi, Pandit Nehru (1889–1964) became very influential in the Congress Party. Educated in Britain at Harrow public school and Cambridge University, Nehru was truly a man of two worlds; sophisticated, charming and witty in European company but also a dedicated Indian nationalist. His political activities resulted in his being imprisoned by the British several times between 1921 and 1945. He became Prime Minister of India in 1947.

ATS

The women soldiers of Britain's ATS (Auxiliary Territorial Service) soon took over many of the jobs previously done by men, thus releasing them for more active war service. Here trainee cooks are marching to their own kitchen garden.

The Forces' sweetheart

The voice of Vera Lynn (1917–   ) was known to troops all over the world from her programme *Sincerely Yours*. The signature tune, and the song which made her famous, was *We'll Meet Again*.

The Warsaw ghetto

Mass starvation haunted the Jewish ghetto in Warsaw, the Polish capital, which had been taken by the Germans in 1939. This baby – and many others – simply starved to death under the murderous Nazi regime.

Stalingrad – mass grave

These were the words repeated over Soviet loudspeakers to the German Sixth Army trapped in Stalingrad and, with a German soldier dying every seven seconds, they were not far from the truth. The Germans had reached Stalingrad on August 26th and made increasingly desperate attempts to take the city. But the Soviets steadily built up their forces and by November they had surrounded what was left of the city. Hitler's generals begged him to let the besieged troops break out, but he stubbornly ordered his soldiers to fight on. By December the Germans were in desperate straits, with little food and inadequate ammunition and medical supplies reaching them by air. By late January 1943 the Soviets were clearly assured of victory and on January 31st Field Marshal von Paulus surrendered.

Above: German soldiers at Stalingrad make their way through a shattered turbine factory.
Left: Soviet soldiers advance through the ruins of Stalingrad.

1943

Jan	14	Churchill, de Gaulle and Roosevelt meet at Casablanca
	15	Japanese retreat from Guadalcanal
	18	Luftwaffe raids on London begin again
	23	Eighth Army captures Tripoli
	31	German Field Marshal Paulus surrenders at Stalingrad
Feb	8	USSR: Soviets recapture Kursk
	10	Eighth Army reaches border of Tunisia
	28	RAF bombs Berlin in first daytime raid
Mar	15	Soviets forced from Kharkov by Germans
	29	N Africa: Montgomery breaks through Mareth Line
Apr	1	US: Rationing begins on meats, fats and cheese
	10	Tunisia: Eighth Army takes Sfax
	20	Poland: Jews massacred in Warsaw ghetto
	11	US forces land in Aleutian Islands
	12	Tunisia: German Army surrenders
	17	Germany: Ruhr dams bombed by RAF
Jul	5	USSR: German offensive at Kursk
	23	Sicily: Allies occupy Palermo
	26	Mussolini resigns and is arrested

Aug	5	USSR: Soviets capture Orel
	10	Quebec: Churchill, Roosevelt and Mackenzie King meet
	16	Sicily: US troops take Messina
	23	Soviets retake Kharkov
Sep	3	Allies land in Italy
	8	Italy's unconditional surrender announced
	10	Italy: Eighth Army captures Taranto
	25	USSR: Soviets capture Smolensk
	30	Italy: Fifth Army captures Naples
Oct	13	Italy declares war on Germany
Nov	1	US troops invade Bougainville in Solomon Islands
	3	US coal miners end 6-month strike
	6	Soviets capture Kiev
	23	Americans capture Makin in Gilbert Islands
	28	Churchill, Roosevelt and Stalin meet at Tehran
Dec	15	US jazz musician Fats Waller is dead
		The Arts
		Hermann Hesse's novel *The Glass Bead Game*
		Bertolt Brecht's play *Life of Galileo*

Allies invade Sicily

In May, Anglo-American and French troops had defeated the Axis powers in Tunisia, and it was important that the Allies sustained the momentum of their attacks to keep Italy and Germany off-balance. On July 10th, a great armada (more than 3,000 warships and transports) arrived off southern Sicily and began to land troops. The Italian people had lost all appetite for the war and were anxious to end it as soon as possible: not only did Italian troops put up little resistance but some of them actively helped the invading forces. The Germans put up a tougher resistance but

their generals recognised that the island was not defensible and, after some token skirmishes, they retired to the mainland.

For the Allies, the landing on Sicily was symbolic because it meant that they were once more fighting on European ground. They also realised that Italy was no longer seriously in the war and that the Germans were now in retreat on all fronts. Although there would be many more tough battles, the end of the war could at last be foreseen. Below: Allied landing craft are seen loading at a North African port in readiness for the invasion of Sicily.

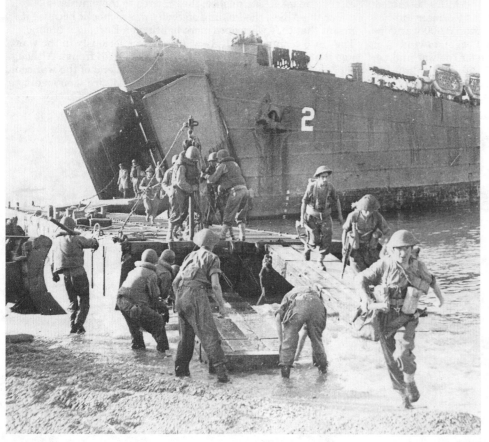

Allies invade Italy

The Sicilian campaign only took a couple of months, and British and Canadian troops crossed the Straits of Messina to land on the Italian mainland on September 3rd. In the meantime, things had moved rapidly in Italy itself. A fortnight after the Allied landing on Sicily, Mussolini was forced to resign with his Fascist Cabinet, and his place was taken by Marshal Pietro Badoglio (1871–1956) who dissolved the Fascist Party and secretly asked the Allies for an armistice. This was duly signed on September 3rd.

Meanwhile, American and English troops prepared to land at Salerno, just south of Naples. They arrived early on September 9th and were met by fierce resistance from the Germans under Field Marshal Kesselring.

Above: Australian troops advance towards a railway station in Sicily.

Left: American and British troops land at Salerno in Italy.

Above right: The Italian town of Ortona is cleared of snipers by Canadian soldiers.

Below right: Sikh troops in action in Italy.

The Battle of Kursk

'The Tigers are burning' was the Soviet
slogan at the end of the greatest tank
battle of all time – referring to the German
tanks which had been destroyed by·Soviet
infantry dropping grenades down their
hatches. The Germans had nearly 3,000
tanks. But the Soviets were expecting
them – with hundreds of mines and anti-
tank guns – and the German assault on
July 5th ground to a halt in the face of
concentrated Soviet fire.

Above left: The Battle of Kursk in progress.
Below left: A German supply column
retreats from Rostov-on-Don.

Guadalcanal

The war in the Pacific also reached a
climax as the increasingly outnumbered
Japanese tried again and again to dislodge
the Americans from Guadalcanal in the
Solomon Islands. Japanese troops
repeatedly threw themselves against
American machine guns, and small
positions sometimes changed hands
several times. The jungle terrain of
Guadalcanal (right) made fighting
gruelling and difficult. There were, of
course, some serious American losses. The
torpedoed American aircraft carrier Wasp
is shown sinking off the coast of
Guadalcanal (above).

Conference at Casablanca

There was not much love lost between the traditionalist French General Giraud and the radical General Charles de Gaulle. At the Casablanca conference in January, Giraud was initially backed by President Roosevelt while Churchill supported de Gaulle.

Conference at Cairo

In November, Roosevelt and Churchill went to Cairo to meet General Chiang Kai-shek, the Chinese leader, to discuss the defeat of the Japanese. Among their staff, shown here, were Anthony Eden and Harold Macmillan.

Bombs over the Ruhr

The year 1943 saw a concentrated aerial attack on Germany's industrial heartland, with four-engined bombers unloading high explosive bombs on the factories of Krupp and other German armament manufacturers. Air Force loaders are seen here preparing heavy bombs for a night raid.

Bomber Harris

Air Chief Marshal Sir Arthur (Bomber) Harris (1892–1984), the man in charge of Britain's Bomber Command, made a habit of visiting his front-line crews. Here, he inspects a Halifax bomber being serviced. Harris had planned the devastating raid on Cologne when he took over Bomber Command in 1942.

The Warsaw ghetto uprising

In spite of three years of starvation, harassment and murder, the Jews in the Warsaw ghetto had managed to acquire and manufacture an impressive array of weapons and ammunition. In April they rose against their Nazi captors and fought them with a courage born of desperation and a ferocity that startled their hated enemies. The Germans had to call in reinforcements to fight the despised Jews. They were forced back, house by house, into the very sewers. Most of the Jewish fighters died in the struggle.

Conscription of French workers

As the German war machine consumed more and more men, German industry became desperate for factory workers. At first the Germans were able to recruit volunteers with stories of good wages and conditions. This sometimes worked in the early days, as shown by these French volunteer workers leaving for Germany. But the truth about wages and conditions soon emerged and the Germans had no choice but to use slave labour. As the people of nations under Nazi occupation saw increasing evidence of German oppression, underground Resistance movements began to develop.

American tanks, British troops

British infantry advance in Tunisia under covering fire from American tanks. Both British and American tanks were markedly inferior to their German counterparts – in fact they were sardonically known to their crews as 'Ronsons' (after the famous cigarette lighters) because of the ease with which they caught fire. Nevertheless they were very welcome to the hard-pressed foot soldiers who valued any armoured support, however inadequate.

Scharnhorst sunk

Although the damage done to Allied shipping by German surface raiders was minor compared to the depredations of the U-Boats, the British Admiralty was obsessed with the prospect of German battleships loose in the Atlantic. When, in late December, news reached London that the German battleship *Scharnhorst* had left port, there was much concern for the convoys to the Soviet Union which were her obvious prey. She was trailed, intercepted and sunk on December 26th by a much bigger British battleship. Here, German sailors service the *Scharnhorst*'s main armament.

Betty Grable

Bouncy, brassy, blonde bombshell Betty Grable was every American GI's favourite pin-up girl – her famous legs were insured for over $200,000. In the '40s she starred in a number of light-hearted musicals, starting with *Tin Pan Alley* (1940) and including *Moon Over Miami* (1941) and *Coney Island* (1943).

1944

Jan 22	Italy: Allies land at Anzio
27	USSR: Siege of Leningrad ends after 2 years
Feb 15	Solomons cleared of Japanese by US troops
Mar 6	US bombers begin daylight bombing of Berlin
Apr 2	Soviets cross Rumanian border
11	Soviets begin liberation of Crimea
22	Allies land in New Guinea
May 9	Soviets recapture Sebastopol in the Crimea
18	Allies bomb Monte Cassino
Jun 4	Fifth Army marches into Rome
6	D-Day: Allies invade Normandy
10	Soviets open offensive against Finland
19	Pacific: US Marines take Saipan
27	France: Allies capture Cherbourg
Jul 3	USSR: Soviets recapture Minsk
9	France: British Army takes Caen
18	Japanese Prime Minister Tojo resigns
20	German generals' attempt on Hitler's life
28	Poland: Soviets capture Brest-Litovsk

Aug 1	Poland: Rising in Warsaw begins
19	Italy: British Eighth Army captures Florence
25	Charles de Gaulle follows Allies into Paris
30	Rumania: Soviets capture Bucharest
Sep 5	Belgium: Brussels freed by Allies
11	US troops enter Germany
17	Airborne landings at Arnhem and Nijmegen
28	France: Canadians capture Calais
Oct 14	Rommel forced to commit suicide
19	US troops land in Philippines
20	Yugoslavia: Soviets and partisans capture Belgrade
Nov 7	US: Roosevelt wins election for 4th term
12	RAF sink Germany's last big warship, the *Tirpitz*
Dec 16	Germans begin Battle of the Bulge in the Ardennes
	The Arts
	Somerset Maugham's novel *The Razor's Edge*
	Aaron Copland's music *Appalachian Spring*
	Laurence Olivier's film *Henry V*
	T.S. Eliot's poems *Four Quartets*

D-Day

Years of careful preparation bore fruit when American, British and Canadian troops landed on the coast of Normandy on June 6th, under General Eisenhower and General Montgomery. Allied planners had kept the Germans guessing as to where the actual landing would be, which meant that the Germans had no choice but to position major defences along the whole of the northern coast of France. Even when they received news of the landing Hitler remained convinced that Normandy was a diversion and the main invasion would be at Calais.

The Germans knew that once a landing had been successfully achieved it would be difficult to defeat, and concentrated their resistance on the beaches. A heavily mined and obstructed beach in northern France is shown here at low tide. The Germans believed – correctly – that the attack would be at high tide and these curious structures were armed to tear the bottoms out of the Allied landing craft.

Anti-aircraft balloons, used to protect the Allied fleet.

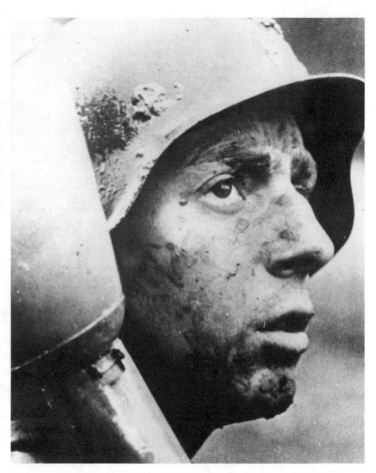

An exhausted Panzer-Grenadier during the Normandy battle.

An Allied amphibious truck loaded with ammunition for heavy guns prepares to beach in Normandy.

This bridgehead in Normandy has an American naval signal post in the foreground.

Normandy suffered heavy damage in the battles following the Allied landing.

Frenchmen versus Frenchmen

A group of French Nazi sympathisers in the south of France gather local people suspected of sheltering Resistance fighters. By early 1944 the French Resistance was highly organised and contributed to the Allied invasion by sabotaging German communications. Frenchmen who had actively helped the Germans usually ended up before the firing squad.

American forces in Normandy

Once the Allied beachheads had been established, the build-up of troops, tanks and artillery was rapid. The German coastal defences were breached and Allied forces broke through into the Normandy countryside.

Collaborators

The French girlfriends of German soldiers – their heads shaven – are led barefoot through the streets.

The Far East

The American planners in the Far East had developed a strategy of 'island-hopping': carefully selecting a number of island targets on the approach to Japan, attacking and taking them, but leaving other heavily armed islands behind them 'to wither on the vine'. This strategy, rather than trying to take every island in their path, meant great savings in men and munitions.

However, the islands they chose to attack had all been heavily armed for years by the Japanese, with mines, tank traps and hundreds of concealed bunkers with machine guns – a nightmare for attacking troops. Every foot had to be fought for. Moreover, the Japanese troops had no fear of death. Hundreds of them were killed in hopeless 'Banzai' charges, led by officers waving ceremonial swords. Very few prisoners were ever taken in the early part of the war.

Japanese losses

The Japanese suffered terrible losses in this island war. The Americans landed on the island of Saipan on June 19th and it took them more than three weeks to defeat the Japanese. About 3,000 Americans were killed and more than 13,000 were wounded, but almost 27,000 Japanese died. An American bulldozer (above) scoops out a mass grave on Saipan for the hundreds of Japanese corpses which lie in tangled heaps beside it. The bodies of Japanese soldiers are shown (left) on the island of Guam. They had defended the burning buildings behind them for two hours against overwhelming odds, and finally charged to their deaths.

Grinding through Italy

The war in Italy had become a slow grind, with the Germans holding on to one carefully prepared defensive line, while they built another in the rear, making the Allied troops pay dearly for every foot they advanced. It was an excellent strategy and very expensive for the Allies.

Heavy bombing was no help either: the German troops retreated into deep shelters while it was going on, and when they emerged the rubble gave them good cover against advancing Allied troops. The ruins of Cassino (above right) provided German paratroop snipers with useful hiding places.

The Germans regarded their Italian ex-allies with great suspicion, believing that they helped the Americans and British whenever they could. A northern Italian prisoner of war camp for British soldiers is shown (top). British prisoners found it relatively easy to escape from and the local population were generous and helpful.

Above left: The Allied landing at Anzio, south of Rome, on January 22nd.

Miners' strike

On March 8th, 9,000 Welsh miners went on strike over pay differentials. They stayed out until the government met their demands.

Conscription of children

The Germans were so desperate for labour that they even conscripted children. This is a Polish children's work camp near Lodz.

Evacuees

The new German V-weapons caused a second wave of evacuation from southern England.

V-weapons

For some years Nazi scientists had been working on a number of secret weapons including a pilotless flying bomb and a rocket with a high-explosive warhead. British intelligence had learned a great deal about both these projects but had not discovered where they were being made or when they might be used.

Enlightenment came when the first V1 flying bomb (or 'doodle bug' as Londoners soon began to call it) fell on London. Here, firemen are shown putting out a blaze caused when a V1 hit a block of flats in London. The flying bombs were so fast that anti-aircraft guns could only hit them by chance and their warheads were so powerful that fighter aircraft which shot them down could easily be blown up with them. In the end, they were only stopped when Allied troops overran their launching sites.

The V2 rocket was quite different. It could be launched from anywhere and it travelled at 3,600 miles per hour – several times the speed of sound. It could not be intercepted and it arrived totally without warning. The prospect of thousands of these so alarmed the government that there was talk of evacuating the whole of the south of England. Luckily the Germans could only produce them in small numbers, and the rapid advance of the Allied soldiers meant that London was soon out of their range.

The film *National Velvet* was a great favourite towards the end of the war. It was the first starring role for Elizabeth Taylor (1932–   ). British-born, she went to Los Angeles in 1939 with her American parents.

On December 16th, Glenn Miller (1904–1944), the popular American bandleader, disappeared on a flight to France.

1945

The horror of Dresden

The citizens of London, Coventry, Bristol, Liverpool and other British cities had suffered badly during the German Blitz. On a few occasions, more than 1,000 people died in a night under the Luftwaffe bombers. But these horrors pale into insignificance beside the catastrophe that struck the beautiful city of Dresden when it was wiped out by British and American bombers.

The first wave of 800 Bomber Command Lancasters arrived on the night of February 13th. They deluged the city centre with high-explosive and incendiary bombs. The next day 400 American Flying Fortresses appeared to add their hail of destruction. The number of dead is impossible to calculate but figures as high as 130,000 have been quoted. Certainly the German authorities had to heap up corpses in the public streets and burn them by the thousand.

In retrospect there seems little military reason for destruction on so vast a scale. The city had no strategic importance and was in fact crowded with refugees fleeing from the Soviets. Dresden raised questions about the effectiveness – to say nothing of the morality – of strategic bombing.

Below: Soviet auxiliaries deal with corpses while a funeral pyre burns in the background.

The final destruction of Germany

The Nazis had sowed the wind in the first years of the war and now the people of Germany were reaping the whirlwind as destruction visited the length and breadth of their battered country. In the course of the war the Allies dropped 2,700,000 tons of bombs on Germany. Among the worst-hit cities were Hamburg, Essen, Berlin and Dresden. The people of Dresden are shown (above, far left) flocking to the only transport left in their ruined city.

Above, near left: During the bombing of Munich, birthplace of Nazism, the famous Frauenkirche was badly damaged.

Left: Nuremberg, home of the Nazi mass rallies of earlier years, was also visited by Bomber Command.

Top: Most of the water mains had been destroyed in the East German industrial city of Magdeburg and civilians had to queue at this single stand-pipe.

Right: This dejected German officer knows that the war is lost.

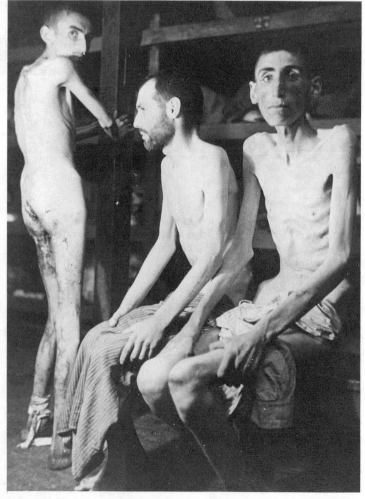

Final solution

American troops overran the East German Buchenwald
concentration camp on April 11th. The liberators found 21,000
starving survivors (left) and thousands of corpses. Right: A day's
output of ash and bone from the Buchenwald incinerator (above).

Many dozens of such camps were discovered throughout
Germany and the occupied territories but even these cannot be
compared with the camps of mass human extermination such as
Treblinka, Belsen (above far right and bottom far left) and, above
all, Auschwitz (top far left) where 12,000 victims were gassed
each day for months on end.

The official estimated death toll for the Jews is 6,000,000.
Slavs, gypsies, homosexuals, the retarded and the insane were
also victims of Hitler's 'Final Solution'. Top: Blocks which victims
were made to stand on when being hung. They were too short to
ensure that the victim's neck would be broken when knocked
away.

The Germans had taken care to destroy as much as they could
of these camps as they retreated, but in the piles of human ashes,
the warehouses full of shoes, jewellery (top right), spectacles and
human hair, there was simply too much evidence of their
mechanised atrocities.

Death of Mussolini

On April 28th, at Dono on Lake Como, Italian partisans halted a convoy of German lorries in which Benito Mussolini, his mistress Clara Petacci and a number of government officials were fleeing to Switzerland. All were summarily tried and shot in the nearby village of Giuliano di Mezzegere, the Committee of National Liberation, a Milan-based partisan group, later claiming responsibility for the killings.

The bodies were loaded into a truck and taken to Milan, where, in a display of medieval barbarism, they were hung upside down from the roof of a petrol station in the Piazza Loreto (left). Large crowds gathered in the square, where 15 partisans had been executed by the Fascist authorities the previous year, and a number of people vented their spleen on the corpses of the former *Duce* and his mistress by pummelling them, spitting on them and shooting at them.

The gruesome exhibition ended in the evening when the disfigured bodies were cut down and buried in unmarked graves. In a final indignity, Mussolini's brain was removed for examination by criminologists before he was interred with his mistress.

Yalta Conference

On February 12th, the leaders of Great Britain, the USA and the Soviet Union announced the results of discussions which were to change the face of Europe. Winston Churchill, Franklin Roosevelt and Joseph Stalin had agreed on the announcement after eight days of intensive talks at the Crimean health resort of Yalta. Here, they decided on the terms of the unconditional surrender, occupation and control of Germany, as well as the future of Poland, Yugoslavia and the Balkans. The 'declaration on a liberated Europe' was widely seen as a recognition of Soviet strength. The conference also laid plans for the creation of the United Nations.

Iwo Jima

The American flag was raised on Mount Suribachi on the Pacific island of Iwo Jima (above) on February 23rd. This strategically crucial island had been strongly defended by Japanese forces during heavy fighting, and its capture brought Japan's major cities within range of American bombers.

The war ends in the Far East

The war in the Far East drew to its close as Allied troops pushed the retreating Japanese Army down through Burma. The Japanese had advanced the length of Burma in a few months in the heady days of early 1942, pushing a demoralised and defeatist British and Indian Army before them. Now they were experiencing the same thing themselves. New commanders with new confidence and new weapons had put heart into the Allied armies and it was the Japanese turn to retreat. Mandalay fell to the Allies in March and by early June they had retaken the Burmese capital, Rangoon.

One measure of the Japanese loss of confidence was the increasing number of prisoners taken. This had been an extremely rare phenomenon early in the war; now increasing numbers of Japanese were giving themselves up – although suicide was still common.

Top: British gunners pound their retreating Japanese foe on the advance through Burma.

Above: American troops prepare to cross the Shweli River in Burma.

Left: Infantry advance towards the ancient pagodas of Mandalay in northern Burma.

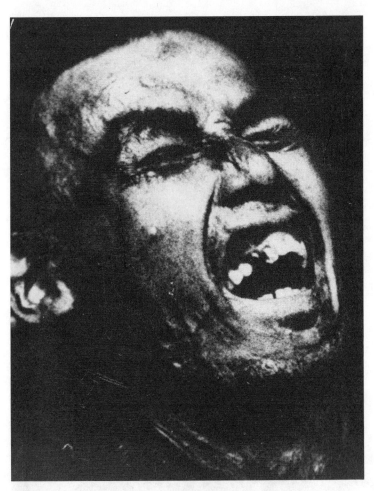

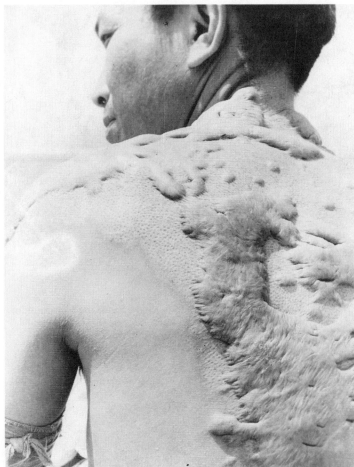

The atom bomb

The 'Manhattan Project' culminated in the detonation of the first atom bomb in the New Mexico desert on July 16th. With this new weapon President Truman could shelve 'Operation Olympic', the proposed invasion of Japan in November 1945 which would be costly in lives. Taking Iwo Jima, an island with an area of eight square miles, had cost 25,000 casualties in February 1945, while Okinawa took nearly three months to subdue.

'Olympic' required a simultaneous Soviet invasion. Many US officials did not want the Soviet Union involved in the post-war settlement in Japan and Churchill and Truman had agreed not to share the results of the Manhattan Project with Stalin. Thus when news of the bomb test arrived as the Allies met at Potsdam in July 1945, Truman decided to use the bomb as soon as one was ready, to try to shock Japan into submission.

At Potsdam the Allies, excluding Stalin, demanded unconditional surrender from Japan, darkly threatening 'prompt and utter destruction'. Capitulation not forthcoming, Hiroshima was devastated by the A-bomb on August 6th. Above left: The anguish of Hiroshima. Above right: An example of the scars caused by radiation.

The Soviet Union declared war on Japan on August 8th, and began to seize Japanese territory. On August 9th, with the original target Kokura obscured by cloud, Nagasaki was laid waste by the bomb 'Fat Boy' (right).

Elements in the Japanese Army resisted moves to surrender and it required an intercession from Emperor Hirohito for the war to be ended; Japan surrendered on August 14th.

Victory

The end of the war in Europe was celebrated around the world.
Top Left: Winston Churchill is cheered by the crowds on his way to the House of Commons to announce the defeat of Germany.
Centre left: The mood was one of euphoria.
Below left: The crowds in Trafalgar Square, London on VE Day.

The final surrender

General Douglas MacArthur (1880–1964), Supreme Commander of the Allied Forces, accepted the surrender of the Japanese aboard the *Missouri* in Tokyo Bay on September 2nd 1945.

The Allies confer

In July President Truman, who had succeeded Roosevelt on his death on April 12th, British PM Churchill (soon succeeded by Attlee) and Stalin met at Potsdam to discuss the future.

Goering taken prisoner

Hermann Goering (1893–1946) was the most senior surviving Nazi to be tried at Nuremberg for war crimes. He was to cheat his captors by poisoning himself with a concealed cyanide capsule.

Anne Frank

This young Jewish girl and her family hid in occupied Amsterdam between 1942 and 1944, until they were betrayed. Anne died at Belsen concentration camp but her diary survived.

Churchill's defeat

One of the great political surprises in Britain was the return of a Labour government with a large majority in July. A jubilant Clement Attlee, the new Prime Minister, is shown with some colleagues. He was to introduce a programme of sweeping nationalisation and a wide range of social reforms.

Churchill was much admired as a world statesman and war leader, but his popularity did not carry over to the Conservative Party as a whole, which was widely held responsible for the pre-war depression and policy of appeasement towards Germany. Also, the returning soldiers wanted fundamental changes in the social structure of Britain and believed that this was more likely to happen under a Labour administration.

1946

Jan	7	The West recognises the Austrian Republic
	11	Albania deposes King Zog; declares a People's Republic
	20	France: De Gaulle resigns; Gouin becomes President
	30	London: UN General Assembly meets for first time
Feb	1	UK: 1st civilian test flights from Heathrow airport
	1	Norwegian Trygve Lie elected UN Secretary General
	1	Hungary declares itself a Republic
	7	Germany: Hess on trial at Nuremberg for war crimes
	14	UK: Bank of England is nationalised
	24	Argentina: Juan Perón is elected President
Mar	5	Winston Churchill speaks of an 'Iron Curtain'
	10	Britain and France start to withdraw from Lebanon
	15	USSR embarks on fourth 5-year plan
Apr	18	Geneva: League of Nations Assembly is dissolved
	21	E Germany: Social Democrats merge with Communists
May	5	Italy: Victor III abdicates; Umberto II is King
	25	Transjordan proclaims its independence
Jun	2	Italy: Referendum in favour of a Republic
	3	Italy: King Umberto II leaves the country
	28	Italy: Enrico de Nicola becomes President
Jul	4	Philippine Republic established
	7	Mexico: Miguel Alemán is elected President
	21	UK: Bread is rationed
	27	US author Gertrude Stein dies in Paris
Sep	1	Greece: Plebiscite in favour of a monarchy
	28	King George II returns to Greece
Oct	15	Cardinals win World Series in St Louis
	15	Goering commits suicide
Nov	4	China and US sign friendship pact
	5	US Republicans regain control of Congress
	6	UK: British National Health Act comes into force
	15	Holland recognises Indonesian Republic
Dec	5	New York chosen as permanent site for UN
	16	France: Socialist Léon Blum forms goverment

The Arts

Nikos Kazantzakis' novel *Zorba the Greek*

Eugene O'Neill's play *The Iceman Cometh*

William Wyler's film *The Best Years of Our Lives*

India pays the price of freedom

In September 1945, Clement Attlee, the new Labour Prime Minister, had promised India her independence at the earliest possible date. But this prospect, instead of uniting the nation in nationalistic rejoicing, ended up splitting it asunder. With the common enemy departing peacefully, the various sects and religions that had united against Britain now began to regard each other with suspicion, fear and hatred.

In February there was a mutiny in the Indian Navy. The mutiny was quickly suppressed but the turmoil in this well-disciplined force boded ill for the more volatile population of the sub-continent. More riots broke out later in February and the following months saw even more violence. The Muslims refused to join with the Hindus and demanded their own State of Pakistan. Massacres took place as neighbouring communities turned on each other in murderous sectarian rage.

Below left: Riots in East Bengal forced many villagers to abandon their homes and flee from affected areas. Here, an evacuee from Ibrahimpur waits with his household possessions to be ferried to safety, while one of the women carries a shotgun.

Below right: M. A. Jinnah, President of the All-India Muslim League and future leader of Pakistan (right) with Mr Chundragar, President of the Bombay Provincial League.

Riots in Calcutta

Top: Dead bodies were a common sight on the streets of Calcutta during the clashes between Muslims and Hindus. These corpses are lying on the main thoroughfare in north Calcutta.

Left: A dead Hindu lies among the Muslims who have killed him. They carry *lathis* – wooden sticks that can be lethal in trained hands.

Above: This was once a crowded and prosperous shopping centre in Calcutta, but Muslim–Hindu clashes have left it looking like a bomb site.

Mao's new war

The Chinese Communists had always regarded the Sino–Japanese war as an interruption in their long struggle to take over China. The Japanese were therefore no sooner defeated than Mao (top left) renewed his old war against Chiang Kai-shek and the Chinese nationalists. Mao was now in a much stronger position, with a million men in uniform, a straightforward strategy and tactics refined in 20 years of battle. The Kuomintang Nationalist Party under Chiang Kai-shek was divided and uncertain. Mao was so confident of the outcome that in August he declared war on his old enemy.

Above: Chiang Kai-shek (1887–1975) accompanied by his wife, greets an American WAC supply sergeant during a tea at their summer home in Chungking.

Strange fruit

Because it was not possible to import 'luxury' items during the war, a whole generation of British children had never seen an orange or a banana and the arrival of these mysterious fruits caused great excitement in most families. Many of the children did not know how to cope with them at first, and tried to eat them skin and all!

Dockers are shown handling the first bananas to reach Britain since before the war. They arrived from the West Indies at London's West India Dock on the banana boat *Jamaica Producer* and were on sale in the streets of London within hours.

We demand Pakistan!

This was the slogan that greeted British and Indian politicians on the streets of London and Delhi when they attended talks on Indian independence. The Muslims were convinced that they would not get a fair deal from the Hindus who made up the majority of the population of the sub-continent. They therefore wanted their own Muslim country. There was a large contingent of Muslim Indians in London at the time, many of them students and passionate nationalists, so these Muslim marches became a common sight on the streets of the capital. Here, a group from the All Indian Muslim League make their way to a meeting in Kingsway Hall after the police refused them permission to call on the Prime Minister in Downing Street.

Strike at General Motors

Workers at General Motors picketing the headquarters in Detroit give a wild welcome to news of the wage increases which will end their strike. The 113-day strike, which was the longest and most costly in the automobile industry's history, brought work to a standstill at hundreds of plants in 18 states. The settlement between management and the United Automobile Workers was for a wage increase of just over 18 cents an hour.

The company was founded in 1908 by William Crapo Durant. He acquired 75 per cent of Oldsmobile stock which, combined with Buick Motors which he had bought in 1904, became the General Motors Company.

The trade union movement

Members of the National Group of the Amalgamated Furnishings Trades Association march from Shoreditch Church (in London's East End) as a protest against the Board of Trade's decision to allow imports of processed glass from the beginning of the following year – a striking demonstration of the determination of working people to protect their jobs at any cost.

Bikini Atoll

Bikini Atoll, one of the American Marshall Islands in the Pacific Ocean, was almost unknown until the Americans decided to use it for testing their nuclear weapons. They removed the entire population to another island and conducted their first test, shown here, on July 25th. As targets, they used some of their own obsolete warships, such as the old battleship *Arkansas* and some warships captured from enemy navies such as the German cruiser *Prinz Eugen*. None of the ships survived the bomb and Bikini continued to be used as a testing site for many years. Its original inhabitants still want to return some day.

Spaak listens

The veteran Belgian statesman Paul-Henri Spaak (1899–1972) was elected President of the United Nations and presided at its very first session, shown here. He then went on to become Secretary-General to the North Atlantic Treaty Organisation (NATO) ten years later.

GI brides

Many thousands of American soldiers had fallen in love with British girls and a great number of them eventually married their sweethearts. These British girls are shown on the transatlantic liner taking them to their new homes in the USA. Unfortunately some were to find their new homes a great deal less desirable than the Hollywood-style houses they had expected.

Cocteau's *Beauty and the Beast*

The French novelist and playwright Jean Cocteau (1889–1963) is here seen presenting the Swedish film actress Ingrid Bergman with the French equivalent of an Oscar for best female performance (she had already received an Academy Award for her part in Cukor's *Gaslight* in 1944). Cocteau's fantasy film *Beauty and the Beast*, acknowledged as one of the masterpieces of his extraordinarily versatile career, was released this year, and his play *The Eagle Has Two Heads* opened to considerable acclaim at London's Haymarket Theatre in February the same year. It was in 1946, too, that Ingrid Bergman had a sensational success in Alfred Hitchcock's *Notorious*: in her role as an espionage agent driven to drink and despair she gave one of the best performances of her career.

Marcel Pétiot found guilty of murder

Dr Marcel Pétiot, a wealthy physician with a successful Paris practice, was convicted this year for the murder of 27 people at his home at 21 rue Lesueur. Here, he is seen in court hearing the death sentence pronounced; he was guillotined on May 26th. Pétiot horribly abused his position as a Resistance worker, promising to arrange escape routes out of occupied France for wealthy Jews, then robbing them of their possessions, murdering them and burning their remains in a grisly basement furnace at his home.

W. C. Fields dies

W. C. Fields (1879–1946), whose real name was William Claude Dukenfield, seen here enjoying the racing at Santa Anita, California with Jane Fowler, daughter of scenario writer Gene Fowler, died this year. Fields brought laughter to millions with films like *Never Give a Sucker an Even Break*, in which he played a misanthropist with a particular dislike of children.

History of Western Philosophy

Bertrand Russell (1872–1970), the great British philosopher, mathematician and radical social reformer – champion of women's suffrage, pacifism and the Campaign for Nuclear Disarmament – published one of his most important works this year, his *History of Western Philosophy*. He won the Nobel Prize for literature in 1950.

1947

Jan	1	Britain nationalises its coalmines
	7	George Marshall appointed US Secretary of State
	16	Vincent Auriol becomes President of France
Feb	7	Arabs and Jews reject UK plans for Palestine's partition
Mar	3	Bulganin replaces Stalin as Soviet Defence Chief
	19	Paul Spaak forms coalition government in Belgium
	19	Communist HQ at Yunan falls to Chinese Nationalists
	29	Nationalist uprising against France in Madagascar
Apr	2	Britain passes Palestine problem to United Nations
	7	Death of Henry Ford
	19	Explosions in Texas City kill 377
May	23	British govt agrees to partition India
	29	Indian Parliament bans 'untouchables'
Jun	5	US: George Marshall calls for 'Marshall Aid' in speech
	17	Burma opts for independent Republic
Jul	6	Spain to have a King when Franco dies
	20	Dutch troops attack Indonesian forces in Java
Aug	1	UN Security Council asks for ceasefire in Indonesia
	15	India becomes independent, with Nehru as PM
	15	Pakistan comes into being with Ali Khan as PM
	27	British govt announces cuts to deal with economic crisis
	31	Communists win Hungarian elections
Sep	14	Concordat with Catholic Church denounced in Poland
	16	John Cobb breaks world land speed record at 394 mph
	30	Pakistan and Yemen join United Nations
Oct	5	Warsaw: Communist conference establishes Cominform
	26	Kashmir joins India despite Pakistan's protests
	29	Belgium, Netherlands and Luxembourg set up Benelux
Nov	14	United Nations recognises independence of Korea
	20	UK: Princess Elizabeth marries Philip Mountbatten
	22	Iran renounces oil agreement with USSR
	25	USSR demands war reparations from Germany
	27	Australian banks nationalised
	29	UN announces plans for partition of Palestine
Dec	19	Friendship pact between Rumania and Yugoslavia
	22	New constitution in Italy offers elected Senate
	27	Greek government bans Communist Party
	30	Kashmir problem goes to United Nations
	30	King Michael of Rumania abdicates

The Arts

Discovery of the Dead Sea Scrolls

Malcolm Lowry's novel *Under the Volcano*

Albert Camus's novel *The Plague*

Robert Graves's book *The White Goddess*

Tennessee Williams's play *A Streetcar Named Desire*

End of Empire

Lord Louis Mountbatten (1900–1979) was appointed the last Viceroy of India on February 20th. He and his wife arrived in India to find that the leaders of the two great religious groups, Hindu and Muslim, had informally agreed to partition the country into India and Pakistan. But their people were divided by hatred and religious bigotry. Worse, the religious groupings were inextricably mixed, with many pockets of Muslims in what was to become India and many pockets of Hindus in what was to become Pakistan.

Now the long trek of these displaced persons to their new countries began – and with it the indiscriminate slaughter. Towns and villages where the two religious groups had once lived in peace under the British Raj, became bitterly divided. Families who had lived side by side as neighbours were now deadly enemies. In spite of the most earnest pleas of the new Viceroy and the leaders of Congress, both Hindu and Muslim, the defenceless convoys slowly making their way across India continued to suffer ambushes and armed attacks.

A nation in turmoil

Horror stories abounded. Whole trainloads of refugees were stopped and their passengers hacked or beaten to death. Parties of children were ruthlessly murdered. Neither age nor sex was any protection against the senseless rage that had suddenly overtaken previously peaceful people. No count was ever made of the dead, although the final estimate ran into many hundreds of thousands.

Above: Lord and Lady Louis Mountbatten are enthroned as the last Viceroy and Vicereine of India.
Below: The Mountbattens had excellent relations with the leaders of both parties in India. Here, they talk to Mahatma Gandhi.

Left: In spite of anguished pleas from the leaders on both sides, communal violence continued all over India. This burnt-out police lorry in Lahore is a symbol of the terrible times.

Below left: Some of the worst rioting took place in the Punjab, as these burnt-out shells of buildings bear witness.

Right: After the riots the city of Amritsar looks as though it has been bombed.

Below: These refugees from murderous riots found temporary safety in the outskirts of Delhi. Feeding and sheltering them gave the government enormous problems.

Bottom: Rioting took place even in the centre of Delhi. Here, a lone soldier mans a Bren gun at a key crossing.

Soviet Union's five-year plan

The first post-war five-year plan for the reconstruction of the Soviet Union's war-torn infrastructure was halfway through when these patriotic posters appeared on the walls in the Soviet zone of Berlin. The one on the far left exhorts Soviet citizens to produce more and better food. The one in the centre proclaims

'Our Will and our Effort is the Essence of Our Five-Year Plan'. And the one on the right is aimed at steelworkers and encourages them to produce more steel. Although the designs are very powerful, their practical effect on the workforce was difficult to measure.

The royal wedding

The gloom of post-war Britain was briefly lightened by a fairytale royal romance. Princess Elizabeth had first met Philip at her parents' coronation. His father was Prince Andrew of Greece and his mother was the sister of Lord Louis Mountbatten, so there was a strong family connection.

Philip and Elizabeth met again when they were both grown-up, and he was a lieutenant in the Royal Navy. Their romance had flowered very quickly and the King and Queen were delighted that their daughter had chosen such a suitable match. They became engaged on July 9th and were duly married on November 20th, immediately after Philip had been ennobled as the Duke of Edinburgh by King George at a private ceremony.

Above: The Princess and her husband on honeymoon.

Left: The Princess's coach passes through Admiralty Arch on the Mall on its way back to Buckingham Palace after the wedding.

The big freeze

The miseries of post-war Britain were made even worse by one of the worst winters in living memory. From the end of January until the beginning of April, Britain was in the grip of arctic weather. Hundreds were stranded in trains stuck in snow drifts. Channel shipping was halted and air travel was restricted.

Troops and even prisoners were brought in to clear snow and help rescue cut-off villages and farms. Fuel shortages led to power cuts, both industrial and domestic, which became a way of life.

Top: The frozen lake in St James's Park, London.

The Chicago Cardinals

The big story of the NFL in 1947 was the first championship for the Chicago Cardinals, who had struggled for years in the shadow of the Chicago Bears. In this year they signed a four year contract with Charley Trippi, from the University of Georgia, a major prize.

Trippi was at his best in this game: he gained 206 total yards and scored touchdowns on a 44-yard run and a 75-yard punt return. Above: Charley Trippi is tackled during a first-quarter punt return.

Al Capone

Born in New York of Italian immigrants, Capone early gained his nickname 'Scarface' while working as a bouncer for a Brooklyn brothel. Driven out of the city under suspicion for the murder of a policeman, he went to Chicago and joined mafia gangster Johnny Torrio. They soon headed the city's underworld along with the rival gang of 'Deanie' O'Banion. In the gangland war for supremacy during the Twenties, more than a thousand were wiped out. O'Banion was killed, and Torrio 'retired' leaving Capone to take over a thriving $5 million-a-year empire built on prostitution, bootlegging, extortion and gambling. He escaped attempts on his life but was finally caught on a tax evasion charge. Eleven years in prison broke him. Sliding into madness from syphilis, he went into hiding on his Florida estate on his release. He died on January 25th.

The return of Eros

On June 28th London's best-loved statue returned to its rightful place at the centre of Piccadilly Circus (top left). The graceful winged figure which was said to symbolise the Angel of Christian Charity, tops an elaborate bronze fountain. It was designed by Sir Alfred Gilbert as a memorial to the 7th Earl of Shaftesbury.

Kokoschka's choice

The Austrian-born artist and dramatist Oskar Kokoschka (1886–1980) became a British citizen in 1947. He had studied at the Vienna School of Applied Art and was a pupil of Gustav Klimt before moving to Berlin in 1907, where he worked on portraits and as an avant-garde illustrator produced some striking posters and lithographs. He was wounded during the First World War. In the early 20s he taught at Dresden Academy, but the vigorous and highly individual expressionist style that he developed eventually earned him the antagonism of the Nazis. After some extensive travelling he settled in Britain in 1937.

1948

Jan	1	British railways nationalised
	4	Burma becomes an independent Republic
	30	US aviator Orville Wright dies
	30	Mahatma Gandhi assassinated in India
Feb	4	Self-governing Dominion status for Ceylon
	7	Omar Bradley succeeds Eisenhower as US Army Chief
	25	Communists seize power in Czechoslovakia
	28	Last British troops leave India
Mar	7	Juan Perón wins election in Argentina
	11	Offices of Jewish Agency in Jerusalem blown up
	15	US coal miners go on strike for better pensions
	29	Chiang Kai-shek elected President of China
	31	US Congress passes 'Marshall Aid' bill
Apr	1	Britain nationalises electricity industry
	12	Roosevelt memorial unveiled Grosvenor Square, London
	16	Organisation for European Economic Cooperation set up
	19	Americans test new type of atom bomb
May	5	Ben-Gurion chairs provisional Israeli govt in Tel Aviv
	14	Arab Legion invades 'Palestine' from Jordan
	15	British leave Palestine; Egyptian troops enter
	16	Chaim Weizmann named first President of Israel
	26	Jan Smuts defeated in S African elections
Jun	3	Malan forms new Nationalist government in S Africa
	7	President Beneš resigns in Prague
	19	Selective Service Bill in US for men aged 19 to 25 years
	24	Russians stop road and rail traffic to and from Berlin
Jul	15	UN Security Council orders ceasefire in Palestine
Aug	15	South Korea becomes a Republic
Sep	4	Queen Wilhelmina abdicates in Holland
	9	North Korea becomes a Republic
Nov	2	Harry S. Truman wins US Presidential election
	15	Canada: Mackenzie King retires; Louis St Laurent PM
Dec	15	Indonesia: Dutch troops seize Jakarta
		The Arts
		Alan Paton's novel *Cry the Beloved Country*
		Vaughan Williams' *Sixth Symphony*
		Laurence Olivier's film *Hamlet*
		Jackson Pollock's *Composition No. 1*

The Berlin airlift

The Berlin airlift was not only concerned with bringing supplies in, it was also concerned with flying people out, thus reducing the number of mouths to be fed. Here, on one of Berlin's many lakes, a Sunderland flying boat is about to take a party of children to the safe and well-supplied haven of Hamburg.

When the Soviets began to slow down and then to halt all surface transport to West Berlin, the Western powers had a clear choice – to supply the city by air or to abandon it. They chose the first alternative but were immediately faced with enormous logistic problems. By means of careful planning, almost continuous work by pilots, loaders and air traffic controllers, and the use of flying boats as well as conventional aircraft, food and other essential supplies began and continued to flow into the beleaguered city, at one point reaching 7,000 tons a day.

The Berlin airlift lasted about a year; in May 1949 the Soviets allowed trains and lorries through again and the airlift finally ended in September. The airlift had a symbolic importance to the people of Berlin: their freedom would not be threatened again.

Above left: Apart from the airlift, a certain amount of food got into Berlin on barges, which were carefully searched for forbidden West German currency by Soviet border guards. Here, German dockers unload the first barge allowed in by the Soviets.

Above: The destruction of all Berlin's bridges during the last days of the war proved an embarrassment to the Western powers when they were needed to transport supplies from Gatow airport to the centre of West Berlin. The British provided a Bailey Bridge (made from interlocking units) at the site of the ruined Frey Bridge, over the River Havel. However this proved inadequate, and so a totally new bridge had to be constructed.

Left: When the Soviets isolated West Berlin they cut off the electricity. Improvisation therefore became the order of the day, until a proper supply of electricity could be organised. Here, the headlights of a jeep illuminate the unloading of an aircraft.

Formation of Israel

Thirty-one years after Britain's endorsement in the Balfour Declaration of the Jewish right to a national home in Palestine, and only hours before the expiry of the British Palestinian Mandate, the formation of the State of Israel was proclaimed by David Ben-Gurion on May 14th. Ben-Gurion himself became Prime Minister in the new State's provisional government, and Chaim Weizmann (above), for many years an embodiment of the Zionist cause, was named as its first President.

Zionism had drawn great strength from the genocidal persecution of the Jews under Nazism, but Israel's birth pangs were marked by terrorist outrages perpetrated by both Jews and Arabs. Events such as the terrorist group Irgun's bombing of the King David Hotel in Jersualem in 1946 and the Arab-organised explosion in the same city in 1948 (above left) created deep unrest, and the mass exodus of Arabs after Irgun's massacre in the village of Deir Yasin sowed the seeds of the Palestinian refugee problem.

The international reaction to the declaration was not slow in coming. President Truman immediately recognised the provisional government, as did Stalin. Egypt, Syria, Lebanon, Iraq and Jordan instantly mobilised their troops against the new State (left), but the Arab attack was uncoordinated and by the end of the year the Israeli Army, by now 100,000 strong, had achieved conclusive victory.

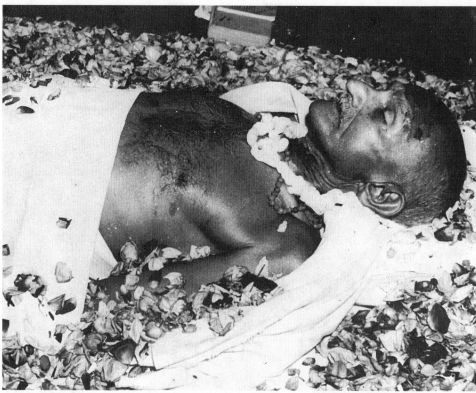

Gandhi assassinated by Hindu fanatic

On January 30th, Mahatma Gandhi, who had been seriously weakened by a fast for Hindu–Muslim friendship, was shot dead as he was helped towards a prayer meeting. His assassin, Nathuram Godse, was a Hindu member of an extremist sect who totally rejected Gandhi's message of goodwill, peace and love.

Gandhi had been heartbroken by the death and violence that had so badly stained the birth of India and Pakistan, and he would have been even more grieved if he could have foreseen the further violence caused by his death. Riots erupted the moment the news reached Bombay, and the police had to fire on the rioters before order could be restored. In the event, the new leaders of India and Pakistan managed to contain the unrest. Under no circumstances did they want a return to the horrors of 1947.

Gandhi had won the affection and loyalty of gifted men and women, old and young, of Europeans of every religious persuasion and of Indians of almost every political line.

Above left: The man who, more than any other, had been responsible for persuading the British to leave India was a familiar figure at 10, Downing Street, and at other seats of political power.

Top right: The Mahatma's petal-strewn body lies in state shortly before his cremation.

Above right: The Governor-General is escorted by his bodyguard on his way to Gandhi's funeral.

The austerity Olympics

The 14th Olympic Games, the first to be held since 'Hitler's Games' in Berlin in 1936, took place in London in the post-war atmosphere of austerity and reconstruction. The Games were declared open by King George VI on the afternoon of July 29th, as a British athlete lit the Olympic flame at Wembley Stadium (top left). Despite the absence of the Soviet Union, Germany and Japan, the Games were a success, especially for the United States who won a total of 38 gold medals.

Three stars particularly outshone their competitors: 17-year-old Bob Mathias (top right), who won the decathlon event for the USA, the great Emil Zatopek, who won four gold medals for Czechoslovakia and the 30-year-old Mrs Blankers-Koen, here shown taking the first hurdle in the 80-metres women's final (above). Perhaps with British rationing in mind, the Indian team brought their own eggs (left).

Smuts voted out

The South African Prime Minister Field Marshal Jan Smuts, leader of the United Party, was ousted in the country's first general election since the war.

Fred Astaire

Fred Astaire (1899–1987) starred with Judy Garland in the film *Easter Parade*. Irving Berlin wrote the music and lyrics.

Before the election

A rare meeting, at the New York St Patrick's Day parade in March, of rival candidates for the American presidency, President Truman and New York Governor Dewey. Dewey was odds-on favourite, so Truman's re-election, in a close result, for a second term of office was an unexpected and personal triumph.

1949

Jan	7	Marshall succeeded by Acheson as US Secretary of State
	10	US introduces 45 and 33.3 rmp records
	12	Britain hangs Margaret Allen, 1st woman for 12 years
	15	Chinese Communists capture Tientsin
	21	Chiang Kai-shek resigns as Nationalist President
	22	Chinese Communists capture Peking
	25	Ben-Gurion's Mapai Party wins Israeli elections
Feb	1	Clothes rationing ends in Britain
Mar	1	US: Joe Louis retires as world heavyweight
	4	Vyshinsky replaces Molotov as Soviet Foreign Minister
	31	Newfoundland becomes Canada's 10th province
Apr	4	NATO Treaty signed in Washington, DC
	18	Ireland becomes a Republic
May	5	Council of Europe established
	11	Siam renames itself Thailand
	12	Berlin blockade lifted by Soviets
	23	German Federal Republic formed with capital at Bonn
	26	Chinese Communists capture Shanghai
Jun	2	Transjordan changes name to Kingdom of Jordan
	16	Big Communist purge in Hungary
Jul	16	Chinese Nationalists begin retreat to Taiwan

Aug	5	US stops aid to Nationalist China
	25	US: 1st experimental colour TV transmission
Sep	15	Konrad Adenauer is new Premier of West Germany
	18	UK: Pound devalued by 30%
	27	Russia denounces pact with Yugoslavia
Oct	1	Mao forms Communist People's Republic of China
	7	German Democratic Republic established in E Germany
	14	US Communist leaders convicted for conspiracy
	16	Greek Civil War ends with defeat of rebels
Nov	7	1st meeting of Council of Europe with Spaak as Chairman
	15	Nathuram Godse hanged in India for murder of Gandhi
	26	India stays inside Commonwealth as Federal Republic
Dec	15	Full membership of Marshall Plan for West Germany
	26	Einstein's new general theory of relativity announced
	27	Holland recognises independence of Indonesia
	30	Sovereignty transferred to Vietnam by France

The Arts

George Orwell's novel *1984*

Arthur Miller's play *Death of a Salesman*

Jacob Epstein's sculpture *Lazarus*

Carol Reed's film *The Third Man*

The Berlin airlift goes on . . . and on

Snow held up the Berlin airlift for a while but groups of German workers were recruited and the runways were soon cleared so that aircraft could land and take off again. Here, a DC3 aircraft waits for the runway to be cleared (below left). Women workers (below right) helped clear rubble from the ruined roads in Berlin so that food convoys were able to get through from the airport to the central distribution points in the city.

The enormous damage done to Berlin by the Allied bombing raids during the war made transport between Gatow airport and central Berlin very difficult. The work done by these old women not only helped to solve the immediate problems of the airlift, but also represented the beginning of the rebuilding of Berlin itself.

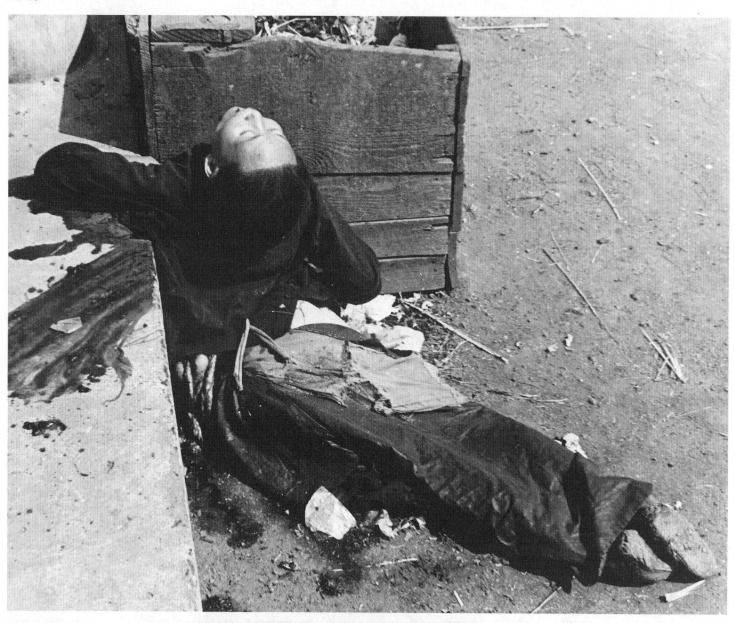

The Communists take over in China

Things went badly for the Chinese Nationalists from the very beginning and by 1949 Mao Tse-tung was on a tidal wave of victory. By January the Communists were at the gates of Peking and the Nationalists were in full retreat. As Peking fell, Chiang Kai-shek resigned and called for an armistice and an immediate ceasefire. This was rejected out of hand and the Communists took the great city of Shanghai in May. By September it was all over and Mao was elected Chairman of the People's Republic of China. On October 1st, a triumphant Mao was able to proclaim China a Communist Republic with Chou En-lai its first Prime Minster.

Above: Mute evidence of the arbitrary violence that was part and parcel of the long agony of China's civil war.

Left: A Chinese Nationalist is held at gunpoint by a Communist soldier.

Israel tidies up

Nationhood and the apparent acquiescence of her Arab neighbours meant that Israel had time to make and mend her infrastructure, to repair war damage and begin to build much-needed houses, factories and public buildings. Here (above left), soldiers have checked that the building is safe for civilian workers to clear the debris and begin to rebuild.

In Jerusalem (above right), the area between the New City and the Arab Quarter had been particularly badly hit during the fighting. In the distance is the old wall surrounding the Old City, and along the wall is the Tower of David. Jerusalem was to remain divided until 1967 when the Israelis took the whole city in the Six-Day War.

The dockers are on strike again

Old-fashioned work processes were still the norm in British docks and trouble had been brewing for some time. The London dockers had a particularly tough reputation and on June 29th some of them came out on strike. They were quickly followed by others and within a few days work on half the ships in London Docks had stopped. The Labour Prime Minister, Clement Attlee,

immediately condemned the strikes but soon 13,000 London dockers were out. On July 22nd the strike ended as suddenly as it had begun. Here, after a rousing speech by one of their leaders, the dockers decide not to go back. Few could have imagined that within a generation the London Docks – and dockers – would disappear for ever.

The young Sinatra

Frank Sinatra (1915–   ), son of immigrant Italian parents, became a singing idol in the 1940s when he was nicknamed 'Swoonlight Sinatra'. One of the most successful of his early films was *On the Town* in 1949, the story of three sailors on a shore leave spree in New York.

Wealth and beauty

The gossip columnists had a field day when one of the world's richest men married one of the world's most beautiful women. Aly Khan, heir to the enormously wealthy Aga Khan, married Rita Hayworth, one of Hollywood's most dazzling stars. They are seen here at the races, hoping for a win from one of Aly Khan's horses.

Good news for children

After seven sour years, sweets and chocolates finally came off the British ration books and children could go into a sweetshop and buy as many of their favourite sweets as they wanted.

Above: Two youngsters from Hackney, London, have their first liberated taste of lollipops and chocolates.

World's biggest telescope

Fifty miles north-east of San Diego, California, the 200-inch Hale telescope at the Mount Palomar observatory enables us to see galaxies a billion light-years away. The instrument weighs 500 tons in total. Finally installed in 1948, it was still attracting large crowds of people the following year. The telescope is named for George Ellery Hale, the American astronomer.

Don't be frightened!

Grotesque masks like these were popular on the cocktail party circuit. Here, a New York businessman shows off his latest acquisition outside the Rockefeller Center.

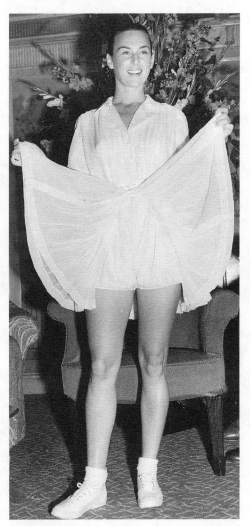

'Gorgeous Gussie'

The summer was brightened by the dazzling outfits of tennis star Gussie Moran, who arrived from America to play in the championships at Wimbledon.

Kicking Picasso's backside

The forthright words of Sir Alfred Munnings, President of the Royal Academy in London, caused a furore when he spoke out against modern art.

Comet's first flight

On July 27th, the De Havilland Comet, the world's first jet airliner, made its maiden flight from an English airfield with war hero and test pilot Group Captain John Cunningham at the controls. The Comet subsequently went into commercial service in 1952 but a series of crashes due to the previously unknown phenomenon of metal fatigue soon brought the airliner's brief career as a world leader to a close.

The strengthened and redesigned Comet went into scheduled service some years later but by then the Boeing 707 was in operation and had taken a commanding lead in the world's airliners, a lead that Boeing and a whole generation of airliners based on the 707 design were never to lose.

1950–1959

The 1950s

The Second World War was over, but despite the ever-present threat of the new atomic weapon, peace still seemed to elude the world. The 1950s were the decade of Korea and of the French war in Vietnam. They were the decade of Suez – that last flexing of British imperial muscles in the Middle East – and of the Hungarian uprising. The first stirrings of those winds of change of which the British Prime Minister Harold Macmillan was to speak so memorably in the 1960s were making themselves felt in Africa and Cyprus, and in the United States the reverberations of black consciousness gave new impetus to the civil rights movements of the deep South.

In the Soviet Union the death of Josef Stalin after years of unchallenged supremacy led to a political power struggle in the upper echelons of the Soviet hierarchy from which the mercurial Nikita Khrushchev emerged victorious. The process of de-Stalinisation began, but the cold war between East and West remained unthawed.

MacArthur and McCarthy

In 1947 President Harry S. Truman of the United States had pledged himself 'to support free peoples who are resisting attempted subjugation by armed minorities or by outside pressures'. For many in the United States and elsewhere the Korean War, which broke out with the invasion of South Korea by the Communist forces of the North in 1950, was the Truman Doctrine in action. For General Douglas MacArthur, commanding the US troops on the ground, however, it rapidly became a crusade against Communism itself. A serious rift developed between MacArthur, who favoured an all-out assault on China, and Truman, who saw the war as a limited action, designed to preserve the security of South Korea. In the end, as international tension mounted and the war threatened to develop into a major superpower confrontation, MacArthur was dismissed from his post.

The early 1950s were also the years of McCarthyism, an extraordinary witchhunt against Communists and Communist sympathisers in all walks of American life, led by Senator Joseph McCarthy of Wisconsin. Movie actors, writers and intellectuals, scientists, and even senior members of the armed forces, were summoned to appear before the Permanent Subcommittee on Investigations.

East and West

The emergence of a new leadership in the Soviet Union after the death of Stalin in 1953 produced changes both at home and in the international arena. However, the cold war continued to divide East and West, such episodes as the Burgess–Maclean–Philby espionage ring and the spying charges brought against the Rosenburgs bearing witness to the highly-charged atmosphere of uncertainty and distrust. The tensions that would lead, in the early years of the next decade, to the very brink of nuclear war pervaded the 1950s. At the same time the stakes were raised by the creation of a new generation of nuclear weapons, with America's first testing of the hydrogen bomb and the Soviet Union's development of its own nuclear capability. The arms race began in earnest, bringing in its wake the first popular campaigns for nuclear disarmament.

Colonial unrest

The independence movements which were to change the face of the less developed world in the 1960s were already challenging the assumptions of colonial rule in the 1950s. Kenya was racked with violence as the Mau Mau acted on their oath to drive the white man out of the country. In the Gold Coast Kwame Nkrumah became sub-Saharan Africa's first black prime minister and, by the end of the decade, head of the new republic of Ghana. There was serious unrest in the French colonies of Morocco and Tunisia as nationalist groups campaigned for independence. Most far-reaching of all in its effects, the situation in the French territory of Algeria erupted into violence, threatening to engulf mainland France itself and sweeping General Charles de Gaulle into power from the political wilderness of Colombey-les-Deux-Eglises. There was bloodshed too in Cyprus, where EOKA terrorists claimed many lives in support of their demands for freedom from British rule and for union with Greece. Whatever remained of British power on the international stage was dealt a severe blow by the Suez fiasco of 1956.

Civil rights in the US

Another movement which was to attain its maturity in the 1960s was born in America during the decade. A young Baptist minister and civil rights campaigner called Martin Luther King came to prominence during a black boycott of segregated bus services in Montgomery, Alabama. Demands for racial integration grew louder in the Southern states, finding their echo in the White House itself.

Science and technology

It was an exciting time in the scientific world. In Cambridge Watson and Crick unveiled their epoch-making discoveries about the structure of DNA and Sanger was awarded a Nobel Prize in Chemistry for his work on insulin. The horizons of medicine were opened up by the first human kidney transplant and the first shot of a business revolution was fired by IBM, who put on the market the first electronic computing machine. A new form of transport – the hovercraft – was put through its paces by the inventor Christopher Cockerell.

Pages 278–9: The State Coach returns to Buckingham Palace after the Coronation of Elizabeth II, 1953.

1950

Korean War

At the end of the Second World War Korea had been arbitrarily divided at the 38th parallel, with a Soviet-supported regime in the north and an American-supported regime in the south. Although they had originally wanted a united democratic republic, both sides remained bitterly opposed and as the USA and the Soviet Union removed their occupying forces, both declared themselves to be independent republics.

On June 25th, North Korea invaded South Korea, which was still unofficially under the auspices of the United Nations and strongly influenced by the USA. The UN called for an immediate withdrawal of North Korean forces. This call was ignored and the USA moved to support its client state of South Korea with General Douglas MacArthur as Commander-in-Chief of UN forces.

By now, North Korean forces had occupied most of the peninsula and the United Nations forces (nearly all American) were cooped up at Pusan in the south-east. The United Nations immediately initiated a powerful counter-attack aided by a bold amphibious landing at Inchon. By the end of September the North Koreans were back at the 38th parallel. Here, American Marines embark for Korea.

China joins in

General MacArthur did not stop when he reached the 38th parallel but drove on into North Korea with no objections from the United Nations. Within three weeks he had driven the North Korean forces almost back to the Manchurian border and had reached the River Yalu at several points. Here the North Koreans began their own counter-attack and soon began to drive the UN forces back south. Here too, some Chinese 'volunteers' were captured.

In November General MacArthur began another big push, this time to end the war once and for all. But at the end of the month, Chinese forces crossed the Yalu River in large numbers and had soon driven the UN forces back to the 38th parallel.

The Korean war had now polarised itself along East–West lines, with the two great ideologies which produced the Cold War facing each other. To the north were the Communist forces of China and Korea with large numbers of Soviet 'advisers'. To the south were the forces of the West, mainly American and South Korean, but with contingents from Britain and the Commonwealth and other Western States.

Top left: Mud-bespattered American troops retreat from Yongsan.

Centre left: South Korean refugees return to Inchon after the city had been recaptured by UN forces.

Bottom left: UN soldiers use metal detectors to check that refugees are not carrying concealed arms.

Below: Victims of war, this homeless brother and sister warm themselves at a small fire.

Above right: American Marines use a 3.5 bazooka to flush out a Communist position.

Below right: American troops reassemble after a bitter battle with the Chinese Army.

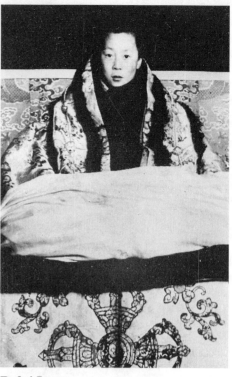

Chinese inside Tibet

On October 24th, China announced the movement of Peking forces into Tibet, penetrating as far as Lhasa, the Tibetan Holy City. On November 13th, Tibet appealed to the United Nations for aid against Chinese aggression.

Dalai Lama

His Holiness the 14th Dalai Lama, ruler of Tibet until the Chinese Communist occupation.

The Kon-Tiki Expedition

Thor Heyerdahl, the Norwegian anthropologist who sailed from Peru to Tahiti on a balsa-wood raft in 1947, published his account of the journey for the first time in English in his book *The Kon-Tiki Expedition*. Together with five men and a parrot, he made the voyage to prove that Polynesia could have been settled by South American Indians. The book was a spectacular best-seller.

Guys and Dolls

Guys and Dolls, Damon Runyon's immortal short stories about the colourful characters of New York 'low life' – gangsters, bookies, gamblers and chorus girls – were first published as a collection in 1932, then became a smash hit musical and film.

Sugar Ray Robinson

It was a happy Christmas for Sugar Ray Robinson (1920–1989) when he beat the German, Hans Stretz in the fifth round, on December 25th. This was the fifth win in a triumphant European tour. He won the middleweight championship two months later.

Coronation Stone stolen

On Christmas Day, Scottish Nationalist activists stole the Stone of Scone from under the Coronation Chair at Westminster Abbey. The stone had been in the Abbey for over 690 years.

Shaw dies

George Bernard Shaw (1856–1950), Britain and Ireland's most famous and controversial playwright and social philosopher, died at his home in Ayot St Lawrence, Hertfordshire, at the age of 94.

Tollund Man

In one of the most remarkable archaeological finds of recent years, the 2,000-year-old body of a man was discovered in a peat bog in Denmark. The corpse was excavated by Professor Glob from the Tollund Mose, a bog near Aarhus in Jutland. It was that of a man, wearing only a leather belt and skull-cap, who had apparently been killed by hanging or garrotting with a braided leather rope, remains of which were found around his neck, perhaps as part of a sacrificial ritual. The body was extraordinarily well preserved by the peat. Scientists were able to establish that he had had his last meal some 12 to 24 hours before he died, had eaten no meat for three days, and had lived on a thin gruel of grain and wild plant seeds. He had three days' growth of stubble on his chin.

George Orwell

The English writer George Orwell (1903–1950) died on January 21st after a long struggle with tuberculosis. Born Eric Arthur Blair in Bengal, Orwell was educated at Eton and served for some years as a policeman in Burma. He began to write in earnest after spending time as a vagrant in France and England, an experience recorded in *Down and Out in Paris and London*, published in 1933. His unorthodox socialist beliefs dictated the shape of much of his later work, including *The Road to Wigan Pier* (1937), *Homage to Catalonia* (1938), which was written after he was wounded in the Spanish Civil War, and his last novel *Nineteen Eighty-Four*, a bleak anti-Utopian view of a totalitarian future. Perhaps his most popular work was the allegorical novel *Animal Farm* (1945), which was later to be made into an animated film (left).

Christian Dior

The influential French fashion designer Christian Dior (1905–1957) gave his first display in London at the Savoy Hotel on April 25th (left). Dior, 45, emerged from years of obscurity to become an overnight household name in 1947 when he presented Paris with his first collection, the revolutionary 'Corolle' line. Christened the 'New Look' by the press, the fashions were a sensational success. Dior's hallmark was a return to the lines of the Edwardian age, with gathered skirts, low necklines and long flowing dresses. After the sparse fashions of the War years, his extravagant use of fabrics – one of his lines containing some 50 yards of material – was seen as representing a return to a more glamorous ideal. He was awarded the Nieman-Marcus Award in 1947.

1951

Jan	10	US writer Sinclair Lewis dies	20	British Hawker Hunter jet fighter makes maiden flight
Feb	14	Ben-Gurion dissolves Parliament after defeat in *Knesset*	Aug 14	US newspaper tycoon Hearst dies
	21	British bomber crosses Atlantic in record 4 hrs 40 mins	31	West Germans introduce 33 rpm long-playing records
	26	US: Presidents to be restricted to 2 terms	Sep 5	Maureen Connolly wins US Tennis Championships at 16
Mar	2	Purge of Czech Communist Party	8	US signs peace treaty with Japan in San Francisco
	7	Iranian Premier Razmara assassinated	13	UN talks on Palestine with Jews and Arabs fail
	8	Iranian oil industry nationalised	19	Attlee calls general election in Britain
	14	Korea: UN troops recapture Seoul	20	NATO asks Greece and Turkey to join it
	20	Montgomery to be Eisenhower's Deputy at SHAPE	Oct 9	Ben-Gurion forms government in Israel
Apr	5	Rosenbergs sentenced to death in US for spying	16	Ali Khan, President of Pakistan, assassinated
	11	Truman sacks MacArthur as military supremo in Korea	26	Winston Churchill is British PM again
	11	UK: Stone of Scone found 3 months after theft	27	Egypt denounces Treaty of Alliance with Britain
May	14	South Africa disenfranchises 'coloured' voters	Nov 11	Perón is re-elected President of Argentina
	18	Vickers *Valiant*, UK jet bomber, makes maiden flight	Dec 24	Libya becomes independent
	23	US Generals Bradley and Marshall condemn MacArthur		*The Arts*
	28	Festival of Britain Pleasure Gardens open at Battersea		J. D. Salinger's novel *The Catcher in the Rye*
Jun	13	De Valera reassumes power in Eire		Igor Stravinsky's opera *The Rake's Progress*
Jul	3	India complains to UN about Pakistan re Kashmir		John Huston's film *The African Queen*
	20	King Abdullah of Jordan assassinated		Alfred Hitchcock's film *Strangers on a Train*

The Chinese advance in Korea

Once more the seesaw war in Korea went against the United Nations forces. In January the Chinese mounted a major offensive and the UN–American forces were again forced to retreat. The Communists soon broke through and four days after the offensive they had captured Seoul, the capital of South Korea.

General MacArthur was growing impatient with the progress of the war but President Truman was aware of the symbolic importance of this East–West conflict and made it clear that the Americans would fight on. And not everything was going according to plan for the Chinese: their lines of communication were stretched and the American Air Force was mounting massive bombing attacks. The Chinese were being pushed back towards the 38th parallel and the UN forces once more prepared to fight for Seoul.

Below: American Marines near the 38th parallel.

Korean War draws to a close

In January, the United Nations forces were able to stem the joint Chinese North Korean Army sweeping down from the north and hold them near the 38th parallel. The uneasy stalemate was abruptly broken when General Douglas MacArthur, the UN Commander in Chief, threatened to invade China. As he was already on record as having wanted to use the atom bomb against his opponent, this threat gave the war an alarming new dimension. It also infuriated President Truman who wanted to contain the conflict and had been increasingly annoyed by MacArthur's political statements. He sacked MacArthur in April. This caused an enormous outcry in America but at least focused the minds of both sides on the dangers of the situation. Soon they both began to look for ways to end the war.

Left: Korean refugees make their weary way from yet another battleground.

Below: General MacArthur inspects North Korean prisoners of war in their stockade.

The Festival of Britain

The post-war gloom in Britain was temporarily but effectively lifted for a few months by the new Festival of Britain on the South Bank of the Thames. It was opened by the King and Queen at the beginning of May and was an immediate success not only with Londoners, who flocked to it in their thousands, but with people from all over the country and, indeed, all over the world.

The Festival's architectural style was very influential and changed public tastes permanently. 'Skylon' was the name suggested by poet Margaret Sheppard Fidler for the vertical feature of the South Bank. Symbolising the spirit of new hope it was illuminated from within at night and appeared to hang in the sky with no visible means of support.

Trouble at Suez

In a speech the previous year, King Farouk had ordered the British to leave Egypt. The British ignored this but made a pretence of placating him. They said they were willing to leave. However they omitted to make any firm promises. This prevarication sparked off anti-British rioting and, in September, led to Egypt's decision to rescind the 1936 Anglo-Egyptian Alliance.

Britain's response was swift. At dawn on October 19th, British troops occupied the key points on the Suez Canal and abruptly stopped the peace talks. Britain also took the wise precaution of removing all civilians from the Canal Zone and in November 2,000 women and children who had been threatened by the continuous riots were evacuated.

Left: British officers and men interrogate Egyptian workers while searching for arms in the troubled Canal Zone.

Below: When Egyptian workers were threatened by the police, camels were abandoned, like this one seen outside a deserted local 'shopping parade'.

Don't cry for me

With her husband General Juan Perón (1895–1974) certain to win the presidency of Argentina, Eva Perón (1919–1952), at the height of her popularity, promised to stand as Vice-President. She was to die within the year of ovarian cancer. Eva, the one-time film and radio actress, had become a powerful though unofficial political leader. She organised women workers, secured the vote for women, pushed for government spending on welfare, and introduced compulsory religious education in schools.

Testing the H-bomb

A further series of atom bomb tests took place on Eniwetok Atoll in the Pacific Marshall islands. The H-bomb being developed by the Americans would be triggered by an atom bomb.

A familiar sign

Winston Churchill did not forget his famous wartime 'V' sign as he campaigned for the Conservative Party in the October election. He was to win by a very narrow margin.

Guy Burgess

Homosexual, drunkard, British Foreign Office favourite and Soviet spy Guy Burgess (1910–1963) caused a sensation when he defected to Moscow.

Donald MacLean

Donald MacLean (1913–1983) was linked with Burgess – he was less flamboyant and more diffident but another British traitor and spy nonetheless.

The Rosenbergs

Julius Rosenberg (1918–1953) and his wife Ethel (1915–1953) were condemned to the electric chair on April 5th for passing secrets to the Soviet Union.

The Shah of Iran marries

The Shah married the beautiful Princess Soraya.

Margaret Hilda Roberts

This unusual picture of the future British Prime Minister Margaret Thatcher (1925–   ) was taken when she was the youngest Conservative candidate at the 1951 election. After an uncharacteristically brief political argument she accompanied four voters on the piano in a sing-song.

The Cruel Sea

This screen adaptation of the famous novel by Nicholas Montsarrat (1910–1981) was among the most popular films of the year. It starred Jack Hawkins as the Captain of the *Compass Rose*, here seen sinking after a torpedo attack in one of the most dramatic scenes of the film.

1952

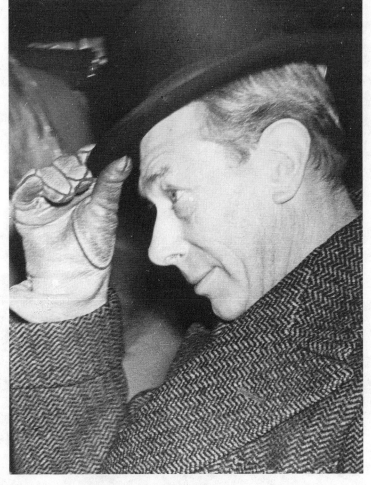

One of the last pictures taken of George VI.

Death of a King

In September 1951, surgeons operating at Buckingham Palace removed one of the King's lungs. He was, they said, 'as satisfactory as could be expected'. These bland words were meant to reassure people and they succeeded. But to most doctors they carried a much more ominous warning. The King had cancer. Like so many of his generation he had been a heavy cigarette smoker all his life and the connection between this and lung cancer was only just beginning to be suspected.

On February 6th, a brief bulletin on the railings of Buckingham Palace announced that the King had died peacefully in his sleep. Britain now had a new Queen.

George VI had been a good and conscientious ruler. He had accepted his fate with a good grace when his elder brother Edward VIII abandoned his throne in 1936 for the love of Wallis Simpson, an American divorcee. He had performed all his public functions admirably, and had been ably supported by a loving wife who had grown with him in popularity and public esteem.

Shortly after his reign began, he found himself monarch of a nation at war and he threw himself into an even more arduous round of public duties. When it was suggested that he and his family should live in Canada for the duration of the war, he turned down the suggestion contemptuously, preferring to share the dangers of London with his people. His house was hit and badly damaged just like theirs. His family's rations were the same as theirs and he and his family scrupulously observed all the rules and regulations imposed by a wartime government, sharing all the privations and hardships that were visited on his subjects.

Long live the Queen

The young Princess Elizabeth and her husband the Duke of Edinburgh were on a tour of the Commonwealth, including Australia, when her father died. They had to cut their tour short immediately and return to Britain. She was 25 and had inherited one of the most demanding jobs in the world.

Left: Princess Elizabeth and Prince Philip are seen off on their Commonwealth tour by King George and Queen Elizabeth.

Right: The new Queen Elizabeth returns to be greeted by the Prime Minister, Winston Churchill, and Leader of the Opposition, Clement Attlee.

Below: The funeral procession of King George VI on its way to Windsor.

Mau Mau

The struggle for freedom in British colonial Africa took many forms but in most cases the transition was peaceful. Only in Kenya did a particular freedom movement – Mau Mau – use violence, killing white settlers. The British used counter-violence and concentration camps.

Top: The British even used African magic against the freedom movements. Here, a witch doctor curses Mau Mau.
Above: Suspected Mau Mau terrorists are held in a Kenyan concentration camp.

Ending the Korean War

Although peace was very much in the offing, the Korean War went on, with each side taking advantage if a favourable situation arose. Some savage air and ground battles were fought out in Korea while world statesmen attempted to find a satisfactory solution. The end finally came in the following year, a year which also saw the beginning of conflict in Vietnam.

Top: New South Korean troops line up before embarking on a tank landing craft.
Above: American Marines bring back three prisoners of war in a jeep.

Harrow rail disaster

A horrifying British train disaster took place on October 8th at Harrow just outside London when two trains crashed and a third, travelling at high speed, hit the wreckage seconds later (above). An early-morning commuter train just leaving Harrow station was struck on the rear by an express from Scotland which had somehow got on the wrong line. An express from Euston, London, then ploughed into the other two trains and brought an overhead bridge down. A total of 112 people died, over 200 were injured and it took days to clear the tracks.

'Ike' rules OK!

Dwight Eisenhower won a resounding victory in the American presidential election, completely wiping out his Democrat opponent, Adlai Stevenson. General Eisenhower, who until a few months earlier was Supreme Commander of the Allied Forces in Europe, won the largest ever popular vote of more than 33 million. The Republican win brought California's senator Richard Nixon into the office of Vice-President.

Albert Schweitzer at home

The great doctor, Albert Schweitzer (1875–1965), set up his hospital at Lambaréné, Gabon, in equatorial Africa in 1913 after a successful career as a musician and author. He spent the rest of his life as a missionary doctor in this obscure corner of Africa but it became a place of pilgrimage for many – not always appreciated by Schweitzer. Here (right), he is seen in the grounds of his hospital. He was awarded the Nobel Peace Prize in 1952.

The *Flying Enterprise*

In January, in one of the most amazing salvage attempts in naval history, Captain Henrik Carlsen tried to save his ship, the *Flying Enterprise*.

'Evita' dies

The enormously popular Eva Perón, wife of Argentinian President Juan Perón, died of cancer on July 26th. She had married him at the age of 16.

Tito visits London

Prime Minister Tito, the Yugoslav leader, paid an official visit to London. He is seen here leaving Westminster Pier, central London, at the end of his visit.

War over Mexican peace mural

Controversy ensued after a mural commissioned by Mexico's Fine Arts Institute mysteriously disappeared shortly after it was completed. The Mexican government had planned to send the mural, entitled *Nightmare of War and Dream of Peace*, to Paris as part of an exhibition, but changed its mind when it saw the work, on the grounds that it could be 'offensive to friendly nations'. The artist Diego Rivera (1886–1957) accused the government of censorship and theft.

1953

Jan	5	Churchill visits new US President Eisenhower	Jul	4	International Confederation of Free Trade Unions meets
	8	Pakistan: Rioting in Karachi		5	Hungary: Ministry formed by new PM Imre Nagy
	10	First meeting of European Coal and Steel Community		20	USSR and Israel restore diplomatic relations
	14	Tito elected President of Yugoslavia		27	Armistice in Korea signed at Panmunjom
	16	Egypt dissolves all political parties	Aug	20	Dr Mussadiq, Iranian Prime Minister, arrested
Feb	10	Egypt: General Neguib takes dictatorial powers		20	Sultan of Morocco deposed by France
	12	Agreement on Sudan between Britain and Egypt		30	Yugoslavia and Hungary resume relations
	12	USSR breaks off relations with Israel	Sep	6	W Germany: Christian Democrats win election
Mar	5	Stalin, Premier of USSR, dies aged 74		12	USSR: Khrushchev appointed First Secretary
	5	Russian composer Prokofiev dies		28	Polish government arrests Cardinal Wyszynski
	26	US: Salk vaccine successful in tests against polio	Oct	8	Portugal: Salazar wins all seats in elections
Apr	6	German Chancellor Adenauer visits New York	Nov	27	US playwright Eugene O'Neill dies
	10	Dag Hammarskjöld becomes UN Secretary-General	Dec	23	USSR: Ex-Minister of Interior Beria executed
	13	British West Indian Federation Conference in London			*The Arts*
May	12	General Gruenther is Supreme Commander in Europe			Arthur Miller's play *The Crucible*
Jun	17	Anti-Communist riots in East Berlin			Dylan Thomas' radio play *Under Milk Wood*
	18	Egyptian Republic proclaimed; Neguib is 1st President			Fred Zinnemann's film *From Here to Eternity*
	19	Atomic spies J. and E. Rosenberg executed in US			Ian Fleming's novel *Casino Royale*

The Queen is crowned

In a ceremony seen for the first time by millions of her subjects on television, Queen Elizabeth II was crowned in Westminster Abbey by the Archbishop of Canterbury on June 2nd. It was a ritual going back centuries, with all the pomp and splendour of the greatest royal occasions. The Duke of Edinburgh was at her side and was the first of her family to pay her homage.

All the ritual implements of majesty were to be seen: the orb, the sceptre, the anointing oil and the great Crown of St Edward.

Perfectly rehearsed, the new Queen played her central role with great natural dignity, making the necessary responses during the ceremony in a cool, clear voice.

After the ceremony and the celebratory trumpet music written by Sir Arthur Bliss, Master of the Queen's Musick, she made her way to Buckingham Palace in a gold coach accompanied by the cheers of thousands of people – most of whom had waited up all night to see her.

The Coronation

At the climax of the ceremony the Archbishop of Canterbury lifts the Crown of St Edward high in the air before lowering it onto the head of 'Your undoubted Queen'. Later, a kneeling subject pays homage to the new Queen (below).

Outside, despite the cold wet weather, two million people waited. At least 30,000 spectators had camped overnight in the Mall. Tickets for seats in the stands changed hands on the black market for £40–£50, while a balcony in a choice site overlooking the route cost as much as £3,500.

Meanwhile history was also in the making – round two and a half million television sets in living rooms up and down Britain where half the nation gathered to watch the day's events. From then on, sales soared. Mass television had arrived.

Korea – the final flicker

The Korean War did not end with a bang or a final heroic gesture but fizzled out when both sides got tired of the sporadic, one-off operations which took place over the early months of the year.

Above: American 'Flying Boxcars' drop supplies to embattled US Marines.

Top right: Drums of aviation fuel wait in readiness for the first Marine Air Wing.

Centre right: Korean prisoners await the end of the war behind barbed wire.

Right: An American howitzer blasts away in the final weeks of the war.

A new war in the Far East

The guns of the Korean War were scarcely silent when the rumbles of a new conflict began. The North Vietnamese, under their charismatic leader Ho Chi Minh, were making life difficult for the French with a series of brilliant guerrilla forays. But the tough French legionnaires and paratroopers were accustomed to winning pitched battles where firepower and weapon superiority could be brought to bear. The shadowy hit-and-run tactics adopted by their opponents puzzled and irritated them.

Top: French paratroopers march to battle in enemy territory.
Left: Villagers wait behind their bamboo defences.
Above: French paratroopers watch their companions arrive for the fatal battle of Dien Bien Phu.

Revolt in East Berlin

The East German authorities and their Soviet superiors got a nasty shock in June when the workers of East Berlin rose in a spontaneous protest against the continuing Soviet presence in the city. After two days it became apparent that the uprising had got out of hand and that the East German authorities could not cope with it by themselves. More powerful and persuasive measures were needed. These were provided by Soviet tanks. The numbers killed were never disclosed but many hundreds were badly injured.

Top: Soviet tanks move into East Berlin to help put down the workers' riots.
Above: East Berliners publicly burn the Soviet flag.

Everest conquered

Everest, at 29,028 feet the world's highest mountain, was finally scaled by Sir Edmund Hillary (1919–   ) of New Zealand and Sherpa Tenzing Norgay (1914–1986) of Nepal on May 29th. The mountain, which the Tibetans call Chuomo-Lungma (Mother Goddess of the World), had defeated nine previous attempts, including the ill-fated Mallory–Irvine expedition of 1924. Working with the very latest equipment, including portable radio and closed-circuit oxygen systems, Sir John Hunt's expedition, sponsored jointly by the Royal Geographical Society and the Joint Himalayan Committee of the Alpine Club, approached the mountain from the south-west and established eight camps on the ascent. Hillary and Tenzing left the Union Jack, the Nepalese flag and the flag of the United Nations on the summit (above).

Stalin dies

Joseph Stalin dead cast about as heavy a pall of fear over his people as Stalin alive. This photograph (left) shows part of a six-mile queue of people who had come to pay their last respects to the tyrant's corpse, almost as if they were frightened he would notice if they did not. It took the Soviets many months to get used to the idea that Stalin, instigator of the Great Purge (1936–1938), had finally and irrevocably gone from their lives.

Comet crash

The revolutionary Comet jet airliners had a most encouraging debut and looked set to change the face of air transport when, after four months' scheduled service, they began to fall out of the sky. After three unexplained crashes, the Comet had to be grounded while the jets underwent a complex series of tests. The cause of the trouble was found to be the previously unknown phenomenon metal fatigue. This could easily be rectified but by then it was too late, as American rivals to the Comet were coming into commercial service. The strengthened Comets were used by BOAC with some success but the world lead established by the first jet airliner could never be regained.

Left: Indian workers examine the wreckage of a Comet that crashed outside Calcutta.

Colonel Nasser

During the year it became apparent that General Neguib was only the puppet ruler of Egypt and that the real power was held by Colonel Gamal Nasser (1918–1970).

Kennedy marries Bouvier

John Fitzgerald Kennedy (1917–1963) married the beautiful society photographer Jacqueline Lee Bouvier on September 12th. He had been elected Senator for Massachusetts the previous year.

Joseph R. McCarthy

Senator Joseph R. McCarthy (1909–1957) was at the height of his anti-Communist witch-hunt. He even accused ex-President Truman. Next year would see McCarthy's inevitable downfall.

1954

Jan 11	British Comet jet airliner falls into Mediterranean		31	Yugoslav President Tito on state visit to Greece
24	New coalition in Israel formed by Moshe Sharett		31	State of emergency in Bugandan province of Uganda
Feb 25	Nasser takes temporary control in Egypt		Jun 18	Pierre Mendès-France becomes French Premier
Mar 1	Organization of American States holds conference		Jul 3	End of all rationing in Britain
8	US and Japan sign mutual defence pact		15	Maiden flight of Boeing 707
12	Kenya: British arrest 700 Mau-Mau activists		17	Theodor Heuss is new President of West Germany
22	US H-bomb irradiates Japanese fisherman		Sep 9	Algerian earthquake kills 1,500
23	Israel pulls out of UN Armistice Commission		15	All China People's Congress held in Peking
31	USSR offers to join NATO		Oct 8	Hanoi taken by Communist troops
Apr 18	Nasser takes full control in Egypt		Nov 3	Outbreak of terrorism in Algiers
27	Georgi Malenkov elected Premier in USSR		5	Burma and Japan sign peace treaty
29	R. Oppenheimer, father of A-bomb, is 'security risk'		17	Nasser becomes official Head of State in Egypt
May 6	Roger Bannister runs mile under 4 minutes		Dec 1	US signs pact with Nationalist China
7	Communists capture Dien Bien Phu in Vietnam		2	US Senate censures Senator McCarthy
8	France proposes Vietnam truce		23	20,000 French troops sent to Algeria
13	President Eisenhower signs St Lawrence Seaway Bill			*The Arts*
15	Queen Elizabeth and Philip start Commonwealth tour			William Golding's novel *Lord of the Flies*
17	US Supreme Court outlaws racial segregation in schools			Elia Kazan's film *On the Waterfront*
19	US composer Charles Ives dies			J. R. R. Tolkien's fantasy *The Lord of the Rings*

Indo-China war continues

With the beginning of 1954 the French war in Indo-China entered its seventh year. It was to mark the final climax of a long and bitter conflict between the French and Vietnamese forces under General Navarre and the Viet Minh guerrillas under their commander General Vo Nguyen Giap, waged in a landscape that was to become all too familiar to television viewers throughout the world in the 1960s and 1970s. As the French dug themselves into their stronghold at Dien Bien Phu, there was intense diplomatic activity by the international powers. By the time the Geneva conference on Indo-China and Korea began in April, the French garrison was already under heavy siege.

End of the Indo-China war

The French garrison of Dien Bien Phu, a cornerstone of her Indo-Chinese defences, became the focus of the fiercest fighting of the entire war during the early months of the year. Despite some defensive successes, such as the capture of a number of Viet Minh prisoners (far left and above), the stronghold fell to the besieging Communist forces of General Giap on May 7th. The defeat was a bitter blow to French morale and proved to be the final nail in the coffin of her Indo-Chinese interests.

In June the French government fell and in July the new Prime Minister, Pierre Mendès-France (1907–1982), reached a peace agreement under which the French withdrew their forces from Indo-China and Vietnam was partitioned along the 17th parallel. As the Communist regime of Ho Chi Minh assumed control of North Vietnam, thousands of refugees fled from their villages and made for the south (left).

H-bomb tested

The nuclear arms race entered a new and more terrifying phase on March 1st with the testing of America's first true hydrogen bomb on Bikini Atoll in the Pacific. Both the Soviet Union and the United States had been working on thermonuclear devices for some years and the US Atomic Energy Commission had already tested precursors of the new device in the Pacific in 1952 and in the Nevada desert (above, insert) in 1953. However, whereas 'Mike', the 1952 bomb, used liquid deuterium, the new H-bomb used the solid lithium deuteride, making it much more practicable as a military weapon. The bomb was some 500 times more powerful than the one which destroyed Hiroshima in 1945. Above: Weather balloons used during nuclear tests.

Algeria

November saw the most serious outbreak of anti-French violence in Algeria since the end of the Second World War. Many people were killed in terrorist attacks by the nationalist Movement for the Triumph of Democratic Liberties (MTLD) before the security forces were able to restore order in the Algiers and Oran areas. There were hundreds of arrests and arms seizures (above).

The unrest followed one of the most powerful earthquakes of the century, which had devastated the Algerian city of Orléansville on September 9th. Some 1,500 people died and thousands had been left homeless (top and left).

Crowds mob Nasser

Wildly enthusiastic crowds climb up to the Presidency's balcony to embrace Prime Minister Nasser as he broadcasts to the nation. In his first major success since taking over from Naguib, Nasser managed to negotiate for the withdrawal of British troops from the Suez Canal Zone. After hard bargaining, a draft agreement was signed in July for the phased evacuation by the British over a period of 20 months. However, British 'civilian contractors' were to keep a base in the zone in case of any danger to Middle East security.

The British government honoured its agreement and evacuation was completed. But in the eyes of purist Egyptian nationalists, 'unconditional evacuation' was the only acceptable solution and Nasser and his colleagues were soon to be under attack for selling out to the British. The extremist Muslim Brotherhood made an unsuccessful assassination attempt on Nasser in October which led to the outlawing of the organization and the execution of six of its leaders.

Billy Graham

On May 22nd a mass meeting at Wembley stadium in London marked the climax of a three-month mission to the UK by the American evangelist Billy Graham (1918–   ). Born in North Carolina, he was ordained as a Southern Baptist minister, and launched a worldwide evangelical campaign. He became very influential around the world, presenting a persuasive and enthusiastic image of Christianity.

Highly charismatic in his delivery, Graham made numerous television appearances and toured widely. He wrote a number of books, including *Peace with God* (1953) and *The Seven Deadly Sins* (1955). His 1954 visit to the UK was a resounding success, with a reported attendance of some 1,300,000 and over 28,000 conversions or 'decisions for Christ', to use Graham's expression.

Bill Haley

American musician Bill Haley (1927– 1981) and his Comets brought the new rock beat to country music – an exciting combination which ensured that the group achieved immense popularity. They scored some of the earliest and most resounding hits of the rock 'n' roll years – *Shake, Rattle and Roll* (1954) was followed by *Rock Around the Clock* (1955) and *See You Later, Alligator* (1956). The group continued playing and touring into the 1970s, and had considerable influence on the development of rock music.

The Flying Bedstead

August 3rd saw the first test flight at Hucknall in Nottinghamshire of the Rolls-Royce Thrust Measuring Rig (TMR) jet-lift vehicle, popularly known as the 'Flying Bedstead'. The ungainly-looking aircraft (left), more closely resembling a Heath Robinson contraption than a piece of advanced military hardware, was the first to be capable of vertical take-off from a horizontal position and created something of a sensation when pictures were released. The plane was powered by two Rolls-Royce engines set horizontally in opposition on each side of the frame and ducted so that they discharged vertically downwards. The pilot sat on a platform above the engines and controlled its movements by means of compressed air jets.

Roger Bannister

Roger Bannister (1929–), a medical student, a former President of Oxford University Athletics Club and the British one-mile record holder, became the first man in athletics history to run the mile in under four minutes – in three minutes 59.4 seconds to be precise. This remarkable achievement took place on May 6th 1954 during an athletics match at Oxford between the Amateur Athletics Association and the University of Oxford.

Churchill's 80th birthday

On November 30th, Sir Winston was presented with a Birthday Book of signatures and his portrait, painted by Graham Sutherland, RA. The painting was commissioned by both Houses of Parliament. Unfortunately Lady Churchill disliked the painting intensely and it was later destroyed.

Errol Flynn

The one-time Hollywood heart-throb Errol Flynn filmed *Lilacs in the Spring* with actress Anna Neagle (1908–1986).

1955

Jan	18	Government in Kenya offers terms to Mau Mau	23	Donald Campbell breaks water speed record at 202 mph
	25	USSR officially ends war with Germany	24	Bulganin and Khrushchev visit East Germany
Feb	5	Mendès-France resigns as French Premier	Aug 1	Warsaw hosts Communist Youth Congress
	8	Malenkov resigns; Bulganin becomes Soviet Premier	11	Muslim right-wing government takes over in Indonesia
	24	Turkey and Iraq sign Baghdad pact	12	German writer Thomas Mann dies
Mar	2	Egypt and Syria sign defence pact	13	UK: IRA raids training centre in Berkshire
	11	Germany, Italy and France ratify European pact	15	Indians attempt to enter Goa
	27	Pakistan declares state of emergency	20	Riots in Morocco
	28	Israel raids Gaza Strip in reprisal attack	Sep 6	Anti-Greek riots in Istanbul and Izmir
	31	Chinese Communist Party purged	19	Juan Perón resigns and leaves Argentina
Apr	5	Churchill resigns as PM; replaced by Eden	24	US President Eisenhower has minor heart attack
	18	Albert Einstein dies	25	Field Marshal Harding appointed Governor of Cyprus
May	5	Official occupation ends in West Germany	30	Young American actor James Dean killed in car crash
	6	Britain goes to International Court over Falklands	Oct 23	S Vietnam becomes a Republic under Diem
	8	Hiroshima victims arrive in US for plastic surgery	30	Abdication of Sultan of Morocco
	9	West Germany joins NATO	Nov 2	Ben-Gurion forms government in Israel
	14	Warsaw Pact signed	26	State of emergency in Cyprus
	26	Khrushchev and Bulganin visit Yugoslavia		*The Arts*
Jun	11	Le Mans car race crash kills 70		Vladimir Nabokov's novel *Lolita*
	15	US and Britain sign agreement on atomic energy		Tennessee William's play *Cat on a Hot Tin Roof*
Jul	4	British dock strike ends after a month		Nicholas Ray's film *Rebel Without a Cause*
	4	Britain will return Simonstown base to South Africa		Bill Haley's pop song '*Rock Around the Clock*'
	18	Disneyland opens in Los Angeles		Michael Tippett's opera *The Midsummer Marriage*

Big Four Summit

The Geneva Summit brought together, in October, the foreign ministers of the world's four most powerful nations: the United States, England, France and the Soviet Union. They were represented by John Foster Dulles, Harold Macmillan, Antoine Pinay and Vyacheslav Molotov. The meeting opened with the three Western ministers tabling proposals for the reunification of Germany and for protecting the Soviet bloc from German aggression. The talks quickly reached deadlock however, when Molotov managed to postpone the publication of the suggestions until he could put forward the Soviet view. He ruled out German reunification, and called for the dissolution of NATO and the Warsaw Pact. Harold Macmillan said that he failed to see why in ensuring Russia's security the West had to abandon its own defences. John Foster Dulles tried to convince Molotov to recognise the significance of the US offer to underwrite European non-aggression treaties.

Riots in Cyprus

Serious rioting broke out in Nicosia on the Mediterranean island of Cyprus when the traditional parades to celebrate Oxi Day (the day when Greece entered the Second World War) were banned by the newly appointed British Governor Sir John Harding. Cyprus police were assisted by British troops in bringing the situation under control, and there were many casualties on both sides (left).

The unrest marked another stage in the deepening crisis in Cyprus. Intercommunal fighting between the majority Greek population and the Turkish minority worsened when Prime Minister Anthony Eden attempted to strengthen the British position on the island. The situation was fuelled by the terrorism of the Greek Cypriot insurrectionary movement EOKA (above) and the increasingly draconian counter-insurgency methods employed by the authorities. During 1955 EOKA, led by Colonel Grivas, stepped up its campaign of bombings, murder and civil disobedience in the cause of *enosis* or union with Greece, while Harding pursued negotiations with the leader of the Greek Cypriot community, Archbishop Makarios.

Khrushchev in Yugoslavia and India

Nikita Khrushchev, the Soviet leader, and the Prime Minister Nikolai Bulganin made remarkable visits to Yugoslavia and Asia during the course of the year. Both trips were widely seen as expressing the new style of leadership in the Soviet Union.

In Yugoslavia in May Khrushchev met the President Marshal Tito (far left) for talks in Belgrade, and in an extraordinary radio speech he apologised to his host country for the break in relations between the two Communist regimes of Yugoslavia and the Soviet Union which had taken place under his predecessor, Joseph Stalin, in 1948.

In November the Soviet leader flew to India for discussions with the non-aligned government of Pandit Nehru. The visit aroused enormous popular interest and huge crowds gathered in Calcutta (near left) and elsewhere to catch a glimpse of Khrushchev.

Crisis in the Formosa Strait

In an atmosphere of mounting international tension, the Chinese Nationalist forces of Chiang Kai-shek were finally driven out of the Tachen Islands to their one remaining stronghold, the island of Formosa (Taiwan). The evacuation of the Tachens (left) which formed part of a fringe of Nationalist-controlled islands just off the Chinese coast, took place under heavy fire from Mao Tse-tung's Communist government forces on the mainland. During the crisis, which subsided later in the year, Sino-American relations reached a new low, the US government having committed itself to defending the Nationalists' position in Formosa.

Industrial unrest in Britain

1955 was a year of industrial disputes and strike action in the United Kingdom. In March production of national newspapers was halted when members of the Electrical Trades Union and the Amalgamated Engineering Union took strike action over a pay claim. In May 65,000 railwaymen went on strike and in June striking dockers from Merseyside came to London to persuade their London colleagues to continue their industrial action. The dock strike was held in support of an attempt by the Stevedores' Union to gain representation on provincial port joint committees. It was finally called off after 40 days.

Le Mans disaster

On June 11th 1955 a very serious accident took place on the famous track at Le Mans in France during the 24-hour race. A Mercedes car crashed into the crowd of spectators, killing 70 people and injuring more than 100. This disaster caused the sport of motor racing to be curtailed for some time afterwards.

Grandma Moses

Anna Mary 'Grandma' Moses (1860–1961) emerged late in life as one of America's best-known and most prolific primitive painters. Her vivid portrayals of the farm life she knew so well such as this one, *McDonell Farm*, became very popular.

Princess Margaret

Princess Margaret announced that she had decided not to marry Group-Captain Peter Townsend, a divorcee.

Australian floods

After torrential rain in the north of New South Wales, several tributaries of the River Darling burst their banks simultaneously. This caused serious flood damage in New South Wales in February and March 1955, and inundated tens of thousands of square miles.

It was the worst natural disaster in Australian history. Nearly 100 people died, over 50,000 lost their homes and there were extensive losses of livestock. A massive airlift operation saved many stranded people and a flood relief fund was set up, with substantial contributions from Britain and other Commonwealth countries.

London smog

Air pollution became a serious cause for concern in the early 1950s. After an exceptionally severe incidence of London smog a committee was set up under Hugh Beaver in July 1953 to investigate the problem. The Beaver Committee came up with a Clean Air Scheme, recommending that emission of industrial smoke should become an offence, that industries themselves should be responsible for removing it, and that smokeless fuel should be used in the home. On February 4th 1955, Duncan Sandys, Minister of Housing and Local Government, proposed a comprehensive Bill for the Prevention of Air Pollution, along the lines of the Beaver Report.

Disneyland

The great Walt Disney (1901–1966) founded Disneyland as a base for his television productions in 1954. Among the intensely popular television shows made there were *The Mickey Mouse Club*, *Zorro*, *Walt Disney Presents* and *Walt Disney's Wonderful World of Color*.

On July 15th 1955, Disneyland, which was based in Anaheim (California), opened to the public as the world's most elaborate amusement park. There were four main areas: Adventureland, Frontierland, Fantasyland and Tomorrowland. Equally popular with adults and children, it attracted millions of visitors each year, and in 1967 (a year after Disney's death) work began on an East Coast counterpart – Walt Disney World, at Orlando, Florida.

Albert Einstein

Albert Einstein (1879–1955), who formulated the theory of relativity, died on April 18th.

Kim Philby

British intelligence officer and diplomat, Kim Philby (1912–1988) spied for, and later defected to, the Soviet Union.

The bebop bird

Black jazz saxophonist Charlie 'Bird' Parker (1920–1955) was acknowledged as the king of bebop.

1956

The Suez War

On July 26th, the Egyptian President Colonel Nasser responded to the Anglo-American withdrawal of funding for his Aswan Dam project by seizing all revenues from the Suez Canal, the West's commercial lifeline to the Middle East. The move effectively nationalised the Anglo-French Universal Maritime Suez Canal and closed it altogether to shipping going to or from Israel.

Britain's Prime Minister Sir Anthony Eden favoured a military response but the US was less enthusiastic and the crisis was referred to the United Nations. In October, however, talks took place in Paris between Eden and the French Premier Guy Mollet and were quickly followed by the launching of an Israeli attack against Egypt. Amid rumours of collusion with Israel, British and French naval forces were despatched to Suez in 'Operation Musketeer' (below). Despite the UN's attempt to impose a ceasefire, the Anglo-French attack, supported by bombers based in Cyprus, was launched on November 5th. However it was called off almost immediately when the Americans failed to support it.

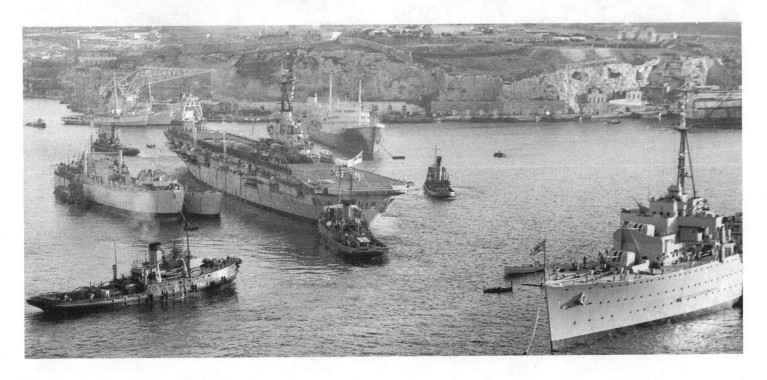

'Operation Musketeer'

Top left: Sir Anthony Eden caricatured in the British press as a sheep in wolf's clothing. Many felt that the cartoonist was proved right by the outcome of the crisis.

Top right: A building burning as British troops take up their positions in Port Said.

Above left: Feelings ran high over the crisis in Britain, with street demonstrations and arrests. Divisions of opinion among the general public were reflected in Eden's own Cabinet.

Above right: Egyptian blockships at the mouth of the Suez Canal at Port Said. British naval salvage ships began clearing the obstructions as soon as the invasion was launched.

Left: Arab children searching through the rubble of buildings left by the British bombing raids on Port Said.

The Hungarian Rising

Nowhere did the policy of de-Stalinisation proclaimed by Khrushchev at the Party Congress in Moscow in 1956 have more dramatic effects than in the troubled Communist State of Hungary. In pursuing the 'Malenkov new course' of economic decentralisation and de-collectivisation, the Hungarian Communist Party leadership had released popular forces for change which were to prove beyond its control.

In October the people of the capital, Budapest, rose against the Soviet regime which had replaced the reforming Imre Nagy as Premier. Barricades appeared in the streets, the statue of Stalin was torn down in the city centre (above) and the revolution seemed to involve all sections of society, including women (near left), industrial workers, and intellectuals of the influential Petöfi circle (far left). The recall of Nagy only fanned the flames and in November Soviet tanks appeared on the streets of Budapest to put down the rising by force.

Makarios deported from Cyprus

There was a significant escalation in terrorist and counter-terrorist activities in Cyprus following the sudden and unexpected deportation to the Seychelles of the Greek Cypriot leader Archbishop Makarios. The deportation was ordered by the British Premier Sir Anthony Eden on the grounds that Makarios was encouraging the anti-British campaign of Colonel Grivas' EOKA movement. British troops stationed on the island sought to extirpate EOKA and its sympathisers, but arms searches in Cypriot streets and villages (above), internment and restrictions on freedom of movement only served to alienate public opinion still further from the authorities (right).

Eden drew up plans for phased self-determination and for constitutional reforms involving partition of the island, but the proposals became bogged down in disputes between the Greek and Turkish governments. While the politicians talked and failed to talk, the bloodshed and unrest continued.

Israeli reprisals in Jordan

Tension along the border between Israel and Jordan heightened significantly during the last few months of the year as sporadic Jordanian attacks were met with ever more determined reprisal raids by the Israelis. In the first major raid, on the night of September 11th, a battalion of Israeli soldiers attacked the police post at Rahwa in Jordan, killing five policemen and ten soldiers and destroying the building.

The cycle of retaliation continued with further Jordanian incursions and Israeli reprisal attacks on Gharandal and Husan. October 10th saw the largest reprisal raid, at Qalquilya, where two Israeli regiments bombarded a police barracks for three hours. King Hussein of Jordan personally directed the Jordanian forces and at least 48 Jordanians and 18 Israelis died in the fighting.

Riots in Kowloon

Fifty-one people were killed and 358 injured when serious anti-European rioting broke out in Kowloon, the mainland area of Hong Kong, in October. The disturbances took place on October 10th, the anniversary of the foundation of the Chinese Republic, and were sparked off when officials removed illegal Nationalist flags which had been put up for the celebrations of the Chinese National Day.

Mobs rampaged through the streets attacking Europeans, looting shops and setting fire to vehicles and buildings. The unrest escalated the following day with pitched battles being fought between Nationalists and Communists. Troops with tanks and armoured cars were sent into Kowloon to restore order and a curfew was imposed. Police broke up the demonstrations with teargas and baton charges and also used live ammunition on the crowd. Some 4,500 arrests were made.

Grace Kelly's wedding televised

On Thursday April 19th, the American-Irish actress Grace Kelly (1928–1982), star of such films as *Dial M for Murder* and *Rear Window*, married Prince Rainier III of Monaco in the clifftop cathedral of St Nicholas, Monaco, before a congregation which included the Aga Khan, Ava Gardner and Aristotle Onassis. The wedding was an international media event with an estimated 1,800 journalists staying in the tiny principality for the occasion. After the televised ceremony, at which the bride wore a dress presented to her by MGM studios, the couple drove to the royal palace in a cream and black open-topped Rolls-Royce for the wedding lunch. Prince Rainier and Princess Grace then left for their honeymoon on his yacht the *Deo Juvante*.

The Millers' tale

Actress and sex-symbol Marilyn Monroe married Pulitzer Prize-winning playwright Arthur Miller on June 29th.

Elvis Presley

Elvis Aron Presley, the former truck driver from the Deep South, rocketed to fame as the undisputed 'king' of rock 'n' roll. It all began for Elvis in 1956, at the age of 21, with 'Heartbreak Hotel', followed the same year by two more greats, 'Hound Dog' and 'Love Me Tender'.

Dali and Olivier

Laurence Olivier sat for the Spanish surrealist painter Salvador Dali in his latest film role as Shakespeare's Richard III at Shepperton Studios (above left). The portrait was commissioned by a Mr Robert Dowling of New York. The work (above right) was completed at Dali's Spanish home and combines profile and full-face perspectives.

1957

Little Rock, Arkansas

One of the ugliest confrontations between blacks and whites in the civil rights struggle in the United States took place in the southern State of Arkansas in September. A Federal district court order had decreed that nine black students should be admitted to the previously segregated Central High School in the town of Little Rock. However, the segregationist Governor of Arkansas, Orville Faubus, took every available step to prevent the students being enrolled at the school, including mobilising the National Guard to bar the doors to them (above).

At President Eisenhower's insistence, the Guard was finally withdrawn, but its place was taken by a white mob who continued to keep the black students out. In an extraordinary move, the President sent 1,000 Army paratroopers to Little Rock and removed the National Guard from Faubus' control. Only with this military escort could the nine blacks enter the school.

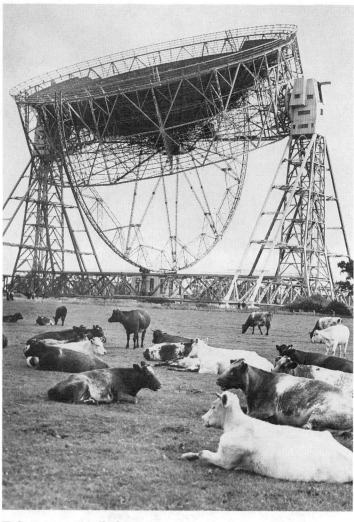

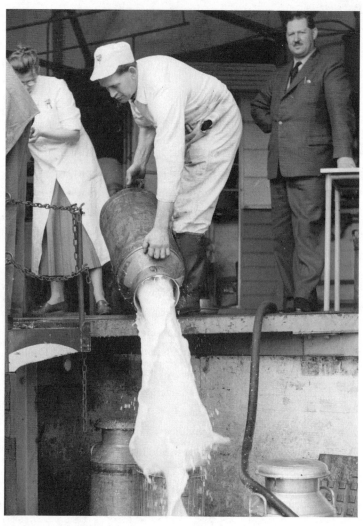

Telescope unveiled

The largest radio telescope in the world was unveiled at Jodrell Bank, England, on October 11th. It was completed ahead of schedule to track the first Soviet satellite, which had been launched the previous week.

Leak at Windscale

Thousands of gallons of contaminated milk had to be thrown away after a fire at the Windscale atomic plant in England resulted in radioactive iodine escaping over some 200 square miles of the surrounding countryside.

Lord Hailsham

The right Honourable Quintin Hogg QC, 2nd Viscount Hailsham and former Minister of Education, was elected Chairman of the British Conservative Party in September. He showed every sign of keeping his head above water in the new job. The exercise would prove useful for the future too, since he was Minister with special responsibility for sport from 1962 to 1964.

Rebellion in Cuba

During the last months of the year, the rebel '26th July' movement, operating from its base in the eastern mountains of Cuba, stepped up its campaign of guerrilla attacks on communications centres and sugar plantations throughout the country. The rebel leader Fidel Castro (above) declared 'total war' on the dictatorial regime of President Batista in the hope of precipitating economic collapse. On September 5th, the government faced a serious challenge when rebel fighters and Cuban Navy officers tried to seize the naval base of Cienfuegos, but the attempt failed and the ringleaders were executed.

Malayan independence

Widespread celebrations in Kuala Lumpur, the Federal capital, including the largest military review in the country's history (above), followed the granting of independence to Malaya by its former rulers, the British, on August 31st. The new constitution provided for a revolving presidency to be held in turn by the Malay sultans.

US ballistic missiles

Shown being lowered onto the first stage is the troublesome second stage of the US Navy's Vanguard missile at the launching pad at Cape Canaverel. The Vanguard rocket carrying the satellite exploded two seconds after take-off on December 6th. The following February the US Army successfully launched the Explorer 1 satellite into orbit around the earth with a Jupiter C rocket. Although the Explorer had a peaceful mission, it was a military rocket that made the launch possible.

First £5,000 premium bond prize

On June 1st, the fourth anniversary of his government's introduction of the first premium bond, the British Prime Minister Harold Macmillan inaugurated the improved Bond Scheme and set in motion the process of deciding who would win the first ever £5,000 prize in the monthly draw. The numbers were chosen by ERNIE (more formally, the electronic random number indicator) in Lytham St Anne's, Lancashire, which Macmillan set running by remote control from the National Savings Headquarters in London. The Prime Minister is seen writing up the number of the first lucky winner.

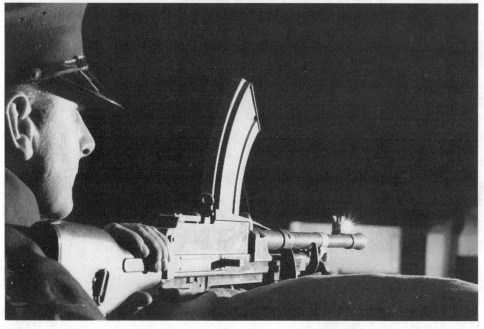

Internment in Ireland

The border between Northern Ireland and the Republic of Eire became the focus of a renewed campaign of Republican violence in the early months of the year. Operation Harvest, the IRA's third major campaign of bombing and sabotage, had as its targets a number of administrative and industrial installations, as well as the buildings and personnel of the Royal Ulster Constabulary, seen (left) patrolling the border with light machine guns. In a highly controversial move to contain the situation, the new Eire government of Eamon de Valera reintroduced internment in July. Under Part 2 of the Offences Against the State Act, terrorist suspects could be arrested and detained without trial, and by the end of the year there were some 100 people in detention in the South and 200 in the North.

Sibelius

Finland's greatest composer, Jean Sibelius (1865–1957), died at the age of 92. A government pension had allowed him to devote himself to music from the age of 32, but he had written nothing since 1926. He is best known for his seven great symphonies.

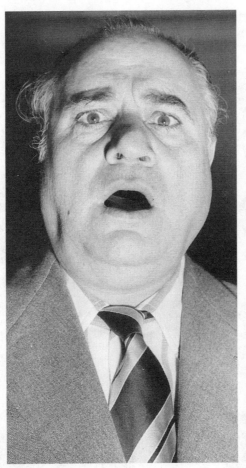

Gigli

November saw the sudden death at 67 of the great Italian tenor Beniamino Gigli (1890–1957) at his home in Rome. Gigli, the son of a shoemaker, became famous for his operatic and concert performances and was particularly known for his interpretations of Puccini and Verdi.

Toscanini

The world of music lost another of its titans with the death in New York of Arturo Toscanini (1867–1957) after a musical career spanning some 70 years. Toscanini was one of the most gifted and uncompromising conductors of the century, always conducting entirely from memory.

The Entertainer

Lawrence Olivier (1907–1989), best known for his Shakespearian and Hollywood roles, reached new heights of versatility with his performance as the seedy song-and-dance comedian Archie Rice in John Osborne's play *The Entertainer*.

Dog in space

On November 3rd, Laika the dog became the first living creature in space. She suffered no ill-effects from acceleration or weightlessness, but died when oxygen in the Soviet Sputnik 2, which was not designed to return to Earth, ran out.

President Eisenhower

President Eisenhower was sworn in for a second term in January this year. He is seen here broadcasting on *Voice of America*, explaining his policy on Communist aggression in the Middle East.

Parking meters in London

The arrival of parking meters in London's Mayfair in July marked the end of all-day parking for motorists. The scheme was officially launched by the Mayor of Westminster. With the new meters, seen being prepared for duty, two hours' parking cost sixpence (2½p) and a further two hours 10 shillings (50p).

Drink-drive campaign in Hungary

Tighter traffic control measures were introduced in Budapest following the October 1956 rising, including the use of the breathalyser, to catch drunken drivers.

The Long Goodbye

Humphrey Bogart (1899–1957), famous for his 'tough guy' roles in films such as *The Big Sleep* and *The Maltese Falcon*, lost his battle against cancer at the age of 56.

1958

Jan	1	European Economic Community (EEC) formed
	1	West German forces join NATO
	3	West Indian Federation formed
	8	USSR: Bulganin proposes summit conference
Feb	1	Egypt and Sudan unite as United Arab Republic
	3	Benelux economic pact signed
	11	French warships no longer allowed to use Bizerta, Tunis
	19	Anglo-Spanish trade agreement
Mar	2	Antarctica: Vivien Fuchs completes 1st overland crossing
Mar	14	British suffragette Christabel Pankhurst dies
	21	China and Hungary sign economic treaty
	27	Khrushchev succeeds Bulganin on Council of Ministers
Apr	2	US embargoes arms shipments to Cuba
	5	Castro begins 'total war' against Cuban dictator Batista
	17	S Africa: Nationalists win big victory in elections
May	2	State of emergency declared in Aden
	3	President Eisenhower proposes demilitarised Antarctic
	13	European settlers riot in Algiers
	27	Sri Lanka: State of emergency declared
Jun	1	Iceland extends fishing limits to 12 miles
	17	Hungarian ex-PM Imre Nagy executed after secret trial
Jul	6	Alaska becomes 49th State of US

	14	King Feisal of Iraq murdered in coup
	24	First life peerage awarded in Britain
	31	Khrushchev visits Britain
Aug	9	US reaffirms refusal to recognise Red China
Sep	3	Verwoerd becomes South African Premier
	5	Martin Luther King arrested for loitering in Alabama
	14	General de Gaulle meets Chancellor Adenauer
Oct	9	Pope Pius XII dies
	9	Yankees defeat Braves to win World Series
	24	Pakistan: Ayub Khan forms Cabinet
	28	Cardinal Roncalli elected Pope John XXIII
Nov	2	Last British troops leave Jordan
Dec	3	Indonesia nationalises Dutch businesses
	12	Algiers: General Galan appointed Inspector-General
	16	NATO rejects Soviet proposals for Berlin
	21	De Gaulle elected President of France
	22	British trade pact with Egypt
	31	Amnesty declared in Lebanon

The Arts

Satyajit Ray's film *The Unvanquished*

T. H. White's novel *The Once and Future King*

Truman Capote's *Breakfast at Tiffany's*

Campaign for Nuclear Disarmament

In February a new pressure group was set up, in the words of its founders, 'to demand a British initiative to reduce the nuclear peril and to stop the armaments race, if need be by unilateral action by Great Britain'. The Campaign for Nuclear Disarmament, or CND, was launched under the presidency of the philosopher and veteran peace campaigner Bertrand Russell, with Canon L. J. Collins as the chairman of its executive committee. The Labour politician Michael Foot and the writer J. B. Priestley were also among its founder members.

One of CND's first acts was to organise a protest march from London to the Atomic Weapons Research Establishment at Aldermaston in Berkshire. A crowd of some 4,000 people gathered in London's Trafalgar Square on April 4th to hear speeches by Canon Collins and other CND leaders before setting out to walk the 50 miles to Aldermaston. Many of the marchers carried banners bearing the distinctive CND logo (left). By the time the demonstration reached the research establishment it was 5,000 strong.

First of the big jets

Before 1958 intercontinental travel by jet airliner was not the commonplace phenomenon that it is today. The introduction of the Boeing 707 changed all that forever. The 707, the first of the big jets, was larger and faster than any rivals. Described at the time as a 'giant', it weighed 311,000 pounds and its long, wide cabin could accommodate up to 189 passengers and carry them at cruising speeds of over 600 miles an hour. It rapidly transformed the image and use of international air travel.

Under the polar ice

The USS *Nautilus* was welcomed at Portland, Dorset, England, after a 6,100-mile trip that included the first voyage under the ice cap of the North Pole. The 2,980-ton *Nautilus*, built in 1954, was the world's first nuclear-powered submarine.

GI Elvis

In 1958 Elvis was drafted into the US army and served overseas in Germany, to intense media attention. His experiences formed the basis of one of his most popular movies, *GI Blues*.

Unrest in Cyprus

There was a serious escalation of violence in Cyprus during 1958.

Top left: Five people were killed when British troops opened fire on rioters in the streets of Nicosia.

Centre left: There were many women among the demonstrators who took to the streets in April to protest against detention of political prisoners.

Left: A mother weeps at the village funeral of Greek Cypriot victims of the violence.

Top right: A Greek victim of gunmen in a passing car, at a café on the outskirts of Nicosia.

Above: British paratroopers embarking from Cyprus on their way to Jordan in July.

Return of de Gaulle

On June 1st, General Charles de Gaulle, who had held no public office since 1946, took over from Pierre Pflimlin as Prime Minister of France. His emergence from the political wilderness took place amid rumours that the insurrectionary French settler administration in Algeria (the Committee of Public Safety) which was increasingly impatient of the Pflimlin regime and increasingly Gaullist in its sympathies, was planning an airborne invasion of Paris to install a military government.

One of the new Prime Minister's first acts was to visit Algeria (left), where he was greeted with enormous enthusiasm by crowds of *pieds noirs*. His message, however, was less to their taste, and some of those who had been instrumental in returning him to power felt that his commitment to the European cause was less whole-hearted than they had hoped.

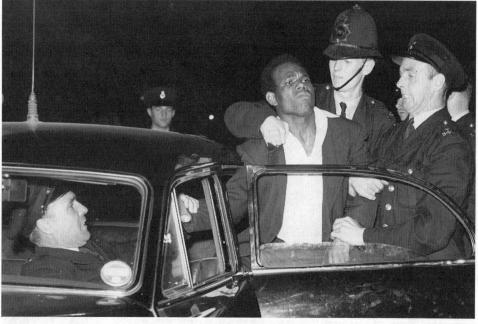

Race riots in London

Police made more than 150 arrests during three days of serious rioting in the Notting Hill district of North London. The trouble flared up after five black men were beaten up by white youths on August 24th. On the night of August 30th, some 200 white and black people fought in the streets, property was damaged and one black household was petrol-bombed. The following evening saw some of the worst disturbances, with four hours of continuous running battles between 400 black and white people, during which police were attacked and injured. On September 1st, gangs of up to 2,000 youths and children attacked black houses, breaking windows and causing extensive damage. Police suspected the involvement of extreme political groups.

US Marines in Lebanon

Holidaymakers on the beaches of Beirut helped the US Marines pull their equipment ashore from landing craft (left) when President Eisenhower responded to the pro-Western Lebanese President Chamoun's request for American assistance by sending some 3,500 troops to the Lebanon. The move came two days after an Arab Nationalist uprising in neighbouring Iraq had resulted in the murder of the Iraqi King Feisal and his Prime Minister. The arrival of the Marines was condemned by the Soviet Union and for a time the situation threatened to escalate into full-scale war.

Munich air crash

One of the greatest tragedies ever to strike the world of soccer occurred in February when eight English footballers were among the 21 passengers killed in an air crash in West Germany. The accident happened as the plane taking the Manchester United team back to the UK from Yugoslavia, where they had just drawn with Red Star Belgrade to qualify for the semi-finals of the European Cup, failed to clear a fence on take-off from Rhiem airport in Munich. Among the dead were the England regulars Roger Byrne, Duncan Edwards and Tommy Taylor. The Manchester United manager Matt Busby, after whom the team had been popularly known as the 'Busby Babes', was also seriously injured in the disaster. The plane, a BEA Ambassador, was reduced to a tangled heap of wreckage. Rescue workers (above) had to do their best in driving snow.

Manned space flight tests

In the United States a programme was launched to test the likely effects of space travel on human beings. Administered by the National Advisory Committee on Aeronautics, the US Air Force and Navy and the manufacturers of the X-15 rocket plane (whose first flight was planned for 1959), the programme involved the use of a huge centrifuge (left).

Entering the capsule, the pilot could fly the machine as it revolved on its giant arm, simulating the degree of acceleration likely to be experienced in actual space flight. The programme was used to train the X-15 pilots for their mission and to carry out medical tests on them to find out how the human body would react to the unfamiliar stresses of space travel.

Hovercraft breakthrough

The British inventor Christopher Cockerell finally succeeded in getting official funding to develop his new 'hovercraft' after submitting film of a working model to the National Research Development Corporation in April. The world's first air-cushion vehicle (AVC), the blue and silver SR-N1 (left), was built by Saunders-Roe, an Isle of Wight aircraft firm, in less than eight months and was unveiled to the public in sea-trials the following year. Its success proved that a heavy vehicle can be supported just above the ground on a cushion of air produced by a thrust much less than the vehicle's weight.

Miles Davis

Miles Davis (1926–1991), the black trumpeter and leading exponent of 'cool jazz', recorded *Porgy and Bess*, a highly original reinterpretation.

Boris Pasternak

The Soviet authorities forced Russian novelist Boris Pasternak (1890–1960) to retract his acceptance of the Nobel Prize for Literature.

Vaughan Williams

English composer and folksong collector Ralph Vaughan Williams (1872–1958) died in London at the age of 86.

1959

Jan	1	Batista, dictator of Cuba, flees to Dominica
	2	Cuba: Fidel Castro proclaims new government
	4	Rioting in Belgian Congo
	8	General de Gaulle is President of France
	17	Senegal and French Sudan unite to form Mali
	21	American film director Cecil B. de Mille dies
Feb	1	Swiss referendum turns down votes for women
	3	American singer Buddy Holly dies
	4	UK and Euratom explore peaceful use of atomic energy
	9	US supplies arms to Indonesia
	21	British PM Macmillan and Selwyn Lloyd visit USSR
	23	European Court of Human Rights has first meeting
	26	State of emergency in Southern Rhodesia
Mar	1	Archbishop Makarios returns to Cyprus
	16	Iraq receives loan from USSR
	17	Dalai Lama flees to India
	18	Hawaii becomes 50th State of US
	24	Iraq pulls out of Baghdad pact
	26	American author Raymond Chandler dies
	28	Kenya: Mau Mau prisoners die at Hola Camp
	28	US: 2 monkeys return alive from space trip
Apr	17	Malaya and Indonesia sign friendship pact
	26	Cuba invades Panama
May	6	UK protests to Iceland re violence in cod war
	25	Khrushchev visits Albania
Jun	3	Self-government for Singapore
	4	American sugar mills in Cuba nationalised
	17	De Valera becomes President of Eire
	26	Canada: Queen Elizabeth opens St Lawrence Seaway
Jul	5	Ghana to boycott all South African products
	6	German artist George Grosz dies
Sep	18	Khrushchev addresses United Nations on disarmament
	22	United Nations refuse to admit Communist China
	25	Khrushchev visits China
Nov	10	United Nations condemn apartheid and racism
	20	7 nations sign European Free Trade Association pact
Dec	9	Britain resumes relations with United Arab Republic
	10	US begins to pull troops out of Iceland
	13	United Nations not to intervene in Algerian problem
	14	Makarios elected first President of Cyprus

The Arts

Henry Moore's bronze *Two-piece Reclining Figure*

Frank Lloyd Wright's Guggenheim Art Museum

Tony Richardson's film *Look Back in Anger*

Carol Reed's film *Our Man in Havana*

Makarios elected President

After years of escalating unrest in Cyprus, the Greek and Turkish governments met in Zürich in February to discuss the future of the island and agreed that it should become independent. Under the proposed arrangements, the British government would keep its sovereign military bases on the island, but a joint Greco-Turkish administration would be set up to govern the new State. The constitution made provision for a Greek President and a Turkish Vice-President and ruled out union with Greece (*enosis*).

Even though *enosis* was the goal for which he and the EOKA movement had been fighting, Archbishop Makarios, seen (above) with EOKA's Colonel Grivas, accepted the proposed settlement, and on March 1st he returned to Nicosia after three years of exile. Elections were announced and in December Makarios became the first President of the new Republic.

Revolution in Cuba

On January 1st, the beleaguered regime of the dictator Fulgencio Batista finally collapsed and he fled to the Dominican Republic. After six years of revolutionary struggle the way was clear for the rebel guerrillas of Dr Fidel Castro, who already controlled most of the east of Cuba, to take up the reins of power. Amid general rejoicing at the fall of Batista, Dr Manuel Urrutia was declared President of the new government and named Castro his Commander in Chief. On January 8th, Castro himself, together with 5,000 of his troops, made a triumphant entry into the capital Havana along streets lined with thousands of cheering citizens.

The new regime was immediately recognised by the governments of the United States, Great Britain, France, the Soviet Union and most of Cuba's Latin American neighbours. Some doubts were expressed internationally, however, when the round-up of Batista officials was followed by swift trials and on-the-spot executions by firing squad.

Voyage of discovery

On February 21st, the British Premier Harold Macmillan made what he described as a 'voyage of discovery' to the Soviet Union. This was the first peacetime visit of a British Prime Minister, and he was met at the airport (above left) by Khrushchev and a welcoming crowd, who liked

Macmillan's gesture of wearing a white fur hat in true Soviet style. While in the Soviet Union the British team had talks with Khrushchev, attended the Bolshoi Ballet and visited Leningrad and Kiev. Arms limitation was discussed, but only limited agreement was reached.

A fortnight later Macmillan was in Washington, DC to report on his Soviet trip to President Eisenhower (above right). Talks at the presidential mountain lodge at Camp David resulted in a communiqué which spoke of 'complete agreement between our two governments'.

Riots in Durban

On June 18th, violent disturbances broke out in the South African town of Durban. Days of serious rioting were sparked off when police destroyed illicit stills during a slum clearance operation designed to resettle some 100,000 blacks. Hundreds of black women attacked beer-halls and other property in the black shanty town of Cato Manor on the outskirts of Durban. They were joined by thousands of other rioters who ran through the streets setting fire to offices, clinics, schools, shops and vehicles. Outside Durban a crowd of some 4,000 blacks blocked the main road and stoned cars as they tried to pass.

The rioting continued throughout the month, leaving buildings and vehicles smouldering (left). Four black people died in the unrest, and damage to property was estimated at some £250,000. The situation in Durban remained tense for some months afterwards and more deaths occurred in September when police opened fire on protesters.

De Gaulle in Italy

The newly inaugurated President of France, General Charles de Gaulle, made a state visit to Italy in June, where he attended a large military parade in Milan.

Indira Gandhi

In February Mrs Indira Gandhi (caricatured above), the daughter of India's Prime Minister Jawaharlal Nehru, was elected President of the ruling Congress Party, a post her father held until 1955.

Dalai Lama in India

The 14th Dalai Lama went into exile in India following the Tibetan revolt against the Chinese, who installed the Panchen Lama as ruler in his place.

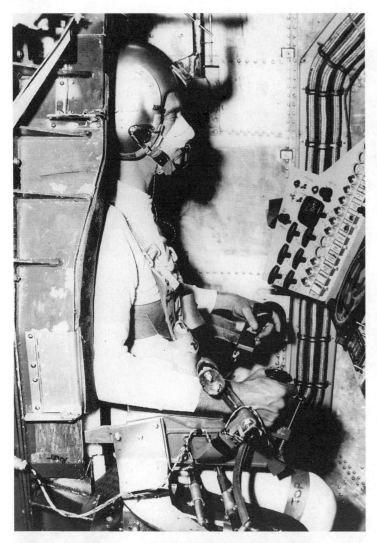

Ben Hur

One of the greatest of the Hollywood epics, famous for the technical splendour of the action scenes, such as the sea battle and the exciting chariot race. This film was to win William Wyler his third directing Oscar. Above: One of the best-known scenes from the film – the chariot race in which Ben Hur (Charlton Heston) rides against his Roman enemy Messala (Stephen Boyd).

On the way to space

Preparations for putting the first man into space continued in the United States. In 'Project Mercury' at the end of the year a monkey called Sam was launched into space to test the effects of acceleration forces and weightlessness. After a 13-minute trip he was parachuted back to Earth, and landed in the Atlantic apparently suffering no ill-effects. Top left: Astronaut Alan Shepard at the controls of a simulated space vehicle.

Classic folk opera

The lavish movie version of George Gershwin's negro folk opera *Porgy and Bess* won the Oscar for the best scoring of a musical for 1959. Set in the slums of Catfish Row in South Carolina, it tells the tragic love story of the crippled beggar Porgy (Sidney Poitier) and the beautiful, reckless Bess (Dorothy Dandridge). The stage version was first launched in New York by the Theatre Guild in 1935.

Frank Lloyd Wright

The world of architecture mourned the passing of Frank Lloyd Wright (1869–1959), who died on April 9th. One of the giants of modern architecture, his work often divided critics. Fallingwater (left), a house built over a waterfall in Bear Run, Pennsylvania, was one of his masterpieces – a living space in perfect harmony with its natural surroundings. The Guggenheim Museum art gallery (above left), opened to the public in October, was described by the *New York Times* as 'the most controversial building . . . in New York'. The pictures were displayed on the walls of a vast spiral ramp.

The Seer of Cookham

This year also saw the death of the British artist Sir Stanley Spencer (1891–1959), who had been knighted by the Queen in the Birthday Honours list in June. The son of an organist and music teacher, Spencer received little formal education before going to the Slade School of Art in 1908 at the age of 17. There he developed the techniques which formed the basis of his highly distinctive work.

A true visionary, Spencer created paintings which fused the divine and the commonplace, often transfiguring the scenes of everyday life he saw around him in the Thames-side village of Cookham, where he was born and spent most of his life. He reached the apex of his creative powers in the 1920s with his murals in Burghclere Chapel in Berkshire and paintings such as *Resurrection Cookham* (1922–1927). His last work, an altarpiece dedicated to his first wife Hilda, remained unfinished when he died.

1960–1969

The 1960s

More than almost any decade before it, the 1960s saw the pace of change quicken in international, social and cultural affairs to the point where many of the older generation felt that the world in which they were living was becoming barely recognisable. Advances in technology that would have seemed unimaginable ten years earlier made possible such giant leaps forward as the exploration of space and the development of heart transplant surgery. The last vestiges of empire disappeared in Africa as Britain, France and Belgium relinquished their colonial interests to the seemingly unstoppable tide of black nationalism. At the same time changes in the leadership of the world's superpowers seemed unable to slow the gathering momentum of the Cold War, which in 1962 brought the human race closer to nuclear war than at any time before or since. And throughout it all, a youth culture was emerging with values that seemed to contradict all that had been assumed by the generation born between the two World Wars.

Winds of change

It was perhaps in the vast and diverse continent of Africa that the greatest changes were felt. In the opening days of the decade the British Prime Minister Harold Macmillan made his famous speech about the 'winds of change' blowing through Africa. In the years that followed, country after country was to attain independence, many after a protracted period of unrest and bloodshed. In Algeria the birth pangs of the new State threatened mainland France itself with collapse and brought the veteran General Charles de Gaulle out of the political wilderness. In the Belgian Congo the very speed with which independence had been granted created the conditions for the tragedy which ensued. In some countries what began in a spirit of hope and liberty declined into despair and totalitarianism as groups that had been united in their desire for independence fragmented into warring factions on achieving power. In Nigeria this factionalism led to the appalling human tragedy of Biafra. In South Africa and Southern Rhodesia the continuing white hold on the organs of power seemed destined to loosen under the onslaught of black unrest.

Civil rights

The black nationalism of the former colonial states found its echo in the developed world too. In the United States the black civil rights movement, under the leadership of Martin Luther King, fought for recognition against the combined forces of prejudice and inertia. Despite the passing of important civil rights legislation under President Kennedy and his successor Lyndon B Johnson, the segregationist instincts of the Governors of some Southern states still sought to maintain the old order. Nonetheless, by the time of King's untimely death at the hands of a white gunman in 1968, the black struggle for equality in the United States had made more progress in a few years than in the whole of the preceding generation.

The superpowers

The era of hope that seemed to be dawning in the United States with the youthful presidency of John F Kennedy came to an abrupt end on the streets of Dallas in 1963, but not before the relationship between the USA and the Soviet Union had been put under unprecedented strain. The attempted US invasion of Cuba and the missile crisis of 1962 left permanent scars on East–West relations and helped fuel the development of the new protest groups springing up to campaign against the proliferation of nuclear weapons. In Berlin the newly erected Wall stood as a potent symbol of confrontation and misunderstanding. In Vietnam the ugly spectacle of American involvement served daily to undermine the high moral ground claimed by the US government in the battle of democracy.

In the Middle East the uneasy stand-off between Israel and its Arab neighbours threatened the powderkeg of US–Soviet relations with the spark of military conflict. The Arab–Israeli war in 1967 changed the map of the region in just six days and established its political contours for the next 20 years. The Palestinian cause also gave impetus to the growing phenomenon of international terrorism which was to dominate the 1970s.

The space race

Even the startling achievements of the space programme derived their momentum from the East–West divide. The world watched in astonishment as the American and Soviet programmes vied to outdo each other in the very public arena of the space race. The decade began with the first man in space and ended with the first men setting foot on the moon. By the time the 'giant leap for mankind' fulfilled President Kennedy's determination to put a man on the moon by 1970 the American space programme alone had cost some $24,000 million. It had also allowed a television audience of 600 million people to watch one of the greatest scientific achievements in the history of mankind.

Beatles and barricades

A revolution in fashion, music, literature and the arts took place as the opening up of mass communications helped create and sustain a worldwide youth market. Mini-skirts and caftans made their appearance on the streets of London and San Francisco. The music of bands such as the Rolling Stones and the Doors came to symbolise their young audiences' rejection of parental values, while the 'pop art' of Andy Warhol and his bizarre entourage drew a cult following for its parodies of the images of mass-production. The word 'permissive' entered the household vocabulary as sexual and social taboos were eroded by the contraceptive pill and the marijuana joint.

Pages 340–1: Edward White's spacewalk outside Gemini 4, June 3rd 1965.

1960

Jan	1	Independent Republic of Cameroons proclaimed
	9	Egypt: Work begins on Aswan Dam
Feb	2	Blacks begin lunch counters sit-in campaign in US
	17	Martin Luther King is arrested in US
	21	Castro nationalises private business in Cuba
Mar	1	Morocco: Agadir is devastated by earthquake
	5	President Sukarno suspends Indonesian Parliament
	13	British government scraps Blue Streak missile project
	30	State of emergency in S Africa after Sharpeville
Apr	1	S African govt bans ANC and Pan-African Congress
	21	Brasilia inaugurated as new capital of Brazil
	27	Synghman Rhee resigns from Presidency of S Korea
May	1	US U-2 aircraft shot down by USSR
	7	Brezhnev replaces Voroshilov as USSR President
	16	Summit meeting in Paris
	23	Israelis arrest former Gestapo chief Eichmann
	27	Turkey: Premier A. Menderes ousted in military coup
	30	Soviet writer Boris Pasternak dies
Jun	9	Hong Kong struck by typhoon
	30	Lumumba becomes first Prime Minister of Congo .
Jul	1	USSR shoots down US aircraft
	7	Belgium sends troops to Congo
	8	U-2 pilot Gary Powers indicted as spy by USSR
	11	Congo: Tshombe proclaims Katanga independent
	18	Malcolm Campbell's *Bluebird* car has first UK test
Aug	7	Castro nationalises all US-owned property in Cuba
	16	Cyprus gains independence under Archbishop Makarios
	22	Two dogs return to Earth from Soviet space trip
	25	Olympic Games open in Rome
	31	East Germans close border with West Berlin
Sept	1	Nyerere becomes Tanganyika's first Prime Minister
Oct	5	S African referendum favours Republic
	19	US imposes embargo on shipments to Cuba
Nov	7	Moscow: missiles first appear in Red Square parade
	9	John F. Kennedy is elected US President
Dec	2	Britain refuses independence for Bugunda
	21	King Saud takes over Saudi Arabian government

The Arts

Hitchcock's film *Psycho*

Ionesco's play *Rhinoceros*

Fellini's film *La Dolce Vita*

Robert Bolt's play *A Man for All Seasons*

Kennedy elected to White House

On November 9th, a new period of American history, and a new era in international relations, was ushered in with the election of the Democrat John F. Kennedy (1917–1963) as the 34th President of the United States of America.

Kennedy, a 43-year-old Senator from Massachusetts, had been groomed for the presidency since childhood by his ambitious father (a one-time US Ambassador to Britain) and stood for many people as the living embodiment of the 'new generation of Americans'. His youth, his charismatic style, his harnessing of the Black vote and to some extent his Catholicism sustained his popularity through a vigorous campaign against the Republican Richard Nixon, which also saw the introduction of the first televised debates between candidates.

The vote itself was a cliff-hanger. Despite carrying 23 states with 303 electoral votes, as against Nixon's 219 votes from 26 states, Kennedy in fact gained only 0.1 per cent more of the popular vote for his dream of a 'New Frontier'.

The Sharpeville massacre

On March 21st, what began as a peaceful protest ended in tragedy in the South African township of Sharpeville when police opened fire on a black crowd, killing 67 people and wounding 186.

The shootings happened on a day of mass demonstrations against the white government's hated pass laws. In a campaign organised by the Pan-African Congress, a breakaway group from the African National Congress, black people all over the country left their passes at home and gave themselves up at their nearest police station to be arrested. Thousands took part in the protests, which were peaceful in the majority of places.

However, at Sharpeville, a township five miles north of Vereeniging, police officers confronted the crowd outside the police station and opened fire, apparently without warning. Official statements claimed that the shootings took place in self-defence, when a crowd of 20,000 tried to storm the station. Black witnesses at the subsequent inquiry said that only 5,000 people were involved and that they had gone peacefully to the police station to discuss the pass laws. A medical expert testified that some 70 per cent of the victims had been shot from behind.

Revolt in Algeria

Among the European community in Algeria, simmering unease with General de Gaulle's Algerian policy, which seemed destined to lead to Muslim rule of the country, boiled over into open revolt on January 24th, after de Gaulle dismissed the *pieds noirs'* hero General Massu. Crowds of demonstrators took to the streets of Algiers to protest against Massu's dismissal and the lack of protection they felt had led to the deaths of increasing numbers of French settlers in FLN terrorist outrages. People who only two years before had cheered de Gaulle's return to power in France now chanted anti-de Gaulle slogans, distributed insurrectionary propaganda from their cars (near right), and dug up roads to make barricades against the police (far right and above). A general strike was declared.

De Gaulle ordered the Commander in Chief in Algeria, General Challe, to restore order, and paratroopers surrounded the barricaded insurgents. The atmosphere became extremely tense as the government in Paris debated whether or not to order the paratroopers to open fire against their fellow Frenchmen. The order was never given and by the beginning of February the stalemate ended with the collapse of the revolt, and the surrender and arrest of many of the insurgents.

Chaos in the Congo

Within days of the hasty transfer of power from Brussels to the independent government of Patrice Lumumba in Léopoldville on June 30th, conflict between the Congo's many political groupings, seen (left) on the eve of independence, plunged the country into lawlessness. A mutiny of the Congolese Army led to attacks on Europeans, and many reports of beatings and rape resulted in Belgians being sent in to restore order.

The most widespread violence ensued when the provinces of Katanga and South Kasai declared themselves independent States. United Nations troops were sent to the Congo and, to US horror, Lumumba sought Soviet military aid. As the bloodshed and chaos mounted, an Army colonel, Joseph Mobutu, staged a military coup on September 14th and by the end of the year the country was torn between four separate regimes.

Macmillan's African tour

In January the recently elected British Premier Harold Macmillan, seen (left) in Basutoland, became the first serving British Prime Minister to set foot in Africa when he began a six-week tour of the continent. The visit – during which he visited Ghana, Nigeria, the Central African Federation and South Africa – marked British recognition of the growth of nationalism in Africa and the need for moves towards independence from colonial rule. In the Ghanaian capital, Accra, Macmillan spoke memorably of 'the winds of change blowing through Africa', a theme to which he returned in Cape Town in February, where he also spoke of the British government's disapproval of apartheid in South Africa.

Cuba and the United States

Relations between the Eisenhower administration and the new revolutionary regime of Fidel Castro in Cuba deteriorated badly after initial US recognition of the Castro government in 1959. Despite having disclaimed all personal presidential ambitions when his movement first took power, Castro had declared himself President in July 1959.

During the course of 1960 he began buying oil and arms from the Soviet Union and when the US exerted economic pressure by stopping its purchases of Cuban sugar, he responded by nationalising American businesses in Cuba. Tension increased still further when Cuba set about 'exporting revolution' to its Latin American neighbours, conducting clandestine operations in the Dominican Republic, Nicaragua and Panama.

However, despite the US government's growing distrust of the Cuban regime, Castro and his right-hand man 'Che' Guevara aroused enthusiastic support among many young Americans (left).

The Royal Family

1960 was marked by three major royal events: on February 19th, the Queen (left) gave birth to Prince Andrew – the first time a child had been born to a reigning British sovereign since the birth of Princess Beatrice, Queen Victoria's youngest child, in 1857. A week later, Princess Margaret took the world by surprise with her engagement to Antony Armstrong-Jones (top left), whom she married in Westminster Abbey on May 6th (top right). Finally, in August Queen Elizabeth the Queen Mother celebrated her 60th birthday and is seen (above) with her grandchildren in the gardens of Clarence House.

U-2 incident

On May 1st, an American U-2 reconnaissance plane piloted by Francis Gary Powers (above) was shot down over the Soviet Union.

Death of Camus

The French existentialist novelist Albert Camus (1913–1960), author of *La Peste* (*The Plague*) and *L'Étranger* (*The Outsider*), was killed in a car crash near Villeneuve-la-Guyard on May 4th. The car in which he was travelling as a passenger, was written off when it collided with a tree.

A weather eye

The world's first weather satellite, Tiros, was launched by the United States from Cape Canaveral on April 2nd.

Lasers demonstrated

The first laser, a device which can generate and focus a highly intense beam of light, was demonstrated by scientists working in California. Laser is an acronym for **L**ight **A**mplification by **S**timulated **E**mission of **R**adiation.

1961

Jan	3	US severs diplomatic and consular relations with Cuba
	17	Congo: Former PM Lumumba murdered
	20	Queen Elizabeth tours India, Pakistan, Iran and Cyprus
	20	John F. Kennedy becomes President of the US
	30	Riots in Sri Lanka
Feb	4	Civil war begins in Angola
	16	Cyprus will apply to join Commonwealth
	22	W German Chancellor Konrad Adenauer visits London
	26	Morocco: Hassan II becomes King
Mar	1	US President Kennedy sets up Peace Corps
	26	British PM Macmillan meets Kennedy in Florida
Apr	12	Soviet Cosmonaut Yuri Gagarin is 1st man in space
	17	Failed 'Bay of Pigs' invasion of Cuba
	22	Right-wing rebellion in Algeria threatens France
	27	Sierra Leone is independent member of Commonwealth
May	1	Tanganyika independent with Nyerere as leader
	8	British spy George Blake sentenced to 42 years
	24	Cyprus becomes member of the Council of Europe
	28	Last journey of Paris–Bucharest Orient Express train
	31	Kennedys welcomed in Paris
	31	S Africa becomes a Republic
Jun	16	Soviet ballet dancer Rudolf Nureyev defects to West
Jul	2	Author Ernest Hemingway commits suicide
Aug	10	Britain applies to join European Economic Community
	13	E Germany closes frontier between E and W Berlin
	17	E Germany erects Berlin Wall
	31	Morocco: Last Spanish troops withdraw
Sep	18	Head of UN, Dag Hammarskjöld, is killed in air crash
	28	Syria: Army coup in Damascus
	29	Syria secedes from United Arab Republic
Oct	9	NY Yankees win World Series for 26th time
	15	Turkey: General Gürsel is elected President
Nov	2	Israel: Ben Gurion forms new coalition govt
	3	U Thant becomes interim Secretary-General of UN
	16	UK: Commonwealth Immigration Bill is introduced
Dec	9	USSR severs relations with Albania
	13	US painter Grandma Moses dies
	19	India takes Goa from Portuguese after 400 years

The Arts

Benjamin Britten's opera *A Midsummer Night's Dream*

Jean Anouilh's play *Becket, Or the Honour of God*

Lionel Bart's musical *Oliver*

Joseph Heller's novel *Catch-22*

Film of *West Side Story*

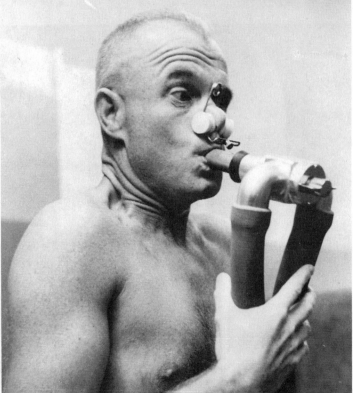

First man in space

On April 12th, the Soviet Union won the race to put the first man in space. That man was Major Yuri Alexeyevich Gagarin (1934–1968) (top), who instantly became a household name throughout the world. The spacecraft in which he was launched from the Baikonur Cosmodrome in Kazakhstan, the 4.7-tonne Vostok 1, orbited the Earth once at an altitude of 327 kilometres before re-entering the atmosphere and landing 108 minutes after take-off. Five weeks later President Kennedy inaugurated the Apollo programme, but it was another nine months before John Glenn (training above) became the first American in orbit.

The Bay of Pigs

A mere three months after the inauguration of the new President, the Kennedy administration was plunged into crisis by an unsuccessful attempt to invade the island of Cuba. On his election in November 1960, Kennedy discovered that the Central Intelligence Agency (CIA) had been training a small army of Cuban exiles in Guatemala with a view to invading Cuba and overthrowing the revolutionary regime of Fidel Castro. Despite his doubts about the plan Kennedy allowed it to proceed, but the outcome was to be one of the greatest humiliations of his presidency.

On the night of April 14th, American B56 bombers took off from bases in Nicaragua to provide air support for the invasion, and 48 hours later a force of some 1,400 men, the majority of them partly trained civilians, landed at the Bay of Pigs. They were met by a stronger Cuban defence than had been anticipated (above left) and fierce fighting ensued. Further American military support was not forthcoming and to make matters worse, the expected risings in Cuba itself failed to materialise. The invasion was a complete failure and within 72 hours had been roundly defeated, leaving the Bay of Pigs littered with the debris of battle (above right). Despite the façade of friendship preserved at the Vienna summit in June (left), relations between America and the Soviet Union were severely strained by the incident.

The Generals' revolt in Algeria

The Algerian War moved into its final phase in January when de Gaulle held a referendum on the future of Algeria, in which French and Algerian people voted overwhelmingly in favour of talks on self-determination. Negotiations were proceeding towards talks at Evian-les-Bains between the French government and the FLN's so-called provisional government of Algeria when suddenly, on the morning of April 22nd, a division of paratroopers (below left) surrounded Government House in Algiers and arrested the French Delegate-General. The Generals' revolt had begun.

Troops took over the major civil and military installations in the city and announced over the radio that the Army was now in control of the country. The four leaders of the military coup, Generals Challe, Jouhaud, Zeller and Salan, declared that they had saved Algeria for France and imposed a state of emergency. By the evening, as rumours circulated of an airborne invasion of Paris by the rebels, General de Gaulle assumed special powers and the capital prepared to repel any attack (top).

In Algeria itself, however, support for the revolt proved to be limited and on April 26th it collapsed. Police set about recovering arms that had been handed out to the paramilitary OAS during the coup (above left) and ringleaders were arrested and tried, with Challe and Zeller being sentenced to imprisonment and Salan and Jouhaud to death.

The Berlin Wall

The political map of Europe was changed literally overnight on August 13th. At 2.30 a.m. the East German government sealed the border between East and West Berlin and began the building of the wall that has divided the city ever since.

As steel-helmeted border guards and People's Police rolled out the barbed wire and the prefabricated concrete blocks that were to form the basis of the wall (bottom, far left), many East Germans made desperate last-ditch attempts to reach the West. In all some 1,500 people, taking only the bare minimum of possessions with them (above right), escaped during the day across back yards or through the city's many bomb sites. Others swam canals or the River Havel, or ran the gauntlet of border guards in their cars (above left). But these were to be virtually the last of the 2,600,000 refugees who had fled to the West since 1949, an exodus that had left East Germany dangerously short of professional people to staff its hospitals and industries.

Over the following days the wall was reinforced (left), and on August 22nd a 100-metre no-man's-land was created on both sides (top, far left), with warnings being given to West Berliners not to approach 'in the interests of their own safety'. There was a chorus of Western condemnation at this violation of freedom of movement, but no action was taken to reopen the border.

The banality of evil

In April the trial began in Jersualem of the Nazi war criminal Adolf Eichmann (1906–1962). Eichmann stood accused of crimes against the Jewish people and crimes against humanity for his part in the extermination of the Jews in Hitler's 'Final Solution'. During the trial, which took place amid unprecedented security, Eichmann, whose appearance of sheer ordinariness surprised and unsettled many people, listened impassively to the evidence against him from behind a bullet-proof glass screen. He pleaded 'not guilty' to the indictment, claiming only to have been following orders. Despite the mounting evidence of his involvement in the organisation of the Holocaust, he insisted that there was 'no blood on my hands'. On December 12th, however, the three judges delivered a unanimous verdict of guilty and Eichmann was sentenced to death.

Kenyatta released

Following the Lancaster House conference on the future of Kenya in January 1960, black demands for the release of the Kenya African National Union (KANU) leader Jomo Kenyatta (top) mounted both in Kenya and elsewhere. Kenyatta had been sentenced to seven years' hard labour in 1953 for his part in the activities of the Mau Mau movement but had not been allowed to return to Nairobi at the end of his term. His continued detention became increasingly embarrassing for the authorities after KANU won a clear majority in the first elections to be held under the new Kenyan constitution in February 1961. Eventually, despite strong opposition from the white community, Kenyatta was allowed to return to his home near Nairobi on August 14th, to be greeted by an enthusiastic crowd of more than 3,000 people (above).

The pill

Despite opposition from religious groups, conservatives and others, the female oral contraceptive pill was launched on to the market after extensive trials.

Adenauer meets Kennedy

Konrad Adenauer, Chancellor of the German Federal Republic, held talks with President Kennedy at the White House in November. They discussed East-West tensions since the Berlin Wall.

Ban the Bomb

1961 was a year of demonstrations in London against the nuclear arms race. Many members of CND were arrested, including the 89-year-old philosopher Bertrand Russell.

Dag Hammarskjöld

A year of intense diplomatic activity in Africa was tragically cut short for the United Nations Secretary-General Dag Hammarskjöld (1905–1961) in September when he was killed in a plane crash while flying to Northern Rhodesia for talks with the Katangan leader Moise Tshombe. Earlier in the year he had met the South African Premier H. F. Verwoerd to discuss apartheid.

Rudolf Nureyev

Nureyev (1938–1993), a leading dancer with Leningrad's Kirov Ballet, caused a sensation by defecting to the West just before the opening of the company's season at Covent Garden in June.

From stage to screen

The smash hit Broadway musical *West Side Story*, the modern-day *Romeo and Juliet*, was translated into a spectacular movie in 1961. Bitter gang rivalries mean that love between Natalie Wood and Richard Beymer is doomed.

Bridget Riley

Bridget Riley (1931–   ), the most exciting young British artist of the 1960s, is seen here with an example of her highly distinctive 'op art'. After her first one-woman exhibition in 1962 she exhibited in 1964 in the New Generation show at the Whitechapel Gallery, in London, and Painting and Sculpture of a Decade at the Tate, then in the Responsive Eye at New York's Museum of Modern Art the following year. In 1969 she won the international prize for painting at the 34th Venice Biennale.

1962

Jan	1	W Samoa becomes an independent Polynesian state
	9	Soviet-Cuban trade treaty signed
	14	EEC agrees on Common Agricultural Policy
Feb	10	US exchanges Soviet spy for captured pilot Gary Powers
Mar	2	UK applies to join European Coal and Steel Community
	2	Burma: Ne Win overturns U Nu in coup
	5	UK applies to join European Atomic Energy Community
Apr	18	W Indian Federation dissolved
May	13	Indonesia: Assassination attempt on President Sukarno
	31	Nazi war criminal Adolf Eichmann hanged in Israel
Jun	14	European Space Research Organisation formed in Paris
Jul	1	Ruanda and Burundi become independent states
	3	Independence of Algeria proclaimed by France
Aug	6	Jamaica independent within Commonwealth
	6	US writer William Faulkner dies
	13	Ghana expels Archbishop of W Africa
	15	Holland and Indonesia agree over West New Guinea
	22	President de Gaulle escapes assassination attempt
	31	Trinidad and Tobago independent in Commonwealth
Sep	1	Earthquake disaster in Iran
	2	USSR to supply Cuba with weapons
	8	China steps up border dispute with India

Oct	9	Uganda an independent state within Commonwealth
	10	Ceasefire in Congo civil war
	20	China attacks Indian border positions
	22	Kennedy says USSR has missile bases in Cuba
	28	US pledges to send arms to India
Nov	2	Tanganyika: Nyerere elected President
	2	Kennedy announces dismantling of Cuban missile bases
	5	Saudi Arabia breaks with United Arab Republic
	10	Eleanor Roosevelt dies
	14	Negotiations with EEC resumed by UK
	21	Sino-Indian ceasefire declared
	30	U Thant to be UN Secretary-General
Dec	5	Dean Acheson, US diplomat, says Britain is 'played out'
	8	Revolt in Brunei ends as British intervene
	9	Tanganyika an independent state in Commonwealth
	10	Crick and Watson win Nobel Prize in DNA work

The Arts

Solzhenitsyn's *One Day in the Life of Ivan Denisovich*

Orson Welles' film *The Trial*

David Lean's film *Lawrence of Arabia*

Edward Albee's play *Who's Afraid of Virginia Woolf?*

Arnold Wesker's play *Chips with Everything*

MISSILE READY TENT FOUNDATIONS (TENTS REMOVED)

ABANDONED LAUNCH POSITION

The Cuban missile crisis

In October the world seemed closer to nuclear war than at any time before or since. Following the previous year's Bay of Pigs fiasco, the Kennedy administration obtained conclusive proof that the Soviet Union was building offensive missile bases in Cuba (left) which could have doubled the number of American cities and bases threatened by Soviet attack. After rejecting the option of an immediate military strike against the installations, Kennedy ordered a naval blockade against Soviet ships bringing military equipment to the island, with the threat of retaliation if the blockade was broken.

The situation threatened to escalate into full-scale conflict between the superpowers as Khrushchev considered whether to accept the challenge thrown down by the Americans. In the end, six days after the US ships moved into the path of the Soviet vessels, Khrushchev ordered his convoy to turn back and agreed to dismantle the Cuban bases.

Independence for Algeria

Despite the intensification of terrorist activity in Algeria in the early months of 1962, with OAS bombs killing many police and civilians and Muslim terrorist organisations staging bloody reprisals, talks on the future of the country continued between the French government and the FLN's provisional government of Algeria, now headed by Ben Khedda, at Evian-les-Bains. They ended on March 18th with the declaration of a ceasefire which came into effect at noon the following day. Plans were also announced for a referendum on the question of independence, under the terms of which France agreed to withdraw its troops over the next three years except from its bases in Mers-el-Kebir and in the Sahara, where it had already begun a nuclear testing programme.

The OAS, which had come to prominence during the Generals' revolt of 1961, responded by stepping up its campaign of propaganda (left) and terrorism still further. The prospect of a Muslim state drew closer, and a mass exodus of Europeans began, as the bombings and murders continued (above left). On April 8th, a referendum in metropolitan France came out strongly in favour of the Evian proposals for independence and large numbers of Muslims began to return to Algeria for the referendum there on July 1st (above right).

The result was an almost unanimous vote for President de Gaulle's independence plan and on July 3rd the French High Commissioner officially handed over the reins of power to the provisional government of Ben Khedda, who became the new Prime Minister. With the raising of the Algerian flag over the capital, eight years of war and 132 years of French rule came to an end. Algeria became an independent sovereign state for the first time in its history.

East–West tension in Berlin

Tension remained high throughout 1962 in the divided city of Berlin, where the recently built Wall had become a potent symbol of East–West confrontation. The sound of gunfire at night bore witness to the continuing attempts of East Germans to escape to the West. Meanwhile, West Berliners were leaving for West Germany at an alarming rate. Propaganda patrols paraded on both sides of the Wall (left) in a 'loudspeaker war' of words.

In February the crisis moved into a new and potentially more dangerous phase when the Soviet Union announced that it was reserving the air corridors between West Germany and West Berlin for use by its own military aircraft at specific times. A campaign of harassment began. Soviet jets buzzed commercial aircraft in the corridors and dropped tin foil to interfere with their radar equipment. Searchlights were trained on Western airliners as they came into land at Berlin's Tempelhof airport, blinding the pilots and seriously increasing the risk of crashing. Western fighter aircraft in West Germany were put on alert but no military action was taken.

In August the first anniversary of the building of the Wall was marked by violent demonstrations in West Berlin.

Bomb attacks in Ghana

On August 1st a hand grenade was thrown at Ghana's President Nkrumah, who narrowly escaped injury: further bomb attacks followed in September, when a curfew was imposed in the capital, Accra.

Here, coffins with the effigies of Nkrumah's three former associates who were charged with the assassination attempt are burnt by loyal supporters in Accra's Black Star Square.

Danish physicist dies

Professor Niels Bohr (1885–1962), the Danish atomic scientist regarded as the greatest physicist since Einstein, died in November this year. Here Bohr is inspecting the atomic plant at Roskilde.

A spy at the Admiralty

On October 22nd a British Admiralty clerk, William Vassall, was sentenced to 18 years' imprisonment for spying for the Soviet Union.

Racism in the Deep South

Racial violence erupted in America's Deep South when attempts were made in September to block Negro James Meredith's registration at the University of Mississippi.

Eleanor Roosevelt

Eleanor Roosevelt (1884–1962) died on November 10th. Besides supporting her husband in politics, she was a writer, journalist, delegate to the United Nations and human rights activist.

Sophia Loren

Seen here with her husband Carlo Ponti, Italian film actress
Sophia Loren (1934–   ) starred in several outstanding films in
the 1960s, including *The Millionairess* (1960), *Two Women* (1961),
Yesterday, Today and Tomorrow (1963) and *Marriage Italian
Style* (1964).

A new school for Prince Charles

On April 2nd 1962, Prince Charles arrived as a new pupil at
Gordonstoun school, near Elgin, Scotland. Accompanied by his
father Prince Philip, himself a former pupil of Gordonstoun, he is
seen here being greeted by the headmaster, Mr Robert Chew.

Marilyn Monroe

Seen here in one of her last films, George Cukor's *Let's Make Love*,
in which she starred with Yves Montand, Marilyn Monroe (1926–
1962), the ultimate sex symbol, combining voluptuousness with
vulnerability, died on August 5th. Her death was ruled a possible
suicide, but is still surrounded by mystery.

First American in orbit

Colonel John Glenn (1921–   ) was the first American to orbit
the Earth. He made three successful orbits in February, with full
media coverage, and his return to the USA was marked by
national celebrations. New York gave him the biggest tickertape
reception ever recorded.

Coventry Cathedral consecrated

Britain's new Coventry Cathedral, designed by Sir Basil Spence to replace the cathedral destroyed in the war, was consecrated on May 25th. The cathedral features work by Jacob Epstein (above left) and other leading artists. Above right, a huge metal crown of thorns frames the entrance to the side chapel of Christ in Gethsemane.

Brazil's World Cup victory

On June 21st, the Brazilian football team, playing without their star striker Pele, beat Czechoslovakia 3–1 at Chile's Santiago stadium to retain the World Cup trophy.

1963

Jan	14	Britain's entry to EEC blocked by de Gaulle of France
	29	US poet Robert Frost dies
	30	French composer Francis Poulenc dies
Feb	1	Autonomy for Nyasaland under Hastings Banda
	19	USSR agrees to pull troops out of Cuba
	20	UK: Lord Beveridge, founder of the Welfare State, dies
Mar	17	Volcano erupts in Bali, killing 11,000
Apr	2	Black civil rights campaign begins in US
	6	Anglo/US Polaris weapons agreement signed
	9	Winston Churchill given honorary US citizenship
	17	Canada: Diefenbaker's Prog. Con. govt resigns
	22	Canada: Lester Pearson forms Liberal Govt
	28	Cuban President Fidel Castro visits USSR
May	22	Formation of Organisation for African Unity
Jun	3	Pope John XXIII dies
	20	US and USSR agree on 'hotline' link
	21	France pulls her navy out of NATO
	29	President Kennedy visits British PM Macmillan
Jul	1	Kim Philby, British spy, revealed as 'third man'
	26	Big earthquake at Skopje in Yugoslavia
Aug	8	UK: Armed gang rob train, netting over £1 million
	22	Lord Nuffield, founder of Morris Motors, dies
	28	200,000 US blacks demonstrate for civil rights
	31	French Cubist painter Georges Braque dies
Sep	4	US: Desegregation riots in Birmingham, Alabama
	4	Death of French statesman Robert Schumann
	16	Malaysia is formed as a new nation
	19	Channel Tunnel agreed in Anglo-French report
Oct	1	Nigeria becomes a Republic within the Commonwealth
	3	Army takes control in Honduras
	6	Los Angeles Dodgers win World Series
	7	Kennedy signs treaty to limit nuclear tests
	9	Kabaka is 1st President of Uganda; Dr Obote is PM
	11	French writer and poet Jean Cocteau dies
	11	French singer Edith Piaf dies
	15	Ludwig Erhardt becomes German Chancellor
Nov	22	President Kennedy is assassinated
	24	L. H. Oswald, accused of killing Kennedy, is shot
Dec	10	Linus Pauling wins Nobel Peace Prize
	12	Kenya becomes a Republic; Kenyatta as President
	The Arts	
		British National Theatre opens
		Thomas Pynchon's novel *V*
		Tony Richardson's film *Tom Jones*
		Mankiewicz's film *Cleopatra*

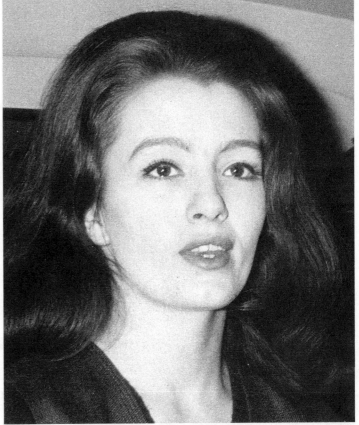

The Profumo affair

On June 5th, John Profumo (1915–   ) (top) resigned from his parliamentary seat and post as British Secretary of State for War, admitting that he had misled the House of Commons following an investigation into his relationship with model Christine Keeler (above), whose favours he was alleged to have shared with the former Russian naval attaché Captain Ivanov. The Profumo affair, with its grave implications for national security, rocked the country and the scandal almost brought down the government.

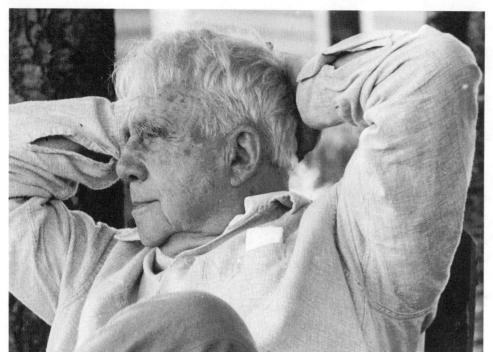

Poet of nature

It was only in the second half of his life that Robert Frost (1874–1963) was able to win recognition for his poetry and in his later years he established himself as a major literary figure. He had worked as a New England shoemaker, teacher and farmer and his poetry, based on themes drawn from that rural life, had more in common with 19th century poets than with the modern drive towards realism.

He won the Pulitzer Prize four times: for *New Hampshire* in 1924, *Collected Poems* in 1931, *A Further Range* in 1937 and *A Witness Tree* in 1943. On his 75th and 85th birthdays he was honoured in the US Senate and he played a prominent role at the inauguration of John F. Kennedy in 1961, reciting the poem 'The Gift Outright', specially written for the occasion.

Protests in Saigon

Saigon's two faces of protest. (Left), given the day off for the occasion 50,000 people demonstrate their support for President Diem's crackdown on the Buddhists.

A young Buddhist priest (right), burned himself to death in Saigon's market square neither moving nor uttering a sound during his ordeal. He was the fifth to commit ritual suicide since May when Vietnamese government soliders fired on a Buddhist demonstration killing nine. The United States government, believing in the Buddhist cause, feared Saigon's chances of beating the Viet Cong without first gaining Buddhist support.

'I have a dream'

1963 was a climactic year in the black struggle for civil rights in America. Black rights workers were murdered in Alabama and Mississippi and in June President Kennedy had to federalise the Alabama National Guard when George Wallace, the segregationist Governor of Alabama, tried to prevent two black students from taking up their places at the University of Alabama in Tuscaloosa. Peaceful protest marches in Birmingham were met by force, and weeks of violent rioting ensued on the city's streets (top left) with police using teargas and fire hoses to contain the situation (bottom left). In September a bomb killed four black schoolgirls in the city.

On August 28th, the wave of black protest crested in an enormous peaceful demonstration, when some 200,000 black and white civil rights supporters marched on Washington, DC from all over the United States. The climax to the march came when the crowd gathered at the Lincoln Memorial. There they were addressed by Martin Luther King (above) who told them, in a powerful and moving speech, of his continuing dream of an equal and united America.

President Kennedy assassinated

In one of the greatest political tragedies of the century, US President John Fitzgerald Kennedy was gunned down in Dallas, Texas, on Friday November 22nd. The shooting took place as the presidential motorcade drove through the city's main business centre. Three shots were fired from the sixth floor of a building near the junction of Elm Street and Houston Street, below, and the President slumped forward, hit in the head and neck. With Mrs Kennedy cradling her husband in her arms, the car sped to the Parkland Hospital where the President died half an hour later without regaining consciousness.

Within two hours (far right) Vice-President Lyndon Baines Johnson, who had been travelling in the car behind the President's, was sworn in as the 35th President of the United States at Dallas airfield. Also within hours of the killing, police had arrested Lee Harvey Oswald, a 24-year-old former Marine, and charged him with the President's murder. Two days later, below right, television viewers throughout the world saw Oswald himself gunned down at point blank range as he was being transferred to the county jail from the basement of Dallas police headquarters. The gunman, a 42-year-old Dallas nightclub owner called Jack Ruby, was immediately arrested.

Kennedy's funeral was held in Washington, DC on November 25th, right, in the presence of the greatest gathering of heads of state in the history of the USA. More than a million mourners lined the route as the coffin, draped in the American flag, was taken to St Matthew's Roman Catholic Cathedral.

Above: Only five months earlier Kennedy had seemed to signal new hopes for Western unity when he visited Berlin and made his famous 'Ich bin ein Berliner' speech at the Berlin Wall.

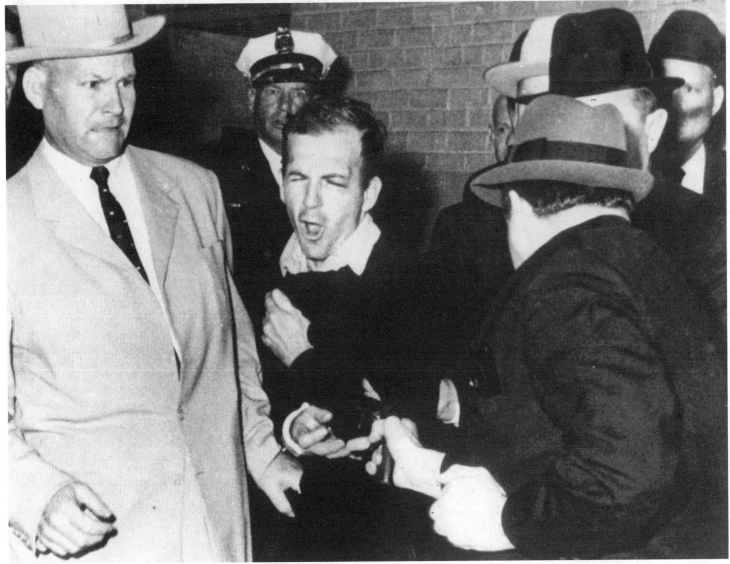

Kenyan independence

Colourful tribal dancing (above) and widespread celebrations followed the end of 68 years of British rule in Kenya with the granting of independence at midnight on December 12th. The following day, on behalf of the Queen, Prince Philip handed the Kenyan Prime Minister Jomo Kenyatta the constitutional instruments of power in a ceremony attended by thousands of people at the Uhuru Stadium in Nairobi (left). In a moving speech Kenyatta described it as 'Kenya's greatest day' and spoke of the 'British principles and justice' on which the new state would be built.

The Great Train Robbery

One man was badly injured and mailbags worth more than £2½ million were stolen on August 8th in what became known in Britain as the Great Train Robbery. The crime took place in the early hours of the morning near Linslade in Buckinghamshire when an armed gang held up an overnight Royal Mail train travelling from Glasgow to London. In a meticulously planned operation, the 15 raiders used four six-volt batteries to simulate a red stop signal. When the train stopped, they coshed the driver, Jack Mills, decoupled the engine and some of the carriages and drove them to Bridego Bridge further along the line. Here, the mailbags were loaded into a waiting lorry. Police quickly found the gang's hideout in a nearby farm and Charlie Wilson, the first of the Great Train Robbers to stand trial, was arrested and charged later the same month.

First woman in space

Two years and two months after Yuri Gagarin became the first man in space, the Soviet space programme scored another coup when it put the first woman cosmonaut into orbit. Twenty-six-year-old Lieutenant Valentina Tereshkova (left) achieved this distinction on June 16th when the spacecraft Vostok 6 joined its immediate predecessor Vostok 5 in orbit around the Earth. Feminist groups in the United States claimed that the Soviet Union was demonstrating a more enlightened attitude to women than the United States, but NASA showed less immediate enthusiasm for this new challenge than they had when Gagarin pipped them to the post in 1961.

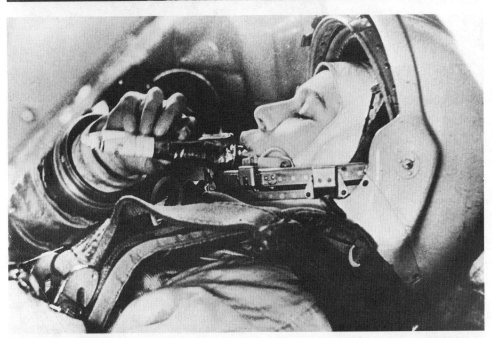

Regrets for Edith Piaf

The death was announced of the French singer Edith Piaf (1915–1963). Piaf, known as 'The Little Sparrow', was born Edith Giovanna Gassion in Paris. She began her singing career in the bars, cafés and streets of the French capital at the age of 15 and was soon discovered and transferred to the cabaret circuit by her first husband. After the Second World War she went on to international stardom with her deeply emotional performances of such songs as 'Milord', 'La Vie en Rose' and 'Je Ne Regrette Rien'. She also appeared in films, including *Le Bel Indifférent* (1940) which was written for her by her close friend Jean Cocteau.

1964

US support for Vietnam

Throughout 1964 President Lyndon Johnson's administration debated how best to support their allies in the Republic of Vietnam. The Republic was on the verge of collapse, with mounting support for the Communist revolution and a succession of unstable civil and military governments. For the US, failure to maintain a pro-western government in Saigon would destroy their credibility as a dependable ally and possibly represent the first 'domino' in a chain of losses feared in the area.

Johnson (above) continued the policy of the 'pacification' of the south. Millions of peasants were moved into 'strategic hamlets', the defences of one of which are shown (right), in order to deny the PLAFSVN (the southern Communist forces) their sources of supply. Top right: A Viet Cong ambush victim is carried away.

In August American involvement was increased in controversial circumstances. On August 2nd, the USS *Maddox* was attacked by North Vietnamese vessels in the Gulf of Tonkin close to the Democratic Republic's coast. Two days later it was involved in another incident which some have suggested was staged to justify an escalation in the war. In retaliation the US bombed targets inside North Vietnam and Johnson secured the authority to use American troops to aid any State in S. E. Asia.

Although there were only 23,000 US military personnel in Vietnam at year's end, most in an advisory capacity, the Resolution provided the basis for the subsequent escalation of American involvement in Vietnam. Far right: One of the Haiphong 'Amazons'.

Death of Nehru

Jawaharlal Nehru (top left), the elder statesman of the Commonwealth, died suddenly in New Delhi on May 27th. He was 74 and had been Prime Minister of India since the country became independent from Britain in 1947. An estimated three million people lined the route of the funeral cortège on May 28th. In a moving ceremony attended by many world leaders, Nehru's grandson Sanjay lit the funeral pyre near the Gandhi Mausoleum. Nehru was succeeded as Prime Minister by L. B. Shastri.

Changing course

Khrushchev visited Egypt in May for the ceremonial opening of the Aswan High Dam on the River Nile (above). Together the Soviet Premier and President Nasser detonated an explosion in the dam, diverting the water into a new channel. It was one of Khrushchev's last international visits. In October he was sacked as Soviet leader for reasons including 'undignified personal behaviour' and foreign policy failures. He was replaced as First Secretary of the Communist Party by Leonid Brezhnev and as Chairman of the Council of Ministers by Alexei Kosygin.

Wilson elected

Harold Wilson became Prime Minister after the British general election of October 15th. His Labour government, which ended 13 years of Conservative rule, had a parliamentary majority of only four.

Bob Hayes is fastest man

Bob Hayes (1942–   ), from Jacksonville, Florida, won himself the title of the 'world's fastest human' by gaining two gold medals at the Tokyo Olympics. He set world records in both the 100 yard and 100 metre dashes. He won the 100 metre semi-final in an amazing 9.9 seconds but this was disallowed because of winds. In the final he tied the world record of 10 seconds.

Kenya becomes a Republic

On December 12th, the first anniversary of Kenya's independence, the country officially became a Republic within the Commonwealth. The Queen sent President Kenyatta a message of goodwill and the change in the constitution was marked by days of celebrations throughout the country. In Nairobi's Jamhuri Stadium (above) President Kenyatta and the departing Governor-General Malcolm MacDonald watched colourful displays of tribal dancing.

Conflict in the Congo

The trauma of decolonisation ravaged the former Belgian Congo (now Zaire) in the 1960s. After Belgium's swift withdrawal in 1960 a series of provincial revolts broke out, with UN forces aiding the government in Léopoldville as it struggled to control the situation. In 1964 Prime Minister Tshombe faced opposition from the Chinese-trained former Cabinet Minister Pierre Mulele, some of whose followers, armed with bows and arrows, are seen above right. The capital, Léopoldville, was bitterly fought over, and only recaptured from the rebels after a counter-attack in which no prisoners were taken (above left). Many Europeans were kidnapped during the conflict. The American Protestant missionaries of Kintshua (above), were held for four days.

Greville Wynne is freed

On April 22nd, the British businessman Greville Wynne arrived back in Britain after his release from prison in the Soviet Union on spying charges.

Jean-Paul Sartre

The 59-year-old existentialist philosopher, novelist and playwright Jean-Paul Sartre (1905–1980) declined the Nobel Prize for Literature on the grounds that it gave undue weight to a writer's influence.

Ian Smith in Britain

The Prime Minister of Southern Rhodesia, Ian Smith (above), visited Britain in September for talks on Rhodesian independence with the British Premier Sir Alec Douglas-Home.

Nobel Peace Prize for King

The American black civil rights leader Martin Luther King was awarded the Nobel Peace Prize for 1964 in Oslo, Norway. The award was made in recognition of his work towards racial integration in the United States.

Independence for N. Rhodesia

The former colony of Northern Rhodesia achieved independence in October. Kenneth Kaunda (1924–   ), leader of the United Nationalist Independence Party, became the first President of the new State of Zambia.

Mandela imprisoned

In June the black nationalist leader Nelson Mandela (1918–   ) was sentenced to life imprisonment by a South African court, having been found guilty of conspiring to overthrow the white government.

1965

Jan	4	T.S. Eliot, US poet, dies
	7	Indonesia pulls out of United Nations
	20	US: Lyndon Johnson inaugurated as President
	24	Winston Churchill (British PM 1940-45, 1951-55) dies
	30	State funeral for Churchill
Feb	7	US aircraft bomb N Vietnam
	15	American signer Nat 'King' Cole dies
	18	Independence for Gambia
	21	Black Muslim leader Malcolm X shot dead in the US
Mar	3	Seretse Khama becomes 1st President of Bechuanaland
	8	US steps up military involvement in Vietnam
	18	Soviet cosmonaut makes 1st ever space walk
	28	Big earthquake in Chile
Apr	4	US jets shot down by N Vietnamese
	9	Indian and Pakistani soldiers clash on border
	17	US students protest against bombings of N Vietnam
	23	Heavy US air raids on N Vietnam
	30	Dominican President Cabral deposed in coup
May	12	W Germany establishes relations with Israel
	13	Franz Jonas elected President of Austria
Jun	19	Bloodless coup in Algeria
	19	Nguyen Cao Ky becomes President of S Vietnam
	24	S Vietnam severs relations with France
	30	India and Pakistan sign ceasefire
Jul	14	US statesman Adlai Stevenson dies
Aug	2	UK: White Paper limits Commonwealth immigrants
	7	Singapore leaves Malaysian Federation
	11	Race riots in Los Angeles, US
	27	Swiss architect Le Corbusier dies
Oct	17	Anti-Vietnam War demonstration in US and UK
	25	Harold Wilson goes to Rhodesia for talks with Ian Smith
Nov	9	Death penalty abolished in Britain
	11	Rhodesian unilateral declaration of independence (UD)
Dec	16	British novelist Somerset Maugham dies
	19	France: General de Gaulle is re-elected President
	29	N Vietnam leader Ho Chi Minh rejects US peace talks
	30	Philippines: Ferdinand E. Marcos becomes President

The Arts

UK: MBE for Beatles in Queen's Birthday Honours

Norman Mailer's novel *An American Dream*

The Sound of Music film musical

David Lean's film *Dr Zhivago*

Vietnam escalates

1965 marked the first massive deployment of US forces in Vietnam. To try to force a negotiated settlement a bombing campaign known as 'Rolling Thunder' was begun in February. Because air bases were vulnerable to guerrilla infiltration and sabotage, large numbers of marines were deployed in March to protect them. Below: Marines are shown landing 10 miles north of the vast airfield at Da Nang.

By July 1965, 175,000 US troops were in Vietnam, most assigned to base protection. The Americans relied upon their technological superiority and immense amounts of firepower (right, a village thought to harbour Communist troops is bombed). The helicopter was vital to the notion of 'airmobility'. Below, South Vietnamese soldiers are shown disembarking for an attack.

The helicopter was, however, difficult to maintain and vulnerable to ground fire, while the influx of supplies presented the Americans with immense logistical problems.

The NLFPAVN (northern Communist forces) harried and chased the South Vietnamese forces and their US allies, ensuring that firm control was never established over the Republic of Vietnam. Opposite: Victims of a terrorist bomb outside the US embassy in Saigon.

Churchill's funeral

Sir Winston Churchill's state funeral took place in London on Saturday January 30th. The British elder statesman had died, aged 90, on January 24th. His coffin, draped with a Union Jack, was borne by gun carriage from Westminster Hall, where some 300,000 people had paid their last respects during the lying-in-state, to St Paul's Cathedral, where the funeral service was held. Three thousand people attended, including Queen Elizabeth, who broke with royal precedent by awaiting the arrival of the body in the cathedral.

After the service, the coffin was carried through streets lined with mourning crowds to Tower Pier on the River Thames. From there, to the sound of massed pipe bands and a 17-gun salute, it was taken by river to Waterloo Station for the last leg of its journey to Oxfordshire, where Sir Winston Churchill was laid to rest in Bladon churchyard next to his parents and within sight of Blenheim Palace, the home of the Churchill family for more than two centuries.

First walks in space

Another milestone in the ever-quickening East–West space race was passed on March 18th when the Russian cosmonaut Alexei Leonov became the first man to walk in space. Three months later, astronaut Edward H. White (left) became the first American to walk in space. On June 3rd, he left the Gemini 4 spacecraft and floated outside the ship for a record 21 minutes.

The moors murders

A full-scale search was launched on Saddleworth Moor near Manchester, England (above), after the body of a ten-year-old girl was found buried there in October. The discovery, and the resulting charges of murder against Ian Brady and Myra Hindley (above), opened perhaps the most notorious murder case of the century.

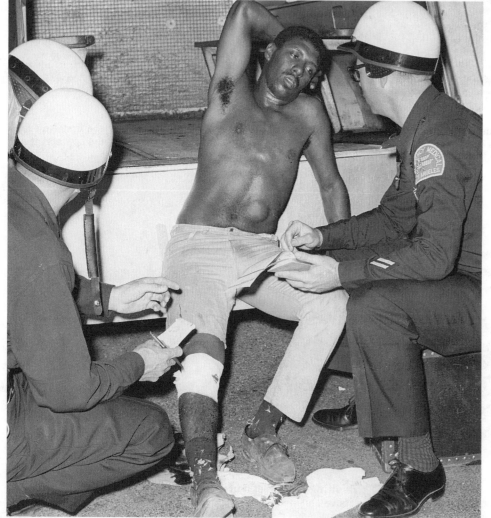

Black civil rights

In the United States the black civil rights struggle moved into a new phase. In the wake of President Johnson's Civil Rights Act of 1964, Martin Luther King concentrated his campaign for black voter registration on the town of Selma in Alabama. Only 335 of the black population of about 14,000 were registered to vote here and attempts to increase this number had been resisted by the local authorities.

On March 7th, a black protest march to the State capital, Montgomery, was violently broken up by State troopers acting on the orders of the State Governor George Wallace, and one of the demonstrators was killed. Two weeks later Johnson federalised the National Guard to give protection to a peaceful march led by King himself. Twenty-five thousand people gathered in Selma in the morning drizzle (above, left and right) to walk the 52 miles to Montgomery, where King addressed the crowd.

Despite the passing of the 1965 Civil Rights Act, which removed further obstacles to black voting, unrest continued and spread to cities outside the South. In August the worst riots in living memory took place in the Watts district of Los Angeles, where 34 people were killed and 35 million dollars worth of property was destroyed in violent disturbances (left).

Rhodesian unilateral declaration of independence

On November 11th, a few days after the British Prime Minister Harold Wilson was greeted by demonstrators while visiting the Rhodesian Premier for talks in Salisbury (above) Ian Smith unilaterally declared Rhodesia an independent State. The minority white government ignored its technical dismissal by the Governor Sir Humphrey Gibbs and the British Labour government rushed legislation through Parliament to impose economic sanctions on the rebel regime.

Kennedy memorial

Queen Elizabeth unveiled a memorial to John F. Kennedy at Runnymede, the meadow by the Thames where the Magna Carta was signed in 1215. The former President's widow Jacqueline and his son John (above) were present at the ceremony.

MBEs for The Beatles

Controversy erupted in Britain when the Queen's Birthday Honours List included MBEs for The Beatles. John, Paul, George and Ringo received their awards at an investiture held at Buckingham Palace in October.

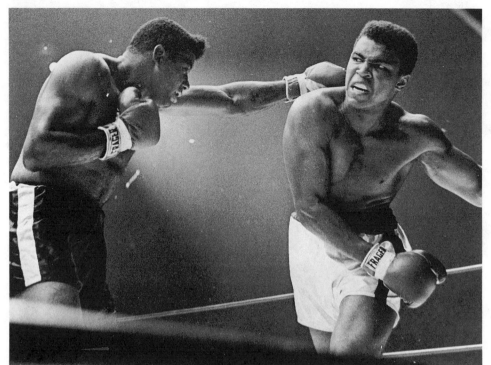

Muhammed Ali

On November 23rd the controversial boxer Muhammed Ali (left) defeated Floyd Patterson in Las Vegas to retain his title as Heavyweight Champion of the World. Ali, who changed his name from Cassius Clay the previous year after his conversion to Islam, retained his heavyweight title after a technical knockout in the 12th round.

Brigitte Bardot

The French actress and sex-symbol Brigitte Bardot (above) became the focus of enormous media attention when she visited the United States in December to publicise her new film *Viva Maria!*, in which she played a gun-toting South American revolutionary. The journalists who followed her everywhere during her stay compared her to Marilyn Monroe.

Le Corbusier

The Swiss-born architect, born in 1887, died on August 27th. A legend in his time, he was a major pioneer of the modern movement in architecture. His major achievements include the Unité d'Habitation at Marseilles, which housed 1,600 people under a single roof. He is seen with the magnificent enamelled door he designed for the Punjab Parliament.

The Spy Who Came in from the Cold

John le Carré's third novel, *The Spy Who Came in from the Cold*, clinched his reputation as the grand master of spy fiction with its complex, gripping plot exposing hypocrisy and betrayal within the intelligence services. It was also made into a memorable film, released in 1965 and starring Richard Burton who gave a remarkable performance in the title role.

1966

Jan	1	Bokassa takes over in Central Africa Republic		31	US: Race riots in Chicago, New York and Cleveland
	8	US launches biggest offensive ever in Vietnam war	Aug	11	Malaysia and Indonesia make peace agreement
	17	US H-bomb accidentally dropped over Spanish coast		13	China: Cultural Revolution announced by Mao Tse-tung
	19	Indira Gandhi takes over as Indian PM		27	Francis Chichester goes on round world voyage in yacht
	19	Australian PM Menzies resigns after 16 years	Sep	6	Verwoerd, S African PM, is assassinated
Feb	8	Freddie Laker forms cut-price transatlantic airline		29	Falkland Islands raided by Argentina
	24	Ghanaian President Nkrumah ousted while in China		30	Bechuanaland gains independence as Botswana
Mar	12	Java: General Suharto assumes power in army coup	Oct	20	UK: Inhabitants of Aberfan buried by coal slag heap
	17	US astronauts dock in space		22	Spy George Blake escapes from jail in London
	23	Pope and Archbishop of Canterbury meet in Rome		26	President Johnson visits US troops in Vietnam
	31	Labour wins landslide victory in British election	Nov	9	Italy: Flood ruins many art treasures in Florence
Apr	4	Soviet spacecraft orbits the moon		9	Jack Lynch becomes new Irish PM
	19	Australia sends 4,500 soldiers to fight in Vietnam		20	Escaped British spy George Blake arrives in E Berlin
	30	1st regular English-Channel hovercraft service begins	Dec	6	Rhodesia: Ian Smith refuses UK proposals to end UDI
May	6	UK: 'Moors Murderers' Brady and Hindley jailed for life		22	Rhodesia leaves the Commonwealth
Jun	2	Eamon de Valera becomes President of Ireland at 83			*The Arts*
	6	Unmanned US spacecraft lands on the moon			Truman Capote's novel *In Cold Blood*
Jul	1	France withdraws armed forces from NATO			Whitney Museum, New York City, completed
	3	Vietnam war protests at American Embassy, London			John Fowles's novel *The Magus*
	20	Harold Wilson, British PM, imposes freeze on earnings			Joe Orton's play *Loot*

US sends more troops to Vietnam

The Republic of Vietnam and their American allies increased their efforts to isolate the southern revolutionaries by stopping the flow of troops and supplies from North Vietnam. Communist leaders were hoping for a mass rising in the towns of the south to topple the fragile government. By now they had infiltrated most rural areas, where government forces were weak. Here (below),

North Vietnamese regulars and southern National Liberation Front guerrillas patrol the Saigon River in South Vietnam.

Meanwhile, US bombing of the north escalated and petrol dumps were attacked to prevent fuel reaching the supply convoys, leading to evacuation of the northern capital Hanoi. The US then flooded South Vietnam with troops and supplies.

Aberfan

At 9.30 on the morning of October 21st tragedy struck the small Welsh mining village of Aberfan, near Merthyr Tydfil, when a slag heap collapsed, engulfing the village school. The disaster left 147 dead, and virtually wiped out an entire generation of schoolchildren.

The children were gathering for morning assembly when the landslide began, and in a matter of seconds both Pantglas Infants' and Junior School, together with surrounding buildings, were buried under two million tons of mine waste, rocks and sludge. From midday the school would have been empty for the half-term holiday.

Rescue work went on all day and throughout the night as more than 2,000 police, firemen, civil defence workers and volunteers tunnelled through 45 feet of slag to recover bodies and search for survivors. Hardened reporters and policemen broke down in tears as the first bodies were carried out of the mud and the full extent of the tragedy began to become clear. Mothers and grandmothers scrabbled at the rubble with their bare hands and miners from nearby pits left their work to help with the rescue operations. The Prime Minister and the Duke of Edinburgh flew to the scene to offer their condolences to the bereaved.

A hundred thousand people were present on October 27th when the first funerals took place. Eighty-one small coffins were lowered into two long trenches in the hillside cemetery. A 100-foot cross of floral wreaths was laid across the graves and throughout Britain flags were flown at half-mast as the burial service was read.

Reagan elected Governor

Former Hollywood actor, Ronald Wilson Reagan (1911–   ), was elected Governor of California on November 8th. Reagan had only joined the Republican Party in 1962.

Truman Capote

The American writer (1924–1984) had a phenomenal success with his best-selling documentary, *In Cold Blood*, an account of the mass killing of a Kansas family.

Dr Martin Luther King

Civil rights leader Dr Martin Luther King sits with his wife in their four-room slum apartment in Chicago after moving in on January 26th. Dr King decided to experience the problems of slum life first-hand as part of his massive anti-slum campaign.

Dylan and Baez

Bob Dylan (born Robert Zimmerman, 1941–   ), and Joan Baez became two of the great cult figures of the 1960s, enthralling huge audiences with their compelling folk music and songs of protest. Baez first introduced Dylan at one of her own concerts.

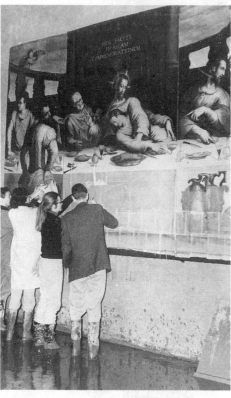

Florence flooded

In November the city of Florence, capital of the province of Tuscany and cradle of the Italian Renaissance, was devastated when severe winter storms brought the worst flooding in its recorded history. Thousands of homes were evacuated and hundreds of works of art damaged as the River Arno broke its banks, claiming more than 100 lives and leaving a trail of mud and destruction. The Santa Croce area was the worst hit, Cimabue's *Crucifixion* being one of the flood's most tragic artistic casualties. Thousands of precious books (above centre) and the pews of the cathedral (above right) also suffered.

Verwoerd assassinated

On September 6th Dr Hendrik Verwoerd (above), Prime Minister of South Africa and leader of the Nationalist Party, was stabbed to death by a white extremist in the House of Assembly.

Top: Forced labour for Africans in Johannesburg.

The Cultural Revolution

In August, Chairman Mao Tse-tung launched the Great Proletarian Cultural Revolution to release the revolutionary fervour of Chinese youth. Millions of young Chinese, brandishing copies of the *Little Red Book*, formed themselves into Red Guards and set about extirpating all revisionism and Westernism.

The Times they are a-changing

The Canadian millionaire publisher Lord Thomson of Fleet bought *The Times* newspaper from the Astor family. The move brought *The Times* and the *Sunday Times* under a single proprietor.

Jack Nicklaus

Another great year for Jack Nicklaus (1940–   ) who won both the US Masters and the British Open Championships. He turned professional in 1961 and went on to become the biggest money-winner golf had known.

Mrs Gandhi

In January Mrs Indira Gandhi (1917–1984) (above), the daughter of former Indian Premier Jawaharlal Nehru, was elected Prime Minister following the death of Lal Bahadur Shastri.

England's World Cup victory

On July 30th, in front of a crowd of 93,000 at Wembley Stadium in London, the England football team defeated West Germany 4–2 to win the World Cup. In what turned out to be a nail-biting match, Germany took the lead after 13 minutes, but six minutes later Geoff Hurst equalised. Martin Peters put England in the lead towards the end of the second half, but in the closing seconds a goal from Weber (above) made it 2–2. In extra time England came into their own with two more goals by Geoff Hurst, the only player to have scored a hat-trick in a World Cup final.

1967

Jan	2	Ronald Reagan sworn in as Governor of California
	3	Jack Ruby, Lee Harvey Oswald's killer, dies
	15	Green Bay Packers win first Super Bowl
	16	George Wallace's wife becomes Governor of Alabama
	27	US: 3 astronauts killed in launch pad rehearsal
Feb	5	Somoza elected President of Nicaragua
	11	Red Army takes over Peking
	14	UK: 100 Labour MPs condemn US bombing of Vietnam
	14	Greek King Constantine flees after attempting coup
	22	Sukarno replaced by Sumarto as President of Indonesia
	26	US steps up war offensive with attack on Viet Cong HQ
Mar	6	Hungarian composer Zoltán Kodály dies
	10	US bombs industrial targets in N Vietnam
	12	Mrs Gandhi re-elected PM of India
	24	Army seizes power in Sierra Leone
	26	10,000 hippies rally in New York's Central Park
Apr	19	Konrad Adenauer, W German Chancellor 1949–63, dies
	21	Stalin's daughter Svetlana defects to US
	21	Right-wing army officers seize power in Greece
	24	Soviet cosmonaut Vladimir Komarov killed in capsule
May	8	US Muhammed Ali indicted for draft evasion
	28	Chichester completes solo yacht trip round world
Jun	1	Moshe Dayan appointed Israeli Defence Minister
	5	The 6-Day War begins with Israeli air strikes
	7	American writer Dorothy Parker dies
	17	China explodes her first H-bomb
Jul	7	Nigerian troops invade Biafra
	23	US President Johnson meets Soviet Premier Kosygin
Aug	3	British poet Siegfried Sassoon dies
	15	Bill passed banning pirate radio stations in Britain
Sep	3	Traffic in Sweden drives on right
	12	Governor Reagan calls for escalation of Vietnam War
Oct	8	Clement Attlee, British Labour PM 1945–51, dies
	9	Cuban revolutionary Che Guevara killed in Bolivia
	16	US: Joan Baez arrested at anti-war protest
	25	Abortion Bill is passed by British Parliament
Nov	27	De Gaulle vetoes Britain's entry to EEC
Dec	9	Nicolae Ceaușescu becomes Rumania's President
	17	Australian PM Harold Holt drowns

The Arts

Gabriel Garcia Marquez' *One Hundred Years of Solitude*

Desmond Morris's book *The Naked Ape*

BBC TV series *The Forsyte Saga*

Bonnie and Clyde film

Beatles' *Sergeant Pepper's Lonely Hearts Club Band*

The *Torrey Canyon* disaster

On March 18th, a giant oil tanker, the *Torrey Canyon*, ran aground on the Seven Stones Reef between the Scilly Isles and Land's End, causing the greatest oil pollution threat to the coasts of Britain this century. The 975-foot tanker, laden with some 117,000 tons of Kuwaiti oil, was bound for Milford Haven when struck the reef. Within six days some 30,000 tons of oil had escaped into the sea, producing a slick covering 260 square miles. Thousands of gallons of detergent were dumped on it, but two days later the tanker broke her back during a salvage attempt (above), releasing a further 30,000 tons of oil.

Emergency measures were taken on March 28th and 29th when Royal Air Force bombers dropped aviation fuel, high-explosive bombs, rockets and napalm on the tanker to sink it and burn off the remaining oil. The six hours' continuous bombardment was a success, but by then 100 miles of Cornish beaches were polluted and irreparable damage had been done to wildlife.

The Six-Day War

In one of the most efficient military operations of modern times, Israeli forces routed the armies of three Arab States and occupied an area larger than the entire State of Israel in just six days.

The Six-Day War began after Colonel Nasser, who had entered a pact with Jordan and Syria, moved his troops into Sinai and closed the Straits of Tiran to Israeli shipping. On June 5th, the Israeli Air Force launched a lightning attack against Arab airbases, and the air forces of Egypt, Jordan and Syria were left in ruins. At the same time three Israeli tank divisions moved into the Sinai desert. They took the Sinai capital of El Arish and by June 6th the Egyptian Army was in total disarray (above).

By June 7th, King Hussein's Jordanian forces had also been routed and most of the West Bank, including the Old City of Jerusalem (top left), was in Israeli hands. On June 9th, amid calls for a ceasefire, Israeli forces pressed on to the Suez Canal (centre and bottom right). At the same time an attack was launched on the Syrian-held Golan Heights and by June 10th, when the war ended, these too had fallen to Israel. Right: Some of the casualties of the war. Top: El Quantowa, on the Suez Canal.

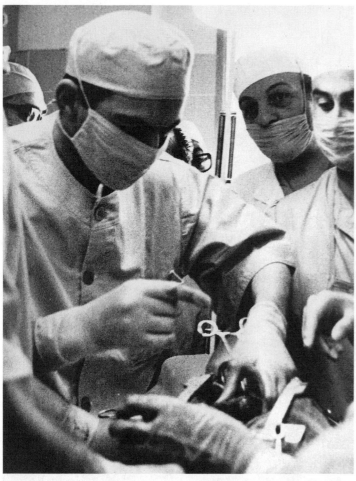

First heart transplant

The first ever human heart transplant was carried out
successfully at a Cape Town hospital by surgeon Dr Christiaan
Barnard. Fifty-three-year-old Louis Washansky received a new
lease of life in the pioneering operation.

Trouble in Aden

Housewives took to carrying sub-machine guns in the colony of
Aden (above) as the pace of nationalist terrorism increased. The
death toll rose sharply as the struggle for independence moved
into its final phase.

Liverpool Catholic Cathedral consecrated

In May a new Catholic cathedral was consecrated in Liverpool.
The work of Sir Frederick Gibberd (1908–1984), it was
constructed around a circle 194 feet in diameter and incorporated
the crypt of an earlier unfinished cathedral.

Anti-Vietnam war rally

New York's First Avenue is filled with demonstrators during an
anti-war rally on April 15th. The 100,000 marchers started their
rally at Central Park and made their way through the streets of
Manhattan to the United Nations.

Pressure on South Vietnam

Throughout the year Communist forces maintained pressure on the South Vietnamese government and their American allies. Above: An American success – a North Vietnamese soldier is captured just south of the de-militarised zone (the 'DMZ') separating North and South Vietnam.

Death of Donald Campbell

Millions of people watched their television sets in horror as Donald Campbell's attempt to break his own world water speed record of 276.33 miles per hour ended in tragedy on Coniston Water in England's Lake District. At 300 miles per hour on his return run, his boat *Bluebird* suddenly somersaulted backwards and sank. Campbell's body was never found.

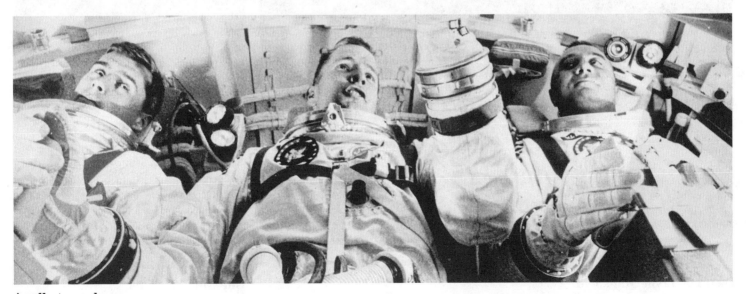

Apollo tragedy

The American space programme claimed its first lives on January 27th when disaster struck the first manned Apollo spacecraft during ground testing at Cape Kennedy. Fire engulfed the command module after an electrical fault on the launchpad and the three astronauts inside – Roger Chaffee, Virgil Grissom and Ed White (who had made the first American spacewalk 18 months earlier) – were killed before they could escape. They are shown during training for the mission.

Svetlana Stalin defects

Svetlana Stalin, daughter of the discredited Soviet dictator, gave a press conference in New York after her defection to the West in April.

QE2 launched

The £25½-million liner, the *Queen Elizabeth II*, seen during preparations at John Brown's yard, was launched by her namesake on September 20th.

Harold Holt

Australia's Prime Minister, Harold Holt (1908–1967), disappeared and was presumed drowned while swimming in the sea on December 16th.

Death of Jayne Mansfield

The Hollywood actress Jayne Mansfield was killed at the age of 35 when the car in which she was travelling collided with a lorry near New Orleans on June 29th (above). She was best known as a blonde sex symbol in such films as *The Girl Can't Help It* and *Kiss Them for Me*. Despite success in publicity, her film career was in a decline by the mid-60s. She never broke out of the sexpot mould.

Che Guevara killed

Bolivian troops displayed the body of Ernesto 'Che' Guevara (above), the guerrilla revolutionary and former lieutenant to Fidel Castro, after shooting him dead in the jungle.

1968

Martin Luther King assassinated

The leading voice of black America was brutally silenced on the night of April 4th when Martin Luther King, the civil rights leader and Baptist minister (top), was gunned down in Memphis, Tennessee, by James Earl Ray, an escaped convict. King, whose campaign for civil rights extended beyond the black community to all the poor of America, was in Memphis to support a strike of the city's dustmen. He had walked out on to the balcony of his motel room for some air when shots were fired from a neighbouring boarding house. His funeral in Atlanta, Georgia (above), was attended by some 150,000 people, including representatives of the US government.

Unrest on the streets of Paris

The worst rioting ever to hit mainland France took place in Paris, leaving scenes of devastation not seen since the Second World War. There was turmoil on May 6th when some 10,000 left-wing students fought CRS riot police, armed with teargas, fire hoses and batons, in the streets of the Latin Quarter. Cars and buses were overturned and burned. There were 600 injuries and 422 arrests. On May 10th, further pitched battles took place between police and students, who dug up paving stones for barricades. The rioting was followed by a five-week student occupation of the Sorbonne University (left) and a general strike, during which rubbish piled up in the streets (above).

Robert Kennedy assassinated

Victory turned to tragedy on June 5th when Senator Robert Kennedy (above) was gunned down after celebrating his success in the California primary election for the Democratic presidential nomination. Kennedy, 42, the brother of the assassinated President, was shot in the head and shoulder by a Jordanian Arab, Sirhan Bishara Sirhan, who was immediately arrested. The shooting happened just after midnight at the Ambassador Hotel, Los Angeles, where the Senator had been making a victory speech to a packed meeting of his supporters. He was rushed to hospital where doctors fought to save him, but he died 24 hours later without regaining consciousness.

Moon orbit by US astronauts

Another milestone in man's journey into space was passed on Christmas Eve when the United States put the first manned spacecraft into orbit around the moon. The ship, Apollo 8, had taken off from Cape Kennedy on December 21st (above) and orbited the moon ten times before returning to Earth. The astronauts – Colonel Frank Borman, Captain James Lovell and Major William Anders – sent photographs and television pictures back to Earth, but the emotional climax of the mission came on Christmas morning with Borman's voice reading from space the opening verses of the Book of Genesis.

The Ronan Point disaster

Three people were killed and others were trapped when part of a block of flats collapsed in the East End of London. The disaster happened on March 16th in Butcher's Road, Plaistow, when a gas explosion brought down all the corner flats in the 22-storey tower block Ronan Point (above). Police and firemen were joined by dock workers and other volunteers as the rescue work began. An inquiry was set up to investigate the construction of the block, which was built to a design common in London and elsewhere in the UK.

The invasion of Czechoslovakia

August saw the end of the 'Prague Spring', a period of liberalisation and reform in Czechoslovakia in which a new leadership, headed by Communist Party chief Alexander Dubček and State President Svoboda, had begun a 'socialist democratic revolution' including a relaxation of censorship and constitutionally guaranteed popular freedoms. The Kremlin, aware of the possible impact of such changes on their position in eastern Europe, sent in Warsaw Pact armies to prevent what they termed a 'counter-revolution'.

In Prague, crowds milled around the Soviet tanks (left and above left). Sporadic fighting broke out but, with over 600,000 troops occupying the country, resistance was futile. The majority could only keep a melancholy vigil like this one (above) in Wenceslas Square on August 28th.

Spring turned to winter as Czechoslovakia underwent a process of 'normalisation'. A new leadership reintroduced curbs on the press, banned the formation of new parties and brought the government back into line with the rest of the Warsaw Pact nations.

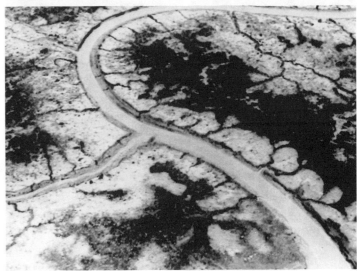

The 'Tet' Offensive

On January 31st, the National Liberation Front (NLF) and North Vietnamese troops launched the 'Tet' Offensive on the major urban areas of South Vietnam. Fierce street fighting continued during February, notably in Saigon where landmarks like the US Embassy and the Presidential Palace were stormed, and in the town of Hue (left) where 113,000 of the 145,000 inhabitants were left homeless. The strength with which the offensive was resisted, seen by millions worldwide on television, cast doubt on the ability of the US and South Vietnamese troops to defeat their enemies. Above left: South Vietnamese casualties in Saigon.

President Johnson initiated the first peace talks by halting the bombing of North Vietnam, the North's precondition for negotiation.

Defoliation

The systematic defoliation of South Vietnam was increasingly being questioned as a military tactic. Designed to deny the NLF food and shelter, South Vietnamese President Thieu concluded in 1968 that its effects on the populace as a whole made it counterproductive. Two areas of mangrove forest are shown (above), before and after defoliation.

Biafran tragedy

While politicians argued and the civil war dragged on in Nigeria, a worldwide relief operation was mounted for the starving people of Biafra.

Hair

The American rock musical *Hair*, now under Tom O'Horgan's direction, opened on Broadway in April. The new, shocking, version was a huge success.

Hancock suicide

The British comedian Tony Hancock (1924–1968), who became a household name with his radio show *Hancock's Half Hour*, committed suicide in a hotel room in Sydney, Australia.

Bridge crosses the Atlantic

London Bridge was sold to an American oil millionaire for £1 million. Every stone was numbered for reassembly before the bridge was dismantled and reassembled in Arizona.

1969

Biafra

The civil war in Nigeria, which had dragged on for 18 months since the secession of Biafra, entered its final phase in 1969. The new State was surrounded by a Federal Nigerian Army of some 250,000 men. Its remaining territory was home to eight million people, a third of them refugees, many of whom were dying of starvation in squalid temporary camps. Thousands of people were dying every day by the middle of the year, and a vast international relief operation was sending 40 flights a night into the country. Despite worldwide sympathy for the plight of the Biafran people, it was fast becoming clear that the forces of their leader Odumwega Ojukwu would not be able to hold out indefinitely against such overwhelming odds.

Man on the moon

A great milestone in human history was passed when man first set foot on the surface of the moon. The moment was broadcast live to an estimated 600 million people, or one in five of the world's population. The lunar landing was the successful culmination of the Apollo space project and fulfilled President Kennedy's ambition to put a man on the moon by the end of the decade.

Apollo 11's historic mission began at Cape Kennedy on July 16th at 9.32 a.m. Three days and 240,000 miles later, the three astronauts (Neil Armstrong, Edwin 'Buzz' Aldrin and Michael Collins) went into orbit around the moon, and at 1.47 p.m. on July 20th Armstrong and Aldrin began their descent in the lunar module 'Eagle'. (Inset: The lunar module photographed from the window of the command module.) The module's three landing probes touched down in the Sea of Tranquillity at 4.17 p.m. and just over six and a half hours later Neil Armstrong became the first human being to set foot on the moon, with the words 'That's one small step for a man, one giant leap for mankind.'

Aldrin joined him shortly afterwards and together the two men set up a television camera to film themselves as they planted the American flag, unveiled a plaque, collected samples from the lunar surface and conducted scientific experiments. During their eight and a half hour moonwalk they received a congratulatory telephone call from President Nixon and demonstrated the effects of one-sixth gravity by jumping in their 16-layer moonsuits.

'Eagle' rejoined the orbiting command module after 21 hours and 37 minutes on the moon. The return to Earth, below, went almost exactly according to schedule and splashdown took place in the Pacific on July 24th.

Jan Palach's funeral

Flowers are heaped upon the grave of Jan Palach, the 21-year-old Prague philosophy student who burned himself to death in protest at the Soviet invasion of Czechoslovakia. Over half a million people paid their respects to the funeral cortège on January 25th. Wenceslas Square's newly painted signs reading *Red Army Square* were replaced by *Jan Palach Square*.

Rioting in Londonderry

Sectarian strife flared up once more in Northern Ireland. After Unionist Orange Day parades on July 12th, rioting broke out in many of the main towns. Above: A burning shop in the predominantly Catholic Bogside area of Londonderry later in the summer of 1969. British troops were brought in at the request of the Ulster cabinet to 'prevent a breakdown of law and order'.

Chappaquiddick

In July Senator Edward Kennedy was given a two-month suspended prison sentence for leaving the scene of an accident in which a woman passenger in his car was drowned. Mary Jo Kopechne died when the car, driven by the Senator, plunged over a bridge on Chappaquiddick Island, Massachusetts. Hours elapsed before Kennedy reported the accident.

Charles Manson

Charles Manson, head of a Californian commune of hippies and drifters, brutally murdered Sharon Tate, pregnant wife of film director Roman Polanski, at their Hollywood home on August 9th, along with four other victims. The trial revealed the power he exerted over his followers. He was sentenced to death – commuted to life imprisonment – along with three others.

Trudeau in London

The flamboyant Canadian Prime Minister Pierre Trudeau (above), whose Liberal Party won a landslide victory in 1968, arrived in London for talks with the British Premier Harold Wilson.

Ho Chi Minh dies

Ho Chi Minh, founder and ideological leader of the Vietnamese Communist Party, died on September 3rd. To commemorate his contribution to the Revolution, Saigon was renamed Ho Chi Minh City.

Judy Garland dies

The singer and actress Judy Garland (1922–1969) died in London a few days after her 47th birthday. Born Frances Ethel Gumm, she was best known for her portrayal of Dorothy in the film *The Wizard of Oz*.

Concorde's first flights

The controversial supersonic jet airliner Concorde 001 had its maiden flight at Toulouse on March 2nd. The flight, which had originally been scheduled for February 1968, began at 3.30 p.m. and lasted about half an hour. At the controls was the chief test pilot of Sud Aviation, André Turcat, who took the plane to a speed of 300 miles per hour.

The British-built Concorde 002 (above) flew for the first time at Filton airfield in Bristol the following month. Brian Trubshaw, the test pilot, attained a speed of around 200 miles per hour and landed the plane at the RAF airfield at Fairford, Gloucestershire, some 20 minutes after take-off. It was a 'wizard flight' he said.

1970–1979

The 1970s

For many people it was the decade of disillusionment, the years in which the heady idealism of the 1960s, the belief of millions of young people that they could really change the world, collapsed into cynicism and bitterness. From the ashes of revolutionary fervour arose the ugly phoenix of terrorism.

In the United States the American dream changed into the reality of Vietnam and Watergate. On the international stage the first overtures of East–West détente were abruptly silenced by the Soviet invasion of Afghanistan. War flared again in the Middle East, where revolutionary changes in Iran and chaos in Lebanon undermined the promise of stability held out by the Egypt–Israel peace settlement. The seemingly insoluble Palestinian problem fuelled international terrorism on an unprecedented scale. Hijacks and hostages became the headlines of the 1970s.

Meanwhile the economies of the Western nations slid inexorably towards recession. As oil prices rose, inflation and unemployment moved towards the top of the political agenda. The scene was set for far-reaching social changes.

International terrorism

Perhaps the most disturbing development of the decade was the spread of international terrorism. Political violence was nothing new. Its history was as long as the history of mankind. What distinguished the terrorist movements of the 1970s from their predecessors was the international scale of their operations. The terrible roll-call of deaths and kidnappings paid eloquent testimony to the failure of governments to find an answer to the problem, as ordinary citizens joined the front-line casualties of an insidious undeclared war. Hijackings brought terror to the airways, with outrages such as those at Dawson's Field in Jordan and Entebbe in Uganda making headline news. In West Germany the Red Army Faction, generally known as the Baader–Meinhof gang, brought chaos to the streets with their campaign of bombings in major cities. In Munich Palestinian guerrillas shocked the world with their murder of Israeli athletes competing in the Olympic Games and in Northern Ireland and mainland Britain the IRA stepped up its nationalistic campaign of terror after the 'Bloody Sunday' shootings. In Italy the Red Brigades proved able to kidnap and murder a former premier at will. Even the relative tranquillity of Canada was not immune: in 1970 the Quebec Liberation Front abducted and killed the Minister of Labour.

Vietnam and Watergate

The decade began with the United States still firmly entrenched in Vietnam, as the war that had provided a focus for so much protest in the 1960s dragged on with no conclusion in sight. Unprecedented television coverage beamed the stark realities of war into millions of homes throughout the world. Its nightly images, showing as they did the effects of military action on the civilian population of Vietnam, helped to turn public opinion against the war in America and elsewhere. The US withdrawal, when it finally came, was soon to be followed by Communist occupation of Saigon and the creation of a worldwide refugee problem as the first Vietnamese boat people fled the new régime. The damage to morale was compounded by the breaking of the Watergate scandal, which swept Richard Nixon from the White House in America's first ever presidential resignation. The disillusionment went very deep. With its apparent helplessness in the face of the Iranian hostage crisis at the end of the decade, America's guardianship of the free world seemed threatened.

The Middle East

The Arab–Israeli conflict continued to make the Middle East the focus of international tension. The powderkeg of Middle Eastern politics was further primed during the 1970s by the outbreak of the Yom Kippur War and the descent of Lebanon into political anarchy as civil war began to turn the city of Beirut from the playground of the Arab rich to the burned-out ruin familiar from so many television pictures. Despite the award of the Nobel Peace Prize to Egypt's Anwar Sadat and Israel's Menachem Begin for their 1978 peace treaty, stability in the region seemed as elusive as ever. In 1979 a new and unpredictable element entered the picture as the Shah's régime was swept from power in Iran on a tide of Islamic fundamentalism and popular dissent. By the end of the decade the Ayatollah Khomeini had returned to Tehran after years of exile and the American hostage crisis had begun.

Economic affairs

It was a decade of economic decline and industrial unrest in the Western democracies. The swingeing OPEC oil price rises that followed in the wake of the Yom Kippur War sent shock waves through the industrial world. In Britain governments of right and left seemed equally unable to arrest the descent into economic chaos, of which the three-day working week and the 'winter of discontent' became potent symbols. Inflation rose inexorably. A wave of strikes paralysed the country in an outbreak of what Britain's European neighbours – whom she joined in the Common Market in 1973 – were to call the 'British disease'. But this was not a British problem alone. By 1977 there were some 15 million people registered as unemployed in the seven countries – the UK, the US, France, West Germany, Italy, Japan and Canada – whose leaders met in London for urgent talks on the economic outlook. Controversial remedies were already being discussed. Many people looked to the 1980s with apprehension.

Pages 406–7: Three hijacked aircraft blown up by the PFLP at Dawson's Field, 1970.

1970

Jan	1	Age of majority reduced from 21 to 18 in UK		18	US rock musician Jimi Hendrix dies of drug overdose
	12	Biafra capitulates to Nigerian forces		28	Egyptian leader Gamal Abdel Nasser dies
Feb	9	PLO leader Yasser Arafat visits Moscow for talks	Oct	5	Anwar Sadat succeeds Nasser as President of Egypt
	25	US painter Mark Rothko commits suicide		9	Cambodia declared a Republic
Mar	2	Israel and Syria in biggest clash since Six-Day War		10	Fiji becomes independent of Britain
Apr	16	Ian Paisley wins Bannside by-election in N Ireland		10	Quebec minister Pierre Laporte kidnapped and killed
	30	US troops sent to Cambodia to attack communist bases		16	Sadat of Egypt is President of United Arab Republic
May	4	4 US students shot dead at Kent State University, Ohio	Nov	3	Allende becomes President of Chile
	12	6 blacks die in racist riots in Georgia, US		9	De Gaulle (French President 1944–5, 1959–69) dies
Jun	4	Tonga becomes independent from Britain		12	US: Court martial of Lt Calley for My Lai massacre
	11	Former Russian statesman Alexander Kerensky dies		13	Syria: General Hafez el-Assad seizes power
	18	Conservatives win election in Britain		27	Gay Liberation Front marches in London for first time
	26	Dubček is expelled from Czech Communist Party	Dec	3	Publication of Industrial Relations Bill in UK
	29	Last US troops withdraw from Cambodia		16	Six killed in Polish riots at Gdansk shipyard
Jul	8	UK: Roy Jenkins elected Deputy Leader of Labour Party		17	*Pravda* attacks Soviet writer Solzhenitsyn as 'hostile'
	20	British Conservative politician Iain Macleod dies		20	Polish leader Gomulka resigns after rioting
	21	Aswan Dam in Egypt is completed			*The Arts*
	27	Portuguese Fascist dictator Antonio Salazar dies			Ted Hughes's poem *Crow*
Aug	2	British army in Belfast uses rubber bullets for first time			Dmitry Shostakovitch's *Symphony No 14*
	9	Police and blacks clash in Notting Hill, London			*Butch Cassidy and the Sundance Kid* film
	24	Radioactivity leaked at Windscale power station, UK			Young Vic Theatre Company formed in London
Sep	4	Salvador Allende is elected President of Chile			Robert Bolt's play *Vivat! Vivat Regina!*
	12	Palestinians blow up 3 hijacked jets in Jordan			Henri Charrière's book *Papillon*

Shootings at US anti-war demonstration

Four students were killed and nine others injured when National Guardsmen opened fire on a student demonstration at Kent State University, Ohio. The shootings occurred during a wave of campus protests against the entry of American troops into Cambodia on May 1st. On May 4th, between 1,500 and 3,000 students gathered on the college campus at Kent State University, contravening an order by the State Governor banning all meetings, whether peaceful or otherwise. At about midday tear gas was used to break up the demonstration. When some students threw back the canisters and started to hurl stones, the National Guard opened fire without warning. The four students killed – two women and two men, aged 19 and 20 – were not involved in the demonstration itself.

US bombs Cambodia

Both sides in the Vietnam War used the small neighbouring states of Laos and Cambodia in their operations. Bases and supply-lines were established (most notably the Ho Chi Minh trail linking southern Communists with North Vietnam) while the United States tried to destroy these facilities by secret bombing.

Once the pro-American General Lon Nol had seized power in Cambodia, US and South Vietnamese forces searched the country for the Communist headquarters directing operations in South Vietnam. The operation failed to remove the insurgents. Their presence, and the continued bombing and covert operations in Cambodia and Laos, only served to destabilise further these already fragile nations. Left: Cambodian villagers await transport from a US helicopter out of the new battle zone.

Riots in Northern Ireland

In the summer, attempts were made to quell widespread civil disobedience in Northern Ireland. Major Chichester Clark, Northern Ireland's Prime Minister, announced the deployment of 3,500 additional troops in the province at the end of June.

And on the night of July 3rd, the reinforced Army made a comprehensive search for arms in the Falls Road area. They encountered fierce resistance, including barricades and gunfire. Over 200 arrests were made and a curfew was established in 50 streets around the Falls Road. Two rioters were reported to have been shot dead by the Army, and a third was killed by an armoured car, leading to complaints that excessive force had been used in the search. Left: Soldiers on alert the day after the most serious disturbances.

Premiership for Heath

In a surprise result, the Conservative Party won the British general election with an overall majority of 31 seats. Their victory, which confounded most of the opinion pollsters, brought to an end almost six years of Labour rule. The election took place on June 18th and was the first one in which 18-year-olds were allowed to vote.

The following day the outgoing Prime Minister, Harold Wilson, tendered his resignation and was succeeded by Edward Heath, a 53-year-old bachelor.He is seen (left) meeting Conservative women MPs, including Mrs Margaret Thatcher (far left), the only woman member of Mr Heath's Cabinet, who was appointed Secretary of State for Education and Science.

Airliners blown up in Jordan

Three airliners were blown up by Arab guerrillas on September 12th after a triple hijack. The British, Swiss and American planes were seized by members of the Popular Front for the Liberation of Palestine (PFLP) who had been holding about 300 passengers hostage at Dawson's Field, a desert airstrip near Amman. After days of negotiation, the hostages were finally released in exchange for seven Arab detainees.

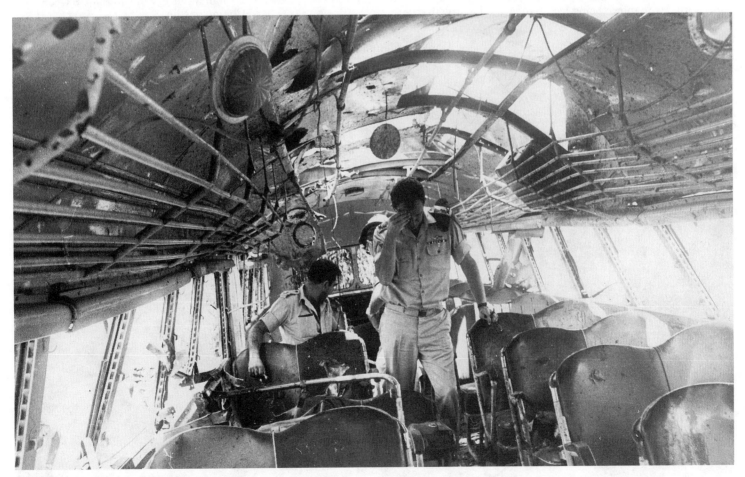

Israeli school bus attacked

There was outrage in Israel when a bus carrying children from school was shelled by Arab guerrillas on the Israel–Lebanon border. Eight children and three adults were killed and 21 were injured (many of them seriously) when the guerrillas fired bazookas at the vehicle from a distance of 20 yards. The PFLP claimed responsibility, and within hours Israeli forces had shelled four Lebanese villages in reprisal.

Victory for Lester Piggott

Champion jockey Lester Piggott (1935–   ) rode Nijinsky to victory in the 2,000 Guineas at Newmarket, England, on April 29th. He is shown being led in after the race.

Jimi Hendrix

Pop star Jimi Hendrix arrives at London's Heathrow Airport on his way to the Isle of Wight Pop Festival. He died in September of a drug overdose.

US Open Championship

In June, 26-year-old Tony Jacklin (1944–   ) became the first British golfer for half a century to win the US Open Championship.

Dirty jobs strike

As plastic bags full of rubbish piled up in the streets and squares of London in October, troops were sent into some areas to break the strike called by the city's refuse collectors. The government action followed growing concern among local councils about the risk to public health from the rotting piles of rubbish.

Mishima commits suicide

Yukio Mishima (1925–1970), the internationally acclaimed Japanese author, killed himself by ritual disembowelment after occupying the Army Headquarters in Tokyo.

Allende becomes President of Chile

Caricatured here, Dr Salvador Allende (1908–1973), the left-wing candidate of the Popular Unity coalition, was elected President of Chile on September 4th.

Death of Nasser

Egyptians throughout the world mourned the death of President Gamal Abdel Nasser on September 28th. He was 52 and had ruled for 14 years when he died of a heart attack.

Funeral of de Gaulle

'France is widowed,' said President Pompidou in his broadcast on the death of Charles de Gaulle on November 9th. Tributes were paid by leaders worldwide as the former President of the French Fifth Republic was buried in his home village of Colombey-les-Deux-Eglises. Some 40,000 French men and women arrived at Colombey to pay their last respects.

Janis Joplin takes drug overdose

The American rock singer Janis Joplin (1943–1970), who was once described as a white woman with a black woman's voice, died of a drugs overdose in Los Angeles on October 4th. She was 27.

Bertrand Russell dies

On February 2nd, Bertrand Russell died at his home in North Wales at the age of 97. His distinguished career as mathematician, philosopher and peace campaigner had a profound influence on the development of Western thought.

Mrs Bandaranaike

On May 27th, ten years after becoming the world's first woman Prime Minister, Mrs Sirimavo Bandaranaike, left-wing leader of the Sri Lanka Freedom Party, was elected Premier of Ceylon (now Sri Lanka) for the second time.

Love, light and peace

Leading figures from the world of popular music were among those seeking spiritual renewal at the feet of the Maharishi in the Himalayas. The Maharishi, leader of the Spiritual Regeneration Movement which practised transcendental meditation, became the guru of Beatles John Lennon, Paul McCartney and George Harrison after they were introduced to him by the latter's wife Patti in 1967. Also learning from the Maharishi's blend of Eastern mysticism and Western materialism were the Scottish singer Donovan (far left) and the young American actress Mia Farrow (third from left).

1971

Jan 10	400 Palestinian guerrillas deported by Jordan	30	US: Supreme Court upholds printing of 'Pentagon Papers'
17	US: Baltimore Colts win Super Bowl	30	USSR: 3 cosmonauts die on return trip
25	Coup in Uganda puts Idi Amin in power	Jul 6	US jazz trumpeter Louis Armstrong dies
Feb 1	Israeli troops cross Lebanese border to defend frontier	29	Tito re-elected as President in Yugoslavia
4	Rolls-Royce declared bankrupt in UK	Aug 12	Syria and Jordan sever relations
5	US spacecraft *Apollo 14* lands on moon	Sep 11	Nikita Khrushchev, Soviet statesman, dies
15	UK: Introduction of decimal currency	14	Duke Ellington gets rapturous reception on Soviet tour
24	UK: Bill to limit Commonwealth immigrants	Oct 7	Israel refuses entry to 21 Jewish black Americans
Mar 8	US comedian Harold Lloyd dies	17	US: Pittsburgh Pirates win World Series
16	US politician Thomas Dewey dies	27	Congo changes name to Zaire
25	Civil war breaks out in Pakistan	28	President Nixon meets President Tito of Yugoslavia
31	US: Lt Calley convicted in My Lai massacre case	Nov 15	Chinese delegates take UN seats for first time
Apr 6	Soviet composer Igor Stravinsky dies	Dec 3	Pakistan and India go to war over Bangladesh
15	UK: Barbican Arts Centre to be built in City of London	20	Zulfikar Bhutto succeeds Yahya Khan in Pakistan
21	Haitian dictator 'Papa Doc' Duvalier dies	21	Kurt Waldheim elected UN Secretary General
May 19	US humorous poet Ogden Nash dies	26	US resumes bombing of N Vietnam
21	Pompidou says way is clear for UK to join EEC		*The Arts*
Jun 4	Hungarian philosopher and critic Georg Lukács dies		Andy Warhol Exhibition at Tate Gallery, London
7	Soviet spacecraft docks with space station		Stanley Kubrick's film *A Clockwork Orange*
16	BBC's first chief, Lord Reith, dies		Visconti's film *Death in Venice*

Civil war breaks out in Pakistan

In March a bitter and bloody civil war broke out in Pakistan after talks on the autonomy of East Pakistan collapsed between Zulfikar Ali Bhutto and Sheikh Mujibur Rahman, leader of the Awami League. On March 26th, Mujibur declared East Pakistan an independent Republic under the name of Bangla Desh (or the Bengal Nation). And there was heavy fighting as General Yahya Khan's Army moved into the province to deal with the rebels. By the end of April it was all over, with Pakistani forces in control of most areas. Amid widespread reports of civilian massacres (below), thousands of refugees began to flee to India.

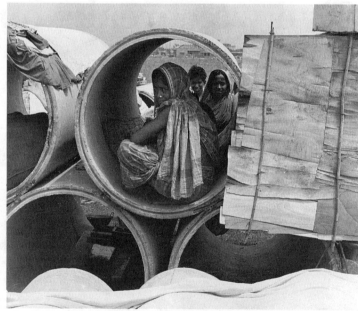

Refugees from East Pakistan

The mass exodus from East Pakistan after the civil war created one of the most serious refugee problems of the century, as well as a tragic spectacle of human misery. By July it was estimated that at least seven million people had fled across the border into India and that refugees were still arriving at the rate of 50,000 a day (top). Those who took refuge in cement sewer pipes in Salt Lake on the northern outskirts of Calcutta were among the luckiest (above). Many others living in the open, or in makeshift camps, faced starvation and cholera as the monsoon season began (left).

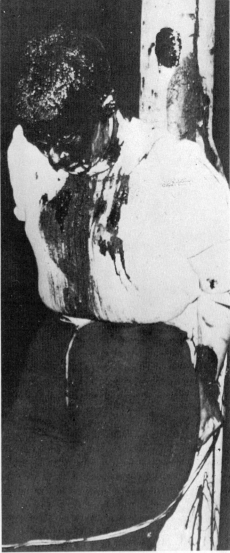

Internment in Northern Ireland

In August 1971 'internment' was introduced in Northern Ireland. Individuals who represented, in the words of Northern Ireland Prime Minister Brian Faulkner, 'a serious and continuing threat to public order and safety' could be held without trial for up to two weeks under the terms of Special Powers Acts dating from the 1920s. The first 300 people were detained on August 9th on the morning of the announcement, and riots broke out in Republican areas of Belfast, Londonderry and Newry. Here (left), British troops survey the aftermath of Belfast street battles in August 1971. On September 7th, the Troubles claimed their 100th civilian fatality when a teenage girl was shot during a gun battle.

Tarring and feathering

In November three women from the Republican Bogside area of Londonderry were 'tarred and feathered' for 'fraternising' with British soldiers. One of them, with head shorn and daubed with red paint and tar, is shown (above). The IRA admitted responsibility at first but the almost universal revulsion expressed at the mutilations caused them to disassociate themselves. One of the women went on to marry her soldier fiancé soon afterwards.

Death of Satchmo

Born with the century in 1900, Louis Armstrong, alias 'Satchmo' to his innumerable adoring fans, died in 1971, after three years of illness. His remarkable career had established him as the greatest of jazz musicians, and undisputed leader of 20th-century popular music, and indeed one of the great musical figures of all time. Loved for the warmth and generosity of his personality as well as his genius on trumpet, Armstrong is seen in characteristic mood in this endearing picture, holding an impromptu performance with young neighbours on the steps of his home in Queen's, N.Y., just a year before his death. The boy is playing a toy trumpet given to Armstrong by nurses in the hospital where he had recently undergone treatment.

Fishermen protest in Britain

The question of fisheries was high on the agenda during the final discussions between British and European delegations over British membership of the Common Market. Under the EEC policy, which came into effect on February 1st, Britain would have had to open its inshore fishing grounds to all member states after a five-year protection period. On September 17th, a fleet of some 100 fishing trawlers (left) from the south and east coasts of Britain sailed up the River Thames to the House of Commons as a protest against the proposed abandonment of Britain's inshore fishing limits. A delegation of fishermen later presented a petition to Prime Minister Edward Heath.

Student riots in Tokyo

Rioting broke out in Tokyo as students protested at the terms of a treaty restoring Okinawa and the Ryukyu Islands to Japanese control. The islands, which had been the scene of fierce fighting between Allied and Japanese forces during the Second World War, had been under American administration since the cessation of hostilities. Under the terms of the reversion treaty, the United States retained its right to military bases on the island of Okinawa. There were serious clashes with police on June 21st, as several thousand left-wing students staged demonstrations demanding that the islands should be handed back unconditionally. Communist students (left) charged police lines with bamboo banner poles and there were 89 arrests.

Driving on the moon

In July David Scott and James Irwin became the first astronauts to drive on the surface of the moon. Using a lightweight battery-controlled Lunar Roving Vehicle, the Apollo 15 team were able to explore a wider area than had been possible before. The men spent two hours covering a five mile area, managing to manoeuvre their vehicle on rear wheels only since the front pair failed to work. Wonderfully clear colour pictures of the astronauts were transmitted back to Earth.

Hirohito in Britain

Emperor Hirohito, the first Japanese sovereign to leave Japan in more than 2,000 years, visited seven Western countries. From October 5th to 7th he was in the UK, where he and the Empress Nagako attended a state banquet at Buckingham Palace.

Tragedy in East Pakistan

Serious flooding in September added to the misery of East Pakistan, which had been devastated by a cyclone towards the end of 1970. As many as half a million people may have died in the disaster, which also left a million people homeless.

Chay Blyth sails round the world

Chay Blyth, (1940–   ) the lone yachtsman, returned to England on August 6th after sailing round the world in 293 days in his 59-foot ketch the *British Steel*. He was greeted by the Prime Minister and members of the Royal Family.

Death of Stravinsky

The musical world was robbed of one of its leading figures with the death in April of the Russian-born composer Igor Stravinsky (1883–1971). His operas, ballets and orchestral works are among the great legacies of modern music.

Etna erupts

As Mount Etna erupted after years of sporadic activity, the people of the Italian village of Sant'Alfio carried relics of saints to the very edge of the river of lava that threatened their homes.

Mother Teresa visits the USA

In the autumn Mother Teresa of Calcutta, who had been active in caring for the refugees from East Pakistan, visited the United States where she set up a mission in the Bronx area of New York City.

Idi Amin gains control in Uganda

On January 25th, Major-General Idi Amin (1925–   ) took power in Uganda after overthrowing the government in a military coup. The President, Milton Obote, was at a conference in Singapore at the time.

'Coco' Chanel

The French fashion designer Gabrielle 'Coco' Chanel (1884–1971) died in Paris at the age of 87. After coming to prominence in the 1920s, she exerted a continuing and powerful influence in matters of style.

1972

Jan	1	French singer and actor Maurice Chevalier dies
	9	Liner *Queen Elizabeth* destroyed by fire in Hong Kong
	12	Sheikh Mujibur Rahman sworn in as PM of Bangladesh
	16	US: Dallas Cowboys rout Miami in Super Bowl
	17	350 Soviet Jews arrive in Israel
	30	Pakistan quits Commonwealth over Bangladesh
	30	N Ireland: British troops fire on civil rights march
Feb	4	Britain recognises Bangladesh
	17	UK: Parliament passes Bill on entry to EEC
	22	US President Nixon visits China for summit
	24	British PM Heath announces direct rule for Ulster
	28	UK: Miners' strike ends after 7 weeks
Mar	30	North Vietnam launches heavy attack on South
Apr	15	US bombers in heavy raids on N Vietnam
	20	American spacecraft *Apollo 16* lands on moon
May	2	US: FBI Director J. Edgar Hoover dies
	9	Israeli commandos rescue 92 hijack victims at Entebbe
	21	Rome: Michelangelo's *Pietà* damaged by maniac
	22	US President Nixon on state visit to USSR
	22	UK: Poet Cecil Day Lewis dies
	28	Duke of Windsor, former British monarch, dies in Paris
Jun	17	US: Attempted bugging of Democrats' Watergate HQ

	27	French Socialist Mitterand and Communists make pact
	29	Supreme Court abolishes death penalty in US
Jul	6	UK: Poulson corruption inquiry set up
	6	Kakuei Tanaka is new PM of Japan
	28	UK: National dock strike
Aug	6	Uganda: President Amin plans to expel 50,000 Asians
	26	20th Olympic Games open in Munich
	28	UK: Air crash kills Prince William of Gloucester
Sep	1	Bobby Fischer becomes World Chess Champion
	5	Arab terrorists kill 11 Israeli athletes at Olympics
	8	Israeli planes raid Lebanon in retaliatory attack
Oct	17	S Korea: President declares martial law
	25	Iceland boycotts British goods as part of cod war
Nov	17	Ex-President Perón back in Argentina after 17 years
	19	SDP govt under Willy Brandt wins German elections
	22	First US B52 bomber shot down over Vietnam
Dec	18	Heavy bombing of Hanoi by American B52s
	24	Huge earthquake in Nicaragua: 10,000 dead
	26	Harry S. Truman (US President 1945–53) dies

The Arts

Lloyd Webber's musical *Jesus Christ, Superstar*

Francis Ford Coppola's film *The Godfather*

Vietnam War nears its end

In March, North Vietnamese forces launched their biggest offensive to date, making inroads on three fronts in South Vietnam. The United States came to the aid of their beleaguered southern allies but, having greatly reduced their troop contingent, they could only resume their bombing of the north and mining of Vietnamese ports. American bombing culminated in a massive Christmas campaign using B52s. The heavy losses suffered by the USAF and the selection of civilian targets drew much domestic and international criticism.

In Paris the lengthy peace negotiations finally began to achieve results. Despite the opposition of South Vietnamese President Thieu, American and Communist negotiators worked on a solution which would leave the North and South Vietnamese to finalise a political settlement after a ceasefire.

The most famous of all Vietnamese war photographs was taken this year. The picture of children (left) fleeing from a napalm raid came to represent the whole conflict in the eyes of the western world.

Munich Olympics

The stunning performances of the young Soviet gymnast Olga Korbut (far left) and the gold medals of American swimmer Mark Spitz (above) and British athlete Mary Peters (left) could not dispel the horror in Munich when the 20th Olympic Games became the setting for an unprecedented terrorist outrage which left 11 Israeli athletes dead.

The tragedy began just before dawn on September 5th when eight hooded terrorists scaled the fence around the Olympic Village. Bursting into the dormitory where the 11 Israeli athletes were sleeping, they shot two dead and took the other nine hostage, threatening to kill them unless 200 Arab guerrillas were released. The German authorities agreed to take the terrorists to Fürstenfeldbruck military airfield where a Lufthansa airliner was waiting on the tarmac to fly them out of the country. There they were ambushed by German marksmen, but in the ensuing gun battle all nine hostages were killed by their captors.

George Wallace

During his campaign in the Maryland primary elections, George Wallace, the Governor of Alabama, was shot by a would-be assassin and left paralysed from the waist down. In the mid-60s Wallace had consistently defied US integration laws by ordering the arrests of thousands of both black and white civil rights protestors.

Shootings in Northern Ireland

In the bloodiest incident of the Ulster 'Troubles' 13 men were shot dead by British paratroopers in Londonderry's Bogside area. After being stoned by some members of a civil rights march the British troops vaulted over barricades (above) and attacked. Allegations of indiscriminate shooting were rejected, and they claimed that individually identified snipers had been fired upon.

Spaghetti Junction

On May 24th, Peter Walker, British Secretary of State for the Environment, opened the Midlands Links Motorways, thus completing the continuous motorway route from London to the Scottish border, a distance of some 300 miles. This final connecting seven-mile stretch – between Great Barr and Castle Bromwich near Birmingham – included the Gravelly Hill Interchange, familiarly known as 'Spaghetti Junction', a very apt name as this aerial photograph shows.

Britain in Europe

In what the British Prime Minister Edward Heath described as 'another great step forward towards the removal of divisions in Western Europe', Britain finally joined the European Community on January 22nd, together with Ireland, Denmark and Norway. In a televised ceremony, delayed by almost an hour when a young German woman threw a bottle of ink at him, Mr Heath signed the Treaty of Accession in the Palais d'Egremont in Brussels.

SALT Treaty signed

The US President Richard Nixon spoke of 'a new age in the relationship between our two great and powerful nations' when he visited the Soviet Union in May. During his visit he and the Soviet leader Leonid Brezhnev signed two treaties limiting and freezing nuclear missile systems in both countries. The leaders shook hands and toasted each other with champagne at the signing ceremony in the St Vladimir Hall in the Kremlin.

Nixon in China

President Nixon had what were described as 'serious and frank' talks with Chairman Mao Tse-tung (above) during a week-long visit to the People's Republic of China in February. The US President attended a banquet for 700 people in the Great Hall of the People in Peking and visited the Great Wall. He and Dr Henry Kissinger (above right) also held lengthy discussions (aimed at normalising relations between the two countries) with the Chinese Prime Minister Chou En-lai (above left).

Chi-chi the giant panda died at London Zoo, where she had been an honoured resident since 1958. She was 15.

Baader-Meinhof arrests

In June leading members of the West German left-wing urban guerrilla group the Red Army Faction, or Baader-Meinhof gang, were arrested in several police raids. The arrests followed a series of bombing incidents in major German cities in which a number of people were killed. Seen from left to right (above) in a sketch made at their trial, Jan Carl Raspe and Andreas Baader were detained after a gun battle in Frankfurt on June 1st, Gudrun Ensslin on June 7th and Ulrike Meinhof on June 16th.

Death of the Duke of Windsor

His Royal Highness the Duke of Windsor died at his home in the Bois de Boulogne on May 28th at the age of 77. As King Edward VIII, the Duke had been the only British monarch to abdicate of his own free will and had lived in self-imposed exile since giving up his throne in 1936 to marry the American divorcee Mrs Wallis Simpson.

The body of the man once described by Lloyd George as Britain's greatest ambassador was flown to Oxfordshire on May 31st and lay in state for two days at St George's Chapel in Windsor, where thousands of people filed past the coffin in silence to pay their last respects. In accordance with the Duke's wish not to be given a state funeral, a simple private service was held in the chapel on June 5th in the presence of the Duchess of Windsor and the Queen (left). After the ceremony the Duke's body was interred in the Royal Family's burial ground at Frogmore in Windsor Great Park, near his great-grandparents Queen Victoria and Prince Albert.

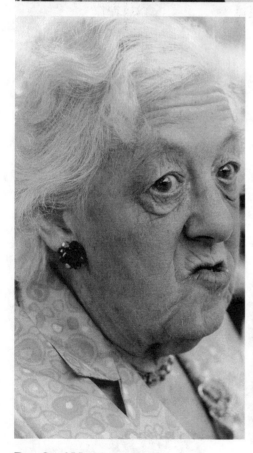

Death of Margaret Rutherford

The British actress Dame Margaret Rutherford (1892–1972) died in May shortly after her 80th birthday. In her latter years she specialised in playing eccentric spinsters and was much loved for her portrayals of Miss Marple.

John Betjeman is Poet Laureate

In October the poet and architectural critic John Betjeman (1906–1984), was appointed British Poet Laureate, a post held before him by Dryden, Wordsworth and Tennyson among others. He succeeded Cecil Day Lewis, who died in May.

First Prime Minister of Bangladesh

Sheikh Mujibur Rahman, leader of the Awami League, was released from detention by President Bhutto of Pakistan in January to become the first Prime Minister of the new state of Bangladesh.

1973

Yom Kippur War

On the religious holiday of the Day of Atonement (Yom Kippur), Israel was invaded by Egypt and Syria in a surprise attack. The first assaults, on October 6th, were soon strengthened by forces supplied by Iraq, Morocco, Saudi Arabia and Jordan. Each side was heavily armed by a superpower patron. Israel suffered substantial losses in the air from Soviet-supplied SAM missiles but American and British-supplied tanks proved to be superior in the decisive confrontations in the desert.

Despite the substantial forces ranged against her, Israel absorbed the attacks and advanced into Egypt and Syria. Israeli troops are shown (above) on the road to Damascus. And a Syrian prisoner is escorted (top) by Israeli soldiers.

This war seriously damaged the détente that had developed between the USA and the Soviet Union. International tension increased when Brezhnev threatened 'unilateral action' if the USA did not help to enforce a United Nations-sponsored ceasefire. This prompted the United States to place its forces on full alert but in the event the ceasefire of October 24th did hold.

London car bombings

One person was killed and nearly 200 injured on March 8th when two car bombs exploded in central London. The IRA claimed responsibility for the bombs, which had been left outside the Old Bailey and in Whitehall (above).

Spanish Premier assassinated

The Spanish Prime Minister Luis Carrero Blanca was killed in Madrid on December 20th when a bomb planted by the Basque separatist organisation ETA destroyed the car in which he was travelling. The blast threw the car 60 feet into the air.

Peace in Vietnam

In Paris a Peace Agreement was signed providing for a ceasefire in Vietnam and the withdrawal of US troops.

Left to right: Xuan Thuy and Le Duc Tho of the North Vietnamese delegation and US Secretary of State Henry Kissinger.

The Watergate hearings

In Washington the 'Watergate Seven' – including Howard Hunt (above right), a security consultant at the White House – were tried on charges arising from the break-in at the Democratic Party National Committee Headquarters.

Noel Coward dies

On March 26th, the gifted writer and musical entertainer Noel Coward (1899–1973) died in Jamaica at the age of 74. His diverse compositions included stage plays, musicals, films and numerous popular songs.

Space station launched

The American space station Skylab 4 was launched into orbit from Cape Kennedy on May 14th. One of the solar shields was damaged shortly after lift-off, but was dramatically repaired in space when a mission manned by Charles Conrad, Joseph Kerwin and Paul Weitz docked with Skylab some ten days later.

Royal wedding

On November 14th, Princess Anne and Captain Mark Phillips were married at Westminster Abbey in London. Thousands of well-wishers, some of whom had camped in the city overnight, lined the streets to wave and cheer as the couple returned to Buckingham Palace after the ceremony.

Death of a great poet

The death of W. H. Auden (1907–1973) in Vienna on September 28th silenced one of the greatest voices of 20th-century poetry. Auden was the leading figure in the group of English poets who came to prominence in the 1930s.

Ben-Gurion dies

The death was announced on December 1st of the veteran Zionist leader David Ben-Gurion (1886–1973). Ben-Gurion was one of the architects of the state of Israel and was its first Premier from 1948 to 1963.

Death of Picasso

April saw the death of the Spanish artist Pablo Picasso (1881–1973), whose restless innovations and often controversial images changed the course of 20th-century art. He was 91.

Student riots in Athens

Sporadic unrest on the streets of Athens erupted into violence at the end of November when police and soldiers broke up a student occupation in the Polytechnic Engineering School (above). Some 5,000 students barricaded themselves in the Polytechnic buildings to demand elections to student unions. Tanks, teargas and live ammunition were used to evict the students when the unrest spread to other groups opposed to the military junta government. At least 23 people died and 200 were wounded.

Konrad Lorenz wins Nobel Prize

The 70-year-old Austrian scientist Konrad Lorenz (1903–1989) was awarded the Nobel Prize for medicine for his work in the field of behavioural research. The prize was shared with Karl von Frisch and Nikolas Tinbergen.

Nixon and Brezhnev

The most significant consequence of President Nixon's visit to the Soviet Union in 1972 was the agreement reached with Soviet leader Leonid Brezhnev. Here, in Washington, they celebrate after signing two Treaty Declarations at a White House ceremony. The signing will eventually lead to a treaty limiting the use and stockpiling of offensive nuclear weapons and the joint cooperation of the countries in research and development of atomic energy, oceanography, transport and agriculture.

Volcanic eruption in Iceland

After lying dormant for thousands of years, the Helgafell volcano off the coast of Iceland suddenly erupted without warning in the early hours of January 23rd. The island of Heimaey was hurriedly evacuated as hot ash and volcanic debris began to rain down on its largest town, Vestmannaeyjar, Iceland's main fishing port. All 5,000 residents were ferried to safety on the mainland, but eruptions continued for some weeks, almost completely blocking the harbour entrance and covering the island with ash.

Ministers in scandal

The British government was rocked by scandal in May following the resignations of two ministers. In apparently unrelated incidents Lord Lambton (left), the Under-Secretary of State for Defence for the Royal Air Force, and Earl Jellicoe, the Lord Privy Seal and Conservative Leader of the House of Lords, resigned after admitting to a 'casual acquaintance' with prostitutes in London.

The affairs had come to light when compromising photographs and tape-recordings of Lord Lambton were sold to a Sunday newspaper by the husband of one of the call-girls involved. Both ministers denied that their activities had caused any risk to national security, a view upheld by the Security Commission set up to investigate the case.

J. Paul Getty kidnapped

On December 14th, J. Paul Getty III, grandson of the American oil billionaire, was released by his kidnappers after being held for five months in hideouts in the mountains of southern Italy. The 17-year-old playboy had been snatched from a street in Rome on the morning of July 15th. Police were initially sceptical about the kidnapping. But there could be no doubt about the authenticity of the ransom demands sent to his mother, Gail Harris, seen here with Getty after his release, when she received a grisly package containing her son's severed ear. The boy was finally released after his estranged grandfather was prevailed upon to pay a ransom of one million dollars.

Brezhnev visit to West Germany

The Soviet leader Leonid Brezhnev made history in May when he became the first General Secretary of the Communist Party of the Soviet Union to visit the Federal Republic of Germany. He was greeted at Cologne airport by the Federal Chancellor Willy Brandt and his wife before beginning four days of talks with West German ministers. The two countries signed a ten-year agreement on economic, industrial and technological co-operation. A joint statement issued by the two leaders at the end of the talks described Brezhnev's visit as 'an historic landmark in relations between the Federal Republic of Germany and the USSR and in European evolution as a whole'. Earlier in the month the Soviet leader had visited Poland and East Germany.

1974

Jan	1	Golda Meir re-elected in Israel		15	Makarios ousted by military in Cyprus
Feb	22	Pakistan recognises Bangladesh		24	Greece: Colonels ousted; Karamanlis new PM
	28	US and Egypt resume diplomatic relations after 7 years	Aug	8	Nixon resigns as US President; Gerald Ford takes over
Mar	24	US spacecraft *Mariner* photographs planet Mercury	Sep	1	General Somoza elected as President of Nicaragua
Apr	2	French President Georges Pompidou dies		12	Emperor Haile Selassie is deposed in Ethiopia
	10	Golda Meir resigns as Israeli Premier		20	Cyclone Fifi kills 10,000 in Honduras
	22	Yitzhak Rabin new Leader of Israeli Labour Party	Oct	11	UK: Labour win second election of the year
May	6	W German Chancellor Brandt resigns over spy scandal		24	Russian violinist David Oistrakh dies
	11	Big earthquake in Sichuan, China, kills 20,000		29	Mohammed Ali regains world heavyweight title
	14	New Archbishop of Canterbury to be Dr Donald Coggan	Nov	29	W German terrorist leader Ulrike Meinhof is jailed
	16	W Germany: Helmut Schmidt becomes Chancellor		29	IRA is outlawed in UK
	18	India tests a nuclear bomb	Dec	8	Greece votes to abolish the monarchy
	19	Valéry Giscard d'Estaing wins French presidency		12	US: Jimmy Carter says he will run for President
	24	US: jazz musician Duke Ellington dies		14	US political commentator Walter Lippmann dies
	31	Israel signs truce with Syria		19	Nelson Rockefeller sworn in as US Vice-President
Jun	3	Yitzhak Rabin is new Israeli Premier		25	Cyclone wrecks northern Australian city of Darwin
	6	Jimmy Connors and Chris Evert win Wimbledon singles			*The Arts*
	26	UK: Labour govt and TUC agree on 'Social Contract'			Tom Stoppard's play *Travesties*
Jul	1	President Perón dies in Argentina			David Hockney exhibition in Paris

IRA bombing campaign

One person was killed and 48 were injured when two bombs exploded in central London on June 17th. The first explosion occurred just before 8.30 a.m. at the Houses of Parliament, causing a serious fire which damaged parts of the 800-year-old Westminster Hall (below). A second and larger bomb went off at the Tower of London later in the day – the Tower was crowded with tourists at the time and the casualties were much more serious. No group immediately claimed responsibility for the bombings, but police said they had all the hallmarks of the IRA.

More IRA bombings

Twenty-eight people died and many more were injured as the IRA's mainland bombing campaign intensified towards the end of the year. On October 5th, bombs exploded in two public houses in Guildford, Surrey killing two Scots Guards and two members of the Women's Royal Army Corps. The Home Secretary Roy Jenkins is shown (left) visiting the scene of the outrage. Later, on November 7th, a bomb studded with nails and pieces of iron killed two people and injured 34 at the King's Arms public house opposite Woolwich Barracks in South London. In both cases the pubs were regularly used by soldiers.

On November 21st, bombs planted in two pubs in the centre of Birmingham claimed 21 lives and caused 182 injuries (above right). Neither of the pubs had any military connections and both were known as regular meeting places for young people. The death toll was the highest ever for a terrorist attack in the UK and caused widespread outrage.

November and December saw other explosions in London, including one in Oxford Street during the Christmas shopping season (above left).

Watergate

The long running Watergate scandal claimed its most senior victim on August 8th, when President Richard Nixon became the first ever President of the United States to resign his office. The announcement came after a series of damaging revelations about the role of the President and his advisors in the break-in at the Democratic Party's National Headquarters, the Watergate Building in Washington, DC on June 17th 1972, and in the cover-up which followed.

The sensational story, which came to light partly as a result of a sustained press campaign by the *Washington Post* journalists Carl Bernstein and Bob Woodward (top left), moved into its final phase in March when a federal grand jury indicted seven former Nixon aides on charges of conspiracy and obstruction of justice. The accused men included the President's former domestic affairs advisor John Ehrlichmann (left) and former chief of staff H. R. Haldeman. Much speculation centred on the contents of tape recordings made at the White House in the weeks following the Watergate break-in, in which the President discussed the implications of the affair with his advisors. When these were finally surrendered to the investigators they were found to have been wiped in parts.

On August 5th, amidst growing demands for his impeachment, Nixon admitted that he had withheld information on the scandal and had made misleading statements. Three days later, with his support in Congress almost evaporated, he announced his resignation in a televised address to the nation (above). Vice President Gerald Ford was sworn in on August 9th as Richard Nixon bade farewell to his White House staff (top right).

Ford is sworn in

Gerald Ford, former Vice-President, is sworn in as the 38th President of the United States, watched by his wife Betty who holds the family bible. Following Nixon's downfall over the Watergate investigations, and his resignation, Ford's accession was greeted with relief and euphoria.

His informal inaugural address was summed up when he said: '. . . I expect to follow my instincts of openness and candour with full confidence that honesty is always the best policy in the end'.

The Flixborough disaster

Twenty-eight people were killed and hundreds were injured when an explosion ripped through a chemical plant at Flixborough in Lincolnshire, UK. The factory was reduced to a mass of tangled wreckage by the force of the blast on Saturday June 1st.

The explosion devastated acres of surrounding farmland, some 2,000 houses were damaged and the village of Flixborough was evacuated as a vast cloud of poisonous cyclohexane gas escaped.

Britain's general election

In an atmosphere of almost unprecedented industrial tension the British premier Edward Heath announced a general election, to be held on February 28th. The results of the poll were inconclusive, with no party winning an overall majority. However, after coalition talks broke down between the Liberal and Conservative Parties, Edward Heath resigned and Harold Wilson (above) became Prime Minister on March 4th.

Turkish invasion of Cyprus

Tension ran high in the eastern
Mediterranean following the overthrow of
President Makarios of Cyprus in a military
coup led by Nicos Sampson, the extreme
Greek-Cypriot leader of the Progressive
Party. The Turkish Premier Bülent Ecevit
claimed that Greek forces were reinforcing
the new regime in Cyprus, and a major
international crisis threatened as Turkish
troops invaded the island at dawn on July
20th. Two days of fierce fighting, involving
some 30,000 Turkish troops, left a triangle
of land between the coast and the capital
Nicosia under Turkish control. Thousands
of residents were evacuated by the Royal
Air Force and Royal Navy. After only a
few days Sampson resigned and was
replaced by the moderate Glafkos Clerides,
and peace talks began in Geneva.

Angola moves towards independence

The Portuguese colony of Angola contained
three major groups fighting for
independence: the MPLA (Popular
Movement for the Liberation of Angola),
the FNLA (National Liberation Front) and
UNITA (National Union for the Total
Independence of Angola). Each had a
different vision for their country, the
MPLA's being the most radical. Dr
Agostinho Neto's Marxist MPLA was
supported by the Soviet Union and
included revolutionary ideology in the
training of its troops. An Instruction
Centre for recruits in the Cabinda
Enclave, north of Angola, is shown (left).

In April the Portuguese right-wing
government of Marcello Caetano was
toppled by a military coup. Successive
changes moved the government to the left,
raising hopes of independence in the
Portuguese colonies of Angola,
Mozambique and Guinea-Bissau.

Air crash in France

In one of the world's worst air crashes, all
346 passengers and crew on a Turkish
Airlines jet were killed when the plane fell
out of the sky shortly after taking off from
Orly airport in France. The wide-bodied
DC10 was on the last leg of its journey
from Ankara to London when the accident
happened.

Eye witnesses said that the jet appeared
to explode in mid-air before plummeting to
the ground in the Forest of Ermenonville,
30 miles north-east of Paris. Rescue
workers and accident investigators found
wreckage and the remains of bodies strewn
over some eight miles of countryside (left).
Among the dead were at least 200 Britons,
40 Turks and 49 Japanese.

Patty Hearst in bank raid

The American newspaper heiress Patty Hearst (1954–   ) was seen taking part in an armed raid in April. Hearst's whereabouts had been unknown since a revolutionary group had kidnapped her in February.

Coup in Ethiopia

After months of instability Emperor Haile Selassie of Ethiopia was deposed by a group of radical Army officers. The Emperor, known as 'The Lion of Judah', was 82.

Solzhenitsyn exiled

On February 13th, Alexander Solzhenitsyn (1918–   ), the Russian dissident author and winner of the 1970 Nobel Prize for literature, became the first Soviet citizen to be expelled from the Soviet Union since Leon Trotsky went into exile in 1929.

Cyclone in Australia

In Australia a cyclone devastated the city of Darwin on Christmas Day, leaving 49 dead. More than half the city's inhabitants were evacuated and the Prime Minister, Gough Whitlam, interrupted a European tour to visit the scene of the disaster.

1975

Jan	10	Portuguese government agrees Angolan independence
	20	Channel Tunnel abandoned by British govt
Feb	11	UK: Margaret Thatcher is new Tory leader at 49
	19	West Indian cricket hero Garfield Sobers knighted
	28	US: 3 Nixon aides sentenced for Watergate cover-up
	28	London: Tube train crash at Moorgate station kills 35
Mar	14	US film actress Susan Hayward dies
	21	Monarchy abolished in Ethiopia
	21	British MP John Stonehouse arrested in Australia
	25	King Faisal of Saudi Arabia killed by mad nephew
Apr	5	Nationalist Chinese statesman Chiang Kai-shek dies
	13	Jack Nicklaus wins 5th Masters golf championship
	16	USSR: Ex-KGB Chief Shelepin expelled from Politburo
	17	Cambodia: Khmer Rouge take Phnom Penh
	30	Vietnam: Saigon falls to N Vietnamese
May	16	Japanese is first woman to climb Everest
	21	Trial starts of Baader-Meinhof gang in Stuttgart
Jun	5	Suez Canal reopens after 8 years
	6	UK: Referendum votes to stay in EEC
	12	Greece applies for membership of the EEC
	13	UK: Ex-Minister John Profumo is awarded CBE
Jul	8	Yitzhak Rabin first Israeli Minister to visit W Germany
Aug	27	Ethiopian ex-Emperor Haile Selassie dies
	29	Irish statesman de Valera dies
Sep	1	Kissinger arranges Israel-Egypt accord on Sinai
	15	Papua New Guinea becomes independent from Australia
	18	Patty Hearst found after 1½ years with Symbionese
Oct	3	UK: Ulster Volunteer Force banned
	22	US: Cincinnati Reds win World Series
Nov	10	Portugal to leave Angola after 320 years
	20	General Franco of Spain dies (Head of State since 1939)
Dec	4	Moluccans seize Indonesian Consulate in Amsterdam

The Arts

Antony Powell's novel *A Dance to the Music of Time*

Anatoly Karpov becomes World Chess Champion

Steven Spielberg's film *Jaws*

Saul Bellow's novel *Humboldt's Gift*

James Clavell's novel *Shogun*

Famine in Ethiopia

Every year areas of Ethiopia were stricken with drought and famine. Haile Selassie had consistently neglected the rural economy and criticism of his failure to acknowledge the existence of famine had contributed to his downfall in 1974. The new regime nationalised land and attempted to remove rural landlords who had exacted onerous dues from their tenants. However the populace still remained at the mercy of the weather.

The desperate plight of the rural poor was worsened by the outbreak of fighting in many areas. Eritrean and Tigrean independence movements were joined by dispossessed landlords and local potentates in challenging the government. This scene of a woman begging for food was reproduced all over the world.

South Vietnam falls

The long war in Vietnam had a swift dénouement. The towns and cities of South Vietnam fell to Communist forces as they swept towards their main objective – Saigon. As each town was approached, a chaotic evacuation of military personnel and civilian refugees took place. The coastal town of Nha Trang fell on April 1st. Here (below left), an American official punches a man away from the door of a plane leaving Nha Trang. On April 21st, Xuan Loc (38 miles east of Saigon) was taken. Refugees are seen (above left), waiting on Highway One for a helicopter to take them to the already crowded capital.

In Saigon US officials and desperate South Vietnamese sympathisers scrambled to leave. By late April it had become impossible to use transport planes to get them out because of the crowds swarming over the runways at Saigon's Ton Son Nhut Airport. Helicopters were therefore used to ferry Americans and what President Ford described as 'high-risk South Vietnamese' out of Saigon. Marines used rifle-butts and tear gas to keep crowds back as evacuation flights took off from the roof of the US Embassy. The last helicopter left at 8 a.m. on April 30th, the day President Duong van Minh surrendered to the provisional revolutionary government of the National Liberation Front (the 'Viet Cong').

The new regime in Saigon entered negotiations with the Hanoi government on the reunification of Vietnam. By the end of 1975 the three states of South-East Asia had Communist governments, a process completed with the victory of the Pathet Lao and the formation of the People's Democratic Republic of Laos in December.

Khmer Rouge overruns Cambodia

On April 17th, Phnom Penh was overrun by the Khmer Rouge, toppling the US-sponsored leader Lon Nol and beginning the most horrific period in Cambodia's history. The Khmer Rouge consisted of dissident Communists who had begun mounting armed opposition to the government from the countryside in the 1950s. With Chinese aid they took over a country weakened by years of fighting which had spilled over from the conflict in neighbouring Vietnam.

When Phnom Penh fell it had already suffered greatly – swollen by over one million refugees and frequently shelled by the Khmer Rouge. Here (left), a man lies dead beside his burning motorcycle after a rocket attack. Under the new régime the population was immediately forced into the fields. For four years virtually every Cambodian worked on the soil in constant danger from suspicious and violent Khmer Rouge soldiers.

The Balcombe Street siege

Police surrounded a London house where four IRA gunmen held two people hostage for six days.

Armed attack

The siege began on December 6th after Martin O'Connell, Edward Butler, Harry Duggan and Hugh Doherty mounted an armed attack on a restaurant in the West End of London. The authorities had been expecting the raid and there was a gun battle with police as the four men made a run for it. They took refuge in a flat in Balcombe Street in the Marylebone area, holding the flat's occupants hostage – Mr John Matthews, a Post Office employee, and his wife Sheila. Hundreds of armed police surrounded the building as the terrorists demanded safe passage to the Republic of Ireland. And a tense waiting game began, with the authorities refusing to give in to the kidnappers' demands.

Surrender

On December 12th, the siege moved into its final phase. A huge screen was erected around the area of operations and it became known that a Special Air Service assault team was about to arrive. At that point the kidnappers released Mr and Mrs Matthews, who emerged on to the balcony and edged their way to a neighbouring flat under cover of police marksmen. Shortly afterwards the four IRA men gave themselves up. Here (left), one of the terrorists surrenders to police.

Kissinger meets Gromyko

US Secretary of State Henry Kissinger meets Soviet Foreign Minister Andrei Gromyko in Geneva. Kissinger's famous shuttle diplomacy culminated in 1974 with a marathon 32-day flying stint, negotiating between Israel and Syria, which resulted in the first signed accord between the two hostile states since 1948. He also mediated in an interim agreement between Israel and Egypt that provided for Israel's further withdrawal from the Sinai Peninsula.

Kissinger's secret missions to China and Russia, during the Nixon administration, paved the way for Presidential visits and a general detente. But by 1975 US–Soviet relations were somewhat strained and strategic arms limitation talks were bogged down with accusations of Soviet violations of the agreements.

In 1973 Kissinger won the Nobel Peace Prize – shared with Le Duc Tho, the North Vietnamese Politburo member. This was largely for his negotiation of the American withdrawal of its troops from Vietnam, and his involvement with the ending of the 1973 Arab–Israeli War.

Reopening of the Suez Canal

During the early months of the year work continued to clear the Suez Canal in time for its reopening on June 5th, eight years after it had been closed during the Six-Day War. By April some ten sunken warships, 120 smaller wrecks (including tanks and aircraft) and 42,000 live explosive devices had been dredged out of the waterway. An additional 750,000 mines were removed from its banks.

Fighting in Angola

As Portugal hurriedly pulled out of Angola, the rival independence movements began fighting. The FNLA and UNITA, backed by South African troops, challenged the MPLA who had declared themselves the government of the new People's Republic of Angola, until Cuban troops were airlifted in to halt the advance. The conflict had repercussions in Portugal, and Angola House in Lisbon was sacked and daubed with pro-FNLA slogans.

King Hassan of Morocco

King Hassan organised 350,000 Moroccans to march into the Spanish Sahara to back his claims on the Spanish colony. Here, women wait at Marrakesh station to join the march.

Hurricane Gladys

Hurricane Gladys threatened the coast of the United States with wind speeds of up to 140 miles per hour, before veering north-east and dissipating over the Atlantic.

Civil war in Lebanon

Fighting between Druze-Palestinian groups and Maronite Christians escalated into full-scale civil war in Lebanon. Barricades in the capital Beirut testified to the failure of numerous peace initiatives.

Starvation in Bangladesh

Thousands of people were dying of hunger in Bangladesh. And Sheikh Mujibur Rahman, founder and President of Bangladesh, was murdered in April – another victim of the political chaos.

Return of Spanish monarchy

Following the death of Generalissimo Francisco Franco on November 20th, Prince Juan Carlos I was sworn in as King of Spain.

Barbara Hepworth

The celebrated sculptor Barbara Hepworth (1903–1975), died on May 21st in a fire at her home in the Cornish village of St Ives. She was 72.

Charlie Chaplin is knighted

The much-loved silent-screen tramp took on a new role as Sir Charles Chaplin when he was knighted by Queen Elizabeth in March.

Streaking

Streaking came to Great Britain in the summer. And streakers, such as this famous one at Lord's cricket ground, gave a whole new meaning to 'getting media exposure'.

John Stonehouse arrested

John Stonehouse, the British Labour Member of Parliament who disappeared after faking his suicide on a Miami beach in 1974, was arrested in Australia on charges of theft and forgery.

Heath replaced by Thatcher

On February 11th, Mrs Margaret Thatcher succeeded the former British Prime Minister Edward Heath as leader of the Conservative Party. She was the first woman ever to hold the post.

1976

Jan	8	Chinese Premier Chou En-lai dies
	12	British writer Agatha Christie dies
	18	US: Pittsburgh Steelers defeat Cowboys in Super Bowl
	23	US singer and actor Paul Robeson dies
Feb	2	US: Daniel Moynihan resigns from UN
	4	US: Trial of Patty Hearst begins
	6	Lockheed says it bribed Dutch Prince Bernhardt
	7	China: Hua Kuo-keng becomes Premier
Mar	14	US musical film director Busby Berkeley dies
	16	UK: PM Harold Wilson announced retirement
	20	US: Patty Hearst found guilty of armed robbery
	24	Argentina: President Isabel Perón is deposed
	24	UK: Ex-Commander Lord Montgomery of Alamein dies
Apr	1	German-born French artist Max Ernst dies
	5	UK: James Callaghan becomes new Labour PM
	5	US: Tycoon Howard Hughes dies
	25	Portugal: Socialist Mario Soares wins free elections
May	6	Earthquake in northern Italy kills 2000
	9	W Germany: Jailed terrorist Ulrike Meinhoff found dead
	24	*Concorde* makes first commercial transatlantic flights
Jun	1	Britain and Iceland end Cod War
	6	US oil tycoon J. Paul Getty dies
	18	S Africa: Over 100 killed after 3 days of rioting

	28	Seychelles become independent Republic
Jul	7	British Queen Elizabeth II starts official visit to US
	4	Israeli commandos storm hijacked plane at Entebbe
	10	Italy: Chemical plant at Seveso leaks toxic dioxin cloud
	13	UK: Roy Jenkins is President of European Commission
	17	Canada: 21st Olympic Games open in Montreal
	21	Eire: British Ambassador to Dublin killed by car bomb
	27	Soviet chess champion Korchnoi defects to West
Sep	9	Chinese leader Mao Tse-tung dies
Oct	11	China: Gang of four arrested, accused of plotting coup
	11	China: Hua Kuo-feng confirmed as Mao's successor
	21	Americans win 5 Nobel Prizes
	25	S Africa: Transkie black 'homeland' given independence
	28	Switzerland: Rhodesia conference opens in Geneva
Nov	2	US: Jimmy Carter is elected President
Dec	3	US: Vance replaces Kissinger as Secretary of State
	4	British composer Benjamin Britten dies
		The Arts
		UK: National Theatre opens
		Marquez's novel *The Autumn of the Patriarch*
		Alex Haley's novel *Roots*
		Alan Pakula's film *All The President's Men*
		Martin Scorcese's film *Taxi Driver*

Riots in South Africa

At least 176 people were killed and 1,228 injured in the worst outbreak of violence between blacks and police in South Africa since the Union was formed in 1910.

Trouble in Soweto

The trouble began in the township of Soweto near Johannesburg which housed more than a million black people. In June some 2,000 secondary school pupils went on strike in protest against the compulsory use of the Afrikaans language in Bantu schools. On June 16th, a procession of demonstrators was broken up by police and one 13-year-old boy was shot dead, sparking off violence in other parts of Soweto, in which a black policeman and a white official were killed. As the unrest escalated police dropped teargas from helicopters in an attempt to disperse angry crowds. Buildings were set alight and vehicles damaged; shops were looted and vigilante groups roamed the streets. A cordon of 1,000 armed police was thrown around Soweto to seal off the township.

Unrest spreads

From Soweto the lawlessness spread to other areas. Rioting broke out in Alexandra Township, Natalspruit, Boksburg and other townships around Johannesburg and Pretoria. There were serious disturbances at black universities in Zululand and in Northern Transvaal, with buildings and cars being burnt. Rioters with rocks, staves and knives clashed in the black homelands and by the time the bloodshed died down, towards the end of June, there had been some 1,298 arrests. The damage to property in Soweto alone was estimated at more than 20 million pounds, with almost every municipal building destroyed. Of the hundreds of dead and wounded only eight were white.

International condemnation

In July M. C. Botha, Minister of Bantu Education, withdrew the Afrikaans language ruling that had sparked off the troubles. But there was international condemnation of the South African government, and the United Nations Security Council passed a resolution describing apartheid as 'a crime against the conscience and dignity of mankind' and upholding the 'legitimacy of the struggle of the South African people'.

Carter wins

Jimmy Carter, one-time peanut farmer from Plains, Georgia, won the November Presidential election bringing back the Democrats to the White House after an eight-year absence. He was the first President from the South since the Civil War.

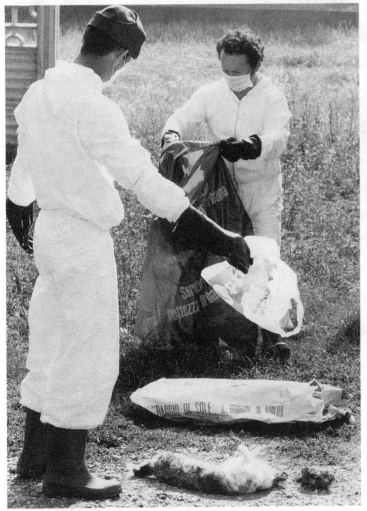

Seveso

One of Italy's worst ever environmental accidents occurred on July 10th, when highly toxic dioxin escaped from a chemical plant in the northern Italian town of Meda near Seveso. The accident, which was caused by a faulty pressure valve, sprayed some two tons of chemicals over the surrounding area, causing burning rashes, headaches, diarrhoea and vomiting in the local population. Many birds and animals died in the contamination (above) and the people of Seveso were not evacuated until more than two weeks after the leak. There were protests at the slowness of the official reaction to the disaster (top).

Drought in the UK

Emergency legislation was rushed through Parliament because of an increasingly serious problem of water supply during the driest summer since records began in 1727. In Gloucestershire the source of the River Thames dried up (top) and in London it reached its lowest level in living memory as week after week passed without rain. As reservoirs turned into arid plains, local authorities were given powers to control many types of water use, from carwashes to hosepipes; and water rationing was introduced in South Wales, south-west England and parts of Yorkshire.

Changes at the top

In a move that came as a complete surprise to his Cabinet colleagues, the British Prime Minister Harold Wilson (far left) announced his resignation as leader of the parliamentary Labour Party, and therefore as Premier, on March 16th. He had apparently made the decision in March 1974 when the Labour Party returned to power, and had told the Queen of his intentions in December 1975.

The ensuing elections for the leadership of the Labour Party were won by James Callaghan (left), the Foreign and Commonwealth Secretary, who defeated Michael Foot by 176 votes to 137 in a ballot of all Labour Members of Parliament. Callaghan, 64, had been Chancellor of the Exchequer and Home Secretary in Wilson's first administration. By the evening of April 5th, when the ballot results became known, he was installed at Number 10 Downing Street as the new Prime Minister.

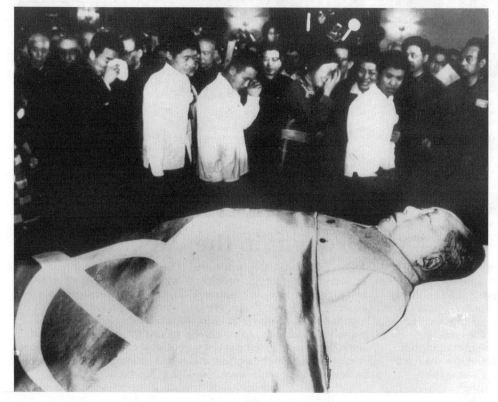

Death of Mao Tse-tung

On September 9th, Mao Tse-tung, Chairman of the People's Republic of China, died at the age of 82. Here, selected 'workers, peasants and soldiers' are seen filing past his body as it lies in state in the Great Hall of the People in Beijing.

The death of the founding father of Communist China sparked a bitter successional crisis. Initially the ultra-radical 'Gang of Four', including Mao's widow, the former film star Chiang Ching, seemed to be gaining control. They promoted a continuation of Mao's 'Cultural Revolution', attacking moderate elements in government as 'capitalist-roaders'. But in October Hua Kuo-feng was appointed Chairman of the Party and the Gang of Four were arrested, accused of plotting to seize power.

By mid-1977, Deng Xiaoping, Mao's Vice-Chairman who had been ousted by the Gang of Four, was restored and Chairman Hua announced eight 'musts' for the economic and political reform of China.

Madame Mao

Chiang Ching, the 62-year-old widow of the former Chinese leader Mao Tse-tung, was arrested in October. She was a member of the notorious Gang of Four who tried to seize power after Mao's death.

Paul Robeson

Paul Robeson (1898–1976) the US bass singer, actor and black rights activist died. His association with left-wing movements brought him before the Un-American Activities Committee in 1950.

Agatha Christie

The doyenne of crime fiction writers, Dame Agatha Christie (1891–1976) died at her home in Wallingford, England, on January 12th at the age of 85. She had some 80 books to her name.

The Entebbe raid

The hijack of a French airliner was brought to a dramatic end when a team of Israeli commandos carried out a daring night raid on Entebbe airport in Uganda. The Air France A 300-B airbus was hijacked shortly after take-off from Athens airport on June 27th by a Palestinian group. They forced it to fly to Entebbe where 98 Israeli and other passengers were detained. Just before midnight on July 4th, three Israeli Hercules C-130 transport planes landed at the airfield. In just 53 minutes, 200 commandos overpowered the Ugandan guards, killed seven terrorists and snatched all but three of the hostages, who were flown back to Israel.

Above: Relatives of one of the terrorists bewail his death in the raid.

Death of a tycoon

J. Paul Getty (1892–1976) the American oil tycoon, died near London on June 6th. A billionaire by the age of 21, he amassed a vast fortune estimated at between 2 and 4 billion dollars – from oil investments and interests in some 200 other concerns. Getty, something of a recluse, married five times and lived the last 25 years of his life outside the United States.

Frank Sinatra

On July 12th, Frank Sinatra, seen with Sammy Davis Jnr in *Robin and the Seven Hoods* (1964), married Barbara Marx, former wife of Marx Brother, Zeppo.

Pictures of Mars

The US spacecraft *Viking* landed on Mars on July 20th and began to send back the first photographs of the surface of the red planet.

Earthquake in Italy

An earthquake left at least 925 dead and as many as 150,000 homeless in the mountains of north-east Italy on May 6th. Above: One of the refugees waits for food.

Scandal in the Netherlands

The Royal Family of the Netherlands was rocked by a scandal connecting Prince Bernhard, the husband of Queen Juliana (above), with irregular payments by the Lockheed Corporation.

Jan	6	Czech intellectuals issue manifesto on human rights		23	Holland: S Moluccans take hostages over independence
	9	US: Oakland Raiders win Super Bowl XI	Jul	2	Death of Russian novelist Vladimir Nabokov
	14	UK: Former PM Anthony Eden dies		5	Pakistan: Zulfikar Bhutto arrested in military coup
	17	Students and workers riot in Cairo over rising prices		21	Cambodians and Thais clash in major border skirmish
	17	US restores death penalty – Gary Gilmore executed		22	'Gang of Four' expelled from Chinese Communist Party
	20	Jimmy Carter sworn in as 39th President of the US		24	Egyptian President Sadat calls ceasefire with Libya
	29	IRA bombs London's West End	Aug	12	US: Space shuttle makes first test flight
Feb	7	El Salvador: General Carlos Romero elected President		16	Elvis Presley found dead, aged 42
	18	Archbishop of Uganda murdered by Amin's troops		19	US comedian Groucho Marx dies
	25	President Idi Amin detains 240 Americans in Uganda	Oct	3	India: Ex-PM Indira Gandhi arrested
	26	El Salvador: Rioters claim electoral fraud	Nov	4	United Nations ban arms sales to S Africa
Mar	7	Pakistan: Bhutto's People's Party wins election		20	Egypt's President Sadat addresses Israeli Parliament
	20	Morarji Desai defeats Mrs Gandhi in Indian election	Dec	5	Egypt breaks with Syria, Libya, Algeria and S Yemen
	27	Major air disaster in Tenerife as 2 jets collide on runway		24	Israeli PM Begin discusses peace with President Sadat
Apr	9	Spain legalises Communist Party after 38-year ban			*The Arts*
	22	Israeli PM Rabin resigns over money scandal			Spielberg's film *Close Encounters of the Third Kind*
	22	North Sea oil well blow-out causes huge slick			John Travolta stars in *Saturday Night Fever*
May	1	Istanbul: 39 people killed in May Day rally			Woody Allen's film *Annie Hall*
	17	Israel: Likud win election; Menachem Begin is PM			George Lucas's film *Star Wars*

Death of Biko

A storm of international protest greeted the announcement that the black consciousness leader Steve Biko had died in police detention in South Africa in September. Biko, 30, was one of a number of black leaders arrested under the 1977 security legislation. A post-mortem revealed brain damage and severe bruising. Denounced by the South African authorities as a violent revolutionary, Biko was described by the liberal journalist Donald Woods as 'quite simply the greatest man I have ever had the privilege to know'. His funeral in King William's Town on September 5th was attended by 15,000 people, including diplomats from 12 Western countries.

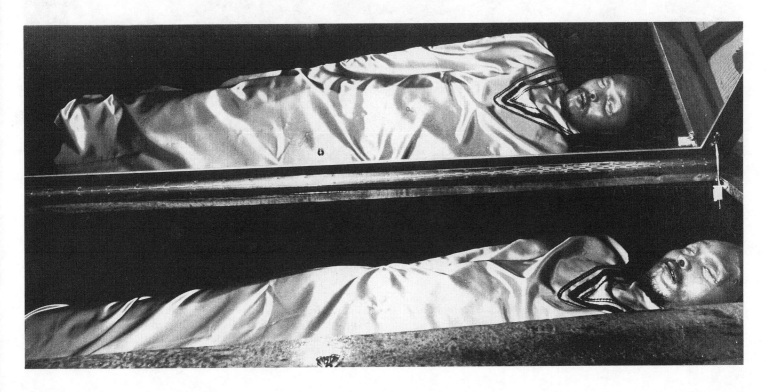

War in Rhodesia

The Rhodesian government had been at war with the Zimbabwean independence movements: ZANU (the Zimbabwe African National Union) and ZAPU (Zimbabwe African People's Union). And the conflict spilled over into neighbouring Mozambique and Zambia in 1977. Rhodesian forces raided Mozambique in search of ZANU fighters (led by Robert Mugabe). They also went into Zambia looking for supporters of Joshua Nkomo's ZAPU and causing widespread destruction.

Above: Refugees rebuild their homes destroyed during a Rhodesian raid on Mozambique.

Fighting continues in Angola

The Angolan civil war continued as the government and their Cuban allies sought to quell opposition outside their only relatively secure stronghold, the capital Luanda. The FNLA (supported by Zaire) claimed to control a third of the country in the north, and UNITA (led by the flamboyant Dr Jonas Savimbi) recovered from a government offensive launched at the end of 1976. By September 1977 they announced that ten of Angola's 16 provinces were in their hands.

Above: Domestic chores in a UNITA camp in southern Angola – cleaning guns and washing babies.

Idi Amin

The oppressive regime of Idi Amin, President of Uganda, came under increasing pressure. Amid accusations of mass murder, including that of the Anglican Archbishop of Uganda, Amin was not invited to the meeting of the Commonwealth Heads of State in 1977.

Bokassa is crowned

With the coronation of the self-styled 'Emperor' Bokassa (1921–), the Central African Republic became an Empire. Bokassa, the Republic's President, crowned himself at a lavish ceremony costing up to 20,000,000 dollars – a quarter of the country's annual income.

Conflict in Ethiopia

With full-scale wars in the Ogaden Desert against Somalia, conflict with secessionists in Tigre and Eritrea, a number of provincial uprisings and bloody civil war in Addis Ababa, Ethiopia was in utter turmoil.
Above: Militiamen parade in Addis Ababa before combat.

Mogadishu hijack

West German commandos ended the hijacking of a Lufthansa 737 in Mogadishu, Somalia, killing three of the four terrorists. The plane, seen here leaving Dubai, toured the Middle East as its captors demanded the release of 11 Red Army Faction members held in West Germany and two Palestinians in Turkey.

Pompidou Centre

The newly opened Pompidou Centre in Paris was already proving a popular attraction in a city known for architectural innovation since Eiffel built his tower there in the 19th century. The Centre, designed by Renzo Piano and the British architect Richard Rogers, consists of an enormous steel cage, constructed in rigid rectangles and supporting floor spaces capable of being used in many different ways. Through and outside the central cage, brightly coloured tubes carry services and convey people around the building, in the latter case often by escalator. This cultural and leisure complex, one of the great achievements of high-technology architecture, was to become the most visited building in Paris.

The boat people

Some 800,000 mainly Chinese and middle-class Vietnamese became refugees from the repressive communist regime of South Vietnam. The 'boat people', as they were known, took to the sea in whatever vessels they could muster for escape to the West. Left, 4000 people cram themselves aboard one ship. Many perished on their long, perilous journeys, falling victim to starvation, disease and piracy. Large numbers ended up in Hong Kong internment camps. The more fortunate landed in any country which would accept them, albeit unwillingly. Given the chance to settle, many not only survived but managed to thrive in various business enterprises.

Bravo blow-out

A serious blow-out in an oil well in the Norwegian sector of the North Sea caused widespread pollution in April. The accident, the first of its kind in almost a decade of offshore drilling in the area, happened at the Bravo Platform in the Ekofisk Field on April 22nd. Over the next eight days some 22,500 tons of oil escaped into the sea, covering about 4,000 square kilometres with a slick 1 to 2 millimetres deep and doing irreparable damage to marine life. A fire-boat sprayed water on to the oil, which was forced out almost at boiling point, in order to avoid an explosion (left). A subsequent inquiry blamed inadequate organisational and administrative systems for the disaster.

Air disaster in Tenerife

Five hundred and eighty-two people died on March 27th when two Boeing 747 jumbo jets collided on the runway at Los Rodeos airport, Tenerife. Both planes had been diverted to Tenerife. One, a Dutch KLM flight from Amsterdam, was taking off without final clearance when the accident happened.

The Grunwick dispute

Police clashed with trade union pickets outside the Grunwick film processing laboratory in Willesden, North London, in some of the bitterest scenes ever witnessed in a British industrial dispute. 'Flying pickets' from the Yorkshire coalfield lent their support to the striking workers. There were over 500 arrests.

Menachem Begin

Following the general election in Israel on May 17th, the right-wing Likud leader Menachem Begin formed a centre-right coalition government, ending 29 years of Labour domination.

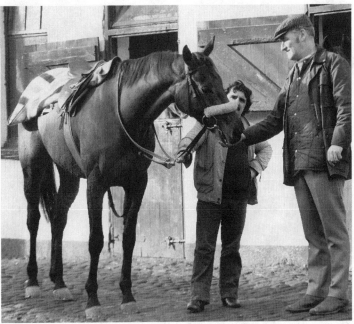

Red Rum

Red Rum made horse-racing history when he won the British Grand National for the third time, ridden by jockey Tommy Stack. Red Rum's previous victories were in 1973 and 1974.

Zia ul-Haq

On July 5th, the Army Chief of Staff General Mohammad Zia ul-Haq (1924–1988) ousted Pakistan's Prime Minister Zulfikar Bhutto in a coup.

Maria Callas

The beautiful American-born operatic soprano Maria Callas (1923–1977) died this year. Born of Greek parents, her most famous roles included *Medea*.

Bing Crosby

The American Bing Crosby (1904–1977), who co-starred with Bob Hope in the famous series of 'road' films, died while playing golf. He was 73.

Queen Elizabeth's Silver Jubilee

Enormous crowds gathered outside the Sydney Opera House in Australia to welcome Queen Elizabeth II during her Silver Jubilee tour of the Commonwealth in February and March. In Britain celebrations for the 25th anniversary of her coronation were held in the summer with great pomp and ceremony. On June 7th, the Queen and Prince Philip attended a service of thanksgiving at St Paul's Cathedral before going walkabout in the streets of London. Street parties were held countrywide.

1978

Jan	3	India: Ex-PM Mrs Gandhi expelled from Congress Party
	4	Chile: Pinochet uses plebiscite to increase his power
	13	Former US Vice-President Hubert Humphrey die
	15	US: Dallas Cowboys win Super Bowl XII
	23	Nicaragua: National strike in protest at Somoza govt
Feb	3	President Sadat visits US and Europe for peace talks
	12	Nicaragua: Sandinistas prepare for civil war
Mar	9	Somalia leaves Ethiopian territory, ending Ogadan War
	16	Rome: Former PM, Aldo Moro, is kidnapped
	18	Ex-PM of Pakistan, Bhutto, is sentenced to death
	21	Rhodesia: first time black ministers sworn into govt
Apr	4	Angolan govt in offensive on UNITA
	18	Second Panama Canal treaty ratified by US Senate
	27	Afghanistan: Govt leaders killed in bloody coup
May	4	S African troops raid SWAPO guerrilla bases in Angola
	11	Riots in Tehran as Muslims call for removal of Shah
	15	Former Australian PM Sir Robert Menzies dies
Jun	23	Italy: 29 members of Red Brigades sentenced to prison
Jul	7	Solomon Islands gain independence from British rule
	11	200 die in Spanish campsite explosion
Aug	6	Death of Pope Paul VI
	12	China and Japan in 10-year peace and friendship treaty
	13	Huge bomb in Beirut kills 150 Palestinians
	19	Iran: Many die in cinema fire begun by extremists
	22	Kenyan President Jomo Kenyatta dies
Sep	8	Iran: Anti-government demonstrations defy martial law
	10	Martial law is imposed in parts of Rhodesia
	16	Pakistan: Zia-ul-Haq becomes new Chief of State
	18	US: Carter, Sadat and Begin at Camp David summit
	25	US: 150 die in air disaster over San Diego, California
	29	Bulgarian defector Markov killed in London
	29	Pope John Paul I dies
Oct	31	Iran: Oil workers' strike halves oil production
Nov	3	USSR and Vietnam sign 25-year friendship treaty
	8	Death of US illustrator Norman Rockwell
	15	Death of US anthropologist Margaret Mead
Dec	5	USSR signs friendship pact with Afghanistan
	6	Spanish voters approve new constitution in referendum
	15	US and China to establish diplomatic relations
		The Arts
		Christopher Reeve in *Superman*
		Robert de Niro in film *The Deer Hunter*
		John Irving's novel *The World According to Garp*
		John Travolta stars in *Grease*
		Isaac Bashevis Singer wins Nobel Prize for Literature

Amoco Cadiz is wrecked

One of the world's worst oil pollution disasters occurred in March when the supertanker *Amoco Cadiz* ran on to rocks off Portsall on the coast of Brittany. The ship was on her way from the Persian Gulf to Rotterdam with 230,000 tonnes of crude oil when her steering gear failed in heavy seas. More than 100 miles of French beaches were polluted by the oil after the tanker broke in two. There was unprecedented destruction of marine and bird life, with millions of marine animals and molluscs being washed ashore. A subsequent inquiry criticised the vessel's captain, Pasquale Bardari, for his 'inexcusable delay' in asking for assistance.

Civil war in Nicaragua

The regime of General Anastasio Somoza came under increasing pressure, as workers and students went on strike and political alliances were formed to confront the government. The FSLN ('Sandinistas') fought Somoza's National Guard in a violent civil war and in August, 25 Sandinistas occupied the National Palace in the capital Managua. After securing the release of a large number of prisoners and a ransom, the Sandinistas fled to neighbouring Panama. They are seen (left) about to embark on their flight out of Nicaragua. The nature of Somoza's rule (described by local Roman Catholic bishops in 1978 as a 'state of terror'), and the depth of opposition to it, led the USA to withhold aid and to encourage a peaceful transfer of power to civilian elements.

Revolution in Afghanistan

Tanks and MiG-21 fighter planes attacked the presidential palace in Kabul as the government of Mohammed Daud was overthrown by a military coup in Afghanistan. The revolution erupted after a clamp-down on political dissent during which one opposition leader had been assassinated and others arrested. The President himself was massacred (together with members of his family) by the insurgents who assumed power as the Armed Forces Revolutionary Council on April 27th.

The Council, led by Colonel Abdul Qadir, appointed Mr Nur Mohammed Taraki as Prime Minister, banned all public meetings and announced that martial law would remain in force indefinitely. The new pro-Communist regime was recognised by the Soviet Union on April 30th and by Britain on May 6th.

The death throes of Rhodesia

After the failure of UDI – the Smith government's declaration of Rhodesian independence within the Commonwealth– pressure increased for an agreement to be reached with the moderate wing of ZAPU, under the leadership of Joshua Nkomo. By 1978 over 6,000 had been killed in the guerrilla warfare tactics of the ZANU, the militant group led by Ndabaningi Sithole. Smith's government and some Nationalist leaders finally agreed to form an interim government which would include black members, with majority rule as the eventual goal (see above right).

Ian Smith agrees timetable

In March Ian Smith, the Rhodesian Premier, agreed with Chief Chirau, Bishop Muzorewa and Mr Sithole a timetable for independence under black rule by December 31st, but civil war continued.

Golda Meir dies

The veteran Israeli leader Mrs Golda Meir died on December 8th at the age of 80. She had been Israel's Prime Minister from 1969 until her resignation in 1974.

P. W. Botha elected

P. W. Botha (1916–   ) was elected leader of the ruling National Party and the ninth Prime Minister of South Africa on September 28th. He succeeded B. J. Vorster who resigned for health reasons.

Ayatollah in waiting

As opposition to the Shah led to increasing unrest in Iran, calls grew for the return of the Ayatollah Ruholla Khomeini (above right), who had been in exile for 16 years. The 77-year-old spiritual leader of Iran's majority Shi'ite Muslims had transferred his headquarters to Pontchartrain on the outskirts of Paris, from where, despite repeated warnings from the French government, he issued regular directives to his militant followers in Iran.

Aldo Moro murdered

The body of the former Italian Prime Minister Aldo Moro was found in the back of a car in Rome on May 9th. He had been shot 11 times. Signor Moro had been kidnapped by members of the Red Brigades on March 16th.

Mass suicide in Jonestown

More than 900 members of a religious cult, the People's Temple, were found dead at their commune in Jonestown, Guyana. They had committed mass suicide by drinking cyanide at the behest of their leader, the Reverend Jim Jones.

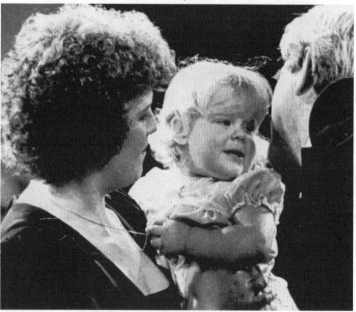

World chess champion

The temperamental chess grandmaster Viktor Korchnoi (1931–   ) (above right), who defected to the West in 1976, lost to fellow-Soviet Anatoly Karpov (1951–   ) in the world championship after a close match in the Philippines.

First test-tube baby

Louise Brown, the world's first test-tube baby, was born in a hospital in Manchester, England, on July 26th. The embryo had been implanted in her mother's womb after *in vitro* fertilisation in a pioneering operation by Dr Patrick Steptoe.

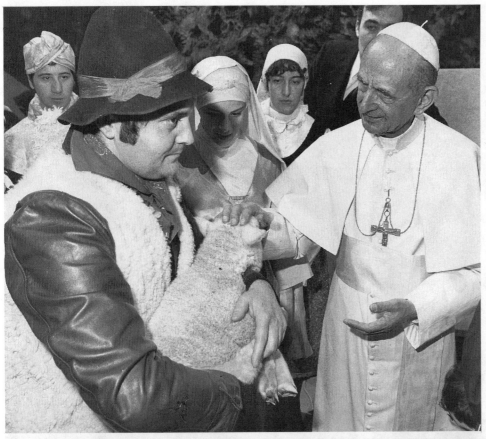

Three Popes in one year

The requiem mass for Aldo Moro was one of the last public appearances of Pope Paul VI (above left), who died of a heart attack on August 6th at the age of 80. In his 25-year reign he had taken an active role in international affairs and his funeral mass was attended by representatives of more than 100 countries.

On August 26th, a secret conclave of cardinals elected Cardinal Albino Luciani, the Patriarch of Venice, as the 263rd Pope (above right). His reign as John Paul I was to be very brief. On September 29th, he was found dead in his bed, apparently from a heart attack, after a pontificate of only 33 days – the shortest since 1605.

For the second time in a year, voting began in the Sistine Chapel to elect a successor to the throne of St Peter. On October 16th, the new Pope was named as Cardinal Karol Wojtyla, the Archbishop of Cracow. The 58-year-old Cardinal (left), the first non-Italian to be elected to the papacy for more than 400 years and the first Pole ever to hold the office, took the name John Paul II. The open-air mass celebrating his inauguration was attended by, among others, Dr Donald Coggan, the first Archbishop of Canterbury to attend the investiture of a Pope since England broke with the Roman Catholic Church in the 16th century.

Björn Borg's triple win

On July 8th the 22-year-old Swede Björn Borg (1956–   ) became the first man since Fred Perry in the 1930s to win the men's singles tennis championship three times in a row at Wimbledon.

Martina Navratilova beats Chris Evert

On July 7th, Martina Navratilova (1956–   ) won the Wimbledon ladies' singles trophy after beating Chris Evert in the finals of the tennis championship.

The Times dispute

Lord Thomson suspended publication of the British newspapers *The Times* and the *Sunday Times* in November as a result of prolonged disputes with printing trade unions.

Donald Woods escapes from South Africa

In January Donald Woods, the banned editor of the *Daily Despatch* of East London (Cape Province), arrived in England with his family after escaping from South Africa in disguise.

1979

Conflict in Afghanistan

Throughout the year the security situation in Afghanistan worsened as government forces battled against Muslim guerrilla rebels in many parts of the country. Half the population were living in areas under rebel control or in disputed regions, ruled by the Army during the day and by the insurgents at night. The largely unco-ordinated Muslim groups, based in neighbouring Pakistan, mounted attacks on Soviet citizens, and the government increasingly turned to the Soviet Union for military equipment and supplies. In December a new Soviet-backed government was installed in Kabul (below), and some 5,000 Soviet combat troops were reported to have entered the country.

Revolution in Iran

Popular opposition to the regime of Shah Mohammed Riza Pahlavi reached fever pitch in Iran during the early months of the year. The streets of Tehran and other major cities became battlegrounds, as opponents of the Shah staged vast demonstrations to protest against poverty and repression, particularly by the hated national intelligence and security organisation Savak. Encouraged by taped messages from the exiled Ayatollah Khomeini (now in Paris) which were circulated among Iran's mullahs, a wave of strikes in major industries brought the country and its economy to a virtual standstill. Statues of the Shah were torn down (above left) and many people were killed as the security forces tried to contain the unrest.

The Shah leaves Iran

On January 16th, the Shah and the Empress Farah left Iran and flew to Egypt for what was described as a 'vacation' but was to become a permanent exile. On February 1st, Ayatollah Khomeini returned to his country after 16 years in the political wilderness to be greeted with adulation by the three million people who had crowded into Tehran to welcome him (left). Ten days later the military withdrew to their barracks and the post-Shah administration of Dr Bakhtiar fell. Revolutionary Islamic government in Iran had begun.

Demands for Shah's extradition

Demands for the extradition of the Shah intensified towards the end of the year. Muslims besieged the hospital in New York City where he had arrived for medical treatment (above right). And in Iran itself a group of revolutionary 'students' occupied the American Embassy (opposite), taking its staff hostage and threatening to kill them unless the Shah was returned to face trial. The stage was set for a dangerous confrontation.

Vietnamese invade Cambodia

In Cambodia the tyrannical rule of 'Pol Pot' (real name Saloth Sar, above), was ended by Vietnamese invasion. The populace had suffered four years of assault from the Khmer Rouge and Pol Pot's legacy was appalling; all the towns had been emptied and the people subjected to psychological and physical torment with up to a quarter of them murdered. Despite this, the Khmer Rouge continued to represent Cambodia at the United Nations while Vietnam and the new Cambodian government were isolated by the international community. Above: Skulls piled up in a mass grave at a Khmer Rouge torture camp.

Nicaraguan revolution

On July 19th, after weeks of bloody civil war, the forces of the left-wing National Liberation Sandinista Front marched triumphantly into the Nicaraguan capital Managua. There were joyful celebrations in front of the Nicaraguan National Palace (top) as the dictator General Anastasio Somoza (1925–1980), deserted by his former allies the United States and by public opinion in Nicaragua itself, finally fled the country after 12 years of authoritarian power. During the bitter conflict Somoza's hated National Guard had been responsible for many atrocities, such as the machine-gunning of this couple's two teenage sons (above).

Fall of Amin

Following the Ugandan dictator Idi Amin's bloody incursion into neighbouring Tanzania in October the previous year, the Tanzanian President Julius Nyerere took spectacular revenge in January. Some 45,000 Tanzanian troops invaded Uganda, destroying the southern towns of Masaka and Mbarara before marching on the capital Kampala.

Despite aid from Colonel Gadaffi of Libya, Amin's forces could not resist for long and were soon routed by Nyerere's so-called 'army of liberation'. Amin himself fled the capital, leaving his incongruously suburban-looking house (above centre) and the

notorious State Research Bureau next door, where the flyblown bodies of Ugandans shot by his retreating men (above left) were only the last in a long line of people to be tortured and murdered there under his regime of terror. Widespread looting and lawlessness followed the arrival of the victorious Tanzanians, who then forged a path northwards into the West Nile district. Such resistance as they met was quickly overcome (top) and by June they had reached Uganda's northern border.

Meanwhile some 100,000 refugees, including many soldiers, had fled across the White Nile into southern Sudan (above).

Disaster at Three Mile Island

A wave of protests followed America's worst nuclear accident at a power station on Three Mile Island in Pennsylvania. Radioactivity was released into the atmosphere and the River Susquehanna when the uranium core of one of the plant's pressurised water reactors overheated in the early hours of March 28th. Thousands of people left their homes in the surrounding area as radiation inside the reactor building reached levels 75 times higher than those required to kill a human being. A subsequent inquiry criticised the National Regulatory Commission for its handling of the crisis.

SALT II

On June 18th, the US President Jimmy Carter and the Soviet leader Leonid Brezhnev signed the SALT II Treaty at the Hofburg Palace in Vienna. The treaty set equal ceilings for both sides on delivery systems for intercontinental ballistic missiles and established limits for the development of new weapons. Its 19 articles also made provision for the reduction of existing stocks of strategic offensive arms. Described by the two leaders as 'a substantial contribution to the prevention of nuclear war and the development of detente', the agreement was welcomed by NATO and the Politburo, but the US Senate refused to ratify it.

Airey Neave killed

On March 30th, Mr Airey Neave, Britain's Opposition Spokesman on Northern Irish affairs, was killed by an IRA car bomb as he was leaving the underground car park at the House of Commons in London.

Mrs Thatcher's triumph

On May 3rd, Mrs Margaret Thatcher, 53, became the first woman Prime Minister of Great Britain when the Conservative Party won the general election with an overall majority of 44.

Seb Coe

In just 41 days the 22-year-old British runner Sebastian Coe (1956–   ) broke three world records, for the 800 metres, the mile and the 1,500 metres, the last in Zürich (above) on August 15th.

Mountbatten murdered

Earl Mountbatten of Burma (1900–1979), the Queen's cousin, was killed on August 27th by an IRA bomb planted on his fishing boat at Mullaghmore in Ireland. He was 79.

Dame Gracie Fields

On February 20th, the much-loved singer Gracie Fields (1898–1979) was invested as a Dame Commander of the Most Excellent Order of the British Empire. She died on September 27th.

Death of a hero

John Wayne (1907–1979) died this year. The celebrated star of westerns and war films played his first major role in John Ford's *Stagecoach* (1939).

1980–1989

The 1980s

History may come to see in the 1980s a turning point not only in the relations between states, but also in the relationship between man and the natural world.

Perhaps the most remarkable changes in the international political scene came as a result of the accession of Mikhail Gorbachev to the leadership of the Soviet Union in 1985. The youngest member of Chernenko's Politburo, he brought with him an astonishingly fresh approach to the domestic and international problems of the Soviet Union, not least in admitting their existence and pledging himself to overcome them. The words *glasnost* and *perestroika* entered the international vocabulary as he launched his crusade for economic revitalisation and freedom from the bureaucratic and ideological shackles of the Brezhnev years, releasing in the process a dramatic tide of popular dissent in the satellite states of the Soviet bloc, which saw one entrenched Communist régime after another collapse in Eastern Europe in the closing months of the decade. The long-term effects of Gorbachev's policies have yet to be seen, especially in the Soviet Union itself, but their immediate effect has been to put East-West relations on a more constructive course than had seemed possible for many years.

Above all, though, the 1980s may come to be remembered as the decade in which concern for the environment soared to the top of the political agenda. The world's worst nuclear catastrophe, research into the so-called 'greenhouse effect' and revelations about the depletion of the world's ozone layer combined to bring green issues into the political mainstream after years of relegation to the margins of debate. Again, it is too early to tell what the long-term effects of this reappraisal will be, but there is now a widespread recognition that it is time to act. More immediate even than the issue of nuclear stockpiles, preserving the environment has become a matter of life and death.

Glasnost, perestroika and Eastern Europe

Glasnost – openness – and *perestroika* – reconstruction – are the terms which have come to be associated most closely with the campaign of the Soviet leader Mikhail Gorbachev to reform the economic and political machinery of the Soviet Union. Many of the traditional obstacles to East-West co-operation have been reduced in the years since he came to power. The release of such leading dissidents as Anatoly Scharansky and Andrei Sakharov reflected a wider relaxation of curbs on human rights – a relaxation that has brought its own problems for the Soviet Union in the upsurge of independence movements in the troubled Republics of Estonia, Armenia, Azerbaijan, Georgia, Latvia and Lithuania. Progress has also been made on the crucial issue of arms control, with the signing of the INF treaty, the first agreement ever to eliminate an entire category of offensive nuclear weapons. President Reagan's cold war rhetoric of the 'evil empire' thawed towards understanding at a series of superpower summits, and another major sticking point was removed with the withdrawal of Soviet troops from Afghanistan at the beginning of 1989.

Most dramatic of all, though, was the collapse of Communist rule in the Eastern European states during 1989 as, one by one, the governments of Poland, Hungary, Czechoslovakia, Bulgaria, East Germany, and even Stalinist Rumania toppled in the face of unprecedented public demand for democratic reform. Perhaps the most telling symbol of this remarkable torrent of change was the opening, after 28 years, of the Berlin Wall, which reunited thousands of East Germans with friends and family in the West and prompted serious discussion of German reunification.

Thatcher and Reagan

In Britain the country's first ever woman Prime Minister gave her name to a political movement. 'Thatcherism' has been defined in different ways by different people, but its effect on the fabric of British society is denied by no-one. Proclaiming the battle against inflation as her government's primary policy objective, Mrs Thatcher launched a campaign to regenerate Britain's recession-hit economy through control of the money supply, restraint of trade union power and a far-reaching programme of 'privatisation' of nationalised industries. Praised by many as achieving a new prosperity, her controversial policies were blamed by others for producing high levels of unemployment and a sharp division between the haves and the have-nots. One of the longest serving of Western leaders, Mrs Thatcher has also played a significant role on the world stage, perhaps most conspicuously in 1982 during the Falklands conflict with Argentina. In the United States the policies of President Ronald Reagan sought to effect a similar rebirth of national self-esteem after the setbacks of the 1970s, and the so-called 'special relationship' gained new life from the two leaders' personal closeness.

The environment

The Chernobyl nuclear accident, which left much of Europe contaminated by radioactivity, made many people realise that environmental crisis is no respecter of national borders. Concern about the natural environment has been further heightened by the discovery that damage to the earth's ozone layer by chlorofluorocarbons (CFCs) and other chemicals is much more serious than had previously been thought. Already there is evidence of an increase in cases of skin cancer as a result of depletion of the ozone layer, which screens out the sun's harmful ultra-violet rays, and concerted action is now being taken to restrict the use of the chemicals concerned. There are also moves to arrest the wholesale destruction of the earth's tropical rainforests. This is held partly responsible for the 'greenhouse effect', which could produce disastrous changes in climate. For the first time, the urgency of the challenge facing mankind has been recognised by the world's governments. It remains to be seen how we shall meet that challenge in the 1990s and beyond.

Pages 470–1: A refugee camp in Ethiopia, October 1984.

1980

Jan	6	Indira Gandhi's Congress Party wins Indian election
Feb	18	Pierre Trudeau is Canada's Prime Minister again
	22	Austrian artist Oscar Kokoshka dies
	24	US Eric Heiden wins 5 Olympic gold medals
Mar	4	Robert Mugabe elected PM of Zimbabwe
	25	UK: Robert Runcie is new Archbishop of Canterbury
Apr	7	US severs relations with Iran
	18	Zimbabwe becomes independent
May	4	Yugoslav President Tito dies
	18	Mt St Helens volcano erupts in US
Jun	2	West Bank Arab Mayors maimed by bombs
	7	US writer Henry Miller dies
	12	Japanese PM Ohira dies 10 days before elections
	13	Auto workers strike in USSR
Jul	5	Björn Borg wins 5th consecutive Wimbledon
	11	Sick US hostage Richard Queen released by Iran
	19	22nd Olympic Games open in Moscow
	27	Deposed Shah of Iran dies in Cairo
	30	Israel makes undivided Jerusalem its capital

Aug	2	Bomb blast in Bologna, Italy, kills 76
	14	Polish workers strike and seize Gdansk shipyard
	15	Wreck of *Titanic* found
Sep	12	Bloodless military coup in Turkey
	17	Ousted President Somoza of Nicaragua assassinated
	21	Iraqui troops cross Iranian border
Oct	3	Terrorists bomb Paris synagogue
	10	Algeria hit by earthquake
	21	US: Philadelphia Phillies win World Series
	23	Soviet Premier Kosygin resigns (dies Dec 19)
	23	Screen actors end 94-day strike in US
Nov	4	Ronald Reagan wins US Presidency
	23	Severe earthquake hits S Italy
Dec	4	Portugal's PM Francisco Sà Carneiro dies in plane crash
	26	Algerian ambassador to Iran visits US hostages
		The Arts
		William Golding's novel *Rites of Passage*
		Robert Redford's film *Ordinary People*
		Umberto Eco's novel *The Name of the Rose*

Oil rig disaster

Tragedy struck the booming North Sea oil industry in March when the semi-submersible mobile rig the *Alexander Kielland* capsized in heavy seas 200 miles off the coast of Norway with the loss of 123 lives. The 10,000-ton rig, which was being used as an accommodation platform for workers on Phillips Petroleum's Edda field at the time of the accident, keeled over and sank in 80 metres of water when one of its five supporting legs collapsed. The death toll made this one of the worst accidents in the history of North Sea oil exploration and urgent checks were ordered on rigs of a similar design. The photograph (below) shows the upturned feet of the rig, which was towed to Haugesund for examination.

Soviet troops in Afghanistan

Following the airlift of Soviet troops into Afghanistan in the closing days of 1979, some 85,000 men were reported to be operational in the country by the end of January. The Soviet intervention, which was denied by Leonid Brezhnev, was met by widespread condemnation in the West and by the imposition of sanctions against the USSR by the United States. As diplomatic activity intensified to try to find a solution to the crisis, Soviet and Afghan troops in Afghanistan itself attempted to consolidate their power over the country beyond Kabul. It was the beginning of what was to prove a long and bitter war against the Moslem *mujahedin* rebels, whose guerrilla tactics were to prove as damaging to the forces of the Soviet Union as those of the Viet Cong had to the United States in Vietnam.

The new US President

Relaxing on board an Air Force DC-9, President-elect Ronald Reagan and his wife Nancy fly across country to Washington, DC for the first time since Reagan defeated President Carter in the elections. Reagan won 489 electoral votes, far more than the 270 needed to win, while Carter got only 49, which was a big drop from the 297 by which he had beaten President Gerald Ford, four years earlier.

Birth of Solidarity

Poland was engulfed in a tidal wave of industrial unrest from July to September after strikes triggered by a rise in meat prices took on a political dimension which threatened the future of the government itself. Stoppages paralysed the shipyards of the Baltic coast, with 17,000 workers occupying the Lenin yard at Gdansk (above left). Panic buying led to food shortages in Warsaw as the strikers demanded the legalisation of independent trade unions, the end of press censorship and the release of imprisoned dissidents. In September the authorities were forced to concede and on September 17th the independent National Committee of Solidarity convened in Gdansk, electing the shipworkers' leader Lech Walesa (1947–   ), shown here (above right), as its Chairman.

The Iran hostage crisis

Relations between the United States and the regime of the Ayatollah Khomeini in Iran reached a new low when American action to end the hostage crisis went disastrously wrong.

Diplomatic measures

The 53 American hostages had been held by a group of revolutionary students in the US Embassy (top left) and the Iranian Foreign Ministry in Tehran since November 1979, their captors demanding the extradition of the Shah. Khomeini threatened to put the hostages on trial as spies and there was a flurry of diplomatic activity on their behalf by the USA, the Palestinian Liberation Organisation and even the Pope. In January the United Nations Secretary-General Kurt Waldheim visited Iran for talks, but the hostages remained incarcerated. On April 7th, President Carter broke off diplomatic relations with Iran and announced a further package of economic sanctions. On April 24th, he launched a raid to release the hostages by force.

The raid

The operation was a catastrophe. Ninety commandos from a special anti-terrorist unit called the 'Blue Light Squad' took off for Iran under cover of darkness with eight Sikorsky helicopters and six Hercules transport planes. However, they were forced to land in a remote desert in the east of Iran when three of the helicopters developed faults. Deciding to abandon the operation, they refuelled for take-off, but in the process one of the helicopters collided with a transport plane, killing eight people. The rest of the team flew out, leaving the desert sands littered with the burnt-out remains of their planes and the bodies of their colleagues (above).

In Iran, reaction to the failure of the raid was jubilant, with crowds chanting and cheering in the streets (bottom left). The remains of the dead men were flown to Tehran, where the Ayatollah Khalkhali displayed and mutilated them at a ghoulish press conference in the Embassy.

The Iranian Embassy siege

This year saw another dramatic operation to rescue hostages, again involving Iranians and again centered on embassy buildings. This time, however, the scene was a cream-washed Georgian villa in the fashionable West End of London and the operation was a striking success.

The terrorists' demands

The rescue was the culmination of six days of tense bargaining between the British authorities and a group of Iranian terrorists who had occupied the Embassy on April 30th. The gunmen, calling themselves the Group of the Martyr, belonged to a minority Arab group and were demanding the release of 91 fellow Arabs imprisoned under the Ayatollah Khomeini's revolutionary regime in the Iranian province of Khuzestan. They threatened to kill their 26 hostages and blow up the Embassy unless their demands, which included a plane to fly them out of the country, were met. Negotiations reached a stalemate, the terrorists extending their deadlines and reducing their demands, until finally they asked only for a safe passage out of Britain. On May 5th, however, the siege entered a new phase when the gunmen shot dead two of the hostages.

The SAS storms the Embassy

The same day astonished television viewers saw a crack squad of the British Special Air Service (SAS) storm the Embassy in a meticulously planned raid. Smoke and flames billowed from the elegant windows as the hooded black-uniformed SAS men used explosive devices to cover their entry, some bursting in from the balcony at the front of the building (above), while others abseiled down the walls and swung in through windows at the rear. In a matter of minutes, five of the six gunmen had been shot dead and all the surviving hostages were released. The building itself was gutted by fire from the explosions (right).

Milton Obote returns to Uganda

Dr Milton Obote (1924–   ), the former President of Uganda, was greeted by cheering crowds when he returned to his country from Tanzania on May 27th. He announced his intention of standing in the forthcoming leadership elections.

Queen Beatrix of the Netherlands

On April 30th, Princess Beatrix (above left) was installed as Queen of the Netherlands in a symbolic coronation ceremony in Amsterdam's Nieuwe Kerk. She succeeded her mother, Queen Juliana (above right), who abdicated on her 71st birthday.

Thalidomide

In November the British newspaper *The Sunday Times* was awarded costs by the European Court in its case against the government ban on an article about thalidomide.

Peter Sellers dies

The British actor and comedian Peter Sellers (1926–1980) died at the age of 54. He rose to fame in radio's *The Goon Show* and went on to a distinguished comic film career.

Daley Thompson wins gold medal

Daley Thompson (1958–) won the first ever British gold medal for the decathlon at the Moscow Olympics in July.

Alexandra Palace fire

Alexandra Palace in North London – which contained the largest concert hall in Europe – was burned out in July. More than 200 firemen fought the blaze.

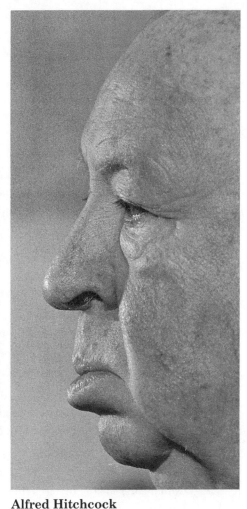

Alfred Hitchcock

The British film director Alfred Hitchcock (1899–1980) died in April at the age of 80. A master of suspense, he was famous for films such as *The Birds* and *Psycho*.

Cecil Beaton

The British photographer and designer Sir Cecil Beaton (1904–1980) died at his home in Wiltshire, England, at the age of 76.

John Lennon murdered

The former Beatle John Lennon (1940–1980) was shot dead in New York City on December 8th. He was 40.

Elton John in Central Park

The colourful British rock musician Elton John (1947–) gave an open-air concert in New York City's Central Park.

1981

Jan	1	Greece joins EEC
	5	UK: Yorkshire Ripper murderer arrested
	25	Mao's widow and 'Gang of Four' sentenced to death
	25	US: Oakland Raiders win Super Bowl
Feb	9	General Jaruzelski becomes Polish Premier
	9	US rock singer Bill Haley dies
	22	Iran frees 3 British missionaries
Mar	2	Pakistanis hijack airliner
	26	UK: Social Democratic Party formed
	30	US: President Reagan shot
Apr	4	Italian Red Brigades leader arrested
	12	US launches first space shuttle *Columbia*
	12	UK: Race riots erupt in Brixton, London
May	5	Hunger striker Bobby Sands dies in Belfast prison
	10	Socialist François Mitterrand elected French President
	13	Pope John Paul II shot in Vatican City
Jun	7	Israel bombs Iraqi nuclear reactor
	22	Bani-Sadr ousted from Iran's Presidency
	29	China: Hu Yaobang replaces Hua as Party Chairman
	30	UK: Blanks fired at the Queen in London
	30	Ireland: Garret Fitzgerald becomes PM
Jul	10	UK: Widespread youth riots
	18	US: 111 killed when hotel collapses in Kansas City
	31	Baseball strike in US ends after 7 weeks
Aug	3	US air traffic controllers begin strike
	19	US downs 2 Libyan jet fighters
Sep	15	President Sadat expels 1,500 Soviets from Egypt
	20	Belize gains independence
Oct	3	Belfast Maze Prison hunger strike ends
	6	President Sadat assassinated in Cairo
	13	Hosni Mubarak elected as Egypt's new President
Nov	9	U San Yu elected President of Burma
	30	US and USSR begin arms talks in Geneva
Dec	10	USSR: Sakharovs end hunger strike
	11	Argentina's President Viola ousted
	13	Martial law imposed on Poland
	27	Songwriter Hoagy Carmichael dies in US
	31	Jerry Rawlings directs successful coup in Ghana

The Arts

Salman Rushdie's novel *Midnight's Children*

Picasso's *Guernica* returned to Spain from New York

Meryl Streep in film *The French Lieutenant's Woman*

Steven Spielberg's film *Raiders of the Lost Ark*

Hugh Hudson's film *Chariots of Fire*

Andrew Lloyd Webber's musical *Cats*

Royal wedding

In the media event of the decade, the Prince of Wales and Lady Diana Spencer were married at St Paul's Cathedral in London on July 29th. An estimated 750 million people worldwide watched the pageantry on television, and the day of the wedding was declared a public holiday in Great Britain.

The big day

The festivities began the previous day when Prince Charles lit the first of a chain of 102 beacons across the British Isles and thousands of people crowded into London's Hyde Park to watch a spectacular firework display in honour of the royal couple. On the morning of the wedding day itself, the streets of the capital were thronged with well-wishers, many of whom had camped out for days beforehand. The Royal Family left Buckingham Palace at about 10 a.m., Prince Charles travelling in the last of a procession of carriages. When they arrived at St Paul's, the bridegroom advanced to his place flanked by his two 'supporters', Prince Andrew and Prince Edward, and preceded by the Admirals of the Fleet. Lady Diana arrived with her father Earl Spencer in the Glass Coach used by King George V at his coronation in 1910. She was accompanied by five bridesmaids and two pageboys who carried the 25-foot train of her ivory silk taffeta dress, the design of which had been a closely guarded secret.

After the event

After the vows the Prince and Princess walked down the red-carpeted aisle together (left) and waved from the cathedral steps (right) before riding back to the Palace in an open carriage. The newly-weds made the traditional appearance on the balcony of Buckingham Palace and delighted their audience with an unprecedented royal kiss (above) before leaving in an open landau for the first stage of their honeymoon.

President Sadat assassinated

On October 6th, President Mohammed Anwar el Sadat of Egypt was murdered by Islamic fundamentalist gunmen in Cairo. The shooting happened at 1 p.m. during the annual military parade to commemorate the beginning of the Egyptian offensive in the 1973 Arab–Israeli war. A lorry in the procession stopped in front of the rostrum where the President and other luminaries were watching a fly-past of Egyptian Air Force jets. Armed men climbed out and ran towards Sadat, hurling grenades and opening fire with automatic weapons. The President and seven others fell, mortally wounded (left). Sadat was flown to the Maadi military hospital where he died an hour and 40 minutes later.

Sadat's funeral on October 10th was attended by only one Arab head of state. He had isolated himself in the Arab world by the rapprochement with Israel which had won him and Menachem Begin the Nobel Peace Prize in 1978 and led to a peace treaty between the two countries in 1979. Iraq, Libya, Syria and the Palestinian Liberation Organisation openly applauded his assassination.

Reagan assassination attempt

Just ten weeks after his inauguration as President of the United States, Ronald Reagan became the victim of a bizarre assassination attempt. As the President left a hotel in Washington D.C., where he had been addressing a trade union convention, six shots were fired. Security men closed ranks around Reagan as he fell to the pavement (above). The President was rushed to the George Washington University Hospital where he underwent a two-hour operation to remove a bullet from his left lung. His assailant, John Warnock Hinckley, the 25-year-old son of an oil executive, was immediately arrested. He had apparently planned the shooting in order to impress the film actress Jodie Foster, whom he had never met but with whom he was obsessed.

Pope shot

Pope John Paul II was seriously wounded in a shooting incident in Rome on May 13th. He was hit in the stomach while driving in his open-topped 'Popemobile' among some 10,000 pilgrims in St Peter's Square. As he was driven to hospital for a five-hour life-saving operation, the gunman (a 23-year-old Turk named Mehmet Ali Agca) was apprehended by police.

Solidarity

Strikes and industrial unrest continued in Poland (top left: Warsaw during a transport strike) where relations between the government and the free trade union Solidarity deteriorated badly towards the end of the year. In September the union held its first national congress in Gdansk (left) and re-elected Lech Walesa (top right) as Chairman. However, it also put forward economic policies which the authorities saw as a bid for political party status. When Solidarity proposed a national referendum on a vote of no confidence in the government, the Polish leader General Jaruzelski (above) arrested almost all the union's leadership and declared martial law.

483

Vietnamese boat people

Refugees continued to risk death and piracy on the high seas in order to flee the new Communist regime in Vietnam. In the first eight weeks of the year, 451 boat people arrived in Hong Kong (left) – twice as many as in the same period in 1980. In neighbouring Macao, 240 refugees were arriving every day. Many of them came from China (which had taken 250,000 refugees since 1979), and the Hong Kong government asked the Chinese authorities to increase surveillance along its coast.

Unrest in Spain

It was a year of political violence in Spain. In February members of the Civil Guard burst into the *Cortes* (Parliament building) in Madrid in an attempted military coup. The following month there was trouble from the military wing of ETA, the Basque separatist movement. Ignoring the ceasefire declared by the political wing at their press conference (left), they murdered a police commissioner and two army officers. Troops were sent into the Basque provinces to assist the police but terrorist incidents continued, including a bank siege in Barcelona, a bomb attack on a car carrying the King's personal staff, and a number of kidnappings.

Bobby Sands dies

On May 5th, Bobby Sands became the first of ten Provisional IRA hunger-strikers to die in the so-called 'H blocks' of Belfast's controversial Maze Prison. Sands was serving a 14-year sentence for firearms offences; his protest was in support of demands for the reintroduction of special category status for Republican prisoners and had lasted 65 days. During that time he had been elected to the Westminster Parliament in a by-election in the Northern Irish constituency of Fermanagh and South Tyrone. On May 7th, he was buried in a Republican plot in West Belfast's Milltown cemetery (left).

US hostages released

Intense diplomatic activity by the Algerian government in the closing months of 1980 led to the release from captivity of the 52 US hostages in Iran (left). The end of their 444-day ordeal came on January 20th after the USA agreed to freeze the assets of the deposed Shah, end trade sanctions and unfreeze Iran's assets in the USA. They were released the day Ronald Reagan was sworn in as US President, but it was ex-President Carter who greeted the released hostages as they disembarked in Wiesbaden, West Germany.

Riots on streets of Britain

Serious unrest broke out on Britain's inner-city streets when police were attacked by black and white youths following an incident in Brixton, South London. Many buildings and vehicles were gutted (above left) and there were 779 reported crimes as Brixton was swept by three days of violence. In July the rioting spread to Southall in West London where fighting broke out between white and Asian groups. In Toxteth (above right), a dockland area of Liverpool, police used CS gas for the first time in mainland Britain to control gangs of youths who ran riot through the streets, throwing petrol bombs.

Tutu meets Runcie

In April Bishop Desmond Tutu of South Africa (1931–   ), General Secretary of the South African Council of Churches, visited London for talks with Dr Robert Runcie (1921–   ), the Archbishop of Canterbury, at Lambeth Palace. Tutu faced confiscation of his passport on his return to South Africa.

The Deptford fire

Thirteen black people died when fire swept through a house in Deptford, South London, during an all-night party on January 19th. Suspicions grew that the incident was a racist attack and the area became the focus of protests by members of the West Indian community. An enquiry began into the causes of the fire.

Yorkshire Ripper arrested

Four years of terror came to an end for women in the north of England when Peter Sutcliffe, 35, a long-distance lorry driver from Bradford, was arrested and charged with the 'Yorkshire Ripper' murders. Sutcliffe, seen here on his wedding day, pleaded guilty to 13 killings.

US space shuttle

The first flight of the US space shuttle *Columbia* began with a successful lift-off from the Kennedy Space Center in Florida on April 12th.

The 'Gang of Four'

In March the new Social Democratic Party was launched in Britain by four former Labour MPs: Roy Jenkins, David Owen, William Rodgers and Shirley Williams.

Natalie Wood

Natalie Wood (1938–1981) began her successful film career at the age of three. She died by drowning – thought to have lost her footing while boarding a dinghy.

Victory for Champion

British jockey Bob Champion, (1948–) who had been given eight months to live when diagnosed as having cancer in 1980, won the Grand National on Aldaniti.

Steve Davis wins

The 23-year-old snooker player Steve Davis (1957–) beat Doug Mountjoy to win the world championship in Sheffield, Northern England, in April.

McEnroe beats Borg

Temperamental young American John McEnroe (1959–) became the new Wimbledon tennis champion, beating Björn Borg.

1982

Israel in Lebanon

Months of mounting tension in the Middle East came to a head in June when Israel launched a full-scale invasion of Lebanon. The operation, code-named 'Peace for Galilee', had the declared aim of driving the Palestinian Liberation Organisation (PLO) out of bases near Israel's northern border. However, the invasion force of some 90,000 troops pushed on to Beirut in house-to-house fighting (above centre), leaving coastal cities in ruins and trapping many PLO fighters, including Yasser Arafat (top), in the capital as they surrounded it. By the time a ceasefire was declared on June 25th, Israeli tanks had advanced to the 'green line' dividing Christian East and Muslim West Beirut.

The Falklands conflict

From April to June the South Atlantic became the focus of world attention as Britain and Argentina went to war over the Falkland Islands. The conflict began on April 2nd when Argentinian forces invaded the islands in support of a long-standing claim to sovereignty. The 70 British Royal Marines stationed on the islands were overwhelmed. On April 3rd, the dependency of South Georgia was also occupied and by April 12th there were some 10,000 Argentinian troops on the islands (opposite top).

Britain took swift action. A large task force was assembled and set sail for the South Atlantic (opposite centre). During the three weeks it took to cover the 8,000 miles to the Falklands there was intense diplomatic activity by the USA and others to find a peaceful solution to the crisis.

At the end of April British forces recaptured South Georgia and imposed a 200-mile total exclusion zone around the Falklands. On May 2nd, Argentina's second-largest warship the *General Belgrano* (top) was sunk 30 miles south of the zone, and on May 4th the British destroyer HMS *Sheffield* (above) was struck by an Argentinian Exocet missile. British troops established a bridgehead on East Falkland on May 21st from which they advanced over the next week to take Goose Green and Darwin after fierce fighting. A second bridgehead was established on June 8th near the capital Port Stanley, which fell after further heavy fighting on June 14th. The same day the Argentinian forces surrendered to the British commander of land forces. The hostilities had cost 254 British and 750 Argentinian lives.

Bombings in London parks

IRA bombs claimed 11 lives and injured more than 50 people in the centre of London on July 20th. The first of the two explosions occurred at 10.43 a.m. in Hyde Park as members of the Queen's Household Cavalry were making their way to Whitehall for ceremonial guard duty. Four soldiers were killed and many civilians wounded by the bomb, which was packed with four- and six-inch nails. The full force of the explosion was taken by the cavalry horses (left), many of which had to be destroyed. The second bomb went off at 12.55 p.m. under a bandstand in Regent's Park where members of the Royal Green Jackets were giving a concert. Seven soldiers died and 28 people were injured.

The Iran–Iraq War

With the beginning of 1982 the war between Iran and Iraq entered its 16th month. The military stalemate which had bogged the two sides down in a series of inconclusive battles, and which may already have claimed as many as 100,000 lives, was broken by a new Iranian offensive in March. The action was one of the most decisive of the war. Iranian troops recaptured some 850 square miles of land in Khuzestan which the Iraqis had gained after their attack on Iran in 1980.

At the end of March Iranian military officials claimed to have taken 15,500 Iraqi troops prisoner, some of whom are shown (left) at a camp outside Tehran. By May the Ayatollah Khomeini's forces had taken the key border town of Khorromshahr and invaded Iraq itself. Over the following months the Iraqis were driven out of Iran almost completely, and President Saddam Hussein reacted to his troops' losses on land by launching a series of air attacks on Iranian oil installations in the Gulf.

Meanwhile, all political and diplomatic efforts to put an end to the fighting seemed doomed to failure. Iraq called for a ceasefire as the war began to turn against it, but Khomeini was now determined to pursue the fight until he brought down President Hussein's regime. As the death toll mounted, and younger and younger recruits were sent to the front, it seemed as if the slaughter would continue indefinitely.

PLO leave Beirut

Some of the 1,500 Palestinian fighters forced to leave the war-torn city of Beirut give victory signs to supporters gathered to greet them at the harbour gate in Larnaca, Cyprus. In further attempts to destroy terrorist bases, Israeli jets had bombed Moslem West Beirut, despite appeals for restraint from the US government. The guerrillas were allowed to go with one gun each, leaving behind rocket-propelled grenade-launchers and other sophisticated weaponry.

It was hoped that the election of Bashir Gemayel, the Christian leader, as Lebanon's President would ease negotiations for the later withdrawal of the Israelis and Syrians, but he was killed by a bomb before he could take up the post. In the end his brother was sworn in as President.

Unrest in Poland

Following the imposition of martial law and the arrest of leading members of the independent trade union Solidarity at the end of 1981, there was continuing unrest in Poland. In May more than 3,000 people were arrested when police used teargas grenades and water cannons to break up anti-government demonstrations in Warsaw (left).

There were also serious disturbances in Szczecin, Wroclaw, the steel town of Nowa Huta and the Baltic port of Gdansk (birthplace of Solidarity) where some 10,000 people clashed with security forces in August. In October Solidarity and Rural Solidarity were outlawed by the authorities, but the Solidarity leader Lech Walesa, who had been held in isolation for almost a year, was finally released on November 12th.

Boat people rescued

On July 26th, the West German rescue ship the *Cap Anamur* (left) entered its home port of Hamburg. On board the converted freighter were 285 Vietnamese boat people, refugees from the Communist regime which succeeded the American withdrawal from Vietnam in 1979.

This was the *Cap Anamur*'s last rescue mission. For three years it had patrolled the South China Seas with a medical team from the Committee of German Emergency Doctors and had rescued a total of 9,500 refugees. It was estimated that as many as 80 per cent of Vietnamese boat people had been victims of acts of piracy on the seas, and stories of robbery, murder, abduction and rape were commonplace among those still arriving in many of the world's ports.

The *Mary Rose*

On October 11th, the *Mary Rose*, the flagship of Henry VIII's fleet, was raised from the seabed off Southsea in Hampshire, England. The operation was the culmination of 17 years of research on the wreck, involving almost 25,000 dives. At 9.03 a.m. the ship's hull emerged from the water for the first time since it sank 437 years earlier. There was a heart-stopping moment when part of the lifting frame gave way, but the ship was successfully mounted on a barge (above) and taken to dry land.

Potomac air crash

More than 70 people were killed when a Florida Air jet plunged into the frozen Potomac River in Washington D.C. during a heavy snowstorm on January 13th.

Birth of a royal heir

On June 21st, the Prince and Princess of Wales celebrated the birth of their first son. The young prince, second in line to the throne, was christened William Arthur Philip Louis.

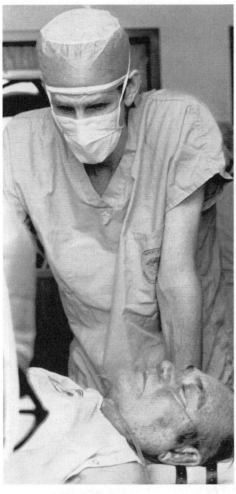

First artificial heart

Dr Barney B. Clark, 61, received the world's first artificial heart in a 7½-hour operation performed by Dr William DeVries in Utah, USA.

Pope at Anglican service

Pope John Paul II made history in Canterbury Cathedral on May 29th as the first Pope to attend an Anglican service in Britain.

Socialist landslide in Spain

Felipe González (1942–   ), aged 40, became Europe's youngest Prime Minister when his Socialist Workers' Party swept to power in Spain's elections on October 28th.

Rainer Werner Fassbinder

The German film director Rainer Werner Fassbinder (1946–1982) died at the age of 36. He had made more than 40 films.

Henry Fonda

The American actor (1905–1982), died in August after winning an Oscar for his last film *On Golden Pond*.

Princess Grace and Ingrid Bergman

The world of show business mourned the deaths of Princess Grace of Monaco (above left) and Ingrid Bergman (above right).

1983

Jan	3	Poland forms new labour unions
	7	Guatemala to get US arms
Feb	2	USSR and US resume START talks in Geneva
	25	US dramatist Tennessee Williams dies
Mar	2	Pope John Paul II visits Central America
	5	Labour leader Bob Hawke wins Australian elections
	8	UK composer William Walton dies
	14	OPEC forced to cut oil prices
	23	US: Reagan proposes 'Star Wars' defence system
Apr	12	US: Chicago gets first black mayor
	24	Turkey restores political parties
May	21	US makes AIDS top health priority
Jun	9	Tory Party led by Thatcher re-elected in UK
	9	Soares named Portuguese Premier
	16	Yuri Andropov elected Soviet President
	18	Sally Ride becomes first US woman in space
Jul	15	Armenians bomb Paris airport
	21	Poland ends martial law
	27	US: Pershing II missile fails test for third time
	29	UK: Actor David Niven dies
	29	Spanish film director Luis Bunuel dies
Aug	4	Bettino Craxi becomes Italy's first Socialist Premier
	5	Bomb kills 19 at Lebanese mosque
	21	Philippines: Benigno Aquino assassinated in Manila
Sep	1	Soviets shoot down S Korean airliner
	2	Israel's Premier Begin resigns; Yitzhak Shamir elected
	10	Peru lifts state of emergency
Oct	5	Lech Walesa awarded Nobel Peace Prize
	19	Grenada's PM Malcolm Bishop killed in coup
	23	Beirut car bomb kills US and French soldiers
Nov	14	First US Cruise missiles arrive in Britain
	24	Israel and PLO swap prisoners
	26	UK: £2.6 million in gold stolen from Heathrow airport
Dec	13	Turkey gets new government with Turgut Ozal as PM
	17	London: IRA bomb kills 5 in Harrods store

The Arts

Philip Roth's novel *The Anatomy Lesson*

Shirley MacLaine in film *Terms of Endearment*

US invades Grenada

In the small Caribbean island of Grenada, a military coup had ousted the moderate faction of the ruling New Jewel Movement. Prime Minister Maurice Bishop and members of his Cabinet had been executed and a 'Revolutionary Military Council' established.

President Reagan described the regime as a 'threat to the security of the United States', claiming that a new airport being built with Cuban assistance was a military facility. In October the United States mounted Operation 'Urgent Fury' and invaded the island, meeting unexpectedly fierce resistance from Grenadan troops. Here (below), a Chinook helicopter has been shot down on a Grenadan beach. American forces then left the island in the hands of a pan-Caribbean force, pending new elections.

Massacres in Assam

Thousands of people died as intercommunal violence swept the Indian state of Assam, focused on the State Assembly elections on February 14th. The bloodshed took place against a background of hostility to the estimated one million Bengali refugees who had fled to Assam before the formation of Bangladesh. Troops were sent into the Nelli area of the Nowgong district after hundreds of villagers were massacred on February 18th (above). Up to 500 Bengalis were reported killed on Oppidaya island and as many as 1,000 in the Mangaldoi district. By the end of March some observers estimated the total death toll as 3,000.

747 jumbo shot down

All 269 passengers and crew were presumed dead after Soviet fighters shot down a South Korean Boeing 747 airliner in Soviet airspace on September 1st. The Soviet Union accused the plane, which had veered off course after leaving Alaska, of spying and failing to respond to warnings. While relatives grieved, there was widespread Western condemnation of the shooting.

Contras in Nicaragua

In Nicaragua the anti-government Contra guerrillas continued their efforts to destabilise the country. The vital oil facilities at Corinto were attacked (above), leading to evacuation of the town and a fuel shortage. President Reagan attempted to increase funding for the Contras, but the House of Representatives reduced the appropriation and sought control over expenditure.

Beirut

Throughout the year anarchy reigned in the Lebanese capital Beirut, as opposing factions fought for supremacy on the streets, reducing the city (which had once been the playground of the wealthy in the Middle East) to a ruined shell.

Bomb attack against US Embassy

The international peacekeeping force, which had been stationed in Beirut since August 1982, was subjected to continual attacks and harassment by militia groups. Resentment at the presence of the US contingent culminated on April 18th in a suicide bomb attack against the US Embassy. Sixty people died and more than 100 were injured when a van packed with explosives was driven into the building, leaving it a smoking ruin (opposite, top left).

Violence escalates

The general lawlessness escalated in May after Israel agreed to withdraw its troops. Druze militiamen stationed in the hills overlooking the city shelled Christian and Lebanese Army positions in the suburbs. Masked Shi'ite fighters put up barricades in the southern suburbs (opposite, top right and bottom) and heavily armed factions battled it out in alleys and burned-out buildings. Kidnappings became commonplace, and the government seemed powerless to control the spiralling violence.

A ceasefire declared in September proved to be only a brief respite from the bloodshed. On October 23rd, in an incident that sent shockwaves through the Western world, more than 300 American and French soldiers were killed in two simultaneous suicide attacks on their headquarters in Beirut. The majority of the casualties occurred at the US Marine Battalion HQ, where 260 men died when a lorry loaded with some 5,000 pounds of explosive crashed through the perimeter fence (above).

Violence in Sri Lanka

Official figures put the death toll at more than 380 as intercommunal violence swept Sri Lanka. There was criticism of President Junius Jayawardene (1906–) for the wide-ranging powers given to security forces to combat the terrorism of Tamil separatist guerrillas, as fighting erupted between the Tamil minority and the Sinhalese majority in July and August. Many Tamil refugees fled to the north as fire, looting and murder devastated parts of the capital Colombo (left). The violence spread to the island's central highlands, with reported revenge attacks by the Sri Lankan Army in the Jaffna peninsula and elsewhere.

Impasse in El Salvador

In the strife-torn Central American Republic of El Salvador, rebels of the FMLN (Farabundo Marti National Liberation Front) continued their campaign against the government. Both sides remained chaotically divided and unable to resolve the impasse. An FMLN offensive (the 'January Revolutionary Heroes' campaign) succeeded in capturing 12 towns in Morazan province. A bridge over the Torola River, bombed by the FMLN to slow government efforts to secure the province, is shown (left).

President Reagan attempted to increase aid to the government while the US Congress wanted assurances that human rights were being respected and that promised elections would proceed. Meanwhile, there were mounting protests at the numbers of deaths at the hands of government troops. The US Ambassador had noted in November 1982 that 30,000 people had been murdered since 1979.

Rebellion in Chad

In 1982 the Libyan-backed President of Chad, Goukouni Queddei had been ousted by the forces of Hissène Habré. Queddei formed a rival government in the north of the vast African nation and made a bid to regain power. Assisted by Libyan military units, the rebels moved south in the second part of 1983.

At President Habré's request, France came to the aid of its former colony and French troops and aircraft helped to repel the rebels. Here (left), a guard watches over captured Queddei supporters in the capital, Ndjaména. But large areas of Northern Chad remained in the hands of Queddei and his Libyan allies.

When the United States became involved on the side of the government, US-Libyan tensions were increased, especially in the Gulf of Sirte on Libya's Mediterranean coast.

The Harrods bomb

The scene outside Harrods, the prestigious London store, on Saturday, December 17 after the explosion of a terrorist car-bomb. Five people were killed and 91 injured on one of the busiest pre-Christmas shopping days. While the IRA claimed responsibility for the bomb, leaders of the organisation denied having given authorisation for the attack.

The America's Cup

Yachting history was made on September 26th when the USA's stranglehold on the prestigious America's Cup was broken for the first time in 132 years. The American defender *Liberty* (above left) was defeated by Australian millionaire businessman Alan Bond's *Australia II* (above right). The seventh and final race of the series was a close-run contest, with *Liberty* maintaining the lead from the early stages.

Klaus Barbie arrested

The former Nazi officer Klaus Barbie (1913–   ) was arrested in Bolivia in January on charges of fraud and organising paramilitary groups. Barbie was wanted in France, where he had twice been sentenced to death *in absentia* for war crimes committed during his time as Head of the Gestapo in Lyon. France demanded his extradition and on February 5th he was sent to Lyon to face trial.

Mass murder in London

Dennis Nilsen, one of the biggest multiple killers in British criminal history, was arrested on February 9th after the remains of human bodies were found at his house in Muswell Hill, North London (above). Police were astonished when Nilsen, a 37-year-old civil servant, openly admitted killing 15 men over four years. Dismembered human remains were found in plastic bags in his wardrobe and in drains under the house.

Neil Kinnock elected leader

On October 2nd, Neil Kinnock (1942–   )
was elected leader of the British Labour
Party at its annual conference in Brighton.
He succeeded Michael Foot, who had been
leader since 1980. Mr Kinnock, 41, had
been Labour MP for Bedwellty in South
Wales since 1970 and Shadow Cabinet
Spokesman on Education since 1979.

Raúl Alfonsín becomes President

Argentina returned to civilian rule on
December 10th with the inauguration of
President Raúl Alfonsín (1926–   ),
following the victory of his Radical Civil
Union Party in the general elections of
October 30th. He vowed to curb the power
of the military and to try those responsible
for the 'dirty war' of the 1970s.

Arthur Koestler

The Hungarian-born writer and thinker
Arthur Koestler (1906–1983) died in
March at his home in London together
with his wife Cynthia. They had both
committed suicide. Koestler, a naturalised
British citizen, was best known for
Darkness at Noon, a searing critique of
left-wing totalitarianism.

Face to face

Amid growing rumours that the Bulgarian security services
might have been involved in the assassination attempt on Pope
John Paul II in 1981, the Pope met his would-be assassin in his
prison cell in Rome on December 27th after conducting a
Christmas service at the gaol. Mehmet Ali Agca, a Turkish
extremist, had been imprisoned for life in 1981 for an attempt on
the Pope's life which led to the deaths of bystanders in St Peter's
Square. The rumours, which resulted in Italy and Bulgaria
breaking off diplomatic relations, originated in statements made
by Agca himself.

1984

Jan 18	Gromyko and Shultz meet in Sweden		25	US author Truman Capote dies
Feb 7	US astronauts first to walk untethered in space		30	Space shuttle *Discovery* makes maiden flight
9	Soviet leader Yuri Andropov dies		Sep 4	Beirut car bomb kills 23 at US Embassy
13	USSR: Konstantin Chernenko succeeds Andropov		4	Canada: Prog. Con. Brian Mulroney is PM
29	Canada: Pierre Trudeau resigns; John Turner PM		Oct 11	Kathryn Sullivan first US woman to walk in space
Mar 15	UK: Miners begin year-long strike		19	Polish priest Popieluszko kidnapped and killed
21	French President Mitterrand visits US		24	French film director François Truffaut dies
Apr 1	US singer Marvin Gaye killed by father		26	US: Baboon's heart implanted in Baby Fae
17	UK: Policewoman killed at Libyan Embassy siege		31	India's PM Indira Gandhi assassinated
May 1	Reagan concludes visit to China		Nov 5	Nicaragua: Daniel Ortega is elected President
7	El Salvador: Jose Duarte wins Presidential elections		6	Ronald Reagan re-elected as US President
19	British poet laureate John Betjeman dies		6	Chile's President Pinochet re-imposes state of siege
Jun 30	John Turner replaces Trudeau as Canadian PM		Dec 3	Toxic gas leak kills thousands in Bhopal, India
Jul 12	US: G. Ferraro first woman to run for Vice-President		7	South African Bishop Tutu meets President Reagan
21	Poland grants amnesty to 652 political prisoners		23	Terrorist bomb kills 29 on train in Bologna, Italy
27	UK: Actor James Mason dies			*The Arts*
28	Olympic Games open in Los Angeles			David Lean's film *A Passage to India*
Aug 5	Actor Richard Burton dies			Roland Joffe's film *The Killing Fields*
22	'Coloureds' allowed to vote in South African polls			Milos Forman's film *Amadeus*

Ethiopia's plight

Although famine ravaged many countries in Africa in 1984 it was the plight of Ethiopia which attracted global attention. The continuing failure of the rains had transformed once bountiful areas into virtual deserts. And as crops failed, families left their farms in search of food. Here (below), the search reaches one of Ethiopia's few roads.

The scale of the catastrophe was immense. The United Nations representative in Ethiopia calculated that between 600,000 and one million people had died by the end of the year and that up to eight million more were at risk. A BBC television report, in which a child died before the camera, finally moved the affluent West to act.

The Ethiopian relief effort

Once the international relief effort was under way it ran into severe difficulties. Lack of transport made distribution difficult and it proved almost impossible to co-ordinate the efforts of a vast array of government organisations and humanitarian agencies. Furthermore, the continuing wars in Tigre and Eritrea hampered supplies to the north of the country.

Relations between the various agencies and the government were often strained. The controversial relocation of villagers from northern to southern regions and the spending of up to $250 million on celebrations of the tenth anniversary of Haile Selassie's overthrow were criticised.

By May 1985, however, up to 500,000 tons of food had been delivered. Thousands of people relied wholly on feeding stations such as this one at Korem (above). For the starving millions, like these children (left), a huge economic investment would be needed to build a more secure future.

The Bhopal disaster

Two thousand people died and 180,000 were treated in hospital after poisonous gas escaped from a pesticide factory in Bhopal in the Indian State of Madhya Pradesh. The leak occurred in the early hours of December 3rd at the Union Carbide (India) plant. (In the photograph, left, the top of the three-flanged steel tank which leaked can be clearly seen.) It contaminated some 40 square kilometres of the city; many people died in their houses or in the streets as the cloud of highly toxic methyl isocyanate (MIC) moved over the shanty town around the plant, causing respiratory difficulties, foaming at the mouth and unconsciousness. The plant was immediately shut down and five Union Carbide officials were arrested for criminal negligence. The decision to reopen the plant a few days later in order to process the remaining MIC led to a mass exodus from Bhopal as up to 200,000 people fled.

Clashes in Amritsar

Sikh movements for greater political and religious autonomy in the Punjab became increasingly militant in the early months of the year. Violent clashes between Sikhs and Hindus claimed many lives throughout the region and the Prime Minister Mrs Indira Gandhi introduced wide-ranging powers of arrest and search.

A group of Sikh extremists led by Sant Bhindranwale took refuge in the Golden Temple at Amritsar (left), which became the focus of fierce gun battles with the security forces. During the night of June 5th, the Army stormed the temple complex and as many as 1,000 people were killed in the assault, including Bhindranwale himself.

The action, seen as sacrilegious by many Sikhs, was to lead to further bloodshed and claimed its most eminent victim in October when Mrs Gandhi herself was assassinated by Sikh members of her bodyguard in New Delhi (below right).

French farmers' protest

French farmers took disruptive action in January and February in protest against the importing of foreign meat into France during a glut in the European meat market. The protests were intensified when President Mitterand's government ended rail subsidies for the transport of agricultural produce from Brittany. Groups of farmers hijacked and burned lorries carrying lamb and pork from other EEC member states or gave their contents away to schools and hospitals. Others blockaded railway lines and Channel ports, and set up road blocks on major haulage routes. In one of the worst outbreaks of violence, a gang of angry farmers ransacked government offices in Brest, Brittany.

Father Popiełuszko murdered

Poland was swept by demonstrations in support of the banned trade union Solidarity after a Roman Catholic priest was found murdered in October. Father Jerzy Popiełuszko (on the right in the photograph), who had often been outspoken in his criticism of the Polish authorities, was kidnapped by three men on a road near Warsaw on October 19th. A full-scale manhunt led to the arrest of three members of the security forces on suspicion of murder, and on October 30th Father Popieluszko's body was found dumped in a reservoir west of Warsaw. He had been tied up, beaten and strangled. His funeral on November 3rd was attended by some 250,000 pro-Solidarity mourners.

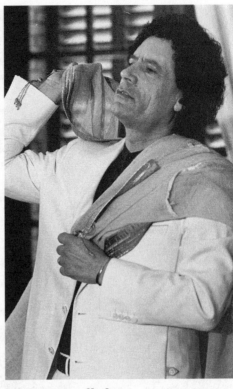

WPC Fletcher shot

Relations between Britain and Libya became very tense after a British policewoman was shot dead in St James's Square in London. The shooting happened on April 17th while WPC Yvonne Fletcher was policing a small demonstration outside the Libyan Embassy, known as the Libyan People's Bureau, by students opposed to the Libyan government. The gunshots came from inside the Embassy, which was immediately surrounded by armed police.

Above: The memorial unveiled to WPC Fletcher on the spot where she fell.

Libyans expelled

As a result of the shooting of Yvonne Fletcher, the British government broke off diplomatic relations with the Libyan regime of Colonel Gadaffi (above) on April 29th. Two days earlier the staff of the Libyan People's Bureau had been deported.

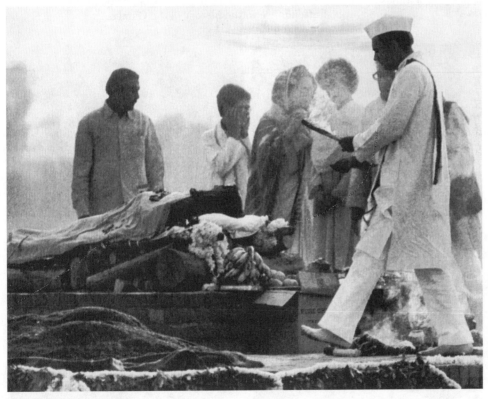

Mrs Gandhi killed

India's new Prime Minister Rajiv Gandhi – until now a commercial airline pilot – about to light the funeral pyre of his mother Mrs Indira Gandhi. Mrs Gandhi was assassinated by her bodyguards in the garden of her home in New Delhi on October 31st. Her killing was a direct response by Sikhs to her storming of their holiest shrine, the Golden Temple at Amritsar, regarded as a desecration even by Sikhs opposed to the extremists who had occupied the temple.

The Brighton bombing

Five people were killed and more than 30 injured when an IRA bomb devastated the Grand Hotel in Brighton, on England's south coast, on October 12th. The Conservative Party Conference was being held there.

Summer Olympics

The Summer Olympics, held at the Memorial Coliseum Stadium in Los Angeles, California, were notable for the absence of almost all the Eastern bloc countries, who decried them as a commercialised US propaganda exercise. But in spite of the boycott the Olympics welcomed more than 7,000 athletes – the largest attendance in the history of the Games.

Torvill and Dean

At the Winter Olympics the British ice-skating pair Jayne Torvill and Christopher Dean won the ice dance gold.

Carl Lewis triumphs

The star of the Los Angeles Games was the American athlete Carl Lewis (1956–   ), who won four gold medals.

Zola Budd

British runner Zola Budd was disqualified from the 3,000-metres after tripping America's Mary Decker.

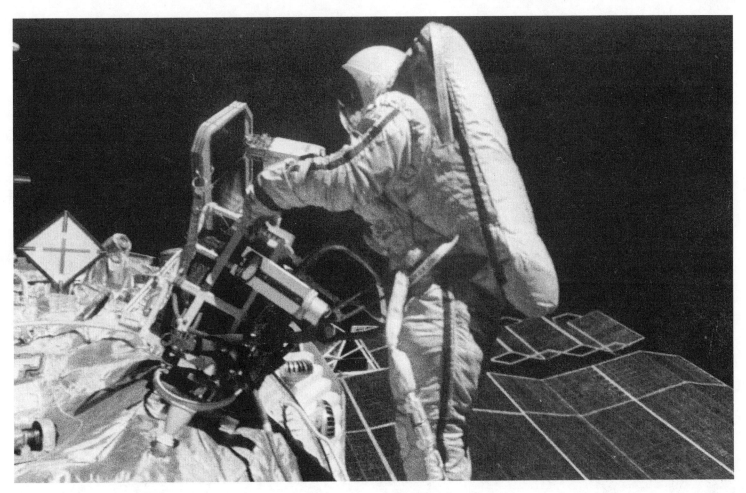

First woman spacewalker

In July the Soviet space programme achieved another 'first' when the cosmonaut Svetlana Savitskaya became the first woman ever to walk in space. She is shown working outside the Salyut-7 space station during the 12-day mission. Savitskaya and her fellow cosmonauts Igor Volk and Vladimir Dzanibekov returned to Earth on July 29th.

J. B. Priestley

England lost one of her grand old men of letters in August with the death, aged 89, of the author, playwright and essayist J. B. Priestley (1895–1984).

Richard Burton

The Welsh actor Richard Burton (1926–1984), seen here with Elizabeth Taylor, whom he married twice, died at the age of 58. His last role was that of O'Brien in the film *1984*.

1985

Jan	3	Ethiopian Jews settle in Israel
Feb	10	Mandela rejects offer of freedom from S African govt
	16	Israel begins withdrawal from Lebanon
Mar	3	UK: coal-miners end strike after 1 year
	10	Soviet Premier Chernenko dies: Gorbachev to succeed
	21	UK: Actor Michael Redgrave dies
	29	Spain and Portugal to join EEC
Apr	6	President Numeiry of Sudan ousted in coup
	11	Albania's Communist leader Elver Hoxha dies
	15	South Africa abolishes racial sex laws
May	10	India: Sikh terrorists kill 59, injure 150
	14	Tamil violence spreads in Sri Lanka
	20	Israel frees 1,150 Palestinian prisoners for 3 Israelis
	25	Lebanon: Hundreds killed in Chatila and Sabra camps
Jun	14	Terrorists seize TWA plane over Middle East
	23	Air India jumbo blown up in mid-air
Jul	1	USSR: Shevardnadze is Foreign Minister
	7	German Boris Becker, 17, is youngest to win Wimbledon
	10	Greenpeace *Rainbow Warrior* ship sunk in New Zealand
	13	US: Reagan undergoes surgery for removal of tumour
Aug	8	South African police kill 18 blacks
	20	Sikh leader Sant Harchand Singh Longowal killed
Sep	1	*Titanic* wreck found off Newfoundland
	2	Kampuchea: Khmer Rouge leader Pol Pot retires
	19	Earthquake devastates Mexico City
Oct	7	Palestinians seize Italian cruise ship *Achille Lauro*
	10	US jets intercept plane carrying hijackers
	10	US actors Orson Welles and Yul Brynner die
	27	El Salvador: President Duarte's kidnapped daughter free
Nov	6	General Jaruzelski elected Poland's head of state
	9	USSR: Gary Kasparov, 22, is world chess champion
Dec	2	UK: Poet Philip Larkin dies
	6	UK joins US Star Wars project
	30	President Zia of Pakistan ends martial law
	31	King Hussein and President Assad hold talks

The Arts

Kurt Vonnegut's novel *Galapagos*

Sydney Pollack's film *Out of Africa*

Live Aid

On July 13th, an estimated 70 million dollars was raised for famine victims in Africa by a huge rock concert organised by the Irish musician Bob Geldof, seen at the event with the Prince and Princess of Wales (below). The all-day concert, which was broadcast to 152 countries by the largest ever intercontinental satellite link-up, took place simultaneously in Philadelphia and at Wembley Stadium in London (below right). It featured appearances by such stars as Mick Jagger and Tina Turner (above right), David Bowie, Paul McCartney, Bob Dylan, Joan Baez, Elton John, Madonna, and Phil Collins (who performed on the same day in both London and Philadelphia). More than 1½ billion people were believed to have watched the telethon worldwide, and switchboards in the UK and the USA were besieged with calls pledging money.

The Geneva summit

On November 19th Ronald Reagan and Mikhail Gorbachev met for the first time in Geneva for the first US–Soviet summit since President Carter met Leonid Brezhnev in Vienna in 1979.

The three-day meeting produced no striking new initiatives, but was generally seen as reducing international tensions by establishing a degree of personal rapport between the two leaders. The tone was set on the very first day when private talks between Reagan and Gorbachev overran their 15-minute schedule by more than three-quarters of an hour. The two men spent two hours in talks accompanied only by their interpreters in the Fleur d'Eau villa on the shores of Lake Geneva, an exchange which became known as the 'fireside chat'.

The talks were described as lively and businesslike, but differences of opinion remained on the crucial issues of arms control – where the US 'Star Wars' project proved a sticking point – regional conflicts and human rights. However, a number of agreements were signed on scientific and cultural matters in a televised ceremony attended by both leaders at the Geneva International Centre. A joint communiqué issued on November 21st pledged both countries to work for peace and the reduction of nuclear arsenals. President Reagan spoke of a 'fresh start' in East–West relations.

The Bradford fire

Fifty-six people died when fire engulfed a wooden stand at Bradford City Football Ground in the UK, on May 11th. The blaze, which began when a cigarette or match ignited accumulated rubbish under the seats, became an inferno within minutes. Many of the dead were trapped at the back of the stand when they found emergency doors locked.

Tragedy at Heysel

Another footballing tragedy occurred at Belgium's Heysel Stadium on May 29th when 41 people died and more than 400 were injured in crowd violence before the European Cup Final between Juventus of Turin and Liverpool. Most of those who died were crushed when a wall collapsed under the weight of supporters trying to escape rampaging British fans.

Colombian volcano

At least 25,000 people were believed dead when the volcano Nevado del Ruiz erupted near the town of Armero in Colombia on November 13th. The town and the surrounding area were devastated by the eruption, which lasted for several days and covered the area in a sea of mud. As rescue operations began (above), a national state of emergency was declared.

Earthquake in Mexico

Thousands of square miles of Mexico City and the surrounding area were devastated on the morning of September 19th by a massive earthquake which claimed the lives of up to 20,000 people. The quake, measuring 8.1 on the Richter scale, also left more than 30,000 homeless. And the rescue operation was hampered by a second earthquake which struck the following day.

Libyan hostages released

Four Britons held in detention in Libya for nine months flew home to England on February 7th. They are shown alighting at Gatwick airport after their ordeal.

TWA hijack

A US Navy diver, Robert Stetham, was murdered by the Lebanese hijackers of a TWA flight from Athens to Rome. Other hostages were released after two weeks of negotiations.

Clive Sinclair's C5

In January the British inventor and entrepreneur Sir Clive Sinclair (1940–   ), launched his electric vehicle, the C5. Looking rather like a large shoe, the C5 ran on a washing-machine motor and could travel at 15 miles per hour.

Pope in South America

Pope John Paul II visited Venezuela, Ecuador, Peru, Trinidad and Tobago during his 11-day tour of Latin America in January and February. He was met by vast enthusiastic crowds, but many clergy were upset by his rejection of 'liberation theology'.

Oil tanker explosions

Thirty people were killed and more than 40 injured when an explosion wrecked the Panamanian oil tanker *Petrogen-One* near the Rock of Gibraltar. The accident happened as the ship was unloading her oil at the Spanish port of San Roque, and set off a second explosion on board the Spanish tanker *Camponavia*, which was loading nearby.

Rainbow Warrior sunk

There was embarrassment among the French authorities after it was found that members of their security services had been involved in blowing up a ship belonging to the international environmental organisation Greenpeace. The attack took place in Auckland Harbour, New Zealand, on July 10th and one crew member died in the explosions from two limpet mines. *Rainbow Warrior* was due to have taken part in a protest against French nuclear tests on Mururoa Atoll in the South Pacific.

Robert Graves

The British poet and novelist Robert Graves (1895–1985) died on December 7th at Deya on the Spanish island of Majorca where he had lived since 1929. Graves, who was 90, was best known for his autobiographical work *Goodbye to All That* and his novels *I, Claudius* and *Claudius the God*.

Joan Collins

The career of 52-year-old Joan Collins (above), the British starlet of the 1950s, reached new heights with her portrayal of Alexis in the American television soap opera *Dynasty*. After her appearance in the series it moved rapidly into the top ten in American viewing ratings.

Marc Chagall

The Russian-born artist Marc Chagall (1888–1985) died in France, where he had lived since 1922. He was 97 and had been working almost to the end of his life. Chagall's brightly coloured paintings were marked by his use of often naive imagery from Jewish folklore and the natural world.

Unrest in South Africa

The South African President P. W. Botha declared a state of emergency in July as violence engulfed black townships in the Transvaal and the Eastern Cape. The rioting claimed hundreds of lives and was sparked off by the new constitution which gave political representation to coloured and Indian people but excluded blacks. There was widespread international criticism of the South African authorities when police shot at least 40 people during a funeral procession near Uitenhage on March 21st, the 25th anniversary of the Sharpeville massacre.

1986

Jan	8	President Reagan freezes Libyan assets in the US
	24	US spacecraft *Voyager 2* probes Uranus
Feb	7	Haitians overthrow President Duvalier
	11	Human rights activist Scharansky freed by Soviets
	25	Cory Aquino defeats Marcos in Philippine elections
	28	Swedish Prime Minister Olof Palme assassinated
Mar	17	US $ reaches lowest post-war rate against Japanese yen
	24	Libyan and US forces clash over airspace
	30	Actor James Cagney dies
Apr	2	Bomb explodes on TWA flight from Rome to Athens
	13	Jack Nicklaus wins US Masters golf, his 18th major
	15	US planes bomb Libya
	15	French dramatist Jean Genet dies
	24	Wallis Simpson, Duchess of Windsor, dies
May	1	1½ million blacks go on strike in South Africa
	14	President Gorbachev reveals Chernobyl facts
Jun	8	Kurt Waldheim elected President of Austria
	13	US jazz clarinettist Benny Goodman dies
	14	Argentine writer Jorge Luis Borges dies
	15	USSR: Chernobyl bosses dismissed
	25	Philippines gets US aid
Jul	2	General strike called in China
	4	US: Celebrations for reopening of Statue of Liberty
Aug	14	Benazir Bhutto of Pakistan is jailed
	31	British sculptor Henry Moore dies
Sep	5	Pakistan: Pan Am jet seized in Karachi
	6	Arab terrorists kill 21 at Istanbul synagogue
Oct	2	US imposes sanctions on S Africa
	7	Nicaragua captures US pilot delivering arms to rebels
	20	Israel: Shamir takes over as coalition PM
	22	US reforms tax code
Nov	3	Mozambique: President Machel killed in air crash
	4	Democrats to control US Senate
	10	Chemical spill pollutes River Rhine
	13	US violates Iran arms boycott
	30	British-born actor Cary Grant dies
Dec	12	Microlite aircraft circles earth non-stop
	19	Soviet dissident Andrei Sakharov freed from exile
	29	Britain's ex-PM Harold Macmillan dies
	30	US begins military exercises in Honduras
		The Arts
		Larry McMurtry's novel *Lonesome Dove*
		Woody Allen's *Hannah and Her Sisters*
		Paul Hogan in film *Crocodile Dundee*
		Oliver Stone's film *Platoon*

Chernobyl

The world's worst ever nuclear accident took place on April 26th when a disastrous fire at the Chernobyl nuclear power station in the Ukraine (top) contaminated much of Europe with radioactive fall-out. There was widespread international criticism of the Soviet Union's secrecy and slow reaction to the disaster, which came to light only after high radiation levels were detected in Sweden.

Meltdown was avoided by sealing the damaged reactor with concrete, but restrictions were imposed on the sale of animal foodstuffs in many countries as tests showed levels of radioactivity well above normal in grazing animals such as sheep, cows and reindeer (above). Doctors differed in their estimates of the number of additional cancer deaths likely to be caused by the disaster in later years.

The Gulf War

Despite diplomatic efforts to end the fighting between Iran and Iraq, the death toll mounted inexorably in what came to be known as 'the forgotten war'. Successes such as Iran's at Al Faw (above) were met by Iraqi counter-offensives and there were mounting rumours that Iraq was using chemical weapons.

Swiss chemical plant fire

Switzerland became the scene of a major environmental disaster in November when a fire at a chemical plant near Basle led to the discharge of thousands of gallons of toxic water into the Rhine. Half a million fish died after water which had become contaminated when it was used to control the fire (above) was pumped into the river.

The *Challenger* disaster

Tragedy struck the US space programme in January when the *Challenger* shuttle exploded shortly after take-off from Cape Canaveral, killing all seven astronauts on board. Well-wishers and relatives of the crew watched in horrified disbelief as the shuttle burst into flames just over a minute into its tenth mission. Media attention focused on the fate of Christa McAuliffe (top left, third from the back), a high school teacher from New Hampshire, who had won a contest to be the first ordinary citizen in space. The accident, which was traced to a fault in one of the twin solid-fuel booster rockets, led to staff changes at the top of the American space agency NASA.

US bombing of Libya

There was widespread criticism after US aircraft, flying from bases in Britain, launched bombing raids on targets in the Libyan cities of Tripoli and Benghazi, apparently in response to alleged Libyan involvement in a Berlin nightclub bombing.

South African pass laws

On April 23rd, President P. W. Botha announced an end to arrests under South Africa's hated pass laws, when a Bill was put before Parliament to abolish the requirement for black people to carry their passes at all times.

The Reykjavik mini-summit

In October President Reagan met the Soviet leader Mikhail Gorbachev for further talks almost a year after their famous 'fireside chat' at the Geneva summit. The meeting in the Icelandic capital Reykjavik took place during two days of talks on bilateral issues. A complete news blackout was observed, but there were rumours of a major agreement on arms control.

The Wapping dispute

Pickets clashed with police outside premises owned by Rupert Murdoch's News International Group after Murdoch moved production of his newspapers to a new plant at Wapping (in London's dockland) with the loss of 5,000 print jobs.

Royal wedding

On July 23rd, Prince Andrew married Miss Sarah Ferguson (known to friends and tabloid headline writers as 'Fergie') at Westminster Abbey in London. The Queen conferred on the royal couple the titles Duke and Duchess of York.

'People's power' in the Philippines

In an extraordinary upsurge of popular support, Mrs Corazon Aquino (1933–   ) (above left), widow of the assassinated Opposition leader Benigno Aquino, swept to power in the Philippines in February. Her inauguration as President followed a widely discredited election in which President Marcos, leader of the country since 1965, had claimed victory.

Kurt Waldheim elected

Dr Kurt Waldheim (1918–) the former United Nations Secretary-General, was elected President of Austria on June 8th after an election campaign dominated by questions about his war record. Dr Waldheim denied allegations that he had been involved in atrocities during his time as a Nazi lieutenant in the Balkans.

Death of Macmillan

Britain lost one of its elder statesmen in December with the death, aged 92, of the Earl of Stockton, who as Harold Macmillan had been Prime Minister from 1957 to 1963. Since acquiring his title in 1984, he had made controversial speeches in the House of Lords criticising aspects of government policy.

Swedish Prime Minister assassinated

Sweden was shocked by the assassination in February of the Prime Minister Olof Palme (1927–1986). Palme was shot dead as he was walking home with his wife after an evening at the cinema in Stockholm. Police investigations were slow to uncover his killer.

Oil and trouble

Oil prices took a battering in world markets in the early months of the year and on April 1st reached record lows after falling through the supposedly critical level of $10 a barrel. Next day trading in gasoline futures on the New York Mercantile Exchange (above) was heavy as prices staged a recovery. Saudi Arabia was alleged to have 'engineered' the price movements.

Andrei Sakharov released

On December 19th, the dissident Soviet scientist Dr Andrei Sakharov (1921–1989) and his wife Yelena Bonner were released from the closed city of Gorky where they had been in internal exile since 1980. Sakharov's return to Moscow on December 23rd was seen as a triumph for Mr Gorbachev's policy of *glasnost*.

Simone de Beauvoir

April saw the death of the French feminist writer and existentialist philosopher Simone de Beauvoir (1908–1986) at the age of 78. A long-time associate of Jean-Paul Sartre, she was the author of the influential works *The Second Sex* and *The Coming of Age*.

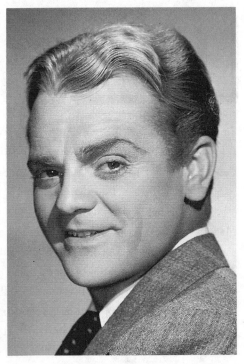

James Cagney

The American movie actor James Cagney (1899–1986) died in March at the age of 86. One of the most frequently imitated stars of all time, Cagney made his name playing tough guy roles in such films as *Public Enemy* (1930), *Angels with Dirty Faces* (1936) and *White Heat* (1949).

Henry Moore

The death of Henry Moore (1898–1986) in August robbed the art world of perhaps its greatest modern sculptor. Moore, seen here with the former British Prime Minister James Callaghan, worked in wood, bronze, stone and cement and was known for his smooth organic forms, often developing variations on the themes of the reclining figure and the mother and child.

1987

Jan 12	Britain's Prince Edward resigns from Royal Marines	25	Pope welcomes Austria's President Waldheim in Rome
21	Archbishop's envoy Terry Waite disappears in Lebanon	28	Death of US film director John Huston
Feb 18	Ireland: Charley Haughey becomes PM	Aug 3	US: Irangate hearings end
19	US lifts sanctions on Poland	Sep 19	Pope concludes US visit
22	US pop artist Andy Warhol dies	21	US seizes Iranian ship in Persian Gulf
Mar 6	UK car ferry capsizes killing 184 at Zeebrugge	Oct 16	Widespread damage as Britain hit by hurricane
16	Michael Dukakis enters US Presidential race	19	Stock markets collapse
Apr 17	US taxes Japanese imports	19	British cellist Jacqueline du Pré dies
27	US bars Austria's President Waldheim from entry	19	US attacks Iranian boat base in Gulf
May 8	Gary Hart drops out of US Presidential campaign	Nov 8	UK: Bomb kills 11 at Ulster Remembrance Day Service
15	Death of US actress Rita Hayworth	29	S Korean Boeing 707 disappears en route to Seoul
17	Iraqi missiles hit US frigate	Dec 8	Reagan and Gorbachev sign arms treaty
28	West German pilot lands in Moscow's Red Square	10	Russian-born US violinist Jascha Heifetz dies
Jun 2	Spanish guitarist Andrés Segovia dies	16	Roh Tae Woo wins Presidential election in S Korea
11	Thatcher wins third term as Britain's PM		*The Arts*
17	New York vigilante Goetz is cleared of murder		Van Gogh's painting *Irises* fetches £30 million
23	Death of US dancer and actor Fred Astaire		Saul Bellow's novel *More Die of Heartbreak*
Jul 4	Nazi war criminal Klaus Barbie convicted in France		Arthur Miller's autobiography *Timebends*
5	Martina Navratilova wins 6th consecutive Wimbledon		Bertolucci's film *The Last Emperor*
11	Australians re-elect Hawke as PM		Richard Attenborough's film *Cry Freedom*

The *Herald of Free Enterprise*

One of the worst peacetime tragedies in the history of English Channel shipping occurred near the Belgian port of Zeebrugge on March 6th when a ferry with more than 500 people on board capsized.

One hundred and eighty-four people died when the 7,951-ton *Herald of Free Enterprise* keeled over in a matter of minutes just outside the harbour wall at Zeebrugge (left). Only a shallow sandbank prevented it from turning over completely. There were many stories of heroism during the rescue operation, one passenger being seen acting as a human bridge to allow others to escape to safety.

The ferry (run by Britain's largest ferry operator Townsend Thoresen) was of the roll-on roll-off kind, and doubts had been expressed in the past about the safety of this particular design. Initial investigations suggested that the ship had gone to sea with her bow doors open and had been destabilised by the resulting inrush of water on to the open car deck.

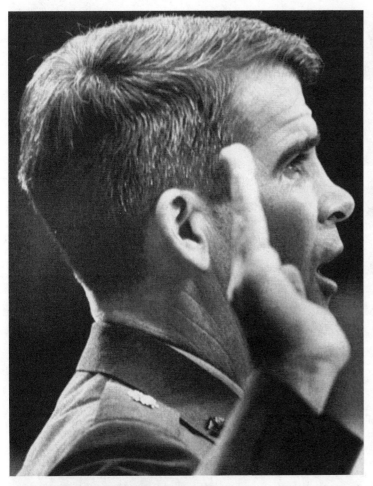

Irangate

Hearings began in May into the Iran–Contra affair which rocked the Reagan administration in the United States. In July the key figures in the case, Colonel Oliver North (top left) and his secretary Fawn Hall (top right) and Admiral John Poindexter (left) appeared before Committees of the House of Representatives and the Senate to answer questions on their part in the affair, in which profits from arms sales to Iran were diverted to support the Contra rebels fighting the Sandinista government in Nicaragua, thus bypassing a Congress ban on aid to the Contras.

The public hearings became a media event, with Oliver North in particular becoming something of a national hero for his uncompromising and unapologetic stance. Admiral Poindexter, who was widely expected to implicate the President himself in the scandal, in fact claimed that he had withheld information from Reagan in order to provide 'deniability' if the affair came to light.

Danny Kaye

Danny Kaye (1913–1987), born David Daniel Kaminsky in Brooklyn, died this year. He had a long career as one of America's best-loved entertainers and comedians, with an amiable, zany brand of humour all his own. He was also extremely popular in Great Britain, where he made frequent appearances at the London Palladium. Among Kaye's many films some of the best known are *The Kid From Brooklyn* (1946), *The Secret Life of Walter Mitty* (1947), *White Christmas* (1954) and *The Court Jester* (1956).

King's Cross fire

Thirty people died and scores were injured when fire engulfed London's busy King's Cross underground station at the end of the evening rush hour.

Survivors described the atmosphere of panic in which passengers ran back down the up-escalators as a fireball roared into the central ticket area, reducing the whole concourse to a mass of charred metal (above). Rescue operations were hindered by the intense heat and toxic fumes released by fittings in the station. Firemen at the scene of the disaster were unable to spend more than a few moments below ground without having to resurface for air as smoke poured down the tunnels.

When a public inquiry was launched into the causes of the tragedy there were indications that safety standards were inadequate, with no sprinkler system in operation and fire extinguishers locked up.

Mathias Rust lands in Moscow

People in Red Square were astonished to see a single-engined Cessna light aircraft land in front of the Kremlin on May 28th. Its amateur pilot, a 19-year-old West German, Mathias Rust, had flown from Helsinki straight through all the Soviet Union's air defences. He was immediately detained.

Mrs Thatcher and Mr Gorbachev

The British Prime Minister Mrs Thatcher and the Soviet leader Mr Gorbachev met twice during the year. In March Mrs Thatcher visited Moscow where talks with the Soviet leader lasted four hours longer than scheduled. She described the occasion as 'a big step forward', and despite their differences on a wide range of policy issues the two leaders evidently established a degree of personal rapport. The new atmosphere of mutual respect was confirmed in December when Mr Gorbachev stopped over in Britain for further talks with Mrs Thatcher on his way to a Washington D. C. summit meeting with President Reagan.

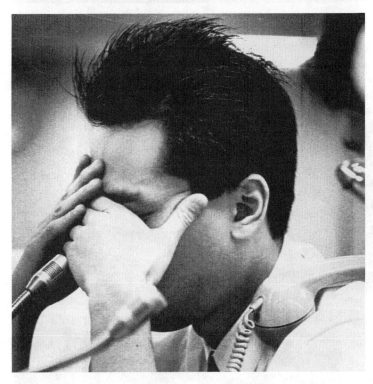

Black Monday

The long bull market in stocks and shares came to an abrupt end on Monday October 19th when the New York Stock Exchange registered a staggering one-day fall in values – twice that of the Wall Street crash of 1929. More than 600 million shares changed hands as investors scrambled to sell. The effects were felt from Tokyo (above) to London (top left), where the FT index fell almost 250 points, threatening the government's privatisation issue of British Petroleum shares.

Enniskillen

Eleven people died and more than 60 were injured when an IRA bomb exploded at a Remembrance Day ceremony in Enniskillen in Northern Ireland. The IRA alleged that the bomb had been detonated by British Army scanning equipment but the claim was dismissed by the British government. There was widespread condemnation of the killings, but many were moved by the words of Mr Gordon Wilson (top right), when he forgave the murderers of his daughter, who died in the explosion.

Tanker war in the Gulf

The Iran–Iraq War entered a new phase with a series of attacks on international shipping in the Gulf. Tension mounted after a Soviet freighter was attacked with machine guns and grenades by Iranian 'revolutionary guards' in speedboats. In May, 37 people were killed when the USS *Stark* was struck by two Exocet missiles from an Iraqi plane. Mines presented an additional hazard, and Britain and France sent minesweepers to the area for the first time.

Storms in Britain

Eighteen people died when unprecedented storms battered the south of England during the night of October 15th. Winds of up to 100 miles per hour tore trees up by the roots and the cost of the damage was estimated at between £100 and £600 million. Gusts of 94 miles per hour were recorded in the centre of London and at the Botanical Gardens at Kew a storm lasting a few hours destroyed trees which would take 200 years to regrow.

Ivan the Terrible trial

The trial began in Jerusalem of John Demjanjuk, who was accused of war crimes committed at the Treblinka concentration camp. The case turned on the question of whether or not Demjanjuk was the guard known as 'Ivan the Terrible'.

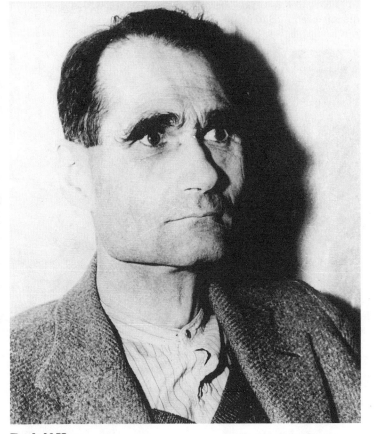

Rudolf Hess

On August 17th, Rudolf Hess (1894–1987), Hitler's former deputy, was found dead in Spandau Prison in Berlin where he was the only remaining inmate. He appeared to have committed suicide. Demolition of the prison began almost immediately.

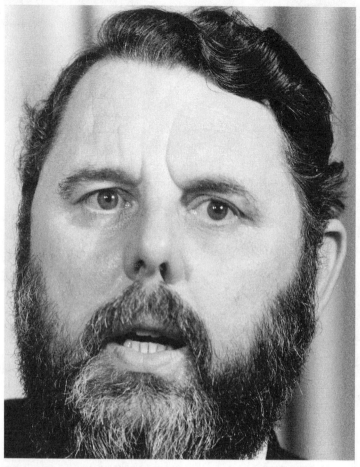

Terry Waite kidnapped

The Archbishop of Canterbury's special envoy, Terry Waite, who had been instrumental in securing the release of many hostages in Lebanon, himself became the victim of kidnappers when he disappeared in Beirut.

Spycatcher

On March 13th, an Australian Court rejected the British government's application for a permanent injunction against former intelligence officer Peter Wright (1917–   ) and the publishers of his controversial book *Spycatcher*.

Death of Andy Warhol

Leading pop art exponent and film-maker Andy Warhol (1931–1987), perhaps best remembered for his silk-screen images such as Marilyn Monroe (above right) and the Campbell's soup tin, died in New York on February 22nd. Despite his determination to remain an enigma, Warhol had a gift for personal publicity, perhaps developed from his background in commercial illustration. He claimed that 'everyone will be famous for 15 minutes' but his fame lasted well over 20 years.

1988

Jan	5	Austrian President Waldheim's war record investigated
	7	UK actor Trevor Howard dies
	15	Arab uprising in Israel begins
	29	Talks break down between Sandinistas and Contras
Feb	5	Panama's General Noriega on drugs charge
	11	UK: Marilyn Monroe's blouse fetches £7150 at Sotheby's
Mar	2	Tension growing between Armenia and Azerbaijan
	7	IRA bombers gunned down in Gibraltar
	19	Belfast: 2 British soldiers lynched at IRA funerals
	21	Nicaragua: Sandinistas open peace talks with Contras
Apr	7	Gorbachev to sign Geneva peace accord on Afghanistan
	16	Deputy PLO leader Abu Jihad murdered in Tunisia
	18	US Navy bombs Iranian oil base
	20	Kuwaiti jumbo hijack over after 16 days and 2 killings
May	10	France: Mitterrand wins 2nd term as President
	16	Soviet troops begin withdrawal from Afghanistan
	31	President Reagan visits Moscow
Jun	2	Ronald and Nancy Reagan visit Queen in London
	21	Western powers summit in Toronto
Jul	3	US warship *Vincennes* shoots down Iranian airliner
	11	Terrorists kill passengers on Aegean cruise ship
Aug	8	Iran and Iraq agree to ceasefire
	8	Angola, Cuba and South Africa agree to ceasefire
	11	Floods devastate Sudan
	14	Enzo Ferrari, Italian car genius, dies
	17	Pakistan's President Zia-ul-Haq killed in plane crash
Sep	4	Floods devastate Bangladesh
	17	24th Olympic Games open in Seoul
	24	Barbara Harris is first US Anglican bishop
Oct	2	Sir Alec Issigonis, inventor of Mini car, dies
	12	USSR offers $600 million reparations to Afghanistan
Nov	2	Israel: Shamir's Likud wins election
	11	George Bush defeats Michael Dukakis as US President
	17	Benazir Bhutto wins election in Pakistan
	23	S Africa: Botha reprieves Sharpeville Six
Dec	6	US rock singer Roy Orbison dies
	7	USSR cuts military strength by 10 per cent
	7	Yasser Arafat recognises existence of Israel
	10	USSR: Terrible earthquake hits Armenia
	22	Pan Am flight explodes over Scotland killing 270
	30	Yugoslav government resigns

The Arts

Bob Hoskins in film *Who Framed Roger Rabbit?*

Salman Rushdie's novel *The Satanic Verses*

Dustin Hoffman in film *Rain Man*

AIDS

Three major conferences in 1988 confirmed the seriousness of the threat posed to mankind by the rapid spread of AIDS (Acquired Immune Deficiency Syndrome). Delegates from all over the world met in London in January and March to discuss the global impact of AIDS. They called for urgent action by all governments to contain the disease which is spread through infected blood and other body fluids.

Another conference, in Stockholm in June, gathered some 6,000 experts from 125 countries, but delegates heard that despite the enormous international research programme scientists were as yet no nearer to finding a cure. Estimates suggested that five million people could be infected with the HIV virus worldwide, of whom 150,000 had already developed the full-blown disease. Experts predicted that this number would double by the end of the year and that there could be as many as a million new cases in the following five years. The largest number of cases had been reported in the United States, but the highest incidence of the disease was believed to be in Africa.

Ben Johnson

The Canadian athlete Ben Johnson (1961–   ) was stripped of his 100 metres gold medal at the Seoul Olympic Games after a drugs test proved positive.

The Eagle has landed

Great Britain's Eddie 'the Eagle' Edwards, seen here making the 120-metre jump in the World Cup ski jumping, came last in both the 89 and the 120 metre events in Thunder Bay, Canada.

The Klosters avalanche

Prince Charles returns to London after surviving an avalanche in the Swiss ski resort of Klosters which claimed the life of his friend Major Hugh Lindsay.

Michael Jackson

The reclusive American rock star Michael Jackson (1958–   ) did a world tour which was a spectacular success.

East and West

President Reagan speaks under a bust of Lenin at Moscow University during his five-day summit meeting with the Soviet leader Mikhail Gorbachev. Agreements were reached on arms control, human rights and regional issues.

Christina Onassis

The death was announced on November 19th of Christina Onassis (1950–1988), daughter of the millionaire Greek shipping magnate Aristotle Onassis (1906–1975). She was 37.

The INF Treaty

During the Moscow summit in June President Reagan and General-Secretary Gorbachev signed the historic INF Treaty. It provided for the elimination of all intermediate-range land-based nuclear weapons over three years. The first cruise missiles left Britain in September (above).

Save the whale

Campaigns by Greenpeace and other environmental organisations to save the whale from the ravages of international commercial whaling programmes met with some success during the year. Whales at Point Alaska were also given a helping hand by conservationists who cut breathing holes in the ice for them.

Clapham train crash

Thirty six people died and more than 100 were injured on December 12th when two trains collided during the morning rush hour near Clapham Junction station in south-west London. The accident happened when an express train ran into the back of a London commuter train which had stopped on the line to report a faulty signal. The impact hurled the two rear carriages of the train into the air and on to an embankment.

Rescue services were on the scene within minutes, but it took four hours to free all the surviving passengers. A third train was derailed and a fourth was stopped by a guard in time to avoid a further collision.

George Bush

George Bush (1924–   ) became the first sitting Vice-President of the United States since 1836 to win a presidential election when he defeated Michael Dukakis in November with 54 per cent of the popular vote.

Death of Zia

General Mohammad Zia ul-Haq (1924–1988), the President of Pakistan, was killed on August 17th when the *Hercules* transport plane in which he was travelling crashed near Bahawalpur in the Punjab. Sabotage was suspected.

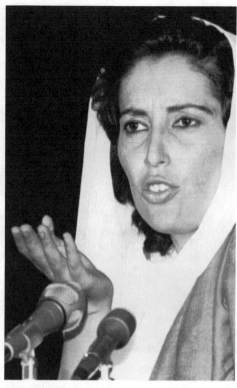

Benazir Bhutto

Benazir Bhutto (1953–   ), leader of the Pakistan People's Party and daughter of the executed former Premier Zulfikar Bhutto, failed to win an overall majority in elections to Pakistan's National Assembly in November but became PM.

Gulf War ceasefire

The Iran–Iraq war neared an end with Iran's acceptance on July 18th of a ceasefire under the terms of the UN Security Council's Resolution 598. Peace talks foundered again in September over Iraq's claim to sovereignty over the Shatt al-Arab waterway.

Baroness Jennie Lee

The death occurred in November of the veteran British socialist Jennie Lee (1904–1988). The widow of Aneurin Bevan, she had been Minister for Education and Science under Harold Wilson and Chairman of the Labour Party from 1967 to 1968. She became a life peer in 1970.

Hurricane Gilbert

Thousands of people were left homeless and millions of pounds' worth of damage was done when Hurricane Gilbert hit Jamaica on September 16th. Here, the wreckage of planes lies scattered around Manley International Airport in the wake of the hurricane.

Australia's bicentenary

There were widespread festivities in Australia as the country commemorated the arrival of the first Europeans in 1788. The high point of the celebrations came on January 26th in Sydney when some two million people watched the arrival of a replica of the fleet (top) which had brought the first white convicts to the colony exactly 200 years before. The Prince and Princess of Wales (inserts) were present at the occasion, which was also marked by a march of 20,000 Aborigines, protesting against the celebrations and their poor living conditions. Above: Rockets light up the night sky in a celebratory fireworks display. Later in the year Queen Elizabeth and Prince Philip visited Australia for a 22-day tour, during which the Queen opened the Expo '88 Exhibition in Brisbane, Queensland.

Lockerbie

Two hundred and seventy people were killed in one of Britain's worst ever air disasters on December 22nd when a Boeing 747 crashed on to the small town of Lockerbie in southern Scotland. The accident happened at 7.19 p.m. as Pan Am flight 103 was on its way from Frankfurt to New York. After a mid-air explosion at 31,000 feet, the aircraft plunged to the ground, crashing across a major road before ploughing into the town. Eye-witnesses described how a fireball engulfed the plane, sending flames roaring 300 feet into the air. The impact demolished some 40 houses and left a crater 50 feet deep and 30 yards long. Many of those who died were Americans returning to the United States for Christmas. Investigations showed that the explosion had been caused by a bomb.

The Piper Alpha tragedy

Disaster struck on July 6th when fire engulfed the Piper Alpha oil rig platform in the North Sea. One hundred and sixty-six people died and many were injured when a series of explosions tore through the 12-year-old rig, which lay 120 miles north-east of Aberdeen. The blasts sent flames some 400 feet into the air above the platform, which was almost completely destroyed. Most of those who died were asleep at the time and there were only 62 survivors, most of whom escaped by leaping into the sea. Rescue operations were hampered by the extreme heat, which could be felt a mile away. The fire took several days to bring under control. An inquiry was launched into the circumstances surrounding the explosion.

Drought in the US

The United States suffered its driest spring since the dust bowl years of the 1930s. Many agricultural regions were designated disaster areas as some 30 states were struck by the worst drought since 1934. The areas most seriously affected were the mid-west and the south. Pasture lands became arid plains and waterways dried up as Montana, Minnesota, North Dakota, Tennessee, North Carolina and Georgia received less than a quarter of their normal level of rainfall. Dust storms scoured off topsoil across more than 13 million acres of land and the giant Mississippi River became unnavigable in places when the water level dwindled to a record low. Commodity prices soared as grain stocks fell, and financial support was planned for stricken farmers.

Earthquake in Armenia

At the end of a year of continued unrest there was tragedy and destruction in the Soviet Republic of Armenia when a massive earthquake devastated the cities of Leninakan and Spitak. As many as 100,000 people were believed to have died in the disaster, which left survivors huddled outside the wreckage of their homes (centre left) and hundreds of coffins piled in Spitak Stadium (centre right). A massive rescue operation was mounted, with many survivors scrabbling at the debris with their bare hands in the hope of finding missing friends and relatives (top left). The Soviet leader Mikhail Gorbachev paid a personal visit to the scene of the earthquake (above right). The disaster came at the end of a troubled year. In February the Southern Republics of Armenia and Azerbaijan were racked by the worst outbreak of ethnic violence in the peacetime history of the Soviet Union after Azerbaijan rejected a call for the predominantly Armenian region of Nagorno Karabakh to be returned to Armenian control. Armenians accounted for more than three-quarters of the population of Nagorno Karabakh, which had been part of Azerbaijan since 1921. There were massive demonstrations and strikes in the Armenian capital Yerevan and throughout the disputed region, and more than 30 people were killed in intercommunal violence in the Azerbaijan city of Sumgait. In September tanks appeared on the streets of Yerevan (above left) as a state of emergency was declared.

1989

Jan	7	Japanese Emperor Hirohito dies, aged 82
	9	British Midland Boeing 737 crashes on motorway
	20	George Bush sworn in as 41st US President
	23	Spanish surrealist painter Salvador Dali dies
Feb	2	Afghanistan: Last Soviet troops leave after 9 years
	3	S African National Party leader P W Botha resigns
	14	Iran: Khomeini orders Moslems to kill Salman Rushdie
Mar	25	Oil spill from Exxon Valdez tanker off Alaskan coast
Apr	15	UK: Football fans die in crush at Hillsborough stadium
	17	Polish Solidarity movement legalised after 8 year ban
	25	Japan: PM Takeshita resigns in corruption scandal
	27	China: Student demonstrators occupy Tiananmen Square
May	16	China: Mikhail Gorbachev and Deng Xiaoping hold talks
Jun	4	Gas explosion on trans-Siberian railway kills hundreds
	4	China: Army massacres pro-democracy demonstrators
	6	Iran: Chaos at Khomeini's funeral as crowds mourn
	22	UK: Bus, tube and rail workers on strike
Jul	4	Hong Kong: Protests against British immigration policy
	11	Actor Laurence Olivier dies, aged 82
	15	France celebrates 200th anniversary of Revolution
Aug	20	UK: Marchioness pleasure boat disaster on River Thames
	25	Voyager 2 spacecraft takes pictures of Neptune

Sep	11	Hungary opens border to East German refugees
	13	S Africa: 20,000 in anti-apartheid demonstration
	22	UK: IRA bomb blasts Royal Marines' School in Deal
	28	Ex-president Marcos of Philippines dies in Honolulu
Oct	19	US: Massive earthquake in San Francisco
	19	UK: Appeal court finds Guildford Four innocent
	23	UK: Ambulance workers begin work-to-rule over pay claim
	29	S Africa: 60,000 in ANC rally
Nov	10	E Germany: Berlin Wall opened
	10	El Salvador: Guerrillas battle with government forces
	24	Czechoslovakia: Communist leadership resigns
Dec	3	Malta: Mikhail Gorbachev and George Bush end summit
	13	Hong Kong: Forced repatriation of Vietnamese
	14	Soviet physicist and dissident Andrei Sakharov dies
	21	US invades Panama and ousts General Noriega
	22	Rumania: Ceausescu flees as civil war grips Bucharest
	26	Irish playwright Samuel Beckett dies in Paris
		The Arts
		Batman film starring Jack Nicholson as Joker
		Andrew Lloyd Webber's musical *Aspects of Love*
		Actors campaign to save Elizabethan Rose Theatre
		Kenneth Branagh's film *Henry V*

George Bush sworn in

On January 20th George Bush became the 41st President of the United States of America. A crowd of thousands cheered enthusiastically in front of the Capitol in Washington as the new President took the oath of office, laying his hand on the same bible on which George Washington had sworn the same oath two centuries earlier.

In what many people regarded as the most passionate and successful speech of his political career to date, Bush devoted his inaugural address to the themes of freedom, economic reform and the battle against crime and spoke of the need for co-operation to achieve these ends. Speaking of the 'new breeze' which he felt blowing, he called on Congress, where there was a substantial Democratic majority, to work closely with the government to reduce the enormous US budget deficit. He also called for a continuation of the war against drugs, crime and homelessness and voiced his confidence in the 'goodness and courage of the American people'.

After the inauguration ceremony, the celebrations continued all day, with a series of receptions and dances.

Soviet withdrawal from Afghanistan

On February 15th the last Soviet troops were airlifted out of Afghanistan ending nine years of bitter war against the *mujahedin* rebels. The previous few days had seen thousands of soldiers leaving the country, many of them crossing the Oxus River frontier in tanks and armoured personnel carriers. The phased operation, which had begun in May 1988, was completed exactly to schedule.

The withdrawal of Soviet troops was seen as another important indication of the new thinking resulting from Mikhail Gorbachev's leadership in the USSR and removed one of the longest standing causes of East-West tension. However, as the returning forces were greeted with a heroes' welcome in the border towns of Uzbekistan, tens of thousands of Afghan rebels were already massing outside Kabul and Jalalabad. The beleaguered regime of President Najibullah imposed virtual martial law in the capital as the first *mujahedin* rockets fell on the city.

Hirohito's funeral

On 24th February the funeral of the controversial Japanese Emperor Hirohito was attended by representatives of 163 countries. Half a million people lined the streets of Tokyo as the Emperor's coffin was taken to the Shinjuku Gyoen Imperial Gardens where he was entombed near his father's mausoleum. There were protests from US and British veterans of World War II, who objected to their countries honouring someone whom they considered a war criminal. His son succeeded him.

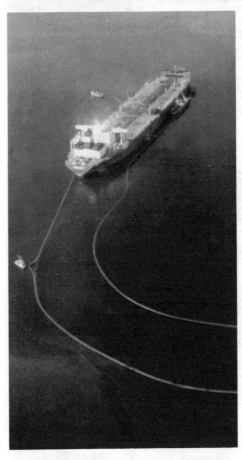

The *Exxon Valdez*

The worst ever oil pollution disaster in American waters took place in March when the 937 foot tanker *Exxon Valdez* ran aground and was holed in Prince William Sound off the coast of Alaska. A massive slick of some 10 million gallons of crude oil polluted 100 miles of coastline, causing irreparable damage to wildlife, including seals, otters and migratory seabirds.

The Salman Rushdie affair

Relations between Britain and Iran deteriorated sharply in February after Ayatollah Khomeini issued a death threat against British novelist Salman Rushdie. This came after months of controversy over Rushdie's novel *The Satanic Verses*, which had seen protests and demonstrations amongst Moslems worldwide. Speaking on Tehran radio, Khomeini urged all Moslems to carry out the death sentence against the author and his publishers, Viking Penguin.

Another football tragedy

Ninety-five Liverpool football fans were crushed to death on April 15th during the semi-final of the FA Cup at the Hillsborough Stadium in Sheffield, England. Fixed steel fences, designed to stop hooligans invading the pitch, had trapped people after police opened the gates.

Earthquake in San Francisco

Disaster struck San Francisco on 19 October when an earthquake, registering 6.9 on the Richter scale, devastated the Bay area of the city. The tremor caused more than 80 deaths, although early reports put the figure much higher. Most of the casualties occurred when the top deck of the double-decker Nimitz freeway fell onto rush-hour traffic travelling on the lower deck. The driver of the truck shown (left) had a lucky escape when the concrete slab poised above his vehicle miraculously failed to collapse.

The M1 air crash

Less than a month after the Lockerbie disaster, Britain experienced another major airline tragedy on 9 January when a Boeing 737 flight from London to Belfast crashed on the M1 motorway near the village of Kegworth in Leicestershire. Forty-four people died when the 12-week old aircraft ploughed into the motorway embankment just 15 seconds' flight from the runway at East Midlands Airport where it was attempting to make an emergency landing after engine trouble. Early reports suggested that the pilot might have shut down the wrong engine.

The Marchioness tragedy

Fifty-one people died when a pleasure cruiser sank after colliding with a massive dredger on the River Thames in the centre of London on 20 August. A birthday party was in full swing aboard the cruiser, the *Marchioness*, when she was struck by the 2000-ton *Bowbelle* under Southwark Bridge in the early hours of the morning. Survivors told of the dredger looming up out of the darkness without warning, prompting calls for urgent improvements in river safety standards.

Ten Years of Thatcher

The year that saw the tenth anniversary of Margaret Thatcher's election as the first woman Prime Minister of Great Britain was a troubled one for her Conservative administration. Opinion polls showed the Labour opposition gaining in popularity as public disquiet over proposed health service reforms, food safety standards and the poll tax seriously damaged the government's standing. Only two months after the anniversary celebrations (right), Mrs Thatcher found herself once more embroiled in controversy when she sacked her long-standing Foreign Secretary, Sir Geoffrey Howe, in a surprise cabinet reshuffle. Then, in October Chancellor Nigel Lawson resigned following differences with the Prime Minister over economic policy and Britain's role in an integrated European monetary system. This led to another significant slump in the government's popularity.

IRA bombing in Deal

This is the spectacle of destruction which confronted the rescue services as they hurried to the scene of a bomb attack on a British Army barracks in Deal, Kent, in September (right). The bomb, which exploded in the early morning at the Royal Marines' School of Music, killed ten soldiers and injured at least twice as many, some of them seriously. Most of the casualties were army bandsmen. The IRA claimed responsibility for the attack, prompting fears that the terrorist organisation was about to mount an intensive bombing campaign against military installations in mainland Britain. After questions were raised about the bomber's ability to gain access to the Deal barracks, there were calls for an urgent review of security procedures at military bases throughout the country.

Trans-Siberian railway disaster

More than 460 people were believed to have died in the Urals region of the Soviet Union after a massive gas explosion destroyed two trains travelling on the Trans-Siberian railway. The explosion, which reduced the trains to a heap of charred and tangled wreckage (right), occurred after a leak of gas from the huge pipeline which follows the railway for long distances as it crosses the wastes of Siberia. The gas was ignited by sparks from the line as the two crowded passenger trains passed each other some 1,200 kilometres east of Moscow. The tragedy shocked the whole country, and the Soviet leader, Mikhail Gorbachev, visiting the scene of the catastrophe, called for a full investigation into its causes.

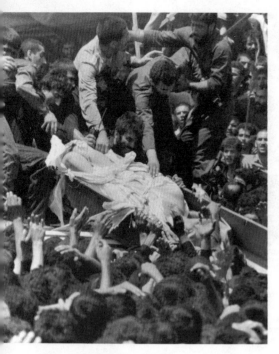

Khomeini's funeral

Crowds of hysterical mourners clutched at the coffin containing the body of the Ayatollah Khomeini as it was carried over the heads of the crowd to its final resting place on the outskirts of Tehran on June 6.

Death of Olivier

Lord Olivier, widely hailed as the greatest actor of the age, died at his Sussex home on 11 July at the age of 82. His roles included memorable interpretations of Richard III, Othello and Henry V (above).

F.W. de Klerk

The election of F.W. de Klerk (above) to the leadership of the South African National Party in February awakened hopes of serious reforms to the apartheid system and of the release from prison of the nationalist leader Nelson Mandela.

Farewell to Noriega

Manuel Noriega, the corrupt Panamanian leader, was finally ousted from power on 21 December when American troops invaded Panama, ostensibly in response to threats and violence against American citizens there. Troops loyal to Noriega staged a counter-attack and the fugitive President himself went to ground in the Vatican Embassy. Noriega, who had strong links with the CIA, originally came to power with the backing of the US government, but had long lost their support. President George Bush made known his desire to see him face drug trafficking charges in the United States.

Tiananmen Square

In the People's Republic of China hundreds of thousands of students, supported by others from all walks of life, gathered in Beijing's central Tiananmen Square to express their dissatisfaction with the country's ageing leadership and to voice their demands for democratic reform. The first mass demonstrations followed the death in April of Hu Yaobang, a former Communist Party leader widely seen as an advocate of reform, and soon developed into a permanent presence in Tiananmen Square. In May, they overshadowed the visit to Beijing of the Soviet leader Mikhail Gorbachev, and later in the same month the students, some of whom undertook a hunger strike for democracy (above left), raised in the square a statue modelled on the US Statue of Liberty (above centre). Similar demonstrations were reported in other major cities throughout China.

On 4 June, the Chinese government decided to end the protests and detachments of the People's Liberation Army closed in on the square. Soldiers fired into the crowds and tanks advanced along the broad main streets of the capital. One brave student succeeded in halting a column of tanks in the Avenue of Eternal Peace (above), but hundreds of others were less lucky. More than 2,000 people are thought to have been killed in the ensuing massacre.

Eastern Europe

1989 witnessed changes in the political map of Europe more far-reaching than any since that map was first drawn in the aftermath of the Second World War. Spontaneous upsurges of popular dissent engulfed country after country in Eastern Europe, rocking to their very foundations the entrenched Communist régimes of the Soviet bloc. Despite the ominous shadow of the Tiananmen Square massacre, vast crowds appeared on the streets of the Eastern European capitals to demand democratic reform, and one by one the governments of the Warsaw Pact – Poland, Hungary, Czechoslovakia, Bulgaria, even East Germany – staggered and fell under the apparently unstoppable tide of their citizens' peaceful mass protest. In November, television viewers throughout the world witnessed emotional scenes in Berlin as the Berlin Wall – for so long the most potent symbol of East-West confrontation – was finally breached and tens of thousands of East German citizens crossed into the West to be reunited with friends and relatives from whom they had been separated by the closing of the border in 1961.

In Rumania, however, the story was tragically different. There the hard-line Stalinist régime of Nicolae Ceausescu met the first wave of street protests not with moderation, but with the gun. Thousands may have died as troops and secret police loyal to Ceausescu battled it out with demonstrators and pro-democracy factions in the army on the streets of Timosoara and Bucharest. In a period of less than two weeks the Rumanian people accomplished a revolution which swept Ceausescu from power, but the cost in human life was high indeed, the many victims including the former dictator and his wife, executed by firing squad in the last days of the year.

Meanwhile in the Soviet Union itself, Mikhail Gorbachev, in many ways the fountainhead of all the changes in Eastern Europe, faced similar demands for greater democracy both among his political colleagues and on the streets of the Soviet republics.

Opposite page, top: Former Czech Prime Minister Alexander Dubcek, exiled after the Soviet crackdown on his reform attempts in 1968, returns in triumph to address crowds in the capital, Prague.

Opposite page, bottom: In December President Gorbachev and Pope John Paul II met, ending 70 years of hostility between the Soviet Union and the Vatican.

Left: Souvenir hunters chip pieces from the newly-opened Berlin Wall.

Below: Polish Prime Minister Tadeusz Mazowiecki calls on Parliament to speed up the democratic process.

Bottom left: Nicolae and Elena Ceausescu shortly before their execution.

Bottom right: Crowds gather under the statue of Lenin in the capital of the Soviet Republic of Azerbaijan to demand independence from Moscow.

1990

Jan	3	General Manuel Noriega surrenders to US military
	27	Dissolution of Polish communist party
	28	East German agreement to form all-party government
Feb	11	Release of Nelson Mandela
	25	Sandinista defeat in Nicaraguan elections
Mar	15	End to CPSU. Gorbachev elected President of USSR
	15	Collapse of Israeli government
	21	Independence for Namibia
	31	Poll tax riots in Britain
Apr	17	International conference on global warming
	19	Victory for pro-democracy in Nepal
May	20	Iliescu elected President in Rumania
	20	*Intifada* rioting in Palestine
	22	NATO Defence Ministers cut budgets
	31	Bush-Gorbachev summit meeting in Washington
	31	Ban on British beef imports in Europe led by France
Jun	21	Massive Iran earthquake
Jul	2	Nationwide strike called by ANC in South Africa
	18	Change of US policy on Indo-China
Aug	2	Iraqi invasion of Kuwait
	7	US troops sent to Gulf

Aug	28	Guinness trial verdicts
	31	De Klerk opens National Party to all races
	31	UN begins talks with Iraq
Sep	6	Death of Sir Len Hutton
	13	Township violence in South Africa
	29	Child summit in New York
Oct	8	Britain joins European exchange-rate mechanism
	8	Arabs killed in rioting on Temple Mount, Jerusalem
	14	Death of Leonard Bernstein
	15	President Gorbachev awarded Nobel Peace Prize
	24	Edward Heath returns to UK with hostages from Iraq
Nov	1	Resignation of Sir Geoffrey Howe
	9	Bush announces doubling of US forces in Gulf
	21	Signing of declaration of end of Cold War in Paris
	22	Bush spends Thanksgiving with troops in Saudi
	22	Resignation of Margaret Thatcher
	27	John Major elected Prime Minister of Britain
Dec	1	Channel Tunnel breakthrough
		The Arts
		David Lynch's film *Wild at Heart*
		A. S. Byatt's *Possession*

German Unification

Amid large-scale celebrations such as the spectacular rock concert in Berlin's Potsdamer Platz during which a giant mock-up of the Wall was demolished (below), the process of German reunification gathered pace throughout 1990. The first two-plus-four talks between East and West German, French, Soviet, US and UK foreign ministers were held at the beginning of May, and a few days later the East and West German finance ministers signed a treaty agreeing to the 'creation of a monetary, economic and social union' between the two countries and setting July 1st as the date for currency union. Full political reunification – a prospect hardly even dreamed of only a year before – officially took place at midnight on October 2nd.

Nelson Mandela Free

After much speculation, African National Congress leader Nelson Mandela finally walked free from Victor Verster prison in South Africa's Cape Province on the afternoon of February 11th. It was the end of 27 years in prison for the 71-year-old Mandela, who had been given a life sentence for treason in 1964. Widespread celebrations were followed by the beginning of serious negotiations between the ANC, of which Mandela was shortly elected Deputy President, and President F. W. de Klerk, but the process of effecting a peaceful transition to a multiracial society was threatened by escalating violence between the ANC and the rival Zulu-based Inkatha movement.

Reed and Polhill Released

In April 1990, the American hostages Robert Polhill and Frank Reed were released from captivity in Lebanon as a result of Syrian and Iranian mediation. Reed (above), a 57-year-old educationist, had been held, blindfolded 24 hours a day, for 3½ years after being kidnapped by the Organisation of Islamic Dawn.

Keenan Released

In August the Irish hostage Brian Keenan (above) was handed over to the Irish Foreign Minister in Damascus after being held for 4½ years by the Organisation of Islamic Dawn who kidnapped him in Beirut in April 1986. The 39-year-old teacher originally refused to leave captivity unless his fellow hostage John McCarthy was also released.

Stefano Casiraghi

On October 3rd Stefano Casiraghi, the husband of Princess Caroline of Monaco, was killed in a speedboat accident near Saint-Jean-Cap-Ferrat in the South of France. The 30-year-old Italian-born financier died instantly when his 5 tonne boat, *Pinot di Pinot*, turned over and sank after striking a wave at more than 125 miles per hour. Casiraghi and his co-pilot Patrice Innocenti, who ejected from the vessel and survived the accident, were defending their title (won the previous year in America) on the second day of the world offshore speedboat championships.

Greta Garbo

Greta Garbo, one of the greatest stars of Hollywood's golden age, died in New York in April at the age of 84. Garbo, whose real name was Greta Gustafsson, was born in Sweden, but moved to Hollywood in the 1920s to make such classic films as *Anna Christie* (her first talkie) and *Anna Karenina*. She went into intensely private retirement after making her last picture, *Two-faced Woman*, in 1930.

Leonard Bernstein

The music world mourned the death in October of the American conductor, composer and pianist Leonard Bernstein. Bernstein, a flamboyant public figure, was one of the greatest conductors of his generation as well as a composer who bridged the worlds of popular and 'serious' music with such scores as *West Side Story*, the Chichester Psalms and numerous orchestral and choral works.

Sammy Davis Junior

The singer, actor and entertainer Sammy Davis Junior died on May 16th after a long battle against throat cancer. He was 64. Davis started in show business at the age of three and became one of America's most successful entertainers in spite of racial prejudice and his own alcohol and drug problems. In addition to a spectacular stage career, Davis made more than 20 films.

The Junk Bond King

In April the American financial executive Michael Milken (right) pleaded guilty to six charges of criminal fraud and conspiracy arising from his time as head of the high-yield bond department at Drexel Burnham Lambert, the Wall Street investment bank. Widely seen as the inspiration behind the multi-million dollar US junk bond market, the 44-year-old Milken was fined $600 million after pleading guilty to the charges as part of a plea-bargaining deal by the prosecution. Part of the case against him derived from conversations secretly tape-recorded by Milken's erstwhile partner in arbitrage, Ivan Boesky. Later in the year Milken faced additional charges, and in November was sentenced to ten years in prison.

Guinness Scandal

In August the defendants in the Guinness trial were found guilty of charges arising from the conduct of Guinness' £2.7 billion takeover of the Distillers group in 1986. Former Guinness chairman Ernest Saunders (left) was sentenced to five years in prison and Gerald Ronson, the garage and property tycoon, was given a fine of £5 million, the largest in British legal history. The judge in the case spoke of 'dishonesty on a massive scale' in the mounting of an illegal share support operation during the takeover. The scandal rocked the City of London.

End of an Empire

On September 26th the Australian entrepreneur Alan Bond (above) finally resigned as chairman and chief executive of his beleaguered Bond Corporation Holdings after a two year battle to save the brewing, mining, media and property group, whose financial position crumbled from a profit of A$403 million in 1987-8 to a loss of A$980 million in 1988-9. A millionaire by the age of 21, Bond became an Australian hero after his boat won the Americas Cup in 1983.

Marion Barry

The problems of drugs, crime and racial tension in America's capital city were thrown into stark relief by the trial of the black Mayor of Washington, Marion Barry, on drugs and perjury charges. In August Barry (above) was cleared of 13 out of the 14 charges arising from a controversial police operation in which a former girlfriend lured him into a hotel room bugged by FBI agents. The case did irreparable damage to Barry's political standing.

Asil Nadir

In October the attempts of the Cypriot-born entrepreneur Asil Nadir (above) to save Polly Peck International, his troubled fruit and electronics company, failed when the company was put into administration. Rumours of financial malpractice at Polly Peck, once the most spectacularly successful share on the UK stock market, were investigated by the regulatory authorities and led to a collapse in investor confidence and the company's share price.

Resignation of Shevardnadze

In a move that shocked both the Soviet Union and the wider world, Soviet foreign minister Eduard Shevardnadze, one of the architects of the East-West détente of the 1980s, resigned on December 20th. In a dramatic speech to the Congress of People's Deputies, he cited the growing influence of conservative hard-liners for his decision, which was described by President Gorbachev as 'unforgiveable'.

Perestroika in the balance

In a grim reminder of the near collapse of the Soviet economy, food rationing was introduced in a number of the country's major cities, including Leningrad (above), in November and December. Despite record harvests, distribution networks had ground to a halt and, while millions of tons of grain rotted in the countryside, the international community, led by Germany, organised an airlift of emergency food aid.

New Prime Minister for Britain

Amid widespread unease about government policy on Europe and local government finance, the resignation in November of the long-time Thatcher loyalist Sir Geoffrey Howe prompted a challenge to Mrs Thatcher's leadership of the British Conservative Party by Michael Heseltine. Thatcher's majority in the first ballot was too small to avoid a second round and, despite her declared determination to fight on, she was persuaded to resign by members of her cabinet. Douglas Hurd and the Chancellor, John Major, then entered the race. Major came out on top in the ensuing vote and, following the withdrawal of Hurd and Heseltine, became the new leader of the Conservative Party and thus Prime Minister, ending 11 years of Thatcher government.

President Walesa

Against a background of soaring unemployment and plummetting living standards, Poland held its first direct presidential elections in November to choose a successor to the resigning President Jaruzelski. Lech Walesa, the leader of the Solidarity trade union, campaigning on a platform of accelerated economic and political reform, gained a narrow majority in the ballot, defeating the Prime Minister Tadeusz Mazowiecki, and the maverick self-made millionaire, Stanislaw Tyminski, whose emergence from exile in Canada to achieve second place in the ballot was a great political surprise. In the second ballot, however, Walesa was elected by a landslide and, at his inauguration on December 22nd, proclaimed the beginning of the 'Third Polish Republic'.

The Gulf Crisis

The cause of world peace, so dramatically advanced by the apparent ending of the Cold War during 1989, suffered a serious setback with the invasion of Kuwait by Iraq in the late summer of 1990. Following the breakdown of talks over territorial and commercial disputes between the two countries, troops loyal to the Iraqi President, Saddam Hussein (left), crossed the Kuwaiti border in force on August 2nd and quickly occupied the whole country, driving the ruling al-Sabah family into exile. Shortly afterwards Saddam Hussein announced the annexation of Kuwait as the 19th province of Iraq.

International reaction

The Iraqi action was met with unprecedentedly unanimous condemnation from the international community, a response no doubt sharpened by the commercial and strategic importance to the industrialised world of the Gulf's oil supplies. This opposition was expressed in the implementation of far-reaching economic sanctions against Iraq and a United Nations resolution demanding the immediate unconditional withdrawal of troops from Kuwait. Meanwhile, Iraqi forces had been gathering along the border with Saudi Arabia and, in response to an urgent request for help from the Saudi Government, the US President George Bush began a massive military build-up in the Gulf area as the spearhead of a multi-national force to defend against further Iraqi aggression and to enforce withdrawal.

Countdown to war

More than 200,000 US troops, supported by British and other contingents and equipped with the most sophisticated military hardware and material, had already been airlifted to the Gulf in Operation Desert Shield when Bush announced at the beginning of November that this force was to be more than doubled over the coming months, creating the potential for a massive counter-strike against Saddam. Thousands of Westerners and other foreign nationals initially held hostage in Kuwait and Iraq as a 'human shield' against UN attack had begun to be released by the end of the year, amid intense diplomatic efforts by individuals and governments to avoid the momentum of war becoming unstoppable. But with sanctions taking longer to bite than had been hoped, and with Saddam attempting to rally both the Islamic fundamentalist and Arab nationalist camps behind his cause by urging holy war against the US (above right) and linking Iraqi withdrawal from Kuwait with demands for Israeli withdrawal from the occupied territories of the West Bank and the Gaza Strip, a diplomatic solution to the crisis seemed more and more elusive. At the end of November United Nations Resolution 678 authorised the use of force by the 28-nation Allied coalition if Iraq had not withdrawn from Kuwait by January 15th, 1991.

1991

Jan	7	Haiti coup defeated
	7	Soviet paratroopers sent to Baltic Republics
	9	Baker-Aziz talks collapse in Geneva
	13	Pérez de Cuéllar meets Saddam Hussein in Baghdad
	15	UN deadline for Iraqi withdrawal from Kuwait passes
	16	Operation Desert Storm begins
	17	Death of King Olav of Norway
	20	Iraq parades captured Allied airmen on TV
	23	High-denomination banknotes withdrawn in USSR
	25	Massive oil slick in Gulf
	29	Nelson Mandela meets Chief Buthelezi in Durban
	29-31	Battle for Khafji in Saudi Arabia
Feb	1	De Klerk promises end of all apartheid legislation
	7	IRA mortar bomb attack on Downing Street
	13	Civilians killed in Allied bombing of Iraqi bunker
	18	Gorbachev-Aziz talks in Moscow to end war in Gulf
	23	Military coup topples government in Thailand
	24	Allied land offensive begins in Gulf
	25	Warsaw Pact military alliance dissolved
	28	Ceasefire in Gulf
Mar	4	Crown Prince returns to Kuwait
	6	Indian PM Chandra Shekkar resigns
	8	Collapse of International Leisure Group
	14	Release of the Birmingham Six
	17	National referendum in USSR votes narrowly for Union
	21	British Government announces end of poll tax
	28	Massive pro-Yeltsin demonstration in Red Square
Apr	2	British businessman Roger Cooper released in Iran
	3	Death of Graham Greene
	12	140 die in Italian ferry disaster
	16	Death of Sir David Lean
	19	Dr George Carey enthroned as Archbishop of Canterbury
	30	Cyclone in Bangladesh leaves millions homeless
May	8	UK scientists discover gene that determines sex
	16	The Queen addresses US Congress
	21	Indian Prime Minister Rajiv Ghandi assassinated
Jun	13	First free presidential election in USSR
Jul	6	BCCI closed by government after huge banking frauds
Aug	8	John McCarthy arrives in UK after release in Beirut
	18	Coup temporarily takes power from Gorbachev
	29	Soviet parliament suspends Communist party
Sep	13	Soviet troops pull out of Cuba

Oct	27	Australia's Wallabies win Rugby World Cup
Nov	5	Robert Maxwell drowns in mysterious circumstances
	8	Basketball star 'Magic' Johnson admits he is HIV positive
Dec	20	Paul Keating becomes Prime Minister of Australia
	21	USSR dissolved; replaced by a commonwealth of states
		The Arts
		Kevin Costner's Dances with Wolves
		Godfather III
		Pavarotti's 30th anniversary concert; Hyde Park, London
		Death of Freddie Mercury, Margot Fonteyn,
		Martha Graham, Graham Greene, Dame Peggy Ashcroft

War in the Gulf

Less than 24 hours after the UN deadline of January 15th passed without seeing an Iraqi withdrawal from Kuwait, Allied forces launched a wave of massive attacks on targets in Iraq and Kuwait, initiating an aerial bombardment of military centres, command and supply networks, and civil infrastructure that was to continue relentlessly for more than a month. The Iraqi response to this phase of the so-called 'air war' was eerily muted, and by the end of January Allied commanders were able to claim air and naval supremacy throughout the Gulf theatre of operations. The effectiveness of the air campaign in eroding Saddam's vast technologically inferior military machine became only too apparent when on February 24th the long-awaited ground war began with a three-pronged attack into Iraq and Kuwait. Fears of enormous Allied casualty rates proved unfounded as Iraqi resistance crumbled before a textbook military operation which saw the complete liberation of Kuwait within three days. On February 28th President Bush called off the bombardment of Iraq's retreating forces and suspended hostilities. Allied casualties amounted to some 250 dead; Iraq's losses will probably never be known, but have been estimated at between 35,000 and 100,000.

Stormin' Norman

As Commander-in-Chief of the Allied forces, US General H. Norman Schwarzkopf (above) was responsible for converting Operation Desert Shield, the defence of Saudi Arabia, into Operation Desert Storm, the campaign to liberate Kuwait.

Scorched earth

Allied forces arriving in Kuwait City saw at first hand the cost of seven months of Iraqi occupation. Property had been looted and destroyed throughout the city and reports of atrocities committed against civilians were widespread. Almost all of Kuwait's 950 producing oil wells had been set on fire (above), leaving a permanent pall of black smoke over the country and an oil-slick over hundreds of square kilometres in the waters of the Gulf. At the same time, members of the al-Sabbah family returning from exile (including Crown Prince of Saad), charged by the Emir with the task of imposing martial law, were greeted by determined demands for democratic reform.

The Kurds

Even before the end of hostilities, factions within Iraq had begun to respond to President Bush's call for the Iraqi people to overthrow Saddam Hussein. A Shia rebellion in the south and a Kurdish uprising in the north were, however, both brutally suppressed by Saddam's remaining forces. The suppression created a massive refugee problem as hundred of thousands of

people fled their homes. International attention was focussed on the plight of the Kurds crowding the inhospitable mountains above the Turkish border (above) in an attempt to escape Saddam Hussein's genocidal reassertion of power. Humanitarian aid was sent but urgent calls for Allied military intervention remained unanswered.

551

The Baltic Republics

Further evidence of the new hard line on domestic dissent in the Soviet Union was provided in January when government troops began a military crackdown in the Baltic Republics. Civilians were killed as tanks appeared on the streets of Vilnius and Riga, the Lithuanian and Latvian capitals, and Black Beret paramilitaries stormed government, press and television offices held by supporters of the nationalist movements. President Gorbachev denied ordering the use of force, but the bloodshed led to massive demonstrations in the Baltics, and in Moscow some 100,000 protestors demanded Gorbachev's resignation. Soviet paratroopers withdrew at the end of January, but tensions remained high in Latvia, Lithuania and Estonia. With Western governments anxious to retain Soviet support for the anti-Saddam coalition, however, international condemnation was muted.

Unrest in Albania

Relatively untouched by events in Eastern Europe at the end of 1989, Albania saw an upsurge of popular demands for democratic reform in 1990 and 1991. In the early months of 1991, President Ramiz Alia imposed presidential rule in an attempt to contain unrest in the capital Tirana, where students tore down a giant statue of the Stalinist leader Enver Hoxha, and, despite some liberalising measures, thousands of refugees fled the country for Greece and Italy.

Mandela and Buthelezi

The long-awaited meeting between ANC Deputy President Nelson Mandela and Chief Mangosuthu Gatsha Buthelezi, head of the rival Zulu-based Inkatha movement, took place in Durban on January 29th (above). The meeting, the first between the two leaders for 30 years, was seen as a vital first step towards the easing of tensions between ANC and Inkatha followers which had claimed thousands of black lives in the townships in the preceding months.

Martha Graham

The world of dance lost two of its most celebrated figures with the deaths of Martha Graham and Margot Fonteyn. One of the most influential dancers and choreographers of the century, Graham was born in Pittsburgh in 1894 and made her independent debut in 1926. Known for her interpretations of primitive or mythological subjects, she became a leading exponent of modern dance techniques, creating some 150 works.

Margot Fonteyn

Born Margaret Hookham in 1913, Margot Fonteyn made her solo debut dancing Giselle in 1937. After becoming prima ballerina of the Royal Ballet in London, she worked closely with its Director, Frederick Ashton, to create roles in a number of ballets, including, in 1963, *Marguerite and Armand*, in which she danced with Rudolf Nureyev in what is considered to be one of the greatest partnerships of modern ballet.

Graham Greene

The death in April of Graham Greene silenced one of the most significant voices of modern English literature. Born in 1904, Greene published his first novel in 1929, but critical acclaim eluded him until the publication of *Stamboul Train* in 1932. Much concerned with loss of faith and the problem of evil, Greene's novels have proved enduringly popular and many, including *The Third Man*, were made into successful films.

Release of John McCarthy

On August 8th, the British hostage John McCarthy, who was kidnapped in Beirut on April 17th 1986, was freed with a message from his captors for UN Secretary General Perez de Cuellar. Much of the press attention focused on McCarthy's reunion with his girlfriend Jill Morrell (above), who had campaigned tirelessly for his release. The release of Terry Waite, who had been held in Beirut since 1987, followed in November.

Robert Maxwell

The Czech-born British tycoon Robert Maxwell died on November 5th after apparently falling overboard from his yacht off the Canary Islands. Despite initial tributes from leading international figures, the event triggered the collapse of his media empire with huge debts, revelations of pension fund plundering on a massive scale and a serious fraud investigation into the financial dealings of Maxwell and his sons Ian and Kevin.

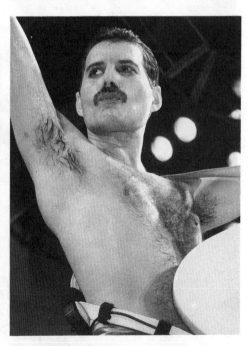

Fighting to the end

AIDS claimed another high-profile victim with the death in November of the British rock star Freddie Mercury. As determinedly outrageous offstage as on, Freddie Mercury, 45, the lead singer of the internationally famous group *Queen*, which shot to fame in the 1970s with such songs as *Bohemian Rhapsody* and *We Are the Champions*, was one of the most flamboyant and popular figures in the world of rock and entertainment.

Rajiv Gandhi assassinated

A political dynasty came to an abrupt and violent end on May 21st when Rajiv Gandhi, former Prime Minister of India and leader of the Congress (I) Party, was murdered in Sriperumpudur, Tamil Nadu. The 46-year-old politician, the son of Indira Gandhi and grandson of India's first premier, Nehru, was about to address a meeting as part of the country's general election campaign when a young woman stepped forward to present him with a bouquet of flowers and detonated explosives strapped to her body. The attack, which was blamed on Tamil separatists, sent shockwaves through the international community. Many heads of state attended Rajiv's funeral in Delhi, at which his son Rahul performed the traditional cremation ceremony (left). Congress (I) elected P. V. Narasimha Rao as its leader after failing to persuade Rajiv's widow to succeed him.

Unrest in Algeria

The Algerian capital, Algiers, was rocked by serious unrest in June after the fundamentalist Islamic Salvation Front (FIS) called for strike action in support of their demands for the resignation of President Benjedid and the creation of an Islamic state. Demonstrations, many of which ended in bloodshed, led to the postponement of general election plans and the creation of an interim non-party government under Sid-Ahmed Ghozali on June 18th. Violent clashes continued between fundamentalists and the security forces, however, and hundreds of FIS supporters were arrested as the government sought to crack down on opposition in and around the capital. The first round of the long-promised general elections finally took place in December, but the result – an unexpectedly large FIS victory – would be overridden by a military coup the following month.

Slovenia and Croatia

The first shots in what was to prove the bloodiest war on European soil since the end of World War Two were fired in the Yugoslavian republic of Slovenia in June. On the 25th Slovenia and Croatia declared their independence from Yugoslavia, a move which led to immediate military confrontation with the Serb-dominated forces of the Yugoslavian National Army (JNA), with the federal airforce bombarding a number of targets in Slovenia (left), including the capital Ljubljiana. International efforts to broker peace made little progress in the face of escalating inter-ethnic tensions, but by early July the success of the Slovenian resistance forces had shifted the focus of the fighting to neighbouring Croatia. Federal planes attacked the Croatian cities of Osijek, Vukovar and Vinkovci in early August, while on the ground JNA-backed Serbian irregulars made sweeping territorial gains.

The last days of the USSR

For three days in August the much-vaunted 'new world order' seemed threatened by a return to the stalemate of the Cold War as hardline Communists in the Soviet Union reasserted their power in a dramatic military coup, deposing President Gorbachev and sending tanks onto the streets of Moscow.

The world held its breath as the Soviet newsagency Tass announced that Gorbachev was 'too ill to perform his duties' and that power had accordingly passed to former Vice-President Yanayev. The new government declared a state of emergency, banning political parties and demonstrations and imposing strict controls on the media. With the military rapidly closing in, Russian Federation President Boris Yeltsin (left) became the focus of widespread popular resistance to the coup, memorably proclaiming his support for democracy from the roof of a tank outside the beleaguered Russian parliament building, the 'White House' (below). Amid mounting tension, barricades appeared on the streets and thousands of demonstrators, defying the government curfew, openly vented their opposition to Yanayev's forces (bottom).

With military support for it patchy, the coup collapsed as suddenly as it had begun. On August 21st a shell-shocked President Gorbachev returned to Moscow from the Crimean *dacha* where he had been held under house arrest. But the balance of power within the country had shifted radically towards Yeltsin, Russia and reform. Within days, most of the former republics had declared independence and the Communist Party was disbanded. On December 21st the USSR ceased to exist and Gorbachev resigned on Christmas Day.

1992

Jan	1	Boutros Boutros-Ghali becomes UN Secretary General
	8	US President Bush collapses on Japanese tour
	15	EC recognises Slovenian and Croatian independence
Feb	1	Presidents Bush and Yeltsin hold talks at Camp David
	10	Airlift of aid to CIS begins
Mar	3	Hundreds killed in Turkish Black Sea mine explosion
	17	South Africa's whites vote for constitutional change
	19	Duke and Duchess of York to separate
Apr	7	EC/US recognise Bosnia-Hercegovina's independence
	9	Conservatives win British General Election
	12	EuroDisney opens in France
	13	Nelson and Winnie Mandela announce separation
May	6	Marlene Dietrich dies
	22	France and Germany form joint defence force
	30	UN agrees wide-ranging sanctions against Yugoslavia
Jun	3	'Earth Summit' begins in Rio de Janeiro
	17	President Yeltsin addresses US Congress
	17	46 die in Boipatong massacre, South Africa
	28	French President Mitterand visits Sarajevo
Jul	6	French lorry drivers bring chaos to roads
	10	Noriega sentenced to 40 years, jail on drugs charges
	16	Bill Clinton accepts Democratic nomination for President
	18	John Smith elected leader of British Labour Party
Aug	19	Right-wing rioting begins in Rostock, Germany
	19	Hurricane Andrew hits southern US
	27	Lord (David) Owen to head EC Yugoslavian peace effort
Sep	7	29 killed in massacre in Ciskei, South Africa
	16	'Black Wednesday': Britain leaves the ERM
	20	France votes yes in Maastricht referendum
	29	Brazilian Congress votes to impeach President Collor
Oct	10	US signs trade agreement with China
	12	Earthquake strikes Cairo
Nov	3	Bill Clinton elected US President
	11	UK: General Synod votes for ordination of women
	24	141 killed in Chinese air crash
Dec	4	US troops land in Somalia
	6	Riots follow Hindu attack on Ayodha mosque, India
	9	UK: PM announces Charles and Diana to separate
	16	Israel orders deportation of 415 Palestinians

The Arts

Expo '92 in Seville

Nobel Prize for Literature: Derek Walcott

Mike Tyson

On March 26th, the former heavyweight boxing champion Mike Tyson was fined $30,000 and sentenced to six years in prison on rape charges by an Indianapolis court. The 25-year-old boxer (above, seen leaving the courtroom) had been found guilty in February of sexually assaulting Desiree Washington, 18, a contestant in the Miss Black America beauty competition, in his hotel room in Indianapolis in July 1991. He had denied the charges. A multi-millionaire whose controversial activities outside the ring had often attracted media attention, Tyson had become the youngest ever heavyweight champion in 1986.

Conservative General Election win

Opinion pollsters were routed as decisively as the opposition parties in the British General Election of April 9th. Contrary to widespread predictions of an inconclusive result or a narrow Labour win, John Major's Conservative Party comfortably held onto power, albeit with a reduced majority, to begin an almost unprecedented fourth consecutive term in office. Four days later, Neil Kinnock (above) announced his intention to resign as Labour leader after nine years in the job. A fiery orator widely credited with making the party electable again after the bitter in-fighting of the early 1980s, he was succeeded by John Smith in July.

Benny Hill and Frankie Howerd

The world of British comedy lost two of its elder statesmen in April with the deaths of Benny Hill and Frankie Howerd. In the later years of his career, Hill (above left), whose comedy relied heavily on slapstick and innuendo, was less popular in Britain than in the US, whereas Howerd, despite superficial similarities in material (above right), gained a more enduring reputation in the UK. Active in film, radio and theatre, he perhaps remains best known for his 1970s television comedy series *Up Pompeii*.

IRA City bomb

Three people were killed and many more injured when a massive IRA bomb exploded in the City of London on April 10th. The 100-lb device, which went off at 9.25 p.m., caused extensive damage, including blowing out every window in the Commercial Union tower (above).

Riots in Los Angeles

In April and May, Los Angeles was rocked by the worst rioting in the US for more than a quarter of a century. The unrest began after four white policemen were acquitted of assaulting a black motorist despite widely televised videotape evidence showing him being kicked and beaten. More than 50 people were killed and some 4,000 injured in four days of violence, looting and arson, which saw 12,000 arrests and more than $1 billion worth of damage. 10,000 troops and National Guardsmen were drafted in to restore order. Riots also occurred in several other cities but on a smaller scale.

1992

Unrest in Thailand

Demonstrations in Thailand against the military-backed premiership of General Suchinda Kraprayoon reached crisis point in May after government troops fired on protestors in the capital, Bangkok. The pace of opposition to the Suchinda régime had quickened when the widely-respected opposition leader Chamlong Srimaung began a hunger-strike in support of his demands for constitutional change. Thousands of people defied a ban on demonstrations to show their support for him, the protests culminating in a 150,000-strong rally in central Bangkok on May 17th (right). The military crackdown, in which a number of protestors were shot, led to days of rioting in the capital. The crisis was only resolved after King Bhumipol Adulyadej, summoned Suchinda and Chamlong to a televised meeting and exhorted them to resolve their differences. A few days later, Suchinda resigned and the National Assembly conceded Chamlong's demands.

The Olympic Games

At the 25th Olympic Games, held in Barcelona in July and August, the controversial British athlete Linford Christie (above) became only the third Briton ever to win the Olympic 100 metres. Christie, 32, who had considered retiring after disappointing performances the previous year, described the victory, in which he set a time of 9.96 seconds, as 'the best race of my life'.

US intervention in Somalia

As factions loyal to rival warlords Mohammed Farrar Aideed and Ali Mahdi Mohammed continued to bring mayhem to the streets of the Somalian capital, Mogadishu, hundreds of thousands of people faced starvation in the countryside. In December, the US dispatched 28,000 troops to Somalia, in an operation codenamed 'Restore Hope', to help support the relief effort.

Right-wing violence in Germany

Weeks of tension erupted into violence in the former East German port of Rostock on the night of August 22nd when hundreds of right-wing youths, throwing paving-stones and firebombs and cheered on by local bystanders, attacked an immigrant hostel in the depressed Lichtenhagen area of the city. Thousands of police were drafted in to contain the unrest, which began when Romanian asylum-seekers, unable to find places in the hostel, camped out in front of it. The asylum-seekers were evacuated, but clashes between police and right-wingers continued for days, spreading from the Baltic port to other cities in both the east and west of the country, where hostels became the focus of attacks often involving neo-Nazi groups. The latest outbreaks of racist violence followed a steep rise both in the number of foreigners seeking asylum in Germany and in unemployment in the east of the country since reunification.
Left: Right-wing youths at a rally in eastern Germany.

Annus horribilis

Speaking after one of the most troubled years for the British monarchy since the Abdication Crisis of 1936, the Queen memorably described 1992 as an 'annus horribilis' in the history of her family. The announcements of the separation of the Duke and Duchess of York and the divorce of Princess Anne attracted unwelcome press attention, but the glare of the media spotlight fell on the Windsors with unprecedented ferocity after the publication in June of a book alleging that marital difficulties had led the Princess of Wales to attempt suicide, and despite condemnation by the Press Complaints Commission, royal exposés continued to provide the shock troops in a fierce tabloid circulation war throughout the ensuing months.

In this fevered atmosphere, the disastrous fire that raged through the royal residence, Windsor Castle, on November 20th, causing extensive damage to rooms, furniture and other treasures, was seen by many as symbolic of the wider fortunes of the family, and further condemnation ensued when it emerged that the costs of restoration were to be met from the public purse. Six days after the fire, the Prime Minister, John Major, let it be known that the Queen was reconsidering the scope of the Civil List and her exemption from payment of personal income tax, an issue on which the Royal Family had recently attracted mounting criticism. The final blow came in December when Prime Minister John Major announced to a hushed House of Commons that the Prince and Princess of Wales were officially to separate. He emphasised that the royal couple had no plans to divorce and that the separation did not affect Princess Diana's constitutional right to become Queen, but both assurances were greeted with considerable public scepticism.

Civil war in Yugoslavia

Throughout the year the former Federal Republic of Yugoslavia continued to tear itself apart in the bloodiest war to be fought on European soil since the end of World War Two. As EC- and UN-brokered peace talks repeatedly failed to achieve a lasting ceasefire, the focus of the conflict shifted from Croatia to Bosnia-Hercegovina, fuelling the worst refugee crisis in Europe for half a century (bottom right).

By January, when EC recognition of Croatian and Slovenian independence sounded the death-knell of the 75-year-old Yugoslav state, a third of Croatia was already under Serbian control. Two months later, Bosnia-Hercegovina's declaration of independence ignited the most volatile ethnic powderkeg in the Balkans. A new and terrible euphemism entered the vocabulary of war as Serbian irregulars and the Serb-dominated federal army began to execute a policy of 'ethnic cleansing' – the forcible mass-expulsion of Bosnian Muslims and other non-Serbs from their towns and villages. Images of skeletal Bosnian detainees (bottom left) revived memories of Nazi concentration camps, outraging public opinion, but still the attempts of the world community to broker peace between the warring parties foundered on the rocks of mutual hatred and distrust. By mid-July the Bosnian capital Sarajevo had been under siege for more than 100 days, with snipers operating freely in the streets and mortar fire from Serb positions in the surrounding hills inflicting appalling casualties on the civilian population. By the end of September, with the international humanitarian relief effort stalled (top right) and the harsh Balkan winter looming for the region's more than a million refugees, the spectre of mass famine reappeared in the heart of Europe.

Deportation of Palestinians

In December, as the *intifada*, or uprising, in the Israeli-occupied territories entered its sixth year, the Israeli Government responded to escalating terrorist activity, particularly by the Islamic Resistance Movement, Hamas, by ordering the summary deportation of more than 400 Palestinians to Lebanon. The Lebanese Government, however, refused to accept the deportees, who were consequently forced to set up a makeshift camp of tents in the inhospitable no man's land between Lebanon and Israel's self-declared security zone. Israel's action attracted widespread international condemnation, but, apart \from allowing the return of 10 Palestinians, the Israeli Government stood by its decision. Concern focused on the effect of the deportations on the fragile peace negotiations that had been taking place in Washington between Israel and the Palestine Liberation Organisation (PLO), whose representatives withdrew from the negotiations in protest on December 17th and pressed for similar action by the rest of the Arab delegation.

Maastricht

The future development of the European community was thrown into doubt in June when a Danish referendum on the Maastricht Treaty on closer economic and political union produced a narrow vote against ratification. A comparably narrow French vote in favour on September 20th failed to dispel the atmosphere of uncertainty, and the issue remained a potent source of political division in Britain, where the government came close to parliamentary defeat at the hands of its backbench 'Euro-sceptics' in November.

The US presidential election

On November 3rd, Bill Clinton (above right),the 46-year-old Governor of Arkansas, won a decisive victory in the United States presidential election, defeating the sitting president George Bush (above centre), who thus became only the fourth incumbent in American history to be voted out of the White House after a single term of office. The result, in which Clinton took 32 states to Bush's 18, marked the end of 12 years of Republican administration and was widely seen as a vote of no confidence in Bush's handling of the US economy. The long and often vitriolic campaign was given extra spice by the on-off candidature of the maverick Texan billionaire H. Ross Perot (above left), whose outsider status and folksy appeal to commonsense earned him an impressive 19 per cent of the popular vote. In the end though, neither Perot's massive expenditure on advertising nor the Republican's concerted campaign of slurs on Clinton's character, among them accusations of draft dodging, were sufficient to deprive the Democrats of victory – a victory made all the more remarkable by the fact that, barely two years earlier, Bush had looked set to coast to reelection on the unprecedented popularity earned by his

1993

Jan	1	European single market comes into operation
	3	Presidents Bush and Yeltsin sign START II Treaty
	12	Albert Reynolds elected Irish Taoiseach
	20	Bill Clinton sworn in as US President
Feb	18	1000 die in ferry disaster off Haiti
	26	Bomb explodes at World Trade Center, New York
Mar	13	Paul Keating wins Australian elections
	19	UN relief convoy reaches Srebrenica
	20	Yeltsin announces presidential rule
	29	Eduard Balladur appointed French premier
Apr	10	Chris Hani assassinated in South Africa
	19	Fire at Waco headquarters of Branch Davidian cult
	24	IRA bomb explodes in City of London
May	2	Bosnian Serb Parliament rejects Vance/Owen peace plan
	4	UK: Tycoon Asil Nadir jumps bail to N Cyprus
	17	Rebecca Stephens first woman to climb Everest
Jun	5	22 Pakistani UN soldiers killed in Mogadishu
	13	Tansu Çiller Turkey's first woman Prime Minister
	13	52 die in Serb attack on hospital in Gorazde
	23	Nigerian President Babangida annuls election results
Jul	6	G7 summit opens in Tokyo

	22	Millions made homeless in Punjab flooding
	25	Israeli air strikes on Hizbullah positions in Lebanon
	28	Car bomb attacks in Rome and Milan
Aug	2	UK ratifies Maastricht Treaty
	15	Pope tours Caribbean, Mexico and US
Sep	13	Israeli-PLO peace accord signed in Washington
	21	President Yeltsin dissolves Russian parliament
	30	10,000 die in Indian earthquake
Oct	4	Rebel leaders surrender at Russian 'White House'
	5	Vatican publishes *Veritatis Splendor*
	15	Nelson Mandela/F. W. de Klerk win Nobel Peace Prize
	25	Conservatives routed in Canadian elections
Nov	1	European Union comes into existence
	17	US Congress votes for NAFTA
Dec	7	South African Transitional Executive Council set up
	12	Strong gains for ultra-nationalists in Russian elections
	15	Downing Street Declaration on N Ireland issued
	15	Completion of GATT Uruguay Round
		The Arts
		Steven Spielberg's films *Jurassic Park*; *Schindler's List*
		Vikram Seth's novel *A Suitable Boy*

Inauguration of President Clinton

On January 20th, William Jefferson Clinton was inaugurated as
the 42nd President of the United States, having defeated George
Bush and Ross Perot. He promised an end to an era of 'deadlock
and drift', but was soon under attack for slowness in filling key
government posts.

Zhirinovsky

Political shockwaves were felt throughout the international
community in December when the ultra-nationalist Liberal
Democratic Party of Russia, under its maverick leader Vladimir
Zhirinovsky (above), gained the largest share of the vote in
elections to the Russian parliament.

Assassination of Chris Hani

On April 10th, the negotiations on constitutional reform in South Africa were seriously jeopardised by the assassination of Chris Hani, the charismatic general secretary of the South African Communist Party. It was claimed Government security forces were responsible.

War in Yugoslavia

Throughout the year, while successive attempts by the international community, to establish a workable peace plan foundered in the face of entrenched intercommunal hostility, fighting continued unabated in the former Yugoslavia. In June, Serb forces besieged Goradze, a United Nations -designated 'safe area', and in July the Bosnian capital, Sarajevo, came under intense bombardment (above). By September, the fiercest fighting was taking place around the Muslim-held town of Mostar, fuelling calls for the lifting of the Bosnian arms embargo.

World Trade Center bombing

On February 26th, six people were killed and hundreds more injured when a bomb exploded in a car park below the World Trade Center building in New York (above). Members of a Muslim fundamentalist group were later arrested and charged.

The Waco siege

72 people were killed when the headquarters of the Branch Davidian sect near Waco, Texas, burnt to the ground following an assault by the FBI, who had besieged the complex for 51 days. The dead included cult leader David Koresh.

Lamont's resignation

In May, Norman Lamont, whose credibility suffered after Britain's withdrawal from the ERM in 1992, was replaced as UK Chancellor of the Exchequer.

Japanese royal wedding

On June 9th, the Crown Prince Naruhito of Japan married Masako Owada, a former diplomat, in a shinto wedding ceremony in the Imperial Palace, Tokyo. The wedding took place against a background of mounting political tensions, culminating in the defeat of the Japanese Government in a confidence vote on June 18th.

Bad?

In November, the pop star Michael Jackson cancelled a projected world tour amid widespread allegations that he had been involved in the sexual abuse of a 13-year-old boy. Multi-millionaire Jackson, whose bizarre lifestyle has been the subject of much comment for some years, denied all the accusations in a televised broadcast from his ranch, Neverland.

Jurassic Park

Steven Spielberg's blockbuster movie *Jurassic Park* grossed an amazing $500 million in box office takings throughout the world during 1993, and clocked up considerably more as a result of a highly sophisticated merchandising campaign. Based on a novel by Michael Crichton, the film included a rare performance by Richard Attenborough.

Power struggles in Moscow

Russian President Boris Yeltsin's decision on September 21st to suspend the Russian Parliament pending elections to a new legislative body, was the signal for an intensification of the already bitter struggles for supremacy between pro- and anti-reform groupings within the political hierarchy of the Russian Federation. Yeltsin's Vice-President, Alexander Rutskoi, a staunch conservative, immediately declared the decree unconstitutional, and on September 24th the Congress of People's Deputies voted to impeach Yeltsin and appoint Rutskoi President in his place. The conflict centred on the Parliament building, known as 'the White House', where the rebels, many of them armed, were soon effectively besieged by Yeltsin's forces.

On October 3rd there were clashes when rebel forces tried to storm the headquarters of the state television company, and the following morning Yeltsin ordered the use of tanks against the White House in a bombardment which left the building burning and blackened (right) and swiftly led to the surrender of the rebel leaders and their supporters.

Israeli-Palestinian peace accord

On September 13th, Israel and the Palestine Liberation Organisation (PLO) signed a historic peace agreement on the lawn of the White House in Washington. The high-profile signing ceremony, overseen by President Clinton was attended by around 3000 invited dignitaries. The agreement came as the culmination of months of secret negotiations conducted under the auspices of the Norwegian Government. The so-called Declaration of Principles made provision for a transition to complete Palestinian autonomy in the West Bank and Gaza Strip. Even as Israeli premier Yitzhak Rabin and PLO leader Yassir Arafat shook hands, however, angry voices were being raised against the agreement in both Israel and the occupied territories.

Frank Zappa

1993 saw the death of the maverick and prolific musician Frank Zappa, once frontman of the *Mothers of Invention*, latterly cultural ambassador.

William Golding

The British novelist William Golding, author of *Lord of the Flies*, died on 19 June aged 82. He won the Nobel Prize for Literature in 1983.

Anthony Burgess

November saw the death of novelist Anthony Burgess, 76, perhaps best known for his controversial 1962 novel *A Clockwork Orange*.

Floods in America

In July, large areas of the American Mid-West were devastated by some of the worst flooding in the history of the United States following weeks of torrential rain. The Mississippi and Missouri rivers, despite emergency shoring-up efforts, broke their banks, inundating more than 40,000 square kilometres of farmland and making 30,000 people homeless. The disaster, which affected some seven states, prompted President Clinton to launch a multi-million dollar federal relief programme.

East meets west

In September, the Dalai Lama, spiritual leader of Tibet, visited the United States. Here, in an apparently incongruous juxtaposition, he is seen with Hollywood star Richard Gere and Gere's wife, model Cindy Crawford, before a fund-raising dinner of the American Himalayan Foundation co-chaired by Gere.

The Hubble Telescope

On December 2nd, the US space shuttle *Endeavour* was launched on a mission to repair the Hubble Space Telescope. The revolutionary telescope, which was launched in April 1990, had developed a major fault in its optical system in June of the same year, but it was not until 1993 that the first opportunity for remedial work became possible. The mission, which returned to Earth on December 13th, involved seven astronauts, who successfully replaced one of the telescope's cameras and its solar panels as well as installing an optics package that corrected the defect thereby fulfilling their operation. Here, in the last of five space walks, astronaut Story Musgrave is seen at the end of the Remote Manipulator System arm, carrying covers for the newly replaced magnetometers.

1994

Jan 13	Italian Prime Minister Carlo Ciampi resigns
17	Earthquake in Los Angeles
Feb 5	70 killed in mortar attack on Sarajevo marketplace
25	29 Muslims massacred at a mosque in Hebron
28	Serbian planes shot down by NATO over Bosnia
Mar 11	Riots in S African homeland of Bophutatswana
28	Silvio Berlusconi gains largest vote in Italian elections
Apr 6	Presidents of Rwanda and Burundi killed in air crash
10	NATO air strikes against Serbs around Gorazde
26	262 die in Chinese Airbus crash in Japan
26	Start of first multi-racial elections in S Africa
May 6	Channel Tunnel opened by Queen & President Mitterand
10	Nelson Mandela sworn in as President of South Africa
12	UK: Labour Party leader John Smith dies
19	Jacqueline Kennedy Onassis dies
27	Alexander Solzhenitsyn returns to Russia
Jun 6	50th anniversary commemorations of D-Day in Normandy
22	Russia joins NATO's 'Partnerships for Peace'
Jul 1	Yassir Arafat enters Gaza Strip
4	Kigali falls to Rwandan Patriotic Front
8	North Korean President Kim Il Sung dies
17	Brazil win World Cup

21	Tony Blair elected leader of British Labour Party
Aug 14	Carlos the Jackal arrested in Sudan
26	Armed Islamic Group forms rebel government in Algeria
31	IRA announces ceasefire in Northern Ireland
Sep 19	US troops land in Haiti
28	900 die in *Estonia* ferry disaster
Oct 5	Switzerland: 50 members of Solar temple cult found dead
15	President Jean-Baptiste Aristide returns to Haiti
17	Queen Elizabeth in state visit to Russia
Nov 8	Republicans gain control of US Congress
17	Irish Taoiseach Albert Reynolds resigns
19	UK: First National Lottery draw
29	Russian aircraft bomb Chechen capital, Grozny
Dec 15	UK: Diane Modahl banned from athletics for drug use
22	Italian Prime Minister Berlusconi resigns

The Arts

Steven Spielberg wins Oscar for *Schindler's List*

Nirvana singer Kurt Cobain commits suicide

Death of UK dramatists Dennis Potter and

John Osborne

Munch's *The Scream* stolen in Oslo

Forest fires in Australia

1994 began disastrously in Australia when forest fires raged uncontrollably through the south-eastern state of New South Wales, destroying everything in their path. More than a 100 fires – among the most devastating to hit the territory for some 200 years – ravaged more than 600,000 hectares of land during the first two weeks of January, leaving four people dead and razing more than 200 homes, 89 of them in a single night on January 8th.

The bushfires were finally brought under control by the middle of the month, and residents who had been evacuated during the emergency were able to return, though some, like the resident of Sydney's southern suburb of Como pictured left, found only the charred remains of their homes awaiting them. The total cost of the damage from the disaster was estimated at more than 150 million Australian dollars.

Elections in South Africa

Between April 26th and 29th, after years of negotiations between F. W. de Klerk's ruling National Party and representatives of the ANC and other parties, South Africa went to the polls in its first ever multi-racial elections. Marking the end of three and a half centuries of white domination of South Africa's black majority, the elections were marred by logistical problems, which resulted in millions of voters having to queue for up to eight hours before polling station officials were ready to receive them, but were conducted in a remarkably peaceful atmosphere and were widely judged to be free and fair. Much media attention focused on the ANC leader Nelson Mandela, who cast his own vote – the first of his life – in the Durban township of Inanda (right).

The result of the elections was an overwhelming victory for his African National Congress party, with 62.6 per cent of the vote to the National Party's 20.4 per cent. Mandela was sworn in as the first President of a multi-racial South Africa in Pretoria on May 10th.

US intervention in Haiti

After months of backstage diplomacy and a mounting tide of refugees from the troubled republic, US troops were dispatched to Haiti on September 19th to oversee the return to power of the democratically elected President, Father Jean-Baptiste Aristide, who had been ousted in a military coup in 1991.

Controversy on ice

In January the US ice skater Nancy Kerrigan was attacked in Detroit by a hitman apparently hired by the ex-husband of her arch-rival, Tonya Harding, who battered her legs with an iron bar. Harding's former bodyguard claimed that Harding herself had helped instigate the assault. Despite repeated denials by Harding, the allegations dominated coverage of the figure skating events at the Winter Olympics in Lillehamme the following month, where, despite her injuries, Kerrigan won a silver medal.

Air strikes in Bosnia

On February 8th, four Serb bombers were shot down by NATO aircraft for infringing a UN-designated no-fly zone near Banja Luka in Bosnia. The engagement marked a hardening of Western attitudes towards continued Serbian aggression in the former Yugoslavia and followed a mortar attack on the city of Sarajevo earlier in the month during which 70 civilians were killed. A few weeks later, in April, NATO warplanes bombed Serb positions around the besieged town of Gorazde.

Deaths of Senna and Ratzenberger

The world of motor racing lost two of its most celebrated figures in two days when the Austrian driver Roland Ratzenberger and the Brazilian champion Ayrton Senna were killed in high-speed crashes on the same stretch of track at the San Marino Grand Prix on April 30th and May 1st, prompting serious re-evaluation of Formula One safety requirements. The funeral of the 34-year-old Senna, the world's leading Formula One driver, was an occasion of national mourning in his native Brazil.

Death of Kim Il Sung

The death in July of North Korea's hardline Communist President Kim Il Sung, stalled nuclear weapons talks with the USA. He was succeeded by his son, Kim Jong Il.

Tragedy in Rwanda

Bloodshed engulfed the central African state Rwanda following a plane crash in April which killed the Rwandan President. His death triggered a tidal wave of violence, which was largely directed against the Tutsi minority. The fighting claimed perhaps half a million lives by the end of May and created some 1.5 million refugees.

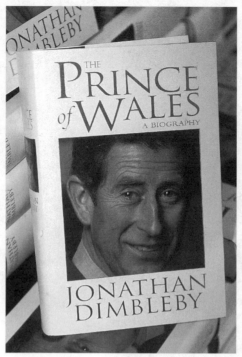

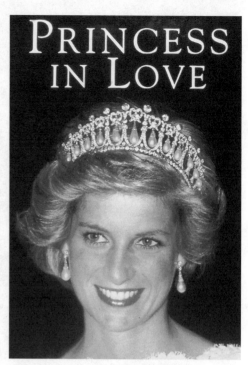

The O. J. Simpson case

In June millions of viewers watched police pursue former US football star O. J. Simpson along the highways of California on live TV. Simpson was later charged with the murder of his ex-wife, Nicole, and a male companion.

The Battle of the Books

1994 saw the publication of two books in a relatively short space of time, which further fuelled speculation about the separated Prince and Princess of Wales: *Princess in Love*, a widely derided account of the Princess' alleged extra-marital activities; and Jonathan Dimbleby's broadly sympathetic biography of Prince Charles, drawing on interviews with the Prince and seen by some people as Charles' attempt to redress the critical balance in coverage of his marriage.

Bad times for Tories

The ruling British Conservative Party was rocked by a series of scandals during the year, which led to a number of highly public ministerial resignations and repeated opposition accusations of 'sleaze' in the ranks of John Major's Government.

Flight from Cuba

The Clinton administration faced a major refugee problem in the summer as thousands of Cuban emigrants took to the seas in makeshift craft to seek asylum in the United States. The exodus followed Cuban President Fidel Castro's mid-August lifting of emigration restrictions in order to exert pressure on the US to lift sanctions. By the end of the month some 20,000 Cubans had made their way to the United States, causing alarm and policy confusion in Washington.

The Irish peace process

Hope was expressed for an end to the 25-year-old 'Troubles' in Northern Ireland when, on August 31st, the IRA announced a 'complete cessation of military activities' from midnight. The announcement, which came eight months after the Downing Street Declaration by the British and Irish governments in December 1993, was cautiously welcomed by the British Prime Minister, John Major. Within a few days, the British Government lifted its broadcasting ban on Sinn Fein, a ban that had been in place since 1981. The IRA's political Wing, and the Sinn Fein leader, Gerry Adams, held talks with the Irish Taoiseach, Albert Reynolds, in a much publicised meeting in Dublin. In October, loyalist paramilitary groups announced their own ceasefire. Talks between Sinn Fein representatives and British officials began at Stormont Castle in December.

Burt Lancaster

October saw the death of the 80-year-old Hollywood actor Burt Lancaster, whose long and successful film career included the 1960 *Elmer Gantry*.

Richard Nixon

On 22nd April Richard Milhous Nixon, the 37th President of the United States (1969–74), died in New York after a stroke. He was 81.

John Smith

On May 12th, John Smith, leader of the British Labour Party since 1992, died suddenly, aged 56. He was succeeded by Tony Blair.

1995

Jan	6	Veteran South African Communist leader Joe Slovo dies
	9	British comedian Peter Cook dies
	15	British troops end daylight patrols in Belfast
	15	2 million attend Pope's mass in Manila, Philippines
	17	5000 die in earthquake in Kobe, Japan
	18	20,000-year-old cave paintings found in Southern France
	19	Russian troops take presidential palace, Grozny
	22	19 Israelis die in Tel Aviv suicide bombing
	23	O. J. Simpson trial opens in Los Angeles
	27	50th anniversary memorial of Auschwitz liberation
	30	Author and naturalist Gerald Durrell dies
Feb	1	UK: Woman anti veal export protester killed, Coventry
	2	British actor Donald Pleasence dies
	3	Mike Foale first British-born astronaut to spacewalk
	12	50th anniversary commemorations of Dresden bombing
	15	English football hooligans riot in Dublin
Feb	26	Barings Bank goes into receivership
Mar	12	Canada seizes Spanish fishing vessel, causes EU dispute
	20	Nerve gas released on Tokyo subway
	20	Queen arrives in South Africa
Apr	14	British troops prepare to leave Northern Ireland
	19	Car bomb in Oklahoma City kills 168, 12 children
May	6-8	50th anniversary of VE Day
	13	Alison Hargreaves first woman to climb Mt Everest, alone, without oxygen
Jun	3	UN rapid intervention force sent to Bosnia
	29	Department store collapses in Seoul, Korea killing 640
	25	South Africa wins Rugby Union World Cup
	30	Military accord to end fighting in Chechyna
Jul	8	Graf wins ladies singles title at Wimbledon, sixth time
	10	Burmese Nobel Prize winner Aung San Kyi released
	11	US resume full diplomatic relations with Vietnam
Aug	7	Jonathan Edwards sets new world record for triple jump
	15	50th anniversary of VJ Day
	17	Air France Concorde sets new round the world record
	30	UN forces attack key Serbian positions in Bosnia
Oct	3	O. J. Simpson acquitted of murder
	18	Grand National winner, Red Rum, buried at Aintree
	27	Quebec disc jockey makes hoax call to the Queen
	29-30	Bill Clinton visits Northern Ireland
	30	Quebec votes to stay in Canada
Nov	4	Prime Minister of Israel, Yitzhak Rabin, assassinated
	11	Nigeria executes dissident writer Ken Saro-Wiwa
	21-2	Rosemary West convicted in Winchester of murder
	25	Ceasefire in the former Yugoslavia
Dec	7	Link revealed between BSE in cattle and CJD in humans

The Arts

Actor Christopher Reeve seriously injured

Riverdance moves from Dublin to London

Tom Hanks stars in the film *Forrest Gump*

Mike Newell directs *Four Weddings and a Funeral*

War in Chechnya

At the end of 1994, President Yeltsin stepped up pressure on the regime of President Dzhokhar Dudayev in the breakaway Caucasian republic of Chechnya by launching air and ground attacks against the Chechen capital, Grozny, in an effort to crush the independence movement. The offensive, which received only lukewarm support from the Russian military and was widely seen as strategically and operationally incompetent, met with stiff resistance from Chechen fighters in and around the capital and with near-universal condemnation from the international community. By February Grozny was a shattered ghost-town, but as Chechen guerrillas vowed to fight on and fears grew that the war could spread throughout the Caucuses, the credibility of Yeltsin's presidency plummeted to an all-time low.

Earthquake in Japan

Some 5000 people died and more than 250,000 were made homeless when an earthquake measuring 7.2 on the Richter scale devastated the Japanese city of Kobe on January 17th. The authorities attracted criticism for the inefficiency of their response to the disaster, Japan's worst quake since the one that destroyed Tokyo in 1923.

'Floods of the century' in Europe

Torrential rains brought widespread flooding to northern Europe during January and early February. Among the worst affected places were the Netherlands, where more than 250,000 people were evacuated from their homes as rising water levels threatened the country's complex system of dykes, and the Rhine, Mosel and Main rivers in Germany, where Cologne was inundated (above).

Not also... but only...

Peter Cook, founder of *Private Eye* magazine a key figure in the 1960s satire boom and best known for his comedy partnership with Dudley Moore, died on January 9th, aged 57.

Queen visits South Africa

The Queen arrived in South Africa on March 20th, her first visit since 1947. President Mandela greeted the Queen and the Duke of Edinburgh as they stepped off HMS *Britannia*, which was docked in the Cape of Good Hope.

Barings Bank

On February 26th London's 200-year-old Barings Bank went into receivership. Derivatives dealer Nick Leeson, trading on the Japanese Futures markets was involved in the loss of £860 million. Leeson, fleeing Singapore, was arrested at Frankfurt Airport. Later, in December, after apparently striking a deal with the Singapore authorities, he began a six-and-a-half-year sentence.

Nerve gas released on Tokyo subway

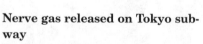

On March 20th canisters of sarin nerve gas were released on several trains of the Tokyo subway by members of the Am Shinrikyo cult. More than 5,500 people were rushed to hospital and 12 died. When the cult's leader, Shoko Asahara appeared in court on multiple murder charges on October 24th more than 8,000 police were on guard in Tokyo. As Japan became the world's richest country, its 'feel-good' factor suffered further blows with the Kobe earthquake and a jumbo jet hijack.

Oklahoma City bomb

In Oklahoma City, on April 19th a truck filled with 4,000 pounds of explosives blew up in front of the Alfred P. Murrah Federal Building, which housed the offices of the Federal ATF (Bureau of Alcohol, Tobacco and Firearms) and a children's nursery; 168 people were killed, including 12 children. The greatest ever act of terrorism on US soil occurred on the second anniversary of the Waco disaster. There were suspicions that far right-wing groups were implicated in the explosion.

South Africa wins the Rugby World Cup

On June 25th 60,000 fans and 43 million TV viewers saw South Africa beat New Zealand 15-12. The win was celebrated joyfully in South Africa as a momentary relief in turbulent times.

Jonathan Edwards
Nice guy Edwards set a new triple jump record on August 7th at the World Athletics Championships, twice breaking the previous world record with jumps of 18.16 metres and 18.29 metres. He was named as BBC Sports Personality of the Year, Champion of Champions by the French sports paper *L'Equipe*, and Athlete of the Year by the International Amateur Athletics Federation.

Burmese Nobel Prize Winner released
Aung San Kyi, leader of the democratic movement in Burma, was released on July 10th after six years of house arrest. The Nobel Peace Prize winner once again began to campaign for dialogue, reconciliation and democracy. Amnesty International reported that the human rights situation in Burma remained 'desperate'.

50th anniversary of VE Day
From May 6-8th celebrations in London and elsewhere marked the 50th anniversary of the end of World War II in Europe. Events included a service at St Paul's Cathedral in the presence of 56 heads of state, a dinner at the City of London's Guildhall, and a huge rally in London's Hyde Park attended by 150,000 people. Among thousands of veterans present were holders of the Victoria Cross and George Cross. The Queen, the 95-year-old Queen Mother and Princess Margaret appeared on the balcony of Buckingham Palace, as they had done 50 years earlier. The 50th anniversary of VJ Day (Victory in Japan) was celebrated on August 15th.

Prime minister of Israel assassinated

Moments after addressing a peace rally in the Square of the Kings, on November 4th, Yitzhak Rabin, Prime Minister of Israel, was assassinated. The perpetrator was a 27-year-old Jewish law student. Mr Rabin had been the target of an on-going hate campaign since the day he shook hands with PLO leader Yasser Arafat on the steps of the White House.

President Clinton visits Northern Ireland

On October 29th-31st Bill and Hillary Clinton visited England, Northern Ireland and the Republic of Ireland. In both London and Dublin Clinton addressed the joint Houses of Parliament. In the first visit of an American President to Belfast he turned on the Christmas tree lights. British forces had begun withdrawing from Northern Ireland in April, and it was hoped that the symbolic visit would galvanize both sides in the conflict to embrace the Anglo-Irish negotiating framework, but gave only a temporary veneer of optimism.

1996

Jan	8	Former French President Mitterand dies
	9	Chechyna insurgents seize 3,000 civilian hostages
	26	Hillary Clinton testifies before Whitewater grand jury
	29	France announces end of current series of nuclear tests
Feb	9	IRA ends ceasefire with bomb at London's Docklands
	28	Russia becomes member of the Council of Europe
Mar	4	UN forces leave Rwanda as UN mandate ends
	13	Dunblane massacre, 16 children and teacher killed
	20	British beef banned in Europe
	31	Unilateral ceasefire in Chechyna
Apr	28	At Port Arthur, Tasmania, 35 people shot dead
May	30	The Duke and Duchess of York divorce
Jun	4	European *Ariane 5* rocket launch fails
	4-7	First official visit of Eire President to Britain
	27	Investigative Irish journalist Veronica Guerin murdered
	30	Germany wins Euro '96
Jul	9-13	Nelson Mandela visits London, first S African state visit
	18	TWA Flight 800 explodes killing all 230 on board
	27	Bomb at Atlanta Olympics; two die, 111 injured
Aug	1	Michael Johnson wins two Olympic golds
	8	Flash floods in the Spanish Pyrennees kill campers
	13	Bread riots in Jordan
	17	Belgian police investigate international paedophile ring
	28	The Prince and Princess of Wales divorce
	29	British forces begin to leave Hong Kong

Sep	19	Second trial of Kevin and Ian Maxwell collapses
	19	NASA's *Atlantis* docks with Russian space station *Mir*
	26	First death following euthanasia legislation in Australia
Oct	13	Damon Hill wins Formula 1 Drivers' Championship
	16	Proposals to ban most handguns in UK
	30	Sale of Jewish art looted in holocaust, held in Austria
Nov	5	Bill Clinton wins US election
	5	Boris Yeltsin undergoes quintuple cardiac bypass
	5	Pakistan Prime Minister Benazir Bhutto dismissed
	10	Evander Hollyfield defeats Mike Tyson
	15	Mass migration as Hutu refugees return to Rwanda
	18	Serious fire in Channel Tunnel train
	30	Stone of Scone placed on view in Edinburgh Castle
Dec	18	Peruvian embassy siege, nearly 500 hostages held

The Arts

Globe Theatre opened in London

Emma Thompson wins Oscars for acting and directing

In Birmingham, UK, largest symphony orchestra perform

Death of Ronnie Scott, Michael Bentine,

Sir Laurens van der Post, Terence Donovan

Docklands bomb ends ceasefire

The IRA marked the end of their 18-month ceasefire with an attack on a high profile British target, London's Docklands. The massive bomb comprising at least half a ton of explosives was planted under a station of the Docklands Light Railway at South Quays. It exploded at 7.01 pm on February 9th. Two people were killed and at least 100 injured. The widespread and extensive damage to houses, shops and offices was costed at more than £100 million and threw the future of the Irish peace process into serious jeopardy.

Dunblane
On March 13th, notoriously unstable misfit Thomas Hamilton entered the gym of Dunblane Primary School in Scotland and shot dead a teacher and 16 children, injuring another teacher and five children, and then killed himself. The nation was plunged into mourning, prompting discussion in the UK and many other countries on the banning of handguns.

BSE
News about the cattle disease BSE grew worse every week, and in March the UK government admitted the link between BSE (Bovine Spongiform Encephalopathy) in cattle and CJD (Creutzfeld-Jacob Disease), the brain disease in humans. British beef was banned in Europe on March 20th. Also in March the government banned SBO (Specified Bovine Offal) from pig and poultry feed.

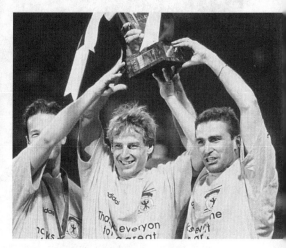

Germany wins Euro '96
On June 30th Germany beat the Czech Republic in soccer's Euro '96 in front of 73,000 fans at London's Wembley Stadium.

Port Arthur massacre
In April at Port Arthur, near Hobart in the island state of Tasmania, Australia, a madman shot dead 35 people including children and a baby. At the tourist resort, the historic ruins of a penal colony, at least another 17 were wounded, some so seriously that limbs had to be amputated. The lone Australian gunman's $1 million in assets were later distributed among his victims and their families, and Martin Bryant received 35 terms of life imprisonment.

Looted Jewish gold and art

In September newly declassified US documents relating to the gold and art seized by the Nazis in World War II contributed to an unravelling story of gold hidden in Swiss and other European banks and of art treasures dispersed all over the world. On October 30th the first sale of Jewish gold and art looted by the Nazis was held in Austria. Reports of confiscated money and collaborations burgeoned.

Damon Hill

At Suzuka, Japan, on October 13th Damon Hill won the Formula 1 Drivers' championship in the last Grand Prix of the season, following in the footsteps of his father, Graham Hill. The BBC Sports Personality of the Year was later sacked by his boss Frank Williams.

Atlantis docks with *Mir*

On September 19th the US space shuttle *Atlantis* docked with the orbiting Russian space station *Mir*, six weeks later than planned. On September 26th the shuttle touched down at the Kennedy Space Centre. American Shannon Lucid, who had been on the space station for six months, thus ended the longest space flight by a woman.

Bomb at Olympics

In a moving opening ceremony at Atlanta, Georgia, the Olympic flame was lit by a trembling Muhammad Ali. Seven days later the Olympic spirit was shattered when a bomb exploded in the Centennial Olympic Park during a rock concert on the warm evening of July 27th. Two people died and 111 were injured. After months of investigation, responsibility for the bombing had still not been established.

Michael Johnson breaks record

In one of many highlights at the 26th Olympic Games American Michael Johnson set new world records on August 1st in both the 200 metres and 400 metres. 'Golden Shoes' ensured his place as the top earner, at $100,000 per run, on the International Amateur Athletics Federation circuit.

Prince and Princess of Wales divorce

On August 28th the marriage of Prince Charles and Princess Diana officially came to an end after 15 years of marriage and the birth of two princes, due to 'irreconcilable differences' and after both had publicly admitted adultery. Diana, Princess of Wales, received £17 million in settlement, but lost her 'HRH' title, after which she immediately resigned as patron of almost 100 charities. On April 30th the Duke and Duchess of York had also divorced after ten years of marriage, but apparently remained good friends for the sake of their two young daughters.

Clinton re-elected

On November 5th, US Democrat President Bill Clinton was returned for a second four-year term. After his challenger Republican Bob Dole ran a lacklustre campaign, President Clinton, nicknamed 'the comeback kid', took 49 per cent of the votes.

Benazir Bhutto dismissed

Prime Minister of Pakistan Benazir Bhutto and her goverment were dismissed on November 5th, amid charges that corruption had prevailed during her three-year government, charges which she totally rejected. Her husband, Asif Ali Zhardari, was for a time held in 'protective custody'.

Hutu refugees

In October, 300 unarmed Hutu refugees were murdered in a church shortly after returning to Burundi. It is believed that at least 1,100 refugees were killed in October and November. In mid-November thousands of Hutus left refugee camps to return to Rwanda in a 25-mile-long march in an on-going saga of unspeakable human misery, starvation and murder.

Fire in Channel Tunnel

On November 18th a serious fire broke out on a freight shuttle in the Channel Tunnel when the train was 12 miles inside the tunnel. The truck-bearing carriages have open lattice-sides, and this may have had a blowtorch effect on the fire some believe started before the train entered the tunnel. Eight people suffered smoke inhalation injuries, and the tunnel was closed to normal traffic for months.

Peruvian Embassy seige

On December 17th, nearly 500 diplomats, politicians and other VIPs were held hostage during a reception at the Japanese ambassador's residence in Lima. The siege by heavily armed left-wing Peruvian rebels was to last for more than four months, although most hostages were released in the early days. On April 22nd, 1997 a 140-man Peruvian assault team ended Latin America's longest hostage seige by force, killing all 14 terrorists, and rescuing the 71 remaining hostages.

1997

Death of Deng Xiaoping

The death was announced on February 19th of China's 'paramount leader' Deng Xiaoping. He was 92, had been suffering from Parkinson's disease for some time and had not been seen in public for three years. Deng was the last major figure from the first generation of Chinese communists, having joined the party at its foundation. He took part in the Long March of 1934-35 and actively supported Mao Tse-tung's bid for leadership, rising to become a senior member of the politburo in the 1950's. He was a great survivor, weathering periods of disgrace and exile to become effective leader of China after Mao's death in 1976, when he set about introducing 'socialism with a Chinese face' - a far-reaching campaign of modernisation which radically transformed China's economy and relations with the West. However, his economic pragmatism went hand in hand with a ruthless approach to political dissent, and his name is indelibly linked with the bloody suppression of pro-democracy demonstrations in Tiananmen Square in 1989. Deng's mantle fell on his chosen successor, Jiang Zemin, who had been President of China since 1993.

Tony Bullimore

In the ill-fated Vendee Global Challenge race, round-the-world yachtsman Tony Bullimore was picked up as he swam out from his upturned boat on his fifth day in the freezing waters of the Southern Ocean. The 'old sea dog', rescued in January in one of the greatest search-and-rescue efforts in maritime history, praised the Australian Navy for 'such a big effort' for 'a little individual like me'.

Tiger Woods wins Masters

With sustained brilliance, Tiger Woods rewrote golf's history books on April 13th. At 21, he became the youngest person, and the first black golfer, to win the US Masters. Additionally, his low 72-hole score of 18-under-par 270 beat the previous record; he had the widest ever winning margin of 12 strokes; his totals broke records for the last 54 holes, as well as the second and third rounds, and for the first 54 holes tied the record.

Dolly the Clone

On February 24th Dolly the sheep was presented to the world. She had been cloned from a single cell of her mother at the Roslin Institute in Edinburgh. While there was widespread moral panic among those who saw Dolly as a stepping stone on the way to human cloning, others saw the opportunities presented by such biotechnical advances for lifesaving medical procedures.

Labour Victory in UK General Election

Records were broken on May 1st when Tony Blair became the youngest Prime Minister for 150 years as he led New Labour to victory. In the largest recorded anti-government swing, the Labour Party gained their biggest ever majority in the House of Commons. They replaced the Conservative Party which had been the longest serving British government of the 20th century.

James Stewart (1908-97) and Robert Mitchum (1917-97)

Hollywood lost two of its most popular screen idols in a single week with the deaths of James Stewart and Robert Mitchum. The two actors could hardly have been more contrasted in their personas. Stewart, who won an Oscar for his performance in *The Philadelphia Story* (1940) and went on to star in such Hollywood classics as *It's a Wonderful Life* (1946), *Harvey* (1950) and *Rear Window* (1954), was seen as the archetypal good guy, while Mitchum's tough on-screen image was reflected in an often scandalous off-screen private life.

Handover of Hong Kong

At midnight on June 30th/ July 1st the Union flag was lowered over Hong Kong for the last time as the colony returned to Chinese sovereignty after 99 years under British administration. Ceremonies in Hong Kong were attended by Prince Charles, Prime Minister Tony Blair and the last governor of Hong Kong, Chris Patten, as well as by the Chinese president Jiang Zemin. There were celebrations throughout China to mark the handover, including a massive firework display in Beijing's Tiananmen Square, attended by some 100,000 people. In his speech President Jiang promised that China would govern the new Hong Kong Special Administrative Region according to the principle of 'one country, two systems' established in the Sino-British Joint declaration of 1984.

Death of a princess

On the morning of August 31st the world woke to the news of the death, aged 36, of Diana, Princess of Wales and to an outpouring of popular grief unprecedented in living memory. The mother of the heirs to the British throne was killed shortly after midnight when the car she was travelling in crashed in the Place de l'Alma underpass in central Paris. Also killed were the princess's lover Dodi Fayed, son of the Harrods owner Mohamed al-Fayed, and the driver of the vehicle Henri Paul, a member of al-Fayed's staff at the Ritz Hotel, Paris, where Diana and Fayed had just dined together. A fourth passenger, bodyguard Trevor Rees Jones, survived but was seriously injured. Eye-witness reports suggested that the car was travelling at around 80 miles per hour in an attempt to outpace paparazzi photographers pursuing it on motorbikes. Later investigations showed that Paul had more than three times the permitted French drink-drive level of alcohol in his blood.

As news of Diana's death spread, hundreds of thousands of people gathered at the royal palaces in London to lay floral tributes and sign books of condolence, and the media devoted itself to blanket coverage of the tragedy. Growing criticism of the royal family's decision not to break their holiday at Balmoral was defused by their return to the capital at the end of the week and by the Queen's public broadcast on the death of her former daughter-in-law.

The funeral, which took place on September 7th, was widely seen as a fitting tribute to the woman memorably described by Prime Minister Tony Blair as 'the people's princess'. More than a million people are estimated to have lined the route by which the coffin, mounted on a gun carriage and followed on foot for the last stages of its journey by Prince Charles, Princes William and Harry, the Duke of Edinburgh and the princess's brother Charles, Earl Spencer, travelled to Westminster Abbey. The service, which took place in the presence of numerous dignitaries and celebrity friends of the princess and was watched by a worldwide television audience estimated at 2 billion, broke with tradition in featuring a specially rewritten version of his song 'Candle in the Wind' performed by Elton John and in the spontaneous applause which greeted Earl Spencer's bitter criticism of press intrusion in his memorial speech. The body was taken from the abbey to the Spencer family home at Althorp in Northamptonshire for a private burial ceremony.

Death of Mother Teresa

Five days after the death of Princess Diana, the death was also announced of her friend and charitable co-worker, the former Nobel Peace Prizewinner Mother Teresa. The Albanian-born nun, best known for her work with the dispossessed of India, died in Calcutta, the city with which she was associated for most of her long career and where she founded her order, the Missionaries of Charity, in 1948. She was 87.

Louise Woodward

On October 30th, at the end of the most closely followed televised trial since that of O J Simpson, the British au pair Louise Woodward was found guilty of the second degree murder of eight-month-old Matthew Eappen at Middlesex Superior Court in Cambridge, Massachusetts. The verdict, which carried a mandatory life sentence of at least 15 years, was the subject of widespread controversy, especially in the UK, with many independent observers questioning the medical evidence and the defending counsel's decision to rule out the possibility of a manslaughter verdict. At a hearing on November 10th, the judge, Hiller Zobel, reduced the conviction to involuntary manslaughter and the sentence to the period Louise Woodward had already spent in custody. She was released the same day but remained in the US pending further hearings.

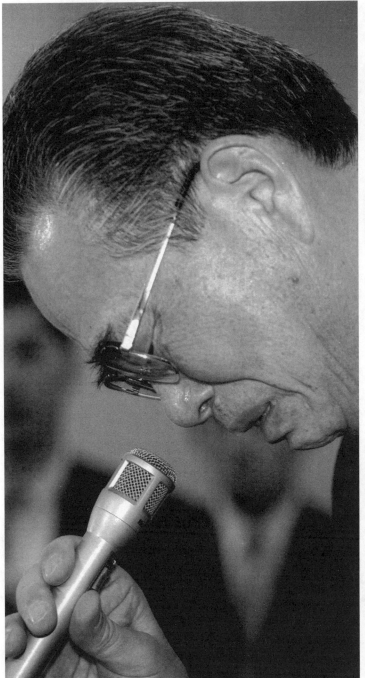

Launch of *Titanic*

December saw the launch in the United States of writer-director James Cameron's film *Titanic*, which was quickly to establish itself as one of the greatest blockbusters in cinema history. Starring the British actress Kate Winslet and heartthrob Leonardo DiCaprio, the movie set personal romance against the epic background of the *Titanic's* fatal maiden voyage and was notable both for its gigantic budget and for its ground-breaking computer-generated special effects. It went on to win numerous Academy Awards.

William Hague

In June, the British Conservative Party acquired its youngest leader for more than 200 years in the person of William Hague, the former Welsh Secretary (above). Following the Tories' crushing defeat in the general election of May 1st, its leader, the former Prime Minister John Major, announced his resignation, igniting a fierce struggle for the leadership of the hugely depleted parliamentary party. The former Chancellor Kenneth Clarke, won both the first and second ballots, but without enough votes to secure an outright victory. On the third ballot, he was overtaken by Hague, who was widely seen as the Eurosceptic candidate of the right. With only 164 Tory MPs remaining to oppose a powerful new government, however, the new leader looked set for a difficult time in opposition.

South East Asian meltdown

The economic problems of South East Asia escalated in November with the collapse of the giant Yamaichi Securities Company, Japan's oldest bank, with the loss of some 7,000 jobs. Earlier in the month two other major Japanese financial service sector companies had also collapsed. Apologising to shareholders and staff for what was the country's biggest ever corporate failure, Yamaichi president Shohei Nozawa (above) wept uncontrollably in front of the world's media. The financial crisis in Japan followed an unravelling of the region's financial markets which began in July with the devaluation of the Thai baht and saw currency crises in Malaysia, the Philippines and Indonesia. A few days before the Yamaichi debacle, in perhaps the most striking evidence of the meltdown effect, South Korea, once the most powerful of the 'tiger' economies of the Pacific Rim and one of the strongest in the world, was forced to seek a $20 billion dollar rescue package from the International Monetary Fund.

Jan	20	President Havel reelected in Czech Republic		
	21	Pope John Paul II visits Cuba		
	21	Monica Lewinsky scandal breaks in US		
Feb	12	Overthrow of Sierra Leone military regime		
	23	Kofi Annan agreement on Iraqi weapons inspection		
Mar	1	200,000 join UK countryside march		
	5	Water discovered on the moon		
	23	Yeltsin dismisses entire Russian cabinet		
	24	Five die in Arkansas school shooting		
Apr	10	Good Friday agreement in Northern Ireland		
	15	Death of former Cambodian dictator Pol Pot		
May	11	India conducts underground nuclear tests		
	15	Death of Frank Sinatra		
	21	Indonesian President Suharto resigns		
	25	Japanese emperor Akihito visits UK		
	28	Pakistan conducts underground nuclear tests		
	30	Thousands killed in Afghan earthquake		
Jun	3	German high-speed train crash kills 98		
	25	Northern Ireland Assembly elections		
	25	President Clinton begins visit to China		
Jul	7	Death of Chief Abiola, Nigeria		
	12	France wins World Cup		
	13	Japanese premier Hashimoto resigns		

Aug	7	Bomb attacks on US embassies in Kenya & Tanzania
	12	Swiss banks settle Holocaust claims
	17	Clinton testifies before Grand Jury
	20	US cruise missile attacks in Afghanistan & Sudan
	23	Yeltsin dismisses government again
Sep	9	Kenneth Starr report submitted to US Congress
	11	Primakov becomes Russian premier
	27	Schrôder replaces Kohl as German Chancellor
Oct	5	Impeachment proceedings begin against Clinton
	6	Tony Blair visits China
	15	Wye summit: Arafat and Netanyahu
	16	General Pinochet arrested in London
	16	John Hume and David Trimble receive Nobel Peace Prize
	29	S African Truth & Reconciliation Commission reports
	29	Death of poet Ted Hughes
	31	Iraq ends cooperation with UNSCOM
		Hurricanes devastate Central America
Nov	23	EU lifts ban on British beef
Dec	4	Cuba restores Christmas holiday
	16	US/UK launch air strikes against Iraq
	21	US acts against EU products in 'banana war'
	23	Peter Mandelson resigns from UK govt
	30	Western hostages killed in Yemen

The impeachment of President Clinton

In January, the White House was rocked by the most serious allegations yet of sexual and ethical misconduct by President Clinton. The claims by 24-year-old Monica Lewinsky, a former White House intern, that the President had had a sexual relationship with her and then ordered her to deny it on oath ignited a media feeding frenzy of an intensity unparalled since Watergate. The President's staunch denials of wrongdoing, together with Hillary Clinton's feisty televised defence of her husband and clear evidence of his continuing popularity among voters, initially seemed to have averted a constitutional crisis, but the relentless momentum of special prosecutor Kenneth Starr's investigation into alleged presidential misdemeanours led, on August 17th, to Clinton becoming the first sitting President to testify before a Grand Jury. In videotaped evidence from the map room of the White House, and later the same day in a televised address to the nation, he finally admitted to an 'inappropriate' physical relationship with Lewinsky. However, the combative tone of his address failed to mollify critics and it soon became clear that his support among Democrats too was leaking away. In September, Starr's report was published and Clinton's videotaped testimony broadcast, and on October 5th impeachment proceedings began in the House of Representatives. By the end of the year, Clinton had become only the second President in US history to have articles of impeachment voted against him. His trial before the Senate on charges of perjury and obstruction of justice began in January 1999, but on February 12th the Senate voted to acquit him, affording the Comeback Kid a new lease of political life for the remainder of his second term.

The final curtain

Fans of popular music throughout the world mourned the death of veteran crooner Frank Sinatra, which was announced on May 15th. The Sinatra phenomenon first gained its hold on the public imagination in the late1930s, when the young former sports reporter sang with the Harry James and Tommy Dorsey bands, establishing a devoted following. His 1954 album *Songs for Young Lovers* became an instant classic, as did his 1969 anthem '*My Way*'. Also a successful film star, in 1953 Sinatra won an Oscar for his performance in *From Here to Eternity*. Despite a turbulent private life and persistent rumours of Mafia connections, Sinatra had by the end of his long life become a national institution in the US. Above all, as even his often derided comebacks proved, he was the consummate popular musician.

Papal visit to Cuba

Between January 21st and 25th, John Paul II became the first pope to visit Communist Cuba, where he held talks with President Fidel Castro, a long-standing opponent of Roman Catholicism, and conducted four mammoth open-air masses in Havana and elsewhere. The Pope used his public appearances in Cuba to combine calls for greater political and religious freedom on the island with demands for an easing of the US embargo against the Castro regime. The visit followed earlier discussions between the Pope and the Cuban President when Castro visited the Vatican at the end of 1996.

Death of Brother Number One

On April 15th the Cambodian Khmer Rouge announced the death of their one-time leader Pol Pot (above) at the age of 73. The former dictator, also known during his four-year reign of terror in Cambodia as Brother Number One, apparently died of a heart attack in the jungle, from which he had conducted a guerrilla war against the government for the last 20 years. Pol Pot, who was born Saloth Sar, seized power in Cambodia in 1975 and set about introducing a collectivist agrarian economy, purged of private property, currency and intelligentsia. In the four years that followed 'Year Zero', the Khmer Rouge regime is estimated to have been responsible for the deaths of up to a quarter of Cambodia's 8 million people. Pol Pot had been purged from his own party in 1997 and had recently faced demands for him to be tried by an international tribunal for crimes against humanity.

The Iraqi weapons inspection crisis

A major new conflict in the Gulf was averted in February by the diplomatic mission to Iraq of the UN Secretary-General Kofi Annan (above, front left). The crisis in relations between Iraq and the US had been building since October, when the Iraqi authorities had threatened to deny the UNSCOM weapons inspection team access to military sites unless UNSCOM expelled all its US personnel from the country. With US and UK forces already massed in the Gulf, and Secretary of State Madeleine Albright engaging in determined shuttle diplomacy to muster support for a military attack on Iraq, Kofi Annan's visit was widely seen as a last chance for a peaceful solution to the crisis. An agreement was hammered out, under which UNSCOM resumed its inspections in return for the UN Security Council's reconsidering the sanctions which had been in place against Iraq since the Gulf War. In April, however, the Security Council decided against reviewing sanctions, and by the end of October the Iraqi authorities had once more suspended all cooperation with UNSCOM. US and UK forces gathered again in the Gulf and although Saddam backed down at the last moment, the next obstruction of UNSCOM's activities was met by air-strikes against Iraqi military installations between December 16th and 20th. The action, codenamed Operation Desert Fox, was criticised in some quarters for its lack of UN sanction, and for the coincidence of its timing with a key vote in the Clinton impeachment process.

Peace in Northern Ireland?

After months of tense negotiations and a flurry of last-minute interventions by British Prime Minister Tony Blair and US President Bill Clinton, leaders of Northern Ireland's political parties announced in the early hours of Good Friday, April 10th, that they had reached agreement on the future development of the peace process in the province. The agreement, which was endorsed by a referendum of all the people of Northern Ireland on May 22nd, made provision for the establishment of a Northern Ireland Assembly, raising the probability that representatives of the mainstream unionist parties and of Sinn Fèin, the political wing of the IRA, would sit together on the governing body of the province. The agreement also provided for the creation of a number of cross-border bodies, and a separate referendum in the Irish Republic showed overwhelming support for abandonment of Ireland's constitutional claim to the north. Elections to the new National Assembly were held on June 25th and at the first meeting of the Assembly on July 1st the Ulster Unionist leader David Trimble was elected First Minister. In October, Trimble and the SDLP leader John Hume were jointly awarded the Nobel Peace Prize for their part in the Northern Ireland agreement, but with the contentious issue of arms decommissioning unresolved, and intense opposition to the settlement among both unreconstructed Unionists and hard-line republicans, the path to peace remained a thorny one into 1999.

(Right: Tony Blair with the Irish Prime Minister Bertie Ahern.)

German high-speed train crash

On June 3rd, Germany suffered its worst rail disaster since the Second World War when a high-speed train left the track in the northern city of Eschede, killing almost 100 of the 350 passengers on board. The intercity express, the Wilhelm Conrad Rôntgen, was travelling at more than 200 kilometres an hour when the derailment occurred, causing the train to collide with one of the supports of a motorway flyover. Many of the casualties were crushed when concrete and other debris from the structure collapsed onto the carriages below. An investigation attributed the accident to a broken wheel.

Embassy bombings

On August 7th, the US embassies in the Kenyan capital Nairobi and the Tanzanian capital Dar-es-Salaam were the subject of massive coordinated bomb attacks which left hundreds dead and thousands more injured. The majority of the casualties occurred in Nairobi, where the bombers drove a truck into the embassy compound; most of the dead and injured were local people. It remained unclear who was responsible for the outrages, but intelligence sources in the US linked the attacks to the Islamic fundamentalist leader Osama bin Laden and on August 20th America responded with cruise missile attacks on alleged terrorist and military bases in Afghanistan and Sudan. President Clinton, who had appeared on national television only three days earlier to admit his relationship with Monica Lewinsky, made a second broadcast address to the nation justifying the action, but it was widely condemned throughout the Middle East and in turn provoked a further bomb attack, this time on the Planet Hollywood restaurant in Cape Town, five days later.

Farewell to Kohl

On September 27th, Chancellor Helmut Kohl became the first German Chancellor since the Second World War to be voted out of office, when his Social Democrat challenger Gerhard Schrôder triumphed in the country's federal elections. Schrôder's accession to the Chancellorship brought to an end 16 years of Kohl's leadership, the most spectacular legacy of which was the reunification of Germany in 1990. The new Chancellor was dependent on Green Party support to form a coalition government, but it soon became clear that tensions within his own SPD party were as likely to cause him political difficulties as those between the coalition partners. In particular, the new SPD Finance Minister, Oskar Lafontaine, quickly established himself as the most controversial figure in the cabinet by appearing to pressure the Bundesbank over interest rate policy.

End of the Rushdie fatwah?

A major stumbling block on the path to better relations between Iran and the West was removed in September with the announcement by Iranian Foreign Minister Kamal Kharrazi that Iran would neither take nor encourage action to endanger the life of the author Salman Rushdie, who had been living in hiding since the fatwah pronounced against him by the Ayatollah Khomeini in 1989. The announcement followed talks with UK Foreign Secretary Robin Cook and was welcomed by Rushdie, who began to appear more frequently in public. With many groups still holding themselves bound by the fatwah, however, the safety of the author of *The Satanic Verses* remained in jeopardy.

Pinochet arrested

On October 16th, General Augusto Pinochet, the former military dictator of Chile, was arrested at a private clinic in London, after application from Spain for his extradition on human rights charges relating to the 'dirty war' which followed his overthrow of President Allende in 1973. The move polarised opinion in Chile and elsewhere, with the former prime minister Lady Thatcher a prominent voice in support of the 82-year-old general, and set in train a complex series of legal hearings to establish the validity of Pinochet's detention. In October, the High Court ruled that Pinochet enjoyed 'sovereign immunity' from prosecution for alleged crimes committed while he was head of state, but this decision was reversed by the House of Lords in December. The Lords' decision was itself overturned, however, when one of the five law lords involved was shown to have undeclared links with the human rights organisation Amnesty International. With further rulings still to come, Pinochet remained in judicial limbo into 1999.

The Wye summit

Moves were made to break the stalemate in the Middle East peace process when Israeli Prime Minister Benjamin Netanyahu and Palestinian President Yassir Arafat met with President Clinton for a special summit at the Wye Plantation, Maryland. Nine days of intensive negotiations, which were joined by King Hussein of Jordan, led to the establishment of a timetable for implementation of some of the stalled key stages of the Israeli withdrawal from the occupied territories, including the reversion of parts of the West Bank to joint control and the strengthening of Palestinian anti-terrorist measures. Both leaders encountered hard-line opposition at home, however, with Netanyahu facing a vote of no confidence in the Israeli parliament, the Knesset.

Gingering up the UN

One of the year's least predictable developments was the appointment in October of former Spice Girl Geri Halliwell to the post of Goodwill Ambassador for the UN Population Fund. Halliwell, whose departure from the girl-power band shocked fans in May, was given special responsibility for the reproductive rights of young women in developing countries. The appointment was widely derided as a populist move unbefitting the gravitas of the United Nations, but Halliwell's evident sincerity and determination to master her brief impressed some doubters.

Death of Ted Hughes

The death of Ted Hughes on October 28th silenced one of the most distinctive voices of post-war British poetry. Hughes, who made his reputation with such collections as *Hawk in the Rain*, *Lupercal*, *Wodwo* and *Crow*, had been Poet Laureate for 14 years and was especially known for his uncompromisingly unsentimental evocations of the natural world. His last collection, *Birthday Letters*, was published when he knew he was dying of cancer, and for the first time addressed in verse the troubled relationship with his first wife Sylvia Plath, whose suicide in 1963 had always shadowed his name. Highly controversial in circles sympathetic to Plath, the book also received wide critical and popular acclaim.

Öcalan detained

Relations between Turkey and Italy came under intense strain in November when the Italian authorities refused to extradite Abdullah Öcalan, the leader of the outlawed Kurdish Workers' Party, to face terrorism charges in Turkey. The decision provoked outrage in Turkish government circles and demonstrations by Turkish and Kurdish groups throughout Europe. Öcalan's search for asylum, which had begun when he was forced out of Syria by Turkish governmental pressure earlier in the year, eventually led him to Nairobi, where in February 1999 he was captured during a secret operation by Turkish government forces and returned to Turkey to stand trial for treason.

Government resignations

Britain's New Labour government was rocked by a series of high-profile scandals and resignations in 1998. In October, the Welsh Secretary Ron Davies resigned after a mysterious sequence of events on Clapham Common, which led to his being robbed at knifepoint of his valuables and his car. Davies, who had been influential in establishing the machinery of devolution for Wales, also later withdrew his candidacy for the post of First Minister in the proposed new Welsh Assembly. In December, the Trade and Industry Secretary Peter Mandelson, a controversial politician widely credited as the principal architect of New Labour's election victory in 1997, resigned following revelations that he had received an undeclared personal loan of £373,000 from the Paymaster-General Geoffrey Robinson towards the purchase of a house in London's Notting Hill. Robinson himself resigned the same day. Given his close personal links with Prime Minister Tony Blair, however, Mandelson's prospects of political rehabilitation were highly rated by many observers.

John Glenn returns to space

On October, US Senator John Glenn became, at 77, the oldest person ever to go into space. It was Glenn's second space record: in 1962 he had been the first US astronaut to orbit the earth. His new mission, which began when the space shuttle Discovery blasted off from Cape Canaveral on the 29th, lasted nine days.

Turmoil in Russia

Russia descended further into political and economic chaos in August when, following a major devaluation of the free-falling rouble, President Yeltsin summarily dismissed the entire government for the second time in a year. Having previously sacked Viktor Chernomyrdin as Prime Minister in favour of Sergey Kiriyenko, he now sacked Kiriyenko in favour of Chernomyrdin. However, the Russian State Duma twice refused to endorse the new appointment, and it was September before a compromise candidate, 69-year-old former Foreign Minister Yevgeny Primakov, was confirmed as Russia's new Prime Minister.

Yemeni hostage crisis

Three British tourists and one Australian lost their lives in December when Yemeni security forces bungled an attempt to rescue them from armed tribesmen who had taken them hostage in a remote area of the country the previous day. Yemen had recently become notorious for kidnappings, but the four were the first hostages to be killed by their captors. Survivors of the massacre spoke of their being used as human shields by the tribesmen, but many observers, including the British government, laid the blame for the tragedy at the door of the Yemeni authorities.

Above: Freed prisoner John Brooke

1999

War in Kosovo

On March 24th, NATO launched air-strikes against targets in the Federal Republic of Yugoslavia in the first major conflict between European states since the end of the Second World War. The move came after a year of escalating tension in Kosovo between Serbian forces loyal to the Yugoslav President Slobodan Milosevic and the majority ethnic Albanian population of the province. Air-strikes had been narrowly averted in October 1998 when Milosevic reined in a Serb offensive against the separatist Kosovo Liberation Army and agreed to the presence of international observers in Kosovo. In December, however, fighting once more broke out in the province and in January ethnic Albanian civilians were massacred in the village of Racak. 'Proximity talks' between Serbian and Kosovar Albanian representatives at Rambouillet in France collapsed in March when Milosevic refused to permit NATO to station a peacekeeping force in Kosovo, and when a further round of talks also failed to reach agreement the international peace monitoring mission withdrew from the province. Serb forces at once began a major offensive in Kosovo, driving tens of thousands of ethnic Albanians from their homes in a systematic campaign of 'ethnic cleansing'. Operation Allied Force began on the evening of March 24th, with NATO forces under the command of General Wesley Clark conducting bombing raids against military installations throughout Yugoslavia. The immediate effect of the action was to trigger an intensification of ethnic cleansing in Kosovo and a refugee crisis on a scale not seen in Europe since the Second World War, as hundreds of thousands of ethnic Albanian Kosovars fled to neighbouring Albania and Macedonia, bringing with them harrowing accounts of massacres by Serb forces. As the bombing campaign continued – and especially as evidence grew of 'collateral damage' to non-military targets, including the Chinese embassy in Belgrade – calls for a diplomatic solution to the crisis mounted.

Not until the beginning of June, however, did Milosevic accept an international peace plan for Kosovo and order the withdrawal of Yugoslavian forces. The bombing stopped on June 9th, and the UN's K-For security force began to deploy in the province to an ecstatic reception from the remaining Albanian population. By the end of June, more than half the estimated three-quarters of a million ethnic Albanian refugees had returned to Kosovo. The toll of human misery continued to escalate, however, with the flight of tens of thousands of Serbs from the province in the face of real and threatened reprisals.

Littleton school massacre

The grim tally of deaths in American high-school shootings mounted further in April when two students at Columbine High School in Littleton, near Denver, Colorado, went on the rampage, killing 13 and leaving more than 20 injured before turning their guns on themselves. Witnesses reported that 'jocks' – successful athletes – were singled out by the killers, who were members of a shadowy group of disaffected right-wing students known as the Trench Coat Mafia. Police operations at the school were hampered by booby-traps and explosives planted by the killers. The massacre led to further calls for a tightening of America's notoriously permissive gun control laws.

Death of Yehudi Menuhin

March saw the death aged 83 of the violinist and conductor Yehudi Menuhin, perhaps the most celebrated virtuoso violinist of modern times. Lord Menuhin, who gave his first public concert at the age of seven and famously recorded the Elgar violin concerto under the composer's baton when he was 16, was well known for the breadth of his musical interests, which extended beyond the classical repertoire to encompass Indian music and jazz. In addition to his classical recordings, many with his pianist sister Hephzibah, Menuhin also made a series of popular records with the jazz violinist Stepan Grappelli. He founded the Menuhin School of Music in 1963 and was awarded the Order of Merit in 1987.

Death of King Hussein

The death was announced on February 7th of King Hussein of Jordan. A pivotal figure in the Middle East peace process, King Hussein, a member of the ancient Hashemite dynasty, had ruled his desert kingdom for 46 years. During that time – and despite such controversial actions as his involvement in the Six Day War of 1967, the expulsion of the PLO from Jordan in 1970, and the backing of Saddam in the Gulf War – he had established himself as an influential and highly respected player on the international stage. The King had been suffering from cancer for some time, and in January had made a dramatic return from treatment in the United States to name his eldest son, Prince Abdullah, as his successor in place of the long-standing heir apparent, Crown Prince Hassan. King Hussein's death plunged Jordan into national mourning, and his funeral in Amman on February 8th was attended by more than 50 heads of state, including President Clinton, Tony Blair, Yassir Arafat, Benjamin Netanyahu and President Assad of Syria.

Devolution in Scotland and Wales

Voters went to the polls in Scotland and Wales on May 6th to elect members of the new Scottish Parliament and Welsh Assembly. The new bodies represented the central element in a far-reaching package of constitutional change initiated by Britain's New Labour government, which included the creation of a Northern Ireland Assembly, reform of the House of Lords and a new unitary authority for Greater London. Labour gained the largest number of seats in each of the new bodies, but failed to secure an overall majority in either, thus ushering in an era of coalition politics in Britain. The Scottish and Welsh Nationalist parties – the SNP and Plaid Cymru – became the official opposition in both assemblies, but low electoral turnout, especially in Wales, led some commentators to question voters' enthusiasm for devolution. Donald Dewar (above) and Alun Michael were elected First Ministers of the Scottish Parliament and the Welsh Assembly respectively.

Launch of the Euro

A new era in the post-war history of Europe began on January 1st with the much-heralded launch of the European single currency – the Euro. Eleven countries adopted the new currency – Austria, Belgium, Finland, France, Germany, Ireland, Italy, Luxembourg, the Netherlands, Portugal and Spain – with Britain the most conspicuous absentee. Each agreed a fixed rate of exchange between the Euro and their national currencies, which were to be phased out by 2002 when Euro notes and coins would come into circulation. The new currency block, known colloquially as 'Euroland', comprised some 300 million people. Trading in the Euro began on January 4th, but the shine was taken off the launch by allegations of fraud and mismanagement in the European Commission and by unseemly squabbling over the 1998 appointment of Wim Duisenberg to the presidency of the European Central Bank. The value of thenew currency fell steadily during its first months of trading.

Death of Screaming Lord Sutch

A large gap was left in the political landscape of Great Britain on June 16th when David – universally known as 'Screaming Lord' – Sutch, the leader of the Monster Raving Loony Party, was found dead in his North London flat, apparently having committed suicide. Sutch, who was 58, had stood for election to Parliament a record 39 times, his trademark top hat, good humour and anarchic behaviour an eccentric and strangely reassuring presence at counts up and down the country. He was succeeded as leader of the party he had formed in his image by a cat called Cat-Mandu.

Earthquake in Turkey

Disaster struck north-western Turkey in the early hours of August 17th when an earthquake measuring 7.4 on the Richter Scale devastated the country's industrial heartland, killing more than 14,000 people and leaving hundreds of thousands more without homes and essential services. The epicentre of the quake, the worst to hit Turkey for more than half a century, was near Korfez, the site of the country's largest oil refinery, where firefighters struggled for weeks to extinguish the resulting conflagration. Shockwaves reached the capital Istanbul, causing the collapse of several residential blocks. As the full extent of the tragedy became clear, there was strong criticism of the Turkish government's rescue efforts. By contrast, Greek rescue teams were quick to respond, setting aside the long-standing antagonism between the two countries and generating hope of a more permanent thaw in relations.

Death of Cardinal Hume

The death was announced on June 17th of the head of the Roman Catholic Church in England, Cardinal Basil Hume, the Archbishop of Westminster. Cardinal Hume, who was 76 and had occupied the archbishopric for almost a quarter of a century, was held in great affection and esteem across the ecumenical divide he had done so much to bridge.

Aitken sentenced

On June 8th, the former Conservative cabinet minister Jonathan Aitken was sentenced to 18 months' imprisonment for perjury. The spectacular fall from grace resulted from Aitken's failed libel action against the *Guardian* newspaper and ended the political career of a man once tipped as a future prime minister. On his release from prison the following year, Aitken, now a bankrupt and separated from his wife, published a book of his experiences, which included an account of his conversion to Christianity.

Has he got news for them

Following Paddy Ashdown's announcement in January that he intended to resign from the leadership of the Liberal Democrats, Charles Kennedy was elected leader of Britain's third-largest party on August 9th. The 39-year-old MP for Ross, Skye and Inverness overcame suspicion of his sybaritic image – partly a legacy of regular appearances on television panel games – to fight off four other candidates for the top job. Political attention focused on his attitude to the close links fostered by his predecessor between the Liberal Democrats and Tony Blair's Labour government.

Paddington train crash

In one of the worst accidents in the history of Britain's rail network, 31 passengers died and more than 200 were injured when a crowded express collided with a local train outside London's Paddington station during the morning rush-hour on October 5th. Most of the fatalities occurred when leaking diesel fuel ignited, engulfing the front carriage of the express. The operation to recover the bodies and to examine the wreckage lasted for days, while investigators' attention focused on the part played in the tragedy by a signal which had been the subject of several safety concerns in the recent past.

Violence in East Timor

On August 30th, the people of the troubled Indonesian province of East Timor voted overwhelmingly in a referendum for independence from Jakarta. Scarcely had celebrations begun, however, than violence erupted across the province, as pro-Indonesian militias, apparently acting in collaboration with the Indonesian military, began a campaign of intimidation and massacre which claimed the lives of thousands of East Timorese and drove up to half a million more to leave their homes. The following month, the UN voted to despatch a multinational peacekeeping force – INTERFET – to the province, and the first detachment of troops, from neighbouring Australia, arrived in the capital, Dili, on September 20th.

Renewed war in Chechnya

At the end of September, three years after its withdrawal at the end of a chaotic two-year war against separatist forces, the Russian army once more invaded the North Caucasian republic of Chechnya. The move followed a series of bomb explosions in Moscow and other Russian cities, which left hundreds dead and were widely, if inconclusively, attributed to Chechnyan separatist terrorists. Air-strikes were launched against targets in the republic on September 23rd, and by the end of the month ground troops too had been deployed. As evidence grew of atrocities committed by both sides, Russian forces closed in on the Chechnyan capital, Grozny, and on December 6th issued an ultimatum to the remaining inhabitants, many of whom had been sheltering for weeks in cellars beneath the shattered city, telling them to leave within five days or risk annihilation. Mounting international pressure failed to dent the popularity within Russia either of the war itself or of the man most closely associated with it, the newly-appointed Russian Prime Minister Vladimir Putin.

602

Hamilton *V.* al-Fayed

On December 21st, after one of the most theatrical hearings in recent legal memory, the former Conservative MP Neil Hamilton lost his libel action against the Harrods owner Mohammed al-Fayed (above). The decision left Hamilton, who had hoped to salvage a reputation sullied by the so-called 'cash for questions' affair of the last years of John Major's Tory administration, facing crippling legal bills of more than two million pounds. Most public interest, however, centred on the performance in court of al-Fayed, who used the occasion to make a series of unrelated allegations, most dramatic among them the accusation that Prince Philip had masterminded the murder of Princess Diana and al-Fayed's son Dodi.

Yeltsin resigns

Ever the master of political surprise, Russian President Boris Yeltsin astonished the world once again with his announcement in the closing hours of the century that he was resigning his presidency six months before the end of his official term of office. Citing his much-publicised ill-health as the reason for bowing out after eight and a half years in the Kremlin, Yeltsin nominated the Prime Minister Vladimir Putin as acting President, a move widely seen as calculated to strengthen Putin's hand in the presidential elections to be held in June 2000. Yeltsin became the Soviet Union's most visible politician when he mounted a tank to oppose the coup against his predecessor Mikhail Gorbachev in 1991, but his reform programme had in recent years become mired in political expediency, social breakdown and allegations of corruption (one of Putin's first acts as acting President was to grant him immunity from prosecution), and his own reputation damaged by serious illness, rumours of heavy drinking, and increasingly erratic public behaviour.

2000

Jan	3	Ex-Chancellor Kohl to face funding scandal probe
Feb	5	Jorg Haider joins Austrian coalition govt
	6	Grozny falls to Russian troops
	7	Ariana 727 hijacked to Stansted Airport
Mar	2	Pinochet returns to Chile
	17	500 members of millennial cult die in Uganda
	20	Pope visits Jordan, Israel and Palestinian territories
	26	Vladimir Putin elected Russian President
	28	Death of novelist Anthony Powell
Apr	14	Shares plummet on NY Stock Exchange
	30	UN peacekeepers taken hostage in Sierra Leone
May	1	Anti-capitalist demonstrations in London
	4	Love Bug virus hits computers worldwide
	7	British troops sent to Sierra Leone
	12	India's population hits 1bn
	21	Death of Sir John Gielgud
	24	Israeli army pulls out of S Lebanon
Jun	3	Clinton meets Putin in Moscow
	10	Death of President Assad of Syria
	18	58 illegal immigrants found dead at Dover
	22	59 die in Yangtze River ferry sinking
	23	15 die in Australian hostel fire
	26	Working draft of human genome completed
Jul	10	200 die in Manila landslide
	11	Barak and Arafat begin peace talks at Camp David
	25	Concorde crashes near Paris
Aug	4	Queen Mother's 100th birthday
	5	Death of Sir Alec Guinness
	12	*Kursk* submarine sinks in Barents Sea
	25	11 British soldiers abducted in Sierra Leone
Sep	7	Fuel protests in UK
	12	EU lifts sanctions against Austria
	15	27th Summer Olympics begin in Sydney
	27	79 die in Greek ferry sinking
	28	Denmark rejects Euro in referendum
	28	Rioting follows Ariel Sharon's visit to Haram-al-Sharif
Oct	5	Milosevic swept from power in Yugoslavia
	11	Death of Scottish First Minister Donald Dewar
	19	Oldest ever cave paintings found near Verona
Nov	7	US elections prove inconclusive
	11	155 die in Austrian funicular fire
	17	Peruvian President Fujimori flees to Japan
	20	EU agree to create Rapid Reaction Force
Dec	13	George W Bush declared US President

Millennium celebrations

Purists may have claimed that the third millennium wouldn't begin for another year, but millions of people all round the world ignored them to stage parties, firework displays and other extravaganzas to celebrate the advent of the year 2000. Not the least cause for celebration was the bug that didn't bite: what had become known as the Y2K problem – the inability of computer systems to recognise the new date – failed to live up to the apocalyptic warnings of some commentators. With billions spent on reprogramming in the months leading up to the New Year, and emergency teams on standby as the 20th century turned into the 21st, not only did the global system fail to collapse, but few problems of moment were reported anywhere.

Harold Shipman sentenced

Britain's most prolific serial killer was sentenced to life imprisonment on January 31st for the murders of 15 women. The victims were all patients of the 54-year-old doctor Harold Shipman, whose crimes came to light only after he made a hamfisted attempt to forge the will of one of them in his favour. All the women had been killed by diamorphine injection and most subsequently cremated on Shipman's instructions. The revelations traumatised the town of Hyde in Greater Manchester where Shipman practised, especially when police disclosed that they were investigating more than 200 other suspicious deaths among Shipman's patients over the previous 15 years.

Farm occupations in Zimbabwe

A crisis developed in Zimbabwe from February when thousands of black protesters, led by veterans of the country's war of independence, began occupying farms owned by white Zimbabweans. The moves followed the rejection by voters of President Robert Mugabe's proposed new constitution, which would have granted him wide-ranging powers including the distribution of white-owned land to blacks, and were widely seen as orchestrated by the ruling Zanu-PF party in an attempt to boost Mugabe's flagging popularity. Despite a decision of the country's High Court ruling the occupations illegal, police declined to act against the so-called 'squatters' or their leader, Chenjerai 'Hitler' Hunzvi, and by April hundreds of Zimbabwe's commercial farms had been occupied and some white farmers murdered. The occupations took place against a background of wider political unrest and violence as Zanu-PF activists attacked supporters of the opposition Movement for Democratic Change in the run-up to elections scheduled for June.

Death of Ian Dury

March saw the death from cancer of Ian Dury at the age of 57. Often described as 'the godfather of punk' or 'punk's Poet Laureate', Essex-born Dury, whose hits with his band The Blockheads included 'Reasons to be cheerful', had a profound influence on the New Wave bands of the 1970s and was one of the most charismatic showmen on the British musical scene.

Riots in Seattle

A meeting of the World Trade Organisation in Seattle at the end of November and beginning of December proved the focus of the largest demonstrations in the United States since the anti-Vietnam protests of the 1970s. Up to 100,000 people took to the streets of the city to protest against the power of international capital and the increasing globalisation of the economic system. The talks, already deadlocked by serious policy disagreements between the US and other trading blocs, were repeatedly disrupted by the demonstrations and ended without agreement. While there was sympathy with the basic concerns of the protesters in many quarters – including the White House, from which President Clinton issued a statement of understanding – the violent actions of a small minority were countered by the imposition of a state of emergency in Seattle, and the deployment of teargas and watercannon brought accusations of overreaction against the city's police force.

Turn again Livingstone

The maverick left-wing MP Ken Livingstone was elected Mayor of London in May, thus returning to the city's helm 14 years after Margaret Thatcher's government abolished the Greater London Council of which he was leader. The race for the mayoralty, intended as a key plank in Tony Blair's policy of devolution of power to the localities, had often bordered on farce. The official Labour candidate, the former Health Secretary Frank Dobson, was widely regarded as a Blair placeman, and the selection procedure for Labour candidate as gerrymandered to secure his nomination. The original Tory candidate, Lord (formerly Jeffrey) Archer, was forced to withdraw from the contest when it emerged that he had asked a friend to lie for him in court during a libel action, and his successor Steven Norris attracted as much interest for his colourful private life as for his policies. Livingstone himself stood as an independent, having vowed to stand as a Labour candidate or not at all,

Flooding in Mozambique

Humanitarian tragedy engulfed southern Africa in February when heavy rains brought catastrophic flooding to the region. Worst affected was Mozambique, a country newly emerging into social stability and economic growth after years of civil war. Thousands of acres of agricultural land were inundated and the infrastructure of large parts of the country washed away. Hundreds of people were killed and up to three-quarters of a million made homeless. Governments and aid agencies responded with helicopters, food and medicine as the world's television services broadcast images of families clinging to the roofs of houses, huddled in treetops or wading through seemingly endless plains of water. The situation was made even worse by the arrival later in the month of Cyclone Eline, which brought further flooding in and around the capital Maputo. Government officials in Mozambique estimated that the floods, the worst in the region for more than 40 years, had set the country's development back by decades.

and was promptly expelled from the party. His immense personal following, and widespread disillusionment with the major parties, secured him a comfortable victory in the polls on May 4th.

Tragedy at Dover

On June 18th 58 Chinese immigrants trying to enter Britain illegally were found dead in the back of a container lorry at the Channel port of Dover. The 54 men and four women had suffocated in extreme summer heat after the driver of the Dutch-registered lorry, which had just made the five-hour crossing from Zeebrugge, closed the air vents to prevent their being detected. He was later found guilty of manslaughter and aiding illegal entry and sentenced to 14 years imprisonment; an accomplice in Britain was also convicted. The tragedy threw into stark relief the risks taken by asylum seekers to enter Britain and the role of organised crime syndicates, such as the notorious Chinese 'snakehead' gangs, in the smuggling of human beings across international borders.

A bridge too far?

Problems continued to dog Britain's showcase millennium projects during the year. In June the much-heralded Millennium Bridge, the first footbridge to be built across the Thames for more than a century, had to be closed two days after its official opening when it began to sway alarmingly under its first pedestrian traffic (above). Meanwhile, attempts to find a buyer for the troubled Millennium Dome suffered a serious setback when the Japanese bank Nomura withdrew its bid for the attraction, and the government were severely criticised for their mismanagement of the whole project in a November report. In the same month, thieves ram-raided the Dome with a JCB in an attempt to steal £350-million worth of diamonds displayed there, but were arrested by waiting police, who had been tipped off in advance.

Football hooligans

In June the image of Britain abroad was once more tarnished by the behaviour of so-called football supporters when English hooligans ran riot in the streets of Charleroi and Brussels during the opening stages of the Euro-2000 championship. Hundreds of English supporters were arrested and deported by Belgian and Dutch police, but the threats of UEFA, the competition's controlling body, to expel England from the championship were forestalled when the team failed to qualify for the quarter-finals a few days later. Only one person was subsequently convicted.

Death of President Assad

The Middle East lost one of its political veterans on June 10th when Hafez al-Assad, the President of Syria, died suddenly of a heart-attack at the age of 69. President Assad had risen to power through the ranks of the military, becoming commander of the Syrian airforce in 1966, the year before Syria's humiliating defeat at the hands of Israel in the Six-Day War. He assumed control of the country after a bloodless coup in 1970 and was elected to the presidency the following year, soon moving ruthlessly to quash internal dissent. Despite his pan-Arab political stance, Assad sided with the UN coalition in the Gulf War against Saddam Hussein in 1990, and his funeral was attended by representatives of the United States and other western powers as well as leaders of neighbouring Arab countries. He was succeeded as President by his son Bashar al-Assad.

Chaos in Sierra Leone

In August there was a further reminder of the grim lawlessness into which Sierra Leone had descended when 11 British soldiers serving with peacekeeping forces were taken hostage by the West Side Boys, the most notorious of the independent militia operating beyond government control in the war-wracked West African state. The soldiers had been patrolling in the Occra Hills, a WSB stronghold some 50 km east of the capital Freetown, when they were abducted. Tense negotiations resulted in the release of five of the officers at the end of the month, but the remaining soldiers were freed only on September 9th when a force of British paratroopers, SAS and Royal Marines stormed the WSB base where they were being held.

Concorde crash

Tragedy struck one of aviation's most famous symbols in July when an Air France Concorde crashed moments after taking off from Charles de Gaulle airport in Paris, killing 109 passengers and crew and four people on the ground. Most of the dead were German tourists travelling to New York on their way to a Caribbean holiday. The crash, the first in Concorde's 31-year history, was attributed to collision with a piece of metal which had fallen onto the runway from another plane.

Fuel protests

The fragility of the supply chain in modern society was dramatically exposed in September when, following similar successful action in France, a small group of hauliers and farmers brought Britain to a near standstill in protest at escalating fuel prices. The protests caught the Labour government unawares and presented it with its greatest domestic crisis since assuming power in 1997. That crisis began on September 7th when protesters set up a blockade of oil refineries, preventing the delivery of supplies to petrol stations. As news of the action spread, queues quickly formed at petrol pumps throughout the country, and within five days more than 90% of UK forecourts had run dry. Schools closed as teachers and pupils found themselves without fuel, and supermarket shelves began to empty under the combined pressures of interrupted supplies and panic-buying of essential foodstuffs. Despite the resulting inconvenience, polls showed substantial public support for the protests, which the co-ordinators called off after a week. Threats to renew their action if fuel taxes were not reduced within 60 days were forestalled by Treasury measures in November.

The fall of Milosevic

In October, amid scenes reminiscent of the popular uprisings in Eastern Europe in 1989, Slobodan Milosevic was swept from power as President of the Federal Republic of Yugoslavia. The momentum of protest had been gathering since the general election of September 24th, in which Milosevic refused to acknowledge defeat despite the evidence of independent observers, which gave him only 33% of the vote as against 58% for his opponent, the leader of the Democratic Party of Serbia, Vojislav Kostunica. On October 1st, in a development of great symbolic importance, thousands of workers at Serbia's largest coalmines, Kolubara and Kostolac - formerly the heartland of Milosevic's support - downed tools in protest at his refusal to resign, and the following day a general strike brought large parts of the country to a standstill. On October 5th, after Milosevic ignored further opposition calls for him to step down, crowds in the Yugoslav capital Belgrade stormed the parliament building (right) and state-controlled television station, with the tacit or active support of the President's security forces. In the evening, Kostunica made a historic broadcast address as the new President of 'liberated Serbia'. However, with Milosevic declaring his intention to remain in politics, and the ethnic powderkegs of Kosovo and Macedonia still primed by years of grievance and conflict, the situation in the Balkans remained critical.

A new intifada

Violence erupted once more in the Israeli-occupied territories at the end of September following a controversial visit to Haram-al-Sharif, a site sacred to both Jews and Moslems, by Ariel Sharon, the veteran hardline leader of Israel's Likud party. Clashes between Palestinian protesters and Israeli troops soon escalated into the worst violence since the peace agreement of 1993, and television pictures of the shooting of a 12-year-old Palestinian boy as his father tried to shelter him from Israeli bullets aroused worldwide condemnation. Despite attempts by the US and the United Nations to broker a ceasefire, the peace process spiralled towards collapse, with Israel launching all-out retaliatory attacks by helicopter gunships after the lynching of two Israeli soldiers by a Palestinian mob at a police station in Ramallah on October 12th. By the end of the year some 350 people, the vast majority of them Palestinians, had been killed and thousands more injured in the West Bank and Gaza, and the Israeli Foreign Minister had pronounced the peace process at an end.

The Hatfield train crash

Tragedy again struck Britain's troubled rail network on October 17th when an express train travelling from London to Leeds was derailed at 115 mph near the town of Hatfield in Hertfordshire, killing four passengers and injuring many more. The crash, which was attributed to a broken rail, triggered months of serious disruption for rail travellers as Railtrack, the rail operating company, launched a programme of intensive repairs and speed restrictions throughout the country.

The US Presidential election

The United States entered uncharted constitutional waters in November after the presidential election proved inconclusive. The media clich 'too close to call' became dramatic reality when Vice-President Al Gore won only a 0.3% majority over his rival, Texas Governor George W ('Dubya') Bush, in the popular vote, and the outcome of the decisive electoral college vote depended on the contested results of a single state, Florida. Early indications were that Bush had won Florida, and Gore telephoned his opponent in the early hours of November 8th to concede the election. An hour later, however, he called back to retract when the extreme narrowness of the margin became clear. With the presidency hanging on a mere 1,500 votes in four disputed counties, the entire election process became mired in accusations of irregularity, manual recounts (above) and ever more abstruse legal challenges and counter-challenges by the Democratic and Republican camps. By December it had descended into near-farce, as commentators introduced a bemused public to the arcana of 'hanging' and 'pregnant chads' - the inconclusively-punched ballot papers on which so much of the controversy turned. Only on December 13th did Gore finally concede the election to Bush. With 102 million votes cast in the country at large, the margin of victory had been just 537 of the 2.9 million votes cast in Florida.

Alpine tragedy

One hundred and fifty-five holidaymakers died on November 11th when fire broke out on a funicular railway carrying them up a mountain at the Austrian winter resort of Kaprun. The tragedy was Austria's worst ever peacetime disaster.

A royal century

On August 4th the 100th birthday of Queen Elizabeth the Queen Mother was marked by a major series of public celebrations in London and elsewhere (and by a minor controversy over which television channels were to broadcast them).

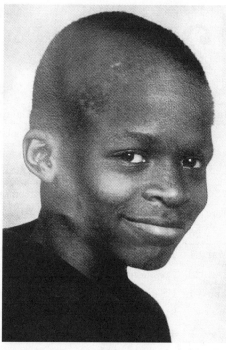

Death of Damilola Taylor

The moral health of Britain was subjected to painful analysis in November after a 10-year-old Nigerian boy was murdered on his way home from school in South London. Damilola Taylor, whose family had come to Britain in search of better healthcare and educational opportunities, was left to bleed to death in a stairwell in Peckham after being stabbed in the leg by unknown assailants.

Sinking of the *Kursk*

The declined state of Russia's post-Cold War defence forces was tragically revealed in August when a nuclear-powered submarine sank with the loss of all its crew during naval exercises in the Barents Sea. The *Kursk* went to the bottom in more than 100 metres of water after a torpedo misfire caused two explosions to rip through the hull. The incident was compounded by days of confusion and Soviet-style misinformation and by the Russian authorities' protracted refusal to accept international help. Repeated Russian attempts to rescue the 118 crew were defeated by heavy seas, and only nine days later was a joint British-Norwegian deep-sea rescue team able to open one of the *Kursk*'s hatches. The disaster severely dented the domestic standing of Russian President Vladimir Putin, who had remained on holiday for almost a week after the sinking.

2001

Jan	16	Tanker Jessica oilspill near Galapagos Islands
	20	George W Bush inaugurated as US President
	24	5m Hindus at Allahabad in largest ever human gathering
	26	Thousands die in Indian earthquake
Feb	7	Ariel Sharon elected PM of Israel
	20	Foot-and-mouth outbreak in UK
Mar	1	Taliban begin demolition of Buddha statues, Afghanistan
	28	President Bush rejects Kyoto treaty on global warming
Apr	1	US spy plane collides with Chinese fighter
		Slobodan Milosevic arrested in Belgrade
May	9	130 die in Ghanaian football stadium collapse, Accra
	27	20 tourists kidnapped in Philippines
Jun	1	Nepalese royal family massacred by Crown Prince
	7	Labour wins UK general election
	11	Oklahoma bomber Timothy McVeigh executed
	16	President Bush meets President Putin for first time
Jul	3	Milosevic appears before UN tribunal
		135 killed in Siberian jet crash
	19	Lord Archer sentenced to prison
	25	Phoolan Devi (the 'Bandit Queen') shot dead
Aug	1	US House of Representatives bans human cloning
	13	Peace agreement signed in Macedonia
	16	New solar system discovered

Sep	2	Death of transplant pioneer Christiaan Barnard
	11	Terrorist attacks kill thousands in New York and Washington
	12	NATO invokes Article 5 of charter
	21	Explosion at fertiliser factory, Toulouse
	26	Arafat and Peres meet for talks
Oct	4	Russian airliner accidentally downed by Ukrainian missile
	5	First victim of anthrax dies in US
	7	Operation Enduring Freedom begins against Afghanistan
		Railtrack declared insolvent
	12	Nobel Peace Prize awarded to Kofi Annan and UN
	17	Israeli tourism minister Rehavan Ze'evi assassinated
	20	350 refugees die in fishing boat sinking off Australia
Nov	7	Concorde resumes passenger flights
	9	Mazar-al-Sharif falls to Northern Alliance
	12	Passenger plane crash kills 260 in New York
	12/13	Kabul falls to Northern Alliance
	23	Milosevic charged with genocide in The Hague
Dec	1	Japanese Crown Princess Aiko born
	7	Khandahar falls to Northern Alliance
	20	National crisis causes collapse of Argentine government
	22	'Shoe bomber' arrested on Paris–Miami flight

Assassination of Laurent Kabila

The chaos already engulfing the Democratic Republic of Congo deepened still further in January with the assassination of the country's president, Laurent Kabila. Kabila (above), a former rebel leader who had assumed power in 1997 after deposing the veteran President Mobuto, was shot by one of his own bodyguards; the gunman was himself shot dead at the scene. He was succeeded as President by his son Joseph Kabila, prompting hopes of a breakthrough in peace negotiations in the Congo, whose civil war had become the focus of regional intervention by Angolan, Zimbabwean, Rwandan and Burundian troops.

Fall of Estrada

'People Power' chalked up a second victory in the Philippines when President Joseph Estrada was swept from power in January. Only days after the collapse of his trial on charges of financial corruption, a coalition of opposition politicians, including former presidents Corazon Aquino and Fidel Ramos, mobilised popular protests of up to half a million people on the streets of Manila, demanding Estrada's resignation. Key members of the beleaguered administration changed sides, and on 20 January, as Estrada fled the presidential palace with his family, the *de facto* leader of the opposition, Vice-President Gloria Macapagal-Arroya, was formally inaugurated in his stead.

Out with the old...

After the prolonged uncertainty of the post-election period, George W Bush was inaugurated as the 43rd President of the United States on 20 January, the first son of a President to take office for more than 175 years. However, the early days of Bush's presidency were overshadowed by controversies generated during the last days of his predecessor. Public attention focused on the unseemly pranks of outgoing White House staff and the Clintons' departure with valuable gifts which they were later required to return. Most damaging of all to the former President's public standing was a flurry of contentious last-minute pardons – among them those of his half-brother Roger Clinton, who had been convicted of cocaine dealing in 1985, and of the fugitive financier Marc Rich, whose wife emerged as a major contributor to Democratic Party funds. *Right:* George Bush eyes his challenger Al Gore and predecessor Bill Clinton at inaugural celebrations.

Earthquake in India

A second term for Labour

The return of Ariel Sharon

Tragedy struck India on 26 January when an earthquake registering 7.9 on the Richter scale left tens of thousands dead and hundreds of thousands homeless in the north-western state of Gujarat. The earthquake, the most powerful to strike the country for more than half a century, devastated the towns of Bhuj, Anjar and Bhachau and triggered a major exodus from what remained of the regional centres of population.

Despite public concern over its handling of the foot-and-mouth crisis, and unease at the second resignation from the government in less than three years of the Northern Ireland Secretary Peter Mandelson — this time over unsubstantiated allegations of improper intervention in the application of an Indian businessman, Srichand Hinduja, for a British passport — Tony Blair's Labour party coasted to victory in the 7 June general election to secure a second term in office. It retained a commanding majority of 167 seats. The Conservative leader William Hague, whose party made a net gain of only one seat, announced his resignation the following day. In September Iain Duncan Smith successfully saw off challenges from a field of contenders, including the former chancellor Kenneth Clarke, to win the leadership, but faced an uphill struggle to revitalise the fortunes of his ailing party.

In February Ariel Sharon, the leader of the right-wing Likud Party, was elected Prime Minister of Israel, defeating the sitting incumbent Ehud Barak by the largest margin in the country's history. The election of Sharon, a veteran hardliner who resigned as Israel's defence minister in 1982 after implication in the notorious massacre of Palestinians at refugee camps in southern Lebanon, threw into doubt the future of a peace process already strained to its limits by months of serious unrest in the West Bank and Gaza Strip.

Violence intensified in April and May with suicide bombings by Palestinian terrorists within Israel and the launching of Israeli military operations in the Gaza Strip. A ceasefire agreed in June had collapsed by the end of July, and in October, in a further escalation of the conflict, the Israeli tourism minister Rehavon Ze'evi was assassinated in Arab East Jerusalem in reprisal for the Israeli assassination in August of Abu Ali Mustafa, the deputy leader of the Popular Front for the Liberation of Palestine.

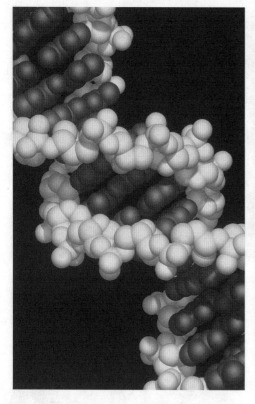

The stuff of life

February saw the publication of findings based on the previous year's mapping of the human genome by two independent research groups in Europe and the United States, the Human Genome Project and the Celera Genomics Group. The most surprising discovery was that human beings have only about 30,000 genes – far fewer than had been expected and little more than twice the number of the humble fruit fly.

A good innings

February saw the death, aged 92, of the legendary Australian cricketer Sir Donald Bradman. 'The Don', as he was widely known, scored 6,996 runs in 52 Test matches during the 1930s and 1940s, notching up an unbeaten record of 29 centuries in 80 Test innings. His other records included the biggest Test score yet achieved – an astounding 334 runs against England at Headingley in 1930.

Ellen MacArthur

A heroine's welcome awaited the 24-year-old British yachtswoman Ellen MacArthur as she crossed the finishing line of the Vendée Globe round-the-world yacht race on 11 February. Tens of thousands of wellwishers greeted her at the French port of Les Sables d'Olonne, as she arrived in her 60-foot vessel, The Kingfisher, after 94 days and 26,000 miles alone at sea. Despite coming in second to the Frenchman Michel Desjoyeaux, who had finished in record-breaking time the previous day, Ellen MacArthur was feted as the star of the race for her determination in the face of numerous dangers, from icebergs and submerged containers to the broken rigging which forced her to spend hours at a time clinging to the top of the mast as she made repairs.

Foot-and-mouth

The UK Labour government faced its worst domestic crisis with the discovery of foot-and-mouth disease in a consignment of pigs at an abattoir in Essex in February. Within weeks the outbreak had reached epidemic proportions, and a policy of wholesale slaughter to contain the spread of the highly infectious disease had led to the culling and burning of hundreds of thousands of cattle, sheep and pigs throughout the country. The crisis – the first outbreak of foot-and-mouth in Britain for more than 30 years – came as a further blow to an agricultural industry already devastated by the effects of the BSE debacle. Exports of livestock, meat and milk were halted, bans placed on the movement of farm animals, and footpaths closed in many rural areas, paralysing the farming and tourist sectors and forcing the government to reschedule elections – including the general election – planned for May. Cases of the disease linked to British exports were also found on mainland Europe.

Death of George Harrison

On 29 November the death was announced of the former Beatle, George Harrison, who had been suffering from cancer. He was 58. Harrison, known as the 'quiet one' of the Fab Four, remained a significant figure in the world of popular music after the break-up of the group in 1970, scoring an international hit with his single 'My Sweet Lord' in the same year, and in 1971 organising a concert for Bangladesh which became a model for later fund-raising pop events such as Live Aid. He was also, with Bob Dylan, Jeff Lynne, Roy Orbison and Tom Petty, a member of the 1980s supergroup the Travelling Wilburys, and made a key contribution to the revival of the British film industry through his production company Handmade Films, which was responsible for such box-office successes as *The Long Good Friday*, *A Private Function* and *Withnail and I*. In 1999 Harrison had survived a frenzied knife-attack by an intruder at his Oxfordshire mansion.

Bush fires in Australia

In December the Australian state of New South Wales suffered its most devastating bush fires for seven years, as flames engulfed more than 500,000 hectares of land, including large areas of the Blue Mountains National Park. On Christmas Day, with firefighters still struggling to bring the blaze under control, the fires threatened the outskirts of the state capital, Sydney, leading to the evacuation of hundreds of homes. Many of the fires were believed to have been started deliberately, and a number of people were arrested and charged with arson. By the time the fires were finally extinguished in mid-January, damage to property was estimated at tens of millions of dollars.

Stranger than fiction

The eventful life of Lord Archer of Weston-super-Mare took another dramatic turn in July when he was convicted at the Old Bailey of perjury and perverting the course of justice. He was sentenced to four years' imprisonment. The millionaire bestselling novelist and former deputy chairman of the Conservative party had withdrawn his candidature for London mayor in 2000 after allegations that he had asked a friend, Ted Francis, to lie for him in his successful libel trial against the *Star* newspaper in 1987.

So long and thanks for all the books...

The world of literature and the media lost one of its best loved figures in May with the death of Douglas Adams at the age of 49. Adams made his reputation in the 1970s as the creator of the radio series The Hitchhiker's Guide to the Galaxy, which formed the basis for a series of bestselling books, including *Life, the Universe and Everything*, *The Restaurant at the End of the Universe* and *So Long and Thanks for All the Fish*. He was also the author of *Dirk Gently's Holistic Detective Agency* and *The Long Dark Tea-Time of the Soul*. An adept of new technology, the fertility of Adams' imagination was tempered only by a lifelong tendency to writer's block.

Massacre in Nepal

The mountain kingdom of Nepal was rocked on 1 June by the massacre of its royal family by the heir to the throne, Crown Prince Dipendra. The Eton-educated Prince apparently became involved in an argument with his parents, King Birendra and Queen Aishwarya, at a family gathering in the royal palace in Kathmandu, and withdrew to his rooms, returning shortly afterwards with automatic weapons. He shot dead eight members of the family, including the King and Queen, before turning a gun on himself. The murders set in train a chaotic process of succession, with Dipendra himself proclaimed King despite being hospitalised and in a coma. When he died, three days after the attack, the throne passed to his brother Gyanendra. The de-stabilising events unfolded against a background of advances made by the Communist Party of Nepal, an underground Maoist group, which had been in rebellion against the ruling regime for five years.

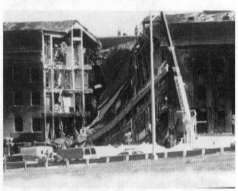

9.11

On the morning of 11 September the United States became the victim of the most destructive single terrorist action in history. At 8.48 a.m. an American Airlines Boeing 767 with 92 passengers and crew on board crashed into the North Tower of the World Trade Center in New York, engulfing the upper storeys in flames. Theories that the crash was a bizarre accident were brutally dispelled fifteen minutes later when a second plane approached the Center and flew into the South Tower. Shortly afterwards reports began to come in of a third strike by a hijacked plane, this time on the Pentagon in Washington DC, and of a fourth plane which had crashed in Pennsylvania, apparently after passengers attempted to overpower the hijackers.

At 9.59 a.m., as emergency services in New York struggled to assist the evacuation of the World Trade Center, the South Tower collapsed, sending clouds of smoke and dust into the air over the city. Half an hour later the north tower also fell. Estimates of the number of dead, initially put at more than 6,000, were later revised to fewer than 3,000, but with the 110-storey twin towers compacted to a heap of blazing rubble at what soon became known as Ground Zero, an exact final figure will probably never be known.

While no group claimed responsibility for the attack, suspicion immediately fell on al-Qaeda ('The Base'), a shadowy Islamic fundamentalist organisation under the overall leadership of the Saudi exile Osama bin Laden, who had been blamed for an abortive attack on the World Trade Center in 1993. As the story of the events of 11

September began to be pieced together, it became clear that many of those involved in hijacking the planes from airports in Boston, Los Angeles and Newark had connections with al-Qaeda, whose main power base was in Afghanistan where bin Laden had been sheltered by the ruling Taliban regime since 1996.

After a period of intense coalition-building, in which Britain took a prominent part and which generated support even among regimes traditionally hostile to the US, President George W Bush, whose handling of the crisis boosted his personal popularity ratings to unprecedented levels, announced on 7 October the beginning of Operation Enduring Freedom to root out al-Qaeda and bin Laden from Afghanistan (above right).

Meanwhile security remained high on the domestic front as packages containing anthrax spores were discovered in government and media offices in the US (above), including, in October, the office of the Democratic majority leader in the Senate, Tom Daschle. The source of the anthrax attacks, which led to a number of fatalities, remained mysterious, but the crash on 12 November of an American Airlines Airbus in the New York suburb of Queens, with the deaths of 260 people, proved to have been a tragic accident.

In Afghanistan itself, allied advances were rapid. With US and UK troops joining forces with the Northern Alliance, a loosely structured federation of groups acting in opposition to the Taliban, the Taliban stronghold of Mazar-al Sharif fell on 9 November. Four days later the Northern Alliance was in control of the capital, Kabul, and an interim government under Hamid Karzai was agreed on 5 December. Khandahar, another key Taliban stronghold, fell on 7 December, and there was intense fighting as alliance troops drove al-Qaeda forces from the Tora Bora cave complex in the White Mountains. Despite these successes, however, neither Osama bin Laden nor Mullah Mohammed Omar, the reclusive one-eyed leader of the Taliban, was apprehended, and military action continued into the New Year.

In the first months of 2002 controversy arose over the deportation of prisoners to 'Camp X-Ray', the Guantanamo Bay holding centre in Cuba (right), and the US government's establishment of secret military tribunals to try foreign nationals captured in the fighting, both of which raised questions about America's compliance with the Geneva Convention on the rights of prisoners of war. Further strain was placed on the unity of the coalition by President Bush's 'axis of evil' speech to Congress in January 2002, which raised the prospect that the 'war against terror' might be extended to other regimes believed to support international terrorism, notably that of Saddam Hussein in Iraq. In May questions also began to be asked about the extent to which intelligence warnings of a major terrorist attack in the US had been ignored in the weeks leading up to 11 September.

2002

A new Europe

The beginning and end of the year saw historic changes in the constitution of the European Union. On 1 January the Euro became legal tender throughout the so-called Euro-zone of twelve countries, providing 300 million people in Europe with a single common currency. Among EU members, only the UK, Denmark and Sweden remained outside it. Euro coins and notes had been issued in December 2001 and dates set for the immediate phasing out of national currencies. At its launch the new currency stood at 1.1177 to the US dollar.

In December EU members convened for a summit in Copenhagen, at which they approved the enlargement of the Union by the accession of ten new states, bringing the total membership to twenty-five. The new members, to be formally admitted on 1 May 2004, were Cyprus (excluding Turkish-occupied territory), the Czech Republic, Estonia, Hungary, Latvia, Lithuania, Malta, Poland, Slovakia and Slovenia. Negotiations continued for the accession of Bulgaria and Romania.

The Oscars

The media spotlight fell on the Oscar awards ceremony in Los Angeles in March when two black stars won top acting awards. Denzel Washington was awarded the Oscar for Best Actor for his role as a corrupt police officer in *Training Day*, and Halle Berry the Oscar for Best Actress for her part in *Monster's Ball*, the first black woman ever to be awarded the honour.

Mixed fortunes for the royal family

A cloud was cast over the Queen's Golden Jubilee year by the deaths of her sister, Princess Margaret, and her mother, Queen Elizabeth the Queen Mother, in the early months of the year, and by allegations surrounding the collapse of the trial of a former royal butler in November. Princess Margaret died on 9 February aged 71, after suffering the latest in a series of incapacitating strokes. The Queen Mother, at whose 100th birthday celebrations the Princess had made a rare public appearance, defied her own ill-health to attend her daughter's funeral. She died on 30 March aged 101. The news set in train a period of national mourning, as some 200,000 people queued to pay their last respects at the lying-in-state in Westminster Hall. The funeral took place at Westminster Abbey on 9 April and more than a million mourners gathered in Parliament Square or lined the route by which the coffin travelled to Windsor, where the Queen Mother was laid to rest next to her husband, King George VI, in St George's Chapel.

Defying the predictions of some commentators that the Golden Jubilee celebrations would be a muted affair, however, at the beginning of June Britain basked in a four-day public holiday to mark the 50th anniversary of the Queen's accession. Local parties in communities throughout the country recalled the atmosphere of the Queen's last jubilee year, 1977, and Union Jacks were much in evidence alongside the English flags of those following England's progress in the initial rounds of the World Cup. The official celebrations were spectacular, beginning with the 'Prom at the Palace' on Saturday 1 June – a classical concert watched by some 40,000 people in the grounds of Buckingham Palace and on giant screens outside. On Monday evening the Palace was again the venue for a concert, this time a three-hour rock extravaganza, with stars including Sir Paul McCartney, Tom Jones and, appropriately enough, the surviving members of the band Queen – whose guitarist Brian May opened the proceedings by playing the national anthem from the Palace roof – serenading the monarch and the millions watching on television worldwide. At the end of the evening the Queen lit the Jubilee Beacon in front of the Victoria Memorial, the last in a chain of hundreds of beacons burning throughout Britain and the Commonwealth. The skies over the capital were filled with a magnificent display of fireworks, and the Palace itself illuminated by a succession of projected images, culminating in the simple but moving message 'God Save the Queen'. The celebrations concluded the following day with a Jubilee pageant, representing the nations of the Commonwealth and the five decades of the Queen's reign, and a flypast of Concorde and the Red Arrows, trailing red, white and blue pennants of smoke.

The festive atmosphere had evaporated by November when the trial of Princess Diana's former butler, Paul Burrell, collapsed at the Old Bailey in bizarre circumstances. Burrell was accused of stealing hundreds of items belonging to the Princess and other members of the royal family. Shortly before he was due to take the witness stand, however, the Queen intervened in the trial, relaying through Prince Charles' solicitor her recollection of a meeting she had had with Burrell four months after the Princess' death in 1997 in which he had told her he was taking some of Diana's possessions into safe keeping. With her intervention the case against Burrell collapsed, and he sold his story to the *Daily Mirror*, triggering an avalanche of lurid tabloid allegations, especially about life in the household of Prince Charles, into which the Prince's private secretary, Sir Michael Peat, was appointed to conduct an internal enquiry.

The right triumphant

Centre-left parties across Europe were shaken in April and May when the far right made significant electoral gains in France and the Netherlands. On 21 April the National Front leader Jean-Marie Le Pen stunned the French political establishment when he defeated the socialist premier Lionel Jospin in the first round of the presidential elections, garnering 16.9 per cent of the vote to Jospin's 16.2 per cent and the sitting President Jacques Chirac's 19.9 per cent. Although in France anti-Le Pen voters closed ranks to re-elect President Chirac by a landslide in the second round, the far right also gained ground in the Netherlands, where the newly formed List Pim Fortuyn party found itself in second place to the centre-right Christian Democratic Appeal party in the elections of 15 May. The List was the creation of populist politician Pim Fortuyn, who was assassinated on 6 May.

The birth of a nation

Stand-off over Kashmir

Release of Suu Kyi

Old enemies joined to celebrate the birth of the world's newest country on 20 May when East Timor became an independent nation after a quarter of a century of struggle against Indonesian hegemony. In a widely reported act of reconciliation, Indonesian President Megawati Sukarnoputri shared a platform with East Timor's new head of state, the former rebel leader Jose Alexandre Gusmao, at an independence ceremony in the East Timorese capital, Dili.

The world held its breath in May as tension escalated between India and Pakistan over the disputed region of Kashmir. On 22 May the Indian Prime Minister, Atal Bihari Vajpayee, called for a 'decisive battle' against terrorism by Kashmiri separatist fighters, whom India claimed were supported by the Pakistani government of Pervaiz Musharraf. With both nations holding nuclear arsenals, there were intense international efforts to broker a solution to the crisis, but despite a lessening of tension in June more than a million troops remained facing each other across the India-Pakistan border.

On 6 May Aung San Suu Kyi, the leader of Myanmar's (formerly Burma) opposition National League for Democracy was released from house arrest in the capital, Yangon, after 19 months in detention. Suu Kyi had spent six years under house arrest by the country's military government between 1989 and 1995, during which time she was awarded the Nobel Peace Prize.

Brazil win the World Cup

Deaths in the world of entertainment

The trial of Milosevic

The early months of the year saw the deaths of three key figures in the entertainment world. On 27 February Spike Milligan, the last remaining member of the team who revolutionised British comedy with the *Goon Show* in the 1950s, died at the age of 83. Milligan, who also wrote a number of books and the anarchically innovative television series *Q*, had been plagued by mental illness throughout his life. On 27 March the deaths were announced of the actor, comedian and musician Dudley Moore and of the film director Billy Wilder. Moore came to prominence in partnership with Peter Cook in the 1960s and went on to have a successful, if not always critically acclaimed, career in Hollywood. Aged 66, he had been suffering for some time from the degenerative condition progressive supranuclear palsy. Billy Wilder's film credits included such classics as *Double Indemnity* (1944), *Sunset Boulevard* (1950) and *Some Like It Hot* (1959).

On 13 February the trial of the former Yugoslav President Slobodan Milosevic began at the International Criminal Tribunal for the Former Yugoslavia at The Hague. Milosevic, who had been arrested in Belgrade in April 2001, refused to recognise the jurisdiction of the court or to appoint lawyers to defend him against charges of genocide, crimes against humanity and war crimes arising from the military action in Bosnia, Croatia and Kosovo which followed the break-up of the federal republic of Yugoslavia. Milosevic was the first former head of state ever to face charges before an international war crimes tribunal and the proceedings were widely seen as the most important war crimes trial since the Nuremberg hearings at the end of the Second World War.

On 30 June Brazil won the World Cup for the fifth time, defeating Germany 2-0 at the international stadium in Yokohama, Japan. Both goals were scored by the 25-year-old striker Ronaldo, whose performance secured him the competition's Golden Boot and confirmed his status as the most exciting player of his generation. The goals also earned him a place in the record-books jointly with the legendary Pelé as the highest scoring Brazilian player, and the third highest scoring player of any nationality, in the history of the World Cup finals. Earlier in the competition, Brazil had crushed England's World Cup hopes, defeating them 2-1 in the quarter-finals, and had gone on to beat Turkey in the semi-finals. The 2002 contest had seen its share of surprises, with Senegal, the USA and the joint home team South Korea outstripping all expectations to reach the later stages. Conversely, favourites France and Argentina fell in the first round, the latter to England, whose captain David Beckham redeemed his sending-off in England's last World Cup encounter with Argentina by scoring the only goal from a penalty just before half-time.

The Soham murders

In August Britain saw one of its most intensive police investigations in recent history as more than 400 officers searched for two missing schoolgirls in Cambridgeshire. The two friends, Holly Wells and Jessica Chapman, both aged ten, disappeared in the small fenland town of Soham on the evening of 4 August. Hopes that they would be found alive faded over the following fortnight as appeals for their return and a thorough search of the town and its surrounding area failed to reveal any clues to their whereabouts. On 18 August their bodies were found in woodland some seven miles from Soham, and two days later Ian Huntley, the caretaker of the local school, was charged with their murder, and his partner Maxine Carr, who had taught the girls, with attempting to pervert the course of justice. The case shocked the country and dominated the news media, leading to angry scenes outside the court in Peterborough when Maxine Carr made her first appearance there on 21 August.

The Washington sniper

Fear gripped the Washington DC area in October as a sniper claimed the lives of ten people in and around the US capital. The killing spree began on the evening of 2 October leaving five people dead by the next morning. Five more people were killed in the next three weeks, most of the victims being shot as they went about such daily tasks as supermarket shopping and filling up with petrol. Three others were injured, including a 13-year-old boy who was shot as he walked to school in Prince George's County, Maryland. In each case only a single shot was fired. Amid mounting criticism of their handling of the case, on 24 October the police arrested John Allen Muhammad, a 41-one-year-old Gulf War veteran, and his 17-year-old protégé, John Lee Malvo, in Frederick County, Maryland, in a car apparently specially adapted for shooting from the tailgate.

Bombings in Bali and Mombasa

The state of uneasy expectation that had prevailed since 11 September 2001 in parts of the world where Western interests are represented was abruptly shattered when terrorists struck the Indonesian tourist resort of Bali. Nearly 200 people were killed and some 300 injured when a huge bomb exploded outside a nightclub in Kuta on 12 October. Many of the dead were Australian holidaymakers. The Indonesian authorities pointed the finger of blame at the radical Islamist group Jemaah Islamiah, which they accused of having links with Osama bin Laden's al-Qaeda movement. The following month another terrorist outrage left thirteen people dead when suicide bombers drove a vehicle full of explosives into an Israeli-owned hotel in the Kenyan resort of Mombasa. At almost the same moment, missiles were fired at an Israeli passenger plane as it took off from Mombasa airport for Tel-Aviv, missing it by inches. Once again, suspicion fell on groups with links to al-Qaeda, who were widely believed to be responsible for the attack on the US embassy in the Kenyan capital, Nairobi, four years earlier.

Moscow theatre siege

The Russian capital was the scene of an extraordinary attack in October, when Chechen separatist rebels took hostage the entire audience at a Moscow theatre. A sequence of events which was to lead to tragedy began on the evening of 23 October when some forty armed militants, led by Movsar Barayev, burst onto the stage of the theatre as a play was about to begin. They threatened to blow up the building with more than 850 people inside unless the Russian authorities called an end to the war in Chechnya. Among the militants were a number of veiled women with explosives strapped to their bodies. A tense stand-off ensued as negotiators sought to bring the siege to a peaceful conclusion, and for three days hostages and hostage-takers alike languished in rapidly deteriorating conditions in the theatre's crowded auditorium. On 25 October Barayev threatened to start executing hostages the following day if his demands were not met, and in the early morning of 26 October Russian special forces pumped a paralysing gas into the auditorium and stormed the building. Most of the rebels were killed in the assault, but more than 100 hostages also died from the effects of the gas, which the Russian authorities declined to identify. Hundreds more were hospitalised. The same day President Putin made a televised address to the nation, in which he asked forgiveness for the civilian deaths.

Earthquake in Italy

Oil spillage off Spain

Twenty-six children and three teachers were killed when their school collapsed after an earthquake measuring 5.4 on the Richter scale struck southern Italy on 31 October. The tragedy occurred in the small town of San Giuliano di Puglia, some 140 kilometres south-east of Rome, and followed a series of earthquakes in Sicily and the eruption of Mount Etna. None of the children was older than six. Attempts to rescue others trapped under rubble were hampered by aftershocks and the remoteness of the Apennine community, where investigations focused on building standards at the school. In all some 10,000 people in the region were rendered homeless by the quake.

Environmental catastrophe and diplomatic wrangling followed the wreck of an oil tanker off the coast of Spain in November. The hull of the 80,000-tonne *Prestige* was damaged in stormy seas on 14 November causing oil spills to threaten the coast around Cape Finisterre. Five days later, while the British and Spanish governments argued over responsibility for the disaster, Spain claiming that the tanker was bound for British Gibraltar, the *Prestige* broke up and sank. Some 300 kilometres of the Galician coast were contaminated by oil driven ashore by high winds.

Jan	2	Two women killed in gang shoot-out in Birmingham		30	US launches Middle East 'road map' to peace
	10	N Korea withdraws from 1970 nuclear non-proliferation treaty	May	2	70 die in Chinese submarine accident
	12	Death of ex-President Galtieri of Argentina		5	Veteran anti-apartheid campaigner Walter Sisulu dies
	28	PM Ariel Sharon returned in Israeli elections		12	Suicide bomb attack kills 59 in Chechnya
Feb	1	Columbia space shuttle lost			34 killed in triple suicide bomb attack in Riyadh, Saudi Arabia
	15	Massive anti-war demonstrations worldwide		14	Second suicide bomb attack near Grozny, Chechnya
	18	196 die in S Korean underground train fire		15	UK–Kenya flights suspended over terrorism fears
	21	Death of Dolly the cloned sheep			Bombs explode at 18 Shell petrol stations, Karachi, Pakistan
	26	Tony Blair faces backbench revolt on Iraq		17	41 killed in bomb attacks in Casablanca, Morocco
		N Korea reactivates nuclear reactor at Yongbyon		21	More than 2,000 die in Algerian earthquake
Mar	12	Serbian PM Zoran Djindjic assassinated		22	UN lifts sanctions against Iraq
	14	France promises to veto a 2nd UN resolution authorising war		26	Australian Governor-General Peter Holingworth resigns
	17	US–UK disarmament deadline for Iraq		29	50th anniversary of first ascent of Everest
	20	War against Iraq begins		30	Bob Hope celebrates 100th birthday
Apr	9	Baghdad falls to US troops		31	Burmese opposition leader Aung San Suu Kyi arrested
	21	Senior Chinese officials resign over SARS under-reporting	Jun	12	Actor Gregory Peck dies
	24	Winnie Madikizela-Mandela convicted of fraud			

Birmingham party shootings

There was a stark reminder of the sharp rise in gun crime in Britain at the beginning of the year when two young women were shot dead as they celebrated the New Year in Birmingham. Charlene Ellis, aged eighteen, and Letisha Shakespeare, seventeen, were caught in crossfire between rival gangs outside a hairdressing studio in the Aston area of the city where they were attending a small party in the early hours of 2 January, Charlene's twin sister Sophie was critically injured. The number of gun-related crimes in Britain almost doubled in the five years from 1997 to 2002.

Death of Roy Jenkins

The death was announced on 5 January of the veteran British politician Roy Jenkins. He was 82. Once thought of as a potential prime minister, Jenkins was home secretary and chancellor of the exchequer in the Labour governments of the 1960s and 1970s. Strongly opposed to the leftward drift of the Labour party in the years after its 1979 election defeat at the hands of Margaret Thatcher, he was a leading member of the so-called 'Gang of Four' who broke away from the party to form the Social Democratic Party (SDP) in 1981. The party formally merged with the Liberals in 1987, but Jenkins' influence with the rising generation of Labour politicians, notably Tony Blair, was widely credited with assisting the development of the New Labour project and the return of the party to power in 1997. Jenkins was also an ardent advocate of closer European political and monetary union, and was the first British president of the European Commission from 1977 to 1981. An eminent historian, he wrote acclaimed biographies of, among others, Gladstone and Churchill, and as Lord Jenkins of Hillhead was chancellor of Oxford University from 1987 until his death.

New Archbishop of Canterbury

Loss of the Columbia space shuttle

Death of a philanthropist

On 27 February Rowan Williams was enthroned as the 104th Archbishop of Canterbury, primate of the worldwide Anglican communion, to which post he had been formally appointed in succession to George Carey at the end of 2002. The colourful ceremony, which took place in Canterbury Cathedral, was a mixture of the old and the new, with traditional fanfares replaced by dancing, and Welsh hymns — including Cwm Rhondda ('Guide me, O thou great Redeemer') — reflecting Williams' love of Wales, of which he was archbishop from 1999; Williams also wore simple vestments made by Welsh craftsmen. Outside the cathedral, however, there were protests by traditionalist evangelicals opposed to the new archbishop's liberal line on issues such as homosexual clergy.

In February the US space shuttle programme suffered its second major disaster when the shuttle Columbia broke up on re-entry into the Earth's atmosphere, with the loss of all seven astronauts on board. The tragedy came seventeen years after the loss of the shuttle Challenger shortly after take-off in 1986. Columbia was returning from its 28th mission on the morning of 1 February when NASA controllers at Houston in Texas lost radio contact. Initial investigations into the accident, which left wreckage strewn across the states of Texas and Louisiana, focused on damage to the heat-shield at the time of take-off.

Sir John Paul Getty, troubled scion of the Getty oil dynasty, died on 17 April at the age of 70. American-born, John Paul Junior was the third son of the billionaire J Paul Getty, and made his home in Britain, becoming a British citizen in 1997. A byword for hedonistic hippydom in the 1970s, his lifestyle led to alcoholism and drug dependency and a long period of reclusive rehabilitation in London. His later years were characterised by philanthropy on a massive scale, as he donated millions of pounds to a variety of arts and other charitable causes, including £50 million to London's National Gallery.

SARS epidemic

A new health scare swept the world in the early months of the year after the identification of a previously unknown disease, severe acute respiratory syndrome (SARS). The highly infectious flu-type illness is thought to have originated in Guangdong province in China in November 2002, but first came to general attention when a number of cases were reported in Hong Kong in February and March 2003. By mid-March cases had been reported in Canada, Indonesia, the Philippines, Singapore, Thailand and Vietnam, and the World Health Organisation (WHO) declared SARS a worldwide health risk. Cases were also soon reported in the US and Europe, and at the end of the month Carlo Urbani, the WHO official who first identified the disease, himself succumbed to it. In April China admitted that the incidence of SARS had been seriously under-reported in her territory, and the health minister and the mayor of Beijing were removed from office. By the beginning of May the number of deaths from SARS was approaching 400, with some 6,000 suspected cases world-wide. While medical researchers struggled to identify the virus and to establish whether the epidemic had peaked, measures were taken throughout the world to restrict travel to South-east Asia and other affected areas, and to quarantine returning travellers.

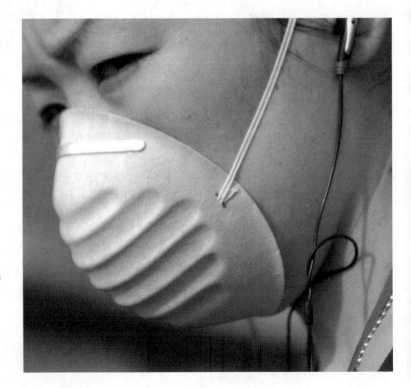

Death of Adam Faith

The singer, actor and businessman Adam Faith died on 8 March at the age of 62, after suffering a heart attack. Born Terence Nelhams, Faith shot to fame as a pop star in the late 1950s with the hit 'What Do You Want' and was an icon of the British pop scene throughout the 1960s. As an actor, he was best known for his creation of the role of 'Budgie' in the long-running TV series of the same name. His later career included a troubled spell as a financial investment advisor.

Nina Simone

The world of jazz lost one of its great names in April with the death of the singer and songwriter Nina Simone at the age of 70. Born Eunice Wayman in North Carolina, Simone studied the piano at the Juillard School of Music before embarking on a career as a performer of the jazz and blues music she described as 'black classical music': her greatest successes included 'Mississippi Goddamn' – a legacy of her intense involvement in the civil rights movement – Gershwin's 'I Loves You, Porgy', which brought her stardom in 1959, 'I Put a Spell on You' and 'My Baby Just Cares for Me'.

Closest Boat Race finish

There was great excitement on the Thames and among the 7.7 million people who watched at home on television as the 149th Oxford and Cambridge Boat Race produced the narrowest finishing margin in the history of the contest. The lead changed three times during the course of the four-and-a-half mile race, with Cambridge coming strongly from behind in the final stages to finish less than a foot behind – a result so close that both crews sat on the water for some time before Oxford's 71st victory in the annual challenge was finally confirmed. The race was also notable for involving two sets of brothers: Matt and Ben Smith (Oxford and Cambridge respectively) and David and James Livingston (likewise).

Living with Michael Jackson

Controversy once more erupted around the reclusive pop star Michael Jackson after the screening in February of the documentary *Living with Michael Jackson*. The programme, which was watched by more than 14 million viewers, provided another glimpse into the bizarre lifestyle of Jackson and his entourage at Neverland, the singer's California ranch, and was based on eight months of filming and interviews by the reporter Martin Bashir, best known for his 1995 television interview with Diana, Princess of Wales. The controversy focused on the fact that children were revealed still to be sleeping overnight at Jackson's house, and followed concerns about Jackson's own three children, one of whom, baby Prince Michael II, Jackson appeared to dangle over a balcony in sight of reporters during the filming of the programme; his other children appeared in public only with protective masks. Jackson, who insisted there was no sexual element to his friendships with children, subsequently claimed to have been betrayed by Bashir, mounting a judicial bid to stop further screenings of the documentary.

Switzerland's America's Cup win

There was excitement on the water in March when Switzerland's *Alinghi* won the sport of yachting's oldest trophy, the America's Cup. The Swiss team's victory against Team New Zealand on 2 March, clinching a 5–0 series of wins in the competition, made them the first European team ever to win the Cup and the first team ever to win at their first attempt. To compound the defending team's defeat, *Alinghi's* skipper, Russell Coutts, is a former Team New Zealand captain, who won the Cup for New Zealand in 1995.

War in Iraq

In the early hours of the morning of 20 March US air strikes against targets in Baghdad marked the beginning of the long expected war against Iraq.

Hawks within the US administration had been pressing for action against the Iraqi regime of President Saddam Hussein ever since the New York and Washington terrorist attacks of 11 September 2001, and in his state of the union address to Congress in January 2002 President George W. Bush had identified Iraq as part of an 'axis of evil', along with North Korea and Iran. Attention focused on Iraq's alleged programmes for developing weapons of mass destruction, which had been the subject of intermittent inspections by the international community up to December 1998 when United Nations weapons inspectors withdrew from the country, citing lack of co-operation from the Iraqi regime. Claims of direct links between the Islamic fundamentalist al-Qaeda movement and Saddam's secularist Ba'ath regime were greeted with greater scepticism.

In September 2002, Bush had addressed the UN to put the case for war against Iraq, and on 8 November the UN security council voted unanimously to support a US–British resolution (Resolution 1441) requiring Iraq to readmit weapons inspection teams. Ten days later inspectors returned to Iraq under the direction of the UN chief weapons inspector Hans Blix. On 7 December, shortly before the UN deadline for an Iraqi declaration on weapons of mass destruction, Iraq submitted to the UN a 12,000-page dossier, after studying which, however, the US judged Iraq to be in 'material breach' of the UN resolution.

By the beginning of the year, against a background of intense international diplomacy, a significant build-up of troops was underway in the Gulf, and the momentum for war began to seem unstoppable. At the same time, differences between the US and Britain on the one hand and many of their key European partners on the other grew ever wider. Escalating demands for a peaceful solution to the crisis were fuelled by Hans Blix's positive report to the UN on the progress of weapons inspections on 14 February and the following day millions of anti-war protestors took to the streets of cities around the world in demonstrations of unprecedented scale. In London, where up to a million people attended Britain's largest ever public protest, prime minister Tony Blair sustained the most

significant parliamentary revolt against a governing party for more than a century as almost 200 MPs voted against the government's case for war. At the international level British-led hopes for a second UN resolution authorising war were torpedoed on 5 March when France, Russia and Germany rejected the idea, and on 14 March the French president Jacques Chirac made himself a hate-figure in the US by confirming that France would veto any attempt to impose an ultimatum on Iraq. Two days later in the Azores, Bush and Blair imposed an ultimatum on the UN itself, giving the organisation 24 hours to enforce its demands for disarmament, failing which a US–British-led coalition would go to war unilaterally. On 18 March, with at least 170,000 coalition troops gathered on the Kuwaiti border with Iraq, Bush gave Saddam 48 hours to leave Iraq or face invasion.

The military operations, once begun, were covered by reporters 'embedded' with front-line troops – despite, or perhaps because of, which the fog of war remained often impenetrable, with claims and counterclaims as to the effectiveness of the coalition's strategy dominating discussion in the media, and the 'shock and awe' promised by US military planners apparently failing to produce the immediate collapse of the Saddam regime that some had predicted. By 24 March, however, with British troops in the south of the country securing the key port of Umm Qasr and besieging Iraq's second city, Basra, American B-52 bombers began to pound Republican Guard positions around Baghdad in preparation for an advance on the capital. Fears of chemical counterattack proved groundless, and by 3 April US troops had advanced to within ten miles of the centre of the city, securing Saddam International Airport. Two days later, as reports came in of the death in an air raid on Basra of 'Chemical Ali' (Ali Hassan al-Majid), the Iraqi general held responsible for the chemical attacks on Kurds in northern Iraq in 1988, US tanks were seen in the suburbs of Baghdad for the first time. On 7 April US forces mounted an air strike

against houses in the al-Mansour area of Baghdad in an apparent attempt to assassinate Saddam himself, and American troops were pictured occupying two of his opulent palaces in the capital. The same day, Basra fell to advancing British forces, but the hoped-for scenes of Iraqi celebration at their 'liberation' were soon matched by an escalating crisis of law and order, with looting and revenge killings rampant. Throughout, the Iraqi information minister, Saeed al-Sahaf, continued to proclaim, in makeshift press conferences, that Iraqi forces were winning the war, gaining grudging, if amused, respect from some foreign observers for his eccentrically unquenchable bravado.

The long anticipated 'tipping point' was given dramatic physical reality on 9 April when, under the eyes of the world's media, US marines helped a crowd of Iraqis to topple a massive statue of Saddam Hussein in one of Baghdad's central squares. In the following days further bastions of the Ba'ath regime fell to coalition forces: the northern city of Kirkuk to a Kurdish advance; Mosul to Kurdish and US forces; and on 14 April Saddam's home town of Tikrit. At the same time, the law and order crisis deepened, with the occupying forces criticised in many quarters for taking an insufficiently authoritarian line against widespread looting, which in the capital included the theft of priceless antiquities from the city's museums. Coalition troops also came under attack by paramilitaries and suicide bombers, taking the conflict into a new phase. As senior members of the Ba'ath administration – America's 'most wanted' list of officials of the Saddam regime – began to be captured or surrender, the whereabouts of Saddam himself remained unknown. By the end of May, with Iraq now under a US-led interim administration, evidence of the scale of the atrocities committed during Saddam's 24-year rule had begun to be unearthed, but no conclusive evidence of his weapons of mass destruction had yet come to light.

Index

Numbers in **bold** type indicate text and illustration references. Numbers in ordinary type refer to entries in the chronology.

Photographic Acknowledgements

The publishers would like to thank all those who have supplied photographs for use in this book and apologise to any whose contribution may have been inadvertently omitted from these acknowledgements.

The majority of the photographs in this book are from the Hulton Deutsch Collection, London. Other sources are as follows:

Archives Idées et Editions, Paris 239b, 245; Archives Photographiques, Paris 13bl; Archives Tallandier, Paris 246b; courtesy of the Art Institute of Chicago (Arthur Heun Fund) 32br; Ashmolean Museum, Oxford, Department of Western Art 50t; Associated Press, London 222bl, 239t, 251c, 421, 466b, 534tr; The Bettmann Archive, Inc., New York/Hulton Deutsch Collection 8, 16t, 16b, 17t, 17br, 34t, 35bl, 38br, 54c, 101tl, 101c, 103br, 113b, 114, 118t, 118bl, 123br, 126bl, 137tr, 138, 141bl, 174t, 175t, 175b; Bildarchiv Preussischer Kulturbesitz, Berlin 211t, 211bl, 214, 222t, 232t; Camera Press, London 544, 547br, Auscape-JPF 533t, 533b, Colman Doyle 545br, Erma 545bl, Snowdon 546bc; Canadian Army 231t; Editions Casterman, Paris and Tournai 144b; The Chrysler Museum Institute of Glass, Norfolk, VA (Gift of Walter P. Chrysler, Jr) 21tc; Colorific, London/Zapruder 366b; Alastair Duncan, New York (photo courtesy of Christie's, New York) 125tl; Mary Evans Picture Library, London 15c, 20t, 21b, 24br, 26tl, 26bl, 26br, 27tr, 28, 31, 33, 37t, 43bl, 44t, 45tr, 51tr, 91l, 92tl, 94bl, 95t, 101tr, 101b, 111tr, 111br, 115br, 116tr, 121bc, 124l, 124r, 125bl, 125br, 135ct, 140br, 142, 143tr; Illustrated London News Picture Library, London 70tl, 72cl, 163tl; Impact/Carolina Alguero 569c; Imperial War Museum, London 46-7, 63t, 69t, 70b, 71t, 71b, 74t, 74b, 78bl, 82t, 83, 86br, 87b, 209tl, 212tl, 218tl, 220t, 224bl, 230t, 231b, 237, 238b, 242br, 251b; David King Collection, London 79; Paul Klee Foundation, Museum of Fine Arts, Berne 136tl; Kobal Collection, London 66br, 84br, 96-7, 103bl, 112tc, 123bl, 123bc, 136br, 137tl, 141tr, 141br, 192br, 193tl, 200bl, 286c, 292br, 322tr, 564br, 573bl; Larousse, Paris 216b, 316br; Larousse, Paris/Signal 216tl; Library of Congress, Washington, DC 17bl, 82b; Magnum Photos, London/Abbas 549b, Ian Berry 569t, Dimitri Erwitt 549tr, Stuart Franklin 541tr, 541b, Philippe Halsman 546br, G. Mendel 545t, Patrick Zachmann 541tl; Mansell Collection, London 20br, 25bl, 27tl, 32t, 42, 56tl; Marconi Company Limited, Chelmsford 15b; permission of MGN-Syndication International Ltd, Los Angeles 212br; Military Archive & Research Services, Stamford 211br; National Aeronautics and Space Administration, Washington, DC 340-1; National Archives, Washington, DC, Navy Department 226b, 233t; National Baseball Library, Cooperstown, NY 105tl; National Film Archive, London 132bl, 162br, 168tr, 168b, 183tr, 219bc, 226tl, 244bl, 338br, 382br, 540tc; Vic Stein/NFL Photos, Los Angeles 265b; National Gallery of Art, Washington, DC, (Chester Dale Collection) 24tc (detail); National Portrait Gallery, London 21tl, 90br; The Octopus Group 18tr, 21c, 37br, 156tc; Phillips Collection, Washington, DC, 314bl; Photri, Alexandria, VA 228b; Popperfoto, London 35t, 35br, 56tr, 59br, 63br, 68t, 68b, 69bl, 69br, 70tr, 72cr, 72b, 73, 75t, 75b, 77 (all), 78br, 80t, 81b, 84bl, 90t, 92cr, 95c, 103bc, 105bl, 105br, 108br, 111tl, 112tl, 115bl, 117tr, 121bl, 127bl, 127br, 128tr, 135b, 137bl, 139bl, 143tl, 143b, 144c, 146-7, 149t, 150t, 151t, 151b, 152t, 153t, 155tl, 155r, 156tl, 157t, 157b, 160c, 162tr, 162bl, 163tc, 163tr, 165t, 165cl, 166bl, 166br, 167b, 169, 170tr, 171br, 172bc, 172br, 173tl, 173tr, 174b, 176tl, 178tl, 178tr, 178b, 186b, 188l, 188br, 191tl, 191br, 192tl, 193tc, 195b, 196t, 212tr, 218tr, 218b, 250 (all), 252c, 252b, 254bl, 258c, 269tl, 271tl, 271tr, 271bl, 276tl, 276bl, 278-9, 284b, 285tl, 285tr, 286t, 286b, 294tl, 296b, 297, 298b, 304bl, 309t, 311, 313c, 316c, 323t, 323b, 324tl, 324tr, 326t, 327bl, 327br, 330t, 330bl, 332c, 332b, 333t, 333b, 338tr, 347tr, 355tr, 356tr, 360bc, 360br, 364 (all), 365c, 365b, 367b, 368t, 368b, 371tr, 372tr, 372br, 373tr, 373b, 374 (all), 375tc, 375bl, 375br, 376, 380 (all), 382t, 382bl, 383, 385tl, 385tr, 385bl, 387tl, 388tc, 392tr, 392br, 394tl, 395t, 396tl, 396tr, 397tl, 397tr, 399r, 400tr, 401, 404tr, 404bl, 404br, 405b, 406-7, 411t, 418t, 422t, 422bl, 423t, 423tr, 424r, 425t, 425b, 431tr, 434tl, 435tl, 440 (all), 443tl, 444tc, 444bc, 447tl, 447br, 449bl, 450tr, 450bl, 453bl, 453br, 454c, 454b, 456tc, 458t, 458b, 460tr, 460br, 463, 464 (all), 465 (all) 466tl, 466tr, 466br, 467cl, 473, 474t, 475t, 476 (all), 478bl, 482t, 484t, 484ct, 487c, 487b, 488tl, 488tr, 489t, 489c, 490 (all), 491 (all), 492t, 493tl, 494, 495t, 495bl, 496 (all), 497t, 497b, 498 (all), 499 (all), 500b, 503 (all), 504 (all), 505bl, 505br, 506bl, 506br, 507t, 508, 509 (all), 510b, 511t, 511b, 512 (all), 513b, 514 (all), 515t, 515b, 516t, 516b, 517 (all), 518 (all), 519b, 520tl, 520tc, 520b, 521tl, 521tc, 521tr, 522, 523tl, 523tr, 523c, 524 (all), 525 (all), 526t, 526b, 527 (all), 528bl, 529, 530 (all), 531 (all), 532tl, 532tr, 532bl, 532bc, 532br, 534 (all), 535 (all); Press Association, London 485br; Punch, London 128tl, 318tl; Range Pictures Ltd/Reuter/Bettman 562r, 562l, 563tl, 563br, 563bl, 563tr, 564bl, 565b, 567b, 568b, 570tr, 570b, 572tl, 572br; Rex Features, London 536, 538b, 547bl, 547bc, 552bl, 554t, 564tl, 566tc, 566b, 572tr, 572bl, 573bc, Tracy Baker/Sipa Press 561b, Deis Cameron 542t, Thierry Chesnot/Sipa Press 548br, Delahaye/Sipa Press 537t, East News/Sipa Press 552t, 574t, Gastaud/Sipa Press 566tr, ITN 549tl, Iwasa 575tr, 575tl, Nils Jorgensen 572tc, 566tl, David Kampfner 573br, Juhan Kuus 552br, Merlet 561tr, Novosti/Sipa Press 539b, Sipa Press 540b, 543br, 546t, 547t, 551tl, 551tr, 575bl, Leon Schadeberg 570tl, The Sun 539t, A. Tavera/Prisma 542b, Today 539c, 547c, Barry Wilkinson 537br, Holine Za Oupar/Sipa Press 554c, Novak/Sipa Press 554b, 555t, East News/Sipa Press 555c, Wojetic Laski/Sipa Press 555b, Today 553tl, Kessler/Sipa Press 553tr, Raj Rama/LGI 553b, Sipa Pool 553tl, 556l, 556r, 557tr, 557tl, The Sun 557bl, Sipa

Press 557br, Voja Miladinovic/Sipa Press 558t, Sipa Press 558bl, Sipa Press/Cham 559t, Sipa Press 560tr, Sipa Press 560c, ITN 560bl, Joker-Sipa Press 560br, Sipa Press 561tr, 561b; H. Roger Viollet, Paris 76t, 125tr, 133br, 235b, 240t; Crispin Rodwell 573t; Royal Geographical Society, London 108bl, 120b, 303r; Soviet Embassy, London 221; Frank Spooner Pictures, London 537bl; Science Photo Library 567t; Sygma/Brooks Kraft 569br, Jon Jones 569bl; Syndication International, London 533tl, 533cr, 538ct, 538cb, 546bl; The Tate Gallery, London 103tr; Topham Picturepoint 575br, Associated Press 564tr, 565t, 571bl, 571br, 574bl; Topham Picture Library, Edenbridge 554bl, Associated Press 409, 537bc, 540tl, 540tr, 543tl, 543bl, 548tl, 548tr, 551b 550, Press Association 538t, 548bl; United States Air Force 253b; United States Army 223t, 238tl, 251t; by courtesy of the Board of Trustees of the Victoria & Albert Museum, London 13tr, 14, 72tr; Yale University Library, New Haven, Connecticut 113tr.

Allsport/Stephen Munday 587bl; Associated Press 576t /The Daily Oklahoman/Jim Argo 577t, /Jacqueline Arzt 579b, /Frank Augstein 581tr,/ Martin Gnedt 582 tl, /Alastair Grant 580, /Eugene Hoshiko 585b, /Ross Setford 577b, /Richard Vogel 578bl, /Xinhua 586t; Press Association News 587bc; Rex Features 581bl, 581br, 582bl, 583tl, 583tr, 584tr, 584tl, 585t, /DPPI 578tl, /Agence DPPI 583bl, /T. Haley 585b, 586cb, 587br, Mauro Carraro 583br, /Tim Rooke 578r, /Leon Schadeberg 576l, /Sipa 587t, /Sipa Press 582r, /Trippett 579tr, /Simon Walker 576c; Whyler Photos 581tl.

Associated Press 591l; Christopher Cormack /Corbis 589 b; UPI /Corbis-Bettmann 590t, 593tr, 588tr, 593tl; Rex Features 588l, 588br, 589c, 589t, 590b, 591tr, 591br, 592r, 592l, 593b, 593tc

Pablo Picasso's Self-portrait, 1900s (detail 13br), and Guernica, 1937 (185t), are © DACS 1989 and Madame Maya Widmaier Picasso, Paris.

René Lalique's Clock Le Jour et La Nuit, c. 1930 (125tl), is © DACS 1989.

Paul Klee's Die Grosse Kuppel, 1927, N 3 (43), pen drawing, German, Ingres/26.8 ¥ 30.4cm, signed below left: Paul Klee Foundation, Berne (detail 136tl), and Oskar Kokoschka's Self-portrait (detail 266bl) are © COSMOPRESS, Geneva/DACS, London, 1989.

Salvador Dali's Laurence Olivier as Richard III, 1956 (detail 322br), is © DEMART PRO ARTE BV/DACS 1989.

Grandma Moses' McDonell Farm, 1943 (314bl), is copyright Grandma Moses Properties Co., New York, 1987.

Andy Warhol's Marilyn, 1967 (detail 528br), is copyright the Estate and Foundation of Andy Warhol, 1989. Courtesy ARS, N.Y.

Stills from Walt Disney's Steamboat Willie, 1928 (141tr), and Snow White, 1938 (192br), are © The Walt Disney Company.

Line illustration by E H. Shepard (132br) copyright under the Berne Convention, reproduced by permission of Curtis Brown, London from Winnie-the-Pooh by A. A. Milne, illustrated by Ernest H. Shepard, copyright 1926 by EPD, renewed 1954 by A. A. Milne. Reproduced by permission of the publisher, Dutton Children's Books, a division of Penguin Books USA Inc.

Lotus Pagoda Lamp Shade and Base, 1906-10 (21tc), is by Tiffany Studios, Corona, NY, impressed 'Tiffany Studios New York 374' on bottom of base, bronze tab impressed 'Tiffany Studios New York' affixed to inside of shade, in leaded glass and bronze, 32" high (Chrysler Museum accession no. 71.8124/ GAT.63.58).

Auguste Rodin's Study for The Burghers of Calais (13bl) is © C.N.M.H.S./ S.P.A.D.E.M.

Paul Cézanne's Sketchbook: Self-Portrait, pencil, 12.4 ¥ 21.7 cm, Arthur Heun Fund; 1951.1 page 37 recto (detail 32br) is © 1989 The Art Institute of Chicago. All Rights Reserved.

Associated Press/Ed Andrieski 599 Top Left, Corbis UK Ltd /Robbie Jack 599 Top Right, /Jean-Pierre Lescourret 599 Bottom Right, Hulton Getty Picture Collection 599 Bottom Left /John Wildgoose 596 Top Centre Rex Features 594 Bottom Right, 594 centre right above, 594 centre right below, 595 Bottom Left, 595 Bottom Centre, 596 Top Left, 596 Top Right, 597, 597 Bottom Right /David Howells 597 Top/Nils Jorgensen 595 Top Right, 596 Bottom, 599 Bottom Centre /Maecke-Gaff 595 Top Left

Mirror Syndication International 600 Top, 600 Bottom

Rex Features 598, 601 Top Left, 601 Top Right, 601 Bottom, 602 Top Left, 602 Bottom Right, 603 left, 603 right, 604 left, 604 right, 605 Top Left, 605 Top Centre, 605 Top Right, 605 Bottom Left, 605 Bottom Right

Corbis/Hulton Getty 613 top/David & Peter Townley 606 bottom; Hulton Getty 613 bottom: Rex Features 606 top, 606 centre left, 606 centre right, 607 top left, 607 top centre, 607 top right, 607 bottom, 608 top, 608 bottom, 609 top left, 609 top centre, 609 top right, 609 centre, 609 bottom, 610 top, 610 bottom, 611 top, 611 bottom left, 611 bottom centre, 611 bottom right, 612 top right, 612 bottom; Science Photo Library/Ken Eward 612 top left.

Popperfoto 615 top, 618 centre, 619 bottom centre, 619 bottom right, 620 bottom right/ Rex Features 614 top, 614 bottom right, 614 bottom left, 614 bottom centre, 615 bottom, 616 right, 616 top left, 616 bottom left, 616 left upper centre, 616 left lower centre, 617 left, 617 top right, 617 centre right, 618 right, 618 left, 619 top, 619 bottom left, 620 top left, 620 top right, 620 bottom left, 620 bottom centre, 621 top, 621 bottom right

Photographic Acknowledgements

ActionPlus/Neil Tingle 623 top right Getty Images/620 bottom right, 623 top centre/Edy Purnomo 619 bottom right/Nick Wilson 623 bottom right/Stefan Zaklin 619 centre left Rex Features/621 right, 624 bottom left/Tony Kyriacou 619 top left/Lou Linwei 622 bottom right/MAC 624 top left/Andrew McCafferty 623 top left/MGG 621 left, 624 centre left/NJ 622 top right/Sipa, 620 top right, 620 bottom left, 623 bottom left, 624 top right, 625 top left, 625 top right, 625 bottom right, 625 centre right top, 625 centre right bottom Topham/PA 622 top left/Photri 622 top centre